Readings in American Political Issues

SECOND EDITION

EDITED BY
*Franklin D. Jones
and Michael O. Adams*
Texas Southern University

KENDALL/HUNT PUBLISHING COMPANY
4050 Westmark Drive   Dubuque, Iowa 52002

Copyright © 1987, 2004 by Kendall/Hunt Publishing Company

ISBN 0-7575-1220-8

All rights reserved. No part of this publication may be reproduced, stored in a retrieval system, or transmitted, in any form or by any means, electronic, mechanical, photocopying, recording, or otherwise, without the prior written permission of the copyright owner.

Printed in the United States of America

10 9 8 7 6 5 4 3 2 1

Contents

Introductory Essay: Michael O. Adams, "Broadening the Scope of American Government," introduces the eclectic collection of articles as an attempt to raise the types of questions that should be added to the traditional coverage of American government. Where appropriate updates are added (e.g. The Ayers Case and Estrada Hearing).

PART ONE—POLITICAL BELIEFS IN THE AMERICAN POLITICAL SYSTEM

American Political Thought—Two Approaches 3
Kenneth Dolbeare

Racism, Multiculturalism, the Black Conservative Movement
and the Post-Civil Rights Era 13
Mack H. Jones

Thinking about Whiteness and American Politics 35
Christopher Deis

Class and Power in America 47
G. William Domhoff

Capitalism and Democracy 57
Gabriel A. Almond

Globalization in the Perspective of Imperialism 69
Robert Went

The Contemporary Black Predicament: Crisis
and Political Obligations 89
Rickey Hill

Framing Pan Africanism for the New Millennium:
The Case of Reparations 105
Charles P. Henry

PART TWO—POLITICAL PARTICIPATION

The Black Population: 2000 136
Jesse McKinnon

The Hispanic Population in the United States 154
Melissa Therrien and Roberto R. Ramirez

2002 National Opinion Poll 164
David A. Bositis

Interest Groups 171
Hanes Walton, Jr. and Robert Smith

The National Urban League in the Development of Leadership
among African American Women 189
Minion K. C. Morrison

Violence, Nonviolence, and the Civil Rights Movement 202
Sally Avery Bermanzohn

Voting Reform in the U.S.: Special Studies and the 2000 Election.... 220
Alex Willingham

The 2000 Florida Election and Its Aftermath:
Voter Disenfranchisement and Political Deals 243
Marcella Washington

Ain't No Party Like a Democratic Party and the Judge from Johnston
County: A Look at North Carolina 2002 Mid-Term Elections 253
Jarvis A. Hall

Proportional Representation and Black Political Representation
and Influence in America: An Alternative to the Single
Member District Strategy 266
Bob Holmes

PART THREE—ISSUES IN INSTITUTIONAL POLITICS

The Federal Courts and Higher Education Desegregation
in Mississippi: The Ayers Case in Perspective 285
Mfanya D. Tryman and Reginald Knight

*The Power of the Jurist: An Examination of Jury Nullification and
Its Use as a Tool for Political Advancement of African Americans* 301
Shaka T. Jones

*Dismantling Racial Profiling: The ACLU's
"Arrest the Racism" Campaign* 307
Nancy C. Cornwell

Report on the Anniversary of Furman v. Georgia 322
American Civil Liberties Union

"Invisible" Latino Youth Find Injustice in the Justice System 342
Francisco A. Villarruel and Nancy E. Walker

*Clarence Thomas and His Latino Clone:
The Dollar's Global Death-Grip* 346

*Post-1994: The New Nadir of African-American
Congressional Participation* 352
Charles E. Jones

Cynthia McKinney's Struggle to Win Reelection Against All Odds ... 370
Marilyn A. Davis

Globalization of Alabama Politics 386
Byrdie A. Larkin

PART FOUR—FOREIGN AND DOMESTIC POLICY

*The Birth of a Global Anti-Racist Community
at the World Conference against Racism, Racial
Discrimination, Xenophobia and Related Intolerance* 397
Hoda M. Zaki

The Universal Declaration of Human Rights—Only a Foundation ... 415
Elisabeth Reichert

Rebuilding America's Defenses 429
Donald Kagan, Gary Schmitt and Thomas Donnelly

War, Terror, the Quest for Domination and Resistance 440
Mack H. Jones

No Matter the Measure, Black Poverty Is High 452
Margaret C. Simms

Politics Mondays: School Vouchers 456
Armstrong Williams

Shoving Vouchers Down D.C.'s Throat 458
The Black Commentator

Opinion in Bakke 465
Thurgood Marshall

Opinion in Grutter 475
Clarence Thomas

Introduction

Broadening the Scope of American Government

Michael O. Adams

There are political realities in American government that deserve closer analysis. The typical American government textbook is designed to be marketable in an increasingly lucrative college textbook industry. Often, to meet that demand textbooks shy away from some of the more controversial topics and issues in American government. Such issues are not isolated thoughts of the disenfranchised, malcontents or the truly revolutionary. They, in many ways, impact the ability of students to reason through the litany of issues they will face as citizens or residents of the United States and the world. To address part of that void we have edited a reader which offers a critical examination of selected issues relevant to the contemporary American political discourse. It is purposely fashioned to include articles that are provocative in an effort to enhance the critical thinking skills of our students.

Often, what is presented in American government textbooks is an examination of institution and policies with limited analysis of the peculiar impact those institutions have on minorities and the poor. Generally, there is a broad sweep of the struggle for equal rights with an obligatory chapter covering the struggles of African Americans, Hispanics, women and the disabled for extension or protection of rights. Achieving the right to vote or access to public accommodations may represent some structural changes but it does not explain the systemic prohibitions for outside groups to become equal partners in the political system. Nor does it generate the necessary discussion that should distinguish between success as defined by political participation and what one can or should expect from participation. Hence, ideology, race and class are relevant to a more comprehensive understanding of American government.

Similarly, the capitalist imperative deserves a more thorough analysis than its triumph over alternative systems. Its implications for both domestic and foreign policy should be a part of that analysis. Issues like job outsourcing, homeland security and wars in Iraq and Afghanistan would become more than issues of American nationalism. A real discussion of who fights wars and why; who benefits materially from such endeavors should be part of the national discourse.

The introductory nature of American government courses is such that many ideas are highlighted in hopes that interests will be sparked for students to seek further knowledge. It is in this vein we have structured this reader.

Part one of the Reader is concerned with political thought and ideology that have been expressed in the American political system.

The American political system has a rich tradition of eclectic political thought. In this section we introduce students of American government to a variety of political thinkers and issues that may not be common. We provide a useful approach to organize American political thought in the article by Kenneth Dolbeare, "American Political Thought—Two Approaches." One approach is the classical approach involving the traditional "liberal-conservative spectrum and its grounding in certain basic values." The second approach focuses on the role of four concepts: dignity, democracy, ideology, and power in the development of American political thought.

Mack Jones in "Racism, Multiculturalism, the Black Conservative Movement and the Post Civil Rights Era" is a critique of the rise of Black conservatism and its intersection with multiculturalism. It also examines the impact of both on American political thought.

Whiteness Studies is a young field of study in American political thought. Chris Deis in "Thinking about Whiteness and American Politics" explores the concept of whiteness and how it impacts the system of racism, racial inequality, and shapes the racial, social, and political boundaries of white Americans. He asks, "How does Whiteness Studies inform our views of American democracy?"

Old questions for political scientists and their students have evolved around issues of class, power, capitalism and democracy. William Domhoff defines social class and power and their usage in American politics in "Class and Power in America." In a presidential lecture for the American Political Association, Gabriel A. Almond explores the historic relationship between democracy and capitalism. He discusses the arguments of those who report of tensions between democracy and capitalism and he argues that both support and subvert a positive relationship between capitalism and democracy.

Another perspective on the nature of capitalism can be seen in the article by Robert Went, "Globalization in the Perspective of Imperialism." Went seeks to update the concept of imperialism in light of the rush to globalization.

Rickey Hill also seeks to update his analysis of political thought in the African American Community. He discusses the role of political thought in shaping politics in the African American community. His thoughtful essay is entitled, "The Contemporary Black Predicament: Crisis and Political Obligation."

Finally, Charles P. Henry provides a brief history of Pan Africanism and explains how as a social movement Pan Africanism could be modernized through the debates on reparations and congressional policies toward Africa.

As most American government texts do, Part Two discusses issues related to political participation. The study of American government will become more complete when there is a greater incorporation of the political lives and interests of African American and other minority groups in the United States. We begin this section with two 2000 census reports on the status of African American and Hispanic populations. Next, David Bositis reports on the one national opinion poll that provides a comprehensive assessment of the opinion of African Americans on key public policy issues viewed as important by the African American community.

What is reflected in the poll is a desire to participate in the political process. Part of that participation is through interest groups. Hanes Walton and Robert Smith identify the major African American interest groups in American politics and explain the roles they play in representing the interests of the African American community. Minnion K. C. Morrison uses the National Urban League to describe how interest groups can develop programs to increase the civic role of African American women as community leaders.

In post 9/11 America, there has been a greater discussion of violence as a means of political participation. But that discussion has been generally limited to terrorism being visited upon the United States by foreign sources. However, Sally Bermazohn in "Violence, Nonviolence, and the Civil Rights Movements," offers the reader the opportunity to study the dynamic between violence and politics in the American south by focusing on the relationship between terror and the state.

Still, the most common method of political participation is voting. But, the 2000 presidential elections and the 2002 mid-term election raised many questions about the legitimacy and accuracy of the election system. Alex Willingham begins the critique of that election period by examining several of the key studies following the 2000 round of elections which sought to explain the voting irregularities in terms of technological problems and how they could be resolved. Marcella Washington (Florida), and Jarvis Hall (North Carolina) describe elections in three states in the aftermath of the 2000 presidential election. Two additional races are later discussed in the institutional section.

Voting and elections are not the only issues. Robert Holmes notes that the present system of voting does not always provide the maximum opportunity for African Americans to represent themselves. He makes his case in the article, "The Use of Proportional Representation."

Part Three focuses on issues related to institutional politics. The conservative state of governmental institutions has never been more prevalent. Institutions of government are led by individuals who are committed to a conservative political agenda, which some perceive as a threat to minority right, health care, employment opportunities and even the election of progressive members of Congress. Moreover, conservatives are now in a position to effect changes to the laws governing civil rights protection and civil liberties by packing the federal courts with more conservative judges.

To help make some sense out of this controversy, we have selected an eclectic group of articles that address some of the challenges facing these institutions today.

Mfanya Tryman and Reginald Knight, "The Federal Courts and Higher Education Desegregation in Mississippi: The Ayers Case in Perspective" examine the history of racial segregation and discrimination in Mississippi in reference to the state's historically black colleges and universities by analyzing the federal courts role in *Ayers v. Fordice*. This article provides interesting insights into the plans and policy recommendations proposed by the federal courts in reference to equal funding and desegregation of Mississippi institutions of higher learning.

Shaka T. Jones, "The Powers of the Jurist: An Examination of Jury Nullification and Its Use as a Toll for Political Advancement of African Americans," analyzes the recent debate over the legal issue of jury nullification. Jones argues that the "knowing and deliberate rejection of evidence or refusal to apply the law either because a jury wants to send a message about some social issue greater than the case itself or because a result dictated by law is contrary to the jury's sense of justice, morality or fairness," may be assessed as a possible tool for the political liberation for African Americans.

While jury nullification is seen as a threat in some quarters, just as racial profiling, before and after 9/11, is seen as a threat in others. Nancy C. Cornwell provides a description and analysis of the constitutional and civil liberties concerns raised by the practice of racial profiling. She does this through the description of the ACLU's campaign against racial profiling in "Dismantling Racial Profiling."

The ACLU is still one of the primary sources to use when discussing the death penalty. One of its reports is reprinted here in its entirety. The 2003 report, *The Anniversary of Furman v. Georgia*, explains through a historical and sociological analysis the reason why the ACLU believes there should be a temporary halt on executions.

The question of fairness in the judicial system is also explored by Francisco Villaruel and Nancy Walker who in "Invisible Latino Youth Find Injustice System," address the disparities and inequalities that exist in the incarceration of Latino youth in America. They reveal that the incarceration rates of Latino youth are often hidden in the official statistics that examine racial disparities in the nation's criminal justice system.

Finally, we end the judicial issue with a discussion of a Bush administration's nominee for the U.S. Court of Appeals. Several nominees have been labeled as holding staunchly conservative views and who differ greatly in their interpretation of the civil rights and civil liberties of minorities and other citizens. The article "Clarence Thomas and His Latino Clone" also projected that the nomination of Miguel Estrada would become as divisive for the Latino community as that of Clarence Thomas was for the African American community. However, this outcome appears to have been averted since Estrada asked that his name be withdrawn from consideration.

We emphasize the role of African Americans in congressional politics in three articles. The first is an update of and article by Charles Jones from the first edition of the reader. "The New Nadir of African American Congressional Participation," is a description and analysis of the role of the Congressional Black Caucus. Jones suggests that the effectiveness of the Congressional Black Caucus may have reached its zenith and is actually on the decline. Marilyn Davis and Byrdie Larkin discuss the failed bids by two incumbent African American members of Congress to retain their seats in Congress in 2002. The defeat of the two candidates is about electoral politics and congressional policymaking particularly in the area of foreign policy.

Marilyn Davis' "Cynthia McKinney's Struggle to Win Reelection against All Odds" analyzes the failure of black Georgia Congresswoman Cynthia McKinney to win reelection in a hotly contested Democratic primary. Davis' article provides an interesting commentary on how a strange coalition of white Democrats, some black Democrats, and crossover Republicans help nominate a centrist black woman, Denise Majette to defeat an outspoken and "controversial" incumbent Congresswoman McKinney. McKinney was criticized for a public statement questioning the role of the George W. Bush administration in the bombing of the World Trade Center and its aftermath.

Byrdie A. Larkin's "Earl Hilliard v. Artie Davis: The Globalization of Alabama State Politics," examines the charge that the Middle East conflict led to the defeat of black incumbent Earl Hilliard in Alabama's 7th Congressional district. Larkin's essay reveals that Arthur Davis received 79 percent of his $1.3 million campaign contributions from out of state donations. More importantly, $200,000 came from Pro-Israeli groups in the state of New York. These contributors did not like Earl Hilliard's position on Israel. Specifically, he was targeted for defeat for his opposition to a non-binding resolution supporting Israel and condemning Palestinian suicide bombers. Larkin argues that the campaign contributions from out of state Arab-American groups contributed to the globalization of Alabama politics.

The last section of the reader, Part Four, introduces students to a number of public policy issues in the domestic and foreign arenas. With the aftermath of the September 11th terrorist attack and the subsequent wars in Afganistan and Iraq and the ongoing "war on terrorism," it is critical to discuss the administration's reasoning and justification behind this foreign policy shift. The implications to the country, both in the manner in which the United States interacts with the other countries of the world as well as for the citizenry of the country, are significant and merit close examination. It is clear that the full effect of the Patriot Act is yet to be seen. Also, with the resulting significant expenditures for the war and security effort, these are sure to be challenging times for the poor and racial minorities.

To help us put things in perspective, we have included several diverse articles that speak directly to the consequence, American foreign and domestic policies.

Hoda Zaki's, **"The Birth of a Global Anti-Racist Community at the World Conference against Racism, Racial Discrimination, Xenophobia and Related Intolerence,"** analyzes the historical and contemporary efforts to convene international conferences to discuss the issue of racial discrimination and inequality. Zaki's article focuses on the Non Governmental Organization Forum she attended as a delegate of the Arab

American Institute. She gives a first person account of the reactions of the U.S. Government and media to the Palestian-Israeli conflict as it was debated at the NGO Forum.

Next is Elisabeth Reichert, "**The Universal Declaration of Human Rights—Only a Foundation,**" *The Journal of Intergroup Relations*, vol. Spring 2002 pp. 34-49. This article is an introduction to the history and development of the Universal Declaration of Human Rights. Reinhert analyzes the Universal Declaration of Human Rights in an attempt to establish a model standard of conduct applicable to every individual and government to basic human rights.

Mack Jones' "**War Terror, the Quest for Domination and Resistance,**" provides a critical assessment of America's "war on terrorism," in the aftermath of the September 11, 2001, attacks on the World Trade Center of New York. Jones' article is particularly useful in placing the September 11th attacks in a theoretical and systematic context that assesses the actions of the terrorists and the U.S. Government's response which included the eventual invasion and occupation of Iraq. Lastly, this article is very useful in the explanation of public opinions held by African Americans in reference to the "war on Iraq."

Margaret Simms, in "**No Matter the Measure, Black Poverty Is High,**" analyzes the latest U.S. Census Bureau's data on income and poverty in the United States. She reveals that in the indices for states in the U.S. with over one million African Americans, current data indicated a reversal of economic progress for African Americans. More importantly, the comparative data revealed that African American households had the highest poverty rate (22.7 percent) of all groups in 2001.

Armstrong Williams, "School Vouchers," and the Black Commentator's "Shoving Vouchers Down DC's Throat," provides an interesting and typical debate on the often divisive issue of school vouchers. The debaters offer a mixture of ideology and negative characterizations of the other side. One can measure the intensity of the support and opposition for a remedy for the mis-education of African American children.

As visible as the discussion of vouchers is in the African American community so is the issue of Affirmative Action. The only African American U.S. Supreme Court justices, Thurgood Marshall and Clarence Thomas, have very different views on Affirmative Action and its possible impact on the status of African Americans. While Marshall accepted affirmative action as one method of ameliorating the effects of racism and racial discrimination, Thomas sees affirmative action as unnecessary and a potential threat to the advancement of African Americans. Both positions can be read in their opinion in two leading affirmative action cases—Thurgood Marshall's opinion in University *of California-Davis v. Allan Bakke* and *Clarence Thomas in Grutter v. Bollinger.*

PART ONE

Political Beliefs in the American Political System

The American political system has a rich tradition of eclectic political thought. In this section we introduce students of American government to a variety of political thinkers and issues that should broaden their appreciation of different perspective of the American political experience. We provide a useful approach to organize American political thought in the article by Kenneth Dolbeare, "American Political Thought—Two Approaches." One approach is the classical approach involving the traditional "liberal-conservative spectrum and its grounding in certain basic values." The second focuses on the role of four concepts, dignity, democracy, ideology, and power in the development of American political thought.

Mack Jones in "Racism, Multiculturalism, the Black Conservative Movement and the Post Civil Rights Era" is a critique of the rise of black conservatism and its intersection with multiculturalism. It also examines the impact of black conservatism and multiculturalism on American political thought.

Whiteness studies is a young field of study in American political thought. Chris Deis in "Thinking about Whiteness and American Politics," explores the concept of whiteness and how it impacts the system of racism, racial inequality, and shapes the racial, social, and political boundaries of white Americans. He asks how whiteness studies informs our views of American democracy.

Old questions for political scientists and their students have evolved around issues of class, power, capitalism and democracy. William Domhoff defines social class and power and their usage in American politics in "Class and Power in America." In a presidential lecture for the American Political Association, Gabriel A. Almond explores the historic relationship between democracy and capitalism. He discusses the arguments of those who report of tensions between democracy and capitalism and he argues that both support and subvert a positive relationship between capitalism and democracy.

Another perspective on the nature of capitalism can be seen in the article by Robert Went, "Globalization in the Perspective of Imperialism." Went seeks to update the concept of imperialism in light of the rush to globalization.

Rickey Hill also seeks to update his analysis of political thought in the African American community. He discusses the role of political thought in shaping politics in the African American community. His thoughtful essay is entitled, "The Contemporary Black Predicament: Crisis and Political Obligation."

Finally Charles P. Henry provides a brief history of Pan Africanism and explain how as a social movement Pan Africanism could be modernized through the debates on reparations and congressional policies toward Africa.

American Political Thought— Two Approaches

Kenneth Dolbeare

The goals of studying American political thought, as suggested in the Preface, include understanding the origins and evolution of today's dominant values and beliefs, what these mean for the way Americans address problems of the present and future, and what any serious challengers may offer in the way of alternatives. We can do this more analytically and efficiently if we first clarify what we are looking for and why—a task that requires some reflection on the nature of political thinking generally. In this essay, I set forth two approaches, each of which (when filled out with careful definitions) I consider capable of providing the analytic depth and perspective that will reveal the essence of evolving American political thought. One is the classical approach, involving the traditional liberal-conservative spectrum and its groundings in certain basic values. The other is a deliberate effort to avoid the confusions and possible datedness of that spectrum by focusing instead on four concepts or themes that have characterized American political thinking and practice from the origins to the present: dignity, democracy, ideology, and power.

The Classical Approach

The classical approach assumes that certain basic assumptions give rise to more or less coherent systems of political values and beliefs, and identifies distinctive mixes of such values and beliefs with long-established labels. Assumptions about *the nature of human beings* and about *the purposes of social life* are fundamentally building blocks of political thinking. If people are assumed to be naturally good, intelligent, reasonable, and mutually concerned with each other's well-being and development, then a community of equals with a minimum of coercion will seem possible and desirable. *Anarchists* think it is. If people are assumed to be self-interested and

---

From *American Political Thought* by Kenneth M. Dolbeare. Copyright © 1998 by Chatham Publishers. Reprinted by permission.

acquisitive by nature, however, ways will have to be found to harness their rational but competitive striving so that the general good can also be provided for, and thus a balance achieved between private and public interests. *Liberals* think they have found such ways. And if people are assumed to be more self-indulgent and emotional than rational, there must be some means of causing them to be guided by the few people who possess wisdom and talent so that the needs of the society as a whole can be served instead. *Conservatives* advocate such means.

In each case, assumptions about human nature have merged with a related sense of the purposes of social order to form the core of well-known systems of political thought. Some of these assumptions and goals also find expression as *political values*, next among the fundamental building blocks of political thinking. In the case of liberalism—the system of thought that has dominated the American tradition—key values include individualism, natural rights (among which property rights have been paramount), freedom, and equality. Each of these values generates powerful loyalties, and together they may come to be viewed as inevitable or beyond question. Anarchists and conservatives hold sharply contrasting values, but they have found it very difficult to be heard in American history. Most of the arguments have been over what specific definitions to affix to the basic liberal values at various periods. Controversy has kept the definitions somewhat blurred, helping to allow change in at least some of their meanings over time. In some cases there have also been changes in the priorities among these values, notably in the rise of equality to challenge freedom. These types of changes are probably the most characteristic of the evolution of American political thought; certainly there have been no outright rejections of treasured values out of the past.

Armed with such insight, we can formulate some questions to ask of political thinkers in our tradition. Foremost is the nature of the thinker's basic assumptions and underlying values. What does he or she assume about human nature, the good society, the best forms of institutions and policies? Why? How do these premises and goals translate into definitions and priorities among political values and beliefs? Few thinkers describe the roots of their values and beliefs neatly, and some may not even state them clearly. That is where the analyst's job begins. From what thinkers advocate and the reasons they give for doing so, the analyst has to reconstruct the fundamental building blocks of their systems of thought in order to see their implications and compare them on grounds more substantial than mere issue positions. The starting point of the classic approach in the American context can only be liberalism.

Liberalism

The dominant system of thought in American political life has been one that sees the individual as a rational, self-interested person, entitled by nature to certain "rights" such as life, liberty, and property. Governments are created by contracts among such individuals to serve such rights and maintain order, and they are otherwise limited in their powers. Rights, contracts, and limits to government are all concepts that suggest a major role for law in organizing the society. An important unstated assumption is that private striving to fulfill needs provides the "best" means (i.e., least coercive and most related to talent and effort) of distributing economic and other rewards of social life.

This familiar litany of values and beliefs is known as liberalism. It has deep roots in Western thought, but it came together and took hold most powerfully in the American colonies in the eighteenth century in a process soon to be examined in detail. Its social base was initially the rising seventeenth-century middle class of artisans, merchants, financiers, and other small entrepreneurs. In Europe it served to defend their prerogatives and property against potential incursions from the land-based power of upper-class aristocrats and from the claims of the peasantry and proletariat. In the United States, where there was no comparable feudal residue to give rise to either a powerful aristocracy or a deprived peasantry of ex-serfs, the liberalism of the dominant middle-class merchants and financiers reigned virtually unchallenged.

Because there were no effective challenges to liberalism, some scholars have seen controversies in American political thought as taking place within an unrecognizedly narrow range.[1] By sharing so many similar commitments and by neither hearing nor perceiving other possibilities, Americans exaggerated differences in positions that were, on any absolute scale of potential viewpoints, not very far removed from each other. Other nonliberal arguments, such as classical conservatism on the right or anarchism or socialism on the left,[2] were either ignored or repressed as un-American.

The principal tension within the liberal tradition has been conflict over the assigning of priorities among the natural rights of individuals. To most liberals, property rights have been paramount, with resulting emphasis on law, contracts, procedural regularity, and stability. To some, human rights and equality in first political and then social and economic dimensions have been uppermost, with commensurately greater concern for participation, justice, and change. All liberals, of course, believe that property rights are important, but some are willing, in most circumstances, to reduce the priority assigned to property in favor of human rights. Much of the conflict in American political history has been over just this issue, and it has been bitter more often than not. That this conflict is real in the eyes of the contestants, however, should not obscure the fact that there is still a large body of agreement between them on other fundamental questions. We should admit the possibility that the American spectrum is relatively narrow, lacking a real conservative or radical alternative to the centrist liberal tradition. What looks to us like a wide range of political viewpoints in the United States may simply be our own failure to perceive the real range of possible alternatives.

It may be argued that the differences between American liberals who emphasize human rights and those who emphasize property rights are so great that it is not meaningful to characterize both groups as liberals. It seems to me that this is a question of what frame of reference we want to employ. If we are content to consider only what Americans have actually argued about in their politics, in a kind of culture-bound acceptance of self-imposed limitations, then the definition is indeed only a meaningless preliminary to decisive specifics. But if we wish to consider the entire range of possibilities and to see the implications for past and future of those very self-limitations, we must work with definitions that both provide such comparative dimensions and permit local subcategorization for what people have actually said in this context. I demonstrate the importance of defining liberalism this way and the extent to which liberalism has predominated in the United States by contrasting liberalism with a definition of conservatism drawn from its modern source, Edmund Burke, and somewhat modified to fit with Clinton Rossiter's *Conservatism in America*.[3]

Conservatism

Conservatism begins from quite a different focus, which leads to a different view of the relationship between people and their governments. Conservatism posits that society comes first—that it has an existence apart from the individuals who make it up. This independent entity is a continuing organism with a life of its own, progressing through centuries. The individuals who happen to make up its population at any given time are but transients, changing from day to day as deaths and births take place. People have no claims prior to those of society and no rights except those society gives them in furthering its own needs. Because people are emotional and frequently irrational, they need order; liberty is the product of an ordered society in which people are able to do what is right and desirable for them to do.

Conservatism does not deny the inevitability of change, but neither does it believe that change has merits for its own sake; the kind of change that is appropriate is what the society is ready for and what fits the established traditions of the society. If one imagines a long line moving from the past through the present and into the future, change that fits on the line is the appropriate kind: this same analogy may be used to connect generations—a partnership of the living with the dead and the unborn—and to suggest the relative consideration given to the needs of individuals and society. Government in this design cannot be either the creature or the servant of the people who happen to make up the society at any given moment, for it is an agent of the society.

Further, because of the inherent inequalities in distribution of talents, some people are better qualified than others to decide what government policies should be; therefore, either the franchise should be limited or other means should be devised to ensure that people of talent predominate. Both political equality and majority rule are therefore considered illusory or undesirable. Only those with the requisite talent decide what government must do on behalf of the society, and individuals' lives are directed accordingly. Because one of the purposes for which the society exists is the betterment of the culture and the attainments of the society, individuals frequently derive very significant benefits and satisfactions from their lives within such a system; conservatives would argue that this is the only way, given the realities of human characteristics, that the amenities of life can ever be realized.

Does it not now appear that liberalism is a distinctive set of beliefs? And that we have indeed had few conservatives in the American political tradition? We do gain perspective on our past and present from comparison with a different pattern of beliefs. To view the main body of American thinkers as representing a wide range of opposing political positions is to miss the whole remaining spectrum of what might have been and, at least theoretically, could still be. And it is good to bear in mind that conservatism is only a moderately differing variant of liberalism in Western political ideas.

We *have* had a few conservatives in the United States, although they are sometimes not recognized as such. One reason for this is that, at any given moment, their views on particular issues (for example, how to reform Congress to make it perform more effectively as a representative institution) may coincide with those of liberals. Another reason may be that dominant liberalism has simply ignored or failed to understand conservatives' arguments. Or it may be that, in their efforts to conserve the hallowed traditions of the society, they look back and find nothing to conserve but elements of liberalism. Not only is this frustrating for conservative thinkers, but it confuses observers as well. Nevertheless, we shall try to point up those rare thinkers and positions throughout American political history who show signs of being conservative in character, if only to mark the boundaries and occasions where liberalism has not been uniformly endorsed.

Radicalism

On the opposite side of liberalism from conservatism runs a small but frequently freshening stream of radicalism. Its impact has often exceeded its visible successes, for, while it has achieved real redistributive and participatory victories for numbers of people, it has done so in return for supporting liberalism. The American radical tradition can be understood only by recognizing that liberalism was not initially democratic and that what we know today as "democracy" is a special version powerfully affected by liberalism. As we see in several of the selections that follow, claims for wider participation and rights (for example, for women, blacks, immigrants, labor, the poor, and Indians) have continued from the earliest days of our history to the present. In almost every case, economic redistribution from the "haves" to the "have nots" has also been part of the challenge mounted in the name of democracy against the established economic, social, and political order of things. As capitalist industrialization began to rigidify social classes and exacerbate inequalities, various protests demanding greater equality arose. Gradually, the franchise was expanded, some redistributions were accomplished, and a sometimes precarious social unity maintained. In the process, liberalism came to wear the label of democracy in many people's minds; our system was democratic, and whatever the United States did defined *democratic*. But for some, true democracy still required greater equality (in social and economic matters, for example), fuller and more meaningful participation in public affairs, and other qualities in social and personal relationships. It is these people who, generation after generation, have raised the radical banner.[4]

Radicalism means going to the roots of problems in search of causes and cures, and here it has been used in connection with egalitarianism—as a counterbalance on the left to conservatism on the right. Two criteria mark the ideas and thinkers who are *radical* in this sense. First, they emphasize the good qualities in human nature and the potential inherent in all people. Solely by the fact of their existence, people are entitled to a variety of human rights and opportunities. This will enable them to transcend selfish acquisitiveness and develop both a fraternal sense of community and satisfying interpersonal relations. Second, they believe that drastic reconstruction of the economy and society is necessary in order to achieve these goals. Government should be employed to create the conditions for realizing these goals and then reduced to minimal functions consistent therewith.

Dominant thinkers and other pragmatic and property-conscious Americans have impatiently rejected (or, even more devastatingly, ignored) such apparently "unrealistic" arguments. But the essence of the claim for greater equality, participation, and respect continues to rise in yet another form, decade after decade, and normally as a version of democracy. It has a continuing effect on liberalism, particularly when the conflict with the inequality fostered by liberalism's commitments to liberty and property rights becomes clear, as it recurrently does.

Changes in Liberalism

One of the consequences of this tension has been the way liberalism has evolved over time. Imagine liberalism as having two parts: a central core of unchanging basic values and purposes and a penumbra of time-specific issue positions and tactically flexible orientations toward the use of government. In the central core of unchanging values are the key elements already described, such as individualism, limited government, natural rights (emphasizing property rights), and legalism. Also in this central core is the assumption that the individual is more important than government and that government exists for the purpose of permitting that individual to serve best his or her own needs and attain personal fulfillment. These values and commitments have remained essentially constant from the earliest days of the Republic to the present.

But there has been change in the surrounding issue positions and orientations toward the use of government. Indeed, these changes, made unconsciously (at least in some cases) in response to perceived changes in social, economic, and political conditions, have amounted to an almost complete reversal of the view of some liberals toward the propriety of the use of government. Most of the early liberals believed that the chief threat to individuals' capacities to develop themselves to the utmost lay in government action, and so they bound government with prohibitions on the one hand and practiced laissez-faire as a basic policy on the other. This position endured for at least the first hundred years, with some exceptions made by those who found government a convenient device for advancing their own interests. These people were able to rationalize that their use of government was necessitated by particular circumstances without raising questions about the basic general policy of laissez-faire.

Toward the end of the nineteenth century, however, two related developments led some liberals to question the desirability of following a nearly absolute policy of laissez-faire. One development was the rise of corporate and personal economic power to the point where it became clear to many that government was no longer the chief threat to individual attainment. The presence of accumulations of "private" power and the leverage that this power gave to some to direct and affect the lives of others led some liberals to feel that government could be used to redress the balance and restore for the individual some semblance of equal opportunity. Granger laws, rate regulations, and trust-busting are examples of such uses of government, and they are entirely consistent with the core values of seeking to promote the individual's capacity to serve his or her own ends and reach personal fulfillment.

The second development was the awakening of concern for human rights and social welfare as opposed to an exclusive emphasis on property rights. All liberals acknowledged the importance of property and economic rights—the rights of individuals to maximize the profit attainable from use of their property and the propriety of economic motivations generally. Classic economic liberalism of the Adam Smith brand had legitimated individual profit-seeking as the best way to advance the economy and ultimately to raise the standard of living for all. In addition, property had always been seen as the basis of individual political independence. The person who owned land would be dependent on no one else's favor and would be able to vote freely in elections; sufficient property would give individuals a stake in the society and lead them away from rash acts toward moderate and stable political behavior.

But toward the end of the nineteenth century the emphasis by some liberals on individual profiteering and self-aggrandizement, rationalized by the application of Darwinian natural selection analogies, produced a reaction from others not so exclusively devoted to property and economic rights. For one thing, the conditions of existence for many people were so marginal that action seemed necessary merely to preserve their existence. The byproducts of industrialization, urbanization, and monopoly control included impoverishment, unemployment, and severe practical limitations on economic opportunities. In addition the pre-Civil War agitation over women's rights and the plight of blacks had contributed to a focus by some on the conditions of the less successful individuals within the society. For these reasons a split developed between the liberals who saw natural rights in terms of civil rights and human rights or social welfare and those who continued with a more exclusively property-rights view.

The first group began to see government as a useful tool for freeing individuals from the external forces that limited them from attaining their ends, and it has used government more and more for this purpose in the twentieth century. The second group, which has continued to place its priorities on economic rights—frequently due to the conviction that this remains the best way to advance the standard of living for all in the long run, not just to advance personal self-interest—have steadily resisted government "interference." Aside from the acknowledged difference in relative priority of economic and human rights, however, all remain steadfast in holding the core values of individualism, limited government, and so forth. Issue positions have shifted among the majority of liberals to produce an almost complete reversal in their view of the propriety of the use of government, but there has been little or no change in the core values or in the basic commitments to the individual and to the attempt to make self-development possible. This is indicative of the flexibility inherent in liberal thought, on the one hand, and part of the explanation of the present confusion in the use of the terms *liberal* and *conservative*, on the other.

Liberal is often used to refer to the first group, those who accept the use of government to help people, and *conservative* to the second group, those who stress economic rights and noninterference by government. But both are liberal in their core values, and from outside the American context, their differences seem minor. For the sake of clarity, I propose to use the term "welfare state liberal" for the first, and "classical" or "1890s liberal" for the second, reserving the term "conservative" for the approach contrasted with liberalism above. Much conflict over political ideas and public policy among Americans occurs between the welfare state liberals and the classical liberals, but our analysis cannot be allowed to be that narrow; there are many other possibilities, and a wider perspective is essential.

This realization raises the question whether the straight-line spectrum, in which the two brands of liberalism are clustered at the middle and only a few thinkers scattered out to the left and right, is still a useful analytic tool. I think it has utility, if only because it is so traditional a means of talking about political ideas. But I acknowledge that the changing nature of some American ideas is also making that spectrum less appropriate and/or comprehensive every day. That is why I next tentatively offer an alternative to the classical approach.

The Four Themes Approach

The problems with the classical approach are inherent in its strengths—long usage and the distinctive but changing American context have muddied definitions and blurred analytical lines. Moreover, the complexity of recent thought and the new and often internal dimensions of concern that have surfaced (gender, place, participation, ecology, spirituality) appear to make the straight-line spectrum of the past seem out of date. One way of incorporating the internal and external aspects of these new dimensions and simultaneously simplifying the analytical task is by focusing on four concepts, or themes, that have been present throughout the evolution of American political thought. These are not exclusive—thinkers do not fit easily into one focus on another. Instead, the four themes imply continuing areas of interest and aspiration and serve to organize our understanding of what is happening in the evolution of American ideas over time. While this approach may be less demanding than the classical, it appears to be more flexible and accepting of new ways of grappling with the eternal questions. Some further explanation of each concept/theme now follows, and the reader is encouraged to choose the approach that seems most useful—or to employ both if preferred.

Dignity

The related notion of "equality" is more familiar, with its multiple and expanding definitions (legal equality, equality of opportunity, equality of condition) and tension with the notion of "freedom." The concept of dignity includes but is not limited to equality: it encompasses the same sense of aspiration and struggle against obstacles, often involving race, gender, class, or national origin. But it is more fluid, more internal, in the sense of being determined not by external measures but by the subjective feelings of the aspirants. Legal forms of equality and objective measures are much less important than how the aspirant group or individuals *feel* about their status—perhaps a more subtle way of understanding the roots of ideas and motivation in politics. We see many examples of the struggle for dignity in the selections that follow.

Democracy

Too often in American experience, "democracy" has been defined by the culture, structure, and practice of American politics—whatever *is* in the United States is automatically to be understood as democratic. This has meant that we can think and talk about only a strictly limited form of democracy, one in which liberal values (individual rights, particularly property), and by now the great inequalities produced by modern capitalism, come first and shape what "democracy" can become. Majoritarianism is in this view illegitimate—"the tyranny of the majority."

Here, we seek to free democracy of all such limits and see an ongoing struggle on the part of many diverse groups of people to achieve a full version of democracy. Expertise, whether scientific or legal, or distant bureaucracy, can be as important as property or inequality as barriers to genuine participation and control on the part of ordinary people. The goal of civic engagement, of sharing in the public life of the community and realizing personal development as a citizen, can now be accepted as a motivating factor in politics. So can the notion of legitimacy for the purposeful use of government on behalf of majoritarian goals. In short, the frame of reference for understanding what is going on in politics can be made much wider.

Ideology

The concept of ideology envisions a set of beliefs about how the world does and should work—beliefs that are grounded in underlying political values and affected by day-to-day perceptions of the "reality" of politics. Such beliefs are coherent with beliefs in ostensibly nonpolitical areas such as science, religion, morality, the understanding of "nature," psychological identity as a person, and notions of the good society. Ideology that explains and justifies the status quo can help to make even the disadvantaged members of the society more accepting of their lot, and thereby to stabilize the polity. At times, a new and different ideology can motivate serious challenges to that same status quo.

Therefore, there is always a major effort (sometimes unrecognized) on the part of the reigning social elements to shape and inculcate a dominant ideology that justifies the way things are: the social-class system, the truths of science and religion, what it means to be an American, the proper uses of nature, the pattern of inequality, and so forth. But it is not a simple or easy process. There are always challenges, and a focus on the ongoing struggle is a revealing way to understand what is happening in the evolution of a country's political thinking. For example, we shall see many instances in which notions of science are used to justify particular forms of inequality in American social life.

Power

The final and most visible concept or theme is that of power, by which I mean the powers of institutions of government and the purposes that can or should be served by government. The principle of limited government (or laissez-faire—"leave alone," or "hands off"), for example, is intended to keep government from taking action, particularly in areas relating to the economy. Much of the continuing struggle over the powers of institutions and the purposes of government has to do with the question of whether and how much government should be doing with respect to the economy. Should slavery be allowed or protected by the national government? Should economic distribution be shaped by the government in any way, and if so, what way?

These and many other issues have engaged the political thinkers and activists of our history and resulted in almost continuous revision of the Constitution, that fundamental allocation of powers between the nation and the states and between the institutions of the national government. The subtle and changing interpretations of the Supreme Court are too complex to be addressed in this book, except for the basic statement of the powers of the Court and the nature of the union, which are found in Part II. But the formal amendments to the Constitution tell a great deal about how the American consensus has evolved, both in terms of the powers added to the national government and those denied it.

In every time period, therefore, we shall take note of such formal changes in the scope and character of government powers.

Conclusion

There is no magic to be found in these four concepts or themes. They do not lead in any single direction, nor do they offer a coherent interpretation of American political thought. But they do provide a focus on four of the most important ongoing lines of development of American political thought, and they do give a sense of what has been happening—what the struggles have been about, and who has won and lost. This is the essence of what we address in this book, and in American political thought: struggle, winners and losers, noninevitability, and never-ending choices about what is to be done.

Notes

1. Louis Hartz, *The Liberal Tradition in America* (New York: Harcourt, Brace and World, 1955).
2. The image of the familiar straight-line political spectrum here can be misleading. What is being measured from left to right is whatever is valued in the society—property, participation, and so on—with distribution wider and more equal on the left and progressively narrower, more limited, and unequal on the right. Simultaneously, conceptions of human nature and the resulting need for order are being arrayed: to the left, humankind is considered cooperative and good, with a minimum of governmentally secured order necessary; to the right, irrationality and emotionalism demand stringent order.

3. Clinton Rossiter, *Conservatism in America* (New York: Random House, 1955, 1962).
4. To be sure, some radicals have not been democrats using any definition of the term. Believing that circumstances required forcing others to be free, they have defended various coercive means. But most American radicals have proceeded from a version of what democracy could and should mean.

Racism, Multiculturalism, the Black Conservative Movement and the Post-Civil Rights Era

Mack H. Jones

. . . . most Americans are simply tired and impatient over our most sinister social problem, the problem, the Negro. They do not want to solve it, they do not want to understand it they want to simply be done with it and hear the last of it.

W. E. B. DuBois, 1906

The elimination of all legal and political barriers to full participation of African Americans in the socio-cultural, political, and economic systems of the country was the primary objective of the modern civil rights movement. Following passage of the Civil Rights Act of 1964, the Voting Rights Act of 1965, and the Fair Housing Act of 1968 legal access had been assured. By 1980, the legal gains along with continued agitation and struggle had yielded noticeable changes in the socio-economic and political conditions of Blacks. They were elected and appointed to political offices in unprecedented numbers, occupied positions in the labor force heretofore closed to them, and Black students were admitted to institutions of higher education that would not have admitted their parents a few decades earlier. Affirmative action and other race specific remedies were employed to facilitate fuller inclusion of African Americans in the life of the country. At the same time, the gap between Blacks and whites on practically all measures of socioeconomic well-being remained exceedingly large. Black unemployment remained consistently twice that of whites, Black family income stagnated at around two-thirds the white figure, and the Black poverty rate continued to be thrice that of whites. As a result of the continuing gap between black and white well being the quest for equal access was transformed into a struggle for material equality as well.

By the early 1980s, the push for material equality had begun to generate considerable negative feedback. Many argued that the

---

Reprinted by permission of the author.

remaining disparities between the races could not be explained by racial discrimination and as such should not be the subject of additional government intervention. More specifically, others argued that inasmuch as race had been designated a constitutionally impermissible category continued use of race-specific remedies even if they are designed to address nagging inequities was unlawful. The country had entered what Robert Smith has called the Post-civil rights era.[1]

Both multiculturalism and the Black conservative movement evolved concurrently with the post-civil rights era. Multiculturalism presented two faces, one as a continuation and broadening of the civil rights movement, the other as a continuation of the historical tradition of white Americans to deny the centrality of race and racial oppression in American society. For groups such as Native Americans, Latinos and women whose consciousness of their status as oppressed people was quickened by the dynamics of the civil rights movement, the call for diversity and multiculturalism represented continuation of the civil rights struggle. On the other hand, the call for diversity and multiculturalism as a response to the perceived need of the country to insure that societal institutions reflect the racial and ethnic diversity of the culture dovetailed with the historical tendency of white Americans to deny the centrality and reality of racial oppression. By defining the problem as the need to insure ample representation of various ethnic and cultural groups rather than the need to undo the legacy of purposeful discrimination against a historically specific group or groups, the inequitable position of Blacks in American society becomes a problem not grounded in any particular material causes and one for which no one or interest is directly culpable. Moreover support for prescriptions for remedial actions that flow from this characterization of the problem would depend on the benevolent sensibilities of the enlightened white majority rather than from societal obligations to redress just grievances of the oppressed. In this context, support for policies promulgated to promote multiculturalism and diversity is determined by the extent to which individuals' commitment to multiculturalism and diversity overrides their devotion to equal protection of the law. Viewed this way, the multicultural focus supports the conservative argument that no substantial race problem remains, and that race-specific remedies are divisive and must be eliminated. This characterization of multiculturalism legitimizes the conservative response that even though diversity and multiculturalism may be laudable goals, as subject of public policies they violate the sacred principle of equal protection of the law. It is at this intellectual pivot that multiculturalism and the Black Conservative Movement (BCM) join to become a significant issue in American life and culture. Multiculturalism legitimizes the deracial focus of the BCM but paradoxically the BCM undermines multiculturalism as a continuation of the struggles of oppressed communities because in the end, the BCM reinforces the tendency of white Americans to deny the reality of race and oppression and imposes an additional barrier to Black progress.

Racism and Denial: The American Tradition

Why would one say that race and racism have always been important systemic factors in American culture and politics and that white America has always been in a state of denial? What evidence is there to support this contention, and moreover, what is the relevance of this claim for understanding and assessing the importance of the rise of the Black conservative movement in the post-civil rights era? To find evidence to support this observation, an examination of the U.S. Constitution as drafted in 1789 and the views of the founding fathers, particularly Thomas Jefferson, is a good place to start.

Americans are taught that the Constitution was a forward-looking document drafted by enlightened freedom loving men. However, the document sanctioned human slavery, obligated the national government to use its power to insure the return of those who managed to escape slavery, and allowed the slave states to count a portion of their enslaved subjects for purposes of representation. It did so without ever mentioning either Blacks or slavery. Nowhere in the document did the founding fathers ever mention slavery or Black people by name. This was a conscious act of denial. Knowing that they were writing a document for posterity and that slavery and racism were repugnant to the human spirit the founding fathers used language that denied the reality of what they were doing. The Constitution reads like a product of an enlightened color blind society. Even today, the uninitiated can read through the entire document without having a clue regarding what lurked behind the high sounding phrases. The founding fathers were in denial about the reality of race and oppression and successive generations of American have followed their lead.

Though they were careful to conceal their racist views in official documents such as the Constitution and the Declaration of Independence, the founding fathers were much more candid in their unofficial documents and other less public discourse. For example, Thomas Jefferson, generally revered as the most enlightened, cosmopolitan and democratic of the group, expressed in his private correspondence the most extreme racist sentiments, suggesting that African people were devoid of practically all of the virtues that made humans human. In one letter explaining why Blacks could not be incorporated as citizens in the American state, he asserted that Blacks were inherently inferior to whites and that this condition was fixed in nature. He went on to say

> And is this difference of no importance? Is it not the foundation of a greater or less share of beauty in the two races? . . . they secrete less by the kidneys, and more by the glands of the skin, which gives them a very strong and disagreeable odor . . . . They seem to require less sleep. A Black, after hard labor through the day will be induced by the slightest amusements to sit up till midnight, or later, though knowing he must be out with the first dawn of the morning. . . . They are more ardent after their female; but love seems with them to be more an eager desire, than a tender delicate mixture of sentiment and sensation. Their griefs are transient. . . . [I]t appears to me, that in memory they are equal to whites; in reason much inferior, as I think one could scarcely be found capable of tracing and comprehending the investigations of Euclid. . . . Some have been liberally educated. . . . But never yet could I find a black had uttered a thought above the level of plain narration; never see even an elementary trait of painting or sculpture.[2]

Jefferson who gave his daughter twenty-five human beings as a wedding present,[3] in keeping with his desire to make the United States a racially homogenous white country, offered an elaborate plan for ridding the country of Black people. His scheme included separating new born Black infants from their mothers and training them in industrious occupations until they reached a proper age for deportation. The separation of infants from their mothers, Jefferson remarked, would produce some "scruples of humanity, [b]ut this would be straining at a gnat, and swallowing a camel."[4]

The lengthy quotation from Jefferson and related discussion above bears directly on the issue of racism and denial. As Americans, we are rarely taught the reality of the history or race and racial oppression. Instead, we are given every reason to deny it. The rise of Black conservatives as a social movement reinforces the legitimacy of and extends the disposition to deny. As such it is a new force in American politics. It is the first social movement led by highly educated and well positioned Blacks who deny the reality of racial oppression in the United States and blame the continuing disparities in Black and white well-being on either the alleged inappropriate behavior of Blacks themselves or interventionist policies of the national government.

This is not to suggest that conservatism is new among African Americans nor is it to suggest that somehow it is an illegitimate political ideology for Black people to hold because African Americans, like their white compatriots have always vacillated between conservatism and liberalism. Rather it is to suggest that a distinction can and should be made between the historical strand of Black conservatism and the new Black conservative movement. It is also to acknowledge that the rise of the Black conservative movement was orchestrated by a segment of the white American elite that has historically opposed all programs for Black advancement and that it is this alliance between the Black conservative movement and traditional white opponents of the civil rights movement that accounts for the failure of the BCM to command significant support within the Black community and why it is viewed with contempt by many within the Black community. I will attempt to explain why this is so by: (1) putting the conflict and competition between liberalism and conservatism in the proper historical and cultural context; (2) explaining how and why liberalism became remains the dominant ideological position among African Americans; (3) describing how beginning around 1980 certain white forces, traditionally unsympathetic to Black interests, orchestrated the rise of the Black conservative movement; and (4) and commenting on the ideology and public policy recommendations of the new Black conservative movements.

Liberalism and Conservatism and Black Political Activity

Few would challenge the assertion that liberalism is the dominant ideology among African Americans. However, as the new Black conservatives are quick to point out, the Black community is not an ideological monolith. There has always been a conservative strand in Black political thought. For example, in addition to Booker T. Washington, historical figures such as Martin Delany, Bishop Henry Turner, Marcus Garvey, Kelley Miller, George Schylur, and even W. E. B. Dubois all expressed views on important issues that would be classified as something other than liberal. Two of the major Black grassroots organizations of the 20th century, Garvey's UNIA and Elijah Mohamed's Nation of Islam, were decidedly conservative on a range of social issues. Minister Louis Farrakhan whose mass appeal has caused consternation in high places espouses a doctrine that is conservative in many respects. Polling data suggest considerable support among Black rank and file for conservative positions on certain social questions. Hamilton reported, for example, that 76 per cent of Black respondents thought courts were not dealing harshly enough with criminals, 41 percent favored the death penalty, 80 per cent thought homosexuality was wrong, and 89 per cent favored a balanced budget.[5]

In spite of the presence of such conservative sentiments, Black support for liberal organizations and political candidates remains overwhelming. For example, in all seven presidential elections from 1972 to 1996 Blacks supported the candidate perceived to be the more liberal, giving an average of 85 per cent of their votes to the nominee of the Democratic party. Of the forty congressional districts represented by Black officeholders in the 1990s only two were represented by black conservatives and both of them represented heavily white districts. Blacks constituted less than five per cent of the population in Connecticut's fifth district represented by Gary Franks from 1990 to 1996, and the fourth congressional district of Oklahoma, represented by J. C. Watts, a leader of the Black conservative movement, had a Black population of approximately six percent. Several Black conservatives challenged incumbent liberal Black congresspersons in the 1998 elections and were defeated soundly. In 2000, two Black conservatives congressional candidates, one in Alabama and the other in Georgia, defeated liberal incumbents.

Black support for liberal candidates for public office is matched by their support for liberal programmatic options, i.e., government intervention, on matters central to the struggle for racial equality. Kinder and Sanders in their sophisticated longitudinal study of public opinion data reported that in each of three domains of race policy, equal opportunity, federal assistance, and affirmative action, "most Blacks pile up on the left" and most whites on the right. "More precisely, the three left-most categories of opinion collect 63 percent of blacks and just 9 percent of whites; meanwhile, the three right-most categories collect 36 percent of whites and just 2 percent of blacks."[6] Black public opinion strongly supports government intervention to address racial inequities while whites firmly oppose them. This the authors refer to as the great racial divide. The Black conservative movement identifies with the position of the white majority in this dichotomy.

So how and why did this great divide come to be? What accounts for the overwhelming identification of African Americans with the liberal ideology? In attempting to forge an answer, we should begin by understanding that both liberalism and conservatism as manifested in American politics are sub-varieties of the Liberal Philosophy that arose in Europe during the seventeenth and eighteenth centuries in response to the strictures of the absolutist feudal and mercantile states. The Liberal Philosophy ushered in the enlightenment and provided justification for the development and consolidation of the modern liberal capitalist state. With its emphasis on the rights of property holders, the sanctity of the individual, the Liberal Philosophy promised to transform the old order into a just and more egalitarian one. In many ways, because of fortuitous historical circumstances, the United States was the ultimate laboratory for the liberal experiment.

By the turn of the twentieth century, the new order promised by the Liberal Philosophy had been firmly entrenched in the United States, but the promise of egalitarian development was far from reality. Moreover, by the 1930s in the United States and other maturing capitalist states the Great Depression signaled that the historical agencies of transformation prescribed by the Liberal Philosophy which had successfully ushered in the new industrial societies were incapable of obviating the new problems that surfaced as the new order began to mature. The problems included, among other things, unregulated, rapacious predatory business practices, endemic unemployment, an unprotected work force, abuse of child labor, substandard housing and health care, and inadequate stultifying as opposed to liberating educational systems. Consequently, new agencies of transformation had to be grafted on existing ones to address the emerging problems of the new order. For the most part, these new agencies of transformation involved some form of government intervention and as the problems of mature capitalism proved to be more and more intractable, interventionist activities by the government proliferated. Collectively they became known as the welfare state.

In due course, the question of the appropriate role of government in addressing social problems became a primary cleavage in American politics and the major point of contention in Liberal Philosophy. Those who assigned primacy to some form of government intervention to ameliorate social problems and the involuntary transfer of resources to those in need became known as liberals, while those opposing such intervention or supporting them only as temporary correctives adjuncts to market forces were characterized as conservatives. Both, however, are firmly within the grand tradition of the Liberal Philosophy and both are committed to maintaining the liberal capitalist state. They differ on the most auspicious means for doing so.

More precisely, in the United States the major points of contention are those post-Great Depression programs which collectively and often pejoratively are referred to as the welfare state. Conservatives argue that such programs are either too expensive, counter productive, or both while liberal adherents suggest that they are necessary to moderate the inherent abrasive dimensions of contemporary capitalism and that they are insurance against mass unrest.

Understood in this fashion, one's position along the liberal-conservative continuum of the Liberal Philosophy is not necessarily a predictor of one's position on the question of the optimum means for ending racial inequalities in the United States; however at least two factors make it appear to be so. The first is the role played by the national government from 1954 to 1980 in reducing racial discrimination. The second is the fact that the systemic debilities which account for much of the expansion of the welfare state, i.e., unemployment, inadequate health care, dependent children, substandard education, etc., are more pronounced among African Americans than among whites, and consequently ameliorative government intervention to address the resulting social problems is often perceived simply as programs designed to assist African Americans, even though non-Blacks may constitute a preponderant majority of the beneficiaries of such programs.

We know, however, that even though the issue of government intervention is the dominant cleavage in American political thought and politics, as political philosophies both liberalism and conservatism deal with much more than government intervention. They each contain a variety of beliefs purporting to explain certain economic, social, cultural, and political dimensions of existence. Moreover, political philosophies are a critical element in the world view that serves as a lens through which one views reality. Individual self-identification as a conservative or liberal, may be based on agreement with any one or any combination of beliefs associated with the liberal or conservative creed. Thus one may identify with conservatism because of that faction's monetary policy while the allegiance of others to the conservative cause may be based on their anti-abortion sentiments. On the other side, the self-identification as a liberal may be based on the perception of an aggressive civil rights policy while agreement with the policy of progressive taxation may be the primary motivating factor for another adherent.

In fact, one may identify strongly with a particular creed, be it liberalism or conservatism, while subscribing to important beliefs associated with the opposite camp, and the ideologically undifferentiated character of American political parties reinforces the probability of such developments. American political parties have vested interest in corralling the loyalty of all potential supporters and accordingly they package their appeals to the broadest public possible even if it means linking logically incompatible ideals and groups. Over time the sum and synthesis of the perception of these appeals come to be accepted as the creed of the ideological faction in question. Individuals are likely to profess loyalty to the formation or party that is identified with the belief or beliefs at the top of their personal ideological hierarchy. For example, the recent realignment of southern whites from the Democratic to the Republican party dramatizes this point. Before passage of the 1965 Voting Rights Act opened electoral politics to southern Blacks, southern whites remained clustered in the Democratic party to which they had retreated following the Civil War. Maintaining white dominance was the paramount element in their ideological hierarchy and the Democratic party for them was the party of white supremacy. When Black political participation accelerated following aggressive implementation of the Voting Rights Act during the 1970s and 1980s and the Democratic party became identified to a certain extent with Black interests, or at least it was perceived to be so, southern whites following the not too subtle entreaties of the southern strategy of the Republican Party leaders switched their allegiance to the latter.

This explains, I think, how in the latter decades of the twentieth century the maintenancc of Black subordination became for many synonymous with conservatism and how liberalism became associated with the cause of racial justice and equal opportunity, and it also explains how liberalism came to be perceived as the consensus political philosophy of African Americans. Let me elaborate.

Throughout the history of the Black presence in the United States, the central concern in Black political thought has been how to end Black subordination and achieve socio-economic parity with white Americans. Political support has been given or withheld from political formations based almost exclusively on the extent to which their promises and actions were perceived as advancing or compromising Black liberation. As an economically weak numerical minority, Blacks have depended on government intervention to augment their power in the political arena. From 1865 to the 1930s, the Republican party enjoyed Black support for that reason. Since the Great Depression, the presidential wing of the national Democratic party has appealed to a diverse set of interests who support government intervention for a variety of reasons. The seemingly almost unanimous loyalty of Blacks to this faction was not necessarily a function of support for all of the constituent elements of what came to be accepted as the liberal agenda. Rather it was a function of the fact that government intervention was seen by Blacks as the crucial factor in the struggle to end racial oppression and economic dominance and the presidential wing of the national Democratic party was seen as more forthcoming on that issue. Black loyalty to that faction to a great extent was the result of the primacy placed on a single item of the liberal agenda, the use of state power to combat political and economic inequities. The Kinder and Sanders study alluded to above makes this abundantly clear. African Americans are firmly committed to the idea that government intervention is essential for racial progress. That commitment, however, runs counter to a paramount element of the conservative creed, the need to minimize progressive government intervention in the economic and social life of the country. Thus the new Black conservative movement with its disdain for government intervention evolved as a direct challenge to the core belief of a preponderant majority of African Americans, and as we shall demonstrate its rise was aided and abetted by forces thought to be hostile to Black interests.

The Rise of the Black Conservative Movement

Although as noted earlier, the rise of conservative Black thinkers in the 1970s and 1980s was not a novel development. Some of its better known advocates such as Walter Williams and Thomas Sowell had published their ideas several years earlier. As Thomas Sowell told a national television audience in 1981, he ". . . had been saying what I am saying for 20 years."[7] However, what warrants discussion is the sudden prominence of Black conservative thinkers and the rise of the BCM as a social force that has had an impact on public discourse that may be considerably greater than its size would suggest. The explanation of their sudden prominence lies at least partially in the widely known if seldom articulated law of American race relations that says that the prominence of Black thinkers is directly proportionate to the power and prestige of their white patrons and in the fact that for the first time in almost half a century the most conservative wing of the national Republican party controlled the White House for a sustained period of time. The prestige of Black thinkers, irrespective of ideology, is always enhanced by having their white benefactors in power.

As for the rise of Black conservatism as an important social movement, there is ample documentation to suggest that it was facilitated by a constellation of white conservative think-tanks, foundations, and publishing outlets that wanted to create an alternative Black leadership class that could serve as a counter weight to the existing liberal oriented traditional Black leaders. Initial efforts to create such an alternative black leadership were undertaken by advisors to President Ronald Reagan in 1980.

The Black conservatives' first national media event of the 1980s, the Fairmont Conference on Black Alternatives held in San Francisco one month after the election of Ronald Reagan was sponsored by the Institute of Contemporary Studies (ICS). Founded in 1972 by Edwin Meese, III, and a group of advisors to then California Governor Ronald Reagan, ICS specializes in book length conservative public policy studies.[8] The Fairmont conference was a seminal development in the BCM. The alliance between Black conservatives and their white patrons was cemented at the San Francisco meeting and several of the participants including Clarence Thomas went on to become major figures in the BCM.

Meese, who followed Reagan to the White House as a principal advisor and cabinet member, made an avuncular if not patronizing address at the Fairmont conference telling the Black conservatives that unlike traditional civil rights leaders who had met with president-elect Reagan a few weeks earlier that the civil rights leaders ". . . were talking about the last ten years and the ideas of the last ten years. You are talking about the ideas of the next ten years or beyond."[9] Later Clarence Thomas cited the Fairmont conference as a watershed development in which Black conservatives ". . . found a home, found each other.[10]

Conservative participants in the Fairmont conference formed the New Coalition for Economic and Social Change and in September 1982 hosted a second national conference entitled "Rethinking the Black Agenda." This conference was co-sponsored by the lead institution in the conservative network, the Heritage Foundation. The New Coalition was announced as a permanent forum for ". . . new ideas and diverse views."[11] The statement of purpose for the conference asserted that:

> Needed are fresh ideas and new approaches to the nagging problems of black poverty, poor education, and government

dependency . . . approaches that reject the notion that American blacks need to be cared for.[12]

Discussions at the 1982 conference were influenced considerably by participants from white conservative institutions. The latter included Edwin Fuelner, Jr., President of the Heritage Foundation who gave greetings and discussed the conference theme, Rethinking the Black Agenda; Charles Murray a research fellow at the Manhattan Institute for Policy Research (another conservative think tank) and author of the controversial *Losing Ground* and later co-author of the even more controversial, *Bell Curve;* and Robert Hawkins, an advisor to President Ronald Reagan and president of the Sequoia Institute, still another institute in the conservative network.

The manipulation of the white conservative network was even more pronounced in the formation of the next national Black conservative organization formed during the early 1980s, The Council for a Black Economic Agenda, that became the action arm of the Black conservative movement. In a colorfully entitled piece, "Inventa a Negro, Inc." Fred Barnes of the *New Republic,* reported that the organization evolved directly out of a plan concocted in the Reagan White House to create a Black leadership class which would be more receptive to and supportive of the conservative policies of the Reagan Administration.[13]

According to Barnes, in late 1984 advisers to President Reagan developed and began implementing a program designed to identify credible Blacks who shared Reagan's philosophy and to sell them as an alternatives to traditional Black leadership. The principle strategists were presidential advisor, James Ciconni, and White House aide, Faith Whittlesey. Ciconni advised the president against meeting with the then current civil rights leadership who he said were more interested in personal publicity and enhancing their status within the Democratic party than in new approaches to the Black problem. Instead of meeting with them, the president was advised to seek out other Blacks ". . . with whom there is a chance of reaching common ground."[14]

Barnes reported further that:

Even as Cicconi was putting the strategy on paper, Faith Whittlesey was pursuing it. . . . Her friend Richard Rahn, the chief economist for the U.S. Chamber of Commerce, convinced her that the White House could make headway with blacks by emphasizing its economic program and dealing with the right blacks. "One thing the White House can do is bestow publicity on people," says Rahn. "If you have credible people, they can be alternative leaders."[15]

Subsequently a list of credible Blacks that included businessmen, professors, policy experts, and conservative activist was put together. Following a meeting sponsored by the administration, they joined together to form the Council for a Black Economic Agenda. After developing an agenda ". . . consisting mostly of sensible free-market proposals to stimulate entrepreneurship in the inner city"[16] the group requested and received an invitation to meet with President Reagan. A decision was made at the White House not to include participants from traditional civil rights organizations.

Stamped with the imprimatur of the White House, the Council for a Black Economic Agenda was to become the major organization of BCM. Several of the participants, including Glen Loury and Robert Woodson soon became nationally prominent spokesmen for their cause.

In addition to supporting the rise of Loury and Woodson as Black leaders, the conservative network was especially instrumental in promoting the ideas to conservative Black intellectuals, economists Thomas Sowell and Walter Williams. Both subsequently spent time at the Hoover Institution, one of the country's older conservative think tanks. The International Center for Economic Policy Studies (ICEPS), a conservative New York based foundation, sponsored Sowell's book, *Minorities and Markets* and organized a lecture tour designed to coincide with its publication. The Manhattan Report, ICEPS periodical, published a special edition which carried the text of some of Sowell's lectures and a discussion of his appearance on the TV talk show, Meet the Press, promoting the book. ICEPS markets the "Sowell Library", a collection of five of Sowell's works. The Hoover Institution Press, another link in the conservative chain, published *Pink and Brown People and other Controversial Essays* which it advertised as a ". . . collection of light essays demonstrating Sowell's deft iconoclastic wit on subjects such as Bakke and the Backlash, Government by Snobs, and Salt II and Munich."[17]

Walter Williams' major work the **State Against Blacks** was sponsored by the Manhattan Institute for Policy Research, a companion structure of ICEPS. The Institute also produced a 30-minute documentary for public television and cable on Williams' views and released it to coincide with publication of the *State Against Blacks*.

Thus, as the foregoing conveys, the white conservative network was instrumental in the launching of the BCM in the early 1980s. Since that time the movement has continued to grow. Faryna, Stetson and Conti's 1997 work lists nine national Black conservative organizations and seven major periodicals as part of the movement. Among the most significant of the new Black conservative organizations is The National Leadership Network of Conservative African Americans, Project 21, founded in 1992, under the aegis of the National Center for Public Policy Research (NCPPR). The latter is a well-funded research and communications organizations created in 1982 initially to provide support for Reagan administration foreign policy initiatives. When the cold war ended, the group turned its attention to a domestic agenda that included economic liberty, the environment, tax reduction, legal reform, campaign finance reform, health care, entitlement reform, cultural issues, the promotion of sound science and economics in regulatory decision-making, *and supporting a new generation of African-American leadership.*[18]

Project 21 was a direct outgrowth of the dismay of the NCPPR with media coverage of the urban unrest following the acquittal of the white policemen who had been videotaped beating the unarmed motorist, Rodney King, in 1992. According to the Center's literature, the media provided extended coverage ". . . to the reaction of liberal civil rights leaders to the events surrounding the Rodney King controversy but made little mention of those in the African-American community who spoke out in favor of law and order and individual responsibility—and against the rioting." The NCPPR decided to convene a meeting of conservative and moderate African-Americans activists ". . . to determine whether it was feasible to construct a program to bring conservative and moderate voices in the black community to the attention of the media. The answer was yes, and Project 21 was born."[19]

Since its inception in 1993, Project 21 has become a major institution for promoting Black conservative views particularly in and around Washington, D. C. According to its literature:

> Project 21 participants have been interviewed by hundreds of news papers, talk shows and television programs throughout the country. Participants have been fea-

tured on such programs as *CNN & Company, CNN Morning News, The Mclaughlin Group, C-SPAN's Saturday Morning Journal, Larry King, Rush Limbaugh, The Michael Reagan Show, BET's Our Voices,* and *America's Black Forum,* as well as in the *New York Times, The Wall Street Journal, The Washington Post, The Washington Times, The Detroit News, USA Today, The Cleveland Plain-Dealer,* and many others.[20]

Project 21 has also released and circulated widely a number of policy papers on problems facing the Black community and a series of annual reports consisting of essays by conservative thinkers. It publishes an annual report on the condition of Black American that can be considered a counter response to the long-standing annual State of Black America published by the National Urban League.

In spite of its extensive media exposure, there is no evidence to suggest that the BCM has developed any significant following among Black rank and file. Nevertheless, as I will argue below, its ideological position has become a significant variable in the discussion of race and public policy.

Ideological Assumptions and Public Policy Choices

An analysis of writing of prominent Black conservatives intellectuals and position papers of the various organizations reveals that they have taken supportive positions on the full range economic, social, political and cultural questions associated with the contemporary conservative creed. These include issues involving fiscal and monetary policies, investments and economic development, relations between church and state, issues of crime and punishment, and other social issues such as adoption, birth control, and abortion. In spite of the breadth of the issues addressed by Black conservatives, it is their position on matters directly related to the race question that commands public attention. To highlight their ideological position on such matters, I will examine the basic argument of three of the new Black conservative thinkers, all economist, who are representative of the group, Walter Williams, Thomas Sowell, and Glen Loury.

Essentially the arguments being advanced by Black conservatives deriding the welfare state and claiming that the major problem confronting Black America is government created dependence are no different than those advanced by their white benefactors and their call for self-help and economic solidarity among Blacks is only a contemporary articulation of one of the oldest and most frequently appearing themes in Black political thought. What is novel is that the new Black conservatives depart from their predecessors and join white conservatives in blaming the Black poor themselves and government intervention for the unhappy plight of African-Americans. This is the central theme of Walter Williams' *The State Against Blacks,* a major contribution to the library of Black conservatives.

Williams argues that "... instead of racial discrimination and bigotry, it is the "rules of the game" that account for many of the handicaps faced by Blacks." These rules, he argues, discriminate against certain people irrespective of race and that Blacks, because of their history, are disproportionately represented "... in the class of people described as outsiders, latecomers, and resourceless".[21]

Williams attempts to build his case by showing that the licensing rules in certain regulated industries, i.e., taxi cabs, plumbers and electricians, railroads, and trucking discriminate against the resourceless. He concludes that the "... reason why blacks are disadvantaged because of government intervention is no mystery. There is a kind of parity in the marketplace that does not exist in the political arena."[22] Thus he argues that when choices are made in the market people have a higher probability of getting some of what they want but "when choices are made through the political arena, they may get none of what they want."[23]

As evidence to support his contention, Williams offers the following explanation which he attributes to Milton Friedman:

> If you go through the ghetto, you will see some nice cars, some nice clothing and some nice foods. In that respect the residents have some of the things that middle class and rich people possess. But you will see no nice public schools. Why not at least some public schools like rich people have? Cars, clothing and food are distributed by the market mechanism. More often than not, if a nice school is found in the ghetto, it is a nonpublic school.[24]

As further evidence of the markets alleged power to thwart discrimination, Williams cites the ability of Blacks during the 1920-1940s to seize use control of housing in the central cities. They did so, he avers, by outbidding whites for the property. He explains

> At first thought, the ability of poor people to outbid nonpoor people may seem as an impossibility, but an example can show how it is possible. Imagine a three story brownstone being rented by a nonpoor white family for $200 per month. Suppose further that the landlord does not like Blacks. But if six Black families suggested that the building be partitioned into six parts to rent for $75 per part the landlord might have to reassess his position. Namely he would have to evaluate the proposal of an income yield of $450, by renting to six Blacks, as opposed to an income yield of $200 by retaining his white tenant. The fact that Blacks have come to occupy neighborhoods formerly occupied by whites demonstrates that the landlord's dilemma was resolved in favor of blacks.[25]

Continuing with the use of housing as an example to demonstrate the claimed efficacy of the market as non-discriminatory force, Williams argues that Blacks were not able to move to suburbia as they did central cities because:

> The power of the state subverted the operations of the market. . . . There are laws that fix minimum lot size, minimum floor space in the house, minimum distance to adjacent houses plus laws that restrict property use to a single family. The combined effect of these laws, independent of de jure or de facto racial discrimination, is to deny poor people the chance to outbid nonpoor people. It is far more difficult for a person to get together the whole house price than one month's rent for a cubbyhole.[26]

I have quoted Williams at length rather than paraphrasing his argument to avoid the charge of misrepresenting his position and creating a strawman that could be easily debunked. Even the moderately attentive reader will see that the strawman is Williams' own creation. Neither of his arguments is compelling. If education were not a public good in a capitalist society characterized by an extreme unequal distribution of income not to mention wealth, would impoverished communities have schools at all? Indeed it would be interesting to know how Williams and his ideological mates explain the rise of public education in the first place.

It is hard to take seriously Williams' argument that the Black presence in central cities as a result of poor Blacks outbidding nonpoor whites demonstrates the tendency of the market to discourage discrimination. Having six poor families pool their resources and pay two and one-half times the old price for what was formerly a single family dwelling and now converted into six cubbyholes hardly seems a goal worthy of pursuing, but that is the analysis that evolves from the ideological assumptions of the conservative creed.

Thomas Sowell shares Williams' ideological thesis that government intervention has been detrimental to Black progress. Responding to the observation that when government failed to take "... responsibilities for upward mobility and equality and justice no one did...." Sowell replied:

> No, I would say just the opposite. The government has been quite active in suppressing the advancement of Blacks in the United States.... The great achievement of the civil rights organization has been getting government off the backs of Blacks, notably in the South with Jim Crow laws, but in other parts of the country with other kinds of laws and other kinds of practices. When these civil rights groups tried to get government to play a positive role, so-called, that's when they've not only failed but when they've had counter-productive results.[27]

The argument that government intervention is a primary cause of the unequal position of Blacks in American life is a central element of the Black conservative ideological creed. It is from this ideological premise that they launch their attack against government programs designed to help blacks and the poor, such as affirmative action, open admissions to colleges and universities, minimum wage and child labor laws, categorical assistance programs, minority set-aside, and the like. As such, their ideas are simply a subset of the broader conservative critique of the post-Great Depression welfare state. Having Black thinkers taking the lead in asserting not only that government intervention is not working but that it is really the cause of much of Black material inequality insulates the conservative movement from the charge that it is indifferent to the conditions of Blacks.

The conservative argument that government intervention has not solved the problems of Black America is obviously true. The continued existence of problems means that all efforts, both public and private sector driven ones, have failed. However it does not logically follow that government intervention is the cause or even a major cause of the problems. Inasmuch as the problems preceded government intervention the law of cause and effect would support the opposite inference. Thus the argument is clearly an ideological one unaccompanied by any effort to demonstrate empirical proof. Indeed, to the contrary, there is ample evidence to suggest that the social, political, and economic advances made by Blacks since the 1930s were greatly facilitated by government intervention and that positive changes in the public sector precipitated changes in the private sector rather than the reverse. Moreover, it was government action in response to militant Black agitation which brought down the racial caste system of the South, the linchpin of the American system of racial oppression.

With more than half of the Black population living in the South, the caste system of the region was the linchpin that held the national racist oppressive order together. It was government intervention in response to societal tensions generated by militant struggle which led to the constellation of court decisions, civil rights statutes, and executive orders that broke the back of the caste system. Reference is being made to the white primary cases of the 1930s and 1940s, the 1954 Brown decision, the Civil

Rights Act of 1964, the Voting Rights Act of 1965, and various executive orders of presidents dealing with equal opportunity.

Contrary to the argument of conservatives, cultural changes did in fact follow in the wake of the legal changes mandated by government intervention. Nowhere was this more pronounced than in the South where as late as the middle 1960s the caste system remained largely undisturbed. Blacks were still treated with derision and contempt in both the private and public sectors and both Blacks and whites were still being socialized to work and function within the prevailing racial order. By the 1980s, Southern culture was undergoing considerable and significant change. For example, the conventional courtesy greetings of Mr. and Mrs. had replaced the patronizing auntie and uncle, Black participation in civic and social institutions had become expected and accepted, Black social activities were routinely covered by local media, and perhaps most important, task segregation in the work force had diminished considerably. These changes were precipitated by state intervention. Cultural changes followed government intervention.

As the southern caste system began to crumble so too did many of the racist practices elsewhere in the country, Blacks, by the 1980s, were found in positions in both private and public sectors heretofore closed to them, positions such as corporate directors, foundation executives, academic administrators, and highly visible elected and appointed government offices.

The confluence of changes in the public and private sectors was not at all surprising because both sectors operate within and are conditioned by the same culture, and as astute students of government and society know, those who make the laws and administer the public sector are the same forces who own and control the dominant structures of the private sector. Racial discrimination and concomitant economic inequities in both sectors resulted from a common source. For example, while racial segregation in public education was mandated by law, task segregation and wage differentials between Black and white workers in the private sector rested squarely on social custom. Thus to separate the public and private sectors analytically and heap blame exclusively on government obscures reality.

A third and perhaps most widely circulated ideological theme of the BCM is the notion advanced by economist Glen Loury in a series of works published during the 1980s and 90s. Although Loury renounced much of his conservative thesis in his latest book, *Anatomy of Racial Inequality* (2002), his initial arguments remain central tenets of the BCM. In his initial formulations, Loury argues that inasmuch as the moral victory of the civil right movement is virtually complete and the disparity between American ideals and racial practices has narrowed dramatically, it is necessary to look beyond racism to explain the compelling problem of the Black poor. The answer, he asserts, is to be found in the values, social norms, and personal attitudes of poor blacks. This, he says, represents the fundamental failure of Black society.

Loury and his ideological companions accuse Black leadership and the middle class from which the leadership comes of not only failing to confront the problem as he has defined it but also with using the presence of the Black poor for political capital to achieve their own self-serving ends through programs such as affirmative action and minority set-asides. To quote Loury:

> The bottom stratum of the black community has compelling problems which can no longer be blamed solely on white racism, and which force us to confront fundamental failures of black society. The social disorganization among poor blacks,

the lagging academic performance of black students, the disturbingly high rate of black-on-black crime, and the alarming increase in early unwed pregnancies among blacks now loom as primary obstacles to black progress. To admit these failures is likely to be personally costly to the black leaders and play into the hands of lingering racist sentiments.[28]

He asserts further:

The growing underclass has become the constant reminder to many Americans of an historic debt owed to the Black community. I suggest that, were it not for this continued presence among us of those worse-off of all Americans, Black's ability to sustain public support for affirmative action minority business set-asides and the like would be vastly reduced. That is the suffering of the poorest Blacks creates a fund of political capital upon which all members of the group can draw in pressing racially based claims.[29]

At first blush Loury's thesis is compelling and seductive. His description of the Black underclass is consistent with other works on the subject. It cannot be denied that well-to-do Blacks benefit disproportionately from affirmative action, minority set-asides and preferential admission to the more highly selective educational institutions. Everyone agrees that greater self-help within the Black community would be a good thing and no one denies that the Black middle class should do more to uplift their poorer kin. All of these ideas are part of an unbroken yet unfulfilled refrain which has always been a central theme in Black political thought, i.e., the need for Black people to depend more on themselves and less on others. Indeed this is the core value of groups such as the Nation of Islam.

If this theme of Black self-help is so commonplace in Black political thought, why does it receive so much attention when articulated by Loury and other Black conservatives? Probably because it is stated as part of a broader ideological argument that portrays Black people themselves as primarily responsible for their unequal position in American society and absolves the broader white community of any culpability in causing it and any responsibility for correcting the problem.

Let me elaborate. Although Loury is careful not to use the word, he describes the culture of the underclass as pathological and argues that it is their culture which prevents members of the group from escaping their depressed condition. However, nowhere does Loury attempt to define or delimit the underclass. Without alerting the reader, he begins to use the terms underclass and poor Blacks interchangeably as when he says that there "... is a keen appreciation among blacks of all social classes that at least one-third of their fellow-blacks belong to the underclass."[30] It is commonly known that one-third of Black families are beneath the poverty threshold but not all poor are considered to belong to the underclass. Certainly there is nothing in the literature to suggest that one-third of Black families are characterized by the description of the underclass given earlier by Loury. However, by explaining the plight of the Black underclass as resulting from their own pathological culture and then equating the Black poor with the underclass, in Loury's analysis, all Black poverty it explained by the alleged pathological culture of the poor.

Further by discussing all of the Black poor as the underclass whose culture explains their plight and then assigning the Black middle class responsibility for rejuvenating the Black poor through ill-defined moral uplift programs and indicting the Black middle class for not meeting this responsibility, Loury and his conservative colleagues reduce the Black problem to a matter internal to the Black community. According to their ideological position, the problem is caused by the aberrant behavior of the Black poor and it continues because the Black middle class fails to meet its responsibility for guiding and uplifting the poor.

Loury goes on to say "... it is virtually beyond dispute that many of the problems of contemporary Afro-American life lie beyond the reach of effective government action, and require for their resolution actions which can be undertaken by the black community itself."[31] He does not tell us why the problems lie beyond effective government action. Is it because the problems are not amenable to collective action? Is it because of the lack of sufficient resources? Or is it because of a lack of will? Or is it a combination of the three? If the problems are not amenable to collective action by government, some discussion of why they are amenable to collective action by the Black middle class would have been helpful. If it is a matter of resources that situate these problems beyond the reach of effective government action, what are the superior resources available to the Black middle class for solving them? We may concede that among the Black middle class there should be a greater reservoir of will to address the problems, but will without the resources and the ability to convert them into effective remedial programs amounts to little.

Public Policy Choices

Starting from the ideological premise that at best government is a necessary evil and the belief that government intervention is a primary cause of the unequal Black predicament, understandably the black conservative movement has a limited public policy agenda.

Project 21, in its 1996 annual report carries a fourteen point Black conservative agenda that, for the most part, reflect the orthodox conservative position. It is more of a list of things that government should cease doing as opposed to a call for positive government action. Specifically it calls for a balanced budget, reduction of the personal income tax and the elimination of capital gains tax for business that invest in "economically depressed areas." The elimination of "public welfare as we know it," minority set-asides and scuttling the minimum wage and the Davis Bacon Act are also on their agenda. Socio-cultural items include a call for the "teaching of history without rewriting it," promoting adoption over abortion, enforcing immigration laws to prevent illegal immigrants from receiving social services and a final item, protecting victims not criminals are also included.

Among the various items on the public policy agenda of the Black conservatives, the three which have been given the most extensive attention because of their relevance to the struggle for racial justice are reducing the role of government in education, ending the minimum wage, and eliminating affirmative action.

Black conservatives argue that the lack of quality education among Blacks account for much of their unequal position. Current federal and state policies, they argue further, only exacerbate the problem. As a solution, they propose a free market educational system characterized by preferential tax laws which would encourage the development of private educational institutions and by a voucher system to assist low income families. Vouchers would be given to children of eligible families to attend schools of their choice. Voucher holders, the argument runs, would gravitate toward schools of demonstrated quality. This, in turn, would force the public schools to either improve their quality or go out of business for a lack of students.

For present purposes we need not speculate on the cost of such a national voucher system nor on the likelihood of government funding for a comprehensive voucher system. We will comment on the probable impact which such a program could have on the Black community. To begin, such a free market education system would of necessity sharpen the already growing class disparities within the Black community. The more prestigious secondary schools with the highest admission standards and tuition costs would be beyond the means for all but a privileged minority of Black families. Inasmuch as there is a direct correlation between the status level of educational institutions and their ability and inclination to exclude outsiders, it is quite likely that the relationship between the value of the voucher and tuition cost would be crafted so as not to change significantly the class homogeneity of the prestigious schools. High status schools might reserve a small number of scholarships for "qualified minorities," i.e., those who score sufficiently well on standardized examinations.

Such a free market education system might have consequences less salutary than those imagined by Black conservatives. One possible outcome would be the siphoning off of the better prepared Black youngsters into a few prestigious secondary schools while the learning environment of the bulk of Black youth remained unchanged. Black graduates of such selective secondary schools would be in line to receive the most prestigious and rewarding positions open to Blacks. As far as they might be concerned, their privileged position would be the result of merit. Conversely and by inference, the subordinate positions occupied by their compatriots who were left behind in inner-city schools would also be explained by racially neutral meritocratic factors. Consequently, both privilege and deprivation would be seen as the result of individual effort. The view that the poor are responsible for their plight would be reinforced.

Furthermore, Black leadership and those who staff and administer the social, economic, cultural, and educational institutions which manage the disadvantaged Black communities would be chosen disproportionately from this privileged group. Having spent their formative years in elite settings in which they were the only Black or one of a few, many might be inclined to accept the interpretation of the Black predicament which prevails in such settings. Consequently they might bring to their work perceptions of the Black poor that differed little from those of their white counterparts. Such Black professionals would serve more as buffers facilitating the continued domination of the poor than as agents for transformation. This would diminish further prospects for Black unity and empowerment.

Elimination of the minimum wage and repealing the Davis-Bacon law seem to be the primary strategy of the BCM for improving the position of Black workers and the Black entrepreneurial class. The Davis-Bacon Act that requires firms engaged in federal construction projects to pay the prevailing wage of the area, according to Black conservatives ". . . was passed in 1931 to keep black workers from competing with whites for construction jobs"[32] and should be repealed. Repeal would not only benefit Black workers ". . . but potential black employers who can't bear the current costs of starting a new business."[33]

Similarly they argue that the minimum wage legislation overprices labor and in the process eliminates many jobs which could be held by Black teenagers and other unskilled persons. Experience in such jobs, it is said, could be parleyed into better paying positions in the future. Consistent with Say's law, this new pool of experienced labor would create its own demand and have a long term salutary effect on the Black labor force.

Critics point out that since 1938 the law has allowed certain categories of firms to pay a sub-minimum wage and that consequently, about 63 per cent of all retail trade and 85 per cent of all service establishments with paid employees can legally pay young people a sub-minimum wage. They also point out that unlike the white labor force, a significant segment of adult Black workers depend on minimum wage jobs.[34]

Opposition to affirmative action programs including preferential hiring, admission to educational institutions, and contract set-asides is perhaps the most controversial element of the Black conservative agenda. Some such as Ward Connerly, who led the successful campaign to outlaw affirmative action in California, argue that race is a constitutionally impermissible category and that its use denies all others equal protection of the law. Some others argue that affirmative action only benefits the Black middle class and as such its social divisiveness outweighs whatever benefits it may bring. Still other Black conservative critics focus on what they believe to be the negative impact that affirmative action has on Black self-esteem. They argue that affirmative action hires or those admitted to universities or other institutions may not command the respect of their white peers who may doubt their qualifications. Finally, some conservatives argue that affirmative action is unnecessary because many blacks have excelled without it and that their performance is sufficient evidence that any individual, no matter their color or previous condition of servitude, can do so if they put their mind to it.

Let us conclude this section with a critical analysis of these arguments against affirmative action. The assertion that race is a constitutionally impermissible category that denies equal protection of the law is consistent with near universal aspirations for a color blind society. However, a convincing case can be made that race is not the pertinent category addressed by affirmative action. The demand is not for special consideration because of the race of the petitioners. Rather the pertinent category is *oppression*. The pertinent question is should special consideration be given to individuals who belong to a group that was singled out for special and unequal treatment by the Constitution of the United States and by statutory law at all levels of American government, national, state, and local, and whose unequal treatment was sanctioned by social custom and reinforced by terror and economic intimidation and who as a result of that government mandated and culturally sanctioned oppression lag behind white Americans on practically every indicator of socioeconomic well-being. *Redress is being sought for the oppression and not because of race.* It so happens that race was used as the basis for oppression but the remedy is being sought for those who fall in the category of the group designated for oppression.

Empirical validity of the claim that affirmative action programs benefit only the Black middle class has not been established. It is true that affirmative action and set-aside programs do not target low-income jobs, but no intervention strategy was necessary to give Blacks access to low-paying dead end jobs. The important question to be answered is who are the people moving into the middle-income positions and university spaces made available through affirmative action.

To the extent that it may be true that set-aside programs benefit the middle class, it should be noted that the United States is a class-based society and in such societies practically all public policies favor those who are better off. Thus the criticism of affirmative action as a class-biased remedy is more a criticism of America as a class-based society than an indictment of affirmative action as an intervention strategy.

Regarding the concern that whites may have negative images of affirmative action beneficiaries and that low Black self-esteem may be the result, it can be said that whites held negative stereotypical attitudes toward Blacks long before affirmative action. For example, even Blacks such as Dr. W. E. B. DuBois, who demonstrated their mettle by earning Ph.D. degrees in the decades immediately following slavery did not receive the respect of their white counterparts. DuBois, a Harvard graduate, found no job in white academia. Furthermore, polling data show that, for whatever it is worth, white attitudes toward Blacks have become more positive since the advent of affirmative action. At any rate, if affirmative action leads to greater representation of Blacks in pivotal American institutions, the lack of white approbation may be a small price for privileged Blacks to pay.

Conclusion

The rise of the Black conservative movement which began in the early 1980s was facilitated by a concerted effort of white benefactors to create an alternative to the traditional liberal Black leadership. That was the theme of the national conference called in the early 1980s and that was the underlying concern of the 1992 call that led to the establishment of the current leading Black conservative group, Project 21.

There is no evidence that the Black conservative movement has generated any significant mass support within the Black community. None of the personalities associated with the Black conservative movement are considered leaders by Black rank and file. The major Black political and economic organizations are still headed by liberal Blacks and the overwhelming preponderance of Black elected officials are identified with liberal causes. However, the Black conservative movement has had a noticeable impact on public discourse on race and public policy. The strategic appointment of Black conservatives by their white patrons to critical positions in what was once considered the civil rights bureaucracy has been a key element in advancing the impact of the BCM. So too has been the extensive coverage given to conservative Black intellectuals by the media.

As appointees of conservative presidents, for example, Clarence Pendelton, Michael Williams, Clarence Thomas, Condoleeza Rice, Gerald Reynolds, and Peter Kirsanov have all had a decided impact on public policy, and Ward Connerly, an appointee of a conservative governor of California has also made his mark.

Pendelton was appointed to the U.S. Civil Rights Commission in 1981 by President Ronald Reagan. A political associate of Edwin Meese, Pendelton was nationally known as an opponent of affirmative action and an acerbic critic of traditional Black leadership. He also served as president of the New Coalition of Economic and Social Change, the Black conservative organization discussed earlier. The Civil Rights Commission had been established by Congress in 1957 and directed to investigate complaints by citizens alleging discrimination because of race, color, religion or national origin, to study and collect information concerning legal developments constituting a denial of equal protection, and to serve as a clearinghouse for information in respect to denial of equal protection of the laws. Until Pendelton's appointment, the Commission was viewed as a friendly port of call by liberal Black civil rights leaders. As a clearinghouse for information related to racial discrimination, it was practically a research adjunct for the civil rights movement with Commission reports often being used to justify support for new civil rights initiatives. All of that changed with the appointment of Pendelton. The Commission soon became an adversarial forum for challenging the legitimacy of traditional Black leadership and both the legality and wisdom affirmative action and other race-specific remedies.

The practice begun by President Reagan of appointing conservative Blacks to positions responsible for enforcing civil right laws including race-specific remedies was continued by presidents George and George W. Bush. In 1990, Bush appointed a former federal prosecutor, Michael Williams, to the position of Assistant Secretary of Education for Civil Rights. The office is responsible for enforcing federal statutes that prohibit discrimination based on race, color, national origin, and gender in education. Williams caused a considerable stir when he declared that scholarships and other forms of assistance earmarked for Black students were unconstitutional. His ruling was one of the early salvos in the argument against programs offering special assistance to minority students.

Ward Connerly, a California entrepreneur, was appointed in 1993 to the University of California Board of Regents by the conservative Governor, Pete Wilson, an earlier associate of both Edwin Meese and Clarence Pendelton. In 1995, Connerly used his position on the board of regents to lead a successful effort to end the use of affirmative action in admissions to the University of California. Later that year he accepted an invitation to chair an ongoing campaign promoting a referendum to end all affirmative action programs in the state of California. Following the success of the California referendum in 1996, Connerly led of a similarly successful campaign in the state of Washington.

The trend continued when George Bush, Sr. nominated Clarence Thomas to serve on the United States Supreme Court. As chairman of the Equal Opportunity Commission and as Assistant Secretary of Education for Civil Rights, Thomas had made known his opposition to practically all forms of race-specific government intervention and to affirmative action programs in particular and as a consequence had incurred the wrath of civil rights leaders for what they perceived as his lack of vigorous enforcement of civil rights laws. His appointment to the Supreme Court meant that the highest ranking Black person in the American political system was diametrically opposed to positions subscribed to by the vast majority of Black people.

Following the lead of his father, President George W. Bush, elected in 2000, appointed a Black conservative, Peter Kirsanov, to fill a vacancy on the Civil Rights Commission and he appointed another, Gerald Reynolds, as Assistant Secretary of Education for Civil Rights. Both Kirsanov and Reynolds were officers in the Center for New Black Leadership. The Reynolds nomination was widely opposed by civil rights organization and President Bush had to resort to a recess appointment when the nomination stalled in the Senate.

Though their views were at odds with those of the Black majority as evidenced by polling data, the ideological positions taken by the high level Black appointees were shared by the collection of conservative Black intellectuals who were also supported by the broader conservative network. Concerted efforts were made to ensure that the writings of conservative Black intellectuals reached as wide an audience as possible. Several members of the BCM have nationally syndicated news column. Project 21, as noted earlier, cites with pride the extensive list of television and radio shows along with numerous newspapers and magazines in which Black conservatives have been featured. The BCM has an extensive inventory of impressive web sites on the internet with several of them being hyperlinks on the home page of the NCPPR. Over all, in spite of their limited support within the Black community, the presence and coverage of Black conservative ideologues in the national media are considerably greater than that of their liberal counterparts. A study of media exposure from 1984 to 1992 using the Nexis database search of major American newspapers and magazines compared the three most exposed conservative ideologues, Thomas Sowell, Glen Loury, and Shelby Steele with three Black progressives, Cornel West, Manning Marable, and Adolph Reed, Jr. and found 901 cites for the conservative trio compared with 122 for the progressives. There were 26 features on the conservatives but only one on the progressives.[35]

To the extent that the goal of the broader conservative movement was to create an alternative Black leadership class, success has not been achieved. However, BCM has been instrumental in recasting the themes around which the discussion of race and public policy revolves. The denial of race as a significant factor now approaches conventional wisdom.

Notes

1. Robert Smith, *We Have No Leaders* (Albany: State University of New York Press, 1996)
2. Richard Bardolph, *The Civil Rights Record* (New York: Thomas Y. Crowell, 1970), 11-12.
3. Ronald Takaki, *A Different Mirror* (Boston: Little Brown, 1993) 71.
4. Jerry Fresia, Toward An American Revolution (Boston: South End Press) 2.
5. Charles Hamilton, "Measuring Black Conservatism," *The State of Black America, 1982* (New York: National Urban League)
6. Donald Kinder and Lynn Sanders, *Divided By Color* (Chicago: University of Chicago Press, 1990), 27.
7. Thomas Sowell on Meet The Press, *Manhattan Report, Special Edition 1 No. 8* (November 1981) 12.
8. John Saloma, lll, *Ominous Politics* (New York: Hill and Wang, 1984) 19.
9. Edwin Meese, lll, quoted in *The Fairmont Papers: Black Alternative Conference* (San Francisco: Institute for Contemporary Studies) 3-4.
10. Stan Faryna, Brad Stetson and Joseph Conti, eds., *Black and Right* (Westport: Praeger, 1997) 6.
11. Excerpted from Conference Recruitment Brochure.
12. *Ibid.*
13. Fred Barnes, "Iventa Negro, Inc." *The New Republic* (April 15, 1985) 9-12.
14. *Ibid.*
15. *Ibid*, 9
16. *Ibid.*
17. *Manhattan Report*, 10.
18. The National Center for Public Policy Research, "A History of the National Center for Public Policy Research," http://www.nationalcenter.internet/ncp-prhist.hmtl
19. Project 21, "History of Project 21," http://www.nationalcenter.org/921history.html
20. *Ibid.*
21. Walter Williams, *The State Against Blacks* (New York: New Press, 1982) xvi.
22. *Ibid*, 142.
23. *Ibid.*
24. *Ibid.*
25. *Ibid*, 143.
26. *Ibid.*
27. Thomas Sowell on Meet the Press, 7.
28. Glenn Loury, "A New American Dilemma," *New Republic* (December 31, 1984) 14.
29. Glenn Loury, "Redirecting Priorities," *Point of View* (Summer 1984) 5.
30. Glenn Loury, *New Republic*, 14.
31. Glenn Loury, *Point of View*, 4.

32. Project 21, "Intro to 1996 Report," http://www.nationalcenter.org/P21Intro96Rpt.html
33. *Ibid.*
34. Robert Hill, "The Economic Status of Black Americans," *State of Black America*, 1981 (New York: National Urban League) 17.
35. Lionel McPherson, "The Loudest Silence Ever Heard", "Black Conservatives in the Media", *Extra* (July/August 1992). Reprinted in *Best of Extra* (n. d) 40.

Thinking about Whiteness and American Politics

Christopher Deis

W.E.B. DuBois' oft quoted observation that "the problem of the twentieth century is the color-line,"[1] has stimulated academic research, reflection, and conversation on questions of race and racial inequality. In the American context, notions of race have often been centered on "the Other"-brown, black, yellow and red communities of color. Consequently, much of the academic and political conversations surrounding issues of race have been focused on fashioning ways that the American polity can better and more fairly include those labeled as "minority groups." However, there is much we can gain from reversing this critical gaze from one focused on the Other, to a perspective that focuses on how systems of racism and racial inequality, impact, benefit and shape the racial, social, and political boundaries of white Americans. A growing body of literature, called critical whiteness studies, has taken up this challenge.[2] This short piece explores several of the theoretical concepts central to critical whiteness studies[3] which include white privilege, whiteness as property, and whiteness as normalcy/invisibility, and asks, how can critical whiteness studies inform our thinking about American democracy specifically, and democratic theory, more broadly?

Before exploring the theoretical concepts outlined above, we need to briefly define the category and concept labeled as "whiteness." Race in this article, is a socially constructed identity that white Americans possess. As applied in critical whiteness studies, race is not a marker that only applies to the Other, but rather is a category that bounds, informs, and describes white Americans as well. However, as all groups are "raced" in the American context, each community experiences the impact of a racial order, which is dependent on hierarchy, quite differently. For white Americans, whiteness is a social category, which is inseparably linked to and contextually dependent on a superior power relationship with other groups:

> Whiteness is a sociohistorical form of consciousness, given birth at the nexus of capitalism, colonial rule, and the emergent relationships among dominant and

subordinate groups. Whiteness constitutes and demarcates ideas, feelings, knowledge, social practices, cultural formations, and system of intelligibility that are identified with or attributed to white people and that are invested in by white people as "white" ... Whiteness can be considered to be a conflictual, sociocultural, sociopolitical, and geopolitical process that animates commonsensical practical action in relationship to dominant social practices and normative ideological productions.[4]

Whiteness is a social location that is not coincidental to a superior position in the American (and Western) social and racial hierarchy. Rather, whiteness is a social location dependent on its superior power relationship to other groups for its very existence. This definition is not based on essentialized notions of racial identity because there is a great degree of diversity in power, resources, influence, and authority among those considered white. Ultimately, whiteness occupies a superior position in the racial and political hierarchy because white citizens in a racialized polity reproduce power arrangements and understandings of social reality that homogenize away difference within the white community in favor of a version of whiteness that encourages and legitimates privilege in power relationships.

This piece is organized as follows. The first section explores the notion of white privilege and its relationship to liberalism and social contract theory. The tension that animates this section of the paper centers on ostensibly universal and democratic notions of democracy in the face of racial inequality and a racial contract critique. The second section of this article explores the concept of whiteness as a type of property within the American and Western polities and how this notion affects citizenship and democratic participation. The third and final section of this piece explores whiteness as a social location, which is constructed as "normal." Because the racial hierarchy in America mandates that whiteness occupy the dominant hierarchical position, the attitudes, beliefs, and behavior of whites are the norm against which other groups are measured. In essence, whiteness becomes an invisible standard against which to assess other groups. This final section explores how this invisibility influences our thinking about democracy and race.

White Privilege, Liberalism and The Racial Contract

Defining and exploring liberalism are difficult tasks that have been the focus of much scholarly work.[5] For the purposes of this paper, I present a highly simplified definition of liberalism. In this piece, liberalism is a political ideology that emphasizes individualism, the need for the state to protect property rights, the responsibility and right of citizens to select their elected officials and type of government, and a notion that the state has some responsibility to secure and encourage the prosperity of its citizens. Furthermore, liberalism in this context proceeds from a tradition of social contract theory and a belief (however metaphorical) in the concept of a state of nature with individuals and communities making "contracts" to form government in the context of natural law to enter into political society. Lastly, liberalism is understood by many theorists to be "raceless" and neutral in its considerations of human difference. For many liberal thinkers, liberalism is a theory that exists outside of the messy business of creating, and sustaining racial hierarchies.[6]

Consequently, basic notions of American democracy rooted in The Federalist Papers, The Constitution, The Bill of Rights, or other documents rest upon relatively "raceless" conceptions of liberalism. A perspective rooted in an abstract version of liberalism does not link citizenship and democracy to any specific notion of race or racial ideology. However, this presents a fundamental dilemma. If we grant that political theories develop in the context of and in response to real world political concerns, how can race not be included and considered within the liberal tradition and by its foundational thinkers? Can we separate liberalism from the Colonial and Imperial projects that rationalized exploitation of Africa and the world outside of Western Europe, which occurred, simultaneously with the development of classic, liberal thought? Can we separate liberalism from understandings regarding the requisite rationality necessary to enter into political society that excluded women, people of color, and others?

Racial Contract theory responds to this puzzle by reading race back into the liberal project.[7] The Racial Contract argues that liberalism, as an ideology, cannot be divorced from the racial hierarchies that produced it and which liberal democratic states have helped to sustain. The notion of a raceless, normative liberalism does not stand up to close inspection:

> No one actually believes nowadays that, of course, that people formally came out of the wilderness and signed a contract. But there is the impression that..the United States were founded on noble moral principles meant to include everyone, but unfortunately there were some deviations. The "Racial Contract" explodes this picture as mythical..non-white exclusion racial exclusion from personhood was the actual norm. Racism, racial self-identification, and race thinking are then not in the least "surprising," "anomalous," "puzzling," incongruent with Enlightenment European humanism, but required by the Racial Contract as part of the terms for the European appropriation of the world.[8]

The social contract theory that lies at the heart of the liberal tradition, is itself closely linked to systems of racial inequality. From a Racial Contract perspective, liberalism as a belief system has historically been linked to the maintenance of white privilege:

> In the first period, the period of de jure white supremacy, the "Racial Contract" was explicit..the expropriation contract, the slave contract, the colonial contract making it clear that whites were the privileged race and the egalitarian social contract applied only to them. . . In the second period. . . the "Racial Contract" has written itself out of formal existence. . . so that persons is no longer coextensive with "whites." What characterizes this period (which is, of course, the present) is tension between continuing de facto white privilege and this formal extension of rights. . . But even apart from these, a crucial manifestation is simply the failure to ask certain questions, taking for granted as a status quo and baseline the existing color-coded configurations of wealth, poverty, property, and opportunities.[9]

The sum effect of a Racial Contract critique is that it demystifies the liberal project. Race is no longer a peripheral phenomenon. Instead, we see that race and the maintenance of a polity in which white group membership was/is privileged, is central to liberal thought. Once we introduce race into our conception of the liberal project, we are able to conceive of the state more properly as a racial polity or racial state:

> States are racial more deeply because of the structural position they occupy in producing and reproducing, constituting and effecting racially shaped spaces and places, groups and events, life worlds and possibilities, accesses and restrictions, inclusions and exclusions, conceptions and

modes of representation. They are racial, in short, in virtue of their modes of population definition, determination, and structuration. And they are racist to the extent such definition, determination and structuration operate to exclude or privilege in or on racial terms.[10]

By reintroducing race to liberalism and placing liberalism's assumptions regarding power and racial group membership at the forefront for analysis, we enhance our understanding of the liberal tradition.

Maintaining white privilege is the central goal of a racial polity. White privilege is understood and described as:

> ... the sets of benefits and advantages inherited by each generation of those defined as "white" in the social process and structure of U.S. society. The actual privileges and the sense that one is entitled to them are inseparable parts of a greater whole. These white advantages can be material, symbolic, or psychological. They infiltrate and encompass many thousands of interactions and other events played out in an individual American's life over the course of a lifetime. . . Stated or unstated, it is a fundamental given of this society. White prerogatives stem from the fact that society has, from the beginning, been structured in terms of white gains and white-group interests.[11]

White privilege is operationalized within a racially ordered, liberal democratic state in a variety of ways. For example, white privilege enables whites to accrue more power and resources than other groups. Whites are able to leverage their group privilege within a state whose boundaries both explicitly and implicitly are organized to both maintain their group privilege and to increase future power. The state, which ostensibly operates in an open and equal fashion in regards to all of its citizens, works via the law, social convention, and political institutions to maintain one group as superior in the social hierarchy and other groups as less so. Historically, the American government and other polities have used measures such as Jim Crow and other laws designed to deny blacks and other people of color, civic, political, and economic opportunities. In the present, we have "color-blind" policies that work to maintain racial inequality by not challenging the social and political processes that maintain white, group privilege under the rubric that for government and social policies to be fair and equal, they must be free of considerations of race.

This section has highlighted the concept of a Racial Contract and liberalism's relationship to maintaining white privilege in a racially ordered polity. A key question to be addressed in the next section of this piece is how white privilege translates into a type of property that racially ordered states (such as America) have historically worked to police and protect. Citizenship and full civic membership in racially ordered states such as the U.S. are not open vessels designed to accommodate all citizens. Rather, citizenship within the racial polity is a highly contested site because of the value whiteness brings to its "owners" and the liabilities accrued by those excluded from full citizenship and white group membership.[12]

Citizenship in a racially ordered society is inseparable from questions of race and power. Race, power relations, and the relationship between national belonging and full civic membership were sites that were intertwined with issues and questions of power and group membership. Citizenship in liberal democratic, racially ordered states such as America was not open equally to all, and the borders, dimensions, and boundaries of that citizenship, were highly policed:

Since the earliest days of colonialism in North America, an identifiable racial order has linked the system of political rule to the racial classification of individuals and groups. The major institutions and social relationships of U.S. society-law, political organization, economic relationships, religion, cultural life, residential patterns, etc. have been structured from the beginning by the racial order.[13]

Joel Olson in his article, "Beyond White Citizenship," contributes further on this point with his observation on the historical relationship between citizenship and race in America that:

> Citizenship was defined against slavery. Blackness and slavery were associated. Black and white were diametrically opposed. All that is left is to complete the square: to be a citizen was also to be white. This is not an empirical observation of who had the vote at the time. Whiteness was not a biological status but a *political* color that distinguished the free from the unfree, the equal from the inferior, the citizen from the slave. Citizenship was not just standing ... but *racialized* standing.[14]

If we accept the Racial Contract's formulation that global systems of racial privilege were created to maintain European (read: white) dominance in power relationships between those labeled as "white" and those labeled as "other," the centrality of whiteness in the American racial order becomes clear. As Jacobson's, *Whiteness of a Different Color*, articulates, America was constructed as a polity where a white majority was to be dominant numerically (and therefore to be dominant, politically) and where, white, Anglo-Saxons were understood to be the racial group most capable of responsible citizenship. To maintain this dominance, whiteness possesses a dynamic quality where it broadened to include heretofore "nonwhite" groups (such as the Irish, Eastern and Southern Europeans, and others) while maintaining exclusion of other, still racially marked groups.[15] White racial group membership is not simply a sense of group belonging or privilege. Rather, white group membership is a type of property that brings economic, social, and political value that is enshrined as social understanding and legal reality.[16]

Whiteness as Property

Cheryl Harris', "Whiteness as Property," describes whiteness as a type of property in the following terms:

> Specifically, the law has accorded "holders" of whiteness the same privileges and benefits accorded holders of other types of property. The liberal view of property is that it includes the exclusive rights of possession, use and disposition. Its attributes are the right to transfer or alienability, the right to use and enjoyment, and the right to exclude others..whiteness conforms to the general contours of property. It may be a "bad" form of property, but it is property nonetheless.[17]

Whiteness as property is a subtle and complex social force. It can work through unacknowledged privilege that whites as a group receive. For example, the psychological advantages of living in a society in which white group sensibilities, culture, and values is the norm. Whiteness as property can work more bluntly. It determined who would or would not be a slave, or who could and could not vote or enjoy full citizenship during Jim Crow. Whiteness can serve as a reward for behavior in service of established racial hierarchies by political elites-the transition of the

Irish in America from non-white in the 18th century to fully white by the 19th and 20th centuries fits this example.[18] Finally, whiteness as a type of property also includes the financial benefits that accrue to those considered white by virtue of benefits denied to others. For example, the eligibility of white Americans for land grants, federal housing loans, differential pay, closed unions, and discriminatory labor markets are historical and contemporary examples of wealth accrued through denial to others. [19]

For this project, whiteness as property contributes an understanding of the intersection between race and the law, and hints at how a concept as apparently value-neutral as "property" can operate in support of racial systems of privilege and power. The sum effect of whiteness as property is that whiteness in a racially hierarchal society clearly brings with it a set of assumptions about what is normal and acceptable that is difficult to separate from an individual's group membership and sense of entitlement.[20] Ultimately, whiteness as property is a concept that details how white privilege brings psychological, material, economic, and political advantages. White racial group membership is not simply a preferential position within a racially ordered society. More broadly, whiteness has a value and is treated as a type of property by the racial state.

How do these concepts play out in the "real world"? The book, *The Tyranny of the Majority*, provides an opportunity to answer this question.[21] Guinier's work focuses on questions of democratic inclusion and how we as citizens can better improve our political institutions by making them more responsive and inclusive. Guinier's primary critique is that rather than be fully participatory and democratic, our political institutions enshrine certain interests at the expense of others. Given the nature of pluralism, this is not a surprise. However, what is theoretically troubling from Guinier's point of view is that fair and open democratic institutions should allow for a "cycling" of preferences. Stated differently, the same interests and combination of interests should not "win" every time. The reality that these winning coalitions of interests often map onto racial, economic, and gender cleavages in society is highly troubling because some citizens are perpetually excluded despite the democratic nature of the procedures applied by political and other decision-making bodies. Guinier labels this perpetual exclusion in Madisonian terms as a "tyranny of the majority":

> In a heterogeneous community, the majority may not represent all competing interests. The majority is likely to be self interested and ignorant or indifferent to the concerns of the minority. In such case, Madison observed, the assumption that the majority represents the minority is "altogether fictitious."[22]

Guinier's solution is what she terms as a "taking turns approach" in which political institutions investigate new techniques and arrangements for registering voter preferences that allow for a more diverse range of voices and political alliances.

Tyranny of the Majority's example of whiteness as a type of property and as privilege, which influences democratic outcomes, appears on the surface to be rather simple and benign. However, her example demonstrates how these concepts can interact to determine democratic outcomes, that are in many respects, unfair and do not register the sentiments and preferences of all participants.

The example highlighted here is taken from the much discussed controversy at Brother Rice High School in which the solution to the discord surrounding the choice of music at the prom was that black and white students would have two separate events. The controversy began when a one person, one vote, voting scheme was used to choose the songs to be played at the prom. On the surface, this seems like an appropriate and fair way of selecting the music for an event in which there would be a large number of students with different preferences. However, the seemingly fair scheme becomes complicated when we acknowledge that musical preferences often correlate closely with race and culture. The black students were in the minority numerically at the school and because voting closely followed racial lines, the black students had few if any of their songs represented in the outcome. The black students found this highly troubling because they are full members and citizens of the school "community," and are paying the same price for a ticket to attend the prom as their white peers, but are not having any of their preferences registered by the "democratic" outcome.

> Black students, by contrast, were angered by what they saw as a business-as-usual approach that legitimates white privilege in ostensibly democratic institutions: For black students at both schools, however, majority decision making was illegitimate because it shut them out. "For every vote we had, there were eight votes for what they wanted . . . [W]ith us being in the minority. . . we're always outvoted. It's as if we don't count."[23]

The response of the white students to the controversy was a predictable one given America's political culture and the way that it has enshrined the notion of one person and one vote:

> Some white students were angry and embittered. They complained that the black students should have gone along with the majority: "The majority makes a decision. That's the way it works."[24]

We need to ask why a white student saw it as reasonable to argue that, "The majority makes a decision. That's the way it works." An initial set of answers to the above question lies in the following passages.

First, whiteness as property and as privilege is visible in a number of ways in this scenario. Primarily, whiteness affords a sense of entitlement in democratic outcomes. Because power relationships and institutions often register preferences by simple majority, (rather than by proportion, for example) the group with a numerical majority will be victorious. In a racial state, with a constructed white majority, this is highly problematic because one group and one group's interests are continually victorious. Whiteness as property and privilege create a sense of self-fulfilling entitlement-because whites as a group are used to "winning" it becomes an expectation, when the interests of whites are not represented then "the system" is suspect and something must be wrong or amiss.

Second, the white students' response to the black student's protests, illustrates how whiteness as property and privilege is able to normalize certain outcomes as being "colorblind." The outcome itself is simply the result of the rules. The intent of democratic procedures, in this case to register all the students' preferences, takes a back seat to a sense of procedural neutrality that continually privileges one group over the other and that masks the unequal, institutional power relationships that determine democratic outcomes.

Finally, whiteness as property and whiteness as privilege, serve to mask the diversity of interests within the white community. As noted earlier in this piece, whiteness is a constructed social category that masks the heterogeneity of its members in the interest of maintaining an apparent conformity of interests. In this example, the simple voting scheme failed to register the intensity of preferences of its participants. In all probability, this voting scheme forced white students who were undecided and/or "fence sitters," to choose one side. This excluded the white students whom preferred the music selected by the black students (or a diversity of music at the prom). In this scenario, whiteness then, can be viewed as limiting the preferences and hurting the interests of the black and white citizens of the school community.

Whiteness as Normalcy

In America, whiteness and white racial group membership occupy an assumed position of normalcy. Whiteness, and the views, cultural expectations, and political values, which are associated with white group membership, are generally taken as the baseline against which other groups are compared.

> Whiteness is so ubiquitous, so habitual, so imbedded that it exists even where and when most whites cannot see it. Stated or unstated, it is a fundamental given of this society. White prerogatives stem from the fact that society has, from the beginning, been structured in terms of white gains and white-group interests. Once this system was put into place in the seventeenth century, white privileges soon came to be sensed as usual and natural.[25]

The centrality of whiteness in American society is hardly surprising given that America is a racial state. Historically, America was constructed as a country with a predominantly European population and its values and political belief systems are taken from The West. Furthermore, as the previous sections demonstrate, whiteness is synonymous with citizen and subsequently requires no explanation or discussion.[26] Although, there is a popular belief in the notion of a melting pot of culture and values, America is predominantly a country where whiteness and white norms and values have been an enforced value system. Ultimately, race, as noted in the introduction to this piece, is a problem of "the Other"-not a condition or social location commonly associated with whites.

The assumption of whiteness as a normal social location has consequences for our notions of democracy and democratic participation. Primarily, the normalcy of whiteness means that other perspectives and values, which may contribute to the polity, are minimized and made illegitimate. Whiteness, when assumed to be a normal (and privileged) social location also assumes a quality best labeled as *universalism*. In this context, universalism refers to the tendency to generalize from the experiences of whites and the expectations rooted in whiteness to other groups. Intergroup differences are washed away by an assumption that whiteness and the experience and expectations of whites holds true for all groups. The sum effect of whiteness as a position of normalcy is that whiteness and *the particular* (not truly universal perspectives) offered by whites acquires a type of invisibility because these views are accepted as the norm to the exclusion of other viewpoints.

Whiteness' invisibility also affects democracy because it allows white racial group membership to become a historical and depoliticized. Whiteness is something "that simply is." Consequently, white racial identity is not linked to privilege or to historical processes that reproduce inequality. For example, when whites are asked about what whiteness means for them, they generally reply that it has something to do with being European, and not with being privileged or benefiting from a racial order.[27] In total, "Whiteness can be considered as a form of social amnesia associated with modes of subjectivity within particular social sites considered to be normative.[28]

This invisibility or "intentional forgetting" serves whiteness by rewriting history to distance the beneficiaries of white privilege from the white supremacist and Herrenvolk ethics that produce inequality. The American context is rich with examples of this intentional forgetting and invisibility surrounding questions of white identity. For example, Thandeka's, *Learning to Be White* details an experiment in which white participants are made aware of their whiteness and find it unsettling and disturbing largely because the category of race "has little conscious meaning for them."[29] *Making Whiteness* details the South's process of historical rewriting and strategic forgetting as central to the creation of a "classless" whiteness as being integrally linked to full membership in the polity before and during the American Apartheid[30] of Jim Crow.[31] Racism's evolution from the violence of dominative racism and a biological explanation of racial difference to the segregation of aversive racism and the institutional and rational discrimination of metaracism can be read as an evolution of privilege as justified by innate, biological difference to one justified in the neo-conservative logic of bad culture.[32] In an American society that extols its "color-blindness" but does not challenge systemic inequality based on race prejudice, we have a terrain where white privilege remains unchallenged because race is no longer central to the public discourse.

The invisibility of whiteness is not static: it is strategically invisible and can be activated and made visible when its beneficiaries and holders are made aware of their race or in response to certain contingencies where group identity becomes salient. Ultimately, whiteness' invisibility serves a normalizing function that homogenizes away internal differences in the white community, creates boundaries on discourse and behavior, and defines an identity as a contextual construct of opposition and difference-with "the Other" as a reference group. In sum, the invisibility and normalcy of whiteness damage democracy because they limit political possibilities that may enhance and improve the equality, vibrancy, and potential of the polity.

Conclusion

This short piece has outlined some key concepts offered by critical whiteness studies and how they complicate our notions of democracy and politics. This work would be incomplete if it did not conclude by exploring, how scholars, activists and others can use the concepts presented to deconstruct whiteness and challenge racial inequality.

The main challenge is to make whiteness visible and remove its universalist qualities and world view. For any anti-racism struggle to be successful, whiteness as a socio-political category that describes a set of behaviors, values, and assumptions relative to power relationships, must be exposed as simply one position (and not the most privileged position) among many. If we take this necessary first step and legitimate the values, concerns, and perspectives of the Other, we will improve the health of the American polity.

Finally, one of the values of critical whiteness studies is that by exposing the role of whites in both maintaining and benefiting from a racial hierarchy, we can begin to discuss the psychological, political, and economic costs of whiteness to white Americans. Returning to an earlier theme, whiteness is a constructed political identity and value system that homogenizes away difference within the white community as it acts to maintain its dominant position in the racial state.[33] By making whiteness visible, we can then move onto the necessary second step in combating the racial order by confronting the costs and damages that whiteness does to white Americans and how whiteness and its exclusionary tendencies damage the polity.

Notes

1. W. E. B. DuBois, *Souls of Black Folk* (Chicago: McClurg, 1903), p. 13.
2. David R. Roediger, *Colored White* (Los Angeles and Berkeley: University of California Press, 2002), pp. 18-24, describes the emerging field of whiteness studies and makes his case for an evolution in the understanding of the boundaries of whiteness that should be represented by a renaming of the field as "critical whiteness studies."
3. This piece uses some of the concepts central to critical whiteness studies, but also draws from other fields in its discussion and examples of these concepts at work.
4. Peter McLaren, "Whiteness is..," in *White Reign: Deploying Whiteness in America,* ed. Joel L. Kincheloe, Shirley R. Steinberg, Nelson M. Rodriguez, and Ronald E. Chennault (New York: St. Martin's Griffin, 1998), p. 66.
5. Several excellent texts that represent the diversity of work on liberalism include: Louis Hartz, *The Liberal Tradition in America,* (New York: Harcourt Press, 1955); David Greenstone, *The Lincoln Persuasion: Remaking American Liberalism,* (Princeton: Princeton University Press, 1993); John Rawls, *Political Liberalism,* (New York: Columbia University Press, 1993); Rogers Smith, *Civic Ideals: Conflicting Versions of American Citizenship*, (New Haven: Yale University Press, 1997); Michael Dawson, *Black Visions,* (Chicago: University of Chicago Press, 2001).
6. For an exploration and discussion of this tendency in liberal thought see, Dawson, *Black Visions,* 239-247.
7. See Charles W. Mills, *The Racial Contract* (Ithaca: Cornell University Press, 1997) for an extended explanation of this theory-that argues for a racial ordering of resources, privilege, and inter-group relationships around a racial hierarchy coexistent with classic liberal social contract theory and modern liberalism.
8. Ibid, 122.
9. Ibid, 73.
10. David Theo Goldberg, *The Racial State,* (Massachusetts: Blackwell Publishers, 2002), p. 104.
11. Joe R. Feagin, *Racist America,* (New York: Routledge, 2000), p. 175.
12. See Matthew Frye Jacobson, *Whiteness of a Different Color* (Massachusetts: Harvard University Press, 1998); Noel Ignatiev, *How the Irish Became White* (Routledge, 1995); Robert G. Lee, *Orientals* (Temple University Press, 1999); Theodore Allen, *The Invention of the White Race: Volume One* (Verso, 1994); Rogers Smith's, *Civic Ideals* (Yale University Press, 1997); David Roediger's, *The Wages of Whiteness* (Verso Press, 1991).
13. Michael Omi and Howard Winant, *Racial Formation in the United States* (New York: Routledge, 1994) p. 79.
14. Joel Olson, "Beyond White Citizenship," *Constellations* (Volume 8, Number 2): 171.
15. Matthew Frye Jacobson, *Whiteness of a Different Color* (Massachusetts: Harvard University Press, 1998), p. 75.
16. See Ian Haney Lopez, *White By Law* (New York: New York University Press, 1996) for an extended historical and contemporary overview and analysis of how the law has worked to reinforce, create, and maintain white privilege.
17. Cheryl Harris, "Whiteness as Property," in David Roediger, ed., *Black on White* (New York: Shocken Press, 1998) p. 108.
18. See David Roediger's, *The Wages of Whiteness* (Verso Press, 1991).

19. See Derrick Bell, "White Superiority in America: It's Legal Legacy, It's Economic Costs," in David Roediger, ed., *Black on White* (New York: Shocken Press, 1998); George Lipsitz, *The Possessive Investment in Whiteness* (Temple University Press, 1998); in economics and sociology see: Melvin Oliver and Thomas Shapiro, *Black Wealth, White Wealth* (Routledge, 1997).
20. On this point, Elizabeth Spelman notes in "Race" and the Labor of Identity," in Susan E. Bobbit and Sue Campbell eds., *Racism and Philosophy* (Cornell University Press, 1999), p. 203, how: Baldwin suggests in *The Fire Next Time* that whatever changes in the meaning of whiteness there may have been historically, many whites have understood being white as not only distinct from but also superior to being black. Using the metaphor of whiteness as property, Spelman translates race privilege into currency on page 213 where she notes: "To be white is to be the bearer of white currency, which by definition, be denomination is worth more than black currency... That is why under long-standing and still current political and social conditions, whites are born with a kind of racial capital blacks cannot possibly accumulate." In framing the American polity as a racial polity, Charles Mills notes in *Blackness Visible* (Cornell University Press, 1998), p. 134, how: "Herbert Blumer argues, racism should be understood not as "a set of feelings" but as a "sense of group position" in which the dominant race is convinced of its superiority, sees the subordinate race as "intrinsically different and alien" has "proprietary feelings about its "privilege and advantage" and fears encroachment on these prerogatives." The sum effect of this sense of majority-right is a sense of entitlement and colour-blindness manifested by appeals to hard work and "just rewards." Frances Rains notes in "Is the Benign Really Harmless?: Deconstructing Some "Benign" Manifestations of Operationalized White Privilege," in Joe Kincheloe, Shirley Steinberg, Nelson Rodriguez, and Ronald Chennault eds., *White Reign: Deploying Whiteness in America* (New York: St. Martin's Press, 1998), p. 84 that: "Implicit in this type of seemingly benign reaction is the perception that some people of color are "taking away" these "earned" rewards from some entitled whites... This "benign" reaction, however, assumes that via location, a.k.a. white privilege, the rewards are somehow *white* rewards to begin with."
21. Lani Guinier, *The Tyranny of the Majority: Fundamental Fairness in Representative Democracy* (New York: The Free Press, 1994).
22. Ibid, pp. 4-5.
23. Ibid, 77.
24. Ibid, 77.
25. Feagin, *Racist America*, 175.
26. See Donald R. Kinder and Lynn M. Sanders, *Divided by Color* (Chicago: The University of Chicago Press, 1996) for a discussion of the concept of symbolic racism and the idea that public opinion research has uncovered that for whites, blacks are believed to violate basic American values of self-reliance, uplift, and patriotism. The idea that blacks are somehow unfit for citizenship by virtue of their behavior explains a great deal of anti-black sentiment.
27. Thomas Nakayama and Judith Martin, *Whiteness the Communication of Social Identity* (Sage, 1999), contains a selection and survey of empirical research regarding whites and white identity and contains the finding that whiteness is

often viewed by whites as a sense of group membership (i.e. European) but not necessarily being an identity that has or brings any privilege.
28. Thandeka, *Learning to be White* (New York: Continuum, 2000), p. 35.
29. Ibid, 16.
30. Douglas Massey and Nancy Denton, *American Apartheid* (Harvard University Press, 1993).
31. Grace Elizabeth Hale, *Making Whiteness,* (New York: Vintage Books, 1998), pp. 43-84.
32. See Etienne Balibar and Immanuel Wallerstein, *Race, Nation, Class* (Verso, 1993), pp. 17-29, 37-69 and Joel Kovel, *White Racism* (Columbia University Press, 1984), pp. 13-41; 177-230.
33. Feagin, *Racist America*, 197-202.

Class and Power in America

G. William Domhoff

What do everyday Americans and social scientists mean when they talk about *social class* or *power,* and how do their views compare? This chapter answers those two questions. It also explains the methods used to study class and power, and presents a preliminary look at the American upper class.

What Is a Social Class?

Most Americans don't like the idea that there might be social classes. Classes imply that people have relatively fixed stations in life. They fly in the face of beliefs about equality of opportunity and seem to ignore the evidence of upward social mobility. Even more, Americans tend to deny that classes might be rooted in wealth and occupational roles. They talk about social class, but with euphemisms like "the suits," "the blue bloods," "Joe Sixpack," and "the other side of the tracks."

American dislike for the idea of class is deeply rooted in the country's colonial and revolutionary history. Colonial America seemed very different from other countries to its new inhabitants because it was a rapidly expanding frontier country with no feudal aristocracy or rigid class structure. The sense of difference was heightened by the need for solidarity among all classes in the war for freedom from the British. Revolutionary leaders from the higher classes had to concede greater freedom and equality for common people to gain their support. One historian states the power equation succinctly: "Leaders who did not fight for equality accepted it in order to win."[1]

Although large differences in wealth, income, and lifestyle already existed in revolutionary America, particularly in port cities and the South, these well-understood inequalities were usually explained away or downplayed by members of the middle classes as well as by the merchants, plantation owners, and lawyers who were at the top of the socioeconomic ladder. As shown by a historical study of diaries, letters, newspapers, and other documents of the period, Americans instead emphasized and took pride in the fact that any class distinctions were small compared with Europe. They recognized that there were rich and poor, but they preferred to think of their country "as one of equality, and

From *Who Rules America? Power and Politics,* 4th edition by G. William Domhoff. Copyright © by McGraw-Hill Companies, Inc. Reprinted by permission.

proudly pointed to such features as the large middle class, the absence of beggars, the comfortable circumstances of most people, and the limitless opportunities for those who worked hard and saved their money."[2]

The fact that nearly 20 percent of the population was held in slavery and that 100,000 Native Americans lived in the western areas of the colonies was not part of this self-definition as a middle-class, egalitarian society. It is clear, however, that the free white majority nonetheless defined itself in terms of the potentially dangerous slaves on the one hand and the warlike "savages" on the other. This made their shared "whiteness" a significant part of their social identity. In fact, race is the first of many factors that make the class-based nature of American society less salient than it might otherwise be.

Even members of the upper class preferred this more democratic class system to what had existed for many centuries in Europe. To emphasize this point, a study of the democratic revolutions in North America and Europe begins with a letter written from Europe in 1788 by a young adult member of a prominent American upper-class family. After the young man registered his disgust with the hereditary titles and pomp of the European class system, and with the obsequiousness of the lower classes, he stated his conviction that "a certain degree of equality is essential to human bliss." As if to make sure the limits of his argument were clear, he underlined the words *a certain degree of equality*. He then went on to argue that the greatness of the United States was that it had provided this degree of equality "without destroying the necessary subordination."[3]

Two hundred years later, in response to sociologists who wanted to know what social class meant to Americans, a representative sample of the citizenry in Boston and Kansas City expressed ideas similar to those of the first Americans. Although most people are keenly aware of differences in social standing and judge status levels primarily in terms of income, occupations, and education (but especially income), they emphasize the openness of the system. They also argue that a person's social standing is in good part determined by such individual qualities as initiative and the motivation to work hard. Moreover, many of them feel the importance of class is declining. This belief is partly due to their conviction that people of all ethnic and religious backgrounds are being treated with greater respect and decency whatever their occupational and educational levels, but even more to what they see as material evidence for social advancement in the occupations and salaries of their families and friends.[4] In short, a tradition of public social respect for everyone and the existence of social mobility are also factors in making class less important in the everyday thinking of most Americans. People are very aware of basic economic and educational differences, and they can size up social standing fairly well from such outward signs as speech patterns, mannerisms, and style of dress, but the existence of social classes is nonetheless passed over as quickly as possible.

People of the highest social status share a general distaste for talking about social class in an open and direct way. Nevertheless, they are very conscious of the fact that they and their friends are set apart from other Americans. In the study of Boston and Kansas City residents, an upper-class Bostonian said, "Of course social class exists—it influences your thinking." Then she added, "Maybe you shouldn't use the word 'class' for it, though—it's really a niche that each of us fits into."[5] In a classic study of social classes in New Haven, a person in the top category in terms of neighborhood residence and educational background seemed startled when asked about her class level. After regaining her composure, she replied, "One does not speak of classes; they are felt."[6] As part of a study of thirty-eight upper-class women in a large Midwestern city, a sociologist bluntly asked her informants at the end of the interview if they were members of the upper class. The answers she received had the same flavor of hesitation and denial:

> I hate (the term) upper class. It's so non-upper class to use it. I just call it "all of us," those of us who are well-born.
>
> I hate to use the word "class." We're responsible, fortunate people, old families, the people who have something.
>
> We're not supposed to have layers. I'm embarrassed to admit to you that we do, and that I feel superior at my social level. I like being part of the upper crust.[7]

Social Class According to Social Scientists

Social scientists continue to debate among themselves at great length about how social classes should be defined and even about the value of theorizing in terms of social classes. While there is considerable overlap on some of the main issues, there is no firm consensus.[8] For purposes of this book, the following general guidelines provide a sufficient starting point.

Class is a two-dimension concept. First and foremost, the term refers to an intertwined economic and power relationship between two or more groups of people who have specific roles in the economic system. Owners of businesses and the employees of those businesses are the most obvious examples of this dimension in the nation-states of the Western world, but not all societies have economies that feature owners and their employees. Second, class is a category that refers to the social institutions, social relationships, and lifestyle within the various economic groups: common neighborhoods, common clubs and recreational activities, and a strong tendency to interact primarily with people from one's own economic class. It is in this latter sense that Americans usually use the term.

However, the degree to which a given *economic class* is also a *social class* can vary widely from place to place and time to time. Class as a relationship is always operating, but the people in any given economic category may or may not live in the same neighborhoods or interact socially. They may or may not think of themselves as being members of one or another class. Historically, it is the members of the most powerful class in a society who organize themselves socially and develop a common class awareness that is an important part of their social identity.[9]

The empirical study of the degree to which a given economic category is also a social class begins with a search for connections among the people and institutions that are thought to constitute it. This procedure is called *membership network analysis*, which boils down to a matrix in which social institutions are arrayed along one axis and individuals along the other. Then the cells created by each intersection of a person and a social institution are filled in with information revealing whether or not the person is a member. This information is used to create two different kinds of networks, one organizational and the other interpersonal. An *organizational network* consists of the relationships among organizations, as determined by their common members. These shared members are sometimes called *overlapping* or *interlocking members*. An *interpersonal network*, on the other hand, reveals the relationships among individuals, as determined by their common organizational affiliations.*

To provide a concrete example of the type of analysis that appears throughout this book, suppose a researcher has the membership lists for several exclusive social clubs. By determining which members are common to each pair

---

*These and other methodological issues are explained in more detail, with the help of diagrams and tables, in Appendix A.

of clubs, it is possible to see which clubs are part of an organizational network defined by the overlapping members. In addition, it can be said that the most central clubs in the network are those with members in common with many other clubs, whereas a peripheral club in the network might have common members only with a club that itself is one or two steps removed from the central clubs. Furthermore, some clubs may have no members in common with any of the others, which reveals they are not part of that social network.

The same procedure can be repeated with alumni lists from preparatory schools and Ivy League colleges, and with guest lists from debutante balls and other social functions. Then the membership overlaps among all these different types of social institutions can be compiled. In effect, this network analysis provides a systematic overview of the social institutions that define the social upper class in the United States.

A membership network analysis is in principle very simple, but it is theoretically important because it contains within it the two types of human relationships of concern in sociological theorizing: interpersonal relations and memberships in organizations. Thus, these networks contain "a duality of persons and groups."[10] For analytical purposes, the interpersonal and organizational networks are often treated separately, and some social scientists talk of different levels of analysis, but in the reality of everyday life the two levels are always intertwined. Hence the phrase, "a duality of persons and groups."

Is There an American Upper Class?

If the owners and managers of large income-producing properties in the United States are also a social upper class, then it should be possible to create a very large network of interrelated social institutions whose overlapping members are primarily wealthy families and high-level corporate leaders. These institutions should provide patterned ways of organizing the lives of their members from infancy to old age and create a relatively elite style of life. In addition, they should provide mechanisms for socializing both the younger generation and new adult members who have risen from lower social levels. If the class is a sociological reality, the names and faces may change somewhat over the years, but the social institutions that underlie the upper class must persist with only gradual change over several generations.

Four different types of empirical studies establish the existence of such an interrelated set of social institutions and social activities in the United States: historical case studies, quantitative studies of biographical directories, open-ended surveys of knowledgeable observers, and interview studies with members of the upper-middle and upper classes. These studies not only demonstrate the existence of an American upper class, they also provide what are called *indicators* of upper-class standing, which are useful in determining the degree of overlap between the upper class and the corporate community or between the upper class and various types of nonprofit organizations. They can be used to determine the amount of involvement members of the upper class have in various parts of the government as well.

In the first major historical case study, the wealthy families of Philadelphia were traced over a period of 200 years, showing how they created their own neighborhoods, schools, clubs, and debutante balls. Then their activities outside of that city were determined, which demonstrated that there are nationwide social institutions where wealthy people from all over the country interact with each other. This study led to the discovery of an upper-class telephone directory called the *Social Register,* published for thirteen large cities from Boston to San Francisco between 1887 and 1975.[11] The guide to the thirteen city volumes, the *Social Register Locator*, contained about 60,000 families, making it a very valuable indicator of upper-class standing.

Using information on private school attendance and club membership that appeared in 3,000 randomly selected *Who's Who in America* biographies, along with listings in the *Social Register*, another study provides a statistical analysis of the patterns of memberships and affiliations among dozens of prep schools and clubs. The findings from this study are very similar to those from the historical case study. Still another study relied on journalists who cover high society as informants, asking them to identify the schools, clubs, and social directories that defined the highest level of society in their city. The replies from these well-placed observers reveal strong agreement with the findings from the historical and statistical studies.[12]

A fourth and final method of establishing the existence of upper-class institutions is based on intensive interviews with a cross-section of citizens. The most detailed study of this type was conducted in Kansas City. The study concerned people's perceptions of the social ladder as a whole, from top to bottom, but it is the top level that is of relevance here. Although most people in Kansas City can point to the existence of exclusive neighborhoods in suggesting that there is a class of "blue bloods" or "big rich," it is members of the upper-middle class and the upper class itself whose reports demonstrate that clubs and similar social institutions as well as neighborhoods give the class an institutional existence.[13]

The specific schools and clubs discovered by these and related investigations are listed in Appendix B [see text]. The *Social Registers* and other blue books are listed as well, but are now utilized primarily for historical investigations because they became less popular and shrank in size in the last third of the twentieth century.

Although these social indicators are a convenient tool for research purposes, they are far from perfect in evaluating the class standing of any specific individual because they are subject to two different kinds of errors that tend to cancel each other out in group data. *False positives* are those people who qualify as members of the upper class according to the indicators, even though further investigation would show that they are not really members. Scholarship students at private secondary schools are one example of a false positive. Honorary and performing members of social clubs, who usually are members of the middle class, are another important type of false positive. *False negatives*, on the other hand, are people who do not seem to meet any of the criteria of upper-class standing because they shun social registries and do not choose to list their private school or their club affiliations in biographical sources.

Private schools are especially underreported. Many prominent political figures do not list their private secondary schools in *Who's Who in America*, for example; even former president George H. W. Bush removed mention of his private school from his entry in the 1980-1981 edition when he became vice president in the Reagan Administration. More generally, studies comparing private school alumni lists with *Who's Who* listings suggest that 40 to 50 percent of corporate officers and directors do not list their graduation from high-prestige private schools. Membership in social clubs may also go unreported. In a study of the 326 members of a prestigious private club with a nationwide membership who are listed in *Who's Who in America*, 29 percent did not include this affiliation.[14]

The factors leading to false positives and false negatives raise interesting sociological questions deserving of further study. Why are scholarship students sought by some private schools, and are such students likely to become part of the upper class? Why aren't private schools and clubs listed in biographical sources by some members of the upper class? Why are some middle-class people taken into upper-class clubs? Merely to ask these questions is to suggest the complex social and psychological reality that lies beneath this seemingly dry catalog of upper-class indicators. More generally, the information included or excluded in a social register or biographical directory is an autobiographical presentation that has been shown to be highly revealing concerning religious, ethnic, and class identifications.[15]

What Is Power?

As might be expected, American ideas about power have their origins in the struggle for independence. What is not so well known is that these ideas owe as much to the conflict within each colony about the role of ordinary citizens as they do to the war itself. It is often lost from sight that the average citizens were making revolutionary political demands on their leaders as well as helping in the fight against the British. Before the American revolution, governments everywhere had been based on the power of legitimacy of religious leaders, kings, self-appointed conventions, or parliaments. The upper-class American revolutionary leaders who drafted the constitutions for the thirteen states between 1776 and 1780 expected their handiwork to be debated and voted upon by state legislatures, but they did not want to involve the general public in a direct way.

It was members of the "middling" classes of yeoman farmers and artisans who gradually developed the idea out of their own experience that power is the possession of all the people and is delegated to government with their consent. They therefore insisted that special conventions be elected to frame constitutions, and that the constitutions then be ratified by the vote of all free, white males without regard to their property holdings. They were steeled in their resolve by their participation in the revolutionary struggle and by a fear of the potentially onerous property laws and taxation policies that might be written into the constitutions by those who were known at the time as their betters. So the idea of the people as the constituent power of the new United States arose from the people themselves.[16]

In the end, the middle-level insurgents only won the right to both a constitutional convention of elected delegates and a vote on subsequent ratification in Massachusetts in 1780. From that time forth, however, it has been widely agreed that power in the United States belongs to "the people." Since then, every liberal, radical, populist, or ultraconservative political group has claimed that it represents "the people" in its attempt to wrest arbitrary power from the "vested interests," the "economic elite," the "cultural elite," "the media," the "bureaucrats," or the "politicians in Washington." Even the Founding Fathers of 1789, who were far removed from the general population in their wealth, income, education, and political experience, did not try to promulgate their new constitution, designed to more fully protect private property and commerce, without asking for the consent of the governed. In the process, they were forced to add the Bill of Rights to insure its acceptance. In a very profound cultural sense, then, no group or class has power in America, but only influence. Any small group or class that has power over the people is therefore perceived as illegitimate. This may explain why those with power in America always deny they have any.[17]

The Social Science Definition of Power

Like social class, the meaning of *power* is still disputed among social scientists, within the context of rough agreement on some issues. For purposes of this book, power can be defined as "the ability to achieve desired social outcomes."[18] This broad definition encompasses two intertwined dimensions. First, power is the overall capacity of a group, class, or nation to be effective and productive. Here, the stress is on power as the degree to which a collectivity has the technological resources, organizational forms, and social morale to achieve its general goals. In that sense, most nations have become more powerful in recent decades than they were in the past.

Second, power is also the ability of a group, class, or nation to be successful in conflicts with other groups, classes, or nations on issues of concern to it. Here, the stress is on *power over*, which is also called *distributive power*. In this book, the distributive dimension of power is the sole concern. More specifically, the book seeks to show that a social upper class of owners and high-level executives, with the help of conservative, single-issue groups and the New Christian Right, has the power to institute the policies it favors even in the face of organized opposition from the liberal-labor coalition.

Unfortunately, it is not an easy matter to study the distributive power of a social class. A formal definition does not explain how a concept is to be measured. In the case of distributive power, it is seldom possible to observe interactions that reveal its operation even in small groups, let alone to see one class affecting another. People and organizations are what can be seen in a power struggle, not classes. It is therefore necessary to develop what are called *indicators of power*.

Although distributive power is first and foremost a relationship between two or more contending classes, for research purposes it is useful to think of distributive power as an underlying trait or property of a social class. As with any underlying trait, it is measured by a series of indicators, or signs, that bear a probabilistic relationship to it. This means that all of the indicators do not necessarily appear each and every time the trait is manifesting itself. It might make this point more clear to add that the personality traits utilized by psychologists to understand individual behavior and the concepts developed to explain findings in the natural sciences have a similar logical structure. Whether a theorist is concerned with friendliness, as in psychology, or magnetism, as in physics, or power, as in the case of this book, the nature of the investigatory procedure is the same. In each case, there is an underlying concept whose presence can be inferred only through a series of diagnostic signs or indicators that vary in their strength under differing conditions. Research proceeds, in this view, through a series of *if-then* statements. *If* a group is powerful, *then* at least some of the indicators of this power should be present.[19]

Three Power Indicators

Since each indicator of power may not necessarily appear in each and every instance where power is operating, it is necessary to have several indicators. Working within this framework, three different types of power indicators are used in this book. They are called: (1) Who benefits? (2) Who governs? and (3) Who wins? Each of these empirical indicators has its own strengths and weaknesses. However, the potential weaknesses of each indicator do not present a serious problem because all three of them have to point to the owners and managers of large income-producing property as the most powerful class for the case to be considered convincing.

Who Benefits?

Every society has material objects and experiences that are highly valued. If it is assumed that everyone would like to have as great a share of these good things of life as possible, then their distribution can be utilized as a power indicator. Those who have the most of what people want are, by inference, the powerful. Although some value distributions may be unintended outcomes that do not really reflect power, the general distribution of valued experiences and objects within a society still can be viewed as the most publicly visible and stable outcome of the operation of power.

In American society, for example, wealth and well-being are highly valued. people seek to own property, to have high incomes, to have interesting and safe jobs, to enjoy the finest in travel and leisure, and to live long and healthy lives. All of these values are unequally distributed, and all may be utilized as power indicators. In this book, however, the primary focus with this type of indicator is on the wealth and income distributions. This does not mean that wealth and income are the same thing as power, but that income and the possession of great wealth are visible signs that a class has power in relation to other classes.

The argument for using value distributions as power indicators is strengthened by studies showing that such distributions vary from country to country, depending upon the relative strength of rival political parties and trade unions. One study reports that the degree of equality in the income distribution in Western democracies varied inversely with the percentage of social democrats who had been elected to the country's legislature since 1945.[20] The greater the social democratic presence, the greater the amount of income that goes to the lower classes. In a study based on eighteen Western democracies, it was found that strong trade unions and successful social democratic parties are correlated with greater equality in the income distribution and a higher level of welfare spending.[21] Thus, there is evidence that value distributions do vary depending on the relative power of contending groups or classes.

Who Governs?

Power also can be inferred from studying who occupies important institutional positions and takes part in important decision-making groups. If a group or class is highly overrepresented or underrepresented in relation to its proportion of the population, it can be inferred that the group or class is relatively powerful or powerless, as the case may be.

For example, if a class that contains 1 percent of the population has 30 percent of the important positions in the government, which is thirty times as many as would be expected by chance, then it can be inferred that the class is powerful. Conversely, when it is found that women are in only a small percentage of the leadership positions in government, even though they make up a majority of the population, it can be inferred that they are relatively powerless in that important sector of society. Similarly, when it is determined that a minority group has only a small percentage of its members in leadership positions, even though it comprises 10 to 20 percent of the population in a given city or state, then the basic processes of power—inclusion and exclusion—are inferred to be at work.

This indicator is not perfect because some official positions may not really possess the power they are thought to have, and some groups or classes may exercise power from behind the scenes. Once again, however, the case for the usefulness of this indicator is strengthened by the fact that it has been shown to vary over time and place. For example, the decline of landed aristocrats and the rise of business leaders in Great Britain has been charted through their degree of representation in Parliament.[22] Then, too, as women, African-Americans, Latinos, and Asian-Americans began to demand a greater voice in the United States in the 1960s and 1970s, their representation in positions of authority began to increase.[23]

Who Wins?

There are many issues over which the corporate-conservative and liberal-labor coalitions disagree, including free trade, taxation, unionization, business regulation, and Social Security. Power can be inferred on the basis of these issue conflicts by determining who successfully initiates, modifies, or vetoes policy alternatives. This indicator, by focusing on relationships between the two rival coalitions, comes closest to approximating the process of power contained in the formal definition. It is the indicator preferred by most social scientists. For many reasons, however, it is also the most difficult to use in an accurate way. Aspects of a decision process may remain hidden, some informants may exaggerate or downplay their roles, and people's memories about who did what often become cloudy shortly after the event. Worse, the key concerns of the corporate community may never arise as issues on the public agenda because it has the power to keep them nonissues through a variety of means.

Despite the difficulties in using the *Who wins?* indicator of power, it is possible to provide a theoretical framework for analyzing governmental decision-making that mitigates many of them. This framework encompasses the various means by which the corporate community attempts to influence both the government and the general population in a conscious and planned manner, thereby making it possible to assess its degree of success very directly. More specifically, there are four relatively distinct, but overlapping processes (discovered by means of membership network analysis) through which the corporate community controls the public agenda and then wins on most issues that appear on it. These four power networks, which are discussed in detail in later chapters, are as follows:

1. The *special-interest process* deals with the narrow and short-run policy concerns of wealthy families, specific corporations, and specific business sectors. It operates primarily through lobbyists, company lawyers, and trade associations, with a focus on congressional committees, departments of the executive branch, and regulatory agencies.

2. The *policy-planning process* formulates the general interests of the corporate community. It operates through a policy planning network of foundations, think tanks, and policy-discussion groups, with a focus on the White House, relevant congressional committees, and the high-status newspapers and opinion magazines published in New York and Washington.

3. The *candidate-selection process* is concerned with the election of candidates who are sympathetic to the agenda put forth in the special-interest and policy-planning processes. It operates through large campaign donations and hired political consultants, with a focus on the presidential campaigns of both major political parties and the congressional campaigns of the Republican Party.

4. The *opinion-shaping process* attempts to influence public opinion and keep some issues off the public agenda. Often drawing on policy positions, rationales, and statements developed within the policy-planning process, it operates through the public relations departments of large corporations, general public relations forms, and many small opinion-shaping organizations, with a focus on middle-class voluntary organizations, educational institutions, and the mass media.

Notes

1. Robert R. Palmer, *The Age of the Democratic Revolution: A Political History of Europe and America, 1760-1800* (Princeton: Princeton University Press, 1959), p. 203.
2. Jackson T. Main, *The Social Structure of Revolutionary America* (Priceton: Princeton University Press, 1965), p. 239, 284.
3. Robert R. Palmer, *The Age of the Democratic Revolution: A Political History of Europe and America, 1760-1800*

(Princeton: Princeton University Press, 1959), p. 3.
4. Richard P. Coleman, Lee Rainwater, and Kent A. McClelland, *Social Standing in America: New Dimensions of Class* (New York: Basic Books, 1978).
5. Richard P. Coleman, Lee Rainwater, and Kent A. McClelland, *Social Standing in America: New Dimensions of Class* (New York: Basic Books, 1978), p. 25.
6. August de Belmont Hollingshead and Fredrick C. Redlich, *Social Class and Mental Illness: A Community Study* (New York: Wiley, 1958), p. 69.
7. Susan Ostrander, "Upper-class Women: Class Consciousness as Conduct and Meaning," in *Power Structure Research*, ed. G. William Domhoff (Beverly Hills: Sage Publications, 1980), pp. 78-79.
8. John Goldthorpe, "Rent, Class Conflict, and Class Structure: A Commentary on Sorensen," *American Journal of Sociology* 105, no. 6 (2000); 1572-1582; Aage Sorensen, "Toward a Sounder Basis for Class Analysis," *American Journal of Sociology* 105, no. 6 (2000): 1523-1558; Erik O. Wright, "Class, Exploitation, and Economic Rents: Reflections on Sorensen's 'Sounder Basis,'" *American Journal of Sociology* 105, no. 6 (2000): 1559-1571.
9. Michael Mann, "Ruling Class Strategies and Citizenship," *Sociology* 21, no. 3 (1987): 339-354; Michael Mann, *The Sources of Social Power: A History of Power from the Beginning to A.D. 1760*, vol. 1 (New York: Cambridge University Press, 1986).
10. Ronald L. Breiger, "The Duality of Persons and Groups," *Social Forces* 53, no. 2 (1974): 181-190.
11. E. Digby Baltzell, *Philadelphia Gentlemen: The Making of a National Upper Class* (Glencoe, Ill.: Free Press, 1958).
12. G. William Domhoff, *The Higher Circles* (New York: Random House, 1970), chapter 1.
13. Richard P. Coleman, Lee Rainwater, and Kent A. McClelland, *Social Standing in America: New Dimensions of Class* (New York: Basic Books, 1978).
14. G. William Domhoff, *Who Rules America Now?* (New York: Simon & Schuster, 1983).
15. Richard L. Zweigenhaft and G. William Domhoff, *Jews in the Protestant Establishment* (New York: Praeger, 1982).
16. Robert R. Palmer *The Age of the Democratic Revolution: A Political History of Europe and America, 1760-1800* (Princeton: Princeton University Press, 1959).
17. David Vogel, "Why Businessmen Mistrust Their State: The Political Consciousness of American Corporate Executives," *British Journal of Political Science* 8 (1978): 45-78.
18. Dennis Wrong, *Power: Its Forms, Bases, and Uses* (New Brunswick, N. J.: Transaction Publishers, 1995), p. 2.
19. Paul Lazarsfeld, "Concept Formation and Measurement," in *Concepts, Theory, and Explanation in the Behavioral Sciences*, ed. Gordon DiRenzo (New York: Random House, 1966), 144-202.
20. Christopher Hewitt, "The Effect of Political Democracy and Social Democracy on Equality in Industrial Societies: A Cross-National Comparison," *American Sociologist Review* 42, no. 3 (1977): 450-464.
21. John Stephens, *The Transition from Capitalism to Socialism* (London: Macmillan, 1979).
22. W. L. Guttsman, *The English Ruling Class* (London: Weidenfeld & Nicholson, 1969).
23. Richard L. Zweigenhaft and G. William Domhoff, *Diversity in the Power Elite: Have Women and Minorities Reached the Top?* (New Haven: Yale University Press, 1998).

Capitalism and Democracy

Gabriel A. Almond, Stanford University

Joseph Schumpeter, a great economist and social scientist of the last generation, whose career was almost equally divided between Central European and American universities, and who lived close to the crises of the 1930s and 40s, published a book in 1942 under the title, *Capitalism, Socialism, and Democracy*. The book has had great influence, and can be read today with profit. It was written in the aftergloom of the great depression, during the early triumphs of Fascism and Nazism in 1940 and 1941, when the future of capitalism, socialism, and democracy all were in doubt. Schumpeter projected a future of declining capitalism, and rising socialism. He thought that democracy under socialism might be no more impaired and problematic than it was under capitalism.

He wrote a concluding chapter in the second edition which appeared in 1946, and which took into account the political-economic situation at the end of the war, with the Soviet Union then astride a devastated Europe. In this last chapter he argues that we should not identify the future of socialism with that of the Soviet Union, that what we had observed and were observing in the first three decades of Soviet existence was not a necessary expression of socialism. There was a lot of Czarist Russia in the mix. If Schumpeter were writing today, I don't believe he would argue that socialism has a brighter future than capitalism. The relationship between the two has turned out to be a good deal more complex and intertwined than Schumpeter anticipated. But I am sure that he would still urge us to separate the future of socialism from that of Soviet and Eastern European Communism.

Unlike Schumpeter I do not include Socialism in my title, since its future as a distinct ideology and program of action is unclear at best. Western Marxism and the moderate socialist movements seem to have settled for social democratic solutions, for adaptations of both capitalism and democracy producing acceptable mixes of market competition, political pluralism, participation, and welfare. I deal with these modifications of capitalism, as a consequence of the

---

From *PS: Political Science and Politics* by Gabriel A. Almond. Reprinted with the permission of Cambridge University Press.

impact of democracy on capitalism in the last half century.

At the time that Adam Smith wrote *The Wealth of Nations*, the world of government, politics and the state that he knew—pre-Reform Act England, the French government of Louis XV and XVI—was riddled with special privileges, monopolies, interferences with trade. With my tongue only half way in my cheek I believe the discipline of economics may have been traumatized by this condition of political life at its birth. Typically, economists speak of the state and government instrumentally, as a kind of secondary service mechanism.

I do not believe that politics can be treated in this purely instrumental and reductive way without losing our analytic grip on the social and historical process. The economy and the polity are the main problem solving mechanisms of human society. They each have their distinctive means, and they each have their "goods" or ends. They necessarily interact with each other, and transform each other in the process. Democracy in particular generates goals and programs.

You cannot give people the suffrage, and let them form organizations, run for office, and the like, without their developing all kinds of ideas as to how to improve things. And sometimes some of these ideas are adopted, implemented and are productive, and improve our lives, although many economists are reluctant to concede this much to the state.

My lecture deals with this interaction of politics and economics in the Western World in the course of the last couple of centuries, in the era during which capitalism and democracy emerged as the dominant problem solving institutions of modern civilization. I am going to discuss some of the theoretical and empirical literature dealing with the themes of the positive and negative interaction between capitalism and democracy. There are those who say that capitalism supports democracy, and those who say that capitalism subverts democracy. And there are those who say that democracy subverts capitalism, and those who say that it supports it.

The relation between capitalism and democracy dominates the political theory of the last two centuries. All the logically possible points of view are represented in a rich literature. It is this ambivalence and dialectic, this tension between the two major problem solving sectors of modern society—the political and the economic—that is the topic of my lecture.

Capitalism Supports Democracy

Let me begin with the argument that capitalism is positively linked with democracy, shares its values and culture, and facilitates its development. This case has been made in historical, logical, and statistical terms.

Albert Hirschman in his *Rival Views of Market Society* (1986) examines the values, manners and morals of capitalism, and their effects on the larger society and culture as these have been described by the philosophers of the 17th, 18th, and 19th centuries. He shows how the interpretation of the impact of capitalism has changed from the enlightenment view of Montesquieu, Condorcet, Adam Smith and others, who stressed the *douceur* of commerce, its "gentling," civilizing effect on behavior and interpersonal relations, to that of the 19th and 20th century conservative and radical writers who described the culture of capitalism as crassly materialistic, destructively competitive, corrosive of morality, and hence self-destructive. This sharp almost 180-degree shift in point of view among political theorists is partly explained by the transformation from the commerce and small-scale industry of early capitalism, to the smoke blackened industrial districts, the demonic and exploitive entrepreneurs, and exploited laboring classes of the second half of the nineteenth century. Unfortunately for our purposes, Hirschman doesn't deal explicitly with the capitalism-democracy connection, but rather with culture and with manners. His argument, however, implies an early positive connection and a later negative one.

Joseph Schumpeter in *Capitalism, Socialism, and Democracy* (1942) states flatly, "History clearly confirms ... [that] ... modern democracy rose along with capitalism, and in causal connection with it ... modern democracy is a product of the capitalist process." He has a whole chapter entitled "The Civilization of Capitalism," democracy being a part of that civilization. Schumpeter also makes the point that democracy was historically supportive of capitalism. He states, " ... the bourgeoisie reshaped, and from its own point of view rationalized, the social and political structure that preceded its ascendancy ..." (that is to say, feudalism). "The democratic method was the political tool of that reconstruction." According to Schumpeter capitalism and democracy were mutually casual historically, mutually supportive parts of a rising modern civilization, although as we shall show below, he also recognized their antagonisms.

Barrington Moore's historical investigation (1966) with its long title, *The Social Origins of Dictatorship and Democracy; Lord and Peasant in the Making of the Modern World*, argues that there have been three historical routes to industrial modernization. The first of these followed by Britain, France, and the United States, involved the subordination and transformation of the agricultural sector by the rising commercial bourgeoisie, producing the democratic capitalism of the 19th and 20th centuries. The second route followed by Germany and Japan, where the landed aristocracy was able to contain and dominate the rising commercial classes, produced an authoritarian and fascist version of industrial modernization, a system of capitalism encased in a feudal authoritarian framework, dominated by a military aristocracy, and an authoritarian monarchy. The third route, followed in Russia where the commercial bourgeoisie was too weak to give content and direction to the modernizing process, took the form of a revolutionary process drawing on the frustration and resources of the peasantry, and created a mobilized authoritarian Communist regime along with a state-controlled industrialized economy. Successful capitalism dominating and transforming the rural agricultural sector, according to Barrington Moore, is the creator and sustainer of the emerging democracies of the nineteenth century.

Robert A. Dahl, the leading American democratic theorist, in the new edition of his book (1990) *After the Revolution? Authority in a Good Society*, has included a new chapter entitled "Democracy and Markets." In the opening paragraph of that chapter, he says:

It is an historical fact that modern democratic institutions ... have existed only in countries with predominantly privately owned, market-oriented economies, or capitalism if you prefer that name. It is also a fact that all "socialist" countries with predominantly state-owned centrally directed economic orders—command economies—have not enjoyed democratic governments, but have in fact been ruled by authoritarian dictatorships. It is also an historical fact that some "capitalist" countries have also been, and are, ruled by authoritarian dictatorships.

To put it more formally, it looks to be the case that market-oriented economies are necessary (in the logical sense) to democratic institutions, though they are certainly not sufficient. And it looks to be the case that state-owned centrally directed economic orders are strictly associated with authoritarian regimes, though authoritarianism definitely does not require them. We have something very much like an historical experiment, so it would appear, that leaves these conclusions in no great doubt. (Dahl 1990)

Peter Berger in his book *The Capitalist Revolution* (1986) presents four propositions on the relations between capitalism and democracy:

Capitalism is a necessary but not sufficient condition of democracy under modern conditions.

If a capitalist economy is subjected to increasing degrees of state control, a point (not precisely specifiable at this time) will be reached at which democratic governance becomes impossible.

If a socialist economy is opened up to increasing degrees of market forces, a point (not precisely specifiable at this time) will be reached at which democratic governance becomes a possibility.

If capitalist development is successful in generating economic growth from which a sizable proportion of the population benefits, pressures toward democracy are likely to appear.

This positive relationship between capitalism and democracy has also been sustained by statistical studies. The "Social Mobilization" theorists of the 1950s and 1960s which included Daniel Lerner (1958), Karl Deutsch (1961), S. M. Lipset (1959) among others, demonstrated a strong statistical association between GNP per capita and democratic political institutions. This is more than simple statistical association. There is a logic in the relation between level of economic development and democratic institutions. Level of economic development has been shown to be associated with education and literacy, exposure to mass media, and democratic psychological propensities such as subjective efficacy, participatory aspirations and skills. In a major investigation of the social psychology of industrialization, a research team led by the sociologist Alex Inkeles (1974) interviewed several thousand workers in the modern industrial and the traditional economic sectors of six countries of differing culture. Inkeles found empathetic, efficacious, participatory and activist propensities much more frequently among the modern industrial workers, and to a much lesser extent in the traditional sector in each one of these countries regardless of cultural differences.

The historical, the logical, and the statistical evidence for this positive relation between capitalism and democracy is quite persuasive.

Capitalism Subverts Democracy

But the opposite case is also made, that capitalism subverts or undermines democracy. Already in John Stuart Mill (1848) we encounter a view of existing systems of private property as unjust, and of the free market as destructively competitive—aesthetically and morally repugnant. The case he was making was a normative rather than a political one. He wanted a less competitive society, ultimately socialist, which would still respect individuality. He advocated limitations on the inheritance of property and the improvement of the property system so that everyone shared in its benefits, the limitation of population growth, and the improvement of the quality of the labor force through the provision of high quality education for all by the state. On the eve of the emergence of the modern democratic capitalist order John Stuart Mill wanted to control the excesses of both the market economy and the majoritarian polity, by the education of consumers and producers, citizens and politicians, in the interest of producing morally improved free market and democratic orders. But in contrast to Marx, he did not thoroughly discount the possibilities of improving the capitalist and democratic order.

Marx argued that as long as capitalism and private property existed there could be no genuine democracy, that democracy under capitalism was bourgeois democracy, which is to say not democracy at all. While it would be in the interest of the working classes to enter a coalition with the bourgeoisie in supporting this form of democracy in order to eliminate feudalism, this would be a tactical maneuver. Capitalist democracy could only result in the increasing exploitation of the working classes. Only the elimination of capitalism and private property could result in the emancipation of the working classes and the attainment of true democracy. Once socialism was attained the basic political problems of humanity would have been solved through the elimination of classes. Under socialism there would be no distinctive democratic organization, no need for institutions to resolve conflicts, since there would be no conflicts. There is not much democratic or political theory to be found in Marx's writings. The basic reality is the mode of economic production and the consequent class structure from which other institutions follow.

For the followers of Marx up to the present day there continues to be a negative tension between capitalism, however reformed, and democracy. But the integral Marxist and Leninist rejection of the possibility of an autonomous, bourgeois democratic state has been left behind for most Western Marxists. In the thinking of Poulantzas, Offe, Bobbio, Habermas and others, the bourgeois democratic state is now viewed as a class struggle state, rather than an unambiguously bourgeois state. The working class has access to it; it can struggle for its interests, and can attain partial benefits from it. The state is now viewed as autonomous, or as relatively autonomous, and it can be reformed in a progressive direction by working class and other popular movements. The bourgeois democratic state can be moved in the direction of a socialist state by political action short of violence and institutional destruction.

Schumpeter (1942) appreciated the tension between capitalism and democracy. While he saw a causal connection between competition in the economic and the political order, he points out "... that there are some deviations from the principle of democracy which link up with the presence of organized capitalist interests.... [T]he statement is true both from the standpoint of the classical and from the standpoint of our own theory of democracy. From the first standpoint, the result reads that the means at the disposal of private interests are often used in order to thwart the will of the people. From the second standpoint, the result reads that those private means are often used in order to interfere with the working of the mechanism of competitive leadership." He refers to some countries and situations in which "... political life all but resolved itself into a struggle of pressure groups and in many cases practices that failed to conform to the spirit of the democratic method." But he rejects the notion that there cannot be political democracy in a capitalist society. For Schumpeter full democracy in the sense of the informed participation of all adults in the selection of political leaders and consequently the making of public policy, was an impossibility because of the number and complexity of the issues confronting modern electorates. The democracy which was realistically possible was one in which people could choose among competing leaders, and consequently exercise some direction over political decisions. This kind of democracy was possible in a capitalist society, though some of its propensities impaired its performance.

Writing in the early years of World War II, when the future of democracy and of capitalism were uncertain, he leaves unresolved the questions of "... Whether or not democracy is one of those products of capitalism which are to die out with it ..." or "... how well or ill capitalist society qualifies for the task of working the democratic method it evolved."

Non-Marxist political theorists have contributed to this questioning of the reconcilability of capitalism and democracy. Robert A. Dahl, who makes the point that capitalism historically has been a necessary precondition of democracy, views contemporary democracy in the United States as seriously compromised, impaired by the inequality in resources among the citizens. But Dahl stresses the variety in distributive patterns, and in politico-economic relations among contemporary democracies. "The category of capitalist democracies" he writes, "includes an extraordinary variety ... from nineteenth century, laissez faire, early industrial systems to twentieth century, highly regulated, social welfare, late or postindustrial systems. Even late twentieth century 'welfare state' orders vary all the way from the Scandinavian systems, which are redistributive, heavily taxed, comprehensive in their social security, and neocorporatist in their collective bargaining arrangements to the faintly redistributive, moderately taxed, limited social security, weak collective bargaining systems of the United States and Japan" (1989).

In *Democracy and Its Critics* (1989) Dahl argues that the normative growth of democracy to what he calls its "third transformation" (the first being the direct city–state democracy of classic times, and the second, the indirect, representative inegalitarian democracy of the contemporary world) will require democratization of the economic order. In other words, modern corporate capitalism needs to be transformed. Since government control and/or ownership of the economy would be destructive of the pluralism which is an essential requirement of democracy, his preferred solution to the problem of the mega-corporation is employee control of corporate industry. An economy so organized, according to Dahl, would improve the distribution of political resources without at the same time destroying the pluralism which democratic competition requires. To those who question the realism of Dahl's solution to the problem of inequality, he replies that history is full of surprises.

Charles E. Lindblom in his book, *Politics and Markets* (1977), concludes his comparative analysis of the political economy of modern capitalism and socialism, with an essentially pessimistic conclusion about contemporary market-oriented democracy. He says

> We therefore come back to the corporation. It is possible that the rise of the corporation has offset or more than offset the decline of class as an instrument of indoctrination.... That it creates a new core of wealth and power for a newly constructed upper class, as well as an overpowering loud voice, is also reasonably clear. The executive of the large corporation is, on many counts, the contemporary counterpart to the landed gentry of an earlier era, his voice amplified by the technology of mass communication.... [T]he major institutional barrier to fuller democracy may therefore be the autonomy of the private corporation.

Lindblom concludes, "The large private corporation fits oddly into democratic theory and vision. Indeed it does not fit."

There is then a widely shared agreement, from the Marxists and neo-Marxists, to Schumpeter, Dahl, Lindblom, and other liberal political theorists, that modern capitalism with the dominance of the large corporation, produces a defective or an impaired form of democracy.

Democracy Subverts Capitalism

If we change our perspective now and look at the way democracy is said to affect capitalism, one of the dominant traditions of economics from Adam Smith until the present day stresses the importance for productivity and welfare of an economy that is relatively free of intervention by the state. In this doctrine of minimal government there is still a place for a framework of rules and services essential to the productive and efficient performance of the economy. In part the government has to protect the market from itself. Left to their own devices, according to Smith, businessmen were prone to corner the market in order to exact the highest possible price. And according to Smith, businessmen were prone to bribe public officials in order to gain special privileges, and legal monopolies. For Smith good capitalism was competitive capitalism, and good government provided just those goods and services which the market needed to flourish, could not itself provide, or would not provide. A good government according to Adam Smith was a minimal government, providing for the national defense, and domestic order. Particularly important for the economy were the rules pertaining to commercial life such as the regulation of weights and measures, setting and enforcing building standards, providing for the protection of persons and property, and the like.

For Milton Friedman (1961, 1981), the leading contemporary advocate of the free market and free government, and of the interdependence of the two, the principal threat to the survival of capitalism and democracy is the assumption of the responsibility for welfare on the part of the modern democratic state. He lays down a set of functions appropriate to government in the positive interplay between economy and polity, and then enumerates many of the ways in which the modern welfare, regulatory state has deviated from these criteria.

A good Friedmanesque, democratic government would be one "... which maintained law and order, defended property rights, served as a means whereby we could modify property rights and other rules of the economic game, adjudicated disputes about the interpretation of the rules, enforced contracts, promoted competition, provided a monetary framework, engaged in activities to counter technical monopolies and to overcome neighborhood effects widely regarded as sufficiently important to justify government intervention, and which supplemented private charity and the private family in protecting the irresponsible, whether madman or child...." Against this list of proper activities for a free government, Friedman pinpointed more than a dozen activities of contemporary democratic governments which might better be performed through the private sector, or not at all. These included setting and maintaining price supports, tariffs, import and export quotas and controls, rents, interest rates, wage rates, and the like, regulating industries and banking, radio and television, licensing professions and occupations, providing social security and medical care programs, providing public housing, national parks, guaranteeing mortgages, and much else.

Friedman concludes that this steady encroachment on the private sector has been slowly but surely converting our free government and market system into a collective monster, compromising both freedom and productivity in the outcome. The tax and expenditure revolts and regulatory rebellions of the 1980s have temporarily stemmed this trend, but the threat continues, "It is the internal threat coming from men of good intentions and good will who wish to reform us. Impatient with the slowness of persuasion and example to achieve the great social changes they envision, they are anxious to use the power of the state to achieve their ends, and confident of their own ability to do so." The threat to political and economic freedom, according to Milton Friedman and others who argue the same position, arises out of democratic politics. It may only be defeated by political action.

In the last decades a school, or rather several schools, of economists and political scientists have turned the theoretical models of economics to use in analyzing political processes. Variously called public choice theorists, rational choice theorists, or positive political theorists, and employing such models as market exchange and bargaining, rational self interest, game theory, and the like, these theorists have produced a substantial literature throwing new and often controversial light on democratic political phenomena such as elections, decision of political party leaders, interest group behavior, legislative and committee decisions, bureaucratic, and judicial behavior, lobbying activity, and substantive public policy areas such as constitutional arrangements, health and environment policy, regulatory policy, national security and foreign policy, and the like. Hardly a field of politics and public policy has been left untouched by this inventive and productive group of scholars.

The institutions and names with which this movement is associated in the United States include Virginia State University, the University of Virginia, the George Mason University, the University of Rochester, the University of Chicago, the California Institute of Technology, the Carnegie Mellon University, among others. And the most prominent names are those of the leaders of the two principal schools: James Buchanan, the Nobel Laureate leader of the Virginia "Public Choice" school, and William Riker, the leader of the Rochester "Positive Theory" school. Other prominent scholars associated with this work are Gary Becker of the University of Chicago, Kenneth Shepsle and Morris Florina of Harvard, John Ferejohn of Stanford, Charles Plott of the California Institute of Technology, and many others.

One writer summarizing the ideological bent of much of this work, but by no means all of it (William Mitchell of the University of Washington), describes it as fiscally conservative, sharing a conviction that the ". . . private economy is far more robust, efficient, and perhaps, equitable than other economies, and much more successful than political processes in efficiently allocating resources. . . ." Much of what has been produced ". . by James Buchanan and the leaders of this school can best be described as contributions to a theory of the failure of political processes." These failures of political performance are said to be inherent properties of the democratic political process. "Inequity, inefficiently, and coercion are the most general results of democratic policy formation." In a democracy the demand for publicly provided services seems to be insatiable. It ultimately turns into a special interest, "rent seeking" society. Their remedies take the form of proposed constitutional limits on spending power and checks and balances to limit legislative majorities.

One of the most visible products of this pessimistic economic analysis of democratic politics is the book by Mancur Olson, *The Rise and Decline of Nations* (1982). He makes a strong argument for the negative democracy-capitalism connection. His thesis is that the behavior of individuals and firms in stable societies inevitably leads to the formation of dense networks of collusive, cartelistic, and lobbying organizations that make economies less efficient and dynamic and polities less governable. "The longer a society goes without an upheaval, the more powerful such organizations become and the more they slow down economic expansion. Societies in which these narrow interest groups have been destroyed, by war or revolution, for example, enjoy the greatest gains in growth." His prize cases are Britain on the one hand and Germany and Japan on the other.

> The logic of the argument implies that countries that have had democratic freedom of organization without upheaval or invasion from longest will suffer the most from growth-repressing organizations and combinations. This helps explain why Great Britain, the major nation with the longest immunity from dictatorship, invasion, and revolution, has had in this century a lower rate of growth than other large, developed democracies. Britain has precisely the powerful network of special interest organization that the argument developed here would lead us to expect in a country with its record of military security and democratic stability. The number and power of its trade unions need no description. The venerability and power of its professional associations is also striking. . . . In short, with age British society has acquired so many strong organizations and collusions that it suffers from an institutional sclerosis that slows its adaptation to changing circumstances and technologies. (Olson 1982)

By contrast, post-World War II Germany and Japan started organizationally from scratch. The organizations that led them to defeat were all dissolved, and under the occupation inclusive organizations like the general trade union movement and general organizations of the industrial and commercial community were first formed. These inclusive organizations had more regard for the general national interest and exercised some discipline on the narrower interest organizations. And both countries in the post-war decades experienced "miracles" of economic growth under democratic conditions.

The Olson theory of the subversion of capitalism through the propensities of democratic societies to foster special interest groups has not gone without challenge. There can be little question that there is logic in his argument. But empirical research testing this pressure group hypothesis thus far has produced mixed findings. Olson has hopes that a public educated to the harmful consequences of special interests to economic growth, full employment, coherent government, equal opportunity, and social mobility will resist special interest behavior, and enact legislation imposing anti-trust, and anti-monopoly controls to mitigate and contain these threats. It is somewhat of an irony that the solution to this special interest disease of democracy, according to Olson, is a democratic state with sufficient regulatory authority to control the growth of special interest organizations.

Democracy Fosters Capitalism

My fourth theme, democracy as fostering and sustaining capitalism, is not as straightforward as the first three. Historically there can be little doubt that as the suffrage was extended in the last century, and as mass political parties developed, democratic development impinged significantly on capitalist institutions and practices. Since successful capitalism requires risk-taking entrepreneurs with access to investment capital, the democratic propensity for redistributive and regulative policy tends to reduce the incentives and the resources available for risk-taking and creativity. Thus it can be argued that propensities inevitably resulting from democratic politics, as Friedman, Olson and many others argue, tend to reduce productivity, and hence welfare.

But precisely the opposite argument can be made on the basis of the historical experience of literally all of the advanced capitalist democracies in existence. All of them without exception are now welfare states with some form and degree of social insurance, health and welfare nets, and regulatory frameworks designed to mitigate the harmful impacts and shortfalls of capitalism. Indeed, the welfare state is accepted all across the political spectrum. Controversy takes place around the edges. One might make the argument that had capitalism not been modified in this welfare direction, it is doubtful that it would have survived.

This history of the interplay between democracy and capitalism is clearly laid out in a major study involving European and American scholars, entitled *The Development of Welfare States in Western Europe and America* (Flora and Heidenheimer 1981). The book lays out the relationship between the development and spread of capitalist industry, democratization in the sense of an expanding suffrage and the emergence of trade unions and left-wing political parties, and the gradual introduction of the institutions and practices of the welfare state. The early adoption of the institutions of the welfare state in Bismarck Germany, Sweden, and Great Britain were all associated with the rise of trade unions and socialist parties in those countries. The decisions made by the upper and middle class leaders and political movements to introduce welfare measures such as accident, old age, and unemployment insurance, were strategic decisions. They were increasingly confronted by trade union movements with the capacity of bringing industrial production to a halt, and by political parties with growing parliamentary representation favoring fundamental modifications in, or the abolition of capitalism. As the calculations of the upper and middle class leaders led them to conclude that the costs of suppression exceeded the costs of concession, the various parts of the welfare state began to be put in place—accident, sickness, unemployment insurance, old age insurance, and the like. The problem of maintaining the loyalty of the working classes through two world wars resulted in additional concessions to working class demands: the filling out of the social security system, free public education to higher levels, family allowances, housing benefits, and the like.

Social conditions, historical factors, political processes and decisions produced different versions of the welfare state. In the United States, manhood suffrage came quite early, the later bargaining process emphasized free land and free education to the secondary level, an equality of opportunity version of the welfare state. The Disraelí bargain in Britain resulted in relatively early manhood suffrage and the full attainment of parliamentary government, while the Lloyd George bargain on the eve of World War I brought the beginnings of a welfare system to Britain. The Bismarck bargain in Germany produced an early welfare state, a post-ponement of electoral equality and parliamentary government. While there were all of these differences in historical encounters with democratization and "welfarization," the important outcome was that little more than a century after the process began all of the advanced capitalist democracies had similar versions of the welfare state, smaller in scale in the case of the United States and Japan, more substantial in Britain and the continental European countries.

We can consequently make out a strong case for the argument that democracy has been supportive of capitalism in this strategic sense. Without this welfare adaptation it is doubtful that capitalism would have survived, or rather, its survival, "unwelfarized," would have required a substantial repressive apparatus. The choice then would seem to have been between democratic welfare capitalism, and repressive undemocratic capitalism. I am inclined to believe that capitalism as such thrives more with the democratic welfare adaptation than with the repressive one. It is in that sense that we can argue that there is a clear positive impact of democracy on capitalism.

* * *

We have to recognize, in conclusion, that democracy and capitalism are both positively and negatively related, that they both support and subvert each other. My colleague Moses Abramovitz, described this dialectic more surely than most in his presidential address to the American Economic Association in 1980, on the eve of the "Reagan Revolution." Noting the decline in productivity in the American economy during the latter 1960s and 70s, and recognizing that this decline might in part be attributable to the "tax, transfer, and regulatory" tendencies of the welfare state, he observes,

> The rationale supporting the development of our mixed economy sees it as a pragmatic compromise between the competing virtues and defects of decentralized market capitalism and encompassing socialism. Its goal is to obtain a measure of distributive justice, security, and social guidance of economic life without losing too much of the allocative efficiency and dynamism of private enterprise and market organization. And it is a pragmatic compromise in another sense. It seeks to retain for most people that measure of personal protection from the state which private property and a private job market confer, while obtaining for the disadvantaged minority of people through the state that measure of support without which their lack of property or personal endowment would amount to a denial of individual freedom and capacity to function as full members of the community. (Abramovitz, 1981)

Democratic welfare capitalism produces that reconciliation of opposing and complementary elements which makes possible the survival, even enhancement of both of these sets of institutions. It is not a static accommodation, but rather one which fluctuates over time, with capitalism being compromised by the tax-transfer-regulatory action of the state at one point, and then correcting in the direction of the reduction of the intervention of the state at another point, and with a learning process over time that may reduce the amplitude of the curves.

The case for this resolution of the capitalism-democracy quandary is made quite movingly by Jacob Viner who is quoted in the concluding paragraph of Abramovitz's paper, "... If ... I nevertheless conclude that I believe that the welfare state, like old Siwash, is really worth fighting for and even dying for as compared to any rival system, it is because, despite its imperfection in theory and practice, in the aggregate it provides more promise of preserving and enlarging human freedoms, temporal prosperity, the extinction of mass misery, and the dignity of man and his moral improvement than any other social system which has previously prevailed, which prevails elsewhere today or which outside Utopia, the mind of man has been able to provide a blueprint for" (Abramovitz, 1981).

References

Abramovitz, Moses. 1981. "Welfare Quandaries and Productivity Concerns." *American Economic Review,* March.

Berger, Peter. 1986. *The Capitalist Revolution.* New York: Basic Books.

Dahl, Robert A. 1989. *Democracy and Its Critics.* New Haven: Yale University Press.

———. 1990. *After the Revolution: Authority in a Good Society.* New Haven: Yale University Press.

Deutsch, Karl. 1961. "Social Mobilization and Political Development." *American Political Science Review,* 55 (Sept.).

Flora, Peter, and Arnold Heidenheimer. 1981. *The Development of Welfare States in Western Europe and America.* New Brunswick, NJ: Transaction Press.

Friedman, Milton. 1981. *Capitalism and Freedom.* Chicago: University of Chicago Press.

Hirschman, Albert. 1986. *Rival Views of Market Society.* New York: Viking.

Inkeles, Alex, and David Smith. 1974. *Becoming Modern: Individual Change in Six Developing Countries.* Cambridge, MA: Harvard University Press.

Lerner, Daniel. *The Passing of Traditional Society.* New York: Free Press.

Lindblom, Charles E. 1977. *Politics and Markets.* New York: Basic Books.

Lipset, Seymour M. 1959. "Some Social Requisites of Democracy." *American Political Science Review,* 53 (September).

Mill, John Stuart. 1848, 1965. *Principles of Political Economy,* 2 vols. Toronto: University of Toronto Press.

Mitchell, William. 1988. "Virginia, Rochester, and Bloomington: Twenty-Five Years of Public Choice and Political Science." *Public Choice.* 56: 101-119.

Moore, Barrington. 1966. *The Social Origins of Dictatorship and Democracy.* New York: Beacon Press.

Olson, Mancur. 1982. *The Rise and Decline of Nations.* New Haven: Yale University Press.

Schumpeter, Joseph. 1946. *Capitalism, Socialism, and Democracy.* New York: Harper.

Globalization in the Perspective of Imperialism

Robert Went

ABSTRACT: A major aspect of economic globalization is the combination of free trade and free movement of capital. This apparently signifies a return to an international regime similar to that existing before World War I, the period generally characterized as imperialism. But globalization is not just a repetition of this previous period of capitalism. Important changes have taken place in the functioning of the world economy, most importantly increased cross-border links among capitals and internationalization of capital. There are, moreover, essential differences in the mechanisms of imperialist domination, which is expressed today mainly in economic and hardly in military rivalry between the main powers.

Introduction

A major aspect of economic globalization is the global push towards the combination of free trade and free movement of capital. This apparently signifies a return to a regime similar to that existing before World War I. And while today the social, political and economic consequences of and driving forces behind the increasing international interconnectedness of economies are heavily debated, the same was true at the beginning of the 20th century. Marxists and others discussed the causes, dynamics and possible future development of capitalism in terms of *imperialism*. This paper sets out some similarities and differences between the capitalism of those days and today's capitalist globalization.

1. Globalization: Myth or Reality?

In the literature on globalization one can, a bit schematically, distinguish three different

---

From *Science & Society*, Volume 66, No. 4, Winter 2002-2003 by Robert Went. Copyright © 2002 by Science & Society. Reprinted by permission of The Guilford Press.

opinions. For authors such as former U.S. Secretary of Labor Reich (1992) and the Japanese business guru Ohmae (1995), globalization is a definite trend that is changing everything, against which national states or trade unions can do very little or even nothing. Partially in reaction, writers such as Kleinknecht (1998) and Wood (1997) strongly question the importance, newness, and effects of globalization. Among other things, these authors stress that companies are not really "footloose"—free to move whenever and wherever they choose around the world—or say that the world economy was at least as internationalized at the end of the 19th century as it is today. The "g-word" has been given many different meanings, they say, and has become ideology.

But there is also a third position that can be summed up in the proposition that *globalization is an exaggeration* (see, *e.g.*, Boyer and Drache, 1996; Hirst and Thompson, 1996; Kitson and Michie, 2000). Authors who subscribe to this position acknowledge that there are significant changes under way with important implications for the organization and functioning of the world economy. But they explain at the same time that we are (still?) far from a truly globalized economy (see *e.g.*, Frankel, 2000; Rodik, 2000), that there are no linear developments, and that many of the claims of globalization ideologues are untenable. This paper can be situated within this current: globalization is often exaggerated but not a myth, because it is impossible to deny that over the last two decades important changes have taken place in the functioning and organization of the world economy. Although it is too brief and too schematic, a list of four especially important elements may be useful:

1. An increase in the number of really integrated global markets for products and trade, and especially for finance.

2. Without going along with the overstatement that big companies are now footloose,[1] there is no denying the growing weight of multinationals in the global economy: companies try to plan and organize the conception, production, and distribution of their products and services preferably not only regionally or bi-regionally but globally, with important consequences for their structures.[2]

3. An increase in problems of governance and regulation on a global level, as a consequence of the fact that national states are becoming—and making themselves—less effective: supranational organizations (G7, IMF, WTO, BIS, OECD, etc.) and regional organizations (EU, NAFTA, MERCOSUR, etc.) get a bigger role to play.

4. A globalization of macroeconomic policies: since the counterrevolution that took place in economics at the end of the 1970s, the monetarist and neoclassical paradigms are almost unchallenged in international institutions and in the political mainstream. Variants of the same recipes (export-oriented growth, fewer social policies and a smaller public sector, free trade and free capital flows, deregulation, flexibilization, privatization, and priority to price stability) are followed or forced through (with the help of international organizations and financial markets) everywhere in the world.

Important for all these aspects of economic globalization is today's dominant combination of free trade and free movement of capital. Indeed free trade and free international capital mobility have not always been coupled. During the post—World War II "golden age of capitalism," for example, cross-border financial flows were heavily regulated (see, *e.g.*, Eatwell and Taylor, 2000). As UNCTAD researcher Felix (1995, 1) puts it:

Is free international capital mobility compatible with free trade and stable exchange rates? The answer of the architects of the Bretton Woods system, who filtered the inter-war experience through the then burgeoning Keynesian theoretical paradigm, was a firm no. The current answer of the chief surviving Bretton Woods institution, the International Monetary Fund, and of the G-7 monetary authorities, who filter post-World War II experience through the New Classical Macroeconomics paradigm, is yes. Their efforts to stabilize the volatile international monetary system is premised on the compatibility, indeed the desirability, of combining free international capital mobility with stable exchange rates and free trade.

It is not by accident that Felix quotes Keynes in describing "proposals to stabilize exchange rates and promote free trade without limiting international capital mobility" as "exercises in squaring the circle."[3] Keynes was one of the principal architects of the Bretton Woods agreement of 1944.[4] And as Boughton (1997, 10) notes:

> The truth is that the founding fathers were downright bullish on capital controls. . . . As drafted at Bretton Woods, Section 1(a) of article VI read: "A member may not make net use of the Fund's resources to meet a large or sustained outflow of capital, and the Fund may request a member to exercise controls to prevent such use of the resources of the Fund. If, after receiving such a request, a member fails to exercise appropriate controls, the Fund may declare the member ineligible to use the resources of the Fund.

After the Second World War, capital controls were broadly considered to be necessary as a means to give governments a certain control over the national economy, to allow for the implementation of national policy goals (Eichengreen, 1996). The background is the basic macroeconomic policy "trilemma" that a country can only have two of the following three features: a fixed exchange rate, full capital mobility and monetary policy independence (Wyplosz, 1998, 4). This means that countries combining a more or less fixed (or pegged) exchange rate with free movement of capital, as is common today and was common before the First World War under the gold standard,[5] are forced to give up control over domestic macroeconomic objectives, such as full employment in Western Europe, either inducing capital formation or dampening inflation in developing countries (Bruton, 1998, 907).[6]

Obstfeld (1998, 8) registers that "the broad trends and cycles in the world capital market over the last century reflect changing responses to the fundamental policy trilemma." There is general agreement that a periodization of the degree of international capital mobility shows a U-shaped pattern:

> Before World War I, controls on international financial transactions were absent and international capital flows reached high levels. The interwar period saw the collapse of this system, the widespread imposition of *capital controls*, and the decline of international capital movements. The quarter-century following World War II was then marked by the progressive relaxation of controls and the gradual recovery of international financial flows. The latest period, starting with the 1970s, is again one of high capital mobility. (Eichengreen, 1996, 3; see also Bordo and Schwartz, 1997.)

Although today national economies are increasingly linked and interwoven, the idea that capital controls are an essential (though insufficient) policy tool to safeguard economies from becoming a plaything for financial markets has now largely disappeared. In a typical editorial, the *Financial Times* (April 18, 1998) explained that everybody should understand that now "at the national level, the emerging global standard consists of liberal trade and open financial market." This "global standard" is promoted, pushed and blackmailed permanently into all corners of the world, by international organizations and lobby groups, national business elites, multinationals and traders on financial markets. It was therefore hardly a surprise that U.S. Treasury Secretary Rubin recently "urged African governments to open goods and financial markets and embrace globalization even at the risk of political difficulties" (*Financial Times*, July 15, 1998).

These and other cases reflect a real change in the policy orientation of major international organizations. Writing about the history of the IMF, Boughton (1997.8) notes that by 1994, "the long-simmering debate over the wisdom of capital controls has been completely overtaken." Echoing the often-heard argument that technological developments leave no choice, he infers that "no country can share in the benefits of international trade unless it allows capital to move freely enough to finance that trade, and modern financial markets are sophisticated and open enough that capital transactions can no longer be compartmentalized as trade-related or speculative." The IMF is one of the best examples of how far this mutation has gone. While its Executive Board reaffirmed in 1956 the right of members to impose capital controls, the Fund's Interim Committee decided unanimously in April 1997 to amend the Articles of the Fund, so that capital controls will only be allowed temporarily in exceptional situations (*IMF Survey*, May 12, 1997). Nor is the IMF the only powerful international organization pushing in this direction. After heavy negotiations and substantial pressure on hesitant governments, in December 1997 more than a hundred countries signed a pact under the aegis of the World Trade Organization (WTO) to liberalize trade in banking, insurance and other financial services. And secret negotiations by the OECD to formulate a Multilateral Agreement on Investment (MAI), to institutionalize globally the right of capital to freely move in and out of countries, has only failed for now because NGOs managed to mobilize broad resistance to such an agreement in various parts of the world, and because doubts about such a far-reaching treaty were even present in governmental circles of some of the OECD member states, notably France.

In sum, the case for globalization as a new phenomenon is often overstated, but nevertheless there appear to be a number of new features of capitalism that need to be accounted for. One important aspect of economic globalization is today's emphasis on the combination of free trade and free capital flows, which apparently signifies a return to an international regime similar to the pre-World War I regime. And while today the social, political and economic consequences of and driving forces behind the increasing international interconnectedness of economies are heavily debated, the same was also the case at the beginning of the 20th century. The next section reviews this debate.

2. *Imperialism*

Like today, at the beginning of the 20th century an extensive discussion took place about important changes in the character and functioning of capitalism. The emergence of big conglomerates and monopolies, the increasing weight of finance capital, the importance of capital exports as a means to raise the profit rate in addition to international trade, and the accompanying drive for, or inevitability of, imperialist policies by national states, were recognized in different parts of the world in very different groups and milieus. This section provides a general impression of the issues debated at that time.

The English sociologist and economist John Hobson, who published his extensive study of imperialism in 1902, was one of the first to distinguish imperialism from the much longer existing colonialism. For Hobson (1902, 94-109), imperialism "implies the use of the machinery of government by private interests, mainly capitalists, to secure for them economic gains outside their country." The economic root of imperialism is "the desire of strong organized industrial and financial interests to secure and develop at the public expense and by the public force private markets for their surplus goods and their surplus capital. War, militarism, and a 'spirited foreign policy' are the necessary means to this end."

For the writing of his classic treatise *Imperialism, the Highest Stage of Capitalism*, Lenin made extensive use of Hobson's monumental work. Lenin formulates the following—now famous—definition of imperialism:

> Without forgetting the conditional and relative value of all definitions in general, which can never embrace all the concatenations of a phenomenon in its full development, we must give a definition of imperialism that will include the following five if its basic features:
>
> (1) the concentration of production and capital has developed to such a high stage that it has created monopolies which play a decisive role in economic life; (2) the merging of bank capital with industrial capital, and the creation, on the basis of this "financial capital," of a financial oligarchy; (3) the export of capital as distinguished from the export of commodities acquires exceptional importance; (4) the formation of international monopolist capitalist associations which share the world among themselves; and (5) the territorial division of the whole world among the biggest capitalist powers is completed. Imperialism is capitalism at that stage of development at which the dominance of monopolies and finance capital is established; in which the export of capital has acquired pronounced importance; in which the division of the world among the international trusts has begun, in which the division of all territories of the globe among the biggest capitalist powers has been completed. (Lenin, 1917, 83.)

The domination of monopolist associations of big employers is for Lenin the principal feature of imperialism.[7] In its economic essence imperialism "is monopoly capitalism," Lenin writes, identifying four principal manifestations of monopolies:

> Firstly, monopoly arose out of the concentration of production at a very high stage. . . . Secondly monopolies have stimulated the seizure of the most important sources of raw materials. . . . Thirdly, monopoly has sprung from the banks. . . . Some three to five of the biggest banks in each of the foremost capitalist countries have achieved the "personal link-up" between industrial and bank capital. . . . A financial oligarchy, which throws a close network of dependence relationships over all the economic and political institutions of present-day bourgeois society—such is the most striking manifestation of this monopoly. Fourthly, monopoly has grown out of colonial policy. . . . To the numerous "old" motives of colonial policy, finance capital has added the struggle for the sources of raw materials, for the export of capital, for

spheres of influence, *i.e.*, for spheres for profitable deals, concessions, monopoly profits and so on, economic territory in general.

As the emphasis he puts on the increasing weight and power of finance capital shows, Lenin leans heavily on the famous study by Hilferding, first published in 1910. The increasing dependence of industry upon bank capital means for Hilferding that the finance capitalist increasingly concentrates "his control over the whole national capital by means of his domination of bank capital." The export of capital makes it possible for the first time "to overcome the harmful effects of a protective tariff on the rate of profit," and the fact that new markets are no longer simply outlets for goods, but also spheres for the investment of capital, brings about a change in the political behavior of the countries that export capital. Direct rule over the area where capital is invested becomes more important, and all capitalists with interests in foreign countries call therefore for a strong state to protect their interests all over the world.

> and for showing the national flag everywhere so that the flag of trade can also be planted everywhere. Export capital feels most comfortable, however, when its own state is in complete control of the new territory, for capital exports from other countries are then excluded, it enjoys a privileged position, and its profits are more or less guaranteed by the state. Thus the export of capital also encourages an imperialist policy. (Hilferding, 1910, 322.)

Both Hilferding and Lenin argue that capital, under the leadership of finance capital, has become the conqueror of the world in an expansionist policy to colonize new foreign markets. One of their main opponents was Karl Kautsky. Like Lenin, Kautsky originally considered war, militarism, imperialism and capitalism as closely linked, but by 1912 his position had radically changed (Geary, 1987, 53). Explaining that imperialist expansion was related to the interests of pre-industrial elites and high finance, Kautsky started defending the idea that finance capital only played a secondary role in the imperialist phase of capitalism. Its most important section was for Kautsky industrial capital, and in his opinion other options were available than the colonization of agrarian territories and war, to guarantee industry the agrarian hinterland for raw materials and foodstuffs (Salvadori, 1979, 187). Later on Kautsky concluded that the interests of capital were best served by free trade and improved communication, and therefore by peace. Considering it likely that this common interest would be recognized by the capitalist nations, he envisaged in 1914 the possibility of a peaceful "ultraimperialism," in which capital would cooperate to organize its worldwide domination:[8]

> From the purely economic standpoint . . . It is not excluded that capitalism may live through another new phase, the transference of the policy of cartels to foreign policy, a phase of ultra-imperialism, which of course we must fight against just as energetically as we fought imperialism. Its dangers would lie in a different direction, not in that of the armaments race and the threat to world peace. (Kautsky, 1915, 90.)

Kautsky (1915, 90-1) maintained that imperialism is a "political system," and neither "an economic phase" nor "advanced capitalism of a higher stage," but "a particular kind of capitalist policy, just like Manchesterism, which it replaces."[9]

This position was heavily criticized by Lenin (1917, 85-6) who argued that "Kautsky detaches the politics of imperialism from its economies," and does not understand that imperialism "strives to annex *not only* agrarian territories, but even most highly industrialized regions," because contrary to what he alleges, the "characteristic feature of imperialism is *not* industrial but *financial* capital." It is interesting to see that not only Marxists made this analysis. Lenin quotes for example a statement to that effect by Cecil Rhodes, a British financial magnate who led colonial expeditions in southern Africa at the turn of the century. Rhodes was of course not the only procapitalist defender of imperialism, and conservative and liberal advocates of imperial expansion such as Bismarck and the French politician Ferry also stressed its economic necessity (Geary, 1987, 47).

Nor were these insights limited to Europe. Parrini and Sklar (1983) suggests that the "Hobson-Lenin theory of imperialism" has "pro-capitalist American origins," and that their thinking was already published and in place in the years 1896 to 1901 by "some neglected turn-of-the-century American economists, who influenced or participated in the formation of U.S. foreign policy." Arthur Twining Hadley of Yale, Jeremiah W. Jenks of Cornell and financial authority and journalist Charles A. Conant "took the lead among American thinkers in laying the theoretical foundations for the break with the classical model of the competitive market," and identified at an early stage the role of monopolies and international investment. They argued that "the condition for a viable national corporate investment was its globalization in an international investment system," and that the economic, political, social, and cultural requirements for such an international system "lay at the heart of modern capitalist imperialism, the root cause of which was surplus capital in the highly developed industrial societies." According to Parrini and Sklar, Conant saw state intervention as necessary "on behalf of an international investment system and imperialism in foreign affairs," and he "frankly affirmed" imperialist relations with the non-industrial societies of the world "as necessary, unavoidable, in the national interest, and, being developmental and 'civilizing,' as enlightened and progressive."

These ideas had a major influence on government policies in the USA. Conant and Jenks served as members of the three-member Commission for International Exchange (CIE), established in 1903 by President Roosevelt, to develop plans for the integration of China and other non-industrial countries on silver standard currencies into an international investment system based on the gold standard. This commission played an important role in the formulation of the so-called Open Door Policy, which was implemented by the McKinley-Roosevelt administrations and by administrations thereafter. Pointing to capital seeking investment but failing to find a profitable rate, the CIE concluded that finding outlets for this capital was in some respects "more important than increasing the annual exports of manufacturing countries." It was therefore considered necessary to construct an international monetary and investment system, which was presented as involving "common benefits for all," but based on the assumption "that the stability, growth, and prosperity of the American economy depended on its ability to expand freely into, and exercise a controlling voice in, the international economy."

In sum, at the beginning of the 20th century the evolution of capitalism, with as important characteristics the coming into existence of big conglomerates and monopolies, an increasing weight of finance capital, and imperial policies by national states, was widely discussed. Financial capital was generally seen as the main driving force behind imperialist state policies, but there were major disagreements about the weight of this sector within the whole of capital. Linked to this question, debates took place about the possibility of capitalist development without militarism and war, involving concepts such as ultra-imperialism (Kautsky) or pointing to substantial equality of economic and educational opportunities (Hobson). The final section compares these analyses to contemporary debates about the character and dynamics of globalization.

3. Capitalism Today

For supporters and opponents of imperialism alike, free trade and capital mobility were essential instruments for the stabilization and extension of worldwide capitalism at the beginning of the 20th century. Since then many things have changed in the structure and organization of the global economy, but after a long detour such policies are today once again dominant and strongly advocated by important international organizations, university and think-tank figures, and governments of OECD countries. Little or no room is left for different policies. And, as was recently demonstrated again in Asia, unwilling or hesitant governments are pushed to comply with the prevalent paradigm by globalized financial markets, the IMF and like-minded organizations, and national business elites (see Bello, 1998; Bullard, 1998; Wade, 1998; Wade and Veneroso, 1998). The defense of these policies is also reminiscent of earlier times. Today, free trade and free capital movement are supposed to lead to an optimal allocation of capital, goods and services, and should therefore bring a better life for everybody. In a similar vein, classical economists such as Mill, Torens and Wakefield once advocated colonization "based on the classical principles of free trade and the free movement of resources," as a means "to ensure continued improvements in living standards for all people, both at home and in the colonies" (Hodgart, 1977, 3-4). As we have seen in the previous section, proponents of imperialist policies at the beginning of the 20th century, as an essential means to guarantee the stability and growth of capitalism, also presented their policies as beneficial for all, civilizing or even progressive.

But numerous empirical studies show that such policies are not at all beneficial for the majority of the world population (*e.g.*, Galbraith, Darity and Jiaqing, 1998; Prichett, 1996; UNDP, 1997). As Rubens Ricupero, Secretary-General of UNCTAD, testified in his overview of the 1997 Trade and Development Report (UNCTAD, 1997, 2-10):

> The big story of the world economy since the early 1980s has been the unleashing of market forces. . . . The "invisible hand" now operates globally and with fewer countervailing pressures from governments than for decades. . . . Since the early 1980s the world economy has been characterized by rising inequality and slow growth. Income gaps between the North and South have continued to widen. . . . Polarization among countries has been accompanied by increasing income inequality within countries. . . . In almost all developing countries that have undertaken rapid trade liberalization, wage inequality has increased.

He notes that these facts fly in the face of the many commentators who are optimistic about the prospects for faster growth and for convergence of incomes and living standards which global competition should bring:

> These trends are rooted in a common set of forces unleashed by rapid liberalization that make for greater inequality by favoring certain income groups over others. . . . Capital has gained in comparison with labor, and profit shares have risen everywhere. . . . In the North there has been a remarkable upward convergence of profits

among the major industrial countries. . . . A new rentier class has emerged worldwide with the substantial expansion of international capital flows and the hike of interest rates. (UNCTAD, 1997, 6.)

So how then can this change in the dominant opinion about the incompatibility of free trade and free capital flows be explained? Not only the empirical evidence but also the theoretical arguments for the gains from free trade and free movement of capital are extremely weak (to say the least), and there is no ground for the suggestion that the theoretical and practical objections of Keynes and others are no longer valid.[10] On the contrary, evidence for the opposite is overwhelming. Calvo and Mendoza (1997, 27-8) conclude that "the global economy is inherently more volatile than a world economy with limited capital mobility," and that this "global market volatility can induce large social costs." Wyplosz (1998, 2) argues that "financial market liberalization is the best predictor of currency crises. This has been true in Latin America in the 1980s, in Europe in the early 1990s and in Asia in 1997." On the social effects, research shows that "developing countries that liberalized and globalized were subject to larger swings in inequality than countries that did not. . . . In most cases, identifiable liberalizations are followed by rising inequality in wages" (Galbraith, Darity and Jiaqing, 1998, 6). One of the reasons for this, Felix (1998, 209) explains, is that "the liberalization of international capital movements has forced macroeconomic policy to react primarily to signals from the financial rather than from the job market. . . . Economists defending the position that liberalizing and globalizing financial markets has improved economic welfare now avert their eyes from the adverse real economic trends." While Obstefeld (1998, 1) notes that "regional financial crises seem to have become more frequent, and the domestic impact of global financial developments has grown—to the alarm of many private citizens, elected officials, and even economists."

One of these economists is free trade champion Bhagwati (1998), who calls the idea that full capital mobility is inevitable and desirable a myth: "claims of enormous benefits from free capital mobility are not persuasive," and "none of the proponents of free capital mobility have estimated the size of the gains they expect to materialize, even leaving out the losses from crises that can ensue." The former Economic Policy Adviser to the Director-General of the GATT also reminds us that such different countries as China, Japan and those of Western Europe have all registered their biggest growth rates without capital account convertibility. In the same vein, mainstream economist Rodrik (1998) finds on the basis of data from almost 100 countries between 1975 and 1989 that free capital mobility has no significant impact on countries' economic fortunes. He concludes: "The greatest concern I have about canonizing capital-account convertibility is that it would leave economic policy in the typical 'emerging market' hostage to the whims and fancies of two dozen or so thirty-something country analysts in London, Frankfurt and New York.

Today's heavy-handed promotion of the combination of free trade and free capital flows cannot be credited to its proven economic advantages. Based on written commentaries and analyses produced by large multinational banks and interviews with some of the major decision makers at these and other private sector financial institutions, Rude (1998, 4) shows for example that since the East Asian financial crisis, even participants in the financial markets tend to agree:

> The severity of the financial implosion that took place in East Asia has prompted many market participants to question the stability of today's globalized financial system.

Market participants have not only lost faith in the prospect of continued robust growth, therefore, but in the merits of financial market liberalization and globalization, indeed, in the viability of free, unregulated international capital markets as well.

Like previous changes of monetary regimes, this shift has to be interpreted as the outcome of political changes. Eichengreen (1996, 42-3) explains that the gold standard could be maintained before World War I, because

> the insulation enjoyed by the monetary authorities allowed them to commit to the maintenance of gold convertibility. . . The extension of the franchise and the emergence of political parties representing the working classes raised the possibility of challenges to the single-minded priority the monetary authorities attached to convertibility. Rising consciousness of unemployment and of trade-offs between internal and external balance politicized monetary policy.[11]

He builds his argument on one advanced by Karl Polanyi, who

> suggests that the extension of the institutions of the market over the course of the nineteenth century aroused a political reaction in the form of associations and lobbies that ultimately undermined the stability of the market system. He gave the gold standard a place of prominence among the institutions of laissez faire in response to which this reaction has taken place. In the same vein, the described changes (but also, *e.g.,* the whole set-up of the EMU) can be interpreted as successful attempts to reduce democratic influence on the economy.

This time the main factor can be summarized as a global change in the relationship of forces between capital and labor since the end of the 1970s. the increased unemployment in the OECD countries since the end of the long postwar expansion and the disappearance of full employment as a policy goal; a number of setbacks and defeats of national and socialist movements and projects in countries in the Third World;[12] and the collapse of the former Soviet bloc in Eastern Europe, have all worked to the benefit of capital. This has resulted in a substantial increase in capital's share of income in all parts of the world, in the earlier described changes in the structure and functioning of the world economy and more generally in a political, social and economic agenda that is more and more dominated by the interests of capital. Bhagwati (1998) argues for example that the current myth of enormous benefits from free capital mobility has been created by "the Wall Street—Treasure complex, following in the footsteps of President Eisenhower, who had warned of the military-industrial complex."

So just as at the beginning of the century, the interests of capital in the countries of the First World can be identified as the motor force behind the current global drive towards free trade and unrestricted capital movement. And this time with even more pernicious consequences: "Walter Wriston, ex-CEO of Citicorp, chortles that the globalized financial markets now hold macroeconomic policy in a tighter grip than under the gold standard" (Felix, 1998, 209). This break with the policies of the first three decades after World War II reflects a fundamental change in the relationship of forces between capital and labor.[13] But today's promotion of free trade and free capital flows, two important economic arms of imperialism just as at the beginning of the last century, is no evidence for the argument that contemporary globalization is just a repetition of this previous period of capitalism.

Although most elements of Lenin's definition of imperialism still hold today, I submit that three important changes have to be taken into account.[14]

First, while Lenin and Hilferding already registered capital flows from imperialist countries to other imperialist countries,[15] this interpenetrating of capitals was at the time a minor tendency. The main trend was the centralization of capital on a national level, "transforming thousands and thousands of scattered economic enterprises into a single national capitalist, and then into a world economy" (Lenin, 1917, 32). There was a general consensus that because the finance capitalist "increasingly concentrates his control over the whole national capital by means of domination of bank capital," the struggle among nations representing their respective capitals "to incorporate parts of the world market into the national market, through a colonial policy which involves the annexation of foreign territories" (Hilferding, 1910, 225; cf 325), was intensifying. But since that time the structure of the world economy has changed considerably, and inter-OECD investments have become much more important. Magdoff (1969, 62) noted that "the internationalization of capital among the giant firms is of a much higher order today than was the case fifty years ago when Lenin wrote his work on imperialism." And Mandel (1972, 64) noticed already before the end of the post-war economic boom that the rise of new industries in the metropolitan countries and the fear of liberation movements in the Third World had led after the Second World War to "an abrupt change in the pattern of long-term capital export. In contrast to the period from 1880-1940, capital now no longer mainly moved from the metropolitan countries to the underdeveloped ones. Instead, it chiefly went from some metropolitan countries to other imperialist countries." This trend has only increased in the decades since then, as can be seen, among other factors, from the multiplication of regional trade blocs and customs unions since the beginning of the 1980s, most spectacularly the EU. Such developments are an important reason why critics of *globalization* argue that *regionalization* (or *triadization*) is a better term to characterize the dominant trend in the world economy, because it expresses where the biggest shares of trade and capital flows are found (see, *e.g.*, Kleinknecht and Ter Wengel, 1998; Ruigrok and van Tulder, 1995; Went, 2000b).

Instead of the national cartels that competed to divide world markets at the beginning of the century, we now see all kinds of international investments, alliances and strategies by multinationals that are competing and cooperating in both developed and developing countries. At the same time, the number of international organizations and fora to coordinate and regulate economic policies has increased dramatically. In these organizations the big countries work together, among others to open up developing countries for trade and capital. None of this means that there is no competition any more among imperialist countries, but that such rivalries are fought out economically rather than militarily.[16] This can also be seen from the fact that the USA, the main imperialist country in the world, is no longer seriously preparing for a possible war with Japan or Europe (cf. Achcar, 1998).

A second difference, connected to the previous one, concerns the role and structure of finance capital. The national bank-dominated financial systems that Hilferding and Lenin saw in their time have made way for a much more integrated worldwide financial system, where global norms for profitability are set.[17] Because of the disappearance of capital controls, globalized financial markets increasingly discipline investors and governments. The space for national differences is being undermined more and more. As Plender (1997, 97) puts it:

> In a world where exchange controls have been abolished, the German and Japanese cross-subsidies from depositors and investors to industry are unlikely in future to be sustainable. At the risk of some slight oversimplification, if a country tries artificially to reduce the financial returns available to depositors and investors, its exchange rate will collapse in the long run as domestic and international capital pours out in pursuit of higher returns elsewhere. Because governments and central banks will act to forestall the inflationary consequences of a collapsing exchange rate, they will, in normal circumstances, raise interest rates, thereby bringing their industries' cost of money back into line with the international norm.

It falls outside the scope of this paper, but this difference is a major reason why one could argue that capitalism has entered a different phase since the beginning of the 1980s.[18]

There is a third difference of a political character. Dominant countries no longer colonize parts of the world with military force, but promote the combination of democracy and a market economy. In fact, according to Robinson (1996a), it is *polyarchy* rather than *democracy* that is being established: "Promoting polyarchy and promoting neoliberal restructuring has become a singular process in U.S. foreign policy."[19] Robinson explains that "authoritarianism increasingly proved to be an untenable mode of domination and an unpredictable means of preserving asymmetries within and among nations as globalizing processes began to assert themselves." He forcefully argues that this is only a shift in the means and not in the ends of policy, which are still "defense of the privileges of the Northern elites and their Southern counterparts in a highly stratified world system."

As I argue more extensively elsewhere (Went, 2001-2) all this does not mean that national states will disappear. While capital is increasingly internationalized, essential state functions are for the moment neither performed by nation-states nor by international institutions and collaborations of states. A prolonged period of trial and error to shift and reorganize responsibilities and tasks between national and international levels is the most likely perspective, with all sorts of conflicts because interests are divergent, and no predetermined outcome. Nation-states will definitely not vanish in the foreseeable future: "at this point in history, the fading away of the nation-state is a fallacy" (Castells, 1997, 307). But neither will the current status quo last forever: "we are not witnessing 'the death of the nation-state,' but its transformation" (Robinson, 1996b, 19). There are powerful pressures for mutations, and regional and global reorganizations in the future or already underway, such as the increasing economic integration of the European Union, will have significant implications for the organization of states.

Nor can contemporary globalization at this stage be interpreted as the vindication of Kautsky. For Burbach and Robinson (1999, 27) the "open-ended and unfinished" process of globalization has by now evolved into a configuration where "for the first time in history . . . we can speak of transnationalization of capital, a world in which markets are truly global and integrated. Capital ownership of the leading enterprises is also internationalized, with shareholders or financial institutions from various parts of the world being able to move their stockholdings in and out of any number of corporations and countries." They go one step further when they argue that "transnational class formation" is occurring and that a "transnational capitalist class" (TCC) is formed. Robinson and Harris (2000, 21) conclude the logic of this argument with the thesis that economic forums such as the IMF, World Bank, WTO, G7 and OECD constitute "an incipient TNS (transnational state) apparatus in formation." Since they also register the dominant role of finance capital, their perspective is very reminiscent of Kautsky's *ultra-imperialism*. The respective authors present their arguments for a TCC and TNS as no more than a tendency, and point to the many contradictions and conflicts of interest that may block the future evolution of such a global-state-in-the-making. But they do seem certain enough about the coming trajectory of the global economy to exclude other possible international structures explicitly (*super-imperialism*, which under the current condition would mean dominance of the USA) or implicitly (continuing competition between the USE, EU and Japan). The present author submits that it is much too early for such a choice, and that the two other models are not only not excluded, but very much in contention.

Summary and Conclusion

A key aspect of today's economic globalization is the emphasis on the *combination* of policies of free trade and free movement of capital, which apparently signifies a return to a similar international regime before World War I. But despite many similarities, economic globalization is not just a repetition of this previous period of capitalism. Policies in the pre-World War I period of imperialism were driven by the interests of *nationally* centralized capital under the control of bank-dominated finance capital, and resulted in the well-known imperial policies of national states to incorporate foreign territories into their national markets for the exports of goods and capital. The interests of capital in the countries of the first world are also the motor force behind the current economic globalization.

But today's world economy is characterized by an increasing number of cross-border links among capitals from different countries, a higher level of internationalization of capital, an integrated worldwide financial system, and a greater role for international organizations and fora to coordinate and regulate economic policies. The idea that nation-states will therefore disappear in the foreseeable future is, however, mistaken: states are not dying but changing. There are enduring conflicts of interests, but these are expressed mainly in economic and hardly at all in military rivalry among the main capitalist powers. Where this will bring us in the future is not predetermined: three models—*a transnational state, USA-dominance,* and *continuing competition among blocs*—are for the moment equally (un)likely.

Notes

1. For a healthy dose of scepticism about such claims see Ruigrok and Van Tulder, 1996; and Doremus, *et al.*, 1998.
2. In its *World Investment Report 1998* UNCTAD estimates that the world counts at least 53,000 transnational companies (TNCs) and at least—in all likelihood it is more—448,000 foreign affiliates. "In 1996, 85 of the top 100 TNCs were headquartered in the Triad, compared to 86 in 1990. The United States, Japan, the United Kingdom, France and Germany alone accounted for three-quarters of the entries in both years. Their dominance has remained roughly unchanged since 1990, regardless of

3. Keynes would have looked at the offspring of the postwar economy, "the global financial markets and the theology of free trade, with a very cold eye," notes Longworth (1998, 47), quoting Keynes' famous passage: "I sympathize, therefore, with those who would minimize, rather than those who would maximize, economic entanglement between nations. Ideas, knowledge, art, hospitality, travel—these are things which should of their nature be international. But let goods be homespun whenever it is reasonable and conveniently possible: and above all, let finance be primarily national."

4. During the negotiations U.S. representative White promised "to respect the priority the British attached to full employment," although controls on international capital movements were "contrary to White's early vision of a world free of controls on both trade and financial flows" (Eichengreen, 1996, 96-8). Clearly the United States did not subscribe to "the darker Kenesian view of the behavior of financial markets, in which volatility is largely endogenously generated because the bandwagon overbidding and herd-like dumping of financial assets result from rational individual behavior under uncertainty" (Felix, 1998, 196).

5. *See e.g.,* Bordo and Schwartz, 1997, and Eichengreen, 1996, on the history and conditions for the functioning of the gold standard. Trade and foreign borrowing were simplified when more and more countries adopted the same monetary standard, and in the final years of the 19th century the system reached into Asia (Russia, Japan, India, Ceylon) and Latin America (Argentina, Mexico, Peru, Uruguay), while silver remained the monetary standard only in China and a few Central American countries (see also Eichengreen and Flandreau, 1996). It should not be forgotten, however, that the necessary cooperation for a gold standard functioned mainly for north-central Europe, led by England, the main economic power, and Germany, and that "problems at the periphery did not threaten systemic stability, leaving Europe's central banks less inclined to come to the aid of a country in, say, Latin America."

6. Capital controls, Eichengreen (1996, 5) argues, "loosened the link between domestic and foreign economic policies, providing governments room to pursue other objectives like the maintenance of full employment. . . . By limiting the resources that the markets could bring to bear against an exchange rate peg, controls limited the steps that governments had to take in its defense. For several decades after World War II, limits on capital mobility substituted for limits on democracy as a source of insulation from market pressures."

7. Describing imperialism interchangeably as the "highest," a "special" or "the latest" stage or epoch of capitalism, Lenin's theory can be seen, as McDonough (1995) shows, as a direct ancestor of later theories of capitalist stages, such as social structure of accumulation and long waves of capitalist development.

8. The fact that this theory of a peaceful imperialism, to be achieved by the workers movement in cooperation with progressive parts of the bourgeoisie, was widely held within the Second International is one of the reasons why Kautsky and so many others were unprepared when the war broke out in August 1914 (Geary, 1987).

9. There are clear similarities with the position of Hobson, who also maintained that imperial expansion is not inevitable to create the necessary outlets for progressive industry, and argued from an underconsumptionist analysis for an alternative (Hobson, 1902, 86-7).
10. Today it is often forgotten that Ricardo already argued that immobility of capital is a necessary condition for his theorem of comparative advantage to work (see Went, 2000a). In 1942 Keynes (1980, 149) wrote to Harrod:

    Freedom of capital movement is an essential part of the old *laissez-faire* system and assumes that it is right and desirable to have an equalization of interest rates in all parts of the world. It assumes, that is to say, that if the rate of interest which promotes full employment in Great Britain is lower than the appropriate rate in Australia, there is no reason why this should not be allowed to lead to a situation in which the whole of British savings are invested in Australia, subject only to different estimations of risk, and until the equilibrium rate in Australia has been brought down to the British rate. In my view the whole management of the domestic economy depends upon being free to have the appropriate rate of interest without reference to the rates prevailing elsewhere in the world. Capital control is a corollary to this.

    See also Bhagwati, 1998, and Rodrik, 1998, on free capital flows; Bruton, 1998, on import substitution policies and "export fetishism."
11. Others have called this *monetary laissez-faire*, "by which they mean limited government intervention" (Flandreau, *et al.*, 1998, 129).
12. The debt crisis in Latin America of the 1980s was used to strangle import substitution strategies and to open up debtor countries to international capital: "In the terminology of Hyman Minsky, Volcker's monetary policy transformed Mexico into a Ponzi financial unit. This ushered in Mexico's debt crisis, and the subsequent demands by the U.S. government, the Bretton Woods institutions, and their private sector allies among the multinational banks and corporations that Mexico undertake a program of free-market restructuring. Two main tenets of the free-market restructuring program were for the state to sell a substantial share of its assets to the private sector and to substantially reduce regulations on capital inflows and foreign direct investment" (Pollin, 1998, 225-6). Note the similarity with the content of the agreements of Asian countries in crisis with the IMF.
13. The *combination* of free trade and free capital flows is a break with the Bretton Woods regime for the countries in the First World, while the orientation towards free trade and export-led growth constitutes an additional break (with the import substitution strategy) for countries in the Third World.
14. I owe some of the following insights partially to an e-mail by James Devine on the Progressive Economists Network List (Pen-L).
15. Hilferding (1910, 326) notes for example that "the United States exports industrial capital to South America on a very large scale, while at the same time importing loan capital from England, Holland, France, etc., in the form of bonds and debentures, as working capital for its own industry."
16. The collapse of the former Soviet bloc facilitated this change, but steps in this direction were already taken after the Second World War, as Magdoff (1969, 40-1) explains:

    While the imperialist powers did not give up the colonies gladly or easily, the main purposes of colonialism had been achieved prior to the new political independence: the colonies had been intertwined with the world capitalist markets; their resources, economies, and societies had become adapted to the needs of the metropolitan centers. The current task of imperialism now became to hold on to as many of the economic and financial benefits of these former colonies as possible. And this of course meant continuation of the economic and financial dependency of these countries on the metropolitan centers. Neither in the period right after the Russian Revolution nor in our own day does the central objective of extending and/or defending the frontiers of imperialism signify the elimination of rivalries among the imperialist powers. However, since the end of the Second World War this central objective has dominated the scene because of the increasing threat to the imperialist system and because of the greater unity among the powers imposed by United States leadership.

17. "Today the cost of capital will tend to equalize between countries after allowing for risk, which means, among other things, that German and Japanese companies now have to meet a global profit criterion. If they fail to do so, their stock markets will in the end fall, thereby raising the cost of equity capital. Because of this they have already been forced to adopt more flexible labor-market policies, including the Anglo-Saxon practice of downsizing" (Plender, 1997, 57). See Coutrot, 1998, for the consequences for workers.

18. One of the more prolific researchers defending this position is the French Marxist economist François Chesnais (1997, 62-3):

> For the time being I will designate this . . . by the somewhat complicated name of "global accumulation regime dominated by finance," or "financialized global accumulation regime," stressing its very marked rentier characteristics. . . . Born from the impasses to which the "thirty glorious years" of prolonged accumulation led . . . this mode is based on transformations of the "wage relation" and a very sharp increase in the rate of exploitation . . . but its functioning is governed mainly by operations and choices of forms of finance capital that are more concentrated and centralized than in any previous period of capitalism.

See also Chesnais, 1994; 1996a.

19. "What U.S. policymakers mean by 'democracy promotion' is the promotion of *polyarchy,* a concept which developed in U.S. academic circles closely tied to the policymaking community in the United States in the post-World War II years. . . . Polyarchy refers to a system in which a small group actually rules and mass participation in decision-making is confined to leadership choice in elections carefully managed by competing elites. . . . Democracy is limited to the political sphere, and revolves around process, method and procedure in the selection of 'leaders.' This is an *institutional* definition of democracy. . . . A caveat must be stressed. U.S. preference for polyarchy is a general guideline of post-Cold War foreign policy and not a universal prescription. Policymakers often assess that authoritarian arrangements are best left in place in instances where the establishment of polyarchic systems is an unrealistic, high-risk, or unnecessary undertaking" (Robinson, 1996a, 49; cf. 112).

References

Achcar, Gilbert. 1998. "The Strategic Triad: The United States, Russia and China." *New Left Review,* 228 (March/April), 91-127.

Bello, Walden. 1998. "The End of the Asian Miracle." *The Nation,* January 12/19, 16-21.

Bhagwati, Jagdish. 1998. "The Capital Myth." *Foreign Affairs,* 77:3 (May/June), 7-12.

Bordo, Michael and Anna Schwartz. 1997. *Monetary Policy Regimes and Economic Performance: The Historical Record.* NBER Working Paper, 6201.

Boughton, James. 1997. "From Suez to Tequila: The IMF as Crisis Manager." *IMF Working Paper*, WP/97/90 (July).

Boyer, Robert and Daniel Drache. 1996. *States against Markets.* London: Routledge.

Bruton, Henry. 1998. "A Reconsideration of Import Substitution." *Journal of Economic Literature*, XXXVI:2 (June), 903-936.

Bullard, Nicholas. 1998. *Taming the Tigers: The IMF and the Asian Crisis.* London: CAFOD.

Burbach, Roger and William Robinson. 1999. "The Fin de Siècle Debate: Globalization as Epochal Shift." *Science & Society*, 63:1, 10-39.

Calvo, Guillermo and Enrique Mendoza. 1997. "Rational Herd Behavior and the Globalization of Securities Markets." Institute for Empirical Macroeconomics, Globalization of Securities Markets." Institute for Empirical Macroeconomics, Federal Reserve Bank of Minneapolis. Discussion Paper, 120.

Castells, Manuel. 1997. *The Information Age: Economy, Society and Culture.* Volume II: *The Power of Identity.* Boston, Massachusetts and Oxford, England: Blackwell.

Chesnais, François. 1994. *La Mondialisation du capital.* Paris: Syros.

Chesnais, François, ed. 1996a. *La mondialisation financiére: Genése, coût er enjeux.* Paris: Syros.

———. 1996b. "Mondialisation du capital et régime d'accumulation à dominante financière." *Agone: Philosophie, Critique & Littérature*, 16.

———. 1997. "L'Emergence d'un régime d'accumulation mondial à dominante financière." *La Pensée*, 309, 61-86.

Coutrot, Thomas. 1998. *l'Entreprise néo-libérale, nouvelle utopie capitaliste?* Paris: Editions la Découverte.

Doremus, Paul, William Keller, Louis Pauly and Simon Reich. 1998. *The Myth of the Global Corporation.* Princeton, New Jersey: Princeton University Press.

Eatwell, John and Lance Taylor. 2000. *Global Finance at Risk. The Case for International Regulation.* New York: The New Press.

Eichengreen, Barry, 1996. *Globalizing Capital: A History of the International Monetary System.* Princeton, New Jersey: Princeton University Press.

Eichengreen, Barry and Marc Flandreau. 1996. "The Geography of the Gold Standard." In Jorge Braga de Macedo, Barry Eichengreen, Jaime Reis and William Coleman, *Currency Convertibility: The Gold Standard and Beyond.* New York: Routledge.

Felix, David. 1995. "Financial Globalization versus Free Trade: The Case for the Tobin Tax." *UNCTAD Discussion Papers*, 108 (November).

———. 1998. "On Drawing General Policy Lessons From Recent Latin American Currency Crises." *Journal of Keynesian Economics*, 20:2, 191-221.

Frankel, Jeffrey. 2000. "Globalization of the Economy." NBER Working Paper, 7858 (August).

Freeman, Allan. 1998. "GATT and the World Trade Organisation." *Labour Focus on Eastern Europe*, 59 (Spring), 74-93.

Galbraith, John Kenneth, William Dairty and Lu Jiaqing. 1998. "Measuring the Evolution of Inequality in the Global Economy." Working Paper, Center for Economic Policy Analysis, III:4.

Geary, Dick. 1987. *Karl Kautsky.* Manchester, England: Manchester University Press.

Grieve Smith, Jonathan. 1997. "Devising a Strategy for Pay." In Jonathan Michie and Jonathan Grieve Smith. *Employment and*

Economic Performance: Jobs, Inflation, and Growth. Oxford, England: Oxford University Press.

Harvey, David. 1995. "Globalization in Question." *Rethinking Marxism,* 8:4 (Winter), 1-17.

Hilferding, Rudolf. 1910 (1981). *Finance Capital: A Study of the Latest Phase of Capitalist Development.* London, Boston, Melbourne and Henley: Routledge & Kegan Paul.

Hirst, Paul and Graham Thompson. 1996. *Globalization in Question.* Cambridge, England: Polity Press.

Hobson, John. 1902 (1965). *Imperialism.* Ann Arbor, Michigan: Ann Arbor Paperbacks.

Hodgart, Alan. 1977. *The Economics of European Imperialism.* London: Edward Arnold.

International Monetary Fund (IMF). 1997a. *World Economic Outlook.* Washington: IMF.

_____. 1997b. *International Capital Markets: Developments, Prospects, and Key Policy Issues.* Washington: IMF.

Kautsky, Karl. 1915 (1983). "the Necessity of Imperialism." In *Selected Political Writings,* edited and translated by P. Goode. London and Basingstoke: Macmillan Press.

Keynes, John M. 1980. *Activities 1940-1944. Shaping the Post-War World: The Clearing Union. Collected Writings,* edited by Donald Moggridge. Vol. XXV. London and Basingstoke: Macmillan Press.

Kitson, Michael, and Jonathan Michie. 2000. *The Political Economy of Competitiveness.* London: Routledge.

Kleinknecht, Alfred and Jan ter Wengel. 1998. "The Myth of Economic Globalization." *Cambridge Journal of Economics,* 22:5, 637-647.

Leiderman, Leonard, and Aharon Razin. 1994. *Capital Mobility: The Impact on Consumption, Investment and Growth.* Cambridge, England: Cambridge University Press.

Lenin, Vladimir. 1917 (1975). *Imperialism, the Highest Stage of Capitalism: A Popular Outline.* Moscow: Progress Publishers.

Longworth, Richard. 1998. *Global Squeeze: The Coming Crisis for First-World Nations.* Lincolnwood, Illinois: Contemporary Books.

Luxemburg, Rosa, and Nikolai Bukharin. 1972. *Imperialism and the Accumulation of Capital.* London: Allen Lane/Penguin Press.

Magdoff, Harry. 1969. *The Age of Imperialism.* New York and London: Monthly Review Press.

Mandel, Ernest. 1972 (1975). *Late Capitalism.* London: Verso.

McDonough, Terry. 1995. "Lenin, Imperialism, and the Stages of Capitalist Development." *Science & Society,* 59:3 (Fall), 339-367.

Obstfeld, Maurice. 1998 "The Global Capital Market: Benefactor or Menace?" NBER Working Paper, 6559.

Ohmae, Kenneth. 1995. *The End of the Nation State.* New York: Free Press.

Oman, Charles. 1997. "Technological Change, Globalisation of Production and the Role of Multinationals." *Innovations, Cahiers d économie de l'innovation,* 5.

Parrini, Carl and Martin Sklar. 1993. "New Thinking About the Market, 1896-1904: Some American Economists on Investment and the Theory of Surplus Capital." *Journal of Economic History,* XLIII: 3 (September), 559-578.

Perraton, Jonathan, David Goldblatt, David Held and Anthony McGrew. 1997. "The Globalisation of Economic Activity." *New Political Economy,* 2:2, 257-277.

Plender, John. 1997. *A Stake in the Future: The Stakeholding Solution.* London: Nicholas Brealey Publishing.

Pollin, Robert. 1998. "Theory and Policy in Response to 'Leaden Age' Financial Instability: Comment on Felix." *Journal of Post Keynesian Economics*, 20:2, 223-233.

Pritchett, Lant, 1996. "Forget Convergence: Divergence Past, Present and Future." *Finance and Development* (June) 40-43.

Reich, Robert. 1992. *The Work of Nations*. New York: Vintage Books.

Ricardo, David. 1970 (1817). *On the Principles of Political Economy and Taxation*. In Piero Sraffa, ed., *The Works and Correspondence of David Ricardo*, Vol. 1. Cambridge, England: Cambridge University Press.

Robinson, William. 1996a. *Promoting Polyarchy: Globalization, US Intervention and Hegemony*. Cambridge, England: Cambridge University Press.

_____. 1996b. "Globalisation: Nine Theses on Our Epoch." *Race & Class*, 38:2, 13-31.

Robinson, William and Jerry Harris. 2000. "Towards a Global Ruling Class? Globalization and the Transnational Capitalist Class." *Science & Society*, 64:1, 11-54.

Rodrik, Dani. 1998. "Who Needs Capital-Account Convertibility?" *Princeton Essays in International Finance*, 207 (May), 55-65.

_____. 2000. "How Far Will International Economic Integration Go?" *Journal of Economic Perspectives*, 14:1, 177-186.

Rowthorn, Robert and Richard Kozul-Wright. 1998. "Globalization and Economic Convergence: An Assessment." *UNCTAD Discussion Papers*, 131 (February).

Rude, Christopher. 1998. *The 1997-98 East Asian Financial Crisis: A New York Market-Informed View*. Paper for Expert Group meeting of the United Nations Department of Economic and Social Affairs, in conjunction with the Regional Commission of the United Nations (July).

Ruigrok. Winfried and Rob van Tulder. 1995. *The Logic of International Restructuring*. London: Routledge.

Salvadori, Massimo. 1976. *Karl Kautsky and the Socialist Revolution 1880-1938*. London: New Left Books.

Semmel, Bernard. 1970. *The Rise of Free Trade Imperialism: Classical Political Economy, the Empire of Free Trade and Imperialism 1750-1850*. Cambridge, England: Cambridge University Press.

_____. 1993. *The Liberal Ideal and the Demons of Empire: Theories of Imperialism from Adam Smith to Lenin*. Baltimore, Maryland and London: John Hopkins University Press.

United Nations Conference on Trade and Development (UNCTAD). 1997. *Trade and Development Report, 1997*. New York and Geneva, Switzerland: UNCTAD.

_____. 1998. *World Investment Report 1998: Trends and Determinants*. New York and Geneva, Switzerland: UNCTAD.

United Nations Development Programme (UNDP). 1997. *Human Development Report 1997*. New York and Oxford, England: Oxford University Press.

Wade, Robert. 1998. "From Miracle to Meltdown: Vulnerabilities, Moral Hazard, Panic and Debt Deflation in the Asian Crisis." Draft paper, Russell Sage Foundation, http://epn.org/sage/asiac3a.html.

Wade, Robert, and Frank Veneroso. 1998. "The Asian Crisis: The High Debt Model Versus the Wall Street-Treasury-IMF Complex." *New Left Review*, 228 (March-April), 3-23.

Went, Robert. 1996. "Globalization: Myths, Reality and Ideology." *International Journal of Political Economy*, 26: 3, 39-59.

_____. 2000a. "Game, Set and Match for Mr. Ricardo? The Surprising Comeback of Protectionism in the Era of Globalized Free Trade." *Journal of Economic Issues*, XXXIV:3, 655-677.

―――. 2000b. *Globalization: Neoliberal Challenge, Radical Responses.* London: Pluto Press.

―――. 2001-2. "Globalization: Towards a Transnational State? A Skeptical Note." *Science & Society,* 65:4 (Winter), 484-491.

Willoughby, John. 1995. "Evaluating the Leninist Theory of Imperialism." *Science & Society,* 59: 3, 320-338.

Wood, Ellen Meiksins. 1997. "'Globalization' or 'Globaloney'." *Monthly Review,* 48:9 (February), 21-32.

Wyplosz, Charles. 1998. "Globalized Financial Markets and Financial Crises." Paper presented at a conference organized by the Forum on Debt and Development in Amsterdam, March 16-17.

The Contemporary Black Predicament: Crisis and Political Obligations

Rickey Hill, Ph.D.
Elizabeth P. Allen Distinguished University Professor
Political Science and Black Studies
DePauw University

This essay is an attempt to assess the contemporary predicament of Black people in the United States. Broadly conceived, it is concerned with those dimensions of Black politics internal to the Black community: the struggle over the optimum strategy for liberation and the struggle for political transformation and emancipation.[1] This essay is an exercise in theory building and political thought. The essay is delimited by five concerns: (1) a survey of Black political and social thought. This survey is provided in order to give conceptual framework to how political and social thought has shaped political and social activity; (2) a characterization of the contemporary Black predicament, as a crisis of everyday life; (3) a descriptive assessment of the structural crisis which shapes the Black predicament. The structural crisis is illustrated by social welfare indicators; (4) an interpretation of the internal crisis which retards political and social development inside the Black community. This internal crisis is characterized as a crisis of identity, politics and philosophy. It is illustrated by the failures of leadership, organization and program; and (5) a statement of political obligations is offered for the Black predicament. Some concluding observations are also made.

The analysis herein is premised on the assumption that philosophic quality of a critical and reflexive nature is absent from polit-

Reprinted by permission of the author.

ical discourse about Black people in the United States. Black political and social theorists are faced with the formative obligation to provide theoretical characterization of the Black predicament. Black political and social thought must explain and interpret the Black predicament; unmask the constraints by which it is structured. In so doing, Black political and social thought not only unmasks the crisis of the modern and post-modern projects, but it comes to confront the failures of the Black community.

It is this writer's hope that the essay will contribute to the restoration of philosophic constraint. Toward this end, any interpretation of the contemporary Black predicament should begin with a treatment of how political and social thought has been fashioned among Black people in the United States.

A Survey of Black Political and Social Thought

Black political and social thought has argued for its own authenticity at least since the early 1800s. "Free men of color" were bothered enough about the status of Black slaves to speculate on how that mass ought to situate itself upon emancipation.[2] Frederick Douglass suggested that freed slaves were an impoverished peasantry, only capable of surviving the struggle of the fittest through social rehabilitation.[3] Alexander Crummell viewed the former slaves as an ethnic group that was in need of cultural revitalization.[4] T. Thomas Fortune argued that the struggle in the South was not between the races, but between labor and capital.[5] The great debate between W.E.B. Du Bois and Booker T. Washington—which involved many intellectuals—became the ground upon which the dominant trends of thought about the nature of the Black condition, after slavery, were argued through the first four decades of the 20th Century.[6] The Du Bois-Washington debate was a juxtaposition of the integration and separation categories, which on both sides could have been characterized as nationalist. The advent of Marcus Garvey occasioned the solidification of separatism among the Black masses, as Garvey was concerned with the removal of the race problem from the American culture, by advocating the transplanting of the African in America to Africa.[7]

From the early 1800s, well into the 1940s, Black political and social thought represented both a will to integrate into American society and a will to separate from American society. Over this period of time, the status of Black people ebbed and flowed in the transformation of the American state; from slavery and domination to segregation and domination.[8] With the "landmark" Supreme Court decisions of 1944[9] and 1954[10], change was made in the legal status of Black people in the United States. However, it was after 1954 that the political theories of the earlier decades unfolded in practical ways.

After the Brown decision of 1954, and beginning with the "Walk to Freedom" bus boycott in Montgomery, Alabama of 1955 to 1956,[11] civil rights activity was ushered in as a "struggle for full socio-economic and political participation."[12] The political and ideological fiat was the Civil Rights Movement. The Movement was ignited by the structural conditions of existence in the 1950s.[13] Shaped by an activist-protest ideology, the Movement was to render Black people free of de jure racial segregation.

The featured ideologue of the Civil Rights Movement was Dr. Martin Luther King, Jr., the preacher, who emerged as leader of the Montgomery bus boycott. The movement was organized by several national (but in programmatic terms, mainly southern) civil rights organizations. Among the organizations were the National Association for the Advancement of Colored People (NAACP), the Congress of

Racial Equality (CORE), the National Urban League (NUL), the Southern Christian Leadership Conference (SCLC), and the Student Non-Violent Coordinating Committee (SNCC).[14]

The ideological character of the civil rights organizations was integrationist. It was based upon the strategy of political appeals and alliances with white liberal and labor groups. Methodologically, legal and judicial forms were used to change the status of Black people, especially in the American South. The integrationist position prescribed a programmatic and practical process of political participation and social integration.

With the passage of the Civil Rights Act of 1964 and the Voting Rights Act of 1965, the Civil Rights Movement had fulfilled its objective of eliminating de jure racial segregation in the American South. The tendency to affirm the American legislative paradigm fit well with the goals and objectives of monopoly capitalism. While the successes or gains, which integrationists wish to recount, are in large measure attributable to a rationalizing monopoly capitalism, the Civil Rights Movement failed to achieve the broad economic gains it needed. The fragmented nature of the Civil Rights Movement's leadership had to finally contend with a rising radicalism and protest typified by Black power and Black nationalism (and Pan-Africanism).

The "Meredith March" in the summer of 1966 seemed to symbolize a new juncture in the political thinking of Black people, especially in the Southern region.[15] Led by SNCC and its chairperson at the time, Stokely Carmichael,[16] the march politicized the ideological slogan Black power.[17] In its political form, Black power represented a break with the traditions of the American paradigm.[18] Black power developed out of the need for control over the political and economic resources and institutions in the Black community.[19]

The test of the philosophical and organizational utility of Black power was never realized. While Black power may have argued against the integrationist agenda, it could not transcend that agenda. Instead, there arose a proliferation of hundreds of cultural and political organizations, with varying Black power agenda. To the extent that Black power solidified the basic civil rights objectives, its moment of historic significance only had been realized in the American South. The general failure of Black power resulted in the emergence of a contemporary Black nationalism.

Contemporary Black nationalism, in form and substance, was an entirely different phenomenon. In large measure, Black nationalism was a northern phenomenon, personified by the theories of Malcolm X. It was naive about the southern experience-characterized by a tendency to romanticize about Black life and culture in the southern region. Black nationalism "mistook artifacts and idiosyncrasies of culture for its totality and froze them into an ahistorical theory of authenticity.[20] The desire for territorial separation and geographical ownership of southern states and the like did not [jibe] with the general understanding that Black people in the southern region had about their conditions. It may be argued that a significant number of Black people in the American South viewed themselves to be as much southern as American. Contemporary Black nationalism, in its ideological and cultural variants, did not transcend the civil rights tendency.[21]

Two final observations can be made about Black power and contemporary Black nationalism: (1) as radical fringes, within the Civil Rights Movement, Black power and Black nationalism failed to develop a systematic critique of civil rights ideology, and (2) organizationally, Black power and Black nationalism were never grounded in the day to day activities of the Civil Rights Movement, especially in the American South.[22] Between 1968 and the early 1970s, these ideologies had given way to Pan-Africanism.

The Pan-Africanism of the late sixties and the early seventies not only rejected the inter-racialist model of the Civil Rights Movement, but it was neo-Garveyist. It posited that the destiny of Black people in the United States was tied to African people throughout the world. The basic argument was clear: Black people in the United States should reject all aspects of the dominant culture and values. African traditionalisms and an African socialism were advocated. While the ideologues established institutions to expound the principles of Pan-Africanism, those institutions were never directed toward Black people in the southern region.[23] Overall, Pan-Africanism was to represent a general ideology that all Black people in the United States could subscribe to the claims that it made were never realized. Like Black power and Black nationalism, Pan-Africanism was never able to contend with or against dominant civil rights ideology.

The early 1970s saw an emergence of a Marxist trend in the U.S. Black community. This trend was initially circumscribed around the African Liberation Support Committee, which had been established in 1972 to organize African-American support for African liberation movements in southern African and Guinea-Bissau. By the mid-1970s, there were numerous Marxist variants, characterized by internecine ideological struggles over the "correct road for Black liberation." However, Marxism suffered the same fate as Black power, Black nationalism and Pan-Africanism.

With failures and the demise of Black radical opposition, dominant civil rights ideology had arrived at its finest hour. In the American South, the acquisition of Black political authority had become the crowning achievement of the Civil Rights Movements. Nationally, affirmative action and equal employment access had become a function of "state-sponsored democratization."

By the late 1970s, Black political activity lost its excitement. Black liberals had by now consolidated their interests around electoral politics with the election of Black mayors in major U.S. cities and increasing numbers of Black persons elected to various local and state public offices. Under President Jimmy Carter, Black liberals enjoyed the presence of two Black Ambassadors to the United Nations. There seemed to have been a "second coming?"

However, with the election of Ronald Reagan to the U.S. presidency, new Black ideologues emerged. For the first time, since Booker T. Washington from the 1890s to his death in 1915 and the Black journalist, George Schuyler (1940s-1950s)[24] an authentic, self-righteous, and passionately ideological Black conservatism had come to identify with a national government administration.[25] The group is personified by economists Thomas Sowell[26] and Walter Williams.[27] The new Black conservatism is explicit in its political and ideological views: it rejects liberal reforms, labor agitation, and racial protests and argues for the "profit-oriented ethos," that emphasizes "the free standing individual" and promotes success in a capitalist system. To date, these new conservatives have proposed public policies that are broadly anti-minimum wage, anti-equal opportunity and anti-affirmative action. While new Black conservatism has found a presence, it has not broken through to dominate political thought inside the U.S. Black community.

Historically, the tends in Afro-American political and social thought have been characterized by activism. While protest activities have continued in episodic forms, Black opposition to racial and class domination has atrophied. Since the mid-1970s, not only has negativity-residual and artificial-receded, but theoretical reflexiveness has been a rare quality.

The advent of the William (Bill) Clinton presidency in 1992 returned Black liberals to the public fore. The Clinton presidency also gave rise to a group of Black intellectuals known as public intellectuals. Black liberals and public intellectuals decided to support the moderate-conservative Clinton despite the fact that the Clinton-Gore campaign had utilized the "Southern racial strategy" to woo Southern white conservative voters and Northern, Midwestern, and Western white middle class Reagan Democrats. Clinton-Gore campaigned extensively in the white suburban fringes of large urban metropolitan regions while largely ignoring the Black urban centers.

Black Democratic party liberals, such as Jesse Jackson, embraced Clinton despite the fact that Clinton left the campaign trail in New Hampshire to return to Arkansas to prove he was a strong prosecutorial governor by presiding over the execution of a brain-dead Black man, Ricky Ray Rector. During his 1992 campaign, Clinton pushed the ideas of "three strikes you are out" and prison boot camps, aiming at fighting crime with a Black face. Clinton also campaigned against public welfare in predominant white suburbs.

As a founding member of the conservative-moderate Democratic Leadership Council, Clinton had fashioned a "New Covenant" to promote conservative public policy emphasizing individual responsibility and opposing public assistance for the disadvantaged. With his campaign mantra being "It's the Economy Stupid," Clinton made the calculation that Black voters had no choice but to vote for him over Republican incumbent George H. W. Bush and the Reform Party candidate, Ross Perot. Clinton also calculated that the white electorate would respond well to an ostracism of Jesse Jackson, the symbolic leader of the Democratic party's "left wing."

Clinton set out to deliberately "bait a prominent African American." Jackson became his victim, as Clinton used the occasion of Jackson's Rainbow Coalition Summit Conference to criticize rapper Sister Souljah for her remarks, carried by the *Washington Post*, that "if black people kill black people everyday, why not have a week and kill white people?" Clinton's objective was to humiliate Jackson while sending a message to white voters that he would not kowtow to Jackson as Walter Mondale had done in 1988. This move proved essential to Clinton's 1992 victory. Clinton outpolled Bush among white voters, and despite overall low Black voter turnout, he received 82 percent of the Black vote.

Perhaps, more significant than the role that the Black liberal political elite played or did not play in Clinton's 1992 victory was the ascendancy of Black public intellectuals. This group was especially typified by such personalities as Harvard University Black studies head Henry Louis Gates, Jr. and Princeton/Harvard Black Studies professor Cornel West. Gates, West, and others became prominent advocates for Clinton-Gore policies to "end welfare as we know it," "mend but not break" affirmative action, and argue for a strategic role for the Black middle class in regulating and managing the so-called Black underclass. The Black public intellectuals enjoyed access to the Clinton White House and great fanfare in white high culture circles.

During the Clinton era, Black liberals and public intellectuals pursued their petty personal and class interests rather than the broad tactical and strategic objective of enhancing the life chances of the "Black masses." Moreover, these groups proved loyal to a party, and a presidential administration who made public policies diametrically antithetical to broad based Black groups and class interests. With the help of the Congressional Black Caucus (which numbered 38 in the House of Representatives in 1992), Clinton pushed through a crime bill that rained down unprecedented persecution upon Black, young, primarily male; first-time and nonviolent offenders. During the two term Clinton regime, the number of Black juveniles charged with crimes went from 456,072 to 535,500. During the same period, the number of Black adults in the criminal justice system went from 1,873,200 to 2,149,900.

Moreover, Clinton's 1196 welfare bill, which "ended welfare as we know it," devastated poor Black families, especially children. With its lifetime limits on benefits, workforce mandates, and little, if any, provisions for child care, Clinton's welfare bill expanded the working poor, and shifted national governmental entitlements to the middle class. The Black liberal political elite complied with Clinton's rightward policies and bamboozled the Black masses into believing novelist Toni Morrison's fantasy that Clinton "is the country's first black president."

The bamboozle seem to be thorough going, as the 1995 "Million Man March," led by Nation of Islam's Louis Farrakhan, rallied nearly one million Black men in Washington, DC but made no demands on the Clinton regime and the American state. The subsequent "Million Woman March" and "Million Youth Marches" were equal impotent in their political rhetoric and protestations. By July 1998, it became apparent that Black people had lost the capacity to make radical demands on the American state as the Black Radical Congress convened in Chicago with an array of individuals and groups from the Black left and the Black revolutionary nationalism of the 1960s and 1970s, but failed to produce an agenda of action for a new Black politics and political thought.

The 2000 election of Republican George W. Bush to the presidency has resulted in the reemergence of Black conservatives from the Reagan-Bush era. However, their vociferousness has been tempered by the roles played by Colin Powell, the first Black person to serve as the Secretary of State, and Condoleezza Rice, the second Black person (Powell was the first) and first Black woman to serve as National Security Advisor; to give the veneer that Black people are finally major players in national and international policy-making. How this impression translates to mass legitimacy remains to be seen in the 2004 national elections and beyond.

Black political theorists are confronted, then, with the task of reconstructing the essential obligations of political discourse. Several questions must be asked and answered. What is the Black predicament? How do we characterize the Black predicament? What political obligations are required to arrest the Black predicament?

In the remainder of this essay, I am going to assess the contemporary Black predicament. I shall proceed by defining and examining the Black predicament as a crisis of everyday life. Then I will prescribe what I take to be some of the critical political obligations that are required to arrest the Black predicament. I will conclude with some tentative observations about the role of Black intellectuals and the responsibility that Black people have for their future.

The Crisis of Everyday Life

Today, we find an economic system that is in crisis. It can no longer ensure job provision, and a level of productivity that will sustain economic growth. The American culture—historically lacking identity and authenticity—is a dying culture. It is typified by a myriad of decadent popular forms. Politics, while remaining trivialized, is characterized by fear and hysteria, as the U.S. government goes about the world making war, invading sovereign nations and instigating nuclear war. Through it all, the wretched of this country remains victimized, as they are taken off the public assistance rolls and asked to die in wars which are "misspoken" of as "peace missions." These are dark times!

The Clinton era economic policies, which made the rich even richer, have ended. The computer technology industry—the "dot coms"—which saw a proliferation of new wealth among post-baby boomers has bottomed out. The economic policies of the current Bush regime have lead to increasing unemployment, a business cycle spiraling out of control, and revelations of longstanding corporate corruption; resulting in historic bankruptcies, resignations, imprisonment, and government bailouts.

These dark times are glaring inside the U.S. Black community. This effort to make an assessment of the Black predicament is cognizant of the variety of problems and questions which characterize discussions of the Black experience in the United States, i.e. race and class dichotomies. It is not the intent of this writer to obscure these problems and questions. They lie at the very center of any discussion of the Black predicament. However, my treatment of the concept 'Black community'[28] suggests that the Black predicament is a group problem. Admittedly, there are determinant class, ethnic and cultural factors which characterize the Black predicament. But these factors are not, in every given situation, dominant factors. I make this specification, because I believe that we cannot reduce the Black predicament to a mere discussion of "ideological" categorizations. Above all, we must look to the structure of everyday life inside the Black community.

The Black community in the United States is in crisis.[29] Externally, this is a crisis of everyday life within a capitalist totality. This external crisis is structural, and is, in part, illustrated by social welfare statistics; describing levels of poverty, unemployment and the life among Black people.[30] More importantly, this external crisis is characterized by the overexploitation of Black labor and the domination of Black life.

Internally, this crisis has a dual nature. The first level of the internal crisis is defined as an identity crisis. The second level of the internal crisis is defined as a political and philosophical crisis. The former is evident by the fact that Black people "still lack a compelling model of themselves, of their purposes in North American society and of the kind of reasoning which can generate such a model.[31] The latter particularizes the incapacity of Black people to define, realize and defend their objective interests as a group and/or class of people. More precisely, this political and philosophical crisis is one of leadership, organization and program.[32]

The problems which now confront Black people are not new. The current state of Black life results from long standing economic and developmental shifts and transformations. The contemporary Black predicament may be similar to that following the Black Reconstruction of the late 19th Century.[33] Then, as is the case now, a restructuring took place in the industrial sector of the economy, which prescribed the political relationship of Black people to southern institutions. The difference is that Black people now have become economically irrelevant,[34] as the current restructuring requires less and less human labor-unskilled, skilled and professional.

The state of Black economic irrelevancy implies a political strategy. At least three concerns must be addressed: (1) a reigning national public policy shaped by a belief that the problems of race and racial, oppression have been eliminated; (2) the need to argue for the obligation of government to provide for the public good; and (3) the Black community's need to recognize its own failure; in part, its inability to come to terms with political obligations, and, in part, its inability to make radical demands on the American state.

The concerns cited above specifies a broader dilemma that Black people have within the political community in the United States. They also underpin the elemental nature of the contemporary Black predicament. This elemental nature is shaped by the fact that the overwhelming majority of Black people in the United States occupy the lowest levels of the socio-economic apparatus. Social welfare statistics, though not the best indicators, glaringly illustrate part of the structural crisis of the Black community.

Structural Crisis: A Survey of Social Welfare Indicators[35]

We need only consider a few of the primary indicators. The rate of poverty which currently exist in the Black population is approximately 24 percent; three times higher than poverty among whites. This percentage represents one out of three Black persons, as compared to one out of ten whites. The Black poverty rate is below the 30 percent level for the first time in nearly fifty years. However, the data indicate that the rate of poverty will rise faster among Black people than among whites.

Poverty is high among Black people in urban inner city and rural communities. Poverty is highest among Black people under 18 years at 33.1 percent. Among Black people 65 years and over the poverty rate is 23 percent. The poverty rate is 21 percent in Black families with and without children under 18 years and 27 percent in Black families with children under 18 years. In each case, the Black poverty rate is at least twice as high as the white poverty rate. Among all Black males the poverty rate is 20 percent, and among all females the poverty rate is 27 percent. In each case, the poverty rate among Black males and females is three times higher than among white males and females. The poverty rate among Black female headed households is an astounding 39 percent; three times that of white female headed households. When the poverty rate of 15 percent among Black male headed households is added to the poverty rate among Black female headed households, the poverty rate among Black single-parent families is 54 percent.

Income levels for Black people also fall markedly behind those of whites. According to the 2000 census, the earnings of Black full-time, year-round workers lag behind whites proportionate to their total numbers in every category except those income levels between $10,000-$34,999. Three times as many white individuals and two times as many white households have incomes of $75,000 and over than do Black individuals and households. Black net-worth is three times less than white net-worth. When correlated with educational attainment, Black net-worth still significantly lags white net-worth. Black people fall below whites in every source of income: labor earnings, property income, transfer income, social security income, retirement income, and public assistance. For every $100 that the average white person has the average Black person has less than $60.

The problem of unemployment among Black people can be understood by first appreciating that the problem of underemployment is a far greater phenomenon. However, there are no underemployment data available. The overall Black unemployment rate stands at 10.3 percent. Black youth unemployment is now at 30.2 percent. In many large urban centers, Black youth unemployment is at least 60 percent.

The mortality rate among Black people, particularly among Black males, is extremely high. The mortality rate for Black men, resulting from homicide is 69.2 percent. For white males, the rate is 10.2 percent. Black mortality by homicide is 6.8 times greater than white mortality by homicide. The mortality rate by homicide is greater among Black males between 25 and 34 years. The rate among this age group is 134.6 percent. For white males, of the same age group, the rate is 15.3 percent. The mortality rate by suicide has steadily increased over the past two decades. This phenomenon is also critically high among Black males; 12.8 percent. It is highest among Black males in the age group 25-34 years; 24.4 percent.

Poverty, low income levels, unemployment, underemployment and mortality among Black people illustrate the problems of everyday life, as well as the problems of a dying culture. These problems, and others, describe an existence of misery, despair and alienation.

The constraints which are imposed by these problems will continue to increase at alarming rates. Anything short of fundamental structural change will only force another adjustment upon the Black community. Regardless of how much any one sector of the Black community is contained in the crisis of the American political community, the structural crisis inside the Black community can only be arrested by Black people. This can be done by first addressing the internal crisis which confront the Black community; the crisis of identity, politics and philosophy. This crisis is manifested by the lack of meaningful, foresighted and effective leadership, organization and program.

Internal Crisis: Identity, Politics and Philosophy

The Black community lacks a critical identity. It does not have a compelling model of itself, framed by a purposive and reflexive political and social theory. Consequently, Black political praxis is without a criteria for evaluating society and a model for prefiguring transcendency and transformation.

The crisis of Black leadership, organization and program is a crisis of politics and philosophy. Today, this is typified by civil rights leadership that leadership that "don't think we need to make any dramatic changes now.[36] While this is a typical view within civil rights ideology, it is also apparent that there is an absence of any identifiable, organized radical force within the Black community.

The way in which Black liberals and conservatives have situated themselves vis-a-vis dominant class interest is no different from any attendant public found among other groups, who ideologically and otherwise align themselves with given national government administrations. The crisis of politics and philosophy among Black people is not peculiar to any given sector, faction or fringe. It is a thorough going crisis. And it has come to acquire a self-righteous posture.

On the leadership side, the problem is not simply one of the lack of leadership, but the lack of socially responsible and effective leadership. Such leadership is framed by a clear, reflexive and purposive political praxis, unambiguous in its claims against its community and the American state. The absence of such praxis is particularized among groups that have been historically weak. Certainly within the Western world and the United States, this has been the situation for Black people. With very few exceptions, Black leadership has been characterized by irresponsibility and mediocrity.

Taken as a monolith, it is difficult to provide criteria for evaluating Black leadership. If we were to gauge the last twenty years, what other Black leader can be identified, who spoke to Black people about Black people's problems, other than Malcolm X. Or a survey of those Black persons who have achieved positions of political authority would reveal individuals who do not understand the bases and the limits of political power, and who would have a rather myopic understanding of the U.S. political economy. What we will find is a leadership incapable of responding to its own failures, because it has bought into the failures of the dominant class—its liberal and conservative wings.

Since organization and program reflect leadership, it is easy to grasp the larger problems inside the Black community. Generally speaking, these problems are shaped by the character of theory and practice or the lack thereof. Black leadership is situated according to style and visibility. The quality of leadership vision and practice is obscured in most criteria. Even ideology is little evaluated.

Black leadership cannot break out of the constraints which have tied it to dominant class interest. Its practice is one of dependency and subordination. It does not understand the Black community, its primary constituency, but yet speaks in its name. Black leadership lacks power and effective control of the stakes which it has in the system. If we evaluate the "new competitive" Black individual, whom Wilson says has ascended with "the declining significance of race,"[37] or the "Afro-American technocratic and business elite," whom Kilson says has resulted from a "status deracialization"[38] or Ebony's annual parade of the "100 most influential Blacks," we will not find power situated within or among this leadership class.[39]

The crisis of leadership, organization and program is a crisis of the Black community. But it is also a crisis which is due to the failures of traditional American liberalism—thus a crisis of politics and philosophy. As a crisis of politics and philosophy it is structured by the failure of vision: the ability to articulate obligations and define organizational and programmatic agenda. This failure of vision cannot be compensated for by affirming the virtues of a society that is incapable of providing a full political and economic life for all its citizens. Vision generates from the capacity to negate the structural and philosophical constraints of domination, that retards the ability of a people to create their own human personality and culture.

The Black community, and its leadership, have not broken out of the constraints, they have adjusted to them. Even more problematic is the "manichean personality"[40] which characterizes much of Black liberal and conservative leadership. It is a leadership that believes it is free of oppression and domination and now accepts the world of the oppressor as its own, and views the oppressor's victims incapable of human volition and creativity.

Finally, the internal crisis of the Black community, is circumscribed by a leadership that wishes to resurrect a liberal ideology which history has passed by.[41] It is incapable of recognizing its own failures and continues to make bad history.

The crisis which structure everyday life inside the Black community can only be arrested when the Black community comes to grips with its failures and the obligations that it has for those failures. This essay will now turn to prescribe a set of political obligations for the Black predicament. These will be more suggestive than exhaustive.

Political Obligations

The above assessment has been an attempt to characterize the contemporary Black predicament. This prescription of a set of political obligations is underlined by two broad questions: (1) How do Black people rediscover their human personality and culture? (2) what is the desired future for Black people? While these questions may ask about the particularity of Black people, they reflect a broader philosophic quality-politically and morally. What follows, then, is not a set of ideological prescripts. As stated above, the contemporary Black predicament is a predicament in Black political and social thought. Therefore, to suggest a set of political obligations for that predicament is an obligation of Black political thought.

Black political thought must explain the world of the Black experience. It is not an autonomous world and it is largely ordered by failure. This is the world illustrated by a structural crisis, as seen through social welfare indicators. By explaining this world, we are obligated to take responsibility for it—at least for its eradication. Thus, the first obligation is to explain the Black predicament and to take responsibility for arresting that predicament. By so doing, the Black community will begin to remove the constraints on its capacity to act with power and to develop its future.

Secondly, the Black community is politically obligated to remove the dependent relationship it has with the dominant class. This can only be done by working out autonomous strategies inside the Black community, that will depend only on the resources—human and otherwise—inside the Black community.

Thirdly, the Black community must become politically obligated to rebellion. Black people must become predisposed toward the defense of their human worth and dignity. Rebellions declare a limit on indignity and dehumanization. The most indignifying and dehumanizing constraints are found inside the Black community. To rebel against the Black predicament is to accept total responsibility for the future of the Black community and to change the world in which the Black community exists. Rebellion opens up the possibility of defining transformation—structurally and philosophically. It obligates Black people to radical change within the cultural and political life of the Black community. Rebellion means that Black people accept responsibility for the failures of the Black community; the poverty, the hunger, the poor health care, the alienation and the political impotency.

Finally, the Black community needs a negative politics. What is a negative politics? A negative politics is the negation of the constraints which have required the Black community to adjust to domination as a matter of survival. Historically, we can identify these constraints from the institution of slavery, through the institution of segregation, up to this post-segregation era, in which the Black community continues to be dominated by racial oppression and class exploitation. A negative politics require the political capacity to rethink the Black predicament and to realize the objective interests of the Black community. It situates a political praxis predicated on a fundamental rejection of dominant class ideas, ideals and institutions. A negative politics necessitates the "seizing of the time"—the political initiative—to define and to redefine the historic moment.

Philosophically and practically, a negative politics requires the acceptance of a very difficult political fact: the reforms that the American state has been forced to make, have not required a rewriting of the social contract. The society is a white male dominated society. Therefore, the accommodations which it has made, have been made in the interest of a white male dominated society. Consequently, it is so easy for this society—in all its "liberal democracy" to accept a public policy which now rationalizes against affirmative action, civil rights enforcement, and the promotion of equal opportunity.

The social and economic wreckage of late-capitalist America will forever burden the masses of Black people. A negative politics is needed, because Black people do not have anything to be positive about within existing social and political arrangements. We cannot get around the need for a negative politics by appealing to the virtues of white liberals, conservatives or left-liberals. All of these groups are now organizing—intellectually and programmatically against the marginal, middle class gains which some Black people have achieved over the last thirty years or so. These same groups are once again describing the predicament of the masses of Black people with such terms as "pathological."[42]

These political obligations point to the most elemental, but yet monumental responsibilities that Black people have to rediscover their human personality and culture, and to define their desired future. It is, in the darkest moments of this present that the Black community must find its hope and its leap of will.

Conclusion

This essay has been an attempt to provide a characterization of the contemporary Black predicament; its crisis and political obligations. The working assumption in the essay is that, the Black predicament is a predicament in Black political and social thought. The essay has not attempted to provide an exhaustive assessment. It has simply delimited some of the variables that structure the contemporary Black predicament.

Black political and social thought must rediscover its "capacity to be dangerous" by reconnecting itself to Black people. The Black community, regardless of how we might define, taxonomize or characterize it, is not an autonomous community. It remains powerless and dependent. The demise of those marginal, middle class gains, which resulted from the struggles of the 'Sixties' is evident that even the "Black middle class" cannot protect its stakes in the system. The 1983 20th Anniversary March on Washington illustrated the critical side of this problem. While that event mobilized tendencies across the political and ideological spectrum, so far, its "agenda for action" and its "coalition of conscience" remains stillborn. Even Jesse Jackson's "rainbow coalition" can only be viewed, at this juncture, as a bastardization of functional integrationism—the ideological Black middle class's "beloved community."

As long as the Black community remains unprepared to stand against the constraints of domination and dependency, it cannot negate political and ideological moments that are defined by the dominant class. This writer is suggesting that, the Black community must force the "frozen circumstances" to dance to its melody. This burden rests with a resolute, militant and pugnacious Black community, not with a politics that drag Black people into the banality of the two major political parties.

The future of the Black community will depend on rethinking history, politics and culture. This rethinking requires the restoration of philosophic constraint. Black intellectuals—especially social and political scientists—must "fulfill the promise of social analysis;" to render impassioned social criticism of the crisis which structures everyday life for Black people, and provide transvaluation toward a humane, meaningful and purposeful future for Black people. In the final analysis, this rethinking requires the development of a political formation that is prepared to generate self-conscious, radical political praxis among Black people.

The above assessment and observations are only suggestive. The political script, which must be written, must negate that which is immediately before us. If we fail, the future will rush to the past. At the edge of history, how shall we move?

Notes

1. See Mack H. Jones, "Black Politics: From Civil Rights to Benign Neglect," in Harry A. Johnson, Negotiating the Mainstream: A Survey of the Afro-American Experience, (Chicago: American Library Association, 1978).

2. See William Toll, The Resurgence of Race: Black Social Theory From Reconstruction to the Pan-African Conferences, (Philadelphia: Temple University Press, 1979). See also Michael C. Dawson, *Black Visions: The Roots of Contemporary African American Political Ideologies,* (Chicago: The University of Chicago Press, 2001) and Dean E. Robinson, *Black Nationalism in American Politics and Thought,* (New York: Cambridge University Press, 2001).
3. See Frederick Cooper, "Elevating the Race: The Social Thought of Black Leaders, 1827-1850," 25 American Quarterly, (December, 1972): 604-625 and Wilson J. Moses, The Golden Age of Black Nationalism, 1850-1925, Hamden, Conn., (1978). See also Dawson (2001) and Robinson (2001).
4. See Howard Brotz, (ed), Negro Social and Political Thought, 1850-1920, (New York, 1966).
5. See T. Thomas Fortune, Black and White: Land, Labor and Politics in the South, (New York: Aron Press, 1968). See also Frederick Cooper, Op cit.
6. Woll, Op cit. See also August Meier, Negro Thought in America, 1880-1915, Radical Ideologies in the Age of Booker T. Washington, (Ann Arbor: University of Michigan, 1964) and W. E. B. Du Bois, The Souls of Black Folk, (Greenwich, Connecticut: 1961).
7. See Theodore Vincent, Black Power and the Garvey Movement, (Berkeley, 1975). Professor Robert Hill at the University of Massachusetts-Amherst has recently published the first volume of the Garvey papers. See also Ula Yvette Taylor, *The Veiled Garvey: The Life and Times of Amy Jacques Garvey,* (Chapel Hill: The University of North Carolina Press, 2002).
8. See Mack H. Jones, "Black Politics" From Civil Rights to Benign Neglect," in Harry A. Johnson, (ed.), Negotiating the Mainstream: A Survey of the Afro American Experiences, (Chicago: American Library Association, 1978), 164-196.
9. Smith v. Allwright, 321 U.S. 649, (1944).
10. Brown v. Board of Education of Topeka, Kansas, 347 U.S. 483 (1954).
11. See Thomas L. Blair, Retreat to the Ghetto, (New York: Hill and Wang, 1977).
12. See Jones, Op cit.
13. The one pungent and concise assessment of this decade is Adolph L. Reed, Jr., "Black Particularity Reconsidered," 39 Telos, (Spring, 1979): 71-93. See also Reed, *Stirrings In the Jug: Black Politics in The Post-Segregation Era,* (Minneapolis: University of Minnesota Press. 1999).
14. SNCC later changed its name to the Student National Coordinating Committee.
15. See Robert L. Allen, Black Awakening in Capitalist America, (New York: Doubleday and Company, 1969).
16. Carmichael is now known as Kwame Ture.
17. Willie "Mukasa" Ricks coined the Slogan Black Power during the Meredith March.
18. See Stokely Carmichael and Charles Hamilton, Black Power: The Politics of Liberation in America, (New York: Random House, 1967). See also Alex Willingham, "The Impact of Activism on Political Thought in Black America: Focus on the Sixties," (Presented at the Symposium on Race, Politics and Culture, Howard University, Washington, D.C., October 7-8, 1977) and Clayborne Carson, In Struggle: SNCC and The Black Awakening of the 1960s,

(Cambridge: Harvard University Press, 1981).
19. Reed, Op cit, 84.
20. Reed, Op cit, 85.
21. It is interesting to note that the nationalist tendency among Black people are found on the right and left. We need only survey the strategies employed by the Republic of New Africa, ant Nation of Islam, and Floyd McKissack's Soul City (North Carolina).
22. The Black Panther Party, in the Bay Area of California, is probably the only exception to these problems. The Party never had a southern base to speak of. Moreover, it may be argued that, a significant sector of the Black community, in the American South were not prepared to take a non-interracialist position.
23. One of the most prominent formations was Malcolm X Liberation University in Greensboro, North Carolina, headed by Owusu Sadaukai (Howard Fuller). Its primary thrust was aimed at training young Blacks to go to various African countries.
24. George S. Schuyler, Black and Conservative, (New Rochelle: Arlington House, 1966).
25. See Alex Willingham, "The Place of the New Black Conservatives in Black Social Thought: Groundwork for the Full Critique," (Paper presented at the 1981 Annual Meeting of the Association for the Study of Afro-American Life and History, Philadelphia). See also Fairmont Papers, Black Alternatives Conference, (San Francisco: Institute for Contemporary Studies, 1980).
26. See among Sowell works Markets and Minorities, (New York: Basic Books, 1981).
27. Walter E. Williams, The State Against Blacks, (New York: New Press, 1982).
28. The concept, Black community, connotes the overwhelming majority of Black people in the United States, who continues to share a common ethos. It is important to clarify this concept for two reasons. First, there is the widespread contention that with the elimination of legal segregation so went the specificity of Black people as a group or community. Secondly, the new currency "underclass" is another, in a variety of concepts, which have been used, more often than not, to remove the specificity of the Black community as a political entity.
29. Alex Willingham, in his essay, "The Place of the New Black Conservatives . . ." suggests that the crisis is "more ideological than structural." The concept crisis, as used herein, connotes both the problems of existence and the risks and possibilities of confronting and eliminating those problems.
30. The National Urban League has done a very good job of organizing the data on the common variables of poverty, unemployment, income, etc., over the past eight years. See The State of Black America, 1983-1986.
31. Alex Willingham, "Ideology and Politics: Their Status in Afro-American Social Theory," 1 Endarch, (Spring, 1975). 4.
32. This political and philosophical crisis is especially manifested among the "embourgeoisified" Black middle class. The Black middle class has leadership, organizations and programs, but it is unable to impose its will, or free itself from domination. In my view, this is a peculiar situation, illustrating the failure of the Black middle class to effectively tie itself to dominant class interests, while holding on to certain political stakes in the system. See E. Franklin Frazier, Black Bourgeoisie, (New York: the Free Press, 1957).

A recent essay supporting this assessment is Maulana Karenga's, "The Crisis of Black Middle Class Leadership: A Critical Analysis," The Black Scholar, (Fall, 1982). 16-32. Martin Kilson's, "The Black Bourgeoisie Revisited: From E. Franklin Frazier to the Present," Dissent, (Winter, 1983): 85-96, differs from this assessment. Kilson agrees with Wilson's theory of the "declining significance of race." However, Kilson uses the term "status-deracialization." According to Kilson, not only is the Black middle class advancing into "mainstream American power structures," but it is characterized by a "split personality." Kilson suggests that, if the Black middle class views social and political issues as "class-linked," it is likely to respond as a conservative class. If the Black middle class views social and political issues as "race-linked," it is likely to respond as a liberal group. Consequently, Kilson suggests that the Black class is in fact "power-seeking." It responds to social and political issues as a "bona fide elite or upper class," and therefore is conscious of its position and the choices that it makes.

33. See C. Vann Woodward, Origins of the New South, 1877-1913, (Baton Rouge: Louisiana State University Press, 1951) and Reunion and Reaction, (Boston: Little Brown and Company, 1966).

34. See Orlando Patterson, "Toward a Future That Has No Past—Reflections On the Fate of Blacks In The Americas," 27 The Public Interest, (Spring, 1972): 25-62 and "The Moral Crisis of the Black American," 32 The Public Interest, (Summer, 1973): 43-69.

35. This treatment of social welfare statistics is not done in isolation from the broader questions which the paper seeks to answer.

36. Drake Clayton's Black Metropolis, (New York, 1962) is an excellent reference. A Visit to Mississippi and Chicago will bear out the dialectical relationship that emigrants from Mississippi have with their relatives in the Mississippi Delta.

37. This statement is attributable to Benjamin Hooks, executive director of the NAACP. See Walter Leavy, "Black Leadership At the Crossroads," Ebony (February, 1984). 38. William J. Wilson, The Declining Significance of Race, (Chicago: University of Chicago Press, 1978).

38. Kilson, Op cit.

39. Robert C. Smith recognizes this lack of power, but can only prescribe "integration" as "the most effective strategy to resolve the central problem of Black leadership—its relative powerlessness." He further observes that this can be done by enacting and fully funding "the liberal agenda of the New Deal/Great Society." See his "Black Leadership In a Neoconservative Era," 7 Urban League Review (Winter 1982/83): 47-52.

40. See Frantz Fanon, The Wretched of the Earth, (New York: Grove Press, 1969).

41. This specifies the continuing problem of dependency. Attention was called to this problem as early as the 1930s and the 1940s. see L.D. Reddick, "A New Interpretation of Negro History," 22 Journal of Negro History, (1937): 17-28, W. T. Fontaine, "An Interpretation of Contemporary Negro Thought from the Standpoint of the Sociology of Knowledge," 25 Journal of Negro History, (January, 1940): 6-13. And Fontaine, "Social Determination in the Writing of Negro Scholars," 49 American Journal of Sociology, (January, 1944): 302-313.

42. See "March to Nowhere," The New Republic, Op cit. See also Theodore H.

White's comments in his piece, "New Powers, New Politics," The New York Times Magazine, (February 5, 1984): 22-51. Left-liberals have now found a way to paint positivistic pictures of a new Black power by finding comfort in their own "responsible Negroes." See Andrew Kopkind. "Jesse's Run: Black Power In the Age of Jackson," The Nation, (November 26, 1983) and Gary Wills, "Jesse Jackson Over the Rainbow: Out on the busting with the man who would be King," 54 Gentlemen's Quarterly, (February, 1984): 144-222.

Framing Pan Africanism for the New Millennium: The Case of Reparations

Charles P. Henry
University of California at Berkeley

Any "Pan" concept is an exercise in self-definition by a people, aimed at establishing a broader re-definition of themselves than that which had so far been permitted by those in power. Invariably, however, the exercise is undertaken by a specific social group or class which speaks on behalf of the population as a whole.

Walter Rodney, Sixth Pan African Congress

The passage of "The African Growth and Opportunity Act" by the United States Congress presents a current example of the basic problem underlying any revival of the Pan African Movement. This legislation represents a fundamental shift in American foreign policy toward Africa replacing the economic development assistance approach with one designed to encourage private enterprise. In many ways the bill parallels the Clinton administration's "reform" of domestic welfare policy by moving welfare recipients from governmental assistance to private payrolls, e.g., a work requirement. Of course, the Clinton shift in development strategies occurred in the context of a Republican led Congress that sharply cut African economic assistance in 1995 and significant levels of economic growth in countries such as Angola, Ethiopia, Rwanda, and Uganda.

Copyright © by Charles P. Henry. Reprinted by permission.

The "African Growth and Opportunity Act" was originally introduced by Representative James McDermott in Spring 1996 and a year later backed by key members of the Congressional Black Caucus (Rangel) as well as leading Republican conservatives (Crane). The three main features of the bill—the accomplishment of a U.S.-Africa Free Trade Area by 2020; the creation of a U.S.-Africa Economic Cooperation Forum; and the establishment of a U.S.-Africa Trade and Investment Partnership modeled on APEC—also came with a significant set of conditionalities. These conditionalities include no trade with Libya, Cuba or Iraq; cuts in government spending, privatization of governmental services; eliminating barriers to trade such as governmental protection regulations; liberalization of trade and movement toward the World Trade Organization Regime; and movement toward democratic institutions and practices. Thus, the "African Growth and Opportunity Act" shared with welfare reform the assumption that recipients of economic assistance were responsible for their economic status rather than the structure of the political economy.

What was most striking, however, was not the content of the bill but rather the split it created between traditional allies on African issues. From the earliest independence movements through the end of apartheid, African American political elites have generally been united. This bill found Randall Robinson of TransAfrica and Ralph Nader of Public Citizen joining labor and Representative Jesse Jackson, Jr., in opposition. The Clinton administration counter-attacked led by Representative Charles Rangel, Assistant Secretary of State for African Affairs, Susan Rice; David Dinkins and Mel Foote of the Constituency for Africa and even Jesse Jackson, Sr., who had been an early opponent of the bill. Perhaps the key voice in framing the issue for the American public came from African ambassadors, including the Assistant Secretary General of the Organization of African Unity, Ambassador Vijay S. Makhan, who supported the bill. In the final House voting, 24 members of the Congressional Black Caucus supported the bill and 12 opposed it (Walters 2000).

The point of this brief discussion of the "African Growth and Opportunity Act" is to illustrate the difficulties of united action in the post-Apartheid, post-Cold War era. The old ideological divides are complicated by class, gender and even generational divisions. This work explores the ways in which Pan Africanism has been framed in this more complex environment. Pan Africanism may be defined as a body of thought and action that regards the people of African descent throughout the world as constituting a common cultural and political community by virtue of origins in Africa and shared racial, social and economic oppression. It maintains that this common oppression is best fought through united action.[1]

In 1772, Arthur Young estimated that only 33 million inhabitants of the world's population of 775 million inhabitants could be called free. Adam Smith along with most intellectuals of the day thought that slavery was unlikely to disappear for ages, if ever (Drescher 1991: 709). A century later most of the world's inhabitants could be called free and a global anti-slavery movement could rightly claim the major role in slavery's demise. As W.E.B. DuBois tried to make sense of the gap between America's democratic ideals and the "peculiar" institution in *The Suppression of the African Slave Trade*, he concluded that economic necessity trumped moral and religious ideals. Yet much current historical research argues the reverse (Keck and Sikkink 1998: 42). In fact, rather than seeing economics and morality as dichotomous explanations as did DuBois, some historians now consider how the rise of capitalism and changes in the market contributed to changing perceptions, conventions about moral responsibility, and techniques of action that underlay the wave of change provided a new "frame" through which people viewed the institution of slavery.

In the United States and Britain, the anti-slavery movement was clearly a mass movement with hundreds of thousands of people signing petitions and the creation of hundreds of local anti-slavery societies. In France, the movement was confined to an elite but the results were equally profound.[2] The backbone of the English and American movements were religious denominations and the networks between the two countries provided a mechanism for reciprocal influence. A vast supply of religious zeal created by the Protestant revival movements of the early 19th century provided a base of sentiment for anti-slavery ideas. The anti-slavery movement invented what is today called information politics promoting change through the reporting of facts. Not only were slave testimonials widely distributed but even fictional accounts like *Uncle Tom's Cabin* were tremendously influential. World anti-slavery conferences held in London in 1840 and 1843 solidified Anglo-American cooperation even as it sharpened internal divisions within the movement. Of course, the American anti-slavery crusade culminated in the Civil War; however, every significant attempt to reform American society after the Civil War grew out of the abolitionist campaign. Moreover, the transnational anti-slavery campaign provided a "language of politics" and organizational and tactical recipes for other transnational campaigns as well.[3]

The development of an international campaign to abolish slavery in the last century is often presented as the precursor of what is becoming commonplace today—international non-governmental organizations or transnational social movements operating in the context of a global civil society. This transnational connection is supported by a world economy made possible by a revolution in communications technology, the same communications technology makes possible transnational collective action and the development of international institutions and organizations that comprise a global civil society (Tarrow 1998: 178; Boli and Thomas: 173; Meyer, et. al. 1997: 146).

The strong thesis for transnational collective action makes five claims:

1. Electronic media and communication can transcend national political opportunity structures, giving way to transnational ones.

2. The national state may be losing its capacity to constrain and control transnational actors from corporations to human rights advocates.

3. As the state's capacity to control global economic forces declines, borders become blurred as individuals and groups gain access to new kinds of resources.

4. As economies globalize, cultures universalize, institutions proliferate and state sovereignty shrinks; "principled ideas" are increasingly adopted as international norms.

5. All of the above developments have prompted the generation of a dense web of new transnational organizations and movements (Tarrow 1998: 181-2).

How does Pan Africanism fit in new theories set forth to explain the explosive organizational growth around such issues as human rights, the environment, women's issues, and religious fundamentalism? Is Pan Africanism a transnational advocacy network or a transnational social movement or neither?

Transnational advocacy networks (TANs) are distinguished by the centrality of principled ideas or values in motivating their formation. By contrast, transnational actors such as banks and corporations are characterized by instrumental/material goals while scientific groups and epistemic communities are motivated primarily by shared causal ideas. Members of TANs believe that individuals can make a difference through the creative use of information and the use of sophisticated political strategies. Generally operating through targeted campaigns, these networks create political spaces in which differently situated actors negotiate—formally or informally—the social, cultural, and political meanings for their joint enterprise (Keck and Sikkink 1998).

In its first phase from 1900 to 1945, Pan Africanism would appear to share many of the characteristics of a TAN. Channels of communication between colonial powers and their domestic subjects were blocked or ineffective. Pan African activists believed that networking with each other would further their goal of anti-colonialism and therefore promoted networks. A series of Pan African Congresses were called and held in various locations outside Africa to form and strengthen networks. These networks included individuals from a variety of political ideologies and thus can be distinguished from solidarity organizations that base their appeals on common ideological commitments.

Activists representative of this early stage of Pan Africanism targeted their action toward the colonial powers using the type of tactics characteristic of TANS. Utilizing *information politics* they generated politically usable information on the conditions of colonial subjects. *Symbolic politics* were prominent in the Pan African Congresses after World Wars I and II. Pan Africanists also used *leverage politics* by allying themselves with powerful allies in the British labor movement. Finally, they practiced *accountability politics* by holding powerful actors to previously stated policies and principles of equality and democracy.

These early Pan Africanists reinforced each other's sense of issues as their interests, rather than interests defining positions on issues. By way of contrast, supporters of the "African Growth and Development Act" might be charged with letting interests determine their position on the issues. What distinguishes principled activists, then, is the intensely self-conscious and self-reflective nature of their normative awareness (Keck and Sikkink 1998: 35).

Unfortunately when employed as an instrument to examine Pan Africanism, the TAN framework has a number of weaknesses. For example, problems whose causes can be assigned to the deliberate (intentional) actions of identifiable individuals are amenable to advocacy network strategies. Thus, institutional racism, which lacks a short and clear causal chain assigning responsibility, makes action more difficult. Moreover, issues involving legal equality of opportunity may be difficult to address in a system that lacks strong international standards (see, for example, Amnesty International's refusal to challenge the system of apartheid).

These structural issues also create a problem of trust. For activists in developing countries, the issue of sovereignty is deeply embedded in the issue of structural inequality. For these activists, justifying external pressure or intervention in domestic affairs is much more problematic than it is for advocacy networks in developed countries. Witness, for example, the reluctance of African activists to suggest a redrawing of national borders established by colonial powers or any consensus on interventions in Angola, the Congo or Uganda.

Is Pan Africanism better viewed as a transnational social movement rather than a transnational advocacy network? Sociologist Sidney Tarrow defines a transnational social movement as sustained contentious interactions with opponents—national or non-national—by connected networks of challengers organized across national boundaries.[4] Using this definition, environmentalism, Islamic fundamentalism and the European and American peace movements of the 1980s are examples of transnational social movements. For Tarrow, TANs lack the categorical basis, the sustained interpersonal relations, and the exposure to similar opportunities and constraints that social movement scholars have found in domestic social networks.

Comparative work in social movement theory has sought to synthesize recent theoretical developments resulting in three broad sets of factors thought to apply internationally. These three factors include: (1) the structure of political opportunities and constraints confronting the movement (political opportunities); (2) the formal and informal forms of organization available to insurgents (mobilizing structures); and (3) the collective processes of interpretation, attribution, and social construction that mediate between opportunity and action (framing processes) (McAdam 1996: 2).

Political opportunity structures may be defined as consistent—but not necessarily formal, permanent, or national—signals to social or political actors that either encourage or discourage them to use their internal resources to form social movements. These signals include the opening up of access to power, shifting alignments, the availability of influential allies, and cleavages within and among elites (Tarrow 1998: 54). It seems clear that World Wars I and II provided the signal for the most significant Pan African meetings in 1919 and 1945 respectively. Most scholars have given little attention to the impact of global political and economic processes in structuring domestic possibilities for collective action.

Mobilizing structures are those collective vehicles through which people mobilize and engage in collective action. Resource mobilization theory and political process modeling have brought a great deal of attention to this factor. Comparative research has attempted to assess the effect of both state structures and national "organizational cultures" on the form that movements take in a given country. When applied to Pan Africanism, this approach is particularly helpful in examining the Universal Negro Improvement Associations (UNIA) led by Marcus Garvey. Like the Pan African Congress of 1919, Garvey's movement took advantage of the political opportunity created by World War I to organize. Yet while the choice of Paris for the Pan African Congress is easily explained, Garvey's choice of the United States in general and New York specifically require further examination. Garvey spent time in London and established the UNIA in Jamaica before moving to New York. Yet it was in New York that Garvey was able to develop the largest Black mass movement in U.S. history. Much work remains to be done on the informal networks Garvey and the UNIA established domestically and worldwide (Fredrickson 1995).

Framing is the conscious strategic effort made by groups of people to fashion shared understanding of the world and of themselves that legitimate and motivate collective action (McAdam 1996: 6). These conscious strategic efforts include the specific metaphors, symbolic representation, and cognitive cues used to render or cast behavior and events in an evaluative mode and to suggest alternative modes of action.

The impetus to action is as much a cultural construction as it is a function of structural vulnerability and political will. Activist frames stress urgency, agency and possibility while those opposed to action emphasize jeopardy, futility and perverse effects. Repertoires of organization are one form of cultural competence that activists can call on. Thus Garvey effectively used a military model of organization that resonated with returning World War I veterans. Also, the appropriation and replication of colonial forms, organizations, protocols, uniforms, and pompous rhetoric of White sources. However, repertoires of organization vary across groups within society, among societies, and over time (Clemens, 1996: 211).

Research on Pan Africanism has generally focused on the content of formal ideologies rather than the collective identities, core discourses and frames of meaning that link members of the social movement and movement networks. Yet it is in the discourse around collective identity that Pan Africanism has revealed its weaknesses. Culture is a system of meaning which people use to manage their daily worlds but it is also the basis of social and political identity which affects whether people support and act also the basis of social and political identity which affects whether people support and act on a wide range of matters. "Natural" or inherited identities are often the basis of aggregation in social movements. These identities are also the site of continual contestation both within movements and between insurgents and authorities.

Since social movements require solidarity to act collectively and consistently, disagreements over group identity are potentially fatal. The tension between the Pan African leaders W.E.B. DuBois and Marcus Garvey is often described as a conflict over racial identity.[5] Moreover, within the Pan African Congress movement ties to colonial powers created conflict between participants. With the advent of state-led Pan Africanism as represented by Nkrumah, geographic identity replaced racial identity as the defining characteristic of the movement. This shift marks a transition from the decentered, lateral connections of DuBois's Pan African Congresses to a more centered linkage articulated primarily through a real (Ghana) or symbolic (United States of Africa) homeland.

In fact, the categorical identity claims of movements often rest on the solidarity of much more intimate and specialized communities (critical communities). A critical community is a self-aware; mutually interacting group who have developed a sensitivity to some problem, an analysis of the sources of the problem and a prescription for what should be done about the problem. It is interested primarily in the development of new values and perspectives and is critical of the status quo without ties to established political institutions. This critical posture distinguishes critical communities from epistemic communities (Ronchon 1998: 223).

Critical communities can also be distinguished from social movements that are interested in winning social and political acceptance for new values. There are many more critical communities than there are movements. For most of its existence Pan Africanism—with the notable exception of the Garvey movement—has existed as a critical community rather than a movement. In short, as with most pan-movements, Pan Africanism has not moved from theory to praxis (Synder 1984: 6). The ties that link the diaspora together must be articulated and are not inevitable.

The issue of reparations is one of the best contemporary examples of a critical community attempting to develop a movement around an old idea. Reparations, which comes from the word "repair," has been defined as a "movement which seeks to identify and redress those wrongs, so that the countries and people that suffered will enjoy full freedom to continue their own development on more equal terms." (Thompson n.d.: 7). It is a claim that has been reinvented—reframed—several times over the past one hundred and fifty years. Each reparations cycle represents an appeal to the African diaspora and the larger community within a particular cultural context.

The call for reparations in the United States is generally viewed as beginning with the end of the Civil War. Africans, however, asked for reparations for enslavement before Blacks arrived in North America. African kings called for the return of their people and payment of damages for breach of international trade agreements. Enslaved Africans in America continually sought to be compensated for their work and free Blacks fought for the release and compensation of enslaved Blacks (Southern Law Review 1997: 261). This, however, was a critical community without a voice. Much of the surviving record is oral and generally discounted by scholars. Thus, history records that the efforts of Civil War generals to provide confiscated Confederate land to newly freed slaves as the beginning of reparations efforts in the United States. President Lincoln favored compensation to former slave-owners for the loss of their "property" but no compensation to former slaves for their labor (DuBois 1964: 150). Lincoln's successor, Andrew Johnson, quickly rescinded the actions of Union generals who had provided land to the new freedman. In 1866, he vetoed legislation passed by Congress that would have provided relief for freedmen who had land warrants or possessory titles to lands in the Sherman Reservation. They were evicted by the thousands as restoration continued. As early as 1865, Pennsylvania congressman, Thaddeus Stevens proposed a massive land redistribution plan and in 1867 he introduced the Slave Reparation Bill, H.R. 29, saying "they have earned for their masters this very land and much more. Will not the who denies them compensation now be accursed, for he is an unjust man?" (Carruthers 2001: 1)

Stevens proposed to confiscate the land of about 70,000 of the "chief rebels" who owned some 394,000,000 acres of land. This confiscation would affect less than five percent[1] of the South's White families and was "far easier and more beneficial" than expatriating 4 million former slaves (as suggested by Lincoln) said Stevens. Each adult freedman would be given forty acres and the rest would be sold to help pay the public debt. Would America do less, stated Stevens, than Russia whose Emperor had set free twenty-two million serfs compelling their masters to give them homesteads upon the very soil which they had tilled for ages (Stampp 1966: 127).

The American government would do less. DuBois notes in *Black Reconstruction* that the seizure of abandoned estates in the South came as a measure to stop war and not as a plan for economic rebirth. "Against any plan of this sort," says DuBois, "was the settled determination of the planter South to keep the bulk of Negroes as landless laborers and the deep repugnance on the part of Northerners to confiscating individual property." (DuBois 1964: 601) To give land to free citizens smacked of "paternalism" and contradicted the American assumption that any American could be rich if he wanted to be rich. Even the first year of the Freedmen's Bureaus existence was funded not by taxation but by rents collected from the ex-slaves who were renting land from the Bureau. Thus, "color-blindness" or the American refusal to recognize the exceptional status of the freed slave began immediately upon emancipation and continues today. This post civil war cycle is characterized by the call for land as a prerequisite for full citizenship for African Americans. There is little Pan African consciousness expressed and an absolute rejection of the notion of a return to Africa.

A second cycle in the call for reparations coincided with the full development of legal segregation in the South. African Americans sought to escape Southern poverty and racism by migrating north or to Africa. The "exoduster movement" created Black towns in the west while Bishop Henry McNeil Turner revived the call of a return to Africa and also demanded $40 Billion in "financial indemnity" for all ex-slaves. Yet it was a White Selma, Alabama businessman, Walter R. Vaughan, who established the first ex-slave pension and bounty organization and lobbied Congress for economic relief. Vaughan's bill was introduced by Congressman William J. Connell in 1890 and provided for maximum pensions of fifteen dollars per month and maximum bounties of five-hundred dollars for each ex-slave. Significantly, the introduction of the bill coincided with the temporary revival of Republican interest in Black voters, as well as Republican support of increased pensions for Civil War veterans, and the maintenance of high protective tariff levels. "In the debate on the tariff revision bill," says historian Mary Berry, "it was apparent to many Congressmen that there was a close connection between pensions, the surplus in the Treasury, and the tariff." (Berry 1972: 221) Once again reparations were a mere sideshow to a Republican political program and not motivated by the economic plight of the ex-slaves.

Perhaps the motivations behind the bill account for the lack of Black press attention given to this bill and subsequent efforts during this period. When three Black Congressmen were asked to support the bill, Berry reports that they wanted "the means of obtaining knowledge and useful information, which will fit the rising generation for honorable and useful employment" rather than "pensions and bounties" for ex-slaves (Berry 1972: 222). Despite their views, Frederick Douglass, who initially thought the idea impractical, came around to the position that the nation owed retribution to the Black man and that if a measure like Vaughan's had been adopted earlier, "untold misery might have been prevented." (Berry 1972: 223) As late as 1934, ex-slaves were still petitioning the president for some compensation for their years of servitude.

Believing that African Americans should not have to rely on Whites to fight for their rights, Mrs. Callie D. House and Reverend Isaiah H. Dickerson, formed the National Ex-Slave and Mutual Relief Bountys Pension Association in 1894. Their promotion of reparations came to an end in 1916 when House and other members of the Association were indicted for mail fraud (Berry 1972: 229). Mail fraud was the same charge that effectively ended the career of Marcus Garvey, the most successful Black organizer of the 20th Century.

Garvey's approach to reparations was to ask the government for support for Lincoln's original plan of repatriation to Africa. Seizing the opportunity created by World War I, Garvey was able to extract promises of support for his "Back to Africa" program from several influential Southern politicians. Senator McCallum of the Mississippi Legislature, for example, introduced a resolution to petition Congress and the President for support in securing from the Allies sufficient territory in Africa in liquidation of the war debt to provide for the establishment of an independent nation for American Blacks. Of course, Garvey's Black Zionism drew some mass support but was opposed by Black leaders like DuBois. Nonetheless, Garvey launched his first mission to Liberia in 1920 in anticipation of U.S. government support (Padmore 1972: 76). This second cycle of reparations may be seen as a return of Pan African consciousness with a call for a return to Africa by Bishop Turner and Marcus Garvey among others. Parallel to this Pan African thrust is a call for pensions or compensation for ex-slaves that grows out of domestic mainstream politics. The overriding cultural context, however, is a loss of optimism concerning equal rights in the United States as "radical reconstruction" comes to an end and a turning toward Africa as a more hopeful future.

The modern civil rights movement is commonly associated with civil and political rights. Yet the call for "jobs and freedom" was the slogan of the movement's symbolic peak in the 1963 March on Washington. In mid-1963, the Urban Leagues' Whitney Young proposed "an immediate, dramatic and tangible domestic Marshall Plan" that would enable Blacks to begin the social race at the same starting line. Carefully distinguishing between his call for a "special effort" and "special privileges," he called for massive compensatory action, over ten years by government, business, and foundations to generate employment, to improve education, housing and health, and to "reverse economic and social deterioration of urban families and communities." (Young 1993: 172).

Martin Luther King, Jr., agreed that compensatory measures were necessary and had been used to benefit other groups, however, when he announced his own program for economic and social advancement that same year, King labeled it a "Bill of Rights for the Disadvantaged." Putting a price tag of $50 billion over ten years on his proposal, King called for "the development of a federal program of public works, retraining and jobs for all so that none, white or black, will have cause to feel threatened." (King 308).

Following Watts and other outbreaks of urban violence, President Johnson called for a White House Conference in June 1966 to address urban conflict. Growing out of that conference was the "Freedom Budget for All Americans" put forth by Bayard Rustin and A. Philip Randolph. They called for outlays of $185 billion over ten years including guaranteed jobs and income. The Freedom Budget itself was drawn up by a team of Black and White economists and intellectuals, including Leon Keyserling, Vivian Henderson, Tom Kaln, Nathaniel Goldfinger, and Michael Harrington. "No matter what you think of the war (Vietnam), whether you favor or oppose the administrations policies," said Randolph in his Senate testimony, "if the war goes on, and if the country makes the Black and White poor pay for it, this will have the most disastrous consequences on our democratic way of life." (Randolph 1966: 1891)

The Johnson administration never seriously considered the "Freedom Budget" or the earlier economic programs put forth by Whitney Young and Martin Luther King. It was the administration's rejection of such proposals—and a lack of support from former liberal and labor allies—that led King to propose the Poor People's Campaign of 1968. The campaign was designed to shut-down Congress unless action was taken on the economic agenda of the campaign. Although the civil rights movement is not generally seen as a call for reparations, a good case can be made that it represents a third cycle of reparations claims focusing on economic rights for African Americans and others who were economically disadvantaged.

King's death effectively ended any hope the PPC had of succeeding, however, the administration along with Republican supporters had already begun to undercut any support for radical economic reform. The "Great Society" programs had co-opted many activists who might favor such reform. Perhaps the coup de grace was the development of affirmative action which not only served to divide middle-class Blacks from lower-class Blacks but also pitted Whites against Blacks. Liberals divided over the issue of preferences while conservatives assumed the moral higher ground of "color-blindness." (Kinder and Sanders 1996: 83-8).

The Black church community was not willing to give up the moral higher ground. In 1968, Black Baptists demanded that the American Baptist Convention devote 10 percent of its investment portfolio to the capitalization of Black-owned businesses. A year later at New York City's Riverside Church, SNCC leader James Forman interrupted Sunday services to read a "Black Manifesto" which claimed that the nation's "racist churches and synagogues" owed Black Americans $500 million in hardship reparations. He later raised the demand to $3 billion (Van Deburg 1992: 246). Thus, what had begun as a broadening of the civil rights movement to include economic rights for all disadvantaged Americans and moved from the local to the national level, was narrowed to a Black demand for private funding in a fourth cycle of reparations.

Contemporary efforts to build a reparations movement may be traced to the Civil Liberties Act of 1988. This congressional act provided $20,000 (1.2 billion total) and an apology to people of Japanese ancestry who were interned during World War II. While African Americans had no objection to redressing the internment of Japanese Americans, they were incensed that their own claims for reparations continued to be ignored at best and ridiculed at worst. The following year, Representative John Conyers, Jr., introduced a bill in Congress to establish a commission to study reparations for slavery. In 1990, the National Coalition of Blacks for Reparations (N'Cobra) was formed to develop a grassroots movement for reparations. Ron Daniels made reparations a central issue in his independent bid for the presidency in 1992.

Internationally, Nigerian President Ibrahim Babangia took the lead in establishing a reparations movement during his tenure as head of the Organization of African Unity (OAU). After the first meeting of the International Conference on Reparations in Lagos, Nigeria, in the winter of 1990, the OAU set up the Group of Eminent Persons.

In 1992, the OAU formally embraced and endorsed reparations as "the last stage in the decolonization process." This summit of African Heads of State meeting in Dakar, Senegal, formally created an international committee called the Group of Eminent Persons and charged it with determining the scope of damages and a strategy for achieving reparations. Jamaican diplomat Dr. Dudley Thompson was chosen to chair the group (Obadele 1996: 247-8). After a second conference in 1993, the OAU issued the Abuja Proclamation that articulated a grievance against the United States and Western European nations linking slavery and colonialism. The Proclamation states:

> . . . Emphasizing that an admission of guilt is a necessary step to reverse this situation (damage to African peoples);
>
> Emphatically convinced that what matters is not the guilt but the responsibility of those states whose economic evolution once depended on slave labour and colonialism and whose forebears participated either in selling and buying Africans, or in owning them, or in colonizing them;
>
> Convinced that the pursuit of reparations by the African peoples on the continent and in the Diaspora will be a learning experience in self-discovery and in uniting political and psychological experiences;
>
> Calls upon the international community to recognize that there is a unique and unprecedented moral debt of compensation to the Africans as the most humiliated and exploited people of the last four centuries of modern history (Robinson 2000: 220).

Since 1994, numerous reparations claims have been filed against the United States government in federal court, none of which have been successful.

In 1994, the Internal Revenue Service (IRS) reported receiving about 20,000 bogus tax-reparation claims. Capitalizing on the publicity around federal payments to Japanese Americans, con artists falsely informed Blacks that the federal government had passed such legislation for African Americans and offered to file their claims for a fee. Again in 2001, the Social Security Administration issued a special alert to senior citizens involving a reparations scam. An investigation by the agency found that more than 29,000 people were duped by the "Slave Reparation Act." (Mayer 2001: A2; Singletory 2001: H1).

Throughout the nineties, a number of individual cities and states have taken some action on reparations. Cities like Tulsa and Elaine, Arkansas, have considered payments to survivors of racist violence against their citizens. Other cities such as Dallas, Atlanta, Nashville, Cleveland, Chicago and Detroit have passed bills that symbolic support reparations. In New York and California, the state legislatures have passed bills dealing some aspect of reparations (Austin 2001: A2).

The United Nation's World Conference Against Racism (WCAR), which met from August 31 through September 8, 2001, provides an excellent opportunity to examine the development of a Pan Africanist social movement through the issue of reparations. Billed as the largest gathering ever devoted to the discussion of race and racial discrimination, the conference was attended by 170 governments and nearly 19,000 individuals. It brought together an unprecedented group of activists (critical community) interested in conceptualizing and implementing a strategy to secure racial reparations. In writing about transnational advocacy networks, Margaret Keck and Kathryn Sikkink cite conferences and other forms of international contact as primary arenas for forming and strengthening such networks (Keck and Sikkink 1998: 12).

Largely as a result of a shift in control of the UN General Assembly to "non-aligned" or "third world" countries, between 1973 and 2003 the UN designated three decades for action to combat racism and racial discrimination. At the mid-point of the first Decade, 1978, the first World Conference was held in Geneva. The conference specifically addressed apartheid and for that reason was opposed by the United States. Delegates characterized apartheid as "[an] extreme form of institutionalized racism," and a crime against humanity. Reparations did not appear in the final conference document. In August, 1983, the second World Conference to Combat Racism and Racial Discrimination was again held in Geneva and reviewed and assessed the activities undertaken during the first Decade. The conference again devoted a good deal of attention to apartheid but also expanded the analytical scope of discrimination to address acts and policies of intolerance faced by women, refugees, immigrants and migrant workers. Item 43 in the final conference declaration states that "[v]ictims of racial discrimination should have the right to seek from tribunals just and adequate reparation or satisfaction for any damage suffered as a result of such discrimination." (Declarations 1999: 22) Once again the conference was opposed by the United States. Thus, United States participation in the third world conference was a question of real speculation.

The 1997 UN decision to convene a third World Conference Against Racism, Racial Discrimination, Xenophobia and Related Intolerance reflected a growing concern with the rise worldwide in incidents of racism. UN High Commissioner for Human Rights, Mary Robinson, was designated as Secretary-General of the Conference and States, regional organizations and non-governmental organizations (NGOs) were requested to participate in the preparations for the Conference by undertaking reviews and studies and submitting recommendations to the Preparatory Committee (Prepcom). Non-governmental organizations were encouraged to hold a forum both before and during the Conference as had been done at other recent UN global conferences such as Vienna in 1993 and Beijing in 1995. The typical procedure for past UN global conferences has been for a series of regional meeting to develop a working document that will be the foundation for discussion and action at the conference. Difficult issues (language) that cannot be agreed to by consensus at the regional meetings is put in brackets and its resolution serves as the major activity of the conference. UN documents must be agreed to by the consensus of all participating countries.

Ambassador Absa Claude Diallo of Senegal was selected by the Prepcom as its Chair. The members of the Bureau for the WCAR included Senegal, Tunisia, Islamic Republic of Iran, Malaysia, former Yugoslav Republic of Macedonia, Georgia, Brazil, Mexico (Rapporteur), France, United States,[6] and South Africa as ex officio.

The Prepcom selected five themes for the conference:

Theme 1.—Sources, causes, forms and contemporary manifestations of racism, racial discrimination, xenophobia and related intolerance.

Theme 2.—Victims of racism, racial discrimination, xenophobia and related intolerance.

Theme 3.—Measures of prevention, education and protection aimed at the eradication of racism, racial discrimination, xenophobia and related intolerance.

Theme 4.—Provision of effective remedies, recourses, redress, [compensatory][7] and other measures, at the national, regional and international levels.

Theme 5.—Strategies to achieve full and effective equality, including international mechanisms in combating racism, racial discrimination, xenophobia and related

intolerance—and follow up (International Human Rights Law Group 2000).

Newly democratic South Africa was chosen as the host country for the conference.

The timeline for the WCAR is presented in Chart 1.

Regional meetings provide the first and often decisive opportunity to frame the major issues of the conference. We will examine the efforts of five constituencies or communities to frame the issue of reparations at the WCAR. These groups are (1) the UN itself; (2) U.S. NGOs; (3) African governments; (4) the U.S. government; and (5) the media.

The Prepcom adopted the slogan of "United to Combat Racism: Equality, Justice, Dignity" as the slogan for the WCAR. It also adopted the definition of racial discrimination as stated in Article I (1) of the International Convention on the Elimination of All Forms of Racial Discrimination (CERD) which states that the term "racial discrimination" shall mean "any distinction, exclusion, restriction or preference based on race, colour, descent, or national or ethnic origin which has the purpose or effect of nullifying or impairing the recognition, enjoyment of exercise, on an equal footing, of human rights and fundamental freedoms in the political, economic, social, cultural or any other field of public life."

Perhaps the first formal attempt to frame the conference agenda came in WCAR Think Paper I entitled "The World Conference Against Racism: A Conference on Racism Worldwide?" The WCAR Think Papers were a joint project of the Human Rights Documentation Centre (HRDC), the International Service for Human rights (ISHR) and the South Asia Human Rights Documentation Centre (SAHRDC). This document expressed the serious concern that the WCAR would not focus on racism worldwide. Expressing the view shared by the United States and some European governments, the authors feared

Chart 1
World Conference Against Racism
TIMELINE

- 1997, UN General Assembly agrees to hold a third world conference to combat racism no later than 2001.
- January 2000, "Bellagio Consultation" held Bellagio, Italy
- May 2000, First PrepCom meeting in Geneva.
- July 2000, U.S. NGO Coordinating Committee meetings held in Philadelphia and Oakland
- September-November 2000, U.S. Interagency Task Force "discussion group" meetings held in Atlanta, Albuquerque, Chicago, and Washington, DC
- October 2000, U.S. NGO Coordinating Committee meetings held in Atlanta, San Francisco and Phoenix
- October 2000 Regional meeting for Europe held in Strasbourg, France
- December 2000, Regional meeting for the Americas held in Santiago, Chile
- January 2001, Regional meeting for Africa held in Dakar, Senegal
- February 2001, Regional meeting for Asia held in Teheran, Iran
- May–June 2001, Second PrepCom meeting held in Geneva
- July–August 2001, Third PrepCom meeting held in Geneva
- August–September 2001, NGO Forum held in Durban, South Africa
- August–September 2001, World Conference Against Racism held in Durban, South Africa

that the conference would be sued by non-western countries to bash the West. It sought to avoid this outcome by asking each State to acknowledge its own struggle with discrimination as the first step in creating an atmosphere that would lead to " a more realistic and constructive manner in discussing their concerns of racism in other parts of the world." (WCAR Think Paper I 2001: 1) While acknowledging that "the pervasiveness of racial discrimination" in both the domestic sphere and the foreign policy of Western States deserves significant attention, "the authors believe that turning the WCAR into a geopolitical dispute may result in a significant setback for the fight against racism.

Unfortunately, the paper predicts such an outcome is likely. First, because Non-western States are likely "to use their numerical superiority—as they do in forums such as the Commission on Human Rights—to push through a political agenda that is concerned more with combating Western States than it is with genuinely addressing all forms of racial discrimination in all areas of the world." (WCAR Think Paper I 2001: 1) Second, the preponderance of NGOs from Western industrialized States with their greater resources and media contacts are likely to focus the attention of the conference on their own countries to the delight of Non-western and developing countries. The paper concludes with a listing of "forgotten issues" ranging from discrimination against Koreans in Japan to the mistreatment of indigenous people in South America.

It is quite unusual for the initial think piece of a global conference to predict failure and even a setback as the likely outcome. Of course this negative framing could be seen as an attempt by the West to launch a pre-emptive strike at those who sought to draw attention to Western racism.

Prior to the first Prepcom meeting a consultation on the WCAR was held in Bellagio,

Italy, with the support of the Rockefeller Foundation in January 2000. The "Bellagio Consultation" included officials of the World Bank, several UN agencies, the Rockefeller Foundation, several academics, and the leaders of several influential NGOs including the International Human Rights Law Group. The participants heard presentations on the issues of globalization, immigration, ethnic conflict, indigenous peoples, the uses of legislation and litigation with the U.S. serving as the model, and the role of national institutions on human rights. Four themes were recommended to the WCAR by the Bellagio Consultation and all four were accepted by the UN. The only theme added after Bellagio was theme three—measures of prevention, education and protection aimed at the eradication of racism, racial discrimination, xenophobia and related intolerance, at the national, regional and international levels. The Bellagio Consultation mentions reparations as a sub-theme under "Remedies, recourse, redress and compensatory measures. However, at the first Prepcom meeting the word compensatory was bracketed after a week of intense debate between the African group of countries and the European Union and the Untied States (LeBlanc 2001: 1). Thus, from the very first meetings the issue of reparations loomed over the conference pitting Western governments against their own NGOs and developing countries.

As might be expected, the strongest support for reparations came from the Americas Regional meeting in December 2000 in Santiago, Chile, and the Africas Regional meeting in January 2001 in Dakar, Senegal. The declaration agreed to by the African governments in attendance in Dakar is replete with references to the transatlantic slave trade and colonialism. It directly links the underdevelopment of Africa to the transatlantic slave trade and colonialism. Delegates ignored the opening plea of the President of Senegal, Abdoulaye Wade, who not only encouraged delegates to "stop weeping over the past and build to the future" but also declared that "racism in the 21st century is not a big deal." (International Possibilities Unlimited 2001: 5) Perhaps wondering why Senegal chose to host the regional meeting since "racism is almost dead," the delegates produced a declaration that asks for recognition of these historic injustices and an explicit apology from ex-colonial powers or their successors. Furthermore, citing Article 6 of CERD and other human rights instruments, it asserts the right to compensation for victims of racist policies or acts, "regardless of when they were committed." The following four specific recommendations to the WCAR are set forth:

33. The setting up of an International Compensation Scheme for victims of slave trade, as well as victims of any other transnational racist policies and acts, in addition to the national funds or any national equivalent mechanisms aiming at fulfilling the right to compensation.

34. The setting up of a Development Reparation Fund to provide additional resources for development process in countries affected by colonialism.

35. The International compensation Scheme and Development Reparation Fund should be financed not only from governmental sources but also by private contributions emanating in particular from those private sectors which had benefited, directly or indirectly, from transnational racist policies or acts.

36. The follow up mechanism of the World Conference will, inter alia, define the modalities of the compensation scheme for victims of slave trade and to that effect work, closely with the Eminent Persons Group established by OAU Council of Ministers' resolution CM/1339 (LIV), mandated to "set out clearly the extent of

Africa's exploitation, the liability of perpetrators and the strategies for achieving reparation." (African Declaration 2001: 4-5)

While the African declaration refers to internal ethnic conflict and the need for human rights education, the overwhelming sense of the document is that "of a victim-oriented approach" linking most of Africa's contemporary problems to the historical legacy of transnational racist practices.

The Draft Declaration and Plan of Action produced at the Americas Regional meeting in Santiago calls for recognition that conquest, colonialism, and slavery created conditions of systemic discrimination "that still affects large sectors of the population." Moreover, it states that slavery, the transatlantic slave trade and other forms of servitude could today "constitute crimes against humanity." To aid in reconciliation it asks for acknowledgement,

> That the enslavement and other forms of servitude of Africans and their descendants and of the indigenous peoples of the Americas, as well as the slave trade, were morally reprehensible, in some cases constituted crimes under domestic law and, if they occurred today, would constitute crimes under international law. Acknowledge that these practices have resulted in substantial and lasting economic, political and cultural damage to these peoples and that justice now requires that substantial national and international efforts be made to repair such damage. Such reparation should be in the form of policies, programmes and measures to be adopted by the States which benefited materially from these practices, and designed to rectify the economic, cultural and political damage which has been inflicted on the affected communities and peoples (Americas Draft Declaration 2001).

Finally, the document recalls that "pursuant to international law, persecution of a group or community with a particular identity for racial or ethnic motives, as well as institutionalized racism, are serious violations of human rights and, in some cases, may qualify as crimes against humanity." The government of Canada objected to applying the modern legal concept of "crimes against humanity" to acts that took place centuries ago. The United States also objected to characterizing slavery a crime against humanity or even a crime.[8]

Once all the regional meetings had been concluded, a special committee met in March in Geneva to merge the regional drafts into one working document. The result of the special committees work, coming two weeks after the America's regional meeting, was notable for what had been excised from the regional drafts. Although there was a separate section on indigenous Native peoples as in the Santiago document, the separate section on persons of African descent had been dropped and there was no mention of reparations. In fact, the entire thirty-one page draft only mentioned "people of African descent" twice. NGO representatives from the Americas and Asia were so dissatisfied that the draft was rejected and the committee was ordered to produce a new draft at an extra pre-conference meeting in Geneva in May 2001.

At this point the U.S. again sought to frame the discussion by producing a "Non Paper for the WCAR" released in a demarche on the conference. Again stating their desire to focus on the current form and manifestations of racism "as it was intended to do by the UNGA," the U.S. states that it hopes the working group will use the Secretariat's text as the basis for negotiation rather than starting from scratch or working only with regional documents. A large part of the "non paper" is devoted to reparations. "We simply do not believe that it is appropriate to address this history (slavery)—and its many and vast aspects—through such measures as international compensatory measures," states the U.S. Once again a focus on this issue will detract, says the U.S. from the problems that affect peoples lives today. The paper then evokes the views of Senegalese President Abdoulaye Wade who opened the Africas Regional meeting by arguing that the approach to the conference must be on practical solutions to current problems. The views of the Rwandan delegate to the Dakar conference are also used to support the U.S. position. Finally, after mentioning efforts in the United States to create an African American Museum and other educational activities, the non paper firmly rejects "anything that suggests present-day liability on the part of one state to another for that historical situation (slavery)."[9] The paper ends by pointing out the "massive debt relief program" the U.S. has undertaken totaling more than one billion dollars in Africa.

Following a lack of agreement around reparations and the Middle East at the Second Prepcom in May, a very late Third Prepcom was held in Geneva less than three weeks before the WCAR was to begin. This last minute attempt to produce a working document for the WCAR resulted in the inclusion of a separate sub-section on "Africans and people of African descent." It also agreed on the following two paragraphs concerning reparations:

191. Urges States to take all necessary measures to address, as a matter of urgency, the pressing requirement for justice for the victims of racism, racial discrimination, xenophobia and related intolerance and to ensure that victims have full access to information, support, effective protection and national, administrative and judicial remedies, including the right to seek just and adequate reparation or satisfaction for damage, as well as legal assistance, where required;

199. Urges States to reinforce the protection against racism, racial discrimination, xenophobia and related intolerance by ensuring that all persons have access to effective and adequate remedies and enjoy the right to seek from competent national tribunals and other national institutions just and adequate reparation and satisfaction for any damage as a result of such discrimination. It further underlines the importance of access to the law and to the courts for complainants of racism and racial discrimination and draws attention to the need for judicial and other remedies to be made widely known, easily accessible, expeditious and not unduly complicated (PrepCom 2001: 49).

The Prepcom, however, could not agree to include the word "compensatory" in the document and it was left in brackets.

Non-governmental organizations regarded the WCAR as a political opportunity to mobilize allies and shape public opinion. Hanspeter Kriesi has identified four types of formal organizations: "social movement organizations" (SMOs), "supportive organizations," "movement associations," and "parties and interest groups." SMOs are distinguished from the other types in their mobilizing a constituency for collective action toward a political goal. Supportive organizations, on the other hand, are service organizations such as churches, media, and educational institutions that contribute to the social organization of the constituency without directly taking part in the mobilization for collective action. Movement associations are self-help organizations, voluntary associations or clubs that service the movement's constituency but do not directly contribute to the mobilization of action. Finally, while parties and interest groups pursue political goals just as do SMOs, they do not normally depend on the direct participation of their constituents for attaining these goals (Kriesi 1996: 152-3).

One of the remarkable aspects of the push for reparations is the broad range of organizational types that came together around the issue. SMOs such as N'COBRA and the Leadership Conference on Civil Rights were joined by supportive organizations connected to Fisk University and church groups like the United Church of Christ, the Mennonite Church and the Quaker Church. While the U.S. government did not officially attend, several members of the Congressional Black Caucus joined the SMOs and supportive organizations in promoting reparations. Thus, the sense of collective Pan African identity served to unite a broad spectrum of organizations.

Within this spectrum of organizational types, one finds differentiation between organizations within types. Obviously, members of the Congressional Black Caucus differed from the mainstream of the Democratic and Republican parties in promoting reparations.[10] SMOs occupied different ideological spaces within the broader movement. Single issue organizations such as N'COBRA and All for Reparations and Emancipation had a more nationalist perspective than groups like the Leadership Conference on Civil Rights or the International Human Rights Law Group (IHRLG). The more mainstream organizations brought increased legitimacy and potential allies to the campaign for reparations while the more radial or militant groups brought a cadre of committed activists and a sense of history to the movement.

No formal hierarchial organization emerged from this mix. However, at the point of contact with opponents, that is at the regional meetings and prepcoms, an African/African Descendants Caucus was formed representing all the organizations supporting reparations. In Durban, this group issued its position in the form of "Ten Priority Action Points of Consensus." These points are as follows:

1. "The slave trade, slavery and colonialism are crimes against humanity;

2. Reparations for Africans and African Descendants;

3. Recognition of the economic basis of racism;

4. Adoption of corrective national (domestic) public policies with emphasis on environmental racism, health care and education;

5. Adoption of culture specific development policies;

6. The adoption of mechanisms to combat the interconnection of race and poverty, and the role that globalization (caused by governments and the private sector) has in this interconnection;

7. Adoption of mechanisms to combat racism in the criminal punishment (penal) system;

8. Reform of the legal system including national constitutional reforms and development of international and regional mechanisms for dismantling racism;

9. Adoption of policies specific to African and African Descedant Women that recognize and address the intersections of race and gender;

10. Support for the adoption of policies that recognize and address the intersection of race and sexual orientation. (Morris 2002: 7)

This caucus won the battle to achieve recognition as a separate sub-category in the final conference document thus validating its collective identity. Whether the connective structures that permitted the caucus to operate effectively will persist remains an open question (Tarrow 1998: 123-4).

On the issue of reparations, SMOs and supportive organizations were the most active. In the United States, the lead organization in coordinating NGO input into the WCAR process was the International Human Rights Law Group (IHRLG) and its executive director, Gay McDougall. Through the Bellagio consultation in January 2000, the IHRLG worked with the UN and other NGOs to create a framework for NGO participation and a working agenda. As we have seen, reparations emerged from the Bellagio meeting as a controversial but not dominant issue. This would change over the course of the year.

An interim U.S. NGO Coordinating Committee for the WCAR held strategy sessions in Philadelphia and Oakland in the summer of 2000. Over 100 people from different organizations participated in the Oakland meeting that was coordinated by the Women's Institute for Leadership Development for Human Rights (WILD) and the American Friends Service Committee. Reparations received a good deal of attention including the precedents of Native American and Japanese-American reparations, the Conyers bill (H.R. 40), and the need for collaboration between groups seeking reparations. A procedure was adopted to select a permanent U.S. NGO Coordinating Committee.

The permanent U.S. NGO Coordinating Committee was based at the IHRLG. Along with its partners the Leadership Conference on Civil Rights, Leadership Conference Education Fund, National Council of the Churches of Christ in the USA, and the Southern Education Foundation, Inc., the coordinating Committee convened a series of U.S. Leadership Meetings. The meetings were held in Atlanta, San Francisco and Phoenix in October 2000. Local partners and hosts for the meetings were the Center for Democratic Renewal, WILD, Changemakers Foundation, World Affairs Council of Northern California, Mexican American Defense and Educational Fund, and the Inter Tribal Council of Arizona. None of these organizations had reparations as a major group goal or objective. Only the Atlanta meeting had representatives from organizations directly involved in the reparations movement—the Southern Human Rights Organizers' Conference (SHROC) and the Race Relations Institute of Fisk University. The call for reparations, however, was not limited to representatives of those groups and each meeting heard from proponents of reparations.

Following the meetings, the U.S. NGO Coordinating Committee submitted a report to the United States government Inter-Agency Task Force on the WCAR. That report had a section on reparations and stated that "[r]eparations for slavery and unpaid slave labor, as well as for dispossession of Indian lands, placed high on the participants' list of priority issues for the U.S. government to address." Moreover, the report added that "debt relief for 'Third World' countries, in particular those in Africa, was fully supported as a form of reparation for slavery and colonialism." (US Leadership Meetings n.d.: 10) While the participants in the Leadership Meetings had no agreed-upon form reparations should take, they expressed "disappointment at the less-than-forthcoming position of the U.S. government with respect to examining the issue of 'compensatory measures' under the agenda item relating to remedies and redress. The report concluded with a series of recommendations to the U.S. government that included an expanded policy of debt cancellation especially in Africa, a national and international dialogue on reparations for slavery and the transatlantic slave trade, and support for the inclusion of "compensatory measures" as a sub-theme on the agenda of the World Conference (US Leadership Meetings n.d.: 16-7).

The message of the U.S. Leadership meetings was supported in another IHRLG report on Roundtables held in preparation for the WCAR and regional meeting entitled "Race and Poverty in the Americas." Under the subheading of "Reparations" it was reported that there was no common understanding across the Americas of what is meant by "reparations." It was suggested that achieving an NGO consensus on meaning was an important step toward inter-governmental consensus. Some emphasized that debt relief could be considered as reparations if released funds were directed toward anti-poverty and anti-discrimination programs. Others stressed that the language of reparations needed to include reference to "group-based" violations of human rights. Reparations were seen as essential in overcoming the systemic poverty experienced by Indigenous Peoples and African descendants (International Human Rights Law Group 2001b: 9).

At the same time the NGO Coordinating Committee was being formed in summer 2000, the U.S. government created an Interagency Task Force to oversee and coordinate planning for U.S. participation in the WCAR. The Task Force was composed of representatives from the Department of State and the Small Business Administration and chaired by Debra Carr, a senior trial attorney in the Civil Rights Division of the Department of Justice. The Task Force conducted a series of meetings with NGOs similar to those of the NGO Coordinating Committee holding gatherings in Chicago, Atlanta, and Albuquerque as well as Washington. To date there is no public report on the participants in those meetings or the issues they asked the U.S. government to address in Durban.

While Betty King, U.S. Ambassador to ECOSOC, represented the United States on the WCAR Bureau and at the Prepcoms and regional meetings, the most complete statement made available to the public on U.S. participation is the testimony of William Wood, Acting Assistant Secretary of State for International Organization Affairs before the House Subcommittee on International Operations and Human Rights on July 31, 2001. In his remarks, Woods notes that the U.S. co-sponsored the 1998 General Assembly resolution against racism, which called for a third World Conference (Wood 2001: 1). He also takes pride in the $250,000 donation the U.S. made to the UN Secretariat to support the conference. Noting the extensive consultation with NGOs and civil society coordinated by the Task Force, Wood does not mention the outcome of those meetings. He does state that the U.S. position has been consistent in every discussion at every level. That is, that while we "acknowledge historic injustices against Africans, Native Americans and others" the focus of the work of the conference should be "on present day manifestations of racism and intolerance, and how best to combat them." "No one should doubt," says Wood, "the profound regret of the U.S. that our Constitution and our society were ever associated with the abomination of slavery." Then Wood adds an important framing perspective, "[t]he fact that slavery was a historical phenomenon and a prevalent practice in virtually all parts of the world does not diminish that regret." After criticizing the UN Commission on Human Rights for not condemning contemporary slavery in the Sudan, Woods states the "selective memory and selective calls for redress are inconsistent with the goals of the WCAR. Thus, while the U.S. is willing to join with other WCAR participants in expressing "regret for historic injustices, such as slavery and the slave trade," it does not support the "extremes and unbalanced language relating to the trans-Atlantic slave trade and calling for reparations or compensation." (Wood 2001: 3)

Moving to a more positive note, Woods said our emphasis has been on encouraging other states to create national legal structures providing remedies and recourse to victims of contemporary racism. He cites both High Commissioner Mary Robinson and UN Secretary Koffi Annan as emphasizing the importance of a contemporary focus. Finally, in the most direct rejection of reparations Woods states:

> The U.S. has consistently opposed the call for reparations for a variety of reasons, and will continue to do so. There is no consensus in the U.S. on payment of reparations. It is not clear what would be the legal or practical effect of a call for reparations for injustices more than a century old. Nor is it clear that such a call would contribute to eliminate racism in the contemporary world." (Wood 2001: 3)

The Assistant Secretary concludes that in "keeping with our future-oriented approach to the situation in Africa, the U.S. has been active in seeking new, more productive ways t assist Africa to develop." (Wood 2001: 3) Following Wood's testimony, Democratic Congresswoman Cynthia McKinney of Georgia characterized the Bush administration's evasive stance toward the conference as a "clear example of their indifference to racism (TransAfrica 2001: 6).

By the time of the NGO Forum at the WCAR, reparations had emerged as one of the two major issues of the conference.[11] From one of many issues highlighted by the Bellagio consultation, reparations became one of five key areas in the NGO program of action. The program challenged Western criticism by acknowledging and condemning any current forms of enslavement in Africa. This position was not achieved without conflict between the African Descendants caucus which favored such a contemporary reference and the African (continental) caucus in which a number of delegates opposed such a reference. The NGOs also insisted that acceptance of a mutually agreed past can be the most significant step in developing a forward looking agenda. Therefore, the document sets forth four specific kinds of relief: restitution, monetary compensation, rehabilitation, and satisfaction (i.e., apology) and guarantees of non-repetition. Moreover, the program recommends both inter-state reparations such as debt relief and an International Compensation Scheme and/or Development Fund and intrastate reparations such as truth commissions, land grants, and monetary compensation (NGO Forum Program 2001: 37-41).

Groups with a history of reparations activity such as N'COBRA, the Black Radical Congress, and the OAU Eminent Persons Group were well represented in Durban. Major human rights organizations such as Human Rights Watch supported the call for reparations while Amnesty International took no position on the issue. Several groups submitted their views on reparations in writing at the various lead up meetings.[12] The NGO Forum held prior to and during the WCAR held a series of workshops devoted entirely to reparations. Many prominent advocates of reparations from the U.S. and from the Caribbean and Africa spoke at these workshops including John Conyers, Manning Marable, Ray Winbush, Dudley Thompson, and Lord Anthony Gifford. The final Durban Declaration and Programme of Action adopted by the WCAR contains much of the language recommended by the African/African Descendants Caucus of the NGO Forum. The final declaration reads as follows concerning reparations:

99. We acknowledge and profoundly regret the massive human suffering and the tragic plight of millions of men, women and children caused by slavery, the slave trade, the transatlantic slave trade, apartheid, colonialism and genocide, and

call upon States concerned to honour the memory of the victims of past tragedies and affirm that, wherever and whenever these occurred, they must be condemned and their recurrence prevented. We regret that these practices and structures, political, socio-economic and cultural, have led to racism, racial discrimination, xenophobia and related intolerance;

100. We acknowledge and profoundly regret the untold suffering and evils inflicted on millions of men, women and children as a result of slavery, the slave trade, the transatlantic slave trade, apartheid, genocide and past tragedies. We further note that some States have taken the initiative to apologize and have paid reparation, where appropriate, for grave and massive violations committed;

The Durban Programme of Action states the following:

165. *Urges* States to reinforce protection against racism, racial discrimination, xenophobia and related intolerance by ensuring that all persons have access to effective and adequate remedies and enjoy the right to seek from competent national tribunals and other national institutions just and adequate reparation and satisfaction for any damage as a result of such discrimination. It further underlines the importance of access to the law and to the courts for complainants of racism and racial discrimination and draws attention to the need for judicial and other remedies to be made widely known, easily accessible, expeditious and not unduly complicated;

166. *Urges* States to adopt the necessary measures, as provided by national law, to ensure the right of victims to seek just and adequate reparation and satisfaction to redress acts of racism racial discrimination, xenophobia and related intolerance, and to design effective measures to prevent the repetition of such acts;

The WCAR has been presented as a political opportunity for proponents of reparations. Reparations advocates are viewed as part of a larger sub-cultural movement historically known as Pan Africanism. Global conferences provide opportunities for access to power, influence, resources and media that might normally be blocked or not exist at the national and local levels. Such conferences also provide an occasion for reproducing a collective identity as well as networking over an issue. In fact, concern over this collective identity may at times overshadow the political feasibility of the issue. According to Doug McAdam, movement scholars have, to date, grossly undervalued the impact of global political and economic processes in structuring domestic possibilities for successful collective action.[13]

At one level, the resistance of the government of the United States to world conferences on race may be seen as an attempt to close off or block political opportunities for race activists. The United States' absence from all three global conferences on race suggests a fear that the government cannot control the outcome or product of such conferences.[14] While the post-colonial world does complicate U.S. participation globally, it is remarkable that a country that claims to be a global leader in race relations chooses not to be present. This position has been consistent over both Democratic and Republican administrations. Moreover, it stands out in contrast to U.S. participation in virtually every other global forum.

The absence of the U.S. in Durban could certainly be seen as a failure to mobilize enough pressure on the government by NGOs. Had race activists mounted the same campaign for inclusion that feminists launched around the Beijing conference, the government might have acted differently.[15] Still, given the extensive efforts by NGOs around the WCAR, the U.S. absence in Durban may be seen more as a failure of pluralist democracy. Citizens spoke but the government did not answer.

Alternatively, the refusal of NGOs and other governments promoting reparations to compromise on the work, compensatory, for example, could be viewed as elevating collective identity or political solidarity over practical necessity. Calling for political flexibility on the part of NGOs and government proponents, however, is not convincing given firm U.S. opposition to any call for reparations from the very beginning.

This work has relied heavily on an examination of the framing process in the development of Pan Africanism as a social movement. Movement scholars have been critical of the lack of attention the resource mobilization perspective attaches to ideas and sentiments. Pan Africanism, with its emphasis on the meaning and identity of movement participants, would appear an ideal candidate for scrutiny by new social movement scholars. Yet this new social movement theory has focused almost entirely on the recent social movements arising in Europe and North America.

The emergence of reparations as a central theme of modern Pan Africanism and by extension the WCAR represents a new "rhetoric of change." According to Albert Hirschman this discourse stresses urgency, agency and possibility. It frequently over estimates the degree of political opportunity (Gamson and Meyer 1996: 285). Raymond Winbush, one of the major NGO proponents of reparations at the WCAR, predicted that African Americans would achieve compensation for the unpaid labor of their enslaved ancestors within the next ten years at a Black Leadership Forum conference in April 2001 (Bivens 2001).

Momentum developed not only around the WCAR but also the advent of a new century and millennium. W.E.B. DuBois's prophecy that the 20th century would be the century of the color line was extended to the 21st century by reparations proponents. The popularity of Randal Robinson's book, *The Debt: What American Owes Blacks* was another indication that the time for action had arrived.

Perhaps the greatest sense of agency and possibility for reparations advocates came as a result of the unifying of Diaspora NGOs with African governments. The result was a final document that applied the international legal terminology of a "crime against humanity" to slavery and the slave trade. Adding debt relief to the call for reparations and compensatory measure assured the support of many African governments. Finally, the addition of a section in the conference declaration on persons of African descent reinforced the notion of solidarity so critical to the Pan African movement.

Of course, any "rhetoric of change" leads inevitably to a "rhetoric of rejection." The United States government led the charge against reparations. Central themes of this discourse are jeopardy, futility and perverse effects. Government officials constantly repeated that a focus on the past would hinder if not destroy any opportunity for the WCAR to address current manifestations of racism. Moreover, the government said such efforts might even set back racial progress. UN Human Rights High Commissioner Mary Robinson and UN Secretary General Koffi Annan were cited as supporting the U.S. view even though both had made public statements supporting an examination of the issue.[16] Senegalese President Wade gave added legitimacy to the U.S. position in his opening speech at the Africas Regional Meeting.

U.S. officials also argued that the reparations effort was futile. They cited a lack of popular support for reparations at home and accused advocates of trying to bash the West. While expressing regret for the past the U.S. refused to apologize or endorse any language indicating slavery or the slave trade was a "crime" or a "crime against humanity." The government attempted to deflect any guilt by citing the widespread nature of the practice in the 18th and 19th centuries.

Media attention on the WCAR was limited largely to the period just prior to and during the conference. The few articles that emerged around the Prepcoms and regional meeting focused on the issues of the Middle East and reparations. However, the articles did not engage the issues but rather whether they would keep the U.S. from attending the conference (Crossette 2001b; Constable 2001; Fears and Sipress 2001).

A July 30, 2001, *New York Times* article implied that UN Secretary General Annan agreed with the Bush administration in its desire to keep the Middle East and compensation for slavery off the agenda in Durban. Annan's support was important in U.S. efforts to gain legitimacy for its position. Yet this interpretation of Annan's speech to the Urban League is not supported by the Secretary General's actual remarks. He acknowledged that those two issues had "opened deep fissures" and he also acknowledged "an acute need for common ground." Most significantly, he stated that the WCAR "must confront the past," but "most important, it must help set a new course against racism in the future." (Becker 2001) Apparently, confronting the past for the *New York Times* excludes consideration of reparations.

Another report circulated in August challenging several articles that had appeared declaring that reparations were off the agenda in Durban. Interagency task Force Chair, Debra Carr, denied that the U.S. government was responsible for this disinformation. *Newsday* and the *Chicago Sun-Times* were the two newspapers accused of spreading this rumor (Winbush 2001).

Washington Post columnist William Raspberry was one of the few media voices to attempt a substantive discussion of reparations. His column elicited a great deal of response from *Post* readers. Raspberry's own position was that the government must do more to overcome the legacy of slavery, especially in education. Raspberry, however, believed better education needed to be provided for all who were failing and not because of a moral debt but "because America needs its citizens to be educated and productive." (Raspberry 2001: A21) Raspberry, then, might favor the approach taken by Martin Luther King, Jr., in his "Economic Bill of Rights for the Disadvantaged."

Another *Washington Post* columnist, Courtland Milloy, specifically raises the race issue in a piece entitled: "Colin Powell: Bush Man Or Black Man?' Milloy discusses the pressures put on Powell by the Leadership Conference on Civil Rights and its chair, Dorothy Height, to lead the U.S. delegation to the conference. Milloy states that "[o]f all the diplomatic dances that America's first black secretary of state has performed so far, none has ever caused him to step on the toes of his fellow blacks." (Milloy 2001: C1) Thus while the conference promoted solidarity for most Blacks involved, it created dissonance for Powell who had expressed enthusiasm for the conference initially.[17]

In a *New York Times* opinion-editorial, Bob Herbert, took the position that the conference had been doomed to irrelevance from the start. Herbert repeated the U.S. government's criticism of African silence on the issue of present-day slavery in Sudan and Mauritania. While this position is an exaggeration, it fits the frame of equating the Western slave trade as part of a widespread practice that continues even today in Africa. Herbert did acknowledge that if slavery is not a crime against humanity, what is? His basic position was that "you can't fight that kind of hatred (Northern Ireland) with a resolution." (Herbert 2001)

The emphasis on the impact of the final document and the absence of the U.S. miss the most important outcomes of the WCAR. First, the WCAR debate represents a shift in the framing of reparations from the mid-sixties cycle that called for reparations for all disadvantaged Americans. The shift began with the development of the "Black Manifesto" in the surge to Black power in the late sixties. While this shift might be seen as reducing the chances of gaining popular support for reparations, it strengthened the collective identity of its advocates. Moreover, the total rejection of the mid-sixties call for economic rights by liberal allies of the civil rights movement encouraged a turn inward toward Black nationalism. Debra Friedman and Doug McAdam argue that "[t]he more inclusive the collective identity, the harder it is to control, and thus the less powerful it is as a selective incentive." (Friedman and McAdam 1992: 165) Yet making participation more exclusive can also raise the cost of participation and thus reduce membership. To date, this has not happened with reparations.

Second, long-time reparations advocates in the U.S. can claim success in broadening support for their issue among mainstream civil rights and human rights organizations. Single issue groups like N'COBRA and the All for Reparations and Emancipation saw their ranks increase as supportive organizations took up the call for reparations.[18] This action represents the coming together of a critical community through frame alignment. Frame bridging and frame extension did not require potential supporters in the mainstream organizations to depart from traditional and widely shared values.[19] In short, the members of groups such as the Urban League, NAACP and the Leadership Conference on Civil Rights were not required to accept the nationalist leanings of the reparations organizations. Framing slavery as "a crime against humanity" promoted the solidarity of the rights based coalitions with the reparations groups.

Third, WCAR helped to move the reparations debate from the limitations on national discourse to an international arena with fewer constraints. Most importantly, Pan Africanist activists from the African Diaspora were reconciled with African government leaders. The break that occurred with the end of African colonialism and was manifest in the debate over "The African Growth and Opportunity Act" were put aside—with minor exceptions—in a united push for reparations. African governments pushing the West for reparations for the descendants of slaves was reciprocated in the call for debt relief on the part of reparations activists. Their combined strength served to draw attention to Africa—the neglected subject in economic discourse over globalization.

Fourth, the call for compensation from both public and private parties demonstrates a new sophistication on the part of the reparations movement. The demands in the U.S. have historically focused on the government. However, the "Black Manifesto" shifted to pressure for private parties to make amends for Black oppression. The current all inclusive demand no doubt owes its inspiration to private payments made to Jewish holocaust survivors and to the revelation that some U.S. insurance companies profited from slavery (Slevin, 2000: A17).

The success of the WCAR in building a collective Pan African identity around the issue of reparations has not come without costs. All evidence points to the success of Japanese Americans in their quest for reparations as the stimulus behind the current cycle of Black reparations. To that extent, the

Japanese American reparations movement may be considered a master cycle of protest.[20] Black legislators supported the Japanese American effort and it seems likely that activists in that struggle would be willing to support African American demands. Yet there has been very little interaction between the two groups and the call for Black reparations may foreclose alliance with other oppressed groups in the United States. Indeed, some Afro-European delegates maintained that the focus on reparations was a result of African American domination of the caucus agenda although these disagreements were eventually bridged. They were overcome, however, by limiting the call for reparations to a general principle and omitting any discussion of particular procedural or material solutions. In fact, the declaration of slavery as a crime against humanity was seen by many as the first step in a process in which material reparations might be one remedy. In her closing statement, the president of the WCAR, South African foreign minister Nkosazana Dalamini Zuma stated, "[w]e also agreed that slavery is a crime against humanity and that an apology is necessary not for monetary gain but to restore the dignity and humanity of those who suffered ... we agreed that a clear and unequivocal apology constitutes a starting point in a long and arduous journey of finding one another." She added, that "an apology restores the dignity, self-worth and humanity of the black body, broadly defined. We also agreed that other remedial actions would have to be adopted to correct the legacy of slavery and colonialism and all other forms of racism." (Zuma 2001: 171) By refusing to acknowledge this past, the United States not only missed an opportunity to begin a sorely needed dialogue at the international level, but it also ignored and even discounted the emotional linkages of its own citizens to the larger Pan African community. While the emphasis on slavery over current discrimination or recently desegregated "Jim Crow" institutions may unnecessarily complicate the demand for accountability,[21] a focus on contemporary U.S. discrimination would have produced an agenda too tailored to African American needs.

Ultimately, the greatest cost may be born by the United States government. Its consistent refusal to participate in global racism conferences and the refusal of European allies to join the U.S. in boycotting Durban point to increasing isolationism between the U.S. and Europe as well as Africa and the "third world." High Commissioner for Human Rights, Mary Robinson, stated that "the text adopted on the past is historic in that it sets out the issues in plain, unequivocal language for the first time in a document of this kind, agreed to by the international community." (Robinson 2001: 174) The events of September 11th, coming two days after the close of the WCAR, highlight the need for the United States involvement in all international forums.

Notes

[1] Walters, in attempting to link Pan Africanism to the concept of the African Diaspora, poses five types of Pan African relationships: (A) among African states; (B) among African states and African-origin states in the Diaspora, as in the Caribbean; (C) among African states and African-origin peoples (communities) in the Diaspora; (D) among African-origin states in the Diaspora and African-origin communities in the Diaspora, and (E) among African-origin communities in the Diaspora. (Walters 1995)

[2] On the differences between the Declaration of Independence and the French Declaration of the Rights of Man and of

[2] the Citizen see Louis Henkin, *The Age of Rights:* 161-7.

[3] Master frames are the complex systems of ideas that inform entire cycles of protest. They are to movement specific collective action frames as paradigms are to finely tuned theories (Keck and Sikkink 1998: 42).

[4] Tarrow also notes that scholars of ethnic nationalism have ignored social movement theory (1998: 184-9, 211).

[5] The early DuBois had a rather mystical conception of race as described in his "Conservation of the Races" paper while Garvey operated from a more biologically defined paradigm. Garvey's experience with mulattos in Jamaica made him suspicious of DuBois. (Hill 1983).

[6] U.S. Ambassador to the UN Economic and Social Council (ECOSOC), Betty king, represented the United States.

[7] There was no consensus on the work "compensatory". All words with no such agreement are bracketed for later resolution.

[8] U.S. participation in the Americas Regional meeting marked the first time that the U.S. had joined the Americas Region at a UN global conference. Prior to this time it had participated in the Western European Region.

[9] Note that the leadership for an African American History Museum on the Mall in Washington has come from the Congressional Black Caucus and not the Clinton or Bush administrations. (U.S. Non Paper for the WCAR 2001)

[10] The House of Representatives passed a resolution urging the administration to boycott the WCAR. Tom Lantos, democrat from California, was the resolution's sponsor.

[11] The other major controversy revolved around Israel's role in the Middle East. Dalits also led a successful effort to see their caste status included in the debate over forms of discrimination over the objection of the government of India.

[12] For example, the International Human Rights Association of American Minorities submitted a document entitled "Toward the Eradication of Racism and Racial Discrimination in the Americas." The group All for Reparations and Emancipation submitted recommendations on the issue of reparations to the WCAR.

[13] See McAdam, 1996:25. Note that Malcolm X often reminded his audiences that while Blacks were considered a minority in the U.S. when compared to Whites, Nonwhites were the majority worldwide.

[14] Steven Krasner notes that developing countries often prefer the international arena rather than bilateral relationships with major powers (Krasner *Structural Conflict: The Third World Against Global Liberalism,* 1981)

[15] While Assistant Secretary of State William Wood noted the $250,000 the U.S. commitment to funding the WCAR, he failed to mention the 6 to 8 million dollars the U.S. contributed to the Beijing conference. First Lady Hillary Clinton and Secretary of State Madeline Albright headed the U.S. delegation.

[16] In March 2001, the *New York Times* reported that UN High Commissioner for Human Rights Mary Robinson "generally supports such demands (reparations), particularly in it's deep, and it hasn't been properly acknowledged," Robinson added "that this exploitation was in real terms a crime against humanity when it took place and that it had an effect into this century." (Crossette 2001)

[17] Note that the Secretary of State did not hear about the WCAR until January 2001, some four years after the UN General Assembly proposed the conference and seven months after the first PrepCom (Perlez 2001)

[18] Not all race activists were pleased to come together in Durban. Dennis Brutus and Ben Cashdan challenged delegates and participants to get out of the conference center and witness the grinding poverty of Blacks and Indians in Durban's townships and throughout South Africa. They noted that while Jubilee South African leaders had supported the call for reparations, South African president Thabo Mbeki had distanced himself from the reparations campaign (Brutus and Cashdan 2001). A number of local groups used the conference and its participants to launch a major protest march concerning South Africa's economic plight during the conference week (Dixon 2001).

[19] Tarrow defines frame bridging as the least ambitious form of framing linking two or more ideologically congruent but structurally unconnected frames regarding a particular issue or problem. Frame amplification tries to clarify and invigorate an interpretive frame bearing on a particular issue. Frame extension attempts to enlarge the movements of potential adherents. Frame transformation is the most radical form of framing as the movement puts forward a radically new set of ideas and seeks to eliminate old meanings and understandings (Tarrow 1992:188).

[20] Master frames affect the cyclicity and clustering of social movement activity by functioning as master algorithms that color and constrain the orientations and activities of other movements associated with it ecologically and temporarily (Snow and Benford 1992: 151).

[21] Several reparations advocates contend that the strongest case for reparations can be made on the grounds of contemporary racism and the legal apartheid ("Jim Crow") that followed slavery rather than slavery itself (Bittker 1973; Human Rights Watch 2001).

References

Draft Declaration of the African Preparatory Regional Meeting for the World Conference Against Racism, Racial Discrimination, Xenophobia and Related Intolerance 2001. Dakar. Jan. 22-24, 4-5.

Program of Action for the World Conference Against Racism. 2001. *NGO Forum*. Durban, South Africa. August 28-September 1.

Race and Poverty in the Americas. 2001. *International Human Rights Law Group*. August.

Report of the PrepCom on its Third Session. 2001. *United Nations*. Geneva. July 30 August 10. 49. A/CONF. 189/PC.3/11.

Report on Informal Government Meeting and Africa PrepCom 2001. *International Possibilities Unlimited* 10 __

Report on the World Conference Against Racism, First Preparatory Committee (PrepCom) Meeting. 2000. *International Human Rights Law Group*. Geneva. May 1-5.

The Declarations and Programmes of Action adopted by the First (1978) and the Second (1983) World Conference to Combat Racism and Racial Discrimination. 1999. *United Nations*. E/CN.4/1999/WG.1/BP.1. March 9. __.

The World Conference Against Racism: A Conference on Racism Worldwide? 2001. *WCAR Think Paper I*.

Austin, Amber. 2001. "Activists Discuss Slave Reparations." *Associated Press*, March 7.

Becker, Elizabeth. 2001. "Annan Says Race Conference Must Chart Way for Future." *New York Times*. July 31.

Berry, Mary F., 1972. "Reparations for Freedman, 1890-1916: Fraudulent Practices or Justice Deferred." *Journal of Negro History 57*:3 (July): __.

Bittker, Borris I., 1973. *The Case for Black Reparations.* __

Bivens, Larry. 2001. "Slave-reparations debate heating up. *The Arizona Republic* April 21.

Boli, John and George M. Thomas. __. "World Culture in the World Polity." *American Sociological Review* 62: __

Brutus, Dennis and Ben Cashdan. 2001. "World Conference Against Racism: South Africa Between a Rock and a Hard Place." *Znet Commentary,* July 11.

Carruthers, Iva E., 2001. *The Church & Reparations: An African American Perspective.* ORITA.

Clemens, Elizabeth S., "Organizational form as frame." In *Comparative Perspectives on Social Movements,* ed. Doug McAdam, et. Al., Cambridge, UK: Cambridge University Press.

Constable, Pamela. 2001. "Many Causes Set Tone for U.N. Summit on Racism." *Washington Post.* August 31, A14.

Crossette, Barbara. 2001a. "Global Look at Racism Hits Many Sore Points." *New York Times.* March 4.

Crossette, Barbara. 2001b. "Rights Leaders Urge Powell to Attend U.N. Racism Conference." *New York Times.* July 11.

Dixon, Norm. 2001. "Thousands to Protest at Racism Conference." *Green Left Weekly.* August 8, Issue #459.

Drescher. 1991. "British Way, French Way: Opinion Building and Revolution in the Second French Slave Emancipation." *American Historical Review* (June):

DuBois, W.E.B., 1964. *Black Reconstruction in America 1860-1916.* Cleveland: Meridian.

Esedebe, P. Olisanwache. 1982. *Pan-Africanism: 1776-1963.* Washington, DC: Howard University Press.

Fears, Darryl and Alan Sipress. 2001. "U.S. Warns it May Skip Conference on Racism." *Washington Post.* July 27, A1.

Fredrickson, George. 1995. *Black Liberation.* New York: Oxford University Press.

Friedman, Debra and Doug McAdam. 1992. "Collective Identity and Activism." In *Frontiers in Social Movement Theory,* ed. Aldon D. Morris and Carol McClury Mueller. New Haven: Yale University Press.

Gamson, William A. and David S. Meyer. "Framing Political Opportunity." In Doug McAdam, et. Al., ed., *Comparative Perspectives on Social Movements.* Cambridge, UK: Cambridge University Press.

Henkin, Louis. 1990. *The Age of Rights.* New York: Columbia University Press.

Henry, Charles P. ed. *and the Black (Inter)national Interest.* Albany, NY: SUNY. Pp.

Herbert, Bob. 2001. "In America, Doomed to Irrelevance." *New York Times.* September 6.

Hill, Robert A. ed., 1983. *Marcus Garvey and the UNIA: Vol. I.* Berkeley: University of California Press.

Human Rights Watch __

Jackson, Thomas F., 1993. "*Recasting the Dream*" Martin Luther King, African-American Political Thought and the Third Reconstruction 1955-1968. Stanford University: unpublished Ph.D. dissertation.

Keck, Margaret, and Kathryn Sikkink. 1998. *Activists Beyond Borders.* Ithaca, NY: Cornell University Press.

Kinder, Donald R. and Lynn M. Sanders. 1996. *Divided by color: Racial Politics and Democratic Ideals.* Chicago: University of Chicago Press.

Krasner, Steven.

Kriesi, Hanspeter. 1996. "the impact of national contexts on social movement structures." In Doug McAdam, et. Al., ed., 1996. *Comparative Perspectives on Social Movements.* Cambridge, UK: Cambridge University Press.

LeBlanc, Phillippe. 2001. "How Can NGOs Be Effective In The World Conference Against Racism?"

Legum, Colin. 1962. *Pan Africanism.* London: Pall Mall.

Mayer, Caroline E. "Flier Offering Slave Reparations Solicits Personal Information." *Washington Post.* 2001. July 9. A2.

McAdam, Doug, et. Al., ed. 1996. *Comparative Perspectives on Social Movements.* Cambridge, UK: Cambridge University Press.

Meeting of the National Conference of Black Political Scientists, Atlanta, GA, March 9.

Meyer, John W., et. Al., 1997. "The Structuring of a World Environmental Regime, 1870 1990." *International organizations* 51:4 (Autumn) __.

Milloy, Courtland. 2001. "Colin Powell: Bush Man or Black Man?" *Washington Post.* July 29, C1.

Morris, Lorenzo, 2002. "Symptoms of Withdrawal." A paper presented at the annual

Obadele, Imari Abubakari. 1996. *The New International Law Regime and United States Foreign Policy.* Baton Rouge, LA: The Malcolm Generation.

Padmore, George. [1956] 1972. *Pan Africanism or Communism.* Garden City, NJ: Anchor.

Perlez, Jane. 2001. "How Powell Decided to Shun Conference." *New York Times.* September 5.

Randolph, A. Philip. 1966. "Testimony." In *The Federal Role in Urban Affairs.* U.S. Senate (Dec.).

Raspberry, William. 2001. "An Education on Reparations." *Washington Post.* September 10, A21.

Robinson, Mary. 2001. "Closing Statement." Report of the WCAR, Durban, South Africa, August 31-September 8 (A/CONF. 189/12).

Robinson, Randall. 2000. *The Debt: What America Owes to Blacks.* New York: Dutton.

Ronchon, Thomas R., 1998. *Culture Moves.* Princeton: Princeton University Press.

Singletory, Michelle. "The Color of Money." *Washington Post.* 2001. March 4. H1.

Slevin, Peter. 2001. "In Aetna's Past: Slave Owner Policies." *Washington Post.* March 9, A17.

Snow, David A. and Robert D. Benford. 1992. "Master Frames and Cycles of Protest." In *Frontiers in Social Movement Theory,* ed. Aldon D. Morris and Carol McClury Mueller. New Haven: Yale University Press. South Africa, August 31-September 8. (A/CONF.189/12)

Southern University Law Review. 1997. "Black African Reparations." (Fall) __.

Stampp, Kenneth M., 1966. *The Era of Reconstruction 1865-1877.* New York: Knopf.

Synder, Louis L., 1984. *Macro Nationalisms: A History of the Pan-Movements.* Westport, CN: Greenwood Press.

Tarrow, Sidney, 1992. "Mentalities, Political Cultures, and Collective Action Frames." In *Frontiers in Social Movement Theory,* ed. Aldon D. Morris and Carol McClury Mueller. New Haven: Yale University Press.

Tarrow, Sidney. 1998. *Power in Movement.* Cambridge, UK: Cambridge University Press.

Thompson, Dudley. n.d., "Facts on Reparations to Africa and Africans in the Diaspora." In *The Legal Basis of the Claim for Reparations* Lord Anthony Gifford. Kingston Jamaica: Gifford.

TransAfrica. 6

Van Deburg, William L., 1992. *New Day in Babylon*. Chicago: University of Chicago Press.

Walters, Ronald. 1995. *Pan Africanism*. Detroit: Wayne State University Press.

Walters, Ronald. 2000. "The African Growth and Opportunity Act." In *Foreign Policy*

Washington, James A., ed., 19__. *A Testament of Hope*. ___.

Wood, William B., 2001. "The UN World Conference Against Racism." *House International Relations Committee, Subcommittee on International Operations and Human Rights*, Washington, DC. July 31.

Zuma, Nkosazana Dalmini. 2001. "Closing Statement." Report of the WCAR, Durban, South Africa, August 31-September 8 (A/CONF.189/12).

PART TWO

Political Participation

The Study of American government will become more complete when there is a greater incorporation of the political lives and interests of African American and other minority groups in the United States. We begin this section with two 2000 census reports on the status of African American and Hispanic populations. Next David Bositis reports on the one national opinion poll that provides a comprehensive assessment of the opinion of African Americans on key public policy issues that are viewed as important by the African American community.

What is reflected in the poll is a desire to participate in the political process. Part of that is through interest groups. Hanes Walton and Robert Smith identify the major African American interest groups in American politics and explain the roles they play in representing the interest of the African American community. Minion K. C. Morrison uses the National Urban League to describe how interest groups can develop programs to increase the civic role of African American women as community leaders.

In Post 9/11 America there has been a greater discussion of violence as a means of political participation. But that discussion has been generally limited to terrorism being visited upon the United States from foreign sources. However, Sally Bermanzohn in "Violence, Nonviolence, and the Civil Rights Movement," offers the reader the opportunity to study the dynamics between violence and politics in the American south by focusing on the relationship between terror and the state.

Still the most common method of political participation is voting. But the 2000 presidential elections and the 2002 mid-term election raised many questions about the legitimacy and accuracy of the election system. Alex Willingham begins the critique of that election period by examining several of the key studies following the 2000 round of elections which sought to explain the voting irregularities in term of technological problems and how they could be resolved. Marcella Washington (Florida), Jarivs Hall (North Carolina), and Michael Adams (Texas) describe elections in three states in the aftermath of the 2000 presidential election.

Voting and elections are not the only issues. Robert Holmes notes that the present system of voting does not always provide the maximum opportunity for African American to represent themselves. He makes his case in the article, "Proportional Representation and Black Political Representation and Influence in America."

The Black Population: 2000

Census 2000 Brief

Jesse McKinnon

Census 2000 showed that the United States population on April 1, 2000 was 281.4 million. Of the total, 36.4 million, or 12.9 percent, reported[1] Black or African American. This number includes 34.7 million people, or 12.3 percent, who reported only Black in addition to 1.8 million people, or 0.6 percent, who reported Black as well as one or more other races. The term Black is used in the text of this report to refer to the Black or African American population, while Black or African American is used in the text tables and graphs. Census 2000 asked separate questions on race and Hispanic or Latino origin. Hispanics who reported their race as Black, either alone or in combination with one or more other races, are included in the numbers for Blacks.

This report, part of a series that analyzes population and housing data collected from Census 2000, provides a portrait of the Black population in the United States and discusses its distribution at both the national and subnational levels. It is based on the Census 2000 Redistricting Data (Public Law 94-171) Summary File, which was among the first Census 2000 data products to be released and is used by each state to draw boundaries for legislative districts.[2]

The term "Black or African American" refers to people having origins in any of the Black race groups of Africa. It includes people who reported "Black, African Am., or Negro" or wrote in entries such as African American, Afro American, Nigerian, or Haitian.

Data on race has been collected since the first U.S. decennial census in 1790. Blacks have been enumerated in every census.

The question on race was changed for Census 2000.

For Census 2000, the question on race was asked of every individual living in the United States and responses reflect self-identification. Respondents were asked to report the race or races they considered themselves and other members of their households to be.

Source: U.S. Census Bureau, Census 2000 Redistricting Data (Public Law 94-171) Summary File, Tables PL1, PL2, PL3, and PL4.

The question on race for Census 2000 was different from the one for the 1990 census in several ways. Most significantly, respondents were given the option of selecting one or more race categories to indicate their racial identities.[3]

Because of these changes, the Census 2000 data on race are not directly comparable with data from the 1990 census or earlier censuses. Caution must be used when interpreting changes in the racial composition of the United States population over time.

The Census 2000 question on race included 15 separate response categories and 3 areas where respondents could write in a more specific race (see Figure 1). The response categories and write-in answers were combined to create the five standard Office of Management and Budget race categories plus the Census Bureau category of "Some other race." The six race categories include:

- White;
- Black or African American;
- American Indian and Alaska Native:
- Asian;
- Native Hawaiian and Other Pacific Islander; and
- Some other race.

For a complete explanation of the race categories used in Census 2000, see the Census 2000 Brief, *Overview of Race and Hispanic Origin.*[4]

The data collected by Census 2000 on race can be divided into two broad categories: the race *alone* population and the race *in combination* population.

People who responded to the question on race by indicating only one race are referred to as the race *alone* population, or the group who reported *only one* race. For example, respondents who marked only the Black, African American, or Negro category on the census questionnaire would be included in the Black *alone* population.

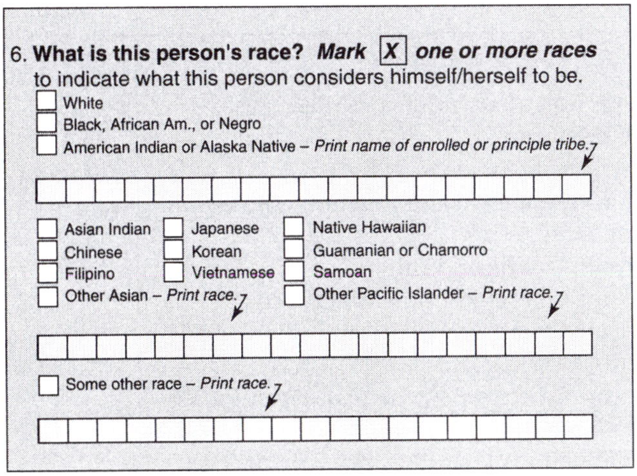
6. **What is this person's race?** ***Mark [X] one or more races*** to indicate what this person considers himself/herself to be.

- [ ] White
- [ ] Black, African Am., or Negro
- [ ] American Indian or Alaska Native – *Print name of enrolled or principle tribe.*
- [ ] Asian Indian
- [ ] Chinese
- [ ] Filipino
- [ ] Other Asian – *Print race.*
- [ ] Japanese
- [ ] Korean
- [ ] Vietnamese
- [ ] Native Hawaiian
- [ ] Guamanian or Chamorro
- [ ] Samoan
- [ ] Other Pacific Islander – *Print race.*
- [ ] Some other race – *Print race.*

Figure 1
Reproduction of the Question on Race From Census 2000

Soruce: U.S. Census Bureau, Census 2000 questionnaire.

Individuals who chose more than one of the six race categories are referred to as the race *in combination* population, or as the group who reported *more than one* race. For example, respondents who reported they were "Black or African American *and* White" or "Black or African American *and* Asian *and* American Indian and Alaska Native"[5] would be included in the Black *in combination* population.

The maximum number of people reporting Black is reflected in the Black *alone or in combination* category.

one way to define the Black population is to combine those respondents who reported only Black with those who reported Black as well as one or more other races. This creates the Black *alone or in combination* population.

Another way to think of the Black *alone or in combination* population is the total number of people who identified entirely or partially as Black. This group is also described as people who reported Black, whether or not they reported any other races.

The Black Population: a Snapshot.

Table 1 shows the number and percentage of respondents to Census 2000 who reported Black alone as well as those who reported Black and at least one other race.

In the total population, 34.7 million people, or 12.3 percent, reported only Black. An additional 1.8 million people reported Black and at least one other race. Within this group, the most common combinations were "Black *and* White" (45 percent), followed by "Black *and* Some other race" (24 percent), "Black *and*

Table 1
Black or African American Population: 2000
(For information on confidentiality protection, nonsampling error, and definitions, see *www.census.gov/prod/cen2000/doc/pl94-171.pdf*)

Race	Number	Percent of total population
Total population	281,421,906	100.0
Black or African American alone or in combination with one or more other races	36,419,434	12.9
Black or African American alone	34,658,190	12.3
Black or African American in combination with one or more other races	1,761,244	0.6
Black or African American; White	784,764	0.3
Black or African American; Some other race	417,249	0.1
Black or African American; American Indian and Alaska Native	182,494	0.1
Black or African American; White; American Indian and Alaska Native	112,207	-
All other combinations including Black or African American	264,530	0.1
Not Black or African American alone or in combination with one or more other races	245,002,472	87.1

- Percentage rounds to 0.0
Source: U.S. Census Bureau, Census 2000 Redistricting Data (Public Law 94-171) Summary File, Table PL1.

American Indian and Alaska Native" (10 percent), and "Black *and* White *and* American Indian and Alaska Native" (6 percent). These four combination categories accounted for 85 percent of all Blacks who reported two or more races. Thus, 36.4 million, or 12.9 percent of the total population, reported Black alone or in combination with one or more other races.

The Black Population increased faster than the total population between 1990 and 2000.

Because of the changes made to the question on race for Census 2000, there are at least two ways to present the change in the total number of Blacks in the United States. The difference in the Black population between 1990 and 2000 using the race alone concept for 2000 and the difference in the Black population between 1990 and 2000 using the race alone or in combination concept for 2000 provides a "minimum-maximum" range for the change in the Black population between 1990 and 2000.

The 1990 census showed there were 30.0 million Blacks. Using the Black alone population in 2000 shows an increase of 4.7 million, or 15.6 percent, in the total Black population between 1990 and 2000. If the Black alone or in combination population is used, an increase of 6.4 million, or 21.5 percent, results. Thus, from 1990 to 2000, the minimum-maximum range for the increase in the Black population was 15.6 percent to 21.5 percent. In comparison, the total population grew by 13.2 percent, from 248.7 million in 1990 to 281.4 million in 2000.

The Geographic Distribution of the Black Population

The following discussion of the geographic distribution of the Black population focuses on the Black alone or in combination population. As the upper bound of the Black population, this group includes all respondents who reported Black, whether or not they reported any other race.[6] Hereafter in the text of this section, the term "Black" will be used to refer to those who reported Black, whether or not they reported any other race. However, in the tables and graphs, data for both the Black alone and the Black alone or in combination populations are shown.

The majority of the Black population lived in the South.

According to Census 2000, of all respondents who reported Black, 54 percent lived in the South (see Figure 2), 19 percent lived in

	Northeast	Midwest	South	West
Black or African American alone	17.6	18.8	54.8	8.9
Black or African American alone or in combination	18.0	18.8	53.6	9.6

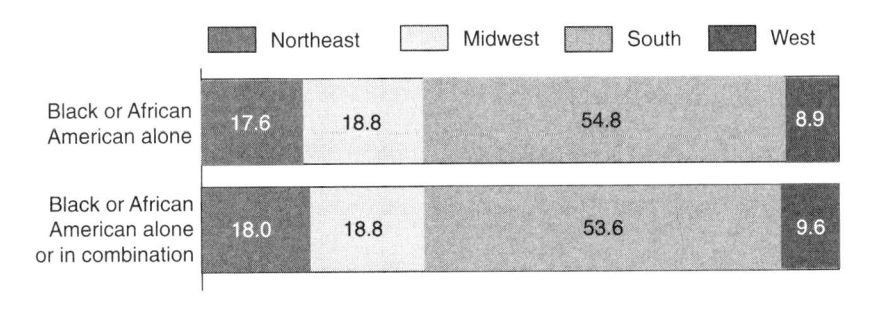

Figure 2
Percent Distribution of the Black or African American Population by Region: 2000
(For information on confidentiality protection, nonsampling error, and definitions, see www.census.gov/prod/cen2000/doc/pl94-171.pdf)

Source: U.S. Census Bureau, Census 2000 Redistricting Data (Public Law 94-171) Summary File, Table PL1.

Table 2
Black or African American Population for the United States, Regions, and States, and for Puerto Rico: 1990 and 2000
(For information on confidentiality protection, nonsampling error, and definitions, see www.census.gov/prod/cen2000/doc/pl94-171.pdf)

	1990			
Area	Total population	Black or African American population — Number	Percent of total population	Total population
United States	248,709,873	29,980,996	12.1	281,421,906
Region				
Northeast	50,809,229	5,613,222	11.0	53,594,378
Midwest	59,668,632	5,715,940	9.6	64,392,776
South	85,445,930	15,828,888	18.5	100,236,820
West	52,786,082	2,828,010	5.4	63,197,932
State				
Alabama	4,040,587	1,020,705	25.3	4,447,100
Alaska	550,043	22,451	4.1	626,932
Arizona	3,665,228	110,524	3.0	5,130,632
Arkansas	2,350,725	373,912	15.9	2,673,400
California	29,760,021	2,208,801	7.4	33,871,648
Colorado	3,294,394	133,146	4.0	4,301,261
Connecticut	3,287,116	274,269	8.3	3,405,565
Delaware	666,168	112,460	16.9	783,600
District of Columbia	606,900	399,604	65.8	572,059
Florida	12,937,926	1,759,534	13.6	15,982,378
Georgia	6,478,216	1,746,565	27.0	8,186,453
Hawaii	1,108,229	27,195	2.5	1,211,537
Idaho	1,006,749	3,370	0.3	1,293,953
Illinois	11,430,602	1,694,273	14.8	12,419,293
Indiana	5,544,159	432,092	7.8	6,080,485
Iowa	2,776,755	48,090	1.7	2,926,324
Kansas	2,477,574	143,076	5.8	2,688,418
Kentucky	3,685,296	262,907	7.1	4,041,769
Louisiana	4,219,973	1,299,281	30.8	4,468,976
Maine	1,227,928	5,138	0.4	1,274,923
Maryland	4,781,468	1,189,899	24.9	5,296,486

	2000				
	Black or African American alone population		Black or African American alone or in combination population		Black or African American in combination population only as a percent of Black or African American alone or in combination population
	Number	Percent of total population	Number	Percent of total population	
	34,658,190	**12.3**	**36,419,434**	**12.9**	**4.8**
	6,099,881	11.4	6,556,909	12.2	7.0
	6,499,733	10.1	6,838,669	10.6	5.0
	18,981,692	18.9	19,528,231	19.5	2.8
	3,076,884	4.9	3,495,625	5.5	12.0
	1,155,930	26.0	1,168,998	26.3	1.1
	21,787	3.5	27,147	4.3	19.7
	158,873	3.1	185,599	3.6	14.4
	418,950	15.7	427,152	16.0	1.9
	2,263,882	6.7	2,513,041	7.4	9.9
	165,063	3.8	190,717	4.4	13.5
	309,843	9.1	339,078	10.0	8.6
	150,666	19.2	157,152	20.1	4.1
	343,312	60.0	350,455	61.3	2.0
	2,335,505	14.6	2,471,730	15.5	5.5
	2,349,542	28.7	2,393,425	29.2	1.8
	22,003	1.8	33,343	2.8	34.0
	5,456	0.4	8,127	0.6	32.9
	1,876,875	15.1	1,937,671	15.6	3.1
	510,034	8.4	538,015	8.8	5.2
	61,853	2.1	72,512	2.5	14.7
	154,198	5.7	170,610	6.3	9.6
	295,994	7.3	311.878	7.7	5.1
	1,451,944	32.5	1,468,317	32.9	1.1
	6,760	0.5	9,553	0.7	29.2
	1,477,411	27.9	1,525,036	28.8	3.1

(continued)

Table 2
continued

	1990			
		Black or African American population		
Area	Total population	Number	Percent of total population	Total population
State				
Massachusetts	6,016,425	300,130	5.0	6,349,097
Michigan	9,295,297	1,291,706	13.9	9,938,444
Minnesota	4,375,099	94,944	2.2	4,919,479
Mississippi	2,573,216	915,057	35.6	2,844,658
Missouri	5,117,073	548,208	10.7	5,595,211
Montana	799,065	2,381	0.3	902,195
Nebraska	1,578,385	57,404	3.6	1,711,263
Nevada	1,201,833	78,771	6.6	1,998,257
New Hampshire	1,109,252	7,198	0.6	1,235,786
New Jersey	7,730,188	1,036,825	13.4	8,414,350
New Mexico	1,515,069	30.210	2.0	1,819,046
New York	17,990,455	2,859,055	15.9	18,976,457
North Carolina	6,628,637	1,456,323	22.0	8,049,313
North Dakota	638,800	3,524	0.6	642,200
Ohio	10,847,115	1,154,826	10.6	11,353,140
Oklahoma	3,145,585	233,801	7.4	3,450,654
Oregon	2,842,321	46,178	1.6	3,421,399
Pennsylvania	11,881,643	1,089,795	9.2	12,281,054
Rhode Island	1,003,464	38,861	3.9	1,048,319
South Carolina	3,486,703	1,039,884	29.8	4,012,012
South Dakota	696,004	3,258	0.5	754,844
Tennessee	4,877,185	778,035	16.0	5,689,283
Texas	16,986,510	2,021,632	11.9	20,851,820
Utah	1,722,850	11,576	0.7	2,233,169
Vermont	562,758	1,951	0.3	608,827
Virginia	6,187,358	1,162,994	18.8	7,078,515
Washington	4,866,692	149,801	3.1	5,894,121
West Virginia	1,793,477	56,295	3.1	1,808,344
Wisconsin	4,891,769	244,539	5.0	5,363,675
Wyoming	453,588	3,606	0.8	493,782
Puerto Rico	**3,522,037**	(X)	(X)	**3,808,610**

X Not applicable.
Source: U.S. Census Bureau, Census 2000 Redistricting Data (Public Law 94-171) Summary File, Table PL1; 1990 Census of Population, General Population Characteristics (1990 CP-1).

	2000				
	Black or African American alone population		Black or African American alone or in combination population		Black or African American in combination population only as a percent of Black or African American alone or in combination population
	Number	Percent of total population	Number	Percent of total population	
	343,454	5.4	398,479	6.3	13.8
	1,412,742	14.2	1,474,613	14.8	4.2
	141,731	3.5	202,972	4.1	15.4
	1,033,809	36.3	1,041,708	36.6	0.8
	629,391	11.2	655,377	11.7	4.0
	2,692	0.3	4,441	0.5	39.4
	68,541	4.0	75,833	4.4	9.6
	135,477	6.8	150,508	7.5	10.0
	9,035	0.7	12,218	1.0	26.1
	1,141,821	13.6	1,211,750	14.4	5.8
	34,343	1.9	42,412	2.3	19.0
	3,014,385	15.9	3,234,165	17.0	6.8
	1,737,545	21.6	1,776,283	22.1	2.2
	3,916	0.6	5,372	0.8	27.1
	1,301,307	11.5	1,372,501	12.1	5.2
	260,968	7.6	284,766	8.3	8.4
	55,662	1.6	72,647	2.1	23.4
	1,224,612	10.0	1,289,123	10.5	5.0
	46,908	4.5	58,051	5.5	19.2
	1,185,216	29.5	1,200,901	29.9	1.3
	4,685	0.6	6,687	0.9	29.9
	932,809	16.4	953,349	16.8	2.2
	2,404,566	11.5	2,493,057	12.0	3.5
	17,657	0.8	24,382	1.1	27.6
	3,063	0.5	4,492	0.7	31.8
	1,390,293	19.6	1,441,207	20.4	3.5
	190,267	3.2	238,398	4.0	20.2
	57,232	3.2	62,817	3.5	8.9
	304,460	5.7	326,506	6.1	6.8
	3,722	0.8	4,863	1.0	23.5
	302,933	**8.0**	**416,296**	**10.9**	**27.2**

the Midwest, 18 percent lived in the Northeast, and 10 percent lived in the West.[7]

The South had the largest Black population, as well as the highest proportion of Blacks in its total population: 20 percent of all respondents in the South reported Black compared with 12 percent in the Northeast, 11 percent in the Midwest, and 6 percent in the West.

About three-fifths of all people who reported Black lived in ten states.

The ten states with the largest Black populations in 2000 were New York, California, Texas, Florida, Georgia, Illinois, North Carolina, Maryland, Michigan, and Louisiana (see Table 2). Combined, these states represented 58 percent of the total Black population, but only 49 percent of the total population. Five of these ten states had Black populations greater than 2 million: New York (3.2 million); California, Texas, and Florida (about 2.5 million each); and Georgia (2.4 million).

In the South, ten states (Texas, Florida, Georgia, North Carolina, Maryland, Louisiana, Virginia, South Carolina, Alabama, and Mississippi) had Black populations over one million and, when combined, they represented 47 percent of the Black population in the country.

In six states, Blacks represented over 25 percent of the total population, and all of them were located in the South—Mississippi (37 percent); Louisiana (33 percent); South Carolina (30 percent); Georgia and Maryland (29 percent) each; and Alabama (26 percent). The District of Columbia, a state equivalent, had the highest proportion of Blacks with 61 percent.

In 13 states, Blacks represented less than 3 percent of the total population. Seven of those states were located in the West—Hawaii, New Mexico, Oregon, Utah, Wyoming, Idaho, and Montana; three in the Midwest—Iowa, South Dakota, and North Dakota; and three in the Northeast—New Hampshire, Maine and Vermont.

The Black population was concentrated in counties in the South.

The Black population is still highly concentrated—64 percent of all counties (3,141 counties) in the United States had fewer than 6 percent Black, but in 96 counties, Blacks comprised 50 percent or more of the total county population (see Figure 3). Ninety-five of those counties were located in the South and were distributed across the Coastal and Lowland South in a loose arc. With the notable exceptions of Baltimore city (a county equivalent) and Prince George's County, in Maryland, generally these counties were nonmetropolitan. St. Louis City, Missouri in the Midwest was the only county equivalent outside the South where Blacks exceeded 50 percent of the total population.

Concentrations of Blacks in the Midwest and West tended to be either in counties located within metropolitan areas or in counties containing universities or military bases or both. Metropolitan concentrations tended to be in central counties containing older central cities.

Although Blacks were not as concentrated in Midwestern counties, in some metropolitan counties, such as around Chicago, Illinois; Gary, Indiana; and Detroit, Michigan, Blacks comprised a sizeable proportion of the population. In the Northeast, Blacks were concentrated in a band of counties extending from Philadelphia, Pennsylvania to Providence, Rhode Island and along the Hudson Valley northward from New York. Western counties with large concentrations of Blacks were located in Southern California, the San Francisco and Sacramento areas, around Denver and Colorado Springs, and in the Seattle and Tacoma area in Washington. Clark County, Nevada (Las Vegas area) also stood out distinctly from surrounding counties in Nevada, Utah, and Arizona.

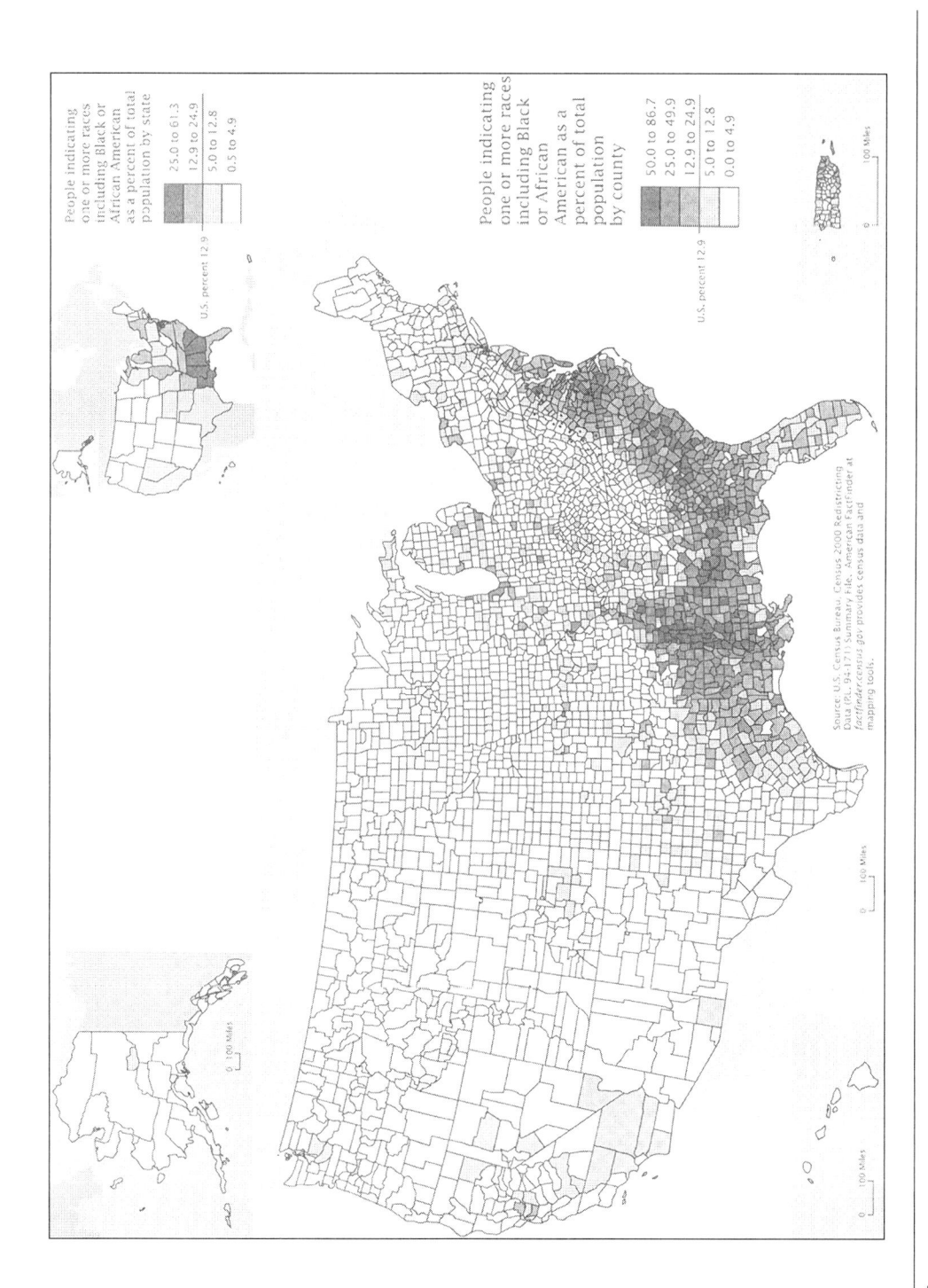

Figure 3.
Percent Black or African American Alone or in Combination: 2000
(For information on confidentiality protection, nonsampling error, and definitions, see *www.census.gov/prod/cen2000/doc/pl94-171.pdf*)

The places with the largest Black populations were New York and Chicago.

Census 2000 showed that, of all places[8] in the United States with populations of 100,000 or more, New York had the largest Black population with 2.3 million, followed by Chicago (1.1 million) as shown in Table 3. Three other places—Detroit, Philadelphia, and Houston—had Black populations between 500,000 and 1 million. Five of the ten places with the largest Black population—Baltimore, Houston, Memphis, Washington, DC, and New Orleans—were in the South.

Of the ten largest places in the United States, Detroit had the largest proportion of Blacks, 83 percent, followed by Philadelphia (44 percent), and Chicago (38 percent). Blacks represented less than 10 percent of the popula-

Table 3
Ten Largest Places in Total Population and in Black or African American Population: 2000
(For information on confidentiality protection, nonsampling error, and definitions, see www.census.gov/prod/cen2000/doc/pl94-171.pdf)

Place	Total population Rank	Total population Number	Black or African American alone Rank	Black or African American alone Number	Black or African American alone or in combination Rank	Black or African American alone or in combination Number	Percent of total population Black or African American alone	Percent of total population Black or African American alone or in combination
New York, NY	1	8,008,278	1	2,129,762	1	2,274,049	26.6	28.4
Los Angeles, CA	2	3,694,820	7	415,195	6	444,635	11.2	12.0
Chicago, IL	3	2,896,016	2	1,065,009	2	1,084,221	36.8	37.4
Houston, TX	4	1,953,631	5	494,496	5	505,101	25.3	25.9
Philadelphia, PA	5	1,517,550	4	655,824	4	672,162	43.2	44.3
Phoenix, AZ	6	1,321,045	60	67,416	53	76,065	5.1	5.8
San Diego, CA	7	1,223,400	36	96,216	32	109,470	7.9	8.9
Dallas, TX	8	1,188,580	11	307,957	11	314,678	25.9	26.5
San Antonio, TX	9	1,144,646	48	78,120	45	84,250	6.8	7.4
Detroit, MI	10	951,270	3	775,772	3	787,687	81.6	82.8
Baltimore, MD	17	651,154	6	418,951	7	424,449	64.3	65.2
Memphis, TN	18	650,100	8	399,208	8	402,367	61.4	61.9
Washington, DC	21	572,059	9	343,312	9	350,455	60.0	61.3
New Orleans, LA	31	484,674	10	325,947	10	329,171	67.3	67.9

Source: U.S. Census Bureau, Census 2000 Redistricting Data (Public Law 94-171) Summary File, Table PL1.

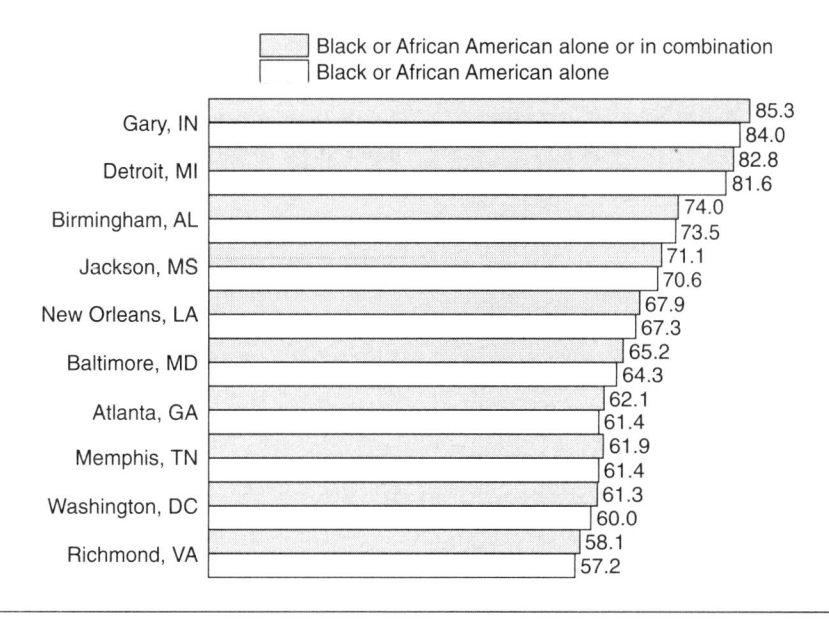

Figure 4
Ten Places of 100,000 or More Population with the Highest Percentage of Blacks or African Americans: 2000
(For information on confidentiality protection, nonsampling error, and definitions, see www.census.gov/prod/cen2000/doc/pl94-171.pdf)

Source: U.S. Census Bureau, Census 2000 Redistricting Data (Public Law 94-171) Summary File, Table PL1.

Place	Black or African American alone or in combination	Black or African American alone
Gary, IN	85.3	84.0
Detroit, MI	82.8	81.6
Birmingham, AL	74.0	73.5
Jackson, MS	71.1	70.6
New Orleans, LA	67.9	67.3
Baltimore, MD	65.2	64.3
Atlanta, GA	62.1	61.4
Memphis, TN	61.9	61.4
Washington, DC	61.3	60.0
Richmond, VA	58.1	57.2

tion in Phoenix (6 percent), San Antonio (7 percent), and San Diego (9 percent).

Two places—New York and Chicago—together accounted for 9 percent of the total Black population. The ten largest places for Blacks accounted for 20 percent of the total Black population.

Among places of 100,000 or more population, the highest proportion of Blacks was in Gary, Indiana, with 85 percent, followed by Detroit, Michigan with 83 percent (see Figure 4). The next eight places with the highest proportion of Blacks had populations over 58 percent Black. Of these 10 places, eight were in the South, and two were in the Midwest.

Additional Findings on the Black Population

What proportion of respondents reporting Black also reported a Hispanic origin?

The Office of Management and Budget defines Hispanic or Latino as "a person of Cuban, Mexican, Puerto Rican, South or Central American, or other Spanish culture or origin, regardless of race." In data collection and presentation, federal agencies use two ethnicities: "Hispanic or Latino" and "Not Hispanic or Latino." Race and ethnicity are considered two separate and distinct concepts by the federal system. Hispanics may be of any race, and Blacks can be Hispanic or not Hispanic.

According to Census 2000, the overwhelming majority of the Black population was non-Hispanic: 98 percent of those who reported only Black and 97 percent of those who reported Black and at least one other race (see Table 4). However, only 82 percent of all respondents who reported Black in combination with one or more other races were non-Hispanic.

The Black non-Hispanic population represented 12.4 percent of people who reported exactly one race and about 12.6 percent of the total population. Of the 6.8 million people who reported two or more races, 21 percent were non-Hispanics who included Black as one of the races reported.

Which other races were Black non-Hispanics most likely to report?

Among Black non-Hispanics who reported more than one race, most indicated they were "Black or African American *and* White" (49 percent), followed by "Black or African American *and* Some other race" (18 percent), "Black or African American *and* American Indian and Alaska Native" (12 percent), and "Black or African American *and* Asian" (7 percent) as shown in Table 5. These four combination categories accounted for about 85 percent of all Black non-Hispanics who reported two or more races.

Which other races were Black Hispanics most likely to report?

Among Black Hispanics who reported more than one race, one-half indicated they were "Black or African American *and* Some other race," followed by "Black or African American *and* White" (27 percent), "Black or African American *and* White *and* American Indian and Alaska Native" (6 percent), and "Black or African American *and* White *and* Some other race" (5 percent)) as shown in Table 5.

Which group was more likely to report more than one race, Black non-Hispanics or Black Hispanics?

Black Hispanics were more likely than Black non-Hispanics to report two or more races. According to Census 2000, 1.0 million people reported Black and Hispanic. Of those, 31 percent reported Black with one or more other races (see Table 6). In contrast, of the 35.4 million Blacks who reported as not Hispanic, only 4.1 percent reported at least one other race.

Were there differences in the age distribution between people who reported only Black or African American and people who reported Black or African American and one or more other races?

People who reported Black as well as one or more other races were more likely to be under 18 than those reporting only Black (see Figure 5). Of the 1.8 million people who reported Black with at least one other race, 54 percent were under 18. This proportion is higher than the Black alone population. Of the 34.7 million people who reported only Black, 31 percent were under 18.

When the Black population is cross-tabulated by Hispanic origin, this pattern persists. For both Black non-Hispanics and Black Hispanics, a higher proportion of those reporting more than one race was under 18 when compared with those reporting Black alone. Among the 1.4 million Black non-Hispanics who reported more than one race, 55 percent were under 18. Of the 33.9 million people who reported Black alone and not Hispanic, 31 percent were under 18. Similarly, among the 325,000 Black Hispanics who reported two or more races, 51 percent were under 18. Of the 710,000 Black Hispanics who reported one race, 39 percent were under 18.

Table 4
Black or African American Population by Hispanic or Latino Origin: 2000
(For information on confidentiality protection, nonsampling error, and definitions, see www.censusgov/prod/cen2000/doc/pl94-171.pdf)

Race and Hispanic or Latino origin	Alone Number	Alone Percent of total	Alone Percent of Black or African American population	In combination with one or more other races Number	In combination Percent of total	In combination Percent of Black or African American population	Alone or in combination with one or more other races Number	Alone or in combination Percent of total	Alone or in combination Percent of Black or African American population
Total population	274,595,678	100.0	(X)	6,826,228	100.0	(X)	281,421,906	100.0	(X)
Black or African American	34,658,190	12.6	100.0	1,761,244	25.8	100.0	36,419,434	12.9	100.0
Hispanic or Latino	710,353	0.3	2.0	325,330	4.8	18.5	1,035,683	0.4	2.8
Not Hispanic or Latino	33,947,837	12.4	98.0	1,435,914	21.0	81.5	35,383,751	12.6	97.2

X Not applicable.
Source: U.S. Census Bureau, Census 2000 Redistricting Data (Public Law 94-171) Summary File, Tables PL1 and PL2.

Table 5
Most Frequent Combinations of Black or African American With One or More Other Races by Hispanic or Latino Origin: 2000
(For information on confidentiality protection, nonsampling error, and definitions, see www.census.gov/prod/cen2000/doc/pl94-171.pdf)

Black or African American in combination	Total Number	Total Percent	Hispanic or Latino Number	Hispanic or Latino Percent	Not Hispanic or Latino Number	Not Hispanic or Latino Percent
Total number reporting Black or African American and one or more other races	1,761,244	100.0	325,330	100.0	1,435,914	100.0
Black or African American; White	784,764	44.6	87,687	27.0	697,077	48.5
Black or African American; Some other race	417,249	23.7	161,283	49.6	255,966	17.8
Black or African American; American Indian and Alaska Native	182,494	10.4	14,472	4.4	168,022	11.7
Black or African American; White; American Indian and Alaska Native	112,207	6.4	18,046	5.5	94,161	6.6
Black or African American; Asian	106,782	6.1	7,269	2.2	99,513	6.9
Black or African American; White; Some other race.	43,172	2.5	15,481	4.8	27,691	1.9
All other combinations including Black or African American	114,576	6.5	21,092	6.5	93,484	6.5

Source: U.S. Census Bureau, Census 2000 Redistricting Data (Public Law 94-171) Summary File, Tables PL1 and PL2.

About Census 2000

Why did Census 2000 ask the question on race?

The Census Bureau collects data on race to fulfill a variety of legislative and program requirements. Data on race are used in the legislative redistricting process carried out by the States and in monitoring local jurisdictions' compliance with the Voting Rights Act. These data are also essential for evaluating Federal programs that promote equal access to

Table 6
People Who Reported Black or African American by Age and Hispanic or Latino Origin: 2000
(For information on confidentiality protection, nonsampling error, and definitions, see www.census.gov/prod/cen2000/doc/pl940-171.pdf)

Age and Hispanic or Latino origin	Black or African American alone or in combination with one or more races — Number	Percent	Black or African American alone — Number	Percent	Black or African American in combination with one or more races — Number	Percent
Total	36,419,434	100.0	34,658,190	95.2	1,761,244	4.8
Hispanic or Latino	1,035,683	100.0	710,353	68.6	325,330	31.4
Not Hispanic or Latino	35,383,751	100.0	33,947,837	95.9	1,435,914	4.1
Under 18	11,845,257	100.0	10,885,696	91.9	959,561	8.1
Hispanic or Latino	442,970	100.0	275,432	62.2	167,538	37.8
Not Hispanic or Latino	11,402,287	100.0	10,610,264	93.1	792,023	6.9
18 and over	24,574,177	100.0	23,772,494	96.7	801.683	3.3
Hispanic or Latino	592,713	100.0	434,921	73.4	157,792	26.6
Not Hispanic or Latino	23,981,464	100.0	23,337,573	97.3	643,891	2.7

Source: U.S. Census Bureau, Census 2000 Redistricting Data (Public Law 94-171) Summary File, Tables PL1, PL2, PL3, and PL4.

employment, education, and housing and for assessing racial disparities in health and exposure to environmental risks. More broadly, data on race are critical for research that underlies many policy decisions at all levels of government.

How do data from the question on race benefit me, my family, and my community?

All levels of government need information on race to implement and evaluate programs, or enforce laws. Examples include: the Native American Programs Act, the Equal Employment Opportunity Act, the Civil Rights Act, the Voting Rights Act, the Public Health Act, the Healthcare Improvement Act, the Job Partnership Training Act, the Equal Credit Opportunity Act, the Fair Housing Act, and the Census Redistricting Data Program.

Both public and private organizations use race information to find areas where groups may need special services and to plan and implement education, housing, health, and other programs that address these needs. For example, a school system might use this information to design cultural activities that reflect the diversity in their community. Or a business could use it to select the mix of merchandise it will sell in a new store. Census information also helps identify areas where residents might need services of particular

152 PART TWO *Political Participation*

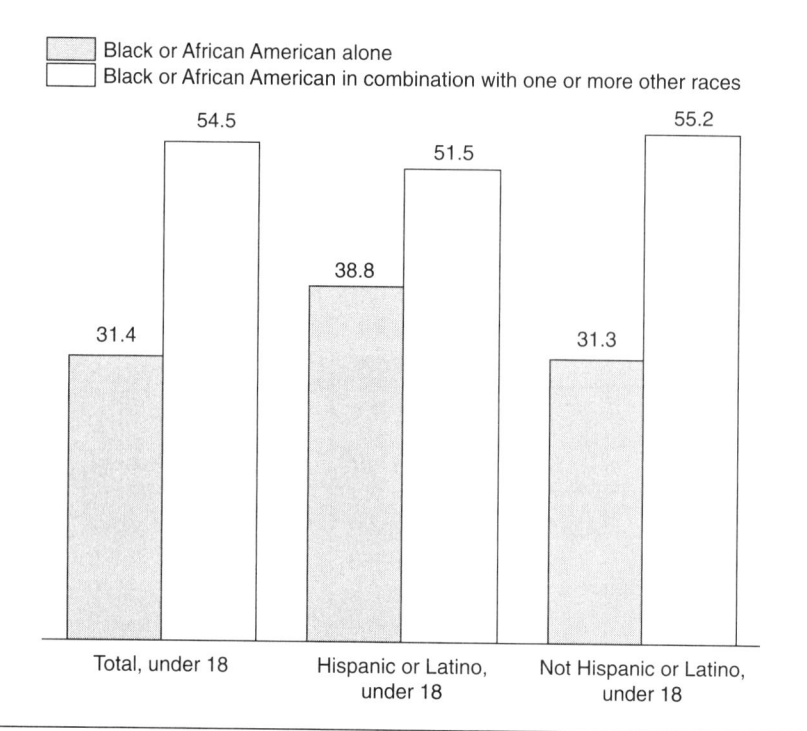

Figure 5

Percent Under Age 18 of People Who Reported Black or African American by Hispanic or Latino Origin: 2000
(For information on confidentiality protection, nonsampling error, and definitions, see *www.census.gov/prod/cen2000/doc/pl94-171.pdf*)

Source: U.S. Census Bureau, Census 2000 Redistricting Data (Public Law 94-171) Summary File, Tables PL3 and PL4.

importance to certain racial or ethnic groups, such as screening for hypertension or diabetes.

Notes

1. In this report, the term "reported" is used to refer to the answers provided by respondents, as well as responses assigned during the editing and imputation processes.

2. This report discusses data for 50 states and the District of Columbia, but not Puerto Rico. The Census 2000 Redistricting Data (Public Law 94-171) Summary File was released on a state-by-state basis in March 2001.

3. Other changes included terminology and formatting changes, such as spelling out "American" instead of "Amer." For the American Indian and Alaska Native category and adding "Native" to the Hawaiian response category. In the layout of the Census 2000 questionnaire, the seven Asian response categories were alphabetized and grouped together, as were the four Pacific Islander categories after the Native Hawaiian category. The

three separate American Indian and Alaska Native identifiers in the 1990 census (i.e., Indian (Amer.), Eskimo, and Aleut) were combined into a single identifier in Census 2000. Also, American Indians and Alaska Natives could report more than one tribe.

4. *Overview of Race and Hispanic Origin: 2000*, U.S. Census Bureau, Census 2000 Brief, C2KBR/01-1, March 2001, is available on the U.S. Census Bureau's Internet site at *www.census.gov/population/www/cen2000/briefs.html*.

5. The race in combination categories are denoted by quotations around the combinations with the conjunction *and* in bold and italicized print to indicate the separate races that comprise the combination.

6. As a matter of policy, the Census Bureau does not advocate the use of the *alone or in combination* population over the *alone* population. The use of the *alone or in combination* population in this section does not imply that it is a preferred method of presenting or analyzing data. It is only one of many ways that the data on race from Census 2000 can be presented and discussed.

7. The South region includes the states of Alabama, Arkansas, Delaware, Florida, Georgia, Kentucky, Louisiana, Maryland, Mississippi, North Carolina, Oklahoma, South Carolina, Tennessee, Texas, Virginia, and West Virginia, and the District of Columbia. The Midwest region includes the states of Illinois, Indiana, Iowa, Kansas, Michigan, Minnesota, Missouri, Nebraska, North Dakota, Ohio, South Dakota, and Wisconsin. The Northeast region includes the states of Connecticut, Maine, Massachusetts, New Hampshire, New Jersey, New York, Pennsylvania, Rhode Island, and Vermont. The West region includes the states of Alaska, Arizona, California, Colorado, Hawaii, Idaho, Montana, Nevada, New Mexico, Oregon, Utah, Washington, and Wyoming.

8. Census 2000 showed 245 places in the United States with 100,000 or more population. They included 238 incorporated places (including four city-county consolidations) and seven census designated places that were not legally incorporated. For a list of these places by state, see *www.census.gov/population/www/cen2000/phc-+6.html*.

The Hispanic Population in the United States

Current Population Reports

Melissa Therrien and Roberto R. Ramirez

This report describes the Hispanic population in the United States in 2000, providing a profile of demographic and socioeconomic characteristics, such as geographic distribution, age, educational attainment, earnings, and poverty status. These characteristics are compared with those of the non-Hispanic White population, and because Hispanics are a heterogeneous group, variability within the Hispanic population is also discussed.[1] The findings are based on data collected by the Census Bureau in the March 2000 Current Population Survey (CPS).[2]

Hispanics reported that their origin was Mexican, Puerto Rican, Cuban, Central or South American, or some other Latino origin on the CPS questionnaire.[3] Hispanics may be of any race.

Population Size and Composition

Approximately one in eight people in the United States is of Hispanic origin.

In 2000, 32.8 million Latinos resided in the United States, representing 12.0 percent of the total U.S. population.[4] As shown in Figure 1, among the Hispanic population, 66.1 percent were of Mexican origin, 14.5 percent were Central and South American, 9.0 percent were Puerto Rican, 4.0 percent were Cuban, and the remaining 6.4 percent were of other Hispanic origins.

Hispanics are more geographically concentrated than non-Hispanic Whites.

Hispanics were more likely than non-Hispanic Whites to reside in the West and less

U.S. Department of Commerce, U.S. Census Bureau.

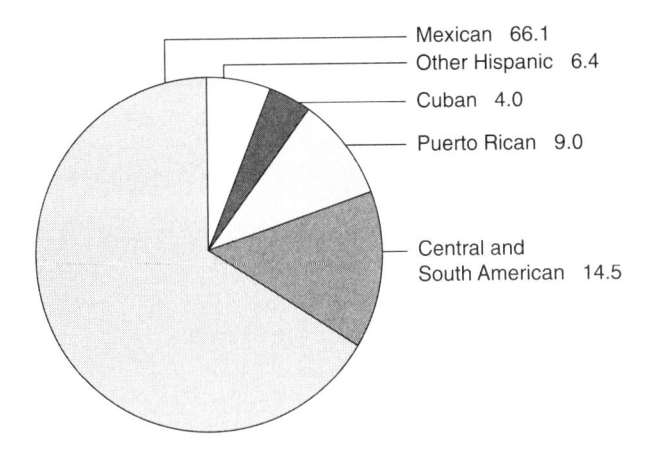

Figure 1
Hispanics by Origin: 2000 (in percent)

- Mexican 66.1
- Other Hispanic 6.4
- Cuban 4.0
- Puerto Rican 9.0
- Central and South American 14.5

Source: U.S. Census Bureau, Current Population Survey, March 2000.

likely to live in the Northeast and the Midwest.[5] Figure 2 shows that the regional distribution of the Hispanic population in 2000 ranged from 44.7 percent in the West to 7.9 percent in the Midwest, while the distribution of non-Hispanic Whites ranged from 32.8 percent in the South to 19.8 percent in the West.

Latinos of Mexican origin were more likely to live in the West (56.8 percent) and South (32.6 percent), Puerto Ricans were most likely to live in the Northeast (63.9 percent), and Cubans were highly concentrated in the South (80.1 percent). Central and South Americans were concentrated in three of the four regions: the Northeast (32.3 percent), the South (34.6 percent), and the West (28.2 percent).

Hispanics are more likely than non-Hispanic Whites to live inside central cities of metropolitan areas.

Nearly half of all Hispanics lived in a central city within a metropolitan area (46.4 percent) compared with slightly more than one-fifth of non-Hispanic Whites (21.2 percent). In 2000, 45.1 percent of Hispanics lived outside central cities but within a metropolitan area compared with 56.2 percent of non-Hispanic Whites. The percentage of Hispanics living in nonmetropolitan areas (8.5 percent) was much smaller than the percentage of non-Hispanic Whites (22.5 percent). Among Latino groups, Puerto Ricans and other Hispanics were most likely to live in a central city within a metropolitan area (61.2 percent and 56.5 percent, respectively) while Cubans were most likely to live outside the central city within a metropolitan area (76.0 percent).[6]

Hispanics are more likely than non-Hispanic Whites to be less than 18 years old.

In 2000, 35.7 percent of Hispanics were less than 18 years of age, compared with 23.5 percent of non-Hispanic Whites. Relatively few Latinos were age 65 and older (5.3 percent) compared with non-Hispanic Whites (14.0 percent). In addition, a smaller proportion of Hispanics were 18 to 64 (59.0 percent) than of non-Hispanic Whites (62.4 percent, see Figure 3). Whereas 32.4 percent of the

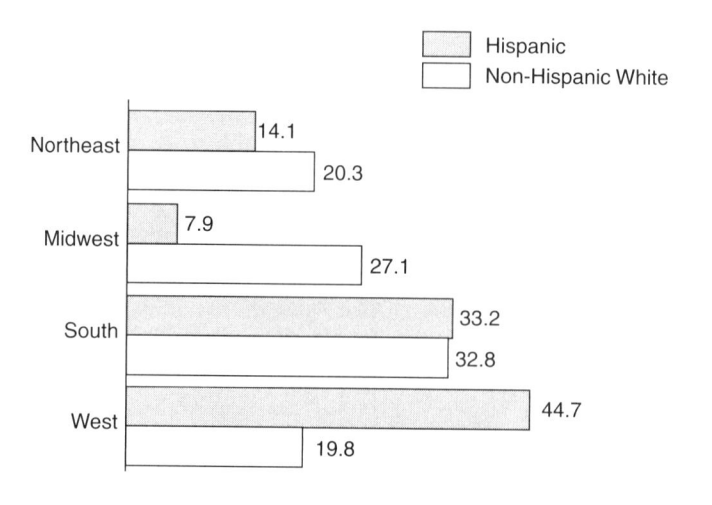

Figure 2
Population by Hispanic Origin and Region of Residence: 2000 (as a percent of each population)

Source: U.S. Census Bureau, Current Population Survey, March 2000.

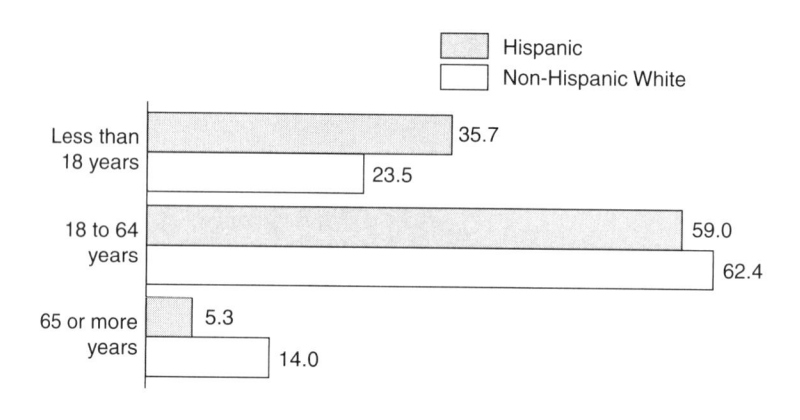

Figure 3
Population by Hispanic Origin and Age Group: 2000 (as a percent of each population)

Source: U.S. Census Bureau, Current Population Survey, March 2000.

Hispanic population were ages 25 to 44, 29.5 percent of the non-Hispanic White population was within this age group. Among Hispanics, 14.5 percent were 45 to 64, while 24.0 percent of non-Hispanic Whites were of these ages (see Figure 4).

Among Latinos, the Mexican origin population had the highest proportion less than 18 (38.4 percent) compared with the Cuban origin population, who had the lowest proportion (19.2 percent). The proportion of elderly (those 65 and older) ranged from

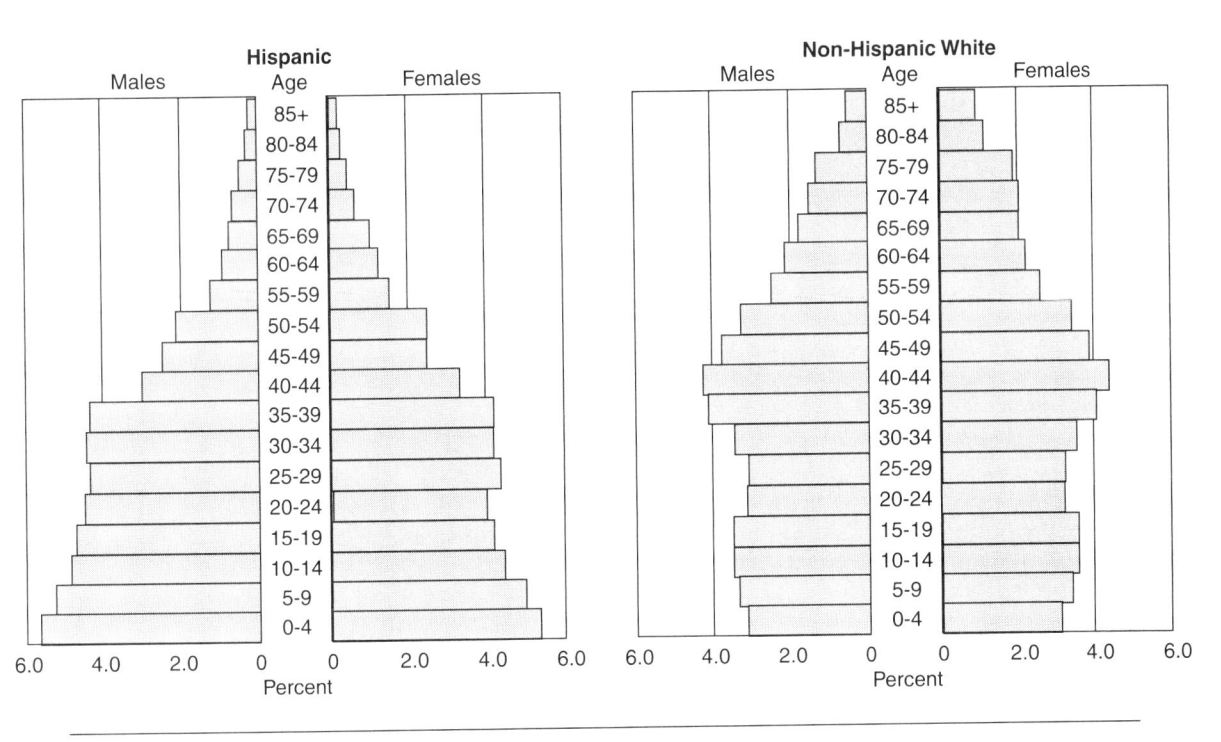

Figure 4
Population by Hispanic Origin, Age, and Sex: 2000 (in percent)[1]

Source: U.S. Census Bureau, Current Population Survey, March 2000.

[1] Each bar represents the percent of the Hispanic (non-Hispanic white) population who were within the specified age group and of the specified sex.

approximately 4.5 percent for both Mexicans and Central and South Americans to 21.0 percent for Cubans.

One in four foreign-born Hispanics is a naturalized citizen.

In 2000, 39.1 percent (or 12.8 million) of the Hispanic population in the United States was foreign born. Of this group, 43.0 percent entered the United States in the 1990s, another 29.7 percent came in the 1980s, and the remainder (27.3 percent) entered before 1980.

Although 74.2 percent of those who entered before 1970 had obtained citizenship by 2000, only 23.9 percent of those who entered between 1980 and 1989 and 6.7 percent of those who entered between 1990 and 2000 had become citizens (see Figure 5).

Family Household Size and Marital Status

Hispanics live in family households that are larger than those of non-Hispanic Whites.

In 2000, 30.6 percent of family households in which a Hispanic person was the householder consisted of five or more people.[7] In contrast, only 11.8 percent of non-Hispanic White family households were this large. Among Hispanic family households,

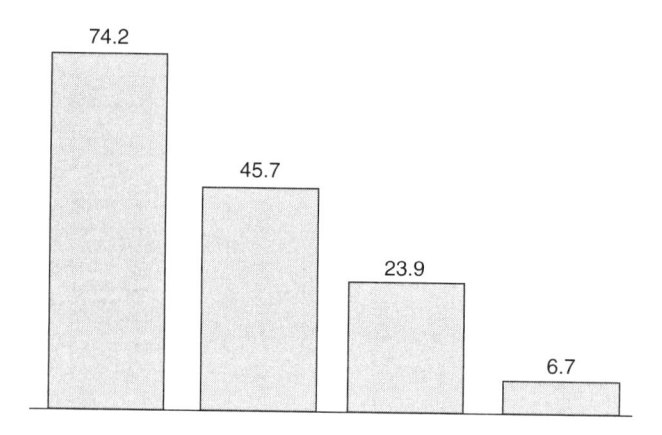

Figure 5
U.S. Citizenship of the Foreign-Born Hispanic Population by Year of Entry: 2000 (in percent)

Bar values: 74.2, 45.7, 23.9, 6.7

Source: U.S. Census Bureau, Current Population Survey, March 2000.

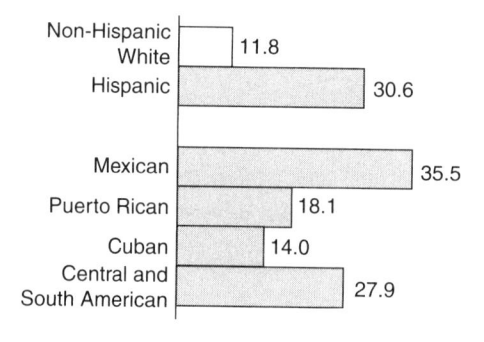

Figure 6
Family Households with Five or More People by Detailed Hispanic Origin: 2000 (in percent)

- Non-Hispanic White: 11.8
- Hispanic: 30.6
- Mexican: 35.5
- Puerto Rican: 18.1
- Cuban: 14.0
- Central and South American: 27.9

Source: U.S. Census Bureau, Current Population Survey, March 2000.

[1] Each bar represents the percent of family households, whose householder was of the specified origin, that consisted of 5 or more people. Data for other Hispanics not shown.

Mexican households were most likely to have five or more people (35.5 percent), as shown in Figure 6.

Family households with only two people represented 21.7 percent of Hispanic family households compared with 46.0 percent of non-Hispanic White family households. Among Hispanic households, Cuban family households were most likely to have only two people (41.3 percent).

For the population aged 15 years and older, Hispanics were more likely to have never been married than non-Hispanic Whites (33.2 percent compared with 24.5 percent). Among Latinos, Cubans were least likely to have never been married (20.4 percent).[8]

Educational Attainment

More than two in five Hispanics have not graduated from high school.

The Hispanic population age 25 and older was less likely to have at least graduated from high school than non-Hispanic Whites (57.0 percent and 88.4 percent, respectively). In addition, more than one-quarter of Hispanics had less than a ninth-grade education (27.3 percent) compared with only 4.2 percent of non-Hispanic Whites. The proportion with a bachelor's degree or more was much lower for Hispanics (10.6 percent) than for non-Hispanic Whites (28.1 percent, see Figure 7).

Educational attainment varies among Latinos.

Among Hispanics, Cubans and other Hispanics were most likely to have graduated from high school (73.0 percent and 71.6 percent, respectively)[9] compared with Mexicans (51.0 percent), as shown in Figure 8. Similarly, the proportion who had attained a bachelor's degree ranged from 23.0 percent for Cubans to 6.9 percent for Mexicans.

Economic Characteristics

Hispanics are much more likely than non-Hispanic Whites to be unemployed.

In March 2000, 6.8 percent of Hispanics in the civilian labor force aged 16 and older were unemployed compared with only 3.4 percent of non-Hispanic Whites.[10] Among Latino groups, 8.1 percent of Puerto Ricans, 7.0 percent of Mexicans, 5.8 percent of Cubans, 5.1 percent of Central and South

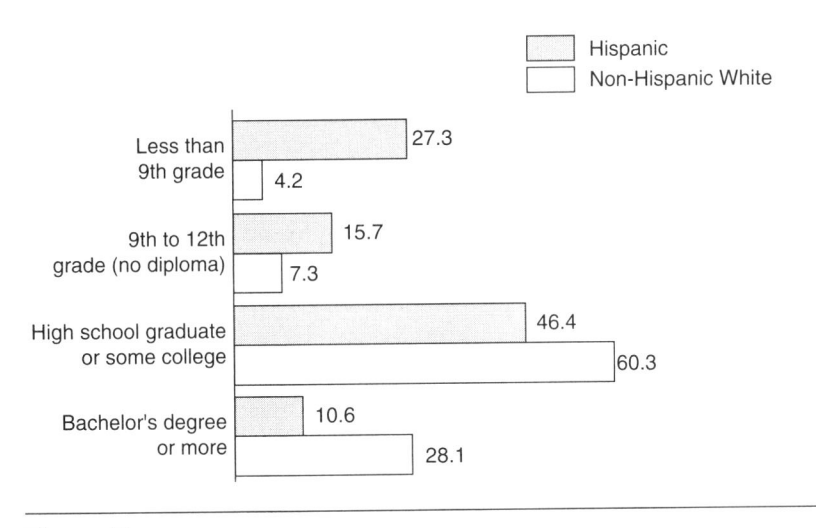

Figure 7
Population by Hispanic Origin and Educational Attainment: 2000 (as a percent of each population 25 years and older)

Source: U.S. Census Bureau, Current Population Survey, March 2000.

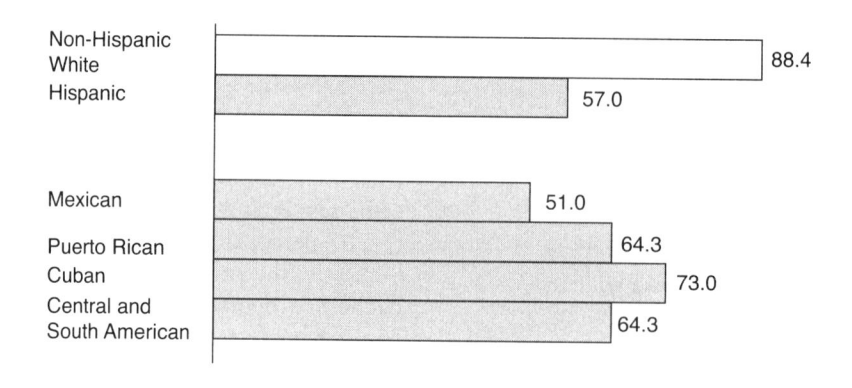

Figure 8
Population with at Least a High School Education by Detailed Hispanic Origin: 2000 (in percent)[1]

Group	Percent
Non-Hispanic White	88.4
Hispanic	57.0
Mexican	51.0
Puerto Rican	64.3
Cuban	73.0
Central and South American	64.3

Source: U.S. Census Bureau, Current Population Survey, March 2000.

[1] Each bar represents the percentage of individuals age 25 and older, of the specified origin, who have at least a high school education. Data for other Hispanics is not shown.

Americans, and 7.8 percent of other Hispanics were unemployed.[11]

Hispanics and non-Hispanic Whites have different occupational distributions.

In 2000, Hispanics were more likely than non-Hispanic Whites to work in service occupations (19.4 percent and 11.8 percent, respectively).[12] In addition, Hispanics were almost twice as likely to be employed as operators and laborers than non-Hispanic Whites (22.0 percent and 11.6 percent, respectively). Conversely, only 14.0 percent of Hispanics were in managerial or professional occupations, compared with 33.2 percent of non-Hispanic Whites. Among Latino groups, Mexicans were least likely to work in managerial or professional occupations (11.9 percent).

Hispanic workers earn less than non-Hispanic White workers.

Among full-time, year-round workers in 1999, 23.3 percent of Hispanics and 49.3 percent of non-Hispanic Whites earned $35,000 or more.[13] Among Latino full-time, year-round workers, Mexicans had the lowest proportion earning $35,000 or more (see Figure 9).

In addition, the proportion of workers making $50,000 or more was 9.6 percent of Hispanics compared with 27.4 percent of non-Hispanic Whites. Mexicans also had the lowest proportion of workers earning $50,000 or more with 7.7 percent.

Hispanics are more likely than non-Hispanic Whites to live in poverty.

In 1999, 22.8 percent of Hispanics were living in poverty, compared with 7.7 percent of non-Hispanic Whites (see Figure 10).[14] Hispanics represented 12.0 percent of the total population but constituted 23.1 percent of the population living in poverty. In addition, Hispanic children under 18 were much more likely than non-Hispanic White children to be living in poverty (30.3 percent versus 9.4 percent). Hispanic children represented 16.2

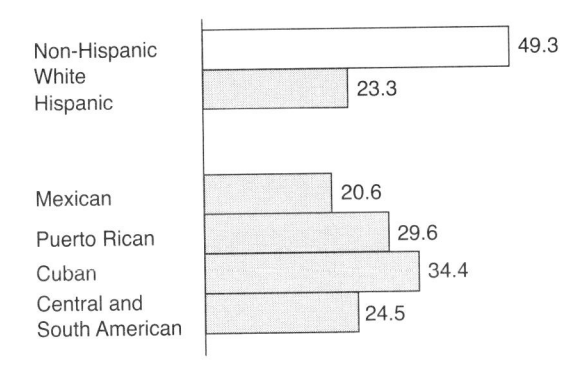

	Percent
Non-Hispanic White	49.3
Hispanic	23.3
Mexican	20.6
Puerto Rican	29.6
Cuban	34.4
Central and South American	24.5

Figure 9
Full-Time, Year-Round Workers with Annual Earnings $35,000 or More by Detailed Hispanic Origin: 1999 (in percent)[1]

Source: U.S. Census Bureau, Current Population Survey, March 2000.

[1] Each bar represents the percentage of individuals, of the specified origin, who earned more than $35,000 for full-time, year-round work. Data for other Hispanics is not shown.

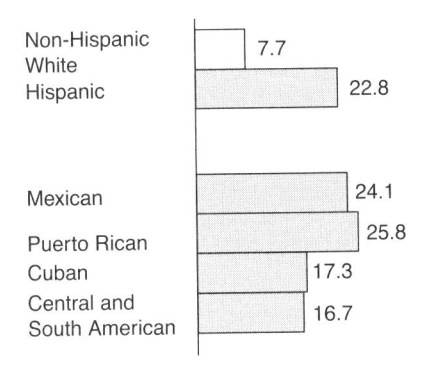

	Percent
Non-Hispanic White	7.7
Hispanic	22.8
Mexican	24.1
Puerto Rican	25.8
Cuban	17.3
Central and South American	16.7

Figure 10
People Living Below the Poverty Level by Detailed Hispanic Origin: 1999 (in percent)[1]

Source: U.S. Census Bureau, Current Population Survey, March 2000.

[1] Each bar represents the percentage of individuals, of the specified origin, who were living in poverty. Data for other Hispanics is not shown.

percent of all children in the United States but constituted 29.0 percent of all children in poverty.

Source of the Data

Estimates in this report come from data obtained in March 2000 by the CPS. The Census Bureau conducts the CPS every month, although this report uses only data from the March survey.

Accuracy of the Estimates

Statistics from surveys are subject to sampling and nonsampling error. All comparisons presented in this report have taken sampling error into account and meet the Census Bureau's standards for statistical significance. Nonsampling errors in surveys may be attributed to a variety of sources, such as how the survey was designed, how respondents interpret questions, how able and willing respondents are to provide correct answers, and how accurately the answers are coded and classified. The Census Bureau employs quality control procedures throughout the production process—including the overall design of surveys, the wording of questions, reviews of the work of interviewers and coders, and statistical review of reports.

The Current Population Survey employs ratio estimation, whereby sample estimates are adjusted to independent estimates of the national population by age, race, sex, and Hispanic origin. This weighting partially corrects for bias due to undercoverage, but how it affects different variables in the survey is not precisely known. Moreover, biases may also be present when people who are missed in the survey differ from those interviewed in ways other than the categories used in weighting (age, race, sex, and Hispanic origin). All of these considerations affect comparisons across different surveys or data sources.

Notes

1. For similar comparisons between the foreign-born and native populations in the United States, see Lisa Lollock, 2000, *The Foreign-Born Population in the United States: March 2000*, Current Population Reports, P20-534, U.S. Census Bureau, Washington DC.
2. The population universe for March 2000 CPS is the civilian noninstitutionalized population of the United States and members of the Armed Forces in the United States living off post or with their families on post, but excludes all other members of the Armed Forces.
3. The terms "Hispanic" and "Latino" are used interchangeably in this report to reflect the new terminology in the standards issued by the Office of Management and Budget in 1997 that are to be implemented by January 1, 2003. For more information, please refer to "Revisions to the Standards for the Classification of Federal Data on Race and Ethnicity," *Federal Register*, Vol. 62, No. 280, October 30, 1997, pp. 58,782-58,790. In addition, being of a particular origin is determined by the respondent. For example, people who indicate that they are of Mexican origin may be either born in Mexico or of Mexican heritage.
4. Puerto Rico is not included in the Current Population Survey.
5. The four regions of the United States for which data are presented in this report are as follows: **Northeast:** Connecticut, Maine, Massachusetts, New Hampshire, New Jersey, New York, Pennsylvania, Rhode Island, and Vermont; **Midwest:** Illinois, Indiana, Iowa, Kansas, Michigan,

Minnesota, Missouri, Nebraska, North Dakota, Ohio, South Dakota, and Wisconsin; **South:** Alabama, Arkansas, Delaware, District of Columbia, Florida, Georgia, Kentucky, Louisiana, Maryland, Mississippi, North Carolina, Oklahoma, South Carolina, Tennessee, Texas, Virginia, and West Virginia; and **West:** Alaska, Arizona, California, Colorado, Hawaii, Idaho, Montana, Nevada, New Mexico, Oregon, Utah, Washington, and Wyoming.

6. The proportions for Puerto Ricans and other Hispanics are not significantly different.
7. Family households consist of two or more people, at least one of whom is related to the householder (the person who owns or rents the housing unit). Hispanic family households have a Hispanic householder.
8. There is no significant difference between the percent never married for Puerto Ricans and Mexicans, Central and South Americans, or other Hispanics.
9. The proportion of Cuban high school graduates does not differ significantly from the proportion of other Hispanic high school graduates.
10. Civilian labor force data shown in this report reflect characteristics of the civilian noninstitutionalized population aged 16 and older for March 2000 and are not adjusted for seasonal changes. Data released by the Department of Labor, Bureau of Labor Statistics, may not agree entirely with data shown in this report because of differences in methodological procedures and their seasonal adjustment of the data.
11. Among all the detailed Hispanic origin groups examined here, statistically significant differences in unemployment rates occur only twice: between Central and South Americans and Mexicans and between Central and South Americans and Puerto Ricans.
12. The occupational classification system used here and by the Bureau of Labor Statistics is the one used in the 1990 Census of Population and is based largely on the 1980 Standard Occupational Classification (SOC).
13. Data on earnings and poverty in this report refer to the calendar year before the survey. In this case, earnings information collected in March 2000 refer to calendar year 1999.
14. Poverty status is determined through a set of money income thresholds that vary by family size and composition (see Dalaker, Joseph, 2000, *Poverty in the United States: 1999*, U.S. Census Bureau, Current Population Reports, P20-207; or *www.census.gov/hhes/www/poverty.html*).

2002 National Opinion Poll

Politics

David A. Bositis

The 2002 Joint Center for Political and Economic Studies National Opinion Poll is a national survey of 1,647 adults, conducted between September 17 and October 21, 2002. The survey's questions cover a broad range of topics including politics and the 2002 midterm elections, education, foreign policy and terrorism, social security, health care, criminal justice, race relations, and globalization.

The survey has two components: a national general population sample of 850 adults and a national sample of 850 adult African Americans. There are 53 African American respondents in the general population sample who are also part of the national sample of African Americans. Thus, in total, there are 1,647 adults, 18 years of age or older, who are included in this study.

This is the first release of the findings from the survey and covers politics and the 2002 elections. In the coming months, the Joint Center will release findings on the other areas identified above. The survey methodology is described in an accompanying appendix.

Politics and the 2002 Elections

The Joint Center for Political and Economic Studies' 2002 National Opinion Poll reveals an interesting mix of continuity and change from its last National Opinion Poll, conducted in the fall of 2000. The black and the (largely white) general populations of the United States continue to be similar in their views on a num-

---

2002 National Opinion Poll Politics by David A. Bositis. Copyright © 2002 Joint Center for Political and Economic Studies, Inc. Reprinted by permission.

ber of subjects but significantly divergent on others.

The Joint Center's 2002 survey was fielded shortly after Labor Day and the start of the political season when Americans usually begin paying more serious attention to the forthcoming election. However, this year many observers have noted that the public has not appeared to be paying much attention to the midterm elections, with Iraq and the Washington area sniper dominating the news.

In rating what are the country's most important national problems, black respondents identified the economy, employment, terrorism, and war at the top of the list; a much larger proportion of whites named terrorism and war the most important national problem, with the economy and employment a distant second. Among both populations, the top issues from 2000—education and healthcare—were judged less pressing in 2002. The survey results provide evidence that African Americans will continue their support for the Democratic party in November 2000. The results also reveal significant differences between blacks and whites on war with Iraq, and on views toward Israel.

In the responses to several questions in the survey, there are clear racial and ideological divides that characterize the 2002 political environment. African Americans, liberals, and Democrats view the current presidential administration and its policies much less favorably than others. Christian conservatives, unlike in the 2000 survey, think that things in the country are generally going in the right direction; African Americans, liberals and Democrats think the country has "gotten off on the wrong track."

The Joint Center's 2002 National Opinion Poll shows that African Americans continue to view former President Clinton very favorably. President George W. Bush is personally viewed more favorably by blacks than in 2000, although his job performance in their judgment is mediocre at best.

In the previous three Joint Center National Opinion Polls (1998-2000), proportionally more African Americans than whites reported that they were financially better off from a year earlier. In the 2002 survey, the black and white responses to that question were statistically indistinguishable.

Finally, black voters indicated a strong preference for a Democratic Congress, with 70.6 percent saying they would vote for the Democratic candidate in their congressional district and only 10.9 percent opting for the Republican candidate.

Most Important National Problem. In the 2002 survey blacks and whites differed more than in 2000 in identifying the most important national problems. Among African Americans the highest rated problems were the economy and employment (23 percent) and terrorism and the potential war with Iraq (23 percent), followed by crime (17 percent) and education (14 percent). Compared with 2000, there were significant declines in the number of respondents identifying prescription drugs and healthcare issues (18 vs. 5 percent) and education(26 vs. 14 percent). Terrorism and foreign affairs were not on the public's radar in 2000; the large increase in the number of African Americans mentioning the economy (23 vs. 14 percent) highlights the decline in the economy since then.

The top mentioned problems among whites were terrorism, war, and foreign affairs, with those responses totaling 35 percent. Among whites, terrorism was followed by the economy (18 percent) and more decline (11 percent). Education declined from 24 percent in 2000 to only 10 percent in 2002.

Presidential and Congressional Job Ratings. President Bush's job approval ratings were comparable to Congress's among blacks, and considerably better among whites. Among blacks, 38.5 percent gave him excellent or good marks, while 59.2 percent rated his job performance as fair or poor. A solid majority of whites (61 percent) rated Bush's job performance as excellent or good, while 37.8 percent gave him fair or poor marks.

Among blacks, seniors (52 percent), Republican identifiers (64.2 percent), and those who thought the country was going in the right direction (58.5 percent) rated Bush's job performance more favorably than others. African Americans who thought the country had gotten off on the wrong track rated Bush's job performance most negatively (70.7 percent fair/poor).

Congress's job ratings were similar to Bush's among all subgroups of African Americans (34.1 percent excellent/good and 61.3 percent fair/poor). Among whites, 36.4 percent rated Congress's work as excellent or good, while 57 percent gave Congress fair or poor marks.

Financial Status. In the 2000 Joint Center National Opinion Poll, African Americans for the third year in a row responded more favorably than whites to this question, with 45 percent indicating that they were financially better off, and 10 percent indicating that they were worse off than a year earlier. In the 2002 survey, only 18.9 percent of blacks said they were financially better off, while 36.7 percent said they were financially worse off; 42.6 percent indicated that their finances were unchanged. Black Republicans (29.6 percent better vs. 22.2 percent worse), those in the West (25.6 vs. 25.6 percent), and those saying the country was going in the right direction (29.6 vs. 17.7 percent) answered this question most favorably. Black seniors (8.1 vs. 35 percent) and black secular conservatives (12.9 vs. 51.6 percent) gave the most negative responses to this question.

The responses by the white respondents were similar to those of black respondents, with 15.9 percent saying their finances had improved in the previous year and 34.7 percent saying their finances had gotten worse. Those in the general population over 50 years old had the smallest proportion of respondents indicating that their finances had improved.

Direction of Country. In the 2000 National Opinion Poll, both black and white respondents, when asked if the country was going in the right direction, generally responded positively (consistent with the generally favorable economic situation at that time). At that time, Christian conservatives were less sanguine about the direction of the country. In 2002, two-thirds of African Americans think the country is on the wrong track, and a plurality of whites (49.7) think so as well. In contrast, Christian conservatives now believe the country is going in the right direction (54.1 percent right direction vs. 36.4 percent wrong track); self-identified Republicans (63.4 vs. 27.2 percent) also believe the country is going in the right direction.

Among all subgroups of African Americans save Republicans, majorities—and usually large majorities—believe the country is going in the wrong direction. Except for Republicans and conservatives, all subgroups of the general population also believe the country is going in the wrong direction.

Feelings Toward Public Figures. The respondents in the survey were asked to rate their feelings toward seven public figures, three of whom were black and four of whom were white. The Joint Center has included these ratings since 1992, with certain prominent national leaders included in each survey (Bill Clinton, Jesse Jackson, Colin Powell), and with others rotated in (Condoleezza Rice and

Dick Cheney) or out (Al Sharpton and Joseph Lieberman) over time. Included in these questions was an explicit name recognition feature; prior to examining how the public feels about these figures, their level of public recognition will be noted. In the black population: Bill Clinton, Al Gore, George W. Bush, Colin Powell and Jesse Jackson are universally known; Dick Cheney is unknown to 13.6 percent of the respondents, and Condoleezza Rice is unknown to 39.7 percent of respondents. In the general population all of the public figures are universally known save Condoleezza Rice who is unknown to 37.9 percent of the general population.

Bill Clinton. Bill Clinton continues to be rated very favorably by African Americans with, 80.9 percent favorable to 11.8 percent unfavorable; these ratings are comparable to his ratings in previous surveys, which have been consistently outstanding. All subgroups of the black population rate Clinton favorably. Among respondents in the general population, Clinton's ratings were essentially unchanged from the 2000 survey, with 51 percent rating him favorably and 43 percent rating him unfavorably.

Al Gore. In the 2000 survey, former Vice President Al Gore was rated very favorably by African Americans, with 86 percent rating him favorably and only seven percent rating him unfavorably. Since his defeat in the 2000 election, Gore's ratings have declined among African Americans, with 66.8 percent rating him favorably, and 20.7 percent unfavorably. In 2002, Gore's favorable to unfavorable ratings declined even more sharply in the general population than among Blacks, with 47.1 percent rating him favorably and 44.2 percent rating him unfavorably; in the 2000 Joint Center survey, Gore's rating among the general population were 62 favorable to 30 percent unfavorable.

George Bush. President George W. Bush's ratings among African Americans increased significantly since 2000. In the 2000 Joint Center survey, Bush's favorable rating among blacks was 29 percent, and he was rated unfavorably by 55 percent. In the 2002 survey, Bush was rated favorably by 50.8 percent of blacks surveyed, and unfavorably by 38.6 percent. Bush continues to be viewed much more favorably by the general population with 72.8 percent viewing him favorably and 23.6 percent viewing him unfavorably.

Dick Cheney. The vice president was viewed somewhat more favorably than not by African Americans, with 43.2 percent favorable and 30.6 percent unfavorable ratings. In the 2000 survey, Dick Cheney's unfavorable ratings were higher than his favorable ratings by a small margin, with 23 percent of blacks rating him favorably and 28 percent rating him unfavorably. Among those in the general population, Cheney's ratings were solid, with 61.3 percent rating him favorably, and 26.8 percent viewing him unfavorably.

Condoleezza Rice. National security advisor Condoleezza Rice was viewed similarly by both blacks and those in the general population. First—and not surprisingly given that she has never run for national office—she is essentially unknown to two-fifths of both population groups. Similar proportions of respondents in both the black (41.1 percent) and general (45.8 percent) population view her favorably; similar proportions in both the black (12.1 percent) and general (9.2 percent) populations also view her unfavorably.

Jesse Jackson. Jesse Jackson's ratings declined significantly among both the black and general populations since 2000. In the 2002 survey, 59.5 percent of African Americans rated Jackson favorably, and 25.5 percent rated him unfavorably. This is a significant decline from the 2000 survey, when Jackson's favorable ratings outnumbered his unfavorable ratings by nine-to-one (83 vs. 9 percent). His ratings among the general population likewise declined, changing from a net positive in 2000 (47 percent favorable to 38 percent unfavorable) to sharply negative in 2002 (31.2 percent favorable to 54.9 percent unfavorable).

Colin Powell. Ret. General Colin Powell continues to be the singularly most favorably viewed figure across all groups and subgroups. Gen. Powell's ratings were quite high among those in both the black (73.3 percent favorable) and the general population (89.3 percent favorable); only 13.6 percent of blacks and 4.9 percent of those in the general population rated Powell unfavorably.

Black Partisanship. There has been a noteworthy change in black partisan identification (away from the Democrats) since the Joint Center's 2000 National Opinion Poll. In 2002, 63 percent of African Americans were self-identified Democrats (down from 74 percent in 2000), 24 percent were self-identified Independents (up from 20 percent in 2000), and 10 percent were self-identified Republicans (up from four percent in 2000). Among African Americans over the past five years, there have been small shifts away from the back toward identifying with the Democratic party. However, African Americans have been voting Democratic at their usual high levels. Among all subgroups of the black population, the most Independent is the 18-25- year-old age cohort, among whom 34 percent identify themselves as Independent. African Americans of retirement age continue to remain Democratic stalwarts, with 75 percent identifying with the Democrats and only 7 percent as Republicans.

Parties and Issues. The respondents were asked which of the two major political parties has the better approach to dealing with a variety of different issues. Among African Americans, while there is some differentiation of the parties on issues, the Democratic party is clearly seen as the party with a better approach to dealing with the issues that were presented. African Americans favor the Democrats over the Republicans on Social Security (52 to 21 percent), race relations (58 to 13 percent), fighting terrorism (34 to 28 percent), keeping unemployment low (59 to 18 percent), health care (61 to 15 percent), immigration (37 to 25 percent), and balancing the federal budget (55 to 19 percent). Among blacks, the Democrats are most favored over the GOP on race relations, and least favored on fighting terrorism.

Respondents in the general population favor the Democrats over the Republicans on Social Security (46 to 25 percent), race relations (45 to 24 percent), keeping unemployment low (39 to 30 percent), health care (46 to 25 percent); the two parties are viewed equally on balancing the federal budget (35 percent). The Republicans are favored over the Democrats on fighting terrorism (51 to 18 percent) and on immigration (33 to 22 percent).

2002 Congressional Vote. When asked their preference in this fall House elections, 70.6 percent of African Americans indicated they would vote Democratic; 10.9 percent said they would vote Republican. The only subgroup of African Americans who supported the GOP were black Republicans. Among those in the general population, the Democrats had a slight edge (though not statistically significant), 38.6 to 37.1 percent; whites favored the GOP over the Democrats by two percentage points (38.9 to 36.7 percent).

Interest in Midterms. The respondents were asked how much the outcome of this year's midterms concerned them, and a slightly higher percentage of blacks (38.6 percent) than whites (35.2 percent) indicated that it concerned them a great deal. African Americans living in the Midwest (50.9 percent) and those with advanced degrees (44.6 percent) indicated the highest level of concern. In the general population, seniors (44.5 percent) expressed the greatest concern for the outcome.

Campaign Issues. The respondents were asked their views on a number of matters that have been raised during the 2002 campaigns, and on the nightly newscasts.

School Vouchers. A majority (57 percent) of African Americans and a majority (52 percent) of those in the general population said they supported school vouchers; 43 percent of blacks and 48 percent of those in the general population oppose school vouchers. Support for school vouchers among Blacks is unchanged from the 2000 survey, and among the general population there has been a slight increase.

War with Iraq. President Bush's policy on Iraq is strongly opposed by African Americans, and while a small plurality of the general population support the president on Iraq, there is substantial uncertainty about the policy. Among African Americans, only 19.2 percent voice support for Bush on Iraq, while 45.3 percent oppose the administration's position. About one-in-three African Americans is uncertain on this issue. In the general population, 39.6 percent agree with the Bush administration, while 25.1 percent oppose Bush on Iraq. As with African Americans, a third of the general population is uncertain about the wisdom of going to war with Iraq.

Rating the U.N. Both African Americans and those in the general population viewed the work of the U.N. in surprisingly similar terms, with a majority of blacks (52.8 percent) and the general population (56.2 percent) rating the work of the U.N. as either fair or poor. Similar propositions from both the black (42.6 percent) and the general (41.5 percent) population rated the work of the U.N. as either excellent or good.

Rating the Leaders of Foreign Countries. In the Joint Center's 2002 National Opinion Poll the respondents were asked to rate their feelings toward the leadership of nine countries that have figured prominently in the news and in U.S. foreign policy. Black and white views on a number of these countries were quite different.

China. A plurality of African Americans viewed China's leadership favorably (46 percent favorable to 34 percent unfavorable), while a majority of the mostly white general population viewed China's leadership unfavorably (50 percent unfavorable to 33 percent favorable).

Cuba. While a majority in both the black and the general populations rated Cuba's leadership unfavorably, African Americans were clearly less negative than whites on Cuba. In the black population, 29.5 percent of respondents rated Cuba's leadership favorably, and 50.5 percent rated it unfavorably. In the general population, only 21.4 percent rated Cuba's leadership favorably, while a substantial 66.2 percent rated it unfavorably.

England. Large majorities in the black (7.2 percent) and general (89.8 percent) population rated England's leadership favorably.

India. African Americans were fairly evenly split on India's leadership, with 39.2 percent viewing it favorably and 34.6 percent viewing it unfavorably. India's leadership fared somewhat better in the general population, with 40.2 percent viewing it favorably, and 26.7 percent viewing it unfavorably.

Israel. A plurality (40 percent) of African Americans rated Israel's leadership unfavorably, with 37.9 percent viewing it favorably. A plurality of those in the general population viewed Israel's leadership favorably (48 percent); 36.6 percent viewed the leadership negatively.

Mexico, Pakistan, Russia, and Saudi Arabia. Blacks and whites shared generally similar views about the leadership in Mexico, Pakistan, Russia, and Saudi Arabia. The Mexican and Russian leadership are generally viewed favorably (though more so in the general population than in the black population), and the leadership in Pakistan and Saudi Arabia are viewed quite unfavorably, with unfavorable ratings outnumbering favorable ones by more than two-to-one.

Interest Groups

Hanes Walton, Jr. and Robert Smith

As late as the late 1960s, with the exception of the NAACP, the Urban League, and to a lesser extent, SCLC and the National Council of Negro Women, there was little organized black interest group influence on the Washington policy-making process. Even the NAACP and Urban League were engaged mainly in rights-based civil rights lobbying rather than in broader material-based public policy concerns.[1] However, since the 1970s blacks have developed a significant presence in the Washington policy-making process, one that focuses on both rights-based and broader, material-based policy interests.

Table 8.1 displays the contemporary structure of black interest groups, illustrating the range of interest and policy concerns of the organized black community. Many of these groups (such as the National Medical Association, the National Association of Black Manufacturers), like their white counterparts, are special interest organizations, generally pursuing their own narrow professional or economic interests. Others, like Trans Africa have a single policy focus—in its case, American foreign policy toward Africa and the Caribbean. Still others have broad, multiple-policy agendas (the NAACP, the Congressional Black Caucus, the Congress of Black Churches), lobbying on the full range of domestic and foreign policy issues.

Black Groups, the "Black Agenda," and the Problem of Resource Constraint

The broad-based policy agenda encompassing both rights- and material-based issues is one of the major problems confronting the African American Lobby in Washington. It is agenda rich but resource poor. Political scientist Dianne Pinderhughes writes,

> The subordinate, dependent status of the black population limits the capacity of black interests to create well funded and

---

Excerpt pp. 116-134 from *American Politics and the African American Quest for Universal Freedom*, 2nd ed. By Hanes Walton, Jr. and Robert C. Smith. Copyright © 2003 by Addision Wesley Longman, Inc. Reprinted by permission of Pearson Education, Inc.

Table 8.1
The Structure of African American Interest Organizations—Selected Groups

Civil Rights	*Economic/Professional*
NAACP (1990)	National Medical Association (1885)
Urban League (1910)	National Bar Association (1925)
Southern Christian Leadership Conference (1957)	National Business League (1900)
NAACP Legal Defense Fund (1939)	National Conference of Black Lawyers (1969)
National Council of Negro Women (1937)	National Association of Black Manufacturers (1970)
	Coalition of Black Trade Unionists (1972)

Public Policy	*Caucuses of Black Elected Officials*
Trans Africa (1977)	Congressional Black Caucus (1969)
Children's Defense Fund (1973)	National Caucus of Black Elected Officials (1970)
National Association of Black Social Workers (1969)	Southern Conference of Black Mayors (1972)
	National Black Caucus of State Legislators (1977)
	National Caucus of Black School Board Members (1971)

Religious

National Baptist Convention (1882)
Nation of Islam (1930)
Congress of Black Churches (1978)

Year in parentheses refers to the year the group was organized. For a fairly comprehensive list of black organizations, their purposes and membership, see *A Guide to Black Organizations* (New York: Philip Morris, 1984)—yes, Philip Morris, the cigarette company.

Strictly speaking, the Children's Defense Fund is an interracial advocacy organization; however, it was founded and is led by a black woman--Marion Wright Edelman-- and much of its advocacy is for poor and disadvantaged minority children.

supported groups capable of the consistent monitoring required in administration and implementation of law. This same status multiplies the number of potential issue areas of importance to black constituencies, but their resource difficulties limit the number of issues they can address, and weaken their likelihood of being taken seriously within any of those areas.[2]

The problem identified by Pinderhughes may be seen by comparing the data in Table 8.2 and 8.3, which show, respectively, the post-Civil Rights Era black agenda of African Americans and the resources of the three major Washington black interest organizations compared with the resources of selected nonblack Washington-based interest groups.

Table 8.2
The Post–Civil Rights Era Black Agenda

Full employment
Welfare reform to include a guaranteed income
Comprehensive national health insurance
Increased federal funding for elementary, secondary, and higher education
Busing for purposes of integrated education
Minority business set-asides
International sanctions on South Africa and repeal of the Byrd Amendment[a]

[a]The Byrd Amendment was an act of Congress permitting the import of chrome from the then-apartheid regime of Rhodesia (now Zimbabwe) in violation of sanctions imposed by the United Nations. It was repealed in 1977.

Source: "Seven Point Mandate," *Focus* 14(1976): 8. *Focus* is the monthly newsletter of the Joint Center for Political and Economic Studies.

Table 8.3
A Comparison of the Resources of the Three Major African American Interest Organizations with Selected Nonblack Organizations

African American Organization	Estimated Membership	Annual Budget
NAACP	450,000; 1,700 local chapters	$11.9[a]
Urban League	118 local affiliates	24
Congressional Black Caucus[b]	39 members of Congress	550,000
Non-African American Organizations		
AFL-CIO	14 million	63
National Association of Manufacturers	2,800 local chapters	17
National Abortion Rights League	400,000	9
Mothers Against Drunk Driving	2.9 million	43
Tobacco Institute	13 companies	38
National Rifle Association	2.6 million	89
Sierra Club	600,000	39
American Israeli Public Affairs Committee	50,000	12
Conference of Catholic Bishops	300 bishops	31
National Gay and Lesbian Tax Force	15,000	1

[a]Unless otherwise noted, the budget figure is in millions of dollars for the year 1995.

[b]The budget for the Congressional Black Caucus is for the Congressional Black Caucus Foundation, a separate, tax-exempt organization formed in 1982 to raise funds to support the group. The amount is as shown: $550,000. Until 1995, the Caucus itself raised $4,000 from each of its members to support its operations. The Republican congressional majority under Speaker Newt Gingrich discontinued this form of member support.

Sources: Various annual reports supplied to the authors by the different organizations or telephone interviews with spokespersons for the groups.

The Joint Center for Political and Economic Studies is a Washington-based think tank devoted to research on African American affairs (Box 8.1). In 1976 it called a bipartisan (Democrats and Republicans) conference of more than 1,000 black elected officials as well as appointed officials then serving in the Carter administration. At the conference's conclusion, the group issued a document, the "Seven Point Mandate," that it said represented a leadership consensus on the post-Civil Rights Era black agenda. The items on that agenda are displayed in Table 8.2.

The agenda includes *rights-based items* (busing for purposes of school desegregation and contract set-asides for minority businesses), but it's main items are *material-based, nonracial issues,* such as universal health insurance and full employment. In this sense, the "black" agenda is not really black but is rather a broad-based liberal reform agenda. It is a consensus agenda. With minor changes in emphasis and specifics, the original items remain the principal issues on the black agenda today. (The minor changes involve less concern with busing and more with affirmative action; the Byrd Amendment has been repealed, and abolition of apartheid has removed the need for sanctions on South Africa.)

Blacks therefore have a broad-based material and rights agenda; yet when compared to other lobby groups in Washington—many with narrow, single-issue agendas—black groups have relatively few resources. Table 8.3 displays data on the membership and financial resources of selected Washington interest groups, including the three most important black groups. With the exception of the gay and lesbian lobby, the trial lawyers association, and the lobby group for Israel, all the nonblack associations have greater resources in terms of membership or local chapters than do the three major black groups. With the exception of the National Abortion Rights League (which has a membership comparable to the NAACP) and the National Gay and Lesbian Task Force, all the nonblack groups have larger budgets than the NAACP, the Urban League, or the Congressional Black Caucus.[3] Also, with the exception of the Conference of Catholic Bishops and the AFL-CIO, most of the nonblack groups are narrow, single-issue groups, focusing their lobbying on one issue such as gun ownership, abortion rights, drunk driving, or U.S. foreign policy toward Israel. Most of these single-issue lobbies, unlike the multiple-issue black groups, have larger budgets. The budget, for example, of Mothers Against Drunk Driving (MADD) is larger than the budgets of the three black groups combined, and the budget of the National Rifle Association (NRA) is three times as great as the budgets of the three black groups combined.

The size of an interest group's membership and budget are important resources. A large membership permits grassroots mobilization by letters and phone calls to the media and members of Congress as well as voter mobilization on election day. Money is, as former California House Speaker Jesse Unruh once said, "the mother's milk of politics." It can be employed in a wide range of activities, such as grassroots organizing, voter mobilization, polling, radio and television ads, and litigation. Critically important, a large financial base permits interest groups to form PACs—political action committees—to raise and give campaign contributions to candidates for office. Since the passage of campaign finance reform laws in the 1970s, PACs have become very important in the lobbying-election process, contributing nearly half the money raised by incumbent congressional candidates (federal law limits PAC contributions to $5,000 per candidate; individuals to $1,000). Several of the nonblack groups (the NRA, the

Box 8.1
The Joint Center for Political and Economic Studies

Think tanks—organizations of scholars and former government officials who do research and planning on domestic and foreign policy issues—are an important part of the policy-making process in the United States.[a] They develop ideas that shape the public policy debate, and unlike university-based scholars, they tend to be directly linked to Washington policy makers, frequently serving in the government for periods of time and then returning to the think tank to do research on policy-related issues. For example, many of the ideas that shaped the Reagan administration's early policy agenda came directly from the Heritage Foundation, a conservative think tank. Other important Washington think tanks include the Brookings Institution, the American Enterprise Institute, and the Urban Institute.

As the Civil Rights Era drew to a close and black politics began its shift from movement-style protests to routine interest group policies, it was early recognized that African Americans needed their own think tank. The Joint Center for Political and Economic Studies was founded to meet this need for policy research and analysis.

The Joint Center's early projects included the collection and dissemination of data on the rapidly growing number of black elected officials (eventually this became its annual *Roster of Black Elected Officials*); the publication of a monthly newsletter; and the provision of technical training, workshops, and publications to black elected officials. The center also from the outset encouraged black elected officials to form caucuses and was instrumental in creating the National Coalition on Black Voter Participation.

In 1972 Eddie Williams became president of the Joint Center. Williams set about to broaden the center's work beyond educational and technical assistance and research support for black elected officials. The result was an announcement that the center would become a "national research organization in the tradition of Brookings and the American Enterprise Institute," rather than simply a "technical and institutional support resource for black elected officials."[b]

Although its budget is modest compared to the budgets of other Washington think tanks, the center has done a remarkable job in facilitating the institutionalization of black politics. Its studies of the growth and development of black elected officials, its work on the implementation of the Voting Rights Act, its work on the development of a consensus black agenda, and its monthly newsletter *Focus* have made the Joint Center the recognized, authoritative source on black politics in the post-Civil Rights Era.[c]

[a]For an analysis of the increasingly important roles played by think tanks in policy making, see James Smith, *Think Tanks and the Rise of the New Policy Elites* (New York: Free Press, 1991).

[b]Joint Center for Political Studies, *Annual Report*, 1991, p. 3.

[c]For a more detailed analysis of the history and development of the Joint Center, see Robert C. Smith, *We Have No Leaders: African Americans in the Post-Civil Rights Era* (Albany: SUNY Press, 1996): 113-20.

trial lawyers, the AFL-CIO) have large PACs that contribute millions of dollars to congressional candidates. None of the black interest groups have PACs, although several unsuccessful efforts were made in the 1970s by a number of black groups to form one.[4]

Given their multiple rights- and material-issue agendas and their relative lack of resources compared to other interest groups, black groups are at a considerable disadvantage unless they can form coalitions with other groups. On most rights-based issues, civil rights lobbying is done through a broad, multiethnic coalition: the Leadership Conference on Civil Rights. (There are, however, tensions within this group; see Box 8.2.) On welfare and poverty issues, the Center for Budget Priorities (a white group) is an effective lobby and advocacy group, and on national health insurance and full employment, the AFL-CIO and the Conference of Catholic Bishops are, with blacks, part of a broad labor-liberal reform coalition. But as shown by the failure to secure effective full employment legislation in the 1970s and by the defeat of President Clinton's universal health care plan in the 1990s, this reform coalition has not been able to effectively counterbalance the power of those interests opposed to universal health and employment.

African American Women and the Quest for Universal Freedom

Although some black male leaders were ardent feminists—supporters of universal freedom for women—most were not and even those who were always were more concerned with ending racism and white supremacism than sexism and male supremacism. Thus, African American women in politics have tended to embrace a more universal version of freedom than African American men; a version encompassing the elimination of both race and gender barriers to equality. But, feminism—the ideology of gender equality and freedom—has historically been an ambivalent phenomenon in the black community and in African American politics. This is because African American women historically have faced the double burden of oppression on the basis of racism, and discrimination on the basis of sexism. This double burden creates dilemmas—whether elimination of racism or sexism is to be the main focus of the struggles of black women and to what extent should black women identify and form coalitions with white women, who frequently are as racist and white supremacist in their thinking as white men. Also, historically in the United States the struggle for women's rights and the struggle for the rights of blacks have been symbiotic and conflictual. The earliest movement for women's rights originated from the activism of white women in the abolitionist movement. However, these largely middle- to upper-class women tended to view sexism as equal or more important than racism. The modern feminist movement that originated in the late 1960s and early 1970s also has its roots in black movements for freedom; specifically in the activism of middle-class white women in the protest phase of the civil rights movement during the 1960s. The modern movement for women's liberation also drew on the black power movement for parts of its militancy in rhetoric, strategies, and organizing principles. But, as during the abolitionist movement, tensions emerged as these middle-class white women also tended to see sexism as equal or more important than racism.

The roots of black feminism go back to the Antebellum Era in the writings and activism of women like Maria B. Stewart and Sojourner Truth, and in the late nineteenth-century writings of women like Anna Julia Cooper, whose 1892 book *A Voice from the South* is an important early work in the development of a distinctive black feminist

Box 8.2

The Leaderhship Conference on Civil Rights

The theory of African American coalitions we have developed in this book suggests that such coalitions, whether rights- or material-based, tend to be unstable and frequently short-lived. While this is generally true, there is one coalition—the Leadership Conference on Civil Rights—that has now lasted almost a half century, although in recent years it too has experienced tensions and conflicts.

The Leadership Conference on Civil Rights (LCCR) is a rights-based coalition. It was founded in 1949 by A. Phillip Randolph, the African American labor leader; Roy Wilkins, assistant director of the NAACP; and Arnold Aronson, a Jewish labor activist. Initially it was a coalition of about 40 black, labor, and Jewish and other religious groups whose principal objective was to secure legislation ensuring the civil rights of African Americans, especially those in the South. This coalition, along with the NAACP, was the principal lobby group for the 1964 Civil Rights Act (at that time, Clarence Mitchell, head of the NAACP's Washington office, also was head of LCCR).

The African American civil rights movement of the 1960s and its successes served as a model for other groups facing various forms of discrimination. These groups (women, gays, and other minorities) joined LCCR, expanding its memberships from about 40 groups in 1949 to more than 150 today. In 1949, most of the organizations in LCCR were black and it was widely viewed as an African American coalition. Today, this is no longer the case, as black organizations constitute little more than a third of LCCR's membership.[a] The expansion of the coalition has inevitably led to tensions and conflicts along racial, ethnic, and gender lines.

From the beginning there were gender conflicts within the civil rights coalition. African Americans, labor leaders, and spokespersons for working-class women opposed the inclusion of a ban on sex discrimination in employment in the 1964 Civil Rights Act. Labor opposed gender equality in favor of preferential treatment for women: laws limiting working hours and the physical burden of work for women and providing such special benefits as rest and maternity leave. African American leaders (mainly men) opposed the inclusion of gender because they argued that it would take jobs from black men—the putative family bread winner—and give them to white women. By contrast, support for the inclusion of gender came from conservatives (the amendment on sex was introduced by Howard Smith of Virginia, an opponent of civil rights, who thought the inclusion of sex would kill the entire bill) and white upper-class women's groups such as the National Federation of Business and Professional Women. Although African Americans and labor leaders now support gender equality in employment, sex-race tensions continue over affirmative action, with some African Americans arguing that white women are the principal beneficiaries of a program originally set up for blacks. Affirmative action has also caused conflict with some Jewish groups in LCCR; these groups tend to object to racial quotas and preferences (especially in higher education) because quotas historically were used to exclude Jews and because some Jewish leaders see them as a violation of merit and the principle of equality for all persons.

(continued)

> **Box 8.2**
>
> **Continued**
>
> Jewish-black tensions in the coalition have also been exacerbated in recent years by conflicts over black support for the Palestinians in the Middle East conflict, Israeli support for the apartheid regime in South Africa, and the antisemitic remarks of the Nation of Islam's Louis Farrakhan.
>
> Another source of tension in LCCR is between African Americans and Mexican Americans. When the 1965 Voting Rights Act was renewed in 1975, the NAACP opposed the inclusion of an amendment to prohibit discrimination against language minorities. Decisions of LCCR require a unanimous vote of its executive committee, thus the NAACP's opposition effectively killed coalition support, forcing Latino groups in the coalition to act alone in a successful effort to get language groups covered by the Voting Rights Act.[b] Although this issue is now settled, it has left a residue of bad feeling between blacks and Latinos. In addition, some African Americans have expressed concerns about the impact of illegal immigration on the employment opportunities of low-income urban blacks, a position that upsets the Asian American and Hispanic American groups in the coalition.
>
> The LCCR is a rights-based coalition that has endured for 50 years, but its successes in the 1960s, the development of new rights groups in the 1970s and 1980s, and the expansion of the coalition have inevitably created some instability. However, as a broad-based coalition that embraces universal rights for all Americans, it is likely to endure, although not without continuing conflicts and tensions.[c]
>
> [a]Dianne Pinderhughes, "Black Interest Groups and the 1982 Extension of the Voting Rights Act," in Huey Perry and Wayne Parent, eds., *Blacks and the American Political System* (Gainesville: University Press of Florida, 1995): 206.
>
> [b]Ibid., p. 211.
>
> [c]Dianne Pinderhughes, "Divisions in the Civil Rights Community," *Political Science and Politics* 25(1992): 485-87.

thought. Black feminism is also rooted in the activities of the black club movement among women. These activities led to the formation in 1896 of the National Association of Colored Women and later the National Council of Negro Women. The National Association of Colored Women, organized a decade before the NAACP, was the first national black organization to deal with race issues, and the National Council of Negro Women led by Dorothy Height dealt with women's issues as well as broader issues of civil rights during the 1950s and 1960s.

In the 1970s, however, it was clearly the feminist movement among white women that revitalized the ideology among black women, in spite of the skepticism and even hostility of many black women to the middle class dominated white feminist movement. The success of the civil rights movement in removing the obvious barriers to racial equality allowed for a renewed focus on gender equality among black women. Shirley Chisholm's election as the first black woman in Congress in 1968 and her 1972 campaign for the presidency were important symbolically in inspiring black female political activism. Finally, the Supreme Court's 1972 decision in *Roe v. Wade* to legalize abortion was a catalyst to action, since the decision was opposed by virtually the entire male dominated black leadership establishment including the NAACP and the Urban League. The National Black Political Convention in 1972 rejected a resolution supporting legal abortions; leading black nationalists denounced the decision as genocidal and Jesse Jackson equated *Roe v. Wade* with the *Dred Scott* decision. (Of major black organizations only the Black Panther Party endorsed *Roe* and a woman's right to choose an abortion.)

In 1973 black women formed the National Black Feminist Organization, which advocated a specifically black agenda of gender equality. In 1974 radical black feminists and lesbians formed the Combahee River Collective (taking its name from a campaign led by Harriet Tubman that freed several hundred slaves), which issued a manifesto defining itself as a group of black women "struggling against racial, sexual, heterosexual and class oppression." (This group is heavily influenced by the writings of Audre Lorde, a young black lesbian feminist and political activist who saw sexuality as an important part of black feminism.[5] In 1984 politically active black women formed the National Political Caucus of Black Women in order to pursue a distinctive gendered role in African American politics, focusing on issues and the election and appointment of black women to office.

Feminism is not a monolithic force in black politics, however. Rather, there are divisions among black feminists based on ideology, and differences based on class, sexual orientation, age, and marital status. Ideologically, there is a liberal feminism, which focuses on things like abortion rights (since *Roe v. Wade* the right to an abortion has become widely accepted in the black community, and supported in public opinion and by almost all black leaders and organizations), equal employment and pay, health and child care, violence against women, and the full inclusion of women in the political process. Radical feminists support these liberal objectives but also focus on the perceived interrelationships between racism, sexism, heterosexism, and capitalism. Thus, unlike liberal feminists they tend to advocate socialism and gay rights. Liberal feminists tend to be advocates of traditional marriage and the strengthening of the traditional family, while the radicals often see marriage and the traditional family as patriarchal structures that inevitably oppress women. These ideological differences are to some extent rooted in and related to age, sexual orientation, social class, and marital status.[6]

Black Nationalist Movements

Black nationalist organizations are movement rather than interest group organizations. Interest groups accept the legitimacy of the system and seek to have it accept their demands for rights and freedoms; movements challenge system legitimacy and seek fundamental system transformation. Historically, black nationalists have certainly challenged the legitimacy of the American system; in their view, it is incapable of delivering universal freedom and equality. This is shown clearly in the system-challenging rhetoric of nationalist leaders. In 1901 Bishop Henry M. Turner caused a national furor when he said "to the Negro in this country the American flag is a dirty and contemptuous rag. Not a star in it can the colored man claim, for it is no longer a symbol of our manhood rights and freedom."[7] Similar controversial remarks about the flag were made by Louis Farrakhan 95 years later in a speech to his followers in Chicago.

Bishop Henry M. Turner and the First Mass-Based Black Nationalist Movement

The ideology of black nationalism is as old as the African American experience in the United States; until the post-Reconstruction Era, however, it was simply the thought of a few intellectuals or the poorly organized efforts of a few remarkable men.[8] The first effort at a nationalist movement on a mass basis was launched by Bishop Henry M. Turner in the 1890s. Faced by the withdrawal of African American freedom, the terrorism of white southern racists, and Booker T. Washington's seeming acceptance of this turn of events, Turner sought to organize blacks for a mass return to Africa. As he frequently said in his speeches and writings, for blacks the choice was simple: "emigrate or perish."[9]

Turner was born a free man of color in 1834. A bishop of the African Methodist Episcopal church, he served as a chaplain in the Union army and as a member of the Reconstruction Georgia constitutional convention. Once Reconstruction ended, Turner attempted to organize a back-to-Africa movement. From 1890 until his death in 1915, Turner organized numerous conferences and filed many petitions with Congress requesting support for his plan. He, for example, was the first African American leader to petition Congress for reparations, calling for a $40 billion payment to blacks for their 200 years of slave labor.

Turner, like most advocates of back-to-Africa schemes, met with little success. Most African American—especially the small middle class—opposed Turner's efforts, apparently preferring to go along with the accommodationist approach of Booker Washington than to risk the perils of emigration across the Atlantic. This is an enduring dilemma of nationalist emigrationists; most African Americans do not wish to leave the United States. In addition, absence of support from middle-class blacks makes it difficult to finance emigration schemes. Turner did organize the Colored Emigration League, publish a monthly newsletter, and establish the Afro-American Steamship Company. For a time he was an honorary vice president of the American Colonization Society, an organization of racists formed in the 1770s shortly after the Revolutionary War. This group favored emigration because, in its view, the United States should be a white man's country. Also, Turner was able to persuade several racist southern congressmen to introduce emigration legislation. This is another dilemma for black nationalist groups: Their potential white coalition partners tend to be racists and white supremacists. Marcus Garvey in the 1920 and more recently Louis Farrakhan have talked to representatives of the KKK and other racist groups about forming coalitions to secure emigration or separation.

Although Turner's movement ended with his death and with little success (it is estimated that perhaps a thousand blacks emigrated to Africa),[10] Turner's rhetoric (he was the first black leader to declare that God was black, a notion later advanced by Marcus Garvey and some sects of the Black Muslims) and strategy of organization was followed by subsequent nationalist leaders and organizations.

Marcus Garvey and the Universal Negro Improvement Association

The second major black nationalist movement was organized in Harlem by Marcus Garvey in 1914. Garvey's organization was called the Universal Negro Improvement Association. At its peak in the 1920s, it claimed a membership of 2 million in the

United States and the West Indies.[11] Like Turner, Garvey declared that God, Jesus, and the angels were black, that whites were an inferior race, and that blacks should return to Africa and restore its past glories. He also founded a steamship company, a newspaper, and a number of small factories and businesses. A charismatic leader and powerful orator, like Louis Farrakhan today he would draw huge crowds to his rallies. An autocratic leader, in 1921 Garvey declared himself provisional president of Africa although he had never set foot on the continent and never would.

Like Turner's movement, Garvey's was opposed by most blacks, with his strongest base of support coming from among the poor and working classes of the big city ghettos of the North. Also, like Turner's movement, Garvey's was opposed by the mainstream, middle-class black leadership establishment (an especially bitter critic was W.E.B. Du Bois). Unlike Turner's movement, Garvey's attracted the attention of the federal government, since its mass following and radicalism appeared to be a threat to internal security. In 1925, Garvey and several of his associates were indicted on federal mail fraud charges of using the mail to sell phony stock in his steamship company. His associates were found not guilty, but Garvey was convicted, sentenced to prison for several years, then deported. He died in London in 1940. With his deportation in 1927, his organization and movement split into a number of small sects and factions and lost its effectiveness.

Louis Farrakhan and the Nation of Islam: The Resurgence of Black Nationalism in the Post-Civil Rights Era

The most influential black nationalist leader and organization of the post-Civil Rights Era is Minister Louis Farrakhan and the Nation of Islam. The Nation of Islam—popularly known as the Black Muslims—was founded by W.D. Fard in 1931. After Fard's disappearance it was led by Elijah Muhammad until his death in 1976.[12] Like Garvey's movement, the Nation was based on racial chauvinism, glorifying everything black and condemning whites as devils.

The Nation grew slowly until the charismatic Malcolm X became its national spokesman in the 1960s. Malcolm helped to build a large following for the group among the urban poor and working class.[13] The Nation, like the Garvey movement, established chapters (mosques) throughout the country, operated small businesses and farms, and published a weekly newspaper. Unlike the Garvey and Turner movements, the Nation did not establish a steamship line since it does not favor emigration to Africa. Instead, it desires the creation of a separate black nation within the boundaries of the United States.

When Elijah Muhammad died in 1976, the Nation of Islam split into a series of sects and factions; the main body of the group, led by Wallace Muhammad, Elijah Muhammad's son, was transformed into a mainstream, integrationist (including whites as members), orthodox Islamic group.[14] For a short time in the 1970s, the Nation of Islam disappeared. This was the objective of J. Edgar Hoover and the FBI. Sometime before the death of Elijah Muhammad (the date is not clear), Hoover sent a memorandum to the special agent in charge of the Chicago office, which in part said:

> The NOI (Nation of Islam) appears to be the personal fiefdom of Elijah Muhammad. When he dies a power struggle can be expected and the NOI could change direction. We should be prepared for this eventuality. We should plan now to change the philosophy of the NOI to one of strictly religious and self-improvement orientation,

deleting the race hatred and the separate nationhood aspects. In this connection Chicago should consider what counter intelligence action might be needed now or at the time of Elijah Muhammad's death to bring about such a change in the NOI philosophy. Important considerations should include the identity, strengths and weaknesses of any contender for NOI leader. The alternative to changing the philosophy of the NOI is the destruction of the organization. This might be accomplished through generating factionalism among the contenders for Elijah Muhammad's leadership or through legal action in probate court.[15]

For a while Minister Farrakhan acquiesced in the transformation of the Nation into a strictly religious, integrationist organization. However, after a year or so, he set about to rebuild the Nation on the basis of the original principles of Elijah Muhammad.[16] However, in his clearest break with the traditions of the Nation, Farrakhan in 1993 abandoned the doctrine of nonparticipation in American Electoral politics. Under Elijah Muhammad, members of the Nation were strictly forbidden to participate in American politics, which he described as the "devil's" system. Farrakhan abandoned this position first by encouraging his followers to register and vote for Chicago mayoral candidate Harold Washington in 1983 and then by supporting Jesse Jackson's campaign for president in 1984.

Unlike most African American organizations, the Nation of Islam receives no money from white corporations or businesses. It has approximately 120 mosques in various cities around the country, operates a series of modest small business enterprises, and has a somewhat effective social welfare system for its members. It publishes a weekly newspaper—*The Final Call*—and Farrakhan may be seen and heard on more than 120 radio and television stations around the country. The organization does not reveal the size of its membership, but it is estimated at no more than 20,000. However, the Nation and Farrakhan have millions of followers. A 1994 *Time* magazine poll found that 73 percent of blacks were familiar with Farrakhan, making him, with Jesse Jackson, the best known African American leader. Most blacks familiar with Farrakhan view him favorably, with 65 percent saying he was an effective leader, 63 percent that he speaks the truth, and 62 percent that he was good for black America.[17] The *Time* poll that produced these figures was taken prior to Farrakhan's success in calling the Million Man March, the largest demonstration in Washington in American history.

Black Nationalism and the Million Man March

Most African Americans are integrationists. That is, they believe that universal freedom and equality are possible in the United States and that blacks should struggle to achieve these goals. Yet, as a sentiment, nationalism is an enduring force in African American society, invoking as it does historical consciousness of race oppression, race solidarity, and collective race responsibility. Aspects of this nationalist sentiment may be observed in the data reported in Table 8.4.

First, although only 23 percent of the African American population accept the fundamental nationalist belief that "equality will never be achieved in America," 77 percent agree that "American society is not fair to blacks." There is strong support for a black political party, for all-male black public schools, and for the idea that blacks should control the economy and government in predominantly black communities. Ironically, support for the most extreme nationalist sentiment—a separate black nation—has nearly doubled since the end of the black power movement. In 1968 at the peak of the black

Table 8.4
Attitudes of Black Americans toward Elements of Black Nationalist Ideology, 1993-1994

Statements from Survey[a]	Percent Agreeing
Equality will never be achieved in America	23
American society is not fair to blacks	77
Blacks should form their own political party	50
Blacks should always vote for a black candidate	26
Blacks should support creation of all-male black public schools	62
Blacks should control the economy in predominantly black communities	74
Blacks should form a nation within a nation	49
Blacks should have their own separate nation	14

Source: Michael Dawson and Ronald Brown, "Black Discontent: The Preliminary Report of the 1993-94 National Black Politics Study," Report #1, University of Chicago. Results are based on a representative, randomly selected sample of the national black population. Percentages are of respondents agreeing with the statements.

power movement only 7 percent of blacks supported the idea of a separate black nation,[18] but in the 1993-1994 survey this support had doubled to 14 percent. While most blacks reject the idea of the creation of a separate black nation, almost half (49 percent) embrace the sentiment that blacks in America are a people apart, a "nation within a nation."

According to Professor Michael Dawson, who conducted the survey reported in Table 8.4, support for black nationalist sentiments has increased in the last decade, especially among middle-class blacks.[19] Sensing this growth in black nationalist sentiments, Minister Farrakhan called on a million black men to march on Washington on October 16, 1995. The figures are in dispute, but it is probable that a million men (and several thousand women) did march on Washington.[20] Most of the mainstream press ignored the march, and many prominent blacks and virtually all whites who made comments attacked the march because it was led by Farrakhan, whom they described as a "racist, sexist, and anti-semitic, homophobic demagogue." Nevertheless, as the day of the march approached, it was endorsed by Jesse Jackson and many other prominent blacks, including the poet Maya Angelou and a number of other well-known black women.

According to Farrakhan, the purpose of the march was moral: a call for atonement, reconciliation, and the acceptance by black men of responsibility for family and community. Farrakhan is usually portrayed in the mainstream press as a radical extremist; but in his emphasis on moral reform and traditional values with respect to family life, sex, and alcohol and drug use, as well as his condemnation of welfare dependency, he is rather conservative. Thus, the moral basis of the march is quite consistent with the philosophy of Farrakhan and the tradition of the Nation of Islam.

On the day of the march, two surveys were conducted: one by the *Washington Post* and the other by a group of Howard University political scientists. Both show similar results in terms of the backgrounds of the marchers and their social and political attitudes.[21] The Howard University survey team interviewed 1,070 men. Its results show that the men who attended the march were primarily from the middle and upper-middle class of the black community, were middle-age, married, and mostly Christian (only 8 percent were muslims).[22] Ideologically, 31 percent identified themselves as liberal, 21 percent as moderate, 13 percent as conservative, 11 percent as nationalist, and 4 percent as socialist (21 percent used some other ideological label).[23] These men were also extraordinarily politically active; 86 percent were registered to vote, 55 percent had lobbied a public official, 87 percent had signed a petition, and 45 percent had worked in political campaigns.[24] When asked why the attended the march, 88 percent cited improving moral values in the black community, 77 percent mentioned moral atonement and reconciliation, but others also expressed nationalist reasons. Eighty-five percent said the march encouraged black self-determination and unity, and 75 percent said they attended as a way to promote independent economic development.[25]

Black nationalist movements tend to come in cycles. Bracey, Meier, and Rudwick suggest that there have been four relatively distinct periods when nationalism was especially salient in African American politics and society, each coinciding with especially difficult or disappointing times for the race.[26] The extraordinary success of the Million Man March (a million men represents more than 10 percent of the black male population), consisting of mostly middle-class and politically active individuals, suggests that we may be on the verge of a new cycle of nationalism (see Box 8.3). The conditions are certainly ripe for such a new cycle. After a period of optimism

---

Box 8.3
The African American Reparation Movement

In the post-Reconstruction Era, Bishop Henry M. Turner was the first African American leader to demand reparation—repayment for the damages of slavery—from the American government. After the Civil War, there was talk of providing a kind of reparation to blacks in the form of "forty acres and a mule." In the 1865 Freedmen's Bureau Act, Congress included a provision granting blacks forty acres of abandoned land in the southern states. President Andrew Johnson, however, vetoed the bill, arguing that to take land from the former slave owners was "contrary to that provision of the Constitution which declares that no person shall 'be deprived of life, liberty and property without due process of law.'"[a] The closest the U.S. government ever came to paying reparation was General William Sherman's Special Order #15 issued on January 16, 1865.[b] It provided 40 acres to black families living on the Georgia and South Carolina coasts (some of the descendants of these families still live or own property on these lands). Blacks, however, never abandoned their claims for reparation, and the recent payment by the Congress and several American cities of reparation to Japanese Americans for their World War II incarceration has led to the rebirth of an African American movement seeking similar renumeration.

The contemporary reparation movement is led by Imari Obadele, a professor of political science at the historically black Prairie View A&M University and the former provision-

(continued)

Box 8.3

Continued

al president of the Republic of New Africa. The Republic of New Africa is a black nationalist organization founded in 1968 by Obadele (who was then known as Richard Henry). The organization favors the creation of a separate, all-black nation in the southern part of the United States. In 1989 Obadele and others formed the National Coalition of Blacks for Reparations (NCOBRA), a nonprofit coalition of black religious, civic, and fraternal organizations. Since its formation the coalition has engaged in a variety of tactics to advance the cause of reparation, including petitions to Congress and the president, lawsuits, and protest demonstrations at the White House.

African American supporters of reparation cite a number of precedents regarding reparation.[c] But the one cited most frequently and the one that gave impetus to this new movement was the decision by Congress in 1988 to issue an apology and pay $20,000 to each Japanese American (or his or her survivors) incarcerated during World War II.[d] Earlier the cities of Los Angeles and San Francisco had taken similar actions. Using the Japanese case as a precedent, NCOBRA has made a proposal to Congress, called "An Act to Stimulate Economic Growth in the United States and Compensate, in Part, for the Grievous Wrongs of Slavery and the Unjust Enrichment Which Accrued to the United States Therefrom." The proposal indicates no dollar amount for payment (suggesting that the figure be established by an independent commission, as was done in the Japanese American case) but requires that one-third of the payment go to each individual African man, woman, and child; one-third to the Republic of New Africa; and one-third to a national congress of black church, civic, and civil rights organizations.[e]

In the Japanese case, the first step was the appointment by the Congress of a commission to study the issue. Thus, in 1995, Congressman John Conyers, an African American, and Congressman Norman Mineta, a Japanese American, introduced a bill to establish a "Commission to Study Reparations for African Americans."[f] Also, in 1995 several African Americans filed a suit in federal court in California asking the court to direct the government to pay reparation. The Court of Appeals of the Ninth Circuit rejected the suit, holding that the United States could not be sued unless it waived its "sovereign immunity" and that the "appropriate forum for policy questions of this sort . . . is Congress rather than the courts."[g]

This new reparation movement is just getting under way, and given the present climate of race relations in the United States, the prospects for its success do not appear good.[h] However, in part because of the publication in 2000 of *The Debt: What America Owes Blacks* by Randall Robinson, the head of TransAfrica, the issue has at least received increased attention. Articles have appeared in leading newspapers and magazines; local and state legislative bodies have taken up the issue; it has been the topic of lively debate on college campuses, on the internet, and local and national talk radio programs; and in 2001 the *Philadelphia Inquirer* published two full-page editorials urging the creation of a national

(continued)

> **Box 8.3**
>
> **Continued**
>
> commission on reparations. Following the 1992 decision of the state of Florida to pay reparations to the survivors and descendants of Rosewood (a black town that was destroyed by a white mob in 1923) the Oklahoma Commission to Study the Tulsa Race Riots of 1921 recommended that the survivors and descendants be paid reparations for the riots in which white mobs attacked a black neighborhood, destroying homes and businesses and killing hundreds of people.
>
> [a]The text of the Freedmen's Bureau bill and President Johnson's veto message are in *The Forty Acres Documents*, Introduction by Amitcar Shabazz (Baton Rouge, LA: The House of Songhay, 1994): 65, 74, 75-94.
>
> [b]The text of Sherman's Order is also in *The Forty Acres Document,* pp. 51-58.
>
> [c]See Boris Bittker, *The Case for Black Reparations* (New York: Random House, 1973) and Daisy Collins, "Reparations for Black Citizens," *Howard University Law Review* 82(1979).
>
> [d]Tom Kenworthy, "House Votes Apology, Reparations for Japanese Americans," *Washington Post,* September 18, 1987, p. A1.
>
> [e]Chokwe Lumumba, Imari Obadele, and Nkechi Taifa, *Reparations NOW!* (Baton Rouge, LA: The House of Songhay, 1995): 67.
>
> [f]The text of the Conyers-Mineta bill is in Lumumba, Obadele, and Taifa, *Reparations NOW!,* pp. 97-107.
>
> [g]*Cato et al. v. United States of America,* United States Circuit Court of Appeals, 9th Circuit #94-17102 (1995): 15162.
>
> [h]An ABC News poll found that overall 77 percent of Americans were opposed to reparation for blacks. Sixty-five percent of blacks supported the idea, while it was opposed by 88 percent of whites. See ABC News *Nightline,* July 7, 1997.

about the possibility of universal freedom and equality following the success of the civil rights movement, many blacks now sense a turning back of the clock, a sense that history may be repeating itself in terms of a second Reconstruction. This sense of pessimism is fueled by the ongoing Reagan revolution as reflected in the election of a Republican congressional majority, the conservative tilt of the Clinton administration, and a series of adverse Supreme Court decisions on affirmative action and the Voting Rights Act. It is also fueled by a growing sense that the mainstream, establishment black leadership of elected officials and civil rights leaders has no plan, program, or strategy to deal with the deteriorating conditions of poor black communities.[27]

Notes

1. Harold Wolman and Norman Thomas, "Black Interests, Black Groups and Black Influence in the Federal Policy Process: The Cases of Housing and Education," *Journal of Politics* 32(November 1970): 875-97.

2. Diane Pinderhughes, "Racial Interest Groups and Incremental Politics" (unpublished paper, University of Illinois, Urbana, 1980): 36.

3. A substantial part of the budgets of both the NAACP and the Urban League comes from contributions by white foundations and corporations. See Robert C. Smith, *We Have No Leaders: African Americans in the Post-Civil Rights Era* (Albany: SUNY Press, 1996), 86-96.
4. Ibid., p. 122.
5. See Audre Lorde, *I Am Your Sister: Black Women Organizing Across Sexualities* (Latham, NY: Kitchen Table Women of Color Press, 1985).
6. On black feminism see Paula Giddings, *When and Where I Enter: The Impact of Black Women on Race and Sex in America* (New York: William Morrow, 1984) and Patricia Hill Collins, *Black Feminist Thought* (New York: Routledge, 1991).
7. Edwin Redkey, "The Flowering of Black Nationalism: Henry McNeal Turner and Marcus Garvey," in Nathan Huggins, Martin Kilson, and Daniel Fox, eds., *Key Issues in the Afro-American Experience*, vol. 2 (New York: Harcourt Brace Jovanovich, 1971): 115.
8. On the historical origins of black nationalist thought, see Sterling Stuckey, *The Ideological Origins of Black Nationalism* (Boston: Beacon, 1972), and Sterling Stuckey, *Slave Culture: Foundations of Nationalist Thought* (New York: Oxford, 1967).
9. Stuckey, *The Ideological Origins of Black Nationalism*.
10. Ibid., p. 114.
11. See Edmund Cronon, *Black Moses: The Story of Marcus Garvey and the Universal Negro Improvement Association* (Madison: University of Wisconsin Press, 1955).
12. Claude Andrew Clegg, *An Original Man: The Life and Times of Elijah Muhammad* (New York: St. Martin's Press, 1997).
13. Bruce Perry, *Malcolm: The Life of a Man Who Changed Black America* (Barrytown, NY: Station Hill Press, 1991).
14. Don Terry, "Black Muslims Enter Islamic Mainstream," the *New York Times*, May 3, 1993.
15. The Hoover memorandum is quoted in Imam Sidney Sharif, "Hoover Plotted against Muslims," *Atlanta Voice*, February 22, 1986.
16. On Farrakhan's strategy to revitalize the Nation of Islam, see Smith, *We Have No Leaders*, pp. 99-100; Lawrence Mamiya, "From Black Muslim to Bialian: The Evolution of a Movement," *Journal for the Scientific Study of Religion* 21(1982): 141; and Mattias Gardell, *In the Name of Elijah Muhammad: Louis Farrakhan and the Nation of Islam* (Durham, NC: Duke University Press, 1996). Gardell's work contains a detailed analysis of the theological underpinnings of the Nation of Islam.
17. William Henry, "Pride and Prejudice," *Time*, February 28, 1994, p. 22.
18. Angus Campbell and Howard Schuman, *Racial Attitudes in Fifteen American Cities* (Ann Arbor: University of Michigan, Institute for Social Research, 1971): 18.
19. Michael Dawson, "Structure and Ideology: The Shaping of Black Public Opinion," paper prepared for presentation at the 1995 Annual Meeting of the Midwest Political Science Association, Chicago, p. 29.
20. "Million Man March Draws More Than 1 Million Black Men to Washington," *Jet*, October 30, 1995, pp. 3-11. A good documentary record of the march including the full program, the major speeches, mission statement, and selected press commentary is in Haki Madhubuti and Ron Karenga, eds., *Million Man*

March/Day of Absence (Chicago: Third World Press, 1996).
21. For the *Washington Post* survey, see "Million Man March Survey," October 17, 1995, p. A23.
22. Lorenzo Morris et al., "Million Man March: Preliminary Report on the Survey" (Washington, DC: Howard University, 1995): 2-3. See also Joseph P. McCormick, "The Message and the Messengers: Opinions from the Million Men Who Marched," *National Political Science Review* 6(1997): 142-64.
23. Morris, "Million Man March: Preliminary Report on the Survey," pp. 4-5.
24. Ibid.
25. Ibid., p. 6. In November 1997 a million black women gathered in Philadelphia to promote unity and community development. See "Million Woman March," *Jet*, November 10, 1997, pp. 5-18.
26. John Bracey, Jr., August Meier, and Elliot Rudwick, *Black Nationalism in America* (Indianapolis: Bobbs-Merrill, 1970): xxx-liii. The four time periods are the 1770s, 1840s, 1880s, and late 1960s.
27. Smith, *We Have No Leaders*, especially chap. 11.

References

Garson, G. David. *Group Theories of Politics*. Beverly Hills: Sage, 1978. A review and critique of the major theories and the research on the interest group basis of American politics.

Giddings, Paula. *When and Where I Enter: The Impact of Black Women on Race and Sex in America*. New York: William Morrow, 1984. One of the earliest and best studies of the subject.

Hamilton, Dana, and Charles Hamilton. *The Dual Agenda: Social Policies of Civil Rights Organizations from the New Deal to the Present*. New York: Columbia University Press, 1996. Although they do not use the terms *rights based* and *material based*, this book is an exhaustive study of the dual agenda of black Americans.

Lowi, Theodore. *The End of Liberalism*. New York: Norton, 1979. An influential study of how interest groups manipulate public policy making in pursuit of narrow, parochial interests.

Pinderhughes, Dianne. "Collective Goods and Black Interest." *Review of Black Political Economy* 12(Winter 1983): 219-36. A largely theoretical analysis of the role of black interest groups in pursuing the multiple policy interests of blacks in an environment of resource constraints.

Pinderhughes, Dianne. "Black Interest Groups and the 1982 Extension of the Voting Rights Act" (pp. 203-24). In Huey Perry and Wayne Parent, eds. *Blacks and the American Political System*. Gainesville: University Press of Florida, 1995. A case study of African American interest group politics in the context of the contemporary civil rights coalition.

Smith, Robert C. *We Have No Leaders: African Americans in the Post-Civil Rights Era*. Albany: SUNY Press, 1996. A detailed study of the transformation of the 1960s African American freedom struggle from movement to interest groups politics, focusing on African American interest groups, the Congressional Black Caucus, black presidential appointees in the executive branch, and Jesse Jackson's Rainbow Coalition.

Stuckey, Sterling. *The Ideological Origins of Black Nationalism*. Boston: Beacon, 1972. A seminal study that includes some of the classic black nationalist writings.

The National Urban League in the Development of Leadership among African American Women

Minion K. C. Morrison
The University of Missouri

This study assesses the role of the National Urban League (NUL), historically one of the major rights organizations, in African American women's leadership development. The League has done this in two principal ways—via a mission at the turn of the century focused on assistance to African American migrant women to urban centers; and through positions as executive officers of League affiliates, the local chapter organizations. This study of these twin roles consists of a historical assessment of women in the NUL, and a comparative analysis of two women who have assumed positions as Executive Directors of NUL affiliates, and their implementation of programs under the direction of the national organization.

The study reveals that historically the NUL has been involved with a series of issues central to the development of African American women as leaders. This first occurred in its fundamental training for and placement of women in the early days of American urbanization. And it has been of singular importance in developing a field of inquiry, social work, whose original focus was issues traditionally associated with women's work in the household. Moreover, the study also reveals the increasing role women play as heads of authoritative positions in affiliates. The two cases analyzed provide illustrative examples of this evolution and process in the NUL.

Copyright © Minion K. C. Morrison. Reprinted by permission of the author.

The General Study of Leadership and Women

Until recent times the general theories and analyses of leadership in the western world reflected the gender bias in social organization that largely barred women from public affairs participation. These early general theories then did not associate women with the traits deemed necessary for leadership. The important factors for focus was an intuitive set of characteristics such as charisma, intelligence, and strength referred to "great men" in history, and not women (Carlyle, 1907). This gender exclusivism was so nearly complete that even when theory improved, such that actual behavior could be described, there was little women's behavior to describe in the "public" sphere. Women's roles were confined to the "personal" area of household and family, and rarely did they occupy traditional positions of power (Flammang, 1997, 101).

Recent times have seen a proliferation of studies from specialists in feminist theory that reveal the greatly expanded participation and leadership of women in politics. This has been done in two ways. First, women have greatly expanded their participation in traditional roles and positions since suffrage. And scholars have greatly expanded the theory of what constitutes the political—demonstrating the importance of the "personal" to organization and processes of politics (Evans, 1979). At the same time, we have learned a good deal about the distinct practices and approaches women's activity add to general theory. Northouse (1997, p. 209) has summarized these as follows: the use of consensus in decision; the view of power as relational; focus on conflict resolution; building a supportive work environment; and support for diversity.

Leadership in the Black Community

Explaining the historical development of leadership among African American women cannot be separated from the general history of leadership within the racial and cultural community. African American women, like men, are products of enslavement and its residual discriminations that led to long-term total and later partial exclusion from routine representation of their constituents in the democratic polity. This had the effect of spawning peculiar types of early leaders within a community where such activity was suspicious or illegal. The earliest public spokespeople (leaders) indigenous to the community were notables who emerged in the subterranean world of the enslaved, given those limited parameters, to organize a community (Blassingame, 1979; Genovese, 1976). Their traits were consistent with those commonly associated with leaders anywhere at the time—drive, motivation, integrity, confidence, cognitive ability and task knowledge (Kirkpatrick and Locke, 1991).

Later these traits were associated with a variety of leaders who were active as abolitionists. These men and women used their notable skills to devise means for defeating the enslavement system and/or for minimizing its impact on the daily lives of Blacks. Some of these leaders like Paul Cuffee sought to challenge the system on its own terms by petitioning for political rights within the U.S. democracy. He also was one of the early exponents of exit for Blacks, a model adopted by other leaders over the years (Bracey, 1970). Then there were other proponents of violent overthrow of the system, like Nat Turner, who led major slave revolts (Aptheker, 1943). Still others used their distinctive traits as orators and community organizers mobilizing the public for action, and spearheading personal relief efforts to spirit Blacks away from the plantations. These classical social movement leaders (Tarrow, 1994) included, among others, men such as Frederick Douglass (Quarles, 1948). But most significantly, some of the most successful social movement leaders in this period were women. The best known are Sojourner Truth, a latter day feminist leader (Painter, 1996); and Harriett Tubman, leader of the "Underground Railroad," (Sterling, 1954). In short, early African American women leaders found themselves equally bound (as were Black men) to efforts to resolve the intractable problem of enslavement and other exclusions based on race.

The resolution of what W.E.B. DuBois called the "problem of the twentieth century," became an abiding focus for African American leaders, and also structured the early scholarly literature that sought to encapsulate ideas about leadership within this racial and cultural community. Not surprisingly, the literature focused on several general themes about how to resolve the problem of racial exclusion—via creation of a national community (here or elsewhere), or via integration into the democratic polity. In assessing early spokespeople for the community one can easily see them trying to work out a resolution in reference to one or the other of these general themes. The classic juxtaposition of the two is best seen in the variations in aims of DuBois (radical integration) (1961) and Booker T. Washington (conservative nationalism) (Harlan, 1972). This occurred in the period when community leadership was still determined by means other than the routine representative system of U.S. government, as most Blacks were still excluded from the franchise. But the variations may also be seen in the approaches of several constituent leaders when Blacks became able to choose their own representative leaders [of the distinct approaches of elected leaders William Dawson (Pinderhughes, 1977) vis-a-vis Adam Clayton Powell (Hamilton, 1992].

Black women were also engaged in leadership activity that was both a product of gendered spaces in public affairs, and of a "feminist" perspective. Being barred from public affairs positions then occupied almost exclusively by white men, women dominated a variety of other community "volunteer" organizations, at the same time that they sought to expand the franchise. The roles of Black women were considerable (far exceeding those of their white counterparts) in both independent community organizations, and auxiliaries of their churches. However, they, like their white cohorts, contributed to activities that built a "political culture of women's organizations" (Guy-Sheftall, 1990, p. 93).

Moreover, there have always been organizations in which Black women were active which had a public affairs function not revealed by organizational titles (Terborg-Penn, 1995). A wealth of typical examples exist in just one region, the South, between 1895 and 1920. Cynthia Neverdon-Morten (1995) identifies scores of urban, rural and national clubs and self-help organizations there. Meanwhile, Hine and Thompson (1998) document women's public affairs roles more broadly during the period between the two world wars. Women were much more connected to each other in the spaces afforded them, and their style of organization and process led to a greater range of networks for cooperation and deployment (Fleammang, 1997). It was from these multiple and overlapping groups that there emerged a political culture of Black women's organizations that defined a broad sector of organized activity in their communities.

The Role of the NUL in Black Women's Leadership Development

The NUL is one of the major organizations dedicated to the improvement of the Black community which has historically been engaged with women and their preparation for leadership roles. Despite an image as a conservative group, dominated by major corporations, the NUL has borne an essential, if partial responsibility, for working with Black women, and for protecting "women's work." Its history in this regard has been very rich. Doubtless our lack of this knowledge reveals much about the gendered character of American political history. And while the particular origins of the NUL are not ignored, studies of the organization have tended to focus on its undeniably important role in the development of major male civil rights leaders (Dickerson, 1998; Weiss, 1989).

In order to fully appreciate the role of the NUL in the training of women, one must look at its roots in two spheres: its target of poor urban communities and its grounding in the social work tradition. Both strands were represented in the two principal figures associated with the founding of the NUL—Ruth Standish Baldwin, a philanthropist to the poor; and George Haynes, one of the earliest trained "social workers" (Moore, Jr., 1981). The organization sought to respond to the peculiar social service needs of African Americans in the urban cities, at the same time that it sought to build the independent capacity of these new communities. While the capacity-building function could be associated with the self-reliance ideology of Booker T. Washington (Harlan, 1972), the then emerging field of social work was much more important. It was the focus of this new field on the provision of assistance to families to alleviate the strains of the urban dislocations (Moore, Jr., 1981, Weiss, 1989) that was a prevailing idea for the NUL. To this end a part of the NUL mission became the development of supports and efficiencies for African Americans as they negotiated their way through the socio-economic and political system, in pursuit of the American dream. This status quo orientation toward the prevailing political ideology was seen as entirely consistent with the broader goal of uplift for the African American community and the full realization of the democratic promise in the broader American social and political experiment. And this continues to be reflected in the current articulation of the mission:

> The mission of the National Urban League is to assist African Americans in the achievement of social and economic equality. The Board of Trustees of the National Urban League and all of its affiliates reflect a diverse body of community, government, and corporate leaders. The League implements its mission through advocacy, bridge building, program services and research.

As the nation was becoming more urban at the turn of the twentieth century, there were an increasing number of strains in the traditional family structure as mass transportation facilitated the movement of people to centers where industrial growth spawned employment opportunities. These economic developments, largely in the North, when combined with continuing racial exclusion in the South, were increasingly attractive to Blacks. However, the strains on these economically more fragile families, were much more dramatic. Often they were not just fragmented, but involved migration of members without partners. This break in the traditional extended family structure was especially critical for single or displaced African American women migrants to the new urban spaces.

The importance of women as a target population for what was to become the NUL occurred at the beginning. An organization then known as the National League for the Protection of Color Women had been founded in 1905 for the purposes its name implies (Weiss, 1974; Hine, 1993). Meanwhile, there were two other organizations with broader purposes—the Committee for the Improvement of Conditions Among Negroes in New York (1906), and the Committee On Urban Conditions Among Negroes (1910) which merged in 1911 to form the organization we know today (Weiss, 1974). This merger brought together the major groups that had formed to work on the conditions of the urban poor. And because a central partner to the merger was specifically focused on women, therein lies the roots of the historical role for the NUL in African American women's training for leadership and social betterment. The new organization now assumed the responsibilities of the National League for the Protection of Women—job location and placement, travel aid, and housing, *inter alia*.

The Role of Women in the Contemporary National Urban League

Hardly anyone would assert that the contemporary NUL is an organization whose principal aim is the preparation of African American women for leadership positions. Yet the organization continues its dedication to a mission that is central to women's roles as partners/breadwinners in families, and as public leaders. And moreover, the NUL is one of the principal organizations whose general mission is dedicated to alleviating the socioeconomic dislocations of African Americans. It is from this vantage point that the subject of this analysis asks how significantly women figure into the life of the present-day NUL and its affiliates. What is the character of women's representation in the hierarchy of the organization; how much of a bearing do issues that specifically relate to lives of African American women have on the organization's activities; and most importantly, in what ways are women involved in the all important affiliates that actually implement the goals of the parent body?

This part of the analysis might best begin by describing the present organization. It has grown over the years in scope, influence, and size. Its fortunes had grown such that by the time of the civil rights movement of the 1960s, the NUL was regarded as one of the "Big Three" traditionally organized African American rights groups—NUL, National Association for the Advancement of Colored People (NAACP), and the Southern Christian Leadership Conference (SCLC). The three men who headed these organizations, Whitney Young (NUL), Roy Wilkins (NAACP) and Martin Luther King (SCLC), were core actors in establishing the civil rights policy agenda, and in serving as bridges to traditional sources of power in government and business. And Whitney Young's position as head of NUL with its links to both government and business may well have had the most extensive connections among the Big Three. By self-description the NUL today is an "organization with strong roots in the community, focused on the social and educational development of youth, economic self-sufficiency and racial inclusion. . . . (and) serves more than two million individuals each year. (NUL Website)" It has grown to 115 affiliates in cities in every region of the country, including an extensive network of affiliates in the previously inhospitable urban South (Strickland, 1966).

The Historical Involvement and Representation of Women in the NUL

The involvement of African American women with the NUL has been substantial from the organization's inception—being both providers of skills and as consumers of the services offered by the organization. Their critical role is explained in part by the "social service" function of the League, a sector in which women in general were more active. At the same time, the strategic niche that Black women occupied in the urban environment, made them more likely candidates for NUL services. Elsa Barkley Brown has stated this deftly:

> Thus the National Urban League in its first three decades provided support for working-class women adjusting to life in the city and for the more well-to-do professional women and artists seeking opportunities and support for their careers. In turn, the support and expertise of Black women in the local Urban League affiliates was crucial to the development of the Urban League, laying the foundation of the reorganization that would emerge in the next decades as a major force in the continuing struggle for civil and economic rights for African Americans (Hine, 1993, p. 871).

Thus while Whitney Young once stated some ambivalence about the role of Black women in public life vis-a-vis Black men (Dickerson, 1998, p. 292), throughout his service to the NUL he always saw women working there in the most important roles. Moreover, he was certainly aware of the seminal contribution women made to the organization throughout its history. He was aware that it was African American women who had the greatest influence in founding, leading and providing structure to the early affiliates. And because the national organization was entirely dependent on these local units for implementation of the mission, in some ways it was women who gave the organization substance. Similarly, Young and every predecessor at the helm of the NUL had been active sponsors of the training of women. For example, eight of the 17 fellowships given by the agency for professional training appropriate to the organization's mission by 1920 went to women (Hine, 1993, p. 871). Many of them later became employees of the organization.

Women achieved League leadership mostly via their highly organized and widely dispersed women's clubs, and through their involvement in the settlement houses. As an example, three of the more important affiliates were dominated by women, many of them African American—those in Chicago, Atlanta and Boston. The Chicago affiliate had its bonafides established on the strength of support from the Black clubwomen of the city who provided the bulk of early funding. They then went on to provide much of the early leadership as both executive director and on the board of trustees (Strickland, 1966). In the early days of the Urban League of Greater Boston women, from their positions as leaders of settlement houses and leaders of clubs, were at parity serving as board members. Then the Atlanta Neighborhood Union, led by Lugenia Hope of Morehouse College, not only became an affiliate of NUL; its structure and organization served as a model for fledgling affiliates in other cities. Lugenia Hope provided more than "good practice," but was an exponent of the new social work theory in an educational setting that was to become home to the Atlanta University School of Social Work (Hine, 1993, p. 870).

Many of the African American women who were NUL leaders were some of the most prominent in the U.S. Their positions within the League were equally visible and influential. In addition to leadership of local affiliates, they served in important posts as national board members, officers of the national secretariat, and in the national Guild. Among those who were members of the national board were Mary McLeod Bethune, Sadie Alexander, and Mollie Moon. Each of these were distinguished women of achievement—respectively an educator/counsel to Presidents, lawyer, and pharmacist. Moreover, they occupied multiple and complex interlocking roles in the NUL. Bethune served as a Vice President in the 1920s, and Alexander was a national secretary for 25 years. But Moon had the most complex role. In addition to being on the board, she founded the National Urban League Guild, a major fundraising arm of the NUL. She was the Guild's prime mover for almost 50 years (Hine, 1993, p. 872). This long service was matched by another woman who virtually made her career with the League: Ann Tanneyhill served for many years in an affiliate (Springfield, Massachusetts) and at the national secretariat. Among her posts in the national office were as Director of Vocational Services, Assistant to Associate Director of Public Relations, and finally as Director of the George Edmund Haynes Fellowship Program (Hine, 1993, p. 1139).

The Contemporary Role of Women in the Urban League

Despite the tremendous changes in women's public roles in the U.S., and their relatively more diverse roles historically in the African American community, a woman has never led the NUL. And in the sheer visibility of women in its other top executive positions, it compares unfavorably with the NAACP, as an example whose most influential role has now been occupied by a Black woman. But does this signal a lessening of women, and especially Black women, in important roles in the organization? The numbers of women as a proportion of the board have increased between 1980 (about 19 percent and 1998 (about 28 percent) (NUL, 1980 and 1998), though not substantially. However, since NUL leadership is more often exercised through its affiliates, it may be more important to assess the roles of women there. And in looking at the leadership patterns of affiliates in the past 15 to 20 years, a significant shift in leadership roles for women is observed. While in 1980 women led just ten of 116 affiliates, today they lead nearly 40, a spectacular shift. And in interviews for this research, African American affiliate executives reported that this shift is significant beyond numbers, but in the distinct training and skills these women bring to the organization.

Therefore, in order to assess the contemporary role of women in the NUL, the balance of this analysis is focused on two recent affiliate executives, who seem to represent an entire class of new leadership for the NUL. These are women who are more likely to fill leadership roles that are increasingly being vacated by older, largely male, affiliate directors. This class of women leaders are described as younger, better educated, and possessing a wider range of training and experience in community networks. They are also said to have proven themselves in previous leadership positions germane to the mission and particular needs of the NUL at this juncture.

Sustained interviews were conducted in 1998 with a present and a former affiliate director of two cities, in traditional areas where the NUL has been strong—the East and Mid-West. These two cities each have a population between 175,000 to 200,000, and were chosen because they seemed illustrative of the places where leadership changes were occurring. They are smaller industrial cities in the

North where shifts in the manufacturing base have caused serious economic displacements for the urban poor, especially for relatively unskilled African Americans and Hispanics. At the time of the research unemployment was high, and there was insufficient job training to help NUL constituents compete successfully in the more service oriented economies.

At the same time, NUL affiliates in cities like these two were also experiencing greater leadership transitions. As older male directors departed, African American women with their variety of training and skills competed more successfully for the vacancies.

One of these cities is in upstate New York. Comparatively, it is a relatively young affiliate, having been founded in 1964. Prior to the selection of the current director, it had not had a woman in its top leadership position (although three women had served as interim). And this old industrial city had seen its economy decline precipitously in the past 25 years, as businesses departed for more favorable climates, or were displaced by technological advances. The level of financial difficulty for the city was acute, threatening the very solvency of the city administration. This made the challenge for this fairly young NUL affiliate especially great. Its constituency of largely unskilled African American migrants from the South was about 15 percent of the population. The affiliate operates with a budget currently just under a million dollars, and chose a local African American, whose roots and career development in the community ran deep, as its first woman executive in 1997.

The second of the cities is in Indiana, and in the heart of the Midwest, and with a population of about 17 percent Blacks. The city is also industrial, and has experienced shifts in its economy with similar consequences to that of the East coast city. Its constituency of African Americans also consists of largely southern migrants, whose skills do not match those required for an increasingly service oriented economy. This affiliate can be described as a fairly old one having started in 1952. It also operates on a budget of about a million dollars. It selected a young African American woman from outside the community who served from 1993-1996, with broad experience in community organizations and local politics.

The affiliates in cities like these were apparently also experiencing acute problems. The field interviews uncovered a general sentiment reflecting transitions in affiliate leadership that were associated with internal organizational and programmatic crisis. For example, both of the subject affiliates were described as in crisis by their new female leaders. They each described some degree of instability in the leadership prior to the succession. They also pointed to a lack of coherence in program, with extraordinary external factors differentially affecting their constituents as the economy shifted. One of the affiliates had three executives in six years, as a permanent successor was being sought. Moreover, it was thought that an absence of programmatic coherence and innovation yielded a lack of credibility for the affiliates among African American constituents and the broader communities as well. Consequently, our women leadership subjects described their challenge as one of major affiliate reconstruction. And they also suggested that some of the distinct skills and strategies they had learned as women were well suited to this task.

Who are these women themselves, and who are those they describe as typical of a new generation of leadership for the NUL as represented in its affiliates? Each has better than a college degree, an achievement they suggest exceeds that for the cohort of leaders being replaced. One of them has a Masters degree in a field related to public policy administration. And, each has come to the NUL with long and very high public profiles.

The upstate New York leader was previously the first woman to serve as a board president of the affiliate that she now heads. She has been on the boards of the Community Foundation and the United Way, the city's well respected symphony orchestra board, and occupied a host of other high level public positions in the community. She was visible both among Blacks and in the broader community of leadership. The midwestern city leader had a similar profile. She served as a United Way executive and board member, on local chapters of the NAACP in several cities, and had been an elected public education official. This leader possessed the widest spectrum of community leadership experience prior to assuming a position as an NUL affiliate executive.

I asked each of the leaders to discuss the evidence of a shift to greater affiliate leadership by women, which my independent census showed as an increase in eighteen years of nearly 30 percent. While each was quick to point out that women had always been involved at the highest levels in the NUL, they noted the sheer increase in the number of women who are holding positions as affiliate executives in the past several years. The interviewees referred to the increased presence of women in the annual NUL leadership training classes, for example. One affiliate leader described the 1977 class of trainees for executive positions as fully half women. Another affiliate leader suggested that this shift has been occurring gradually over the past 15 years. And while they see affiliate leadership as the most substantive in the NUL power hierarchy, reference was also made to considerable increases in women's service as affiliate board chairs.

When asked what contributed to this shift in leadership, the interviewees suggested several factors. In the first place, they see this as a part of a natural transition. As aging executives retire, who tend to be male, the vacancies created simply attract more women competitors. The preference for men as local executive leaders seems to have developed as the NUL became more successful in attracting corporate sponsors, whose executive and board leadership positions were almost entirely devoid of women. And, while the interviewees do not see any particular focus directed at women, it is believed that the generally improved status of women in the society has helped to break down barriers to African American women leadership of NUL executive positions. Indeed it would seem that the NUL has returned to its earlier status when there was actually a preference for or a predominance of women in strategic affiliate positions.

The view was also expressed that now a much larger pool of women with more appropriate skills are bidding for positions as NUL leaders. Like the two affiliate leaders in the subject cases, the new class of women in NUL executive positions are also highly educated. But they also are more likely to have training and experience germane to the mission of social service and community development of NUL. This is consistent with the data which show a spectacular differential between higher education enrollment of African American men and women in general. A long trend where Black women exceed Black men in high school completion continues to the present (Jaynes and Williams, 1989, pp. 336-7). And between 1976 and 1990 Black women's share of college enrollments increased from about 55 percent to 61 percent (Hacker, 1992, p. 178). Therefore, not only are there more women in the workplace, African Americans among them are far better credentialed than African American men.

Similarly, African American women at this juncture appear to possess particularly appropriate experiences. Their experiences from career choices in social service settings is more than comparable to that of their male counterparts. These "new" NUL leaders have been engaged in an array of very visible private, often non-profit, organizations concerned with issues in the African American and other communities at risk. In this regard the affiliate leaders in the eastern and midwestern cities are typical—each was well connected to a host of these organizations and the web of local and national networks that devolved therefrom. Consequently, the leaders in the midwestern and eastern cities believe that they and their cohorts are bringing a wider array of resources to the NUL, specifically as women.

Women's Program Initiatives as Affiliate Directors

It seems evident that women are indeed assuming a wider role in the NUL in their positions as directors of local affiliates. But what difference is this likely to make in an organization whose ties to conservative corporate sponsors may thwart serious departures from status quo interests? The leaders in this study suggest that women are likely to make significant differences not just because of the special skills they bring, but also because of the support they receive from the national headquarters. In the balance of this analysis I discuss their views about program development under crisis circumstances, assess some of their program activity, and review their relations with the national office. It is clear that the women who assumed leadership of the affiliates in this study approached some complex and seemingly intractable problems and turned their organizations around. At the same time, they initiated programs and received sustained support from the national office in doing so.

These affiliate leaders were selected to run organizations that were experiencing crisis. Under these conditions they suggested that innovation and change were necessary and welcomed as the NUL sought the means for restoring these local affiliates to health. Each city had an affiliate where there was leadership instability. In the one city a previous director had departed in the midst of what were termed "gross personal and organizational improprieties". In the other the instability was evident in the extreme high turnover in executives in a short period—three in six years.

Moreover, each affiliate was described as experiencing financial difficulties that resulted from both budget shortfalls, and inefficiencies in management. The one organization had a debt of more than $200,000, which the new executive says she had to resolve. And these problems often contributed to a fundamental loss of credibility among local constituents and corporate and government sponsors as well. Each of the new leaders referred to the major challenge they assumed of revitalizing corporate and government relationships. At the same time they had to restore confidence within the largely African American community the organizations served. The early improvements in organizational stability would seem to suggest that the women enjoyed some success.

Each of these affiliates moved through their crises to a growth in budget and program activity. There was striking similarity in the energy both of these leaders dedicated to management and staffing in their early tenure. Both suggested that they initially worked on reconfiguring their staffs before moving on to expansion. Consistent with the literature on women's managerial style, each of these women referred to their sustained efforts to develop staff, and to bring a human relations perspective to that (Fleammang, 1997). And because there were fiscal concerns, each affiliate also sought additional accounting expertise as the means to greater control and accountability. Subsequently, the staffs and the program budgets for each of these cities was expanded.

The programmatic activity was consistent with the broad areas of the national office. But in each case these affiliates pursued NUL programs not previously available in their cities. Other existing programs were also extended and/or revitalized. A major interest in the East coast city was the integration of technology into its management and training programs. To this end a technology center was created, benefits of which became available for management. However, the most important aim was local community capacity development. One component of the project was the placement of a mini-computer center directly in the community. The executive director described this as the first center of its kind where local NUL constituents who were in job training or preparing for educational advancement have access to an array of information about jobs and education, including online information about college entrance tests like the SAT and ACT. New funds and staff were acquired for this program, some of which came from an NUL allocation of software donated from Microsoft®. The initiative here demonstrates the way the director is determined to compete in the widest range of resource networks for opportunities to strengthen her programs.

The East coast leader's special skills and training were also evident in the emphases and approaches she used in program development. Many of the programs were fairly standard ones found in other NUL affiliates—employment, housing, family support, among others. However, as this director has specific training in management and had served as a long-time program manager, clearly these influenced her directions. There was a lot of emphasis on management and infrastructure, and these were peculiar problems in the local affiliate. A part of this was evident in her almost complete replacement of the staff upon arrival. But she also had to restore several programs for which local funding had been withdrawn. Programs that specifically affected women was another area in which substantial investments were made: training for teenage parents, revolving loans for women, and job counseling. At the same time there was a focus on general family issues: teenage fathers, employment, home ownership, and tenant/landlord relations.

Similarly, the midwestern affiliate aggressively sought funding for new programs and for the revitalization of existing ones. And much of the managerial and program approach here was influenced by the strengths of the director in the areas of education, political leadership, and social advocacy. There were also major efforts to extend affiliate support to a wider spectrum of the constituent community. One of the initiatives that helped to achieve this was the affiliate's acquisition of a youth center previously run by the city. The goal of the affiliate was to strengthen and extend after school, weekend and summer programs for minority youth. A successful capital campaign provided for the renovation of the center and expansion of its programs. This director was significantly aided in sustaining these initiatives because of her previous experience on a school board, developing and overseeing educational programs.

But the director's social and political activism provided a path for tapping into city coffers for human and financial support, even as she championed a strong image for her organization. In part, this was done via collaborative programs with other agencies—e.g. an advocacy program with United Way for African American students concentrated in two city public schools. The advantage, of course, was that this was an organization she knew well, having occupied a senior United Way management position elsewhere. Moreover, her knowledge of city government allowed her to develop and cultivate relationships easily with city leaders and local constituents, as effectively as any politician might. And all of these relationships were fused by a clever public relations or marketing effort. The director wrote a weekly column on local and national issues, and anchored a monthly television program, outlets that gave her high public recognition, even as she contributed to local agenda setting for this community.

Relations with and Support from the National Office

Since neither of these leaders argued that the NUL had any particular priority in the recruitment of women as executive directors, I was curious to understand the nature of the relationship each had with the national office. They described very good relations with the national office, whose support sustained them and the program innovations and expansions undertaken. They were particularly complimentary of the excellent training offered by the national office to new executives. This early training allowed them to establish a rapport with some of the most senior and successful corporate executives in the country. These contacts, they suggested, gave them the opportunity to share their ideas and to obtain new ones for program development in their communities. At the same time the national office was seen as the single most important resource for program support. The affiliates continue to be dependent on the national office for developing many initiatives, and for the accompanying financial backing from its corporate sponsors. Consequently, many templates for programs emanate from the central office and are expected to be picked up by affiliates. These templates are then often expanded via the development of resources, as these women directors have done exceedingly effectively.

In addition, the national office was the chief source of information for the affiliates. This results from the long research tradition of the NUL. The organization began by marshalling data about the socio-economic condition of African Americans as they moved from the southern plantations to the cities. Such data would then be used to develop strategies (in the context of the new social work enterprise) for aiding the urban poor and displaced. The NUL has only strengthened its information base over the years, leading these affiliate directors to cite the current research output as good as any that the national office has ever produced. The NUL produces its independent studies, such as the well respected annual *The State of Black America* (1998), and also amasses and disseminates information produced by others. Each director found the information provided by the national office essential to their local operations.

At the same time that the affiliates felt that the information flow from the national office was critical, it also seemed possible for information to flow upward from local organizations. They felt confident that they had the opportunity to circulate their ideas to the national office and to have these heard and sometimes implemented. In short, they felt fully integrated into the organization.

Conclusion

The NUL remains one of the strongest organizations contributing to the development of African American leadership. It has become in the recent past a significant source for the training and placement of African American women as an increasing number of them are selected as executive directors of NUL affiliates. Though the organization does not appear to have an affirmative program as such for the recruitment of women, the departing older generation of largely male leaders are more often being replaced by women. The applicant pool appears to include a larger number of women, who seem also to have particular training and experiences that comport with current NUL programs. This shift to a greater presence of women in leadership positions actually is consistent with an earlier phase in the history of the NUL when women were more often both leaders and clients of the organization.

References

Aptheker, Herbert. *The American Negro Slave Revolts*. International Publishers, New York, 1943.

Bracey, John, et al, eds. *Black Nationalism in America*. Indianapolis: Bobbs-Merrill, 1970.

Blassingame, John W. *The Slave Community: Plantation Life in the Antebellum South*. Revised. New York: Oxford, 1977.

Carlyle, Thomas. *On Heroes, Hero-Worship, and the Heroic in History*. Boston: Houghton Mifflin, 1907.

Dickerson, Dennis. *Militant Negotiator: Witney M. Young, Jr.* Lexington: University of Kentucky, 1998.

DuBois, William Edward Burghardt. *The Souls of Black Folk*. Greenwich, Conn: Fawsett, 1961.

Fleammang, Janet. *Women's Political Voice: How Women are Transforming the Practice and Study of Politics*. Philadelphia: Temple University, 1997.

Genovese, Eugene D. *Roll, Jordan, Roll: The World the Slaves Made*. New York: Vintage, 1976.

Hacker, Andrew. *Two Nations: Black and White, Separate. Hostile, Unequal*. New York: Ballantine, 1992.

Hamilton, Charles. *Adam Clayton Powell, Jr.: The Political Biography of An American Dilemma*. New York: Collier, 1992.

Harlan, Louis R. *Booker T. Washington: The Making of a Black Leader, 1856-1901*. New York: Oxford, 1972.

Hine, Darlene Clark, et al. *Black Women in American History: An Encyclopedia*. Volume 2. Brooklyn: Carlson, 1993.

Hine, Darlene Clark and Kathleen Thompson. *A Shining Thread of Hope*. New York: Broadway Books, 1998.

Jaynes, Gerald Jaynes and Robin Williams, Jr., eds. *A Common Destiny: Blacks and American Society*. Washington, D.C.: National Academy Press, 1989.

Weiss, Nancy. *Witney M. Young, Jr. and the Struggle for Civil Rights*. Princeton: Princeton University, 1989.

Violence, Nonviolence, and the Civil Rights Movement

Sally Avery Bermanzohn
Department of Political Science Brooklyn College,
City University of New York

Abstract The dynamic between violence and politics in the American South during the Civil Rights Movement is analyzed, focusing on the relationship between racist terror and the state. The study explores how blacks in the rural South tried to defend themselves before civil rights, when white supremacists dominated local government and federal authorities ignored lynch murders. The article traces the development of Martin Luther King, Jr.'s nonviolent resistance strategy, and the long struggle to force the state to combat racist violence, one of the Civil Rights Movement's most significant achievements.

Violence was central to politics during the civil rights era (1950s-1960s) in the United States. For a century following the Civil War, Ku Klux Klan terror and lynch-mob murders had bolstered Southern segregation, and the role of brutality continued during the Civil Rights Movement. Between 1956 and 1966, white supremacists committed more than 1000 documented violent incidents aimed at stopping integration, including bombing, burning, flogging, abduction, castration, and murder.[1] The criminal justice system from the local to the federal government punished few of these crimes.[2]

But at the height of the Civil Rights Movement in the mid-1960s, Congress passed significant civil rights laws and the FBI finally acted against the KKK. Violent racists went underground. How did a grassroots movement achieve such success? Did pure morality win the battle? What was the dynamic between violence, nonviolence and civil rights?

Many historical accounts portray Martin Luther King, Jr. as a saint, and the Civil Rights Movement as a biblical struggle. Coretta Scott King portrayed her slain husband as "an instrument of a Divine plan and purpose."[3] Pulitzer prize-winning biographies emphasized biblical themes through their titles, which compared King to Christ (*Bearing the Cross* by Garrow) and Moses (*Parting the Waters* by Branch).[4] In contrast, this article analyzes King as a master politician who deeply understood the use of terror by Southern racists, and who developed nonviolent resistance as a practical strategy. King was not a pure pacifist. As a young man in divinity school he thought that an armed revolt was the only way to end segregation.[5] As an adult he wrote that sometimes violence could be justified if it was the only means of resisting tyranny. In the last years of his life, he spoke out against the US War in Vietnam and in support of (armed) national liberation movements.[6] King deplored violence for moral reasons, but also because the power structure of the South meant that when violent conflicts occurred, blacks inevitably lost. King knew that gaining the moral upper hand was a practical necessity to gain white liberals' support of the black movement. King and other civil rights leaders skillfully utilized the unique factors that were favorable at that time, including the Cold War and spread of television. Understanding the practical side of King allows activists today to learn from him as a strategist.

Many historical accounts belittle the role of violence, and ignore one of the Civil Rights Movement's greatest achievements: forcing the state to combat racist violence. For example, the *Encyclopedia Britannica* fails to mention violence at all in its description of the Civil Rights Movement as

> ... a mass movement starting in the late 1950s that, through the application of nonviolent protest action, broke the pattern of racially segregated public facilities in the South and achieved the most important breakthrough in equal-rights legislation for blacks since the Reconstruction period.[7]

In contrast, Piven and Cloward in *Poor People's Movements* argue that thwarting racist brutality was the most significant victory of the Civil Rights Movement. They state: "in the South the deepest meaning of the winning of democratic rights is that the historical primary of terror as a means of social control has been substantially diminished." And they criticize scholars, including leftists, for "the tendency to ignore this gain."[8]

Getting the state to protect black lives and punish racist murderers dominated the efforts of civil rights groups for most of the 20th century. Ida B. Wells-Barnett told an audience in 1909, "lynching is color-line murder . . . it is a national crime and requires a national remedy."[9] That same year, blacks and whites founded the National Association for the Advancement of Colored People (NAACP) which campaigned for federal anti-lynching legislation for six decades. Anti-lynching bills passed the House of Representatives in 1922, 1937, and 1940, but Senate filibusters by Southern Democrats defeated each of them. In 1951, 94 African Americans signed *We Charge Genocide*, a petition to the United Nations based on the 1948 Genocide

Convention. In the 1950s, the Ku Klux Klan grew, as did violence against blacks acting on their constitutional rights. During the Montgomery bus boycott Martin Luther King, Jr. developed nonviolent resistance as a way "to continue our struggle while coping with the violence it aroused."[10] A breakthrough occurred in the mid-1960s, at the height of the Civil Rights Movement. In 1964, after the Ku Klux Klan murdered three civil rights activists, President Lyndon Baines Johnson finally ordered the FBI to combat the Klan. In 1968, federal civil rights legislation finally made racist assaults a federal crime. Federal action rippled through state and local law enforcement, in a battle for equal protection in every state and locality, a struggle that continues to this day.

Ignoring or marginalizing violence is a noteworthy phenomenon in recent political discourse. John Keane in *Reflections on Violence* criticizes "the paucity of reflection" on the "the causes, effects and ethico-political implications of violence."[11] Civilization is the opposite of violence, requiring people to settle differences and disputes by peaceful means, yet brutality plagues modern societies. The pattern of violence in society reveals the structure of actual power. The powerful often ignore violence when the victims are poor and/or powerless. Mobs attack racial, religious, or sexual minorities when they feel entitled and believe they can get away with it. (The dynamic is similar when men batter women, or adults batter children.) How government defines crime, and how law enforcement and the judicial system implement the law, affects the prevalence of violence. Authorities perpetuate it when they ignore it, or brutalize those in their custody. Violence grows when the powerful give excuses for it, such as the view that vigilantes provide useful social control through terror.

Keane argues that violence sometimes plagues a population to the point that the community "passes over into the category of uncivil society."[12] In the Old South, good manners often honey-coated a brutal reality. A duality existed between what John Hope Franklin called the "two worlds of race" maintained by "intimidation, terror, lynching, and riots."[13] White Southerners prided themselves on their "civility," their personal grace, courtesy, concern. But William Chafe, in *Civility and Civil Rights,* points out that for African Americans there was:

> . . . the other side of civility—the deferential poses they had to strike in order to keep jobs, the chilling power of consensus to crush efforts to raise issues of racial justice. As victims of civility, blacks had long been forced to operate within an etiquette of race relations that offered almost no room for collective self assertion and independence. White people dictated the ground rules, and the benefits went only to those who played the game.[14]

Moreover, for blacks any "violation of the game" risked brutality that lurked just beneath the smiles and pleasantries. As Robert Williams wrote in 1962, "in a civilized society the law is a deterrent against the strong who would take advantage of the weak, but the South is not a civilized society."[15]

This article analyzes the dynamics of violence and politics in the American South during the Civil Rights Movement. First, it focuses on the relationship between racist terror, Southern government and federal policy, exploring how blacks in the rural South defended themselves when they had no governmental recourse. Second, it traces the development of Martin Luther King Jr.'s nonviolent resistance, and the long struggle to force the federal government to fight the racist violence. John Keane argues that the strategy of nonviolent resistance cannot be understood in isolation from the use of force in society.

For example, Gandhi used nonviolence, according to Keane, to "forcibly obstruct the British imperial government."[16] Can King's strategy be understood as an activist approach that *forcibly* ended segregation and established black political rights?

I

White Violence, Government Complicity, and Black Self-Defense

Until the mid-1960s, the U.S. government allowed racist terror to exist in the South. Lynching is mob murder in defiance of law and established judicial procedures, and after Reconstruction it became commonplace in the South. Between 1882 and 1968, newspapers reported 4742 lynch murders in the U.S. Seventy-three percent of the victims (3445 individuals) were black. Eighty-one percent (3848) occurred in 12 Southern states.[17] A lynch tradition cannot exist without the complicity of authorities. Local and state officials, including police, jailers, mayors, and others, often facilitated, or at least did not impede, racist mobs. The U.S. Congress failed to pass anti-lynching legislation. Federal authorities maintained a hands-off policy, viewing racist violence as a matter for Southern states to handle. Lynch murders declined in numbers over the course of the 20th century. By the 1950s, documented lynchings were rare, but when they occurred, they continued to go unpunished. For example, in 1959 Mack Charles Parker, a black man waiting trial for raping a white woman, was dragged out of his jail cell by hooded white men and murdered. The FBI investigation found that the local police and jailers cooperated with the murderers. Yet a state jury acquitted the white men.[18]

Vigilantism existed alongside "legal" violence, including police brutality and prison conditions so lethal many healthy prisoners succumbed. All-white-male juries condemned black-on-white crimes, while acquitting white-on-black crimes.[19] The structure of violence varied from place to place, varying by tradition and personality of the authorities. In Southern cities, blacks developed their own institutions, including churches and civic organizations that were independent of whites. In the rural South, however, many blacks were economically dependent on whites, and terror continued.[20]

Many Southern whites abhorred violence. Thirty thousand women joined the Association of Southern Women for the Prevention of Lynching in the 1930s, to lobby against the brutality that white men committed in the name of protecting white women.[21] Many business leaders opposed lynching because it created a "bad business climate" and spurred blacks to migrate north.[22] Some political leaders with concerns about their national reputations spoke out against violence, but nevertheless allowed it to continue.[23] Whites who advocated equality of the races could themselves become targets. Violence threatened those whites who violated the social order, perhaps by selling land to a black family, or by having black friends or lovers. These whites risked being labeled "nigger lovers" or "race mixers" and becoming victims of vigilantes.

Public opposition to lynch mobs led to a decline in lynching as a public spectacle after 1920, but violence continued in more subtle forms. Those blacks deemed "uppity" more often had accidents or disappeared. In 1939, the FBI began to investigate lynchings. But when evidence demonstrated white individuals were responsible, courts refused to punish them. Zangrando writes about the change in the tactics of violence:

> Worried that outside pressure might produce a federal antilynching law, some

southern whites found it wise to suppress the news of mob violence . . . select committees might be assigned to abduct, torture, and kill victims without public fanfare . . . Further masking the realities was the phenomenon of "legal lynchings," whereby officials consented in advance to a sham court trial followed promptly by the prisoner's execution.[24]

Washington set the tone of the country's official response to violence. Presidents occasionally spoke out deploring a particular atrocity, but the federal government maintained a hands-off policy from the fall of Reconstruction until 1964. The terror against blacks was considered by national leaders as a problem for state and local authorities.

Black Self-Defense

Defending one's life is a fundamental human instinct. When government fails to protect people, they will do what they can to protect themselves. Rural African Americans' recourse was self-reliance, defending themselves. Many blacks in the rural South used weapons to hunt and to defend their homes and families. People did not openly discuss armed self-defense, but they widely practiced it. James Forman, a 1960s civil rights leader, wrote about the prevalence of "self-defense—at least of one's home." Forman noted that in rural areas "there was hardly a black home in the South without its shotgun or rifle."[25]

To analyze the dynamics of violence and armed self-defense, I interviewed African Americans who grew up poor in the rural South before civil rights. Ronnie Johnson, Willena Cannon, and Thomas Anderson gave detailed descriptions of the impact of violence on the lives of their families. Ronnie Johnson comes from a large family in southern Mississippi.[26] He explained that "behind the front door of every house was a couple of shotguns and rifles. A drawer had shells in it. In the bedroom was another shotgun." Johnson discussed the elaborate measures his family took to protect themselves:

> For my family, the greatest fear was a surprise attack by a group, by the Klan, that would have overwhelming force and drag people from the house. To protect themselves, families like mine tried to have a lot of sons, and teach them how to use weapons. My kinfolk lived in houses that were within shouting distance of each other, so they could gather in time of need. Our house was at the end of a long road that led off the main highway, and everyone kept dogs in the yard. By the time anyone got down that road, everybody knew who they were, what they were, and why they were coming. This close network provided a common defense for ordinary occasions. But if a concerted effort came against one family, then it could be a shoot out.

Johnson explained that the county law enforcement included only a few individuals, the sheriff and a couple of deputies. They made the rounds, in the tradition of Southern civility, acting friendly to keep the peace. "The sheriff seemed real concerned about my grandmother, who he had known all his life," he explained, "but that same sheriff could put on a Klansman's hood." If a white man felt a black violated the social order, whites could form a mob to "take care of the uppity nigger." Law enforcement might or might not be part of the group when it went after an individual. Sometimes the group wore hoods, other times they did not cover their faces. Often they were hooded to protect the identity of the sheriff, landlord, or factory owner in the group.

Blacks' possession of arms deterred white violence. Describing a rural Georgia county in the early 1960s, Melissa Fay Greene writes in *Waiting for Sheetrock*: "one of the reasons for relative peace between the races was that they both were equally armed and each side knew it."[27] Ronnie Johnson agrees, but adds a crucial point: "everybody held their own ground. It was mutual respect, but only to a certain degree—'cause the other side always had more force."

Yet the possession of firearms could not always protect African Americans from violence. A surprise attack by a mob of whites could leave blacks powerless to defend themselves. Willena Cannon grew up in Mullins, South Carolina in the 1940s-1950s, in a sharecropping family.[28] As a child she witnessed the Klan murder of her neighbor. White men lynched her neighbor by trapping him in a barn and setting it on fire. The black man's "crime" was dating a white woman, a consensual relationship that was well known in the area. Willena, her family and neighbors watched in horror as the white men stopped anyone from saving the man in the barn. As smoke engulfed the building, adults carried Willena and the other small children away. The incident terrorized Willena for years. "I heard the man in the burning barn holler," Willena remembered, "and that screaming went on in my nightmares for a long time."

Mob murders, or lynchings, such as the one witnessed by Willena Cannon, relied on fear as the means of social control. As Snead writes in *Blood Justice*:

> . . . the black victim became the representative of his race and, as such, was being disciplined for more than a single crime. Indeed the guilt or innocence of the victim was always far less important than the act of the lynching itself. The lynch mob, in its deadly act, was warning the black population not to challenge the supremacy of the white race.[29]

Authorities reinforced the terrorism by signaling their indifference to these crimes. Willena recalled that shortly after her neighbor burned to death, the sheriff appeared on the scene. He told the stunned sharecroppers that the murder was "the people's business," not his. "The people" were white; black lives were expendable, not "the business" of the sheriff. If a black was suspected of murdering a white, a lynching was in order. But if it was the other way around, "the law" would ignore the incident. For poor rural blacks, legal recourse did not exist. To survive in this environment, Willena's mother taught her children to show no sign of resistance, fearing any protest might lead to them to "disappear."

"People were afraid of appearing arrogant," explained Ronnie Johnson, "but at the same time they had to survive and protect themselves." Blacks were caught in a double bind. They had good reason to not appear "uppity," yet wanted to communicate that if attacked they would fight back. Any disagreement could jeopardize a black person, and most were especially vulnerable because they were economically dependent on working for whites. Getting fair price for farm labor was a challenge; whites could retaliate for a black getting a good price, or for a black complaining about getting cheated. The Johnson family depended on hiring themselves out to whites, and he remembers working in cotton:

> I remember getting on a cotton truck with my family and uncles riding to the fields. Only my grandfather and my grandmother would talk to the white person who owned the property. They worried that the younger folks weren't used to negotiating and would appear arrogant. The elder people did all the talking, and collected all the money, and made all the decisions.

Some individuals deliberately cultivated a reputation for readiness to fight if attacked.

Thomas Anderson grew up on a farm in South Carolina in the 1930s, one of six children born to impoverished sharecroppers.[30] He remembered "the Ku Klux Klan going into people's houses, dragging them out, beating them, hanging them." One of the victims was his cousin. "They drug him out, hung him from a tree, and started shooting. They shot at him 'til there was nothing left but the rope." Anderson's anger overwhelmed his fear. "Being a kid, I was searching myself. Is this the way it's gotta be?" he asked himself. He resolved, "It won't happen to me. Nobody will ever do me the way I don't want them to do. They will have to kill me first." He kept a proud, cool exterior, and learned to use a gun. Thomas Anderson made sure that everyone in the county, white and black, knew that he was an expert marksman. His philosophy was "armed self-defense. You don't go after nobody. But if they come after you, you protect yourself."

Tensions Mount in the 1950s

The tensions between racist violence and civil rights increased throughout the 1950s. Black servicemen had fought and died in the U.S. in World War II, yet state laws and terror continued to disenfranchise Southern blacks. As the United States emerged as a global power, it became harder for the federal government to maintain its "hands-off" policy towards the South. Racist violence and segregation became embarrassing for U.S. foreign policy.[31] In 1954 the Supreme Court found segregated education unconstitutional in a case argued by the NAACP. The unanimous *Brown v. Board of Education* decision placed the Constitution squarely on the side of black political rights. But the Southern power structure yielded nothing. Across the South, political leaders declared they would defy the Court rather than implement integration.

"Constitution or no Constitution, we will keep segregation in Mississippi," Governor Ross Barnett declared defiantly. "I call on every official in the state of Mississippi, every citizen, to use every Constitutional and legal means . . ." Then he paused, took a breath, and added emphatically, *"every possible way . . ."*[32]

Encouraged by the actions of state political leaders, white violence became more audacious. In 1955, two white men in Mississippi killed a 14-year-old boy for "talking fresh to a white woman." Unaware of Mississippi's social order, Emmett Till made a fatal error. He was a young teen from Chicago, vacationing with relatives in Mississippi. He told his cousins about his integrated school, and about his friends, including white girls. Then he said "bye, baby" to a white woman in Mississippi. That night two men took Till from his uncle's home, beat him and threw his battered body into the river. Despite overwhelming evidence, a Mississippi jury (all white men) let the murderers free. The murder of Emmett Till sent shock, fury, and fear through black communities. Ronnie Johnson recalled, "I never will forget the day they pulled Emmett Till's body out of the river. They found him about a half a mile from where we lived. That night all my aunts and uncles came over to our house. The fear, the whispers, the anticipation: what should we do?"

Till's young age and mild nature of his offense shocked the Johnson family. A few days later, Ronnie's teenage uncle came home from his gas station job covered with blood. A local white man didn't like the way he pumped gas, jumped out of the car, and hit him in the face, breaking his nose. Ronnie's father and uncle grabbed weapons, and went to revenge the attack. They knew who the white man was and where he lived, but couldn't find him that night. Despite the family network and elaborate methods of self-defense, Mississippi had become too dangerous for

Ronnie Johnson's father and mother. Quickly, they picked up and left the state.

Outrageous acts against blacks continued. In 1957 Klansmen in Birmingham, Alabama, decided to prove themselves worthy as KKK leaders by "cutting a nigger." They seized a 34-year-old black man, a World War II veteran, interrogated him about voting rights, school desegregation, and that "nigger-loving Communist named Earl Warren." Then they castrated him.[33]

By 1957, three years had passed since the Supreme Court's landmark decision, yet Southern schools remained segregated, and violence maintained the color line. The NAACP filed lawsuits, including a successful one in Arkansas, where the federal court ordered the desegregation of Little Rock High School. Under court order, nine black students were to enter Little Rock High School that September. Instead, Governor Orville Faubus defied the federal government and directed the National Guard troops to prevent the students from entering the building. A mob of several hundred whites gathered in front of the school. A local newspaper editor told the Justice Department, "The police have been routed, the mob is in the streets, and we're close to a reign of terror."[34]

Daisy Bates, president of the Arkansas NAACP, led the campaign to desegregate Little Rock High School. She received many threats to her life and her home was firebombed, but local law enforcement refused to arrest the perpetrators. Bates appealed to federal authorities, who responded that they had "no federal jurisdiction" to protect her. A black neighbor told Bates, "I doubt whether the Negroes are going to take much more without fighting back. I think I'll take the rest of the day off and check my shotgun and make sure it's in working condition."[35] Eisenhower reluctantly sent federal troops to protect the nine students. Troops remained in Little Rock the entire school year.

The inaction of local and state authorities encouraged the Ku Klux Klan, whose ranks swelled to 50,000 in the early 1960s. Wherever civil rights activity developed, Klan violence followed. Bombing became the weapon of choice, as violent racists targeted the homes of scores of "uppity" blacks and "moderate" whites, as well as churches, synagogues, integrated schools, and local government offices. The bomb that killed four little girls in a Birmingham church in 1963 was the 21st bomb in eight years detonated against blacks in that city alone, which became known to many as "Bombingham."[36]

As opposition to the KKK grew, white segregationists developed new organizations that attracted more middle-class membership. White Citizens Councils sprang up across the South in the 1950s, holding rallies of up to 10,000 people. Though the Citizens Councils claimed to use economic pressure to stop integration, rather than violence, often their membership and activities overlapped with the Klan (for example, the Alabama Klansmen who castrated the black man were also members of the Citizens Council). Some referred to the Councils as the "uptown KKK."[37]

State governments established state agencies dedicated to maintaining segregation. The Mississippi State Sovereignty Commission, from 1956 through 1977, "used spy tactics, intimidation, false imprisonment, jury tampering and other illegal methods . . . to maintain segregation at all costs." The Commission gathered intelligence on 60,000 people, one out of every 37 people in Mississippi. Arkansas, Louisiana, Alabama and Florida created similar state investigative commissions. In Mississippi, none of the documents released in 1998 showed a direct connection between the Sovereignty Commission and the deaths of civil rights advocates. But the documents do include plans for using violence. For example, there were multiple discussions of "taking care of" individuals who tried to integrate Mississippi colleges, including having their cars hit by a train or engineering an accident on the highway.[38]

Hovering above the state government efforts to thwart African Americans' civil rights was the FBI. Since its origin in 1908, the FBI had been active in the South, as in the rest of the country. But J. Edgar Hoover, who headed the Bureau from 1919 to 1972, interpreted his mission as hunting down Communists, weeding out anti-American activity, and not protecting civil rights. In 1939, after 4692 people had died in documented lynchings, Hoover directed the FBI in 1939 to carry out formal investigations of mob murders. However, he opposed federal anti-lynching legislation in a 1956 confidential report to President Eisenhower, because he did not see violence against blacks as a significant problem, and he saw the Civil Rights Movement as led by subversives.[39] Thus the FBI gathered information on violence, but punishment required action by local authorities. Racist violence was not Hoover's concern, and he repeatedly dismissed it as a "local issue."[40] James Forman expressed the view of many activists in the South: "the FBI was a farce. It wasn't going to arrest any local racists who violate any and all laws on the statute books. Instead it would play a game of taking notes and pictures."[41]

Although no African American was immune to violence, activists received the most threats. Many individual NAACP leaders and lawyers responded by carrying revolvers. Daisy Bates, head of the Arkansas NAACP who led the Little Rock High School desegregation, carried a handgun in her car, and displayed it to scare off white adolescents who threatened her.[42] NAACP lawyers J. L. Chestnut and Orzell Billingsley wore guns as they pursued legal cases in rural Alabama.[43] Vernon Dahmer, president of the Hattiesburg, MS NAACP, died using a shotgun to defend his family and home, after the KKK firebombed it.[44]

When Martin Luther King, Jr. emerged as a leader during the 1955 Montgomery bus boycott, he received the typical response to civil rights activists. His life was threatened and his home bombed. And in the tradition of the South, after whites firebombed his house, blacks armed themselves and surrounded King's house to protect him.[45]

II

Martin Luther King, Jr. Developed Nonviolence as a Practical Strategy

How does one fight for equal rights when any action, any small gesture, risks brutal retaliation? Blacks rallied against the Klan in Harlem in 1949, but in the South similar tactics were suicidal. In this fearful environment, NAACP court cases dominated the fight for racial justice. But by the mid-1950s, as Southern politicians flagrantly defied the Supreme Court, many blacks questioned the effectiveness of the legal strategy. For example, Connie Lane, a lifelong resident of Greensboro, North Carolina, was 22 years old when the Court overturned segregation in 1954. But nothing changed for her, and she felt great frustration towards the NAACP, which she described as "this grand organization, something for the bourgeoisie black folks, the doctors, the lawyers—not for ordinary people, not for me."[46] She and other African Americans argued over tactics. Was there an alternative to the NAACP's legal strategy? What was the best way to gain equal rights? How could blacks avoid violence directed against them? Anger and fear vied for the upper hand. There were no easy answers.

Martin Luther King, Jr. described the debate in the black community:

> During the fifties, many voices offered substitutes for the tactics of legal recourse. Some called for a colossal blood bath to cleanse the nation's ills . . . But the Negro of the South in 1955 assessing the power of the force arrayed against him, could not perceive the slightest prospect of victory in this approach. He was unarmed, unorganized, untrained, disunited, and most important, psychologically and morally unprepared for the deliberate spilling of blood. Although his desperation had prepared him to die for freedom if necessary, he was not willing to commit himself to racial suicide with no prospect of victory.[47]

King grew up in the South, fearful of the Klan and lynch murders. The first time police arrested King, which was during the Montgomery bus boycott, "panic seized him . . . King gave in to visions of nooses and lynch mobs."[48] King appreciated that blacks' own institutions, their churches, civic groups, schools, were weak compared to the coercive powers arrayed against them. Even where blacks made up a substantial part, or even a majority, of the population, they faced what Morris termed "the iron fist of Southern government."[49]

At first, King assumed violence was needed to win equal rights. He wrote, "when I was in theological school I thought the only way we could solve our problem of segregation was an armed revolt."[50] He met pacifists, but felt they had "an unwarranted optimism concerning man." He felt many were self-righteous, and he never joined a pacifist organization. Instead, he was searching for a "realistic pacifism."[51] Mahatma Gandhi, "the moral appeal to the heart and conscience is, in the case of human beings, *more effective* than an appeal based on threat of bodily pain or violence."[52] Gandhi criticized passive nonviolence and advocated aggressive resistance. King felt that Gandhi's philosophy was "the only *morally and practically* sound method open to oppressed people in their struggle for freedom." He described Gandhi's nonviolent resistance as "one of the most potent weapons available."[53]

It is one thing to study Gandhi in school, and quite another to apply the principles to a different time place and circumstance. Blacks in the American South faced very different conditions than the anti-colonial struggle in India. Would nonviolence work? Or would it just subject black people to more violence? Tactics were a matter of life and death for activists. Many blacks saw nonviolence as passive and ineffectual, as acceptance of the status quo. On the other hand, they realized that any use of arms could be used as an excuse for increased white violence against them. In college and divinity school, King determined through lengthy discussions with his classmates that support from white liberals was possible, if it could be mobilized. Placing the freedom movement on the high moral ground was necessary to gain support outside the black community.

Montgomery Bus Boycott and Nonviolent Resistance

Suddenly in 1955 these questions were no longer theoretical, as King found himself thrust into the leadership of a mass movement. He developed nonviolent civil disobedience as a practical method to cope with segregationists' violence. King wrote in *Our Struggle: The Story of Montgomery* that the boycott developed a way "to continue our struggle while coping with the violence it aroused."[54]

On Thursday, December 1, 1955, Rosa Parks refused to give up her seat on a bus to a white man, and police jailed her for violating state segregation laws. Many other blacks had been arrested for similar violations, but this time the NAACP decided to take her case to court. Even more importantly, Rosa Parks' friends in the Women's Political Council decided to organize a bus boycott, to tap the anger of the black community. They wrote a leaflet and mimeographed thousands of copies, which they distributed through the churches that Sunday. The black ministers quickly organized the Montgomery Improvement Association to lead the boycott, electing a 27-year-old newcomer named Martin Luther King, Jr. as the spokesperson. On Monday morning, no blacks rode the buses.[55]

White officials criticized the bus boycott for having similar tactics to the White Citizens Council. They portrayed African American actions to improve themselves as no different than whites organizing to promote their group's interest.[56] King wanted to distinguish blacks' constitutional demands for equality from the violent tactics of the Klan and White Citizens Council. In a speech on the first night of the boycott, King stated:

> There will be no crosses burned at any bus stops in Montgomery. There will be no white persons pulled out of their homes and taken out on some distant road and murdered. There will be nobody among us who will stand up and defy the Constitution of this nation . . . We are not here advocating violence . . . The only weapon that we have in our hands this evening is the weapon of protest.[57]

King advocated nonviolence, not passivity. King often used the word "militant" or "coercion" to describe their tactics. In one speech, for example, he stated "not only are we using the tools of persuasion—but we've got to use the tools of coercion."[58] He was aggressive in negotiations with the white city leaders, breaking a historical pattern of black leaders caving in because of fear. The boycott continued for a year, and the unity of the black community was remarkable. Unlike court battles that depended on a few brave plaintiffs and their lawyers, the boycott depended for its success on black working people, the maids, the day laborers, every day for a year finding ways other than the bus to get to work.

White racists attacked the homes of the boycott leaders, including the homes of King, Abernathy, Shuttleworth, and Gratz, as well as churches and other locations. The KKK marched trying to intimidate the boycotters. Ten thousand attended the White Citizens Council rally in the Montgomery Colliseum, the largest segregationist rally of the century. But with worldwide interest aroused by the new medium of television, the more violence the blacks endured, the more the press covered the boycott. Terror lost its effectiveness. It took its toll on the victims, but it could no longer derail the movement for equality. Nonviolent resistance emerged as a strategy in the day-to-day activities of the boycott. Taylor Branch, in *Parting the Waters,* points out that "nonviolence, like the boycott itself, had begun more or less by accident." It took six more years for King to fully develop this strategy.[59]

King struggled deeply within himself to provide nonviolent leadership. He knew that as a leader, he was a target for violent whites. His home was assaulted three times, and people protected him with arms. There were weapons inside King's home. Civil rights leader Bayard Rustin visited King in the middle of the boycott, and saw guns in the King household. At one point, Rustin "shouted to stop someone from sitting on a loaded pistol that was lying on the couch."[60] Reverend Glenn Smiley, a follower of Gandhi who visited King to advise him on nonviolent resistance, advised King to "get rid of the guns around his house." King talked intensely to Smiley, describing his fears about violence. King told Smiley, "don't bother me with tactics . . . I want to know if I can apply nonviolence to my heart."[61]

King knew that nonviolent resistance was a strategy that could fail and lead to great bloodshed. John Keane points out that "renunciation of violence" can sometimes result in "tragic annihilation."[62] As a leader, King felt responsible if a demonstration provoked violence against the demonstrators. Mass leaders often face moral dilemmas as they make choices on how to proceed, and King criticized people who saw nonviolent resistance as a pure and simple moral stand. He said "I came to see the pacifist position not as sinless." King criticized self-righteous advocates of peace, stating that "the pacifist would have a greater appeal if he did not claim to be free from the moral dilemmas that the Christian nonpacifist confronts."[63]

In 1963 in Birmingham police used billy clubs, firehouses, and German shepherds against civil rights demonstrators. Eight ministers published a letter blaming King for the violence, stating that grievances should be pursued only in courts, not in the street. King responded in a letter from Birmingham City Jail, declaring:

> . . . the white power structure of this city left the Negro community with no other alternative . . . Its ugly record of police brutality is known in every section of this country. Its unjust treatment of Negroes in the courts is a notorious reality. There have been more unsolved bombings of Negro homes and churches in Birmingham than any city in this nation.[64]

King's nonviolent strategy caught on because it was effective, spurring millions into action and rallying support from around the country and the world. It was the most practical method to deal with racist violence. Some civil rights activists followed King's strategy, even though they themselves personally disagreed with nonviolence. Ella Baker, a leader who worked NAACP in the 1940s and with King in the 1950s, was not a pacifist. She explained, "I frankly could not have sat and let someone put a burning cigarette on the back of my neck . . . If they hit me, I might hit them back."[65] Connie Lane, Greensboro activist, explained that she disagreed with King's philosophy. "I never could get into all this passive resistance, somebody hits you, you fall down on your knees and start praying." She paused, then added, "but I appreciated what Dr. King was doing."

A major challenge to King's strategy came from Robert Williams of Monroe, North Carolina. Williams served in the army in World War II and the Marines in the Korean War. When he returned home to North Carolina, the local NAACP chapter elected him their president. In 1957, a Klan motorcade attacked the house where the Monroe NAACP was meeting, and Williams and others shot at them. The KKK backed off. Williams' NAACP chapter led a variety of civil rights struggles, including a campaign to free two boys, ages seven and nine, who were incarcerated for playing a children's kissing game with the white girls. In 1959, Williams helped a black woman bring suit against a white man who assaulted her, tore off her clothing, and tried to rape her. Williams' frustration rose to the boiling point when the all-white-male jury quickly acquitted the white man. It was yet another example of the double standard of the South. In the name of protecting white women, white men lynched black men and boys, and at the same time felt entitled to violate black women. Just after the verdict, a furious Williams declared on the courthouse steps, "the Negro in the South cannot expect justice in the courts. He must convict his attackers on the spot. He must meet violence with violence, lynching with lynching." For this statement, Williams was kicked out of the NAACP.[66]

An intense debate ensured on the strategy of Robert Williams versus that of Martin Luther King, Jr. In the *Southern Patriot* in 1961, King stressed nonviolent resistance as aggressive action against segregation. In an opposing article, Williams advocated armed self-defense, stating:

> . . . in a civilized society the law is a deterrent against the strong who would take advantage of the weak, but the South is not a civilized society; the South is a social jungle; it had become necessary for us to create our own deterrent . . . we would defend our women and our children, our homes and ourselves with arms.[67]

Williams' words reflected the sentiment of many. But Williams had crossed an unwritten rule about armed self-defense: he publicly advocated it. James Forman pointed out that "self-defense was something people should do and not proclaim." While Forman sympathized with Williams' anger and disillusionment, he also criticized him for openly advocating armed self-defense, which he thought "was a warm invitation for the police to crack down."[68] Forman described the tremendous energy that Robert Williams put into just defending his home; night after night Williams and his supporters had to stay up all night, prepared for an armed attack by the Klan.

Williams' phrase "meeting violence with violence, lynching with lynching" was roundly criticized, because it could be interpreted as a strategy of violence, a justification for blacks lynching whites. The NAACP and King wanted to clearly demarcate themselves from that view. But while criticizing Williams, both the NAACP and King affirmed the right of self-defense. As they removed Williams from membership, the NAACP stated, "we do not deny but reaffirm the right of an individual and collective self-defense against unlawful assaults."[69] King blasted Williams for the "advocacy of violence as a tool of advancement, organized as in warfare, deliberately and consciously." He saw it as an approach with "incalculable perils," whereas nonviolent mass action was a constructive alternative. But King defended the right of self-defense, stating it was accepted as "moral and legal" by all societies. And he acknowledged that pure nonviolence "cannot readily or easily attract large masses, for it requires extraordinary discipline and courage."[70] King's nonviolent strategy won the public debate. But nonviolent resistance continued to coexist with armed self-defense.

King was a "practical pacifist," not a "pure" one. In 1967-1968, he spoke out against the Vietnam War, saying "these are revolutionary times. All over the globe men are revolting against old systems of exploitation and oppression . . . The shirtless and barefoot people of the earth are rising up as never before."[71] He sympathized with the national liberation movements who were using force of arms.

The Movement Forces the Federal Government off the Fence

In the early 1960s, civil rights activists continued to face violence, and the federal government continued its "hands-off" policy. In 1961, black and white Freedom Riders rode on public buses through the South, integrating public facilities. The FBI knew that the Klan planned a "baseball bat greeting" for the Freedom Riders in Alabama, but failed to protect them from a brutal beating. The FBI also stood by while police beat people trying to exercise their right to vote. In 1962, Fanny Lou Hamer, a 45-year-old Mississippi-country woman who would become a nationally recognized civil rights leader, tried to register at the county courthouse. She was arrested, evicted from her home, and shot at.[72] But violence did not stop the movement, as sit-ins, marches, and voter registration drives spread across the South.

Pressure on Washington to end segregation and violence mounted. On the one hand, the failure of the government to protect the exercise of constitutionally protected rights became increasingly embarrassing in the context of the Cold War. The Soviet Union used the South's brutality to batter the U.S. image abroad. On the other hand, American national interests found King's nonviolence useful in international relations. The U.S. promoted King's leadership as an alternative to the armed national liberation struggles in Africa and other parts of the world. For example, the United States Information Agency made a video of the 1963 March on Washington which they showed around the world as evidence of peaceful progress in race relations in the U.S.[73] But that required that there be progress. Such progress depended on the federal government doing something it had failed to do for almost a century: dismantle the stranglehold of white supremacy on local and state government and punish racist violence.

The mounting pressure came to a head in June, 1964. Civil rights activists organized Freedom Summer, attracting Northern white and black students to come South to work on voter registration and other issues. In June the Ku Klux Klan lynched three young civil rights workers, James Chaney, Andrew Goodman, and Michael Schwerner, in Neshoba County, Mississippi. A deputy sheriff drove one of the two cars of the Klansmen. The murders of the young men, one black and two white, became international news. Finally, a president took action: President Johnson directly ordered J. Edgar Hoover to stop the Klan. As a result, the FBI added a counterintelligence program (COINTELPRO) against the Klan to its programs against civil rights activists, the Black Panthers, and Vietnam War protesters. It was the only COINTELPRO initiated under pressure from outside the Bureau and the only one directed at rightwing groups.[74]

Thus in 1964, as the Ku Klux Klan marked its 98th year of working to undermine the U.S. Constitution, the FBI determined that the Klan was "essentially subversive." The Bureau's "war on the Klan" lasted until 1971, when it was disbanded along with the other COINTELPROs. The FBI focused on infiltrating Klan organizations, and by the late 1960s, there were 2000 FBI informants in racist hate groups, comprising perhaps 20% of total Klan membership. Sometimes it was unclear whose side the informants were on. One man on the FBI payroll talked about murdering all black people. Another informant was part of the carload of Klansmen who murdered civil rights worker Viola Liuzzo.[75] Federal involvement, despite its serious shortcomings, was decisive in cutting the link in many places between vigilantes and local law enforcement. There were exceptions, including police complicity with Klan murders in Greensboro in 1979, and police brutality that continues to plague the country to this day. But the Civil Rights Movement, by forcing authorities to punish violent racists, had taken a major step in breaking the white supremacist grip on power.

Conclusion

Nonviolent resistance combined with armed self-defense in the Civil Rights Movement to force the government to do its job: protect people's rights regardless of race. Government actions curtail or encourage violence. In the U.S., from Reconstruction until the height of the Civil Rights Movement, the federal policy of "hands off" towards the South had fostered violence against blacks.

Even in the late 1950s and 1960, whites could brutalize blacks and get away with it. The lynch-mob murders of Emmett Till in 1955, Mack Charles Parker in 1959, and Goodman, Chaney, and Schwerner in 1964 went unpunished. Particularly in rural Southern counties, African Americans often had no recourse to government protection. Some used arms to defend themselves and their homes, but the effectiveness was limited, because violent whites had the power of local and state institutions behind them.

African Americans bent on civil rights coped with the violence used against them in various ways. Many activists routinely carried handguns to protect themselves, as they faced harassment and sometimes murder. When the Montgomery bus boycott launched massive protest action, Martin Luther King, Jr. argued for the boycotters to be nonviolent to differentiate themselves from the tactics of the Ku Klux Klan and White Citizens Council, and to win the support of white liberals. King gradually developed nonviolence into a strategy in the late 1950s and early 1960s, a strategy which helped the Civil Rights Movement grow in size and effectiveness. Pacifism coexisted with armed self-defense: both King and the NAACP officially upheld the right of self-defense.

During the Cold War in the new medium of television, massive nonviolent resistance galvanized national and international attention, as the Civil Rights Movement demanded that the Constitution be enforced throughout the country. U.S. leaders found King's nonviolent strategy useful in foreign diplomacy because it could be promoted as an alternative to armed national liberation movements. In the 1960s, faced with both international pressure and the growing size and scope of the Civil Rights Movement, the federal government finally acted to thwart racist violence in the South. In a dramatic policy shift, LBJ in 1964 ordered J. Edgar Hoover to use the FBI to undermine the Ku Klux Klan, not just gather information on it. The federal government thus began to break the link between violent racists and Southern local and state government, a central victory for civil rights.

As John Keane suggests, strategies of social change may be evaluated based on whether they create or strengthen pluralist peaceful society. Sometimes the use of arms can be constructive, as it was in the American Revolution. Pacifism, too, can be effective or counterproductive based on how it is practiced. Sometimes it has disarmed people who then face increased bloodshed. On the other hand, Keane finds that Gandhi's movement in India "used nonviolence as a means of contesting illegitimate power, for the purpose of strengthening civil society."[76] In the same way, King's nonviolent resistance forced the U.S. government to guarantee civil rights. The Civil Rights Movement succeeded, not because of its nonviolence, but because it was combined with armed self-defense to make the South less violent and more democratic.

Notes

1. The *Ku Klux Klan: A History of Racism and Violence* (Southern Poverty Law Center, Montgomery, Alabama, 1988), p. 23.
2. Unpunished crimes in Mississippi include the murder of Charles Moore in 1964, Ernest Avants in 1966, Benjamin Brown in 1967, Wharlest Jackson in 1967, and Rainy Pool in 1970. The suspected Klansmen were never arrested and still remain unpunished (see Stephanie Saul, "Their Killers Walk Free," *Newsday*, December 15-20, 1998). Other crimes are being punished three decades after they occurred: for example, in 1998 a Mississippi court convicted the man responsible for the 1966 murder of

NAACP leader, Vernon Dahmer (*Associated Press*, August 21, 1998), and in 1994 a court finally convicted the man who assassinated NAACP leader Medgar Evers (*New York Times,* March 18, 1998).
3. Coretta Scott King, *My Life with Martin Luther King, Jr.* (New York: Holt, Rinehart and Winston, 1969), p. 293.
4. David J. Garrow, *Bearing the Cross* (New York: Vintage Books, 1988); Taylor Branch, *Parting the Water: America in the King Years 1954-1963* (New York: Simon & Schuster, 1989).
5. Garrow, *op. cit.*, p. 43; King, *Stride Towards Freedom* (London: Harpers Brothers, 1958), pp. 91-93.
6. Adam Faircloth, "Martin Luther King, Jr. and the War in Vietnam," in M.L. Krenn (ed.), *The African American Voice in US Foreign Policy Since World War II* (New York: Garland, 1998), p. 257.
7. "Civil Rights Movement," in *Encyclopedia Britannica*, 1998.
8. Frances Fox Piven and Richard A. Cloward, *Poor People's Movements* (New York: Vintage Books, 1979), p. 182.
9. Herbert Shapiro, *Whtie Violence and Black Response* (Amherst: University of Massachusetts, 1988), p. 120.
10. Shapiro, *op. cit.*, p. 394.
11. John Keane, *Reflections on Violence* (New York: Verso, 1996), p. 6.
12. Keane, *op. cit.*, pp. 70-71.
13. John Hope Franklin, *Race and History* (Baton Rouge: Louisiana State University Press, 1989), p. 149.
14. William H. Chafe, *Civilities and Civil Rights* (Oxford: Oxford University Press, 1981), p. 8.
15. Robert F. Williams, *Negroes with Guns* (Detroit: Wayne State University Press, 1998; reprinted from 1962), p. 26.
16. Keane, *op. cit.*, p. 64.
17. Robert L. Zangrando, *The NAACP Crusade Against Lynching: 1909-1950* (Philadelphia: Temple University Press 1980), pp. 6-7.
18. Howard Smead, *Blood Justice: The Lynching of Mack Charles Parker* (Oxford: Oxford University Press, 1986).
19. Zangrando, *op. cit.*,
20. Aldon D. Morris, *The Origins of the Civil Rights Movement* (New York: Free Press, 1984), pp. 1-12; Steward E. Tolnay and E. M. Beck, *A Festival of Violence: An Analysis of Southern Lynchings, 1882-1930* (Chicago: University of Illinois Press, 1992).
21. Jacqueline Hall, *Revolt Against Chivalry: Jesse Danial Ames and the Women's Campaign Against Lynching* (New York: Columbia University Press, 1991).
22. Tolnay and Beck, *op. cit.*, p. 5.
23. Smead, *op. cit.*, p. xi.
24. Zandrango, *op. cit.*, p. 4.
25. James Forman, *The Making of Black Revolutionaries* (Seattle: Open Hand, 1990), p. 376.
26. The author interviewed Ronnie Johnson on October 15, 1998, in Brooklyn, New York. Johnson's uncle, Reverend Aaron Johnson, a civil rights activist who lives in Greenwood, Mississippi, was interviewed by Richard Rubin: "Should the Mississippi Files Have Been Reopened?" *New York Times Magazine*, August 30, 1998, pp. 30-37.
27. Melissa Fay Greene, *Waiting for Sheetrock* (New York: Fawcett Columbine, 1991), p. 202.
28. The author interviewed Willena Cannon on November 1, 1989, in Greensboro, North Carolina. See Bermanzohn, "The Greensboro Massacre: Political Biographies of Four Surviving Demonstrators," *New Political Science* 20:1 (1998), pp. 69-89.
29. Snead, *op. cit.*, p. x.

30. The author interviewed Thomas Anderson on August 3, 1990, in Greensboro, North Carolina. See Bermanzohn, *Survivors of the 1979 Greensboro Massacre*, PhD dissertation, City University of New York, 1994.
31. Smead, *op. cit.*, p. 127.
32. "Eyes on the Prize: Fighting Back 1957-1962," Public Broadcasting System.
33. Shapiro, *op. cit.*, pp. 410-141.
34. Shapiro, *op. cit.*, p. 415.
35. Shapiro, *op. cit.*, pp. 415-416.
36. Kenneth O'Reilly, *"Racial Matters": The FBI's Secret File on Black Americans, 1960-1972* (New York: Free Press, 1989), p. 79.
37. Shapiro, *op. cit.*, pp. 410, 434, 468.
38. *New York Times*, March 18, 1998, p. A1.
39. Branch, *op. cit.*, pp. 180-182.
40. O'Reilly, *op. cit.*, p. 5.
41. Forman, *op. cit.*, p. 353.
42. Daisy Bates, *The Long Shadow of Little Rock: A Memoir* (New York: David McKay, 1962).
43. J. L. Chestnut, *Black in Selma: The Uncommon Life of J. L. Chestnut, Jr.* (New York: Farrar, Straus & Giroux, 1990), p. 110.
44. *New York Times*, April 5, 1998.
45. Branch, *op. cit.*, p. 165.
46. The author interviewed Connie Lane on March 10, 1992, in Greensboro, North Carolina.
47. Martin Luther King, Jr., *Why We Cant' Wait* (New York: Harper and Row, 1964), p. 24.
48. Branch, *op. cit.*, p. 160.
49. Morris, *op. cit.*, p. 3.
50. Garrow, *op. cit.*, p. 43.
51. Martin Luther King, Jr., "Pilgrimage to Nonviolence," in Straughton Lynd (ed.), *Nonviolence in America: A Documentary History* (New York: Bobbs-Merrill, 1966), pp. 386-390.
52. Mahatma Gandhi, *Non-Violent Resistance* (New York: Shocken Books, 1951), p. iii (emphasis added).
53. King in Lynd, *op. cit.*, p. 390.
54. Shapiro, *op. cit.*, p. 394.
55. Branch, *op. cit.*, pp. 123-127.
56. This same line of reasoning is used by David Duke in the 1980s-1990s, and the Association for the Advancement for White People.
57. Branch, *op. cit.*, p. 140.
58. Branch, *op. cit.*, p. 140.
59. Branch, *op. cit.*, p. 195.
60. Branch, *op. cit.*, p. 179.
61. Branch, *op. cit.*, pp. 179-180.
62. Keane, *op. cit.*, p. 88.
63. Lynd, *op. cit.*, p. 389.
64. Martin Luther King, Jr., "Letter from Birmingham City Jail," in Lynd, *op. cit.*, p. 463.
65. Susan G. O'Malley, "Ella Baker, " in Mari Jo Buhle *et al.* (eds), *Encyclopedia of the American Left* (Chicago: University of Chicago Press, 1992), p. 82. In 1960, as the sit-in movement of black youth spread across the South, Ella Baker became the advisor to the Student Nonviolent Coordinating Committee (SNCC). When the SNCC debated over whether to take up voter registration in the deep South or to focus on nonviolent resistance, Baker pushed them to combine the two. She thought that nonviolent resistance could be an effective tactic in gaining voting rights in the deep South, explaining that when students "went into these deeply prejudiced areas and started voter registration, they would have an opportunity to exercise nonviolent resistance . . . they wouldn't have to abandon their nonviolence. In fact, they would be hard put to keep it up" (p. 82).
66. Williams, *op. cit.*
67. Williams, *op. cit.*, p. 26.

68. Forman, *op. cit.*, pp. 150, 374.
69. Shapiro, *op. cit.*, p. 460
70. Shapiro, *op. cit.*, pp. 460-461.
71. King, *Where Do We Go from Here?* quoted in Adam Fair, "Martin Luther King, Jr. and the War in Vietnam," in Michael Krenn (ed.), *The African American Voice in U.S. Foreign Policy Since World War II* (New York: Garland, 1998), p. 257.
72. O'Reilly, *op. cit.*, pp. 1-3, 83-90.
73. Forman, *op. cit.*, p. 336.
74. James K. Davis, *Spying on America: The FBI's Domestic Counterintelligence Program* (New York: Praeger, 1992).
75. O'Reilly, *op. cit.*, pp. 217-218.
76. Keane, *op. city.*, p. 64.

Voting Reform in the U.S.: Special Studies and the 2000 Election

Alex Willingham
Williams College

A Legacy of Struggle

When the 2000 presidential election became controversial, it was merely the latest in an oft times contentious debate that had been a part of politics at least since the adoption of the national constitution and the first presidential election 213 years before.[1] Though the U.S. is typically classed as a democracy, certain basic questions persist about the practice. Who should vote? Who should be eligible to hold office? What offices should be elected? How should elected bodies be reapportioned? Is popular participation a priority, where a constitution requires separation-of-powers and checks-and-balances?

The original constitution would encourage such controversy by its own handling of suffrage. Providing for two levels of governing authority, the constitution did not address how officials at one level, the state, were to be chosen and for the federal level it removed major offices—the president, senate and courts—from popular election. It did stipulate that the federal House of Representatives would be chosen "by the people" but left it to the separate states to define who would be eligible to vote. The constitution also guaranteed a "republican form of government," to each state, but that guaranty was mooted in a court opinion rendered early in national history. The result was the absence of an explicit right to vote and an implication, to be sure, that any such denial in the states would meet constitutional standards.[2] This constitutional context would hold over the next two centuries and the development of voting practices would be haphazard as to processes and uneven as to ballot access.

Reprinted by permission of the author.

In the first generation after the adoption of the constitution a suffragist movement—Universal Manhood Suffrage—would be devoted to removing prohibitions on voting. This was, despite the name, exclusively devoted to white male rights which were effectively secured by the time of the Andrew Jackson presidency. There would soon be a movement to secure suffrage rights for women, initiated in the decade before the Civil War. It was not as immediately successful, however, and would require struggle into the early 20th century to the ratification of the 19th amendment. White immigrant voting rights would also be contentious as, first, Irish-Catholic and then other European groups migrated, settled and set up political organization. The movement would peak at the turn of the 20th century.

Race and voting rights would be multiphased and recurring over this entire period. In the early era during slavery, voting rights were often denied to Free Negroes and advocates of Universal Manhood Suffrage often limited their demands to whites only.[3] After the Civil War the citizenships rights of the former slaves were guaranteed by three constitutional amendments including one, the 15th, that explicitly prohibited vote denial. Black voting would be short-lived, however. In a series of state conventions beginning in Mississippi in 1890, Old Slave southern states enacted laws with rigid prerequisites that had the effect of disfranchising the new voters. Southern disfranchisement became the crucial moment in the race area. Though institutionalized in a region of the nation, it disfranchised a whole race and it provoked a serious counter movement under the national constitution. Certain of these laws would be voided in dramatic court opinions. But the system remained substantially in tact until the mid-1960s when congress enacted the Federal Voting Rights Act of 1965.

Finally, there have been "Majority Rule" problems concerned with strictures that broadly limit the power of the vote, but not with reference to race or other suspect classifications. Practices and movements here include direct election of U.S. Senators and Supreme Court justices, presidential veto, state poll taxes, voting age, the Electoral College, and proportional representation. Majority rule issues were raised early in the history of the country—in the ratification debates and in Manhood Suffrage—and given explicit statement in his first term by Andrew Jackson.[4]

The major Majority Rule issue by the mid-20th century was the dilution of the vote resulting from a certain "silent gerrymander." "Silent" because demographic changes caused mal-apportioned election districts with sharp disparities in the number of residents. States laws typically requiring equal sized districts, but few had been dutiful about compliance. In the post-WWII era, demands grew to redress this districting pattern. In a pivotal decision in 1962, the U.S. Supreme Court said such policies were covered under the 14th amendment of the U.S. Constitution. As a result, federal courts could fashion remedies if states refused to act. In a second significant move, the court set standards for the districting that required equality in population.[5]

In a parallel stream of activity, the congress would return to racial restrictions spurred by excesses in the Old South states and the demands of the civil rights movement. First, it would enact an ineffective federal voting law in 1957. The demand to address racial vote discrimination was made again in the 1965 demonstrations at Selma, Alabama. The campaign was organized by the Southern Christian Leadership Conference and drew on the momentum of the civil rights movement. The campaign was brutally attacked by state police forces and by vigilante elements, resulting in three deaths. Congress would respond by enacting the Voting Rights Act of 1965 replacing the 1957 act with strong provisions.

The authority assumed by the court in *Baker* and the racial opportunities guaranteed in the Voting Rights Act would merge in a broad challenge to the suffrage policies of state governments. The key engagement was through reapportionment, now required to be performed timely, and triggered by the federal census. It would be an occasion to monitor the peril of voter dilution either through disparity in relative size of district populations or by racial gerrymandering. This process came to dominate election reform into the last quarter of the 20th century. It was marked by a sweeping reformation of malapportioned election districts and, in the old bi-racial states, a surging litigation movement challenging the racial impact of reapportionment plans and at-large election schemes. Democratic issues were addressed as election districts were equalized to ensure "one-person-One-vote;" racial exclusion was moderated in a quickening of election to state and local offices. The new law—and the movement—brought an end to a hegemonic racial exclusion and came to embody, triumphantly, the values and politics of a tradition of advocacy for democratic rights.[6] Here majority rule and racial exclusion issues are combined in a democratic movement so formidable that many can be forgiven for thinking that all questions had been solved. In this context, election 2000 posed a problem not merely about the rightful winner but also a heritage of discussion on development of Democracy in America.

Special Studies and Election 2000

It may yet be too soon to locate the issues raised by Florida in the larger historical development. It is worthwhile, for purposes of our teaching and research, to examine how the election is being understood. Information about the controversy is extensive. There are writings by journalists in the more attentive newspapers and magazines and the Internet, at least one documentary film, and traditional book texts.[7] In this essay, I will be concerned with yet another set of texts—a mélange of special commissions and research projects that present an additional window on the implications of the election.

They claim a special expertise, often using signature social science tools of investigation. I classify the groups in two broad categories. One, the "study group" was composed of research specialists undertaking a data-intensive study with a formal research question; the other group, the "Task Force," was a mixture of lay and professional persons drawing on public hearings, interviews and textual material. Some of these were convened by public agencies, others by universities and non-profit institutes. Some were state-level studies and others were national in scope. Between December 2000 and late 2002, these groups released special reports often prepared by separate staff and including formal press releases, executive summaries, a main text, recommendations sometimes with data tables and dissenting remarks.

The first document constructing the Florida situation would be the opinion of the U.S. Supreme Court resolving the election by stopping the count check. The majority opinion construed the issue to be one of fairness in the recount process particularly the contrived procedures. This majority was opposed in vigorous dissent and supported in a concurring opinion. But the construction of the problem in the prevailing opinion was focused on the characteristics of the recount and thus on the last stage or "backside" of a larger process.[8]

The special studies started soon after the controversy. On February 1, a report was released by the Voting Technology Project a joint effort of the California Institute of

Technology and the Massachusetts Institute of Technology. The Cal Tech/MIT work initiated a stream of inquiry focused on election technology/voting systems. There would be three reports from Cal Tech/MIT with a final report in July of 2001. In a joint cover letter, the presidents of the schools introduce the final report declaring it to be "evident that problems with counting the votes of the citizens or Florida and elsewhere originated in unsound technology."[9] While the report itself offers less sweeping language, saying that the problems "go well beyond voting equipment," the presidents' statement signaled what was to be given priority as the new voting reform discourse groped toward policy recommendations.

Technology reports would also be produced by two other study groups, a government agency, and two congressional committees.[10] The technology reports are discussed group.

Voting Systems

The Cal Tech/MIT group assembled a county-by-county database on vote distributions and machine type for presidential elections in 1988, 1992, 1996 and 2000. The study sought to "examine the relative reliability of different machines ... to explain changes in the incidence of ballots that are spoiled." The effort focused on the discrete act of balloting and how problems there can relate to "changes in technologies within localities over time."[11]

As these studies began, one issue was the volatility of terminology to specify the problem, or dependent variable, then emerging in popular discussion of the Florida recount. Those terms included "miscounts," "misvotes," "mistaken votes," "spoiled ballots," "uncounted ballots," "unmarked ballots" and the "over-" and "under-vote." The instability of the terminology would plague this entire process and was sustained in part by the lack of consensus definitions and in part because of the way a given definition fed competing claims about blame, motive, and effect.

The project did not standardize the terminology, but it did propose the concept of "residual vote," which came increasingly to be used. The problem occurs when ballots are cast but *no vote is counted* for the office (typically the president in these studies). These are all "combined into a group of uncounted ballots." When that number is determined, they are called "residual votes." They would adjust the residual vote to account for about a third that is intentional and, thus, not a problem in this context.[12] Insofar as those votes represent a positive judgment by the voter—either satisfaction with all options or indecisiveness among them—they speak to Front-side issues. In any case, the effect is to reduce the overall size of the problem votes.

The independent variable in this group of studies was voting system and these too were designated by multiple terms. The Cal Tech/MIT studies used the following categories: *Lever Machine, Hand Marked Paper Ballot, Optical Scans, Punch Card* (Data Vote or VotoMatic), and *Direct Recording*.[13] The study's conclusions have to do with this technology and the "average incidence of spoiled, uncounted, and unmarked ballots." They provide ranking of the quality of the technology saying that optical scan-precinct count machines perform best.[14] Their ranking of electronic voting was unexpected and would prove controversial. The term "Electronic voting" refers to two actions: a method of counting ballots and a method of both casting and counting ballots. This report expects both to expand in the future but points to certain caveats: that ballot-casting DRE machines do not perform notably well and raise substantial security issues. Their observations were especially provocative to the vendors and would occasion a heated reply from another study group funded in part by a vendor.[15]

Conclusions about remedy appear to be contrary. On one hand "simply changing voting equipment" would have major impact—"The U.S. can cut the number of lost votes *due to voting equipment* in half by 2004 using equipment that is already available."[16] On the other hand, they "believe that human factors drive much of the 'error' in voting." The question is just where to locate the problem and how to differentiate appropriate remedies. This is especially confusing because if it where "human" error, is "more of an engineering problem." That would resolve the apparent contradiction in this text but it would also put "human" problems on the margin.[17]

The final report moves away from the quantitative analysis that had been the focus of the preliminary reports to offer a larger set of definitions, and recommendations. Here it is an occasion to conceptualize the components of the act of voting and to anticipate national impact and feasible reform strategies. It is self-consciously (and academically) comprehensive a fact that is reinforced by the national database, effectively placing the Florida story in larger context.[18] One table actually lists residual vote data by state showing Florida was not exceptional nor was the way residual voting *increases* for lower offices on the ballot. They call attention to the emergence of "absentee and early voting" practices as a special characteristic of elections today where many states have moved toward "on demand" absentee balloting before election day. It requires attention not only to traditional absentee balloting "for cause" by mail or at the voting office but to such practices as mail-in ballots.[19]

Yet the analysis comes down to a formalist and mechanical description. The attention of the work is more to the backside on issues of accuracy in counting and recounting.[20] Its picture of the evolution of current voting practices is especially unsophisticated. Thus points in the process that have come to be especially problematic such as "registration," and the "secret ballot," are taken as a given made necessary by "fraud and corruption."[21] But "fraud and corruption" has been merely one leg in the contest over democratic rights, the other one having to do with access and majority rule. In this report, the very categorization wherein constraints on voting are taken as a given, is misleading about the way election rules are implicated in the second process.

Six other reports would deal with election technology. "Election Reform in Detroit" was released April 5, 2001 and prepared by the Staff of the Committee on Governmental Reform of the U.S. House. The short report is focused on "uncounted" ballots in Detroit, Michigan where, between the elections of 1996 and 2000, punch card machines were replaced by optical scan machines. The report was a "before and after" evaluation comparing the uncounted ballots in the two elections and showing a sharp improvement.[22]

The next report was produced by the Institute for Communitarian Policy Studies at George Washington University and titled "Report on Election Systems Reform." They seek to "frame these issues as they might appear to officials and legislators confronted with the practical task of crafting cost-effective solutions to the challenge of election systems reform."[23] They emphasize the goal is to reduce the margin of error, not eliminating them altogether. This is a cost-benefit analysis to estimate the cost of replacing voting systems for the entire nation. They build a database containing prices of election machines based on a survey of vendors. They rely heavily on news media reports to frame their sense of the situation and call on data from the Caltech/MIT study. It would take an expansive view of the place of Florida saying it "brought the question of election reform to the forefront of policy issues facing the nation."[24]

They reach conclusion in three broad areas.[25] First, the costs involved in "a complete overhaul of the nation's voting systems hardware" comes to $1.2 billion and they recommend a $600 million federal grant program to assist this. Second, they determine the preferred machine to be optical scan precinct-count machine. Third, they warn that "technology alone will not provide a complete solution." Their analysis is clearly about technological remedies, however. They say that "problems with electoral systems are at their heart technical," that "the core issues in the Florida recount controversy originated in failures of technology and outmoded technology at that" and that "technical solutions to these problems already exist." They are thus led to ground "the issue of elections systems reform" in "political will and resource allocation."[26] In this, voter education falls under the head of "non-technological measures."[27]

The next technology report came from the group that had prepared the earlier Detroit report. Here they investigate "income and racial disparities in vote counting at the national level" to determine "whether voters in low-income, high-minority districts had their votes discarded in the 2000 election at higher rates than voters in affluent, low-minority districts." It developed a body of data drawn from 40 congressional districts in 20 states, differentiated by race and income, for which they tabulated the uncounted votes and the type of machines used.[28]

The Report made three separate findings: that voters in poor minority districts were more likely to have their votes discarded; that better technology reduced the percentage of uncounted votes in these districts; and that better technology reduced the disparity in uncounted votes between the two classes of districts. They report that the largest reduction in disparities occurred with "precinct-counted optiscan," machine.

The Democratic Investigative Staff of the House Committee on the Judiciary prepared another technology report. The report is a state-by-state survey of voting comparing spoiled ballots, the margin of difference in the presidential vote, and the use of punch card machines. It found that in the 32 states with complete data, some 1.3 million ballots "were discarded with no vote for president." The state results are in a "Spoiled Ballot Table," attached to the report.[29]

Overall this report shifts dramatically to front side issues, going back to campaign tactics in its listing or questions and relevant data. They conclude that there is

> . . . no doubt that serious deficiencies exist in the conduct of elections in virtually every state and that these deficiencies block voters from exercising their constitutionally protected right to vote. What this investigation uncovered was that *Florida is just the tip of the iceberg.* (emphasis in original)[30]

They recommend federal laws mandating machine standards, provisional ballots, sample ballots, and notification of status of registration.[31]

A September 2001 study was devoted to comparing the performance of voting technology. It was based on research conducted between May and September of 2001 by a group at the University of California, Berkeley with partial funding from a voting machine vendor based in Oakland. The study "focuses narrowly," the authors write, on back side issues. It was conducted to "determine which voting systems do the best job of recording and tabulating votes," and the results were published in a final report in September titled "Counting all the Votes: The Performance of Voting Technology in the United States."[32]

The report emphasizes definition and methodology. This report exhibits a refreshing sensitivity to the challenges in collecting data nation wide and they discuss variations in the reliability. They built a database for the 2000 presidential election for county data on type of voting system, total votes cast, total ballots submitted, and certain demographic and political factors (competitiveness). In the final analysis, they would use data from 38 states in the analysis.

They elect to use "residual votes" as their "proxy" for a dependent variable and re-enter the definition process. Here the residual vote is the simple remainder when the total vote for a given office is subtracted from the total ballots submitted on election day. The definition is formally clear: it would be composed of undervotes, overvotes, and "counting errors" (where either a proper ballot was not counted or an improper one was[33]). There are, thus, four types of errors that constitute the residual vote. Type I, the "undervote," is especially troublesome because of the sense that some is intentional and, thus not a problem in the context of the 2000 experience. Their discussion of the minuend is less clear. They would distinguish "total vote," from "total turnout" (or "who shows up") pointing out why the two may differ and/or be reported differently by officials. But the narrative is confusing and about which figure works.[34]

They do find a villain—punch card machines—among the voting systems. They say, however, that "the relative performance of the other systems cannot be determined." They emphasize the poor performance of punch card systems and seek to resurrect the electronic systems for more positive consideration. Here the report seeks to rebut the Cal Tech/MIT study and favor electronic voting systems.[35]

The final technology report was a part of a trio issued in mid-October by the General Accounting Office.[36] This report was devoted to a study of the relationship of the "uncounted" vote to types of "voting equipment." It "statistically analyzed county-level data to investigate relationships among the counties' demographic characteristics, their voting equipment and their percentages of uncounted presidential votes." The demographic variables included race, age, income, and poverty rates and education. The research, started in March, was released in mid-October 2001 in "Elections: Statistical Analysis of Factors That Affected Uncounted Votes in the 2000 Presidential Election."[37]

The GAO study identified the voting equipment as the independent variable and used the five common machine types. The dependent variable was here named the "uncounted presidential votes."[38] The data base was composed of 43 states and the District of Columbia. They find that punch card machines are a main culprit, but do not find that the electronic machinery is as problematic as asserted by the Caltech/MIT study. They found with an unpublished academic report that race and economic status were not associated with the presence of punch card machines although "counties with higher percentages of African-Americans had higher percentages of uncounted presidential votes" and racial difference does not disappear.[39] Like the House Committee report, GAO found that percentages of uncounted votes were higher in high minority communities, "regardless of voting equipment."[40]

This completes a subset of reports focused primarily on technology. The reports were released at different times over the period but are considered together here because of their common subject matter and data focus. We can now turn to the other reports and consider them in chronological sequence starting with early 2001.

IV

In February of 2001, the National Association of Secretaries of State released the first of two statements. Directed to state and local officials, it recommended attention to non-discrimination, equipment, recount standards, training, intergovernmental cooperation on list management, compliance with voting systems standards and collection of data for public awareness. The resolution of July 17, 2001 addressed federal action. It endorsed flexible block grants and discouraged federal mandates and supported provisional balloting. They ask that any study commission include election officials and proposed creation of a special election mail rate.[41]

In March, the General Accounting Office would produce "Elections: The Scope of Congressional Authority," provided information on the constitutional source for congressional authority, statutes where congress had regulated, court opinions responding to those efforts and the use of the funding power to influence local election practices. The thrust of this report is that congressional authority, while not complete, is substantial in five main areas: timing of federal elections, voter registration, absentee balloting, accessibility for elderly and handicapped, and prohibition on discriminatory voting practices.[42] The federal legislation covering these areas is listed in the table.

The next report, also in March, was prepared by the Special Task Force appointed by the Florida governor.[43] Direct, comprehensive and worried, it opens with an ode to First Principles (or "enduring principles of elections"[44]), explores "lessons learned" and concludes with 35 policy recommendations and five "recommended future studies."[45] A central theme is the character of "Florida's Constitutionally-mandated decentralized system of elections administration." The decentralization has to do with authority for the election process as well as budget requests that are "a major factor in the types of voting systems, in voter education, and other important elements, including voter registration records." Decentralization also "made it difficult to obtain reliable information from a single source or assign responsibility."[46]

The Florida report will likely attain a certain historical visibility because of the controversial election that made it necessary. While clearly disturbed, the text conveys a detachment about the experience. It speaks of "voter error," and "allegations" of problems at the polls. It avoids sustained analysis of partisan impact or of race or other conditions that might be expected under the terms of voting law. Recommendations are geared toward a technical fix focusing on selection among alternatives mechanisms and legal reforms. It is informative about the dysfunctionality of decentralized election administration in the state. It says that reform requires better thinking about options involving expensive "voting systems." Recommendations address: voter education, responsibility, and training; "voting system" quality; and "procedures and law," including registration records, voter identification, provisional ballots, scheduling of elections, ballot design, recounts and certification of outcome.

The Civil Rights Commission's Florida report was released in June 2001.[47] "Voting Irregularities in Florida During the 2000 Presidential Election," also concerns one state but it is more centered on troubles in the election process or "voter disenfranchisement." The report is decidedly "front side." It calls attention to distribution of absentee ballots, intimidation by police presence, flaws in the agency-based registration, poor communication at voting precincts, polls closed or relocated, and erroneous registration lists. It attributes these troubles less to intentional scheme than to "ineptitude, and inefficiency" commenting that "the most dramatic undercount in the Florida election was the uncast ballots of countless eligible voters who were wrongly turned away."[48]

The Commission undertook the study to see if the disenfranchisement had a racial impact. It has intensive statistical analysis of two patterns: purges by the felony list and "uncounted ballots." A statewide database was developed using data from counties on election returns, machine type, and a "variety" of demographic variables. A smaller precinct-wide database contained voting returns and registration by race for three counties. They found a racial pattern where African-Americans were more likely than whites to have ballots rejected and to be erroneously listed on the felony purge list. It suggested that formal inquiry by the Justice Department would show a violation under the VRA.[49]

The report takes up the issue of decentralization. The problem is exemplified in several occurrences. The management of lists to certify eligible voters was unreliable. Legitimate registrants were challenged and some turned away; no dependable mechanism was in place to enable proof of registration at the polls. This was complicated by the misuse of the felony listing. It proved unreliable in certifying either the status of those convicted under Florida law or those who migrated there after serving time in another state. Eligible persons were turned away when their name was on the list; some ineligible ex-felons actually voted in the election. Another dramatic consequence of the decentralization is the lack of uniform ballot design over the state. Decisions made by one election supervision resulted in a design that is credited with confusing the choice of thousands of voters.

While the Commission's report is about front side problems it remains top down. The concern with the culpability of high officials, is admirable but labored and the attention to elite responsibility deflects attention from community level activity. The emphasis on formal proof is also unproductive. Detailed discussion of the Voting Rights Act explores whether there is a basis for prosecution under the terms of that Act. This requires attention to legal details of the Act and to inquiry about standards of proof that can confirm a negative result through review of aggregate statistics.

The text of the report also reflects the instability of the emerging terminology. It refers to the counting errors by various terms (unrecorded votes, rejected ballots, uncast ballots, ballot spoilage, vote rejection, as well as overvote and undervote) and seeks to catalogue the impact of the miscounting on a set of victims (again, the terms used here varies, they use "black," as well as "people-" or "communities-" of color) protected under nation's legal and moral authority.

"Election 2000: Review and Recommendations by the Nation's Election Administrators," was released in July 2001.[50] The report came out of a Center based in Houston composed of election professionals in counties and municipalities. They open the report asserting that, despite the 2000 election, "America's election system is *not* in crisis."[51] Overall, the Task Force defined its central concern to be supporting more standardization through federal intervention in election policy in the context of a history and culture of decentralized election administration.

They do write in awareness of the other studies and "recognize and applaud the contributions made by a multitude of committees, task forces and commissions." But they say this Task Force is of particular importance because they are front line professionals concerned with "operational aspects." They are dismissive of some news media and some academic groups—an attitude that was to be registered as well in a survey of their constituency reported three months later.[52] They "disagree directly," with the statement that "by replacing the problem counting system we will eliminate the problem." Indeed, in the text and in a glossary they dispute use of some key terms such as "overvote" and "undervote"[53] and they insist on a distinction between "vote tally devices" and "operational standards" in the process. Finally, they continue a cautious attitude about voter registration not only taking its evolution as a natural but worrying that recent efforts to address that have hampered the work of the professionals.[54]

Wrong Turn: A Dissenting Effort

At this point, we see the completion of a First Round in this process. Seven months had passed since the controversial election. The technology reports had been issued by the Cal Tech/MIT project and by the Congressional Research Service, and the House Committee on Government reform. There had also been reports by the GAO, the Election Center, the Florida Task Force and the Civil Rights Commission. Resolutions had been submitted by the National Association of Secretaries of State, and the National Conference of State Legislators. The Florida Election Reform Act had been enacted May 9.

Cross-referencing is limited but the reports do amount to a fledgling language of reform. They convey some sense of overall significance, how to define the problem, what reforms should be tried and what authority should be responsible. In general, there is ceremonial testimony to a natural—certainly an American—right to vote and a sense that the 2000 incident is significant and involves some "lessons" even if we look only within one state. But these early reports have a legalistic, bureaucratic and mechanistic tone, begging at this stage for some corrective critical response better centered on communities and everyday life and the anxiety of the individual voter. The Commission's report had made a step toward a diverging line of analysis, what with the emphasis on front-side problems, including reports of intimidation, but it would continue to reinforce the developing approach. Yet a certain optimism was created coming less from any expectation that resolution was at hand than that a frame for addressing election problems would emerge in the hurly-burly of activity created by the election outcome.

In a sense, voting activists were at a point where their own assessments were in need of a correction. It was in this context that there is released a "dissenting statement," by two members of the Civil Rights Commission.[55] The Statement was released in mid-July cast in terms that are remarkable given the moment. It is a sharp rebuke to the Commission's report calling it "prejudicial, divisive, and injurious to the cause of true democracy in our society;" saying it "fostered public distrust, alienation and manifest cynicism" and "provides no basis upon which to reform the electoral process in Florida or anywhere else."[56] Broad and bold, it signaled that a critical stance was there to be articulated.

Yet the dissenters would fail to hit target. The strategy was to seize on the racially narrow, lawyer-like report and submit rebuttal. That reinforced a fundamentalist reading that sees the text more as Final Argument than a basis to frame precise charges in more formal litigation (which the Commission acknowledges) and is thus constrained within the parameters of the Commission's report.[57]

The concerns of the Dissenting Statement fall in three main areas: statistical interpretation, alternative explanatory variables, and legal theory of the Voting Rights Act.[58] Here, they respond in kind to the Commission devoting a first portion to arcane discussion of "Statistical Analysis" that takes up 21 of the 55 pages or about 40 percent of the body of the report. In a play on the terminology problems, the dissenters chose to focus not on "spoiled" ballots but on "overvotes" and "undervotes." They maintain that voter intention and especially "voter error" is the main explanation for the ballots not counted.[59] There would be nearly 200,000 of these in that Florida election and the Statement dismisses concern that this may result in disenfranchisement saying that these are matters of choice (the undervote), indecision or voter error (the overvote) and a "machine error," said to be miniscule and randomly distributed among voters.[60]

A more direct statistical criticism has to do with inference rules and the "ecological fallacy." They note that aggregate-level data cannot be used to assign individual characteristics thus it cannot be said that *black* (or *white*) persons cast invalid ballots even if the numbers of such ballots vary positively with the group's population in the aggregate (e.g. county or precinct).[61] The criticism was directed at the Commission's conclusion that the rejection ratio between blacks and whites was 9:1. They dispute the conclusion given the use of county-level data (for the state-wide estimate), and precinct-level data (for three counties), because of the ecological fallacy and they note that the precinct data show a smaller differential.[62]

The third statistical problem concerned how to assess the relationship of race and the pattern of uncounted ballots observed. The Commission had made a central conclusion with a number of formulations: that "the chance of being placed on this (ineligible) list in error is greater for African-Americans;" that there is "a direct correlation between race and having one's vote discounted;" and that "an African American's chance of having his or her vote rejected as a spoiled ballot was significantly greater than a white voter's."[63] The

Dissenting authors disputed the racial connection insisting that the variation in the number of spoiled ballots, while high among the black voters, ought not be explained by reference to their race. At issue here were: (1) interpretation of patterns in the data; and (2) inclusion of other variables. The Dissenters complained that they needed the Commission's data to check the interpretation through separate data runs. That denied, the Dissenters ran a separate analysis and concluded that race does not explain the variation in the spoiled ballots. As an alternative to the racial explanation, the Statement sought to ground the higher spoilage rate in other variables saying, for example, that "the obvious explanation for a higher number of spoiled ballots among black voters is their lower literacy rate."[64] Similarly, differential criminal behavior would account for the misidentifications with the felony list.[65]

The commission report had been inconsistent in two troubling ways. One was its use of terms for the problem ballots and the other its designation of victims in the Florida process. The Statement would criticize the discussion of the victims and went on to impugn the competence of the Commission for failing to include other minority groups, especially Hispanics, and for the limited attention to questions of accessibility. The Statement also criticized the commission for its assessment of the responsibility of state officials. They emphasize the independent constitutional and budgetary status of local voting officials in a decentralized system that removes high state officials from direct responsibility.

In an arresting passage the Statement takes on what it calls "bureaucratic problems." Here it argues that a range of activities prevented voting and these are bureaucratic in nature rather than "actual discrimination." Such an analysis opens an avenue of inquiry and reform that would get around narrow legalistic racializing. They mention establishing eligibility at the polls, stabilizing polling location and hours, accessibility, and ballot design. But the question here is not settled, as the Statement would have, when we determine that there was no racial intent to discriminate or, even, that the offending practices occurred under the management of poll workers who were either simply honest or actually members of the losing political party. Rather there is a need to assess the impact of the overall process (including whether there is a disparate racial impact). Attention to the bureaucratic issue provides a powerful option to expand the discourse that was developing in the new reform movement. The authors of the Statement would themselves say that "by stressing litigation rather than education, the majority report is heading in the wrong direction," but their own comments on this are more seductive than substantive, driven more by the decision to refute than to the challenge to reground a debate then veering toward a crossroad.[66] Indeed after calling attention to the legalist pitfall, the Statement, hewing to Commission themes, moves to dispute the legal analysis of the Voting Rights Act!

There are some cross-references here, but unfortunately, it ignores most of the other reports available by midyear. Their references are almost exclusively to the Commission, which is cited repeatedly for purposes of refutation. It strains the reader's patience with its monotonous counter argumentation much of which involves process within the Commission itself. The monotony is aggravated by a tone of bitterness leaving a harsh edge to the rhetoric and unnecessary contentiousness and petty repetition. Thus several routine points made about the adequacy of statistical inference, were blown out to challenge the politics, motives, and honesty of the statistician employed by the commission. The Statement would have little impact on the developing discourse or policy proposals and remains a missed opportunity.

Consensus, Implementation, Monitoring

The next report came from the highly visible National Commission on Federal Election Reform. The commission was composed of 17 members plus honorary co-chairmen Jimmy Carter and Gerald Ford, the former presidents. Their work involved both formal research and public hearings, but no special data base. Four high profile public hearings were held March-June at the presidential libraries of Carter, Reagan, Lyndon Johnson, and Ford. It collected information through its hearings, from other commission reports and through special task forces of experts. In August 2001, they released "To Assure Pride and Confidence in the Election Process" with 13 recommendations plus concurring and dissenting statements and other appendixes.[67]

Responding to the dynamic context set by the 2000 election studies, the report would display some urgency for consensus and closure. It expressed impatience with the plethora of study groups—"We do not see the need for another blue-ribbon commission of task force," they would write.[68] There is also a dramatic call for non-cooperation with the exit polling so to discourage election projections by the news media. They note that close elections occur often for important national and state offices,[69] that the "electoral system was tested by a political ordeal unlike any in living memory," and "last year's election shook American faith in the legitimacy of the democratic process." National, somber, foreboding, the Florida problem has been substantially extended in this construction.[70]

They note "each generation must nourish and improve the processes of democracy."[71] They do point to constitutional provisions and customs and practices that serve as the framework for voting in the U.S. They note the broad authority of congress in the regulation of federal elections and the central role of states. The overall tone of the report's analysis is cautious. They discuss fears of fraud and give explicit examples yet they say "vote fraud is difficult to discover and prosecute."[72] They do not endorse same day registration, for example and express skepticism about early, absentee, remote and Internet voting. It calls for more centralized administration of elections but would locate that in the state rather than federal government. The 13 Policy Recommendations are:

1. States should enact statewide voter registration
2. States should provide provisional voting by any who claims to be qualified to vote in that state
3. Federal legislation to hold elections on a national holiday
4. Federal legislation to simplify and facilitate absentee voting overseas
5. States should restore voting rights to persons convicted of a felony
6. States and federal governments should take steps to comply with and enforce voting rights laws
7. States should set a bench mark for voting system performance, expressed as a percentage of residual votes
8. Federal government should develop voting systems standards
9. States should define what constitutes a vote on its voting equipment
10. News organizations should not project presidential election results so long as polls remain open in the 48 states
11. Federal funding of $300-$400 million annually with 50-50 state match for election administration
12. Federal responsibilities should be assigned to a new federal agency
13. Federal government should provide assistance for election administration and set policy objectives while states will select strategies at their discretion

The next report would come from the National Council of State Legislators Task Force issued in August 2001. The NCSL Task Force was formed after the election in Florida "on the assumption that states are the appropriate level of government for enacting any election reforms." The Task Force met six times between March and July. It heard testimony from experts, observed presentations from vendors and drew extensively on the other reports. It adopted 36 recommendations directed to state legislatures to be used "in working with the federal government." The priority is on maneuvering to influence any shift in federal power.[73]

The significance of Florida is expansive; they "acknowledge(s) that a national debate on election reform has begun." It emphasizes involvement by states and the NCSL and conditions support on such. They recommended the use of flexible federal block grants in language preferring "broad principles," over "specific mandates." It opposed the creation of any new agency given the FEC. It proposed block grants in six areas: improving election technology, voter registration and list maintenance, improving security and vote counts, voter education, providing greater access to registration and polling places, training for personnel. In the revised version, it recommended amending the NVR to ease removal of names and supported funding for the Office of Election Administration to develop voluntary standards.

The next report would come out of the Constitution Project at Georgetown University, which launched the Forum on

Election Reform in February of 2001. The body would organize itself into five workings groups whose work became the basis for the final report, "Building Consensus on Election Reform." They note that their work developed in the context of a number of other reports and say that "The broad agreement that we found . . . mirrors a comparable unity that is emerging in these major studies."[74] And a good deal of the report is peppered with references to "consensus" or "agreement." The appended statements here, including one by a member of the forum, indicate the more conflicted terrain in which they developed their proposals and, interestingly enough, the limitations of the core proposals advanced. They repeat the now standard line about the autonomy of state policy and make separate recommendations to the states and to congress. "We share with many others the view that primary responsibility for conducting elections should remain at the state and local level."[75]

The next set of reports shift to monitor the reform process. The first of these was prepared by Common Cause and released on the anniversary of the controversial election. "Not Making the Grade: A Year after Florida, Little Action in States on Election Reform" is a survey of the policies in the states to assess conditions. A state-by-state review "shows that very little has been done." A couple of summary numbers sum up their conclusion: only sixteen states received a grade of B or better and only 11 states improved to a higher grade over the year. Two states received "F" and two received "A."[76]

A second monitoring report was released nine months later by the NAACP, titled "Defending the Vote: Holding Officials Accountable." It also focused on election reforms within the states and provided a point scale and letter grade.[77] The NAACP developed two sets of criteria, one to apply to the governor and another to apply to the chief elections officer.[78] Their findings are listed in the Executive Summary and the press release and present a pessimistic picture of the situation then. The six main findings are:

1. Only a few governors signed notable legislation
2. No state explicitly prioritized replacement of oldest machines
3. Governors were "overwhelmingly silent" on felony voting rights
4. No state conducted an audit of its registration list
5. States are avoiding action while waiting on federal leadership
6. Only 14 states provide training from the state office directly to poll workers

The report noted that several states—Michigan and California—"deserve credit for their many innovations." Eight states got a "B" or better, one an "A," and five "F's."

The final major report to be discussed is actually the second of two monitoring reports of the Election Reform Information Project. It is designed to look at policy reforms at the federal, state and local levels to answer the questions what's changed, what hasn't and why? The first was published in October of 2001 and the second a year later.[79] Their initial report is technically the first of the monitoring reports to be issued coming in the weeks before the Common Cause report.

The second report came after the progress reports by the NAACP and Common Cause and followed a flurry of reform activity in the states as well as completion of senate and house negotiations on the new federal law. Its comments on that law identifies the key items of the new consensus: major federal spending, focus on state-level administration, reliance on the reform of voting machines. Respecting the moment of their report, they emphasize that the new federal bill is merely the "end of the beginning," now requiring decisive action in the states. They list state "highlights," but there is no state-by-state grading or basis for comparing this to the other monitoring reports.

Conclusion

In the 21 months between February 1, 2001 and November 2002, special study groups represented a distinctive voice in public discourse about the 2000 election. They conducted highly visible operations that frame the controversial outcome and issued a series of authoritative reports that will surely be significant reference texts for future thinking. "Blue Ribbon" advisory groups are often used, but seldom in such overlapping numbers here so intense that one study report was a review of the "outpouring of reports."[80] It may be a unique event in the nation's history.

The reports convey a complex image of the significance of Florida. Thus a state based focus coexists with a sweeping perspective wherein the problem is nationalized in agonizing terms and localized systems are seen as suspect. In its pivotal opinion, the Supreme Court said its ruling was based on Florida particulars. The Task Force of local election officials would declare that the "system is not in crisis," and in a survey on the anniversary of the 2000 election, they said the Florida events had little or no impact on their work and strongly oppose federal standards.[81] There was dissent in several task forces whose final reports would be accompanied by written attachments, some vigorous and critical, from members of the reporting commission or other stakeholders.[82]

In the end, the reports came to settle at a middling position accommodating key features of the current system. Federal action was needed but it should be directed to funding and formulating voluntary standards. There was a strong preference for state-centralized voting lists and state mandated provisional balloting and felony list regulation. And there was deference to local counties on the selection of machinery despite consensus that the Optical scan/precinct-count machine performed comparatively well on a proposed benchmark.[83] The conclusions of the process are probably best represented in the report of the Carter-Ford Commission listed above. Some notable proposals are not included there including those on the number of elections, voter identification, and reform of the purge rules of the NVR that now amount to an unfounded federal mandate.

It is not certain what the ultimate impact of the special studies will be. Unlike familiar cases with a single blue ribbon body, here there were numerous groups and a myriad of overlapping recommendations and resolutions. Also, pressures to change election policy came from other sources including some states that undertook aggressive review their election procedures, and federal civil rights lawsuits.[84] The impact of the special studies will likely be modest. The areas they cover are expensive, technology-intensive and, in the instance of felony rights, highly politicized. But the greater limit of these studies may be the areas that they do not cover, especially issues that are located in the sphere where mobilization intersects with the quality of the final vote. Community organizations will find these of little use, and, at least in the month preceding the mid terms elections of 2002, they may distract attention to election-day maneuvering and legalistic rights.

As a whole, the reports suggest a three-sector model of the voting problem: A front side centered on the individual voter; a middle part involving human and mechanical machinery (including defining a vote), and a back side focused on the meaning of "residual votes." These studies devote overwhelming attention to the second two sectors, and much of the most authoritative commentary is limited to the backside.[85] But the early reporting of the Florida story was about frustration of the intent of breathing voters, symbolized by the butterfly ballot but reflected in other incidents there and in the off-year elections the following year.[86] It compels careful attention to preparing the communities and individual voters we know to have firm preferences and to identifying "human factors" at the front side. Voter registration itself, and certainly its decentralization into counties and townships, needs to be reassessed more critically. Carter-Ford would acknowledge that voter registration was "a more modern innovation" but the brief history they provide remains sanitized. They do not mention its complicity in serial exclusions and continue a silence, resident in the other reports, about struggles that drove voting reform. It is simplistic, a-historical, and stigmatizing to represent registration as simple protection against fraud and corruption.

The recommendations are overly bureaucratic, managerial and invoke images less of a nimble responsiveness than an authoritarian apparatus. To ensure good lists, they would mandate "coordination" of personal data, including social security, between various government agencies. To prevent fraud, a voter identification number would be required and registrants must swear to citizenship at each vote. By moving away from the complaints raised by real voters in communities, the special studies risk a greater error—rationalization of a system of registration and balloting that eases the inconvenience for the affluent and active and likely would ensure continuation of politics under conditions of limited participation.

Notes

1. Reform proposals and historical background are reviewed in James McGregor Burns, "Beyond How We Cast Ballots to Deeper Issues of Election Reform," *Boston Globe*, January 20, 2001; Arthur Schlesinger Jr, "Not the People's Choice: How To Democratize American Democracy," *American Prospect* 13 (2002).; Frances Piven and Richard Cloward, *Why Americans Don't Vote* (New York: Pantheon, 1988).; and Alexander Keyssar, *The right to vote: the contested history of democracy in the United States* (New York: Basic Books, 2000).
2. See Articles I, II, and III of the Constitution of the United States and the U.S. Supreme Court's opinion in *Luther V Borden*, 48 U S 1 (1849) on the Guaranty Clause.
3. Frederick Douglass, *My Bondage and My Freedom: Life and Times of Frederick Douglass: His Early Life as a Slave, His Escape from Bondage, and His Complete History, Written by Himself* (New York: Collier Books, 1962) See pp. 220-21 for a discussion of the place of race in the Dorr Rebellion.
4. Andrew Jackson, "First Annual Message," in *A compilation of the messages and papers of the presidents*, ed. James D. Richardson (New York: Bureau of National Literature, 1913).
5. *Baker V. Carr*, 369 U.S. 186 (1962) and *Reynolds v. Sims*, 377 U. S. 533 (1964).
6. Lyndon Johnson, "Special Message to the Congress: The American Promise," (1965).
7. The film is William Haugse, Richard Ray Perez, and Joan Sekler, "Unprecedented [videorecording]: the 2000 presidential

election," ed. Joan Sekler and Richard Ray Perez (Santa Monica, CA: L.A. Independent Media Center, 2002).
8. *Bush V. Gore,* 531 U S 98 (2000).
9. Voting Technology Project, "Voting: What Is, What Could Be," (Boston: California Institute of Technology and Massachusetts Institute of Technology, 2001). See cover letter.
10. Stephen Ansolabehere, "A Preliminary Assessment of the Reliability of Existing Voting Equipment," (Boston: California Institute of Technology and Massachusetts Institute of Technology, 2001); Stephen Ansolabehere, "Residual Votes Attributable to Technology," (Boston: California Institute of Technology and Massachusetts Institute of Technology, 2001); Voting Technology Project, "Voting: What Is, What Could Be," (Boston: California Institute of Technology and Massachusetts Institute of Technology, 2001);
11. Ansolabehere, "A Preliminary Assessment of the Reliability of Existing Voting Equipment,", p. 3.
12. Voting Technology Project, "Voting: What Is, What Could Be," p. 21.
13. Ansolabehere, "A Preliminary Assessment of the Reliability of Existing Voting Equipment," Slightly different names are used in listings in the other reports by the Federal Elections Commission at *http://www.fec.gov/elections.html* and see the comment on the "gross categorizations," in Henry Brady et al., "Counting all the Votes: The Performance of Voting Technology in the United States," (Berkeley: University of California, 2001), p. 6.
14. Ibid., See central finding p.3 and ranking table p 10.
15. Voting Technology Project, "Voting: What Is, What Could Be,"
16. Ibid., p. 17. Emphasis added.
17. Ibid., p. 10.
18. Ibid., pp. 6-7, 17 and Table p. 89.
19. Ibid., pp. 36-41.
20. Ibid., p. 58 and page 65-66, for a summation of the problem.
21. Ibid., p. 13, 26 and 43.
22. Committee on Government Reform Minority Staff, "Election Reform in Detroit: New Voting Technology and Increased Voter Education Significantly reduced Uncounted Ballots," (Washington, DC: U.S. House of Representatives, 2001).
23. Ibid., p.2.
24. Norton Garfinkle and Patrick Glynn, "Report on Election Systems Reform,", (Washington: Institute for Communitarian Studies, George Washington University, 2001), p. 1 and p. 5.
25. Ibid. p. 17.
26. Ibid., p. 2.
27. Ibid., p. 3 and 15-26.
28. Committee on Government Reform Minority Staff, "Income and Racial Disparities in the Undercount in the 2000 Presidential Election," (Washington: Committee on Government Reform, U.S. House of Representatives, 2001), p.2.
29. Committee of the Judiciary Democratic Investigative Staff, U.S. House of Representatives, "How to Make over One Million Votes Disappear: Electoral Sleight of Hand in the 2000 Presidential Election," (Washington: Democratic Investigative Staff, Committee of the Judiciary, U.S. House of Representatives, 2001), p. 14 and 121.
30. Ibid., p. 6; and 13-17.
31. Ibid., p. 188-19.
32. Brady et al., "Counting all the Votes: The Performance of Voting Technology in the United States," p. 4. See other statements of the study goal pp. 8; 17 and 47
33. Ibid., p. 8 footnote #16.
34. Ibid., p. 17-19.

35. Ibid., p. 20.
36. General Accounting Office, "Elections: A Framework for Evaluating Reform Proposals," (Washington, DC: General Accounting Office, 2001); General Accounting Office, "Elections: Perspectives on Activities and Challenges across the Nation," (Washington, DC: General Accounting Office, 2001); General Accounting Office, "Elections: Statistical Analysis of Factors That Affected Uncounted Votes in the 2000 Presidential Election," (Washington, DC: General Accounting Office, 2001).
37. Ibid., p. 2.
38. General Accounting Office, "Elections: Perspectives on Activities and Challenges Across the Nation," p. 14.
39. There is no complete cite here but the reference is apparently to Stephen Knack and Martha Kropf, "Who Uses Inferior Voting Technology," ((unpublished) Kansas City: University of Missouri, 2001).
40. General Accounting Office, "Elections: Perspectives on Activities and Challenges across the Nation," pp. 6; 12.
41. National Association of Secretaries of State, "Resolution (Federal), in *National Association of Secretaries of State* (2001); National Association of Secretaries of State, "Resolution (State and Local)," in *National Association of Secretaries of State* (2001).
42. "Elections: The Scope of Congressional Authority," (Washington, DC: General Accounting Office, 2001). *www.gao.gov*
43. A number of other states would become active in the formal study of their elections systems and issue reports. George was especially active. Matt Blunt, "Making Every Vote Count: Report of the Secretary of State Matt Blunt to the People of Missouri," (Jefferson City: Missouri Secretary of State, 2001). Bill Bradbury, Oregon Secretary of State, "Report of the Oregon Elections Task Force," (Salem, OR: Oregon Secretary of State, 2001); Cathy Cox, "The 2000 Election: A Wake-up Call for Reform and Change: Report to the Governor and Members of the General Assembly," (Atlanta: Georgia Secretary of State: Twenty First Century Voting Commission, 2001); Chet Culver, "Iowa's Election 2000: Facts, Findings, and Our Future," (Iowa Secretary of State, 2001); Andrew Galli, Evan Parness, and Damian Delgado, "Building a Better Democracy: A Report of the Commission to Study Rhode Island Election Procedures," (Providence: Commission to Study Rhode Island Election Procedures, 2002); Standards and Technology Governor's 2002 Select Task Force on Election Procedures, "Draft of 2002 Select Task Force on Election Procedures, Standards and Technology," (Tallahassee, FL: Collins Center for Public Policy, 2002); Standards and Technology Governor's Select Task Force on Election Procedures, "Revitalizing Democracy in Florida," (Tallahassee: The Collins Center for Public Policy, 2001); Bill Secretary of State Jones, "A Report on the Feasibility of Internet Voting," (Sacramento: California Secretary of State, 2002). Special Committee on Voting Systems and Election Procedures in Maryland, "Report and Recommendations," (Baltimore: Special Committee on Voting Systems and Election procedures in Maryland, 2001); "Voting Matters in New York: Participation, Choice, Action, Integrity," (Office of Attorney General Eliot Spitzer, 2001).

44. Governor's Select Task Force on Election Procedures, "Revitalizing Democracy in Florida," p. 9.
45. Ibid., pp. 74-85.
46. Ibid., pp. 13; 15 and 50.
47. United States Commission on Civil Rights, "Voting Irregularities in Florida During the 2000 Presidential Election, with Appendix," (Washington, DC: United States Commission on Civil Rights, 2001). The Commission had released an interim report United States Commission on Civil Rights, "Status Report on Probe of Election Practices in Florida During the 2000 Presidential Election," (Washington, DC: U.S. Commission on Civil Rights, 2001).
48. Ibid., Quotes are from p. XII.
49. United States Commission on Civil Rights, "Status Report on Probe of Election Practices in Florida During the 2000 Presidential Election," p. 100.
50. National Task Force on Election Reform, "Election 2000: Review and Recommendations by the Nation's Elections Administrators," (Houston: The Election Center, 2001).
51. Ibid., p. 6, emphasis in original.
52. Election Reform Information Project, "Ready for 2002, Forgetting 2000: Election Officials Oppose Federal Standards and See Only Minor Impact of Election 2000," (Washington, DC: Election Reform Information project, 2002), p. 4.
53. National Task Force on Election Reform, "Election 2000: Review and Recommendations by the Nation's Elections Administrators," p. 26 and 53.
54. Ibid., 45.
55. Abigail Thernstrom and Russell Redenbaugh, "The Florida Election Report: Dissenting Opinion," (New York: Manhattan Institute for Policy Research, 2001). Although both were participating members of the Commission, their work did not amount to a "minority report," due to conflicts about procedures for preparing the statement. See comment in the Commission's report at p. 125 and "dissenting statement," at p. 130 and see pp. 51-52 of the Statement.
56. Ibid. p 1., p. 3.
57. So much so that they would make much of their need for data collected by the statistician that worked on the Commission's report.
58. Thernstrom and Redenbaugh, "The Florida Election Report: Dissenting Opinion," p.10.
59. Ibid., p. 13.
60. Ibid., pp. 11 - 13. And here they do quote the first CalTech/MIT study Ansolabehere, "A Preliminary Assessment of the Reliability of Existing Voting Equipment," at p. 13.
61. See their description in Thernstrom and Redenbaugh, "The Florida Election Report: Dissenting Opinion," p. 14.
62. The Commission's statistician provided additional data that reaffirmed the initial analysis in Alan Lichtman, "Supplemental Report on the Racial Impact of the Rejection of Ballots Case in Florida's 2000 Presidential Election and in Response to the Statement of the Dissenting Commissioners and Report of Dr. John Lott Submitted to the U.S. Senate on Rules and Administration in July 2001," (Washington, DC: Appendix in U.S. Commission on Civil Rights, Voting Irregularities in Florida, 2001).
63. "Voting Irregularities in Florida During the 2000 Presidential Election, with Appendix," (Washington, DC: United States Commission on Civil Rights, 2001), p. 24.
64. Thernstrom and Redenbaugh, "The Florida Election Report: Dissenting Opinion," p. 19.
65. Ibid., p. 46.
66. Ibid., See p. 38, 41.

67. National Commission on Federal Election Reform, "To Assure Pride and Confidence in the Electoral Process," (Charlottesville: Miller Center of Public Affairs, University of Virginia, 2001).
68. Ibid., p. 71.
69. Ibid., p.51.
70. Ibid., quotes from p. 17.
71. Ibid., p. 19.
72. Ibid., p. 27 and note #14, p. 74. and see note #25.
73. National Conference of State Legislatures, "Voting in America: Final Report of the NCSL Elections Reform Task Force," (Denver: National Conference of State Legislatures, 2001), pp. 7-8.
74. Constitution Project, "Building Consensus on Election Reform," (Washington, DC: Georgetown University, 2001).
75. Ibid., pp. 16-18.
76. Common Cause, "Not Making the Grade," (Washington, DC: Common Cause, 2001). P. 5; 8-9.
77. National Association for the Advancement of Colored People, "Defending the Vote: Holding Officials Accountable," (Baltimore: National Association for the Advancement of Colored People, 2002).
78. The criteria differ in separate listings in the report. Compare listings in Ibid., pp. 10 - 12 and 35-37.
79. Election Reform Information Project, "What's Changed, What Hasn't, and Why: Election Reform since November 2000,", (Washington, DC: Election Reform Information Project, 2001) and Election Reform Information Project, "What's Changed, What Hasn't, and Why: Election Reform since November 2001," (Washington, D.C.: Election Reform Information Project, 2002).
80. Election Reform Information Project, "Side-by-Side Comparison of Election Reform Task Force Reports," (Washington, DC: Election Reform Information Project, 2001), p.1. Also included as appendix in Election Reform Information Project, "What's Changed, What Hasn't, and Why: Election Reform Since November 2000". Reports summarized are National Commission on Election Standards and Reform, "Report and Recommendations to Improve America's Election System," (Washington: National Association of Counties, 2001); National Task Force on Election Reform, "Election 2000: Review and Recommendations by the Nation's Elections Administrators," Voting Technology Project, "Voting: What Is, What Could Be;" National Commission on Federal Election Reform, "To Assure Pride and Confidence in the Electoral Process"; The Constitution Project, "Building Consensus on Election Reform;" National Conference of State Legislatures, "Voting in America: Final Report of the Ncsl Elections Reform Task Force."
81. Election Reform Information Project, "Ready for 2002, Forgetting 2000: Election Officials Oppose Federal Standards and See Only Minor Impact of Election 2000," (Washington, DC: Election Reform Information project, 2002); National Task Force on Election Reform, "Election 2000: Review and Recommendations by the Nation's Elections Administrators," (Houston: The Election Center, 2001).
82. See especially the reports from the U.S. Commission on Civil Rights, the Carter-Ford Commission, the Constitution Project and the Berkeley study on voting technology.
83. National Commission on Federal Election Reform, "To Assure Pride and

Confidence in the Electoral Process," p. 54 for one proposed benchmark.

84. A review of the court cases and the disposition are in Election Reform Information Project, "What's Changed, What Hasn't, and Why: Election Reform since November 2000," pp. 12 - 14 and Election Reform Information Project, "What's Changed, What Hasn't, and Why: Election Reform since November 2001," pp. 21-22.

85. Cf. the categories in Voting Technology Project, "Voting: What Is, What Could Be," pp. 58ff.

86. Jon Gould, "Florida Moves North: Electoral Reform in Virginia Post-2000," (New York: The Century Foundation, 2002); Thad Hall, "L. A. Story," (New York: The Century Foundation, 2002); Ronald Hayduk, "The 2001 Election in New York City," (New York: The Century Foundation, 2002); Ingrid Reed, "The 2001 New Jersey Election," (New York: The Century Foundation, 2002).

References

Ansolabehere, Stephen. "A Preliminary Assessment of the Reliability of Existing Voting Equipment." Boston: California Institute of Technology and Massachusetts Institute of Technology, February 1, 2001.

—-. "Residual Votes Attributable to Technology." Boston: California Institute of Technology and Massachusetts Institute of Technology, March 30, 2001.

Baker V. Carr, 369 U.S. 186 (1962).

Blunt, Matt. "Making Every Vote Count: Report of the Secretary of State Matt Blunt to the People of Missouri." Jefferson City: Missouri Secretary of State, January 29, 2001.

Bradbury, Bill, Oregon Secretary of State. "Report of the Oregon Elections Task Force." Salem, OR: Oregon Secretary of State, February 6, 2001.

Brady, Henry, Justin Buchler, Matt Jarvis, and John McNulty. "Counting All the Votes: The Performance of Voting Technology in the United States." Berkeley: University of California,

Burns, James McGregor. "Beyond How We Cast Ballots to Deeper Issues of Election Reform." *Boston Globe,* January 20, 2001, 15.

Common Cause. "Not Making the Grade." Washington, DC: Common Cause, November 6, 2001.

Constitution Project. "Building Consensus on Election Reform." Washington, DC: Georgetown University,

Cox, Cathy. "The 2000 Election: A Wake-up Call for Reform and Change: Report to the Governor and Members of the General Assembly." Atlanta: Georgia Secretary of State, January, 2001.

—-. "Report of the 21st Century Voting Commission." Atlanta: Georgia Secretary of State: Twenty First Century Voting Commission.

Culver, Chet. "Iowa's Election 2000: Facts, Findings, and Our Future." Iowa Secretary of State, March 12, 2001.

Democratic Investigative Staff, Committee of the Judiciary, U.S. House of Representatives,. "How to Make over One Million Votes Disappear: Electoral Sleight of Hand in the 2000 Presidential Election." Washington: Democratic Investigative Staff, Committee of the Judiciary , U.S. House of Representatives, August 20, 2001.

Douglass, Frederick. *My Bondage and My Freedom: Life and Times of Frederick Douglass: His Early Life as a Slave, His Escape from Bondage, and His Complete History, Written by Himself.* New York: Collier Books, 1962.

Election Reform Information Project. "Side-by-Side Comparison of Election Reform Task Force Reports." Washington, DC: Election Reform Information Project, October 1, 2001.

—. "What's Changed, What Hasn't, and Why: Election Reform since November 2000." Washington, DC: Election Reform Information Project, October 22, 2001.

—. "Ready for 2002, Forgetting 2000: Election Officials Oppose Federal Standards and See Only Minor Impact of Election 2000." Washington, DC: Election Reform Information project, January 14, 2002.

—. "What's Changed, What Hasn't, and Why: Election Reform since November 2001." Washington, D. C.: Election Reform Information Project, October 22, 2002.

Galli, Andrew, Evan Parness, and Damian Delgado. "Building a Better Democracy: A Report of the Commission to Study Rhode Island Election Procedures." Providence: Commission to Study Rhode Island Election Procedures, January 9, 2002.

Garfinkle, Norton, and Patrick Glynn. "Report on Election Systems Reform." Washington: Institute for Communitarian Studies, George Washington University, July, 2001.

General Accounting Office. "Elections: A Framework for Evaluating Reform Proposals." Washington, DC: General Accounting Office, October 15, 2001.

—. "Elections: Perspectives on Activities and Challenges across the Nation." Washington, DC: General Accounting Office, October 15, 2001.

—. "Elections: The Scope of Congressional Authority." Washington, DC: GAO,

—. "Elections: Statistical Analysis of Factors That Affected Uncounted Votes in the 2000 Presidential Election." Washington, DC: General Accounting Office, October 15, 2001.

Gould, Jon. "Florida Moves North: Electoral Reform in Virginia Post-2000." New York: The Century Foundation, October 15, 2002.

Governor's 2002 Select Task Force on Election Procedures, Standards and Technology. "Draft of 2002 Select Task Force on Election Procedures, Standards and Technology." Tallahasse, FL: Collins Center for Public Policy, December 9, 2002.

Governor's Select Task Force on Election Procedures, Standards and Technology. "Revitalizing Democracy in Florida." Tallahassee: The Collins Center for Public Policy, March 1, 2001.

Hall, Thad. "L. A. Story." New York: The Century Foundation, October 15, 2002.

Haugse, William, Richard Ray Perez, and Joan Sekler. "Unprecedented [Video-recording]: The 2000 Presidential Election.", edited by Joan Sekler and Richard Ray Perez, 1 videocassette (50 min.). Santa Monica, CA: L.A. Independent Media Center, 2002.

Hayduk, Ronald. "The 2001 Election in New York City." New York: The Century Foundation, October 15, 2002.

Jackson, Andrew. "First Annual Message." In *A Compilation of the Messages and Papers of the Presidents,* edited by James D. Richardson, 1010-25. New York: Bureau of National Literature, 1913.

Johnson, Lyndon. "Special Message to the Congress: The American Promise." 1965.

Jones, Bill Secretary of State. "A Report on the Feasibility of Internet Voting." Sacramento: California Secretary of State, January, 2002.

Keyssar, Alexander. *The Right to Vote : The Contested History of Democracy in the United States.* New York: Basic Books, 2000.

Knack, Stephen, and Martha Kropf. "Who Uses Inferior Voting Technology." (unpublished) Kansas City: University of Missouri.

Lichtman, Alan. "Supplemental Report on the Racial Impact of the Rejection of Ballots Case in Florida's 2000 Presidential Election and in Response to the Statement of the Dissenting Commissioners and Report of Dr. John Lott Submitted to the U.S. Senate on Rules and Administration in July 2001." Washington, DC: Appendix in U.S. Commission on Civil Rights, Voting Irregularities in Florida, August 2001.

Luther V Borden, 48 U S 1 (1849).

Minority Staff, Committee on Government Reform. "Election Reform in Detroit: New Voting Technology and Increased Voter Education Significantly Reduced Uncounted Ballots." Washington, DC: U.S. House of Representatives, April 5, 2001.

—. "Income and Racial Disparities in the Undercount in the 2000 Presidential Election." Washington: Committee on Government Reform, U.S. House of Representatives, July 9, 2001.

National Association for the Advancement of Colored People. "Defending the Vote: Holding Officials Accountable." Baltimore: National Association for the Advancement of Colored People, July, 2002.

National Association of Secretaries of State. "Resolution (Federal)." In *National Association of Secretaries of State,* 2001.

—. "Resolution (State and Local)." In *National Association of Secretaries of State,* 2001.

National Commission on Federal Election Reform. "To Assure Pride and Confidence in the Electoral Process." Charlottesville: Miller Center of Public Affairs, University of Virginia.

National Conference of State Legislatures. "Voting in America: Final Report of the Ncsl Elections Reform Task Force." Denver: National Conference of State Legislatures, 2001.

National Task Force on Election Reform. "Election 2000: Review and Recommendations by the Nation's Elections Administrators." Houston: The Election Center, July, 2001.

Piven, Frances, and Richard Cloward. *Why Americans Don't Vote.* New York: Patheon, 1988.

Reed, Ingrid. "The 2001 New Jersey Election." New York: The Century Foundation, October 15, 2002.

Reynolds V. Sims, 377 U.S. 533 (1964).

Schlesinger Jr, Arthur. "Not the People's Choice: How to Democratize American Democracy." *American Prospect* 13 (2002).

Special Committee on Voting Systems and Election Procedures in Maryland. "Report and Recommendations." Baltimore: Special Committee on Voting Systems and Election Procedures in Maryland, February, 2001.

Thernstrom, Abigail, and Russell Redenbaugh. "The Florida Election Report: Dissenting Opinion." New York: Manhattan Institute for Policy Research, July 19, 2001.

United States Commission on Civil Rights. "Status Report on Probe of Election Practices in Florida During the 2000 Presidential Election." Washington, DC: U.S. Commission on Civil Rights, March 9, 2001.

—. "Voting Irregularities in Florida During the 2000 Presidential Election, with Appendix." Washington, DC: United States Commission on Civil Rights, June 8, 2001.

"Voting Matters in New York: Participation, Choice, Action, Integrity." Office of Attorney General Eliot Spitzer, February 12, 2001.

Voting Technology Project. "Voting: What Is, What Could Be." Boston: California Institute of Technology and Massachusetts Institute of Technology, July, 2001.

The 2000 Florida Election and Its Aftermath: Voter Disenfranchisement and Political Deals

Marcella Washington
Florida Community College at Jacksonville

Florida, an old South state with a history of racial discrimination and intimidation, was at the center of controversy in the 2000 presidential election. Vague and poorly written election procedures, deliberate purging of the voters roll, absentee ballot abuses, confusing ballot designs, intimidation of voters at the polls, voter registration complications were some of the discrepancies uncovered. African Americans and other racial minorities were most adversely affected by the debacle.

Mobilized by the decision of Florida Governor Jeb Bush to end Affirmative Action programs at state universities and colleges, African Americans registered to vote in large numbers and exercised their right on November 7, 2000. They turned out, in part, to send Jeb Bush a message. African American elected officials, led by State Rep. Anthony "Tony" Hill and State Senator Kendrick Meek, mobilized the black vote with the slogans that they "Remember in November" and "Arrive (at the polls) with Five" more voters. African Americans voter turnout reached seventy percent in the 2000 Florida election. But it was to no avail, because Republican operatives had a counter plan. And they used it.

On the day after the election, there was no clear winner of Florida's 25 electoral votes. And for 36 days, Democratic nominee Al Gore challenged Republican nominee George W. Bush for victory in the state.

Purging the Voter Rolls

Under Florida law, all former felons are barred from voting unless they successfully apply to the governor and Cabinet for a

---

Reprinted by permission of the author.

restoration of their civil rights. Many ex-offenders, however, are not even eligible to apply. They include people convicted of certain crimes, or who owe restitution ordered by the court. If felons register illegally, they can be charged with another felony and sentenced to up to five years in prison. The Florida Secretary of State, Republican Katherine Harris, who also served as the state chair of the Bush for President Campaign approved a state contract that would assure that ex-felons would not be able to get their hands on ballots. In 2000, Florida law required that the state Division of Elections[1] maintain a "central voter file."[2] The central voter file was maintained ostensibly to avoid mischief in voting procedures and to ensure that dead people, convicted felons and the mentally incompetent did not vote. Florida law further mandated that a private company contracted by the state validate information regarding voters in the central voter file.[3] The private company annually compared " ... information in the central voter file with available information in other computer databases, including, without limitation, databases containing reliable criminal records and records of deceased persons."[4] The names of the disenfranchised were then sent out to the 67 county supervisors of elections. Upon receipt of any such list, the supervisor was instructed to remove from the registration books the name of any person listed who was deceased, had been convicted of a felony, or had been adjudicated mentally incapacitated. Florida was the only state to pay a private company to review voter rolls in this way.

Florida secretary of state Katherine Harris contracted with ChoicePoint, a company out of Atlanta, to create a "scrub list" that cleansed the Florida voting rolls of those constitutionally barred from the polls. The company records, however, were flawed and some supervisors of elections erroneously purged from the voter rolls thousand of voters who had committed a misdemeanor or had no criminal record at all. Early in the year, ChoicePoint gave Florida officials a list with the names of 8,000 ex-felons to "scrub" or remove from their list of voters. "But it turns out none on the list were guilty of felonies, only misdemeanors. The company acknowledged the error, and blamed it on the original source of the list—the state of Texas."[5] While Florida election officials attempted to put those falsely accused of being ineligible to vote by Texas back on the voter rolls before the election, "the large number of errors uncovered in individual counties suggest that thousands of eligible voters" were turned away from the polls. African Americans were disproportionably scrubbed from the list because in Florida 31 percent of black men are barred from voting because of the ban on felon voting.

A challenge to barring ex-felons from voting was mounted in 2002. Lawyers for tens of thousands of ex-felons barred from voting in Florida asked U.S. District Judge James Lawrence King for a trial so they can try to prove the ban was designed a century ago to dilute the black vote. Nancy Northup of the Brennan Center for Justice in New York argued that the ban on ex-felons voting was synonymous to the poll tax and served as a racial barrier to voting. She noted that blacks make up only 14 percent of Florida's population, but 48 percent of those convicted. The result being that blacks make up a disproportionate number of the estimated 600,000 Floridians barred from voting.

The state countered that the law is, and has been solely based on ex-felons contempt for the law. In July 2002, U.S. District Judge James Lawrence King ruled in favor of the state. "The African-American felon plaintiffs have not been denied the right to vote because of an immutable characteristic, but because of their own criminal acts," King wrote in a 16-page review of the case. "Thus, it is not racial discrimination that deprives felons, black or white, of their right to vote, but their own decision to commit an act for which they assume the risks of detection and punishment."[6] The judge granted the state's request to dismiss the lawsuit, one of several filed in the wake of the 2000 election recount.

Poor and Irregular Ballot Design

The discrimination against voters in the 2000 Florida election was widespread and unyielding. At the time of the election, Florida used punch card ballots. The supervisor of elections in each of Florida's 67 counties was free to design the general election ballot—provided it contained some perfunctory state solicitations. Consequently, ballot design varied from county to county. In Palm Beach County, the Democratic Supervisor of Elections, Theresa LaPore, invented the "Butterfly Ballot." LaPore claimed that the ballot was designed in such a way that the large senior citizen population would be able to understand the ballot because there were 10 presidential candidates qualified for the general election ballot. The ballot designed was a catastrophe, because many voters did not understand the ballot and over 19,000 votes were tossed.

In a suit brought in state court, a number of Democratic voters in Palm Beach County claimed that the butterfly ballot did not meet required state standards and asked the court to void the election and demand another election or a revote. The Florida Supreme Court upheld a lower court ruling that the ballot was not illegal. The Court held that the butterfly ballot did not constitute substantial noncompliance with statutory requirements mandating the voiding of the election.[7]

But it was in Duval County (Jacksonville) where blatant inequities in voting triumphed and prevailed. The Duval County Republican supervisor of elections, John Stafford, designed a poor and irregular ballot that resulted in 27,000 ballots being tossed out and not counted in the presidential tally. The Duval County sample ballot listed all presidential tickets on a single page and instructed voters to "vote all pages," but the actual ballot split the candidates onto two pages to accommodate the punch-card system and contained the instruction, "vote appropriate pages." Needless voter confusion was the result. There were nearly 22,000 "overvotes" and about 5,000 presidential "undervotes" in Duval County. A disproportionate number of these "overvotes" came from precincts with voters who are overwhelmingly Democratic and predominantly black. Black votes were also disproportionately voided in Dade County, Palm Beach County, Madison County and Gadsden County, among others in the state.

As a result of confusing ballots and ill-equipped voting machines, massive voter turnout among African American voters in Florida, which resulted in almost 70 percent more blacks casting votes in Florida than in 1996, was to no avail because a disproportionate number of ballots cast by African Americans were disqualified and thrown out.

Picture Identification Requirements

Florida law required all voters to present picture identification at polling places before voting. The United States Department of Justice raised no specific substantive objections to the requirement. In fact, the DOJ approved or precleared the picture identification requirement in time for the 2000 election.[8] On Election Day, African Americans complained that they were denied the right to vote because they did not have the appropriate picture identification required by state law. Thus, even though these voters had registration cards, they were not allowed to vote because a ballot could not be secured without picture identification.

The practice of turning qualified voters away was excessive and unwarranted because state law actually allows election officials instead to have the persons without proper identification sign an affidavit affirming his or her right to vote. For example, on the sample ballot distributed in Duval County, an admonition to prospective voters stated,

"If you do not provide picture identification, you must complete and sign an affidavit before voting. We strongly encourage you to bring a form of picture identification to the polls since the affidavit procedure will delay voting for you as well as others."

The picture identification requirement thus served as a barrier to voters and as a tool of intimidation used to turn away African American voters.

Absentee Ballot Abuses

The misuse of the absentee ballot process was another voting rights violation in the 2000 Florida election. In 1998, Florida absentee ballot laws were supposedly tightened by the legislature, after thousands of alleged fraudulent absentee ballots were cast in a Miami mayoral election. The new law required voters to provide a long list of identifiers on absentee ballot applications, including Social Security and voter identification numbers. Prior to November's election, both parties sent out applications to make it easier for their supporters to vote. The Republican applications, however, left off the voter identification numbers for thousands of applications.

In Seminole and Martin counties, in clear violation of Florida election law, Republican election officials allowed Republican campaign aides to make corrections to flawed ballot applications. The Republican operatives filled in missing voter identification numbers on ballots that did not include the required information.

Civil suits were brought against both counties over the misuse of the absentee ballot applications. These suits sought to have all of the absentee ballots thrown out. When the cases reached the Florida Supreme Court, the justices agreed with the lower courts rulings and held that there was no evidence of fraud or other intentional misconduct. The Court ruled, "[u]nless a statutory provision specifically states that the lack of information voids the ballot, the lack of information does not automatically void the ballot."[9] The Court further concluded that in both cases there were "irregularities" (relative to the requests for absentee ballots), but the justices denied an appeal to have the absentee ballots invalidated.

The Overseas Ballot Dispute

The counting of overseas ballots was also an issue in the election. More than 1,500 military were rejected because they did not have a proper postmark proving they were sent before Election Day. Republicans contended that most overseas ballots were from military personnel, who were more likely to vote with the GOP. The Florida Attorney General, Bob Butterworth, issued a statement mandating that these ballots be counted:

> It has come to the attention of this office that there may have been some confusion on the part of local canvassing boards in the counting of absentee ballots from U.S. military personnel serving overseas. Based upon news media reports, it appears that some of these ballots may have been rejected due to the lack of a postmark.

This office urges supervisors and canvassing boards in any county which has received such ballots to immediately revisit this issue and amend their reported vote totals, if appropriate.

Most counties agreed to count all the overseas ballots that had no postmark. After these ballots were counted, Bush's popular vote margin increased from 300 to 900 votes.

The Recount

On November 8, 2000, the day after the election, there was no clear winner of the Florida popular vote for president. Because of the narrow margin of votes between George W. Bush and Al Gore a mandatory machine recount was ordered in all 67 counties in the state of Florida. But Democrats requested a manual recount in four counties (Miami-Dade, Broward, Palm Beach and Volusia) where they believed Gore was ahead. Although Palm Beach County announced that it would manually recount all of its votes, Bush sued in U.S. District Court to bar manual counting. The federal court refused to stop the recount, but Florida secretary of state Katherine Harris announced plans to certify statewide results on November 13. Al Gore and the Democrats brought suit in Florida courts to extend the deadline.

A week after Harris' announcement that the election would be certified, and more wrangling by Democrats and Republicans, the Florida Supreme Court ruled unanimously that hand counts in three counties (Broward, Palm Beach and Volusia) were to be included in the final tally. The Court set the date of November 26 as the earliest time for certification. Meanwhile, the Miami-Dade canvassing board had decided to conduct a recount on November 17. But a rowdy and vociferous group of Republican operatives stormed the county court building where the canvassing board was conducting the recount, and demanded entry into the room where the votes were being recounted. The storming of the recount in Miami-Dade paid off for Republicans, because the county's canvassing stopped the recount by rationalizing that it did not have enough time to complete the process.

In a positive development for the Gore campaign, the Florida Supreme Court ruled that manual recounts must be included in the state's vote certification. On November 24, 2000, the United States Supreme Court agreed to hear Bush's appeal to the Florida Supreme Court's decision. Two days later Harris certified George W. Bush the winner in Florida by a margin of 537 votes.

On December 12, the United States Supreme Court in a 5-4 decision rejected the Florida recount. The Court held that the different standards used in the counties for determining a vote violated the Equal Protection Clause of the U.S. Constitution.[10] On December 13, Al Gore conceded the election.

Florida Election Reform

The United States Commission on Civil Rights conducted an investigation and held hearings on voter disenfranchisement in the state. A draft report was issued in June 2001. The commissioners reported that statewide, based upon county-level statistical estimates, black voters were nearly 10 times more likely than non-black voters to have their ballots rejected. And commissioners also found that on Election Day African Americans accounted for approximately 11 percent of Florida voters, however, they cast 54 percent of the 180,000 spoiled ballots. In executive summary, to the "Draft Report: Voting irregularities in Florida", the Commission on Civil Rights asserts, "Potential voters confronted inexperienced poll workers, antiquated machinery, inaccessible polling locations, and other barriers to being able to exercise their right to vote. The Commission's findings make one thing clear: widespread voter disenfranchisement—not the dead-heat contest—was the extraordinary feature in the Florida election."[11]

There were so many voting irregularities and discrepancies in the system that the legislature was forced to act. The 2001 Legislative Session passed the Florida Election Reform Act and it was amended in 2002. The Election Reform Act was a maneuver used by the Republican-controlled state legislature to silence critics and to present an image to the nation that Florida was serious about correcting deficits and irregularities in its election law. But the Republican-controlled legislature was not serious about making major reforms, and only two major changes to the law were enacted: elimination of the punch card voting system and the provisional ballot.

The notorious punch-card voting scheme that was used in 24 of the state's 67 counties was eliminated. The new law prohibits the use of punch card voting. Instead, the Florida Election Reform Act requires counties to move to an optical scan or touch-screen voting system. It is left up to the discretion of local election officials as to which system will be used in their counties.

The discrepancy in voting machines and the lack of trained poll workers resulted in a repeat of the 2000 election fiasco in the 2002 Florida primary. The Florida Election Reform Act bears some responsibility for the 2002 primary debacle. Initially, legislators required poll workers to receive six hours of training. But the number was reduced to three hours of training in 2002.[12]

Poorly trained poll workers and massive breakdown in voting machine technology were the reasons Jeb Bush decided to extend voting hours in the September 2002 Florida primary. Poll workers were not prepared to run the machines and in at least one county, workers simply walked off the job.

Shortly after the primary election, Florida Democratic Chairman Bob Poe listed the irregularities on the party's website:

- Bay County: Ballots jammed in optical scanners and some machines were sent to the wrong polling places.

- Broward County: Dozens of poll workers did not show up. In at least six cities, polls opened late. Democrats received Republican ballots, with no primary in the governor's race.

- Duval County: A precinct at a senior citizen center opened 90 minutes late because poll workers did not realize that they were supposed to turn on machines. Dozen of voters left without casting a ballot. For the first 25 minutes, voters in a precinct in a predominantly black Jacksonville neighborhood distributed Democratic to all voters. Ballots jammed in optical-scanning machines due to rough tears at perforated lines.

- Escambia County: People assigned to new precincts in redistricting went to their old ones. People who moved went to the wrong precinct.

- Hillsborough County: After Governor Jeb Bush extended primary voting by two hours, county election officials has no uniform way to contact precincts to notify them of the decision.

- Miami Dade County: More than 500 voters were turned away before machines were activated nearly five hours late in Miami's Liberty City neighborhood. Machines were inoperable throughout the county.

- Orange County: At more than 100 precincts in the Orlando area, election workers used scissors to cut across flawed ballots before handing them to voters to enable electronic ballots to be read properly. Boxes of ballots had to read by hand.
- Palm Beach County: About 115 poll workers quit on Sunday before the election. Some poll workers did not show up.
- Pasco County: A precinct opened late when a custodian arrived late to unlock the building.
- Seminole County: Election officials ran out of ballots for the new optical scanning machines. Some people left without voting.
- Union County: County workers were forced to count 26,000 ballots by hand because a programming error registered all Democratic votes as Republican.
- Volusia County: Some residents had to vote 20 miles from home because of redrawn precincts. Sample ballots were incorrect.

If a voter's name does not appear on a precinct registration and verification cannot be determined, the voter will be issued a provisional ballot. The county canvassing board will determine the validity of the voter's claim. But a voter intimidation device is written into the law. Before a voter can receive a provisional ballot, he or she must sign a Provisional Ballot Certificate and Affirmation. In part, the oath of affirmation, states: "I understand that if I commit any fraud in connection with voting, vote a fraudulent ballot, or vote more than once in an election, I can be convicted of a felony of the third degree and fined up to $5,000 and/or imprisoned for up to five years."[13] Moreover, a provisional ballot can only be cast at the precinct, and not at any voting precinct in the county.

Oversees military voters will virtually have no restrictions on their right to vote. The Florida Election Reform Act creates Section 101.6592. In part the provision states:

> For absentee ballots received from overseas voters, there is a presumption that the envelope was mailed on the date ... regardless of the absence of a postmark on a mailed envelope or the existence of a postmark date that is later than the date of the election.[14]

Family members of armed service personnel are permitted the right to register after the books close. Again, the law generously considers the voting rights of the military: "An individual or accompanying family member who has been discharged or separated from the uniformed services or the Merchant Marine, or from employment outside the territorial limits of the United States, after the closing date for an election ... may register to vote in such election until 5:00 p.m. on the Friday before the election ..."[15]

Voter fraud is considered a given. In a section of the law titled "Instruction to electors," the supervisor of elections in each county is required to post at each polling place a notice warning voters that voting a fraudulent ballot is a third degree felony, punishable by a fine up to $5,000 and five years in imprisonment. The secretary of state is charged with maintaining a voter fraud hotline. And at the Department of State's website voters are encouraged to report any suspected case of voter fraud. The Florida Administrative Code defines voter fraud as " ... intentional misrepresentation, trickery, deceit, or deception, arising out of or in connection with voter registration or voting ... "

Vigorous attempts by African American and civil rights advocates to register voters resulted in allegations of voter fraud. On the Friday before the 2002 general election, the Florida Times Union ran the front-page story, "More felons receive ballots." The newspaper reviewed registration lists and even obtained a confidential list of absentee requests and returns, election officials are prohibited from giving out by law. The names of the 16 people were printed in the paper, along with the crimes for which they were convicted. The newspaper contended,

> Another 16 felons—a cadre of drug dealers, forgers and thieves—have requested and sometimes cast absentee ballots illegally in Duval County for Tuesday's election. They join 11 other felons who were registered to vote and requested absentee ballots, despite a Florida law prohibiting them from doing so.
>
> A local NAACP registration drive in early October at the county jail and work release site produced 16 of the registrations, election officials said. The others were convicted beforehand or afterward and not expunged.[16]

In 2001, Florida legislators eliminated a requirement that voters sign an affidavit stating that they can't make it to the polls in order to receive an absentee ballot.

And once an absentee ballot is requested it is deemed sufficient to receive an absentee ballot for all elections that are held within a calendar year.

The absentee ballot is now used for early or convenient voting in the state. Once again, uniformity was not applied in election. While early voting was promoted in some counties in the 2002 election, it was not in other counties. There was barely mention of the process in Duval County, but it was promoted heavily in Dade and Broward counties—generally considered to be strongholds for the Democrats. But in the end, it was Jeb Bush, and not the Democrats who were aided by ballots from these counties.

In Broward County, Bush received 21,000 absentee ballots, compared to 17,000 for McBride. In Orange County, the mail-in vote for Bush outnumbered McBride by 2-1. One out of 10 Florida voters chose early voting. Florida Republicans sent thousands of absentee ballot forms to members and watched ballots return. "Volunteers followed up with personal visits, telephone calls and recorded messages from former first lady Barbara Bush."[17] Through November 4, 2002, about 650,000 absentee ballots had been returned, and Florida Republicans claimed more than half of the returned ballots were by registered Republicans.

The process was so successful for Republicans that Florida secretary of state Jim Smith is considering asking the legislature to change state law to allow early voting at satellite stations, instead of just election supervisors' offices.

Still there were hundreds of absentee ballots that were discarded. In Broward County, boxes of votes were trashed because voters forgot to sign them or because they were not returned in the official envelope provided by the supervisor of elections.

In order to challenge the validity of the system, voter fraud was practiced in the 2002 election in at least one Florida county. Palm Beach County elections supervisor Theresa LePore requested the state attorney's office investigate as many as two dozen voters who cast ballots twice in the election. These voters had been sent absentee ballots; they then cast another ballot at the polls. LePore said a reporter from the Palm Beach Post might be among those referred to the state attorney's office. The reporter signed a voter roll list to get a ballot, after he had voted by absentee to verify the county's procedures for stopping someone from voting twice.[18]

In Volusia County, eight absentee ballots were thrown out in the 2002 election because the people who had voted the ballots died before the votes were tallied on Election Day. Fraud among the dead was the rational for discarding the votes. According to Florida law, a ballot cast at an election office and fed into a machine by a person who dies before the election would count. Otherwise, the ballot of the deceased voter would not be counted.[19]

Fearing long lines and voter dissatisfaction with the process, officials in Broward and Duval counties, promoted backup plans for voting a provisional or absentee ballot in the primary and general election. But the state rejected the plans. Ed Kast, the Director of the State Division of Elections, rejected the request by Broward County Democrats for the use of a provisional ballot in the November 2002 general election by stating that the use of the provisional ballot is "a convenience." Because of redistricting, the Jacksonville city council had to approve 46 new polling places in the county's 285 precincts, affecting 60,000 to 80,000 voters. The city council requested that the Republican supervisor of elections John Stafford permit voters to cast absentee ballots in the primary. Stafford stated that he would agree with the plan, if the state of Florida approved it. Seeking an advisory opinion from the Division of Elections, Stafford asked: "Where precinct polling locations have changed, and a voter mistakenly returns to the former location, may election officials provide the voter an absentee ballot for the correct precinct and accept return of that completed ballot on election day at the polling place?" The state responded: "The short answer to your question is no." Election officials maintained that in-person voting can only occur at the offices of the supervisor of elections.[20]

An important victory for Democrats came on November 1, 2002 in Florida. The Democratic Party filed suit to block Republicans from massing poll watchers at voting precincts in Miami-Dade County. Circuit Judge Eleanor Schockett issued a ruling prohibiting the Emergency Campaign to Stop Bill McBride,[21] a Republican political action committee, from placing observers in 450 of 553 Miami-Dade polling places.

Lawyers for the plaintiffs said Democrats had signed about 145 poll watchers. The committee opposing McBride said on its web site that it had submitted 456 signed poll watcher forms.

A statewide voter registration database has been established. All registered voters will be in the database. The supervisor of elections in each county will be able to remove the names of any person who is deceased. The names of ex-felons will be removed, "When the supervisor of elections finds information through the database that suggests that a voter has been convicted of a felony and has not had his or her civil rights restored."[22] A website containing this information was scheduled to be up and running on June 1, 2002. But in June 2002, the Federal Department of Justice (DOJ) ordered the state to delay any purges of suspected felons from local voter lists until the process could be reviewed. Thus far, the DOJ has not pre-cleared the use of the database.

The 2002 Florida was not as problematic as in 2000. But there were still serious errors in voting procedures, and machines that did not work. Florida is still in the process of reforming its election laws. But the reforms so far have not given confidence to voters, especially African American, that the system works for them.

Notes

1. The Division of Elections is under the authority of the Florida Secretary of State and the Secretary of State appoints the Director of the Division of Elections.
2. Fl. Stat., sec. 98.097 (2000).
3. Ibid, sSec 98.0975 (3)(a) (2000).
4. Ibid. Fl. Stat. sec. 98.0975 (3)(a) (2000).
5. Greg Palast, "Florida's flawed 'voter-cleansing' program, available at http://archive.salon.com/politics/feature/2000/

12/04voter_file/ last visited December 23, 2002.

6. Marc Mauer, State disenfranchises those who have paid their debt," (July 28, 2002). Available at http://www.miami.com/mld/miamiherald/2002/07/28/news/opinion/3742792.htm (last visited Dec. 23, 2002.)
7. *Fladell v. Palm Beach County Canvassing Board*, Fl. SC00-23732000.
8. Five counties in Florida remain under the preclearance jurisdiction of Section 5 of the Voting Rights Act: Collier, Hardee, Hendry, Hillsborough, and Monroe counties. The only procedural concern that DOJ expressed to the Florida Department of State was that each of the five covered counties would have to be separately precleared. "The Justice Department seemed to indicate in its August 10, 1998, letter to us that it had no objection to sections 9 and 10 of the new law, which impose identification requirements for voters appearing at the polls ... the Justice Department explained that, because each of the counties subject to preclearance may establish its own list of identification cards which are acceptable, each county's list will have to be separately precleared before the new identification requirements can be implemented." Florida Division of Elections. "Absentee Voting." DE 98-13. (August 19, 1998). *Available at* http://election.dos.state.fl.us/opinions/de1998.shtml#9813 (last visited Dec. 22, 2000).
9. *Jacobs v. Seminole County Canvassing Board* Fl. SC00-2448 (2000) and *Taylor v. Martin County Canvassing Board*, FL. SC00-2448 (2000).
10. *Bush V. Gore*, U.S. 00-949.
11. United States Commission on Civil Rights, "Voting Irregularities in Florida During the 2000 Election," http://www.usccr.gov/vote2000/stdraft1/exsum.htm (last visited Sept. 12, 2001).
12. FL. Sta. sec. 102.014 (4 a, b)
13. Ibid, sec. 101.048, (3).
14. Fla. Stat. sec 101.6592 (2) (2001). The counting of overseas military ballots was another issue in the 2000 presidential election. Although state law required that an overseas ballot would be counted only if it was postmarked on or before Election Day, Bush operatives mounted a campaign to persuade canvassing boards to count these ballots. The votes that were counted included ballots without postmarks and ballots post marked after the election. See, David Barstow and Don Van Natta Jr., "How Bush took Florida: Mining the Overseas Absentee Vote," *The New York Times*, 15 July 2001, 1.
15. Fl. Stat. sec. 978.055, 1.
16. David DeCamp, "More felons receive ballots." Available at http://www.jacksonville.com/tu-online/stories/110102/met_10852645.shtml (last visited Dec. 23, 2002).
17. "Early voting, absentee ballots aided Gov. Bush." Available at http://www.miami.com/mld/miamiherald/news/state/4496950.htm (last visited Dec. 23, 2002).
18. "Two dozen in Palm Beach County accused of trying to vote twice." Available at http://www.centredaily.com/mld/miamiherald/news/state/4478518.htm (last visited Dec. 23, 2002).
19. "8 absentee ballots not alive." Available at http://www.Miami.com/4475527.htm (last visited on Dec. 23, 2002).
20. FL. DE 02-13. Available at http://election.dos.state.fl.us/opinions/new/de_2002/de0213.shtml (last visited Dec. 23, 2002).
21. Bill McBride was the Democratic nominee for governor. Jeb Bush defeated McBride in the November 2002 election.
22. Fl. Stat. sec. 98.0977, (1) (d).

Ain't No Party Like a Democratic Party and the Judge from Johnston County: A Look at North Carolina 2002 Mid-Term Elections

Jarvis A. Hall
North Carolina Central University

As we attempt to understand race and politics in this country, it is always instructive to turn to the states to see what harbingers there are or what interesting trends may be emerging. In general, the 2002 mid-term elections in North Carolina were nearly a mirror image of what happened nationally. Contrary to conventional expectations, Congress, the Republican Party was able to expand their majority in the U.S. House of Representatives and recapture the U.S Senate. Likewise, the North Carolina GOP was able to maintain control of the U.S. Senate seat that was up for grabs, to achieve parity with the Democrats in the North Carolina House of Representatives, and to reduce the Democratic margin in state senate. And perhaps more significantly, Republicans were able to practically dominate the North Carolina judiciary. Thus, North Carolina elections and others challenged significantly our expectations about mid-term elections, however, merely recounting this would not add much to our understanding of the continuing and dynamic role of race in American politics.

Therefore, in this chapter, I suggest that the 2002 North Carolina elections were more instructive because of two important developments that help to illuminate and contextualize the results mentioned above. First, the elections, specifically for the U.S. Senate, exposed some critical strains between the Democratic Party and African Americans, its most loyal constituent group. The intramural cold war, where the party tends to disdain and scapegoat African American office seekers and voters, are merely symptoms of deeper problems within the party. Thus, as I examine the issue of the electability of Dan Blue, an African American candidate for the Senate, and the significance of Black turnout and mobilization, it becomes apparent that, "Ain't no party like a Democratic Party." In the final analysis, the party's inability or unwillingness to directly confront these issues jeopardizes its future. The second development involved a judge from Johnston County. In this election cycle, events in North Carolina opened up a new chapter in redistricting politics when a judge named Jenkins actually drew state legislative maps. I will discuss how and why this happened. Such an occurrence adds a new dimension to a process that is already highly contentious and politicized. Unfortunately, as the stars line up this development is very foreboding for those who look to the redistricting process to advance African American interests.

Before proceeding, I note that the following is not designed to be a comprehensive examination of the developments identified above. However, it is designed to demonstrate how an examination of the North Carolina mid-term elections can be used as vehicle to understand a piece of this important moment in history.

The 2002 North Carolina U.S. Senate Election and Tensions in the Democratic Party

While there was considerable media attention paid to the personalities who ran in the race, the election was more important because it was illustrative of underlying tensions and strains, throughout the country, between African Americans and the Democratic Party. The root cause of these tensions is found in the growing significance of African Americans to the Democratic coalition. Deservedly or not, by 1964, the party was viewed positively by Blacks because of its perceived support for the civil rights agenda. This resulted in a strong and consistent identification of African Americans with the Democratic Party. Thus, the Democratic Party became "blacker" and eventually became identified with other so-called special interests, such as unions, environmentalists, women, and gays, while estranging other groups in the Democratic coalition, such as men, Southerners, business and blue-collar workers. In response to this, many whites began to shift their electoral support to the Republican coalition (Black and Black 2002; Edasll 1992). For instance, since 1974, 80 percent or more of African Americans identified with the Democratic Party. Meanwhile, the number of whites who have identified with the Party has dropped from 58 percent in 1964 to 48 percent in 1996. This has occurred while increasingly Democratic African American office-seekers have sought offices in non-majority Black voting jurisdictions where appeals to white voters are a necessity. Unfortunately, Reeves has shown that white voters, including white Democrats, are hesitant to vote for Black candidates (1997). More specifically, Citrin et al concluded that underlying racial attitudes contributed to the defeat of Black candidates Tom Bradley and Wilson Riles in California. Therefore, the "electability" of African Americans to majority white voting districts is an increasing challenge for Democratic politics.

The strains between Blacks and the Democratic Party are manifest in the different strategic responses each gives to this situation. Many African American candidates have chosen to run deracialized campaigns where office seekers conduct a, " . . . campaign in stylistic fashion that defuses the polarizing effects of race . . . while . . . emphasizing those issues that are perceived as racially transcendent ..." (McCormick and Jones 1993, 76). Only a handful of candidates have employed this strategy successfully. Meanwhile, apparently the party essentially has decided on a dual approach. First, the party engages its own brand of deracialization where party leadership and operatives strategically discourage and impede African American candidates as they seek to win nominations for the party. The other approach stresses appealing to so-called white swing voters while practically ignoring the Black electorate and often scapegoating them when Democratic losses occur. Below, I explain how the 2002 North Carolina U.S. Senate campaign is illustrative of these strains.

The Electability of Dan Blue[1]

Generally, the race for the North Carolina Senate seat was important for two reasons. First, with a razor thin Democratic majority in United States Senate, all of the 2002 races were significant because their outcomes would determine who would control the chamber in the next Congress. Victory for the Republicans would mean that they would have control of the Presidency and majority control over the Congress and the Supreme Court. Second, Jesse Helms, the unreconstructed icon of far right Southern politics, had announced that he did not intend to run again. Thus, the seat, which Helms had held since 1972, became very attractive to a number of potential candidates, some of near celebrity (politically speaking) status. On the Republican side, Elizabeth Dole, wife of former Senator and presidential candidate Bob Dole, former head of the American Red Cross, former cabinet member, and former presidential candidate herself, was directly recruited by President George W. Bush to run. Meanwhile, the Democratic nomination came down to a contest between former African American Speaker of the North Carolina House of Representatives, Dan Blue and former Chief-of-Staff for President Bill Clinton, Erskine Bowles.

There was not much of a contest on the Republican side for the nomination. After some token opposition, the party, including Senator Helms, closed ranks around Dole. The Democratic side, however, was much different. Initially, Bowles announced that he would not seek the nomination. However, he said that the events of 9/11 compelled him to reconsider. But perhaps more persuasive was the strong urging of party leadership after Blue and a white female, Secretary of State Elaine Marshall, emerged as the frontrunners in a crowded field. With such a prime opportunity to win a Senate seat that had been in the Republican camp since 1972, it seemed that party leadership was concerned about whether these candidates could successfully carry the party's banner to victory in the general election. Bowles eventually defeated Blue and the others in the primary but lost to Dole in the November general election.

But the critical question for our purposes is: Was Blue an electable candidate? To say that measuring electability is difficult would be an understatement. It presents an empirical challenge. Ideally one could say, if a candidate is elected, then she or he is electable; meanwhile, if the candidate loses, then she or he is not electable. But as a practical matter, determinations of electability occur before elections. Therefore in the remainder of this section, I speculate about whether Dan Blue should have been considered an electable candidate especially as compared to Erskine Bowles. To do so, I utilize a concept of electability that considers experience, broad appeal within the party, and the ability to get things done.

When Dan Blue decided to run for the U.S. Senate, many considered him the only African American with a chance of winning a seat in the upper house of Congress. After all, he had served for 21 years in the North Carolina House of Representatives, four years as speaker from 1990 to 1994 in a body that was less than 15 percent African American. While speaker, Blue championed progressive politics and policies and among other things pushed for major workplace reforms and led the effort to fund better the state's public Historically Black Universities.[2] In addition, as speaker, he navigated successfully the state through a fiscal crisis without raising taxes on the poor and middle-class. Thus, although Blue represented a predominant Black legislative district in Raleigh, his election as speaker demonstrated that he had broad based appeal as he was chosen by a House Democratic Caucus that had many more conservatives and moderates than progressives. And he did this while being fiscally responsible and not shying away from substantive support of traditional Party values.

Meanwhile, Bowles, an investment banker and son of a former candidate for governor, had never held elected office. Although he maintained residence in Charlotte, he spent much of his time in New York and Washington. Bowles was a millionaire who sat on 17 corporate boards including drug maker Merck and two banks, First Union and Wachovia. At first glance, these business connections may have looked as if they were assets for Bowles, but one must recall that the 2002 elections took place in the shadow of the revelation of a number of corporate scandals. In fact, during the campaign for the general election, Bowles and Republican nominee Dole often traded slurs regarding their corporate connections.

Although Bowles had never held elected office, he was certainly politically connected. In fact, he was most well known because he had been President Bill Clinton's chief of staff. Although Clinton was a Southerner and very popular with African Americans, he was very unpopular with other North Carolinians. In fact, a Democratic presidential candidate had not carried North Carolina since Jimmy Carter did so in 1976. In addition, in a state where Christian fundamentalism is strong, many residents of the state refuse to forgive and forget Clinton's sexual improprieties in the White House. Also, Bowles was hurt because he was in the White House when the North American Free Trade Agreement was passed with strong backing from the Clinton Administration. This crucial piece of legislation was viewed generally as harmful to the North Carolina textile industry.

Who was electable or not? Clearly it is a matter of interpretation as to how to evaluate the political assets and liabilities of the two candidates.[3] Granted, the brief synopses above do not do justice to the qualities of either candidate. But after Blue and Secretary of State Elaine Marshall emerged as the two frontrunners in the Democratic race, Democratic Party leadership had made a decision. At the request of bankers and business interests, former Governor Jim Hunt, U.S. Representative Bob Etheridge and other party leaders urged Bowles to reconsider his decision not to enter the race which he did. Was the decision of the party leadership due to race or some other set of factors?

Admittedly, Blue had a rocky relationship with the party leadership and the North Carolina political mainstream. His progressive politics put him at odds with the conservative direction of both parties. The *Weekly Independent,* a progressive local paper recounts Blue's battle with conservative forces during fiscal crisis mentioned above:

> Blue took office (as speaker) at the height of the 1990-91 recession facing a $1.2 billion budget deficit . . Fighting both a Republican governor and conservative Democrats in the Senate, Blue insisted that business and the rich should shoulder

some of the burden of balancing the budget in '91 . . . Blue stood firmly against the high-powered Senate negotiators who opposed taxing the rich and wanted deeper cuts in education spending. The final deal was largely Blue's way: It cut spending by $600 million and raised taxes the same amount, with most of the money coming from a corporate income tax hike and an income tax hike on family incomes of more than $100,000. Blue had answered yes to the question facing Democrats: "Can a liberal agenda move forward with good, fiscally responsible leadership?" (The Independent Weekly, January 23, 2002)

Blue also angered party leadership when he attempted to regain the speaker's chair in 1998 after the Democrats recaptured control of the House following four years of Republican rule. With the curious coupling of most members of the legislative Black Caucus and House Republicans, Blue lost by one vote to Jim Black of Matthews. Black, a member of the conservative wing of the party, had been the minority leader while the Republicans had been in charge. Democratic Party leadership, including Black and Senate Pro Tempore, Marc Basnight, accused Blue of being disloyal by bargaining with the Republicans. But Blue said the only thing he offered the Republicans was fairness in dealing with them in the House. Besides, Blue and others, especially African American state representatives, Mickey Michaux and Toby Fitch, believed that he should be returned as speaker.

Was Bowles an electable candidate? While avoiding direct acknowledgment of the impact of race in North Carolina elections, some in the Democratic leadership argued that Blue was too liberal for North Carolina and that he had not been loyal. Thus, they surmised that the party needed someone who could raise money, who was more in line with the "mainstream" of the Democratic Party, and who was a loyal Democrat. Hence, Bowles was their choice. The party leadership clearly favored Bowles. In their judgement, he was the electable candidate. However, by making this determination, the party essentially capitulated to anti-Black racial voting and gave tacit acceptance to the racial reasoning that undergirds it. And undoubtedly, this favoritism by the party made the difference in the outcome of the primary. Once the party got behind Bowles, he immediately became the frontrunner. With the exception of condemnations from Representative Mickey Michaux, public complaints about the behavior of the party during the primary season was fairly muted. But it left a fissure in the party that was not repaired prior to the general election.

Confronted with this, Blue was unable to raise enough money to run the grassroots campaign he needed to win. Bowles received 43 percent of the vote in the Democratic primary, while Blue and Marshall received 29 percent to 15 percent respectively. In the general election, although Bowles was able to close the gap with Dole from 20 percent to single percentage points, he lost 54 percent to 45 percent. Notably Bowles performance was not better than that of Harvey Gantt, the African American former mayor of Charlotte, against Jesse Helms in 1990 and 1996.[4] Consequently, the critical question is: All things considered, was Bowles really more electable than Blue? With Blue's political assets and the absence of clear favoritism on the part of the Democratic party leadership for his opponent, one can reasonably conclude that Blue could have won the primary and could have done just as well as Bowles did in the general election. As more and more African American candidates seek Democratic nominations in non-majority Black voting districts, the party must reconsider its knee-jerk and irrational policy of hindering the efforts of these candidates. Eventually, African Americans support for the party will be jeopardized as both candidates and voters consider alternative political strategies.

Black Turnout and Scapegoating the African American Electorate

After, the surprising losses by the Democrats in the 2002 mid-term elections, the blame game started. One recurring recrimination blamed the lack of African American turnout for the inability of the party to make electoral gains. For example, in North Carolina, even in the absence of exit polls, the presumption by most of the mainstream media, supported by party operatives, was that Republicans were able to roll up victories because Black turnout was low. Some of this was somewhat benign; for example, Democratic pollster Celinda Lake, simply mentioned that the lack of turnout by Black voters may explain some Democratic losses. But because it was done so soon after the election and in some cases presented as the only explanation, it angered many Blacks. For example, on BET.com Melanie Campbell, executive director of the National Coalition on Black Civic Participation said, "They always want to blame Black folks. I'm not saying that we had a presidential election turnout, but we didn't have that with any voters." This points to another tension or strain between the Blacks and the Democratic Party: the tendency to blame African Americans for Democratic losses. Of course, this election was not the first time this has happened. Soon after the 1994 mid-term elections Republican victories were attributed to the lack of Black turnout for Democratic candidates. Later analysis showed, however, that Black turnout was actually higher than that for white voters.

The significance of Black turnout to Democratic elections must be examined to answer the following questions: What was Black turnout? How did it compare to general turnout? How did Black turnout impact the 2002 U.S. Senate race? What factors influenced turnout? To answer these questions, I conducted an analysis of North Carolina's 2738 voting precincts with data provided by the North Carolina State Board of Elections. Table 1 provides a summary overview of votes cast in the 2002 U.S. Senate race. It shows that, indeed, Black turnout was lower than that of whites. Statewide, turnout of registered voters stood at 47 percent. Meanwhile, turnout for Blacks and Whites was 41 percent and 49 percent respectively. Although Black turnout was in the low 40s, average turnout of the voting age population in mid-term elections is below 40 percent. Therefore, while white turnout was certainly high, it would be wrong to say that African American turnout was necessarily low.

Interestingly, Republican turnout was slightly higher than Democratic turnout at 51 percent and 49 percent respectively. Moreover, in terms of registered voters, Democrats actually out number Republicans. Taken together this suggests two outcomes that were important to this election. Obviously, Democrats voters, which includes many Blacks but more whites, did not vote at rates high enough to give victory to the Democratic candidate. Also, this suggests that Dole was able to garner a significant number of Democratic votes. Thus, the appropriate questions should have been raised about the Democratic vote in general and not only the Black vote.

Meanwhile, Table 2 shows Black voter turnout in urban areas and in counties, which have a majority black populations. The urban areas had large numbers of African Americans who made up a significant portion of the electorate. They all have large Black middle classes that to varying degrees are educated and politically active. On the other hand, all the counties with majority Black populations are

Table 1
Turnout—2002 North Carolina General Election for U.S. Senate

	Total Registration	% of Registered Voters	Total Voted	% Turnout of Registered Voters
State	5,000,919	100%	2,345,324	47%
Blacks	963,173	19%	396,853	41%
Whites	3,904,906	78%	1,910,610	49%
Democrats	2,415,139	48%	1,190,105	49%
Republicans	1,716,093	34%	877,051	51%

Table 2
Black Turnout and Support for Bowles in Selected Areas

Urban Areas (County/City)	% Population Black	Total # Blacks	2002 Black Turnout	% Vote for Bowles
Mecklenberg/Charlotte	27.9	193,838	42.6	48.7
Wake/Raleigh	19.7	123,820	49.6	44.9
Guilford/Greensboro	29.3	123,253	41.1	49.0
Durham/Durham	39.4	88,109	43.0	63.6
Counties s/ Largest % Black Population				
Bertie	62.3	12,326	34.4	67.7
Hertford	59.6	13,459	33.0	71.6
Northampton	59.4	13,125	46.0	58.3
Edgecombe	57.4	31.349	36.0	65.1
Warren	54.5	10,882	39.5	66.8
Halifax	52.6	30,151	34.7	61.0

rural and located in the northeast part of the state, one of its poorest sections. However, some of the counties, especially, Halifax and Warren, have very active Black communities. Black turnout in the four largest urban areas of the state compared more favorably to overall white turnout. Conversely, with the exception of Northampton County, Black turnout ranged between 33 percent and 39.5 percent. This hints at the possibility that part of explanation for the level of Black turnout can be found in socioeconomic factors. That is, because the Black population is disproportionately poor and rural, turnout is expected to be lower when compared to populations that are less so.

Table 2 also shows that Black turnout was very significant to Bowles' vote totals. With the exception of Wake County where Raleigh is located, Bowles got close to 50 percent or more of the vote in urban areas, all of which had large Black populations. Bowles was much more successful, however, in rural areas in terms of the vote percentage. But, as noted, the Black populations and turnout rates were relatively small in rural counties. Undoubtedly Bowles was very dependent on the Black vote for his vote totals. Blacks, who did vote, voted for him.

But how dependent was he? How much should a Democratic candidate expect from the Black vote? In fact, implied in the questions raised about Black turnout, is question of the dependency of Bowles and other Democratic candidates on Black votes. If the Black vote provided its expected share, is it reasonable to say that Bowles loss can be attributed to the lack of Black turnout? Did the black vote as a portion of the Democrat's total meet expectations? In the absence of knowing how each voter cast their vote, to test this, I looked at the share of candidates' votes that came from counties with 35 percent or more Black population. I compared this share for Bowles in the 2002 general election with Harvey Gantt's run for the Senate in 1996, Al Gore's run for the U.S. Presidency in 2000, and Mike Easley's successful run for Governor of North Carolina, also in 2000. Notably, all of these were deemed high turnout elections. The results are found in Table 3.

Bowles received fewer overall votes than the others did. This is to be expected given that the other races were during presidential years. But the consistency of the candidates' share from these counties was remarkable. About 13 percent of each candidate's total could be attributed to counties with a significant Black population. In this regard, the Black vote met expectations regarding the Bowles vote. However, the portion of the total vote from these counties is less for Bowles that either Gore or Easley in 2000, but it is the same as the Gantt race in 1996. This means that in 2002 other counties with significantly less Black populations made up a higher proportion of the total vote than in the other races. Coupling this with the above finding, I conclude that the vote from these counties did not go significantly for Bowles. In short, while Blacks support Bowles at levels that were comparable to other elections with high turnout, more of the total vote in 2002 came from areas that did not support the Democratic. Before leaving Table 3, I must point out one last matter. The fact that, except for the vote totals, the figures for Bowles and Gantt are identical is especially noteworthy. This simply reinforces the earlier deduction that Gantt, an African American, did just as well as Bowles in the race for Senate.

Although the Black vote was very supportive of, clearly it did not provide him the margin for victory. Could the Black vote have made a difference in this race? To win, all other things remaining equal, Bowles would have had to receive 200,312 additional votes. If Blacks had voted at a rate comparable to whites (49 percent), the total Black vote

Table 3
Share of Democratic Vote from Counties with Significant Black Populations

	Bowles 2002	Gantt 1996	Gore 2000	Easley 2000
Votes in Counties	136,504	155,569	173,096	208,392
% of Candidate Total	13.3	13.3	13.8	13.6
% of Total Vote	6.0	6.0	5.9	7.1

would have gone from 386,853 to 471,955, a difference of 85,102. Even if all of these votes went to Bowles, it would not have made a difference. What would it have taken for the Black vote to make a difference? Assuming that approximately 80 percent of the Black vote would go to the Democrat Bowles, the Black vote would have had to increase to 647,353. This would represent a Black turnout of 67 percent!!

Expecting Blacks to turnout at such high rates would have been asking quite a lot of the Black electorate. But it does point to the significance of mobilization. Both candidates spent a lot of money attempting to mobilize voters. This campaign was the most expensive Senate race in the country in 2002. Dole spent over $12 million while Bowles spent $9.9 million. Drawing on his considerable personal resources, Bowles loaned his campaign $6.8 million dollars. In addition to the tune of over $2 million each, both national parties funneled soft money dollars into the campaign.

But Bowles attempts at mobilization should be questioned. Bowles touted his propensity for bipartisanship[5] while avoiding, even in the primary, his connection to former President Clinton. Prior to the last week in the campaign, little was done in a grand way to mobilize Black voters. During the *last week* of the campaign, Harvey Gantt, former U.S. Labor Secretary Alexis Herman, poet Maya Angelou, and actresses Alfre Woodard and Cicely Tyson campaign on Bowles' behalf. Importantly Dan Blue raised hands with Bowles at a Durham African American church the weekend before the election.[6] However, during the campaign, Bowles failed to engage Black voters with discussion of issues, such as racial profiling and affirmative action, that would resonate with them.

Instead, both Bowles and Dole's stump speeches focused on trade and textile issues, although regarding the latter, textile workers make up less than 10 percent of the state's workforce. Both seemed to be after so-called "Jessecrats." These are white voters who are registered as Democrats but they had voted consistently for Jesse Helms. Moreover, Bowles' campaign seemed to focus especially on so-called "NASCAR Dads." According to Democratic pollster, Celinda Lake, NASCAR Dads are the downscale counterpart to office park dads. They're working class guys with less college and more military experience. What was their defining characteristic? NASCAR Dads are fans of stock car racing, the fastest-growing sport in America (Schneider 2002). Politically they support President Bush but they can be persuaded to vote for Democrats given the right issues.

In the absence of exit polls, it is difficult to determine how well Bowles did with NASCAR Dads; although, it does appear Dole was able to capture the "Jessecrat" vote. But it is clear that Bowles was unable to effectively mobilize Black voters. Although they did get their usual share of the Democrats vote, little was done to get Blacks excited about the race. This along with other creative mobilization efforts (like, perhaps a more electable candidate), to expand the base with unregistered Blacks and others could have made the difference. The above data indicate that certainly Dole and the Republicans excited their electorate and initiated a massive get out to vote effort. Conversely, Bowles and the Democrats failed to mobilize a critical part of their base. Some in the party understand how important this is. In a well-circulated memo, Donna Brazile, head of the Democratic National Committee's Voting Rights Institute and Cornell Belcher, a Democratic consultant said that the party was, "failing to build upon and expand our base." It remains to be seen whether the party will heed this warning and stop alienating an important part of their coalition.

Judge Jenkins and Redistricting[7]

Undoubtedly, redistricting has played a significant role in the election of more Black elected officials, especially in state legislatures and the U.S. Congress. In North Carolina, for example, redistricting has contributed the election of 17 African American members of the North Carolina House, seven African American members of the state senate, and two African American members of the United States Congress. Because the process has become more contentious, the courts play an increasingly important role in determining what is permissible or not regarding how the process is carried out. With cases such as Thornburg v. Gingles (1986), Shaw v. Reno (1993), Shaw v. Hunt (1996), and (Cromartie v. Hunt), North Carolina has been a major arena for court intervention into redistricting. Previously, the role of the courts has been confined to procedural matters, determining the parameters of redistricting and defining such issues as communities of interest, contiguity, compactness, and the use of race. But this round of the redistricting in North Carolina opened up new ground for the courts. A Superior Court judge in Johnston County actually drew the maps that were used for the legislative elections. The politics surrounding this process are potentially significant for the continued role of redistricting to open more opportunities for African American voters.

The Democrats enjoyed (or survived) a 62-58 seat majority in the House and a 35-15 seat majority in the Senate. Not surprisingly, the maps drawn by the legislature favored their party. With few exceptions, the districts protected Democratic incumbents and in some cases, pitted some Republican incumbents against popular Democratic incumbents in districts that favored the Democrats. But in doing so, the plans also divided a considerable number of North Carolina's counties. The House plan divided 70 of the state's 100 counties to form 112 districts. Meanwhile, the senate plan divided 50 counties to form 46 districts. Each created a number of multi-member districts.

This provided an opening for the Republicans, who were embittered by the redistricting process, to challenge legally the plans that had been devised by the Democrats. According to Article II, Sections 3 and 5 of the North Carolina state constitution, "no county shall be divided in the formation of" Senate and House districts. Therefore, the Republicans argued that the plans were unconstitutional. But they had to find the "right" judge to hear the case. Thus, literally, the Republicans, led by Representative Leo Daughtry of Johnston County and Senator Patrick Ballentine of New Hanover County, went judge shopping. They found what they were looking for in Superior Court Judge Knox v. Jenkins. Jenkins was described as a crusty old Jessecrat[8] from Johnston County. In fact, Jenkins was a former political lieutenant and personal friend of Tom Ellis the conservative kingmaker in North Carolina.[9] Also, Jenkins obtained some dubious celebrity because he was the judge in a trial that was the subject of the PBS "Frontline" series in which he allegedly called an African American defendant a "cold-blooded, vicious and a violent juvenile sociopath." These comments were made before a jury was seated.[10] Apparently, for the Republicans, this was the perfect judge.

Democrats and the state, defending the legislative-drawn districts, argued that they did not have to abide by the clause prohibiting splitting counties. The U.S. Justice Department in 1981 objected to the clause, which was added to the constitution in 1968. Moreover, an U.S. District Court ruled in 1983 that the provision was unenforceable because it greatly constrained the ability of the state to avoid the dilution of minority voting as provided for under the Voting Rights

Act. However, Jenkins agreed with the Republicans who had offered alternative plans. The North Carolina Supreme Court, which was composed of five Republicans and two Democrats, upheld Jenkins' decision, saying that the legislature's plan did violate the state constitution and that as much as possible there must be single member districts. Jenkins ordered the legislature to develop plans that did not violate the constitution. However, Jenkins rejected the second round of legislative plans and, without comment and explanation, drew his own maps, which suspiciously resembled plans that had been devised by the Republicans.

The plan developed by Jenkins had 120 single member districts for the House and 50 for the Senate. Importantly the plan had 19 districts in which African Americans made up a majority of the population and 13 in which they made up 40 percent to 50 percent of the population. The legislature's plan had 20 majority-minority districts and seven in which they made up 40 percent to 50 percent. Thus, Republicans claimed that their plan (or Jenkins' plan) actually bolstered minority-voting strength. But several black lawmakers and leaders said that Jenkins' plan was a classic example of "packing" the African American population to the advantage of the Republicans. However, the North Carolina Supreme Court upheld the decision. Moreover, the U.S. Justice Department also approved this plan. The latter had to be done because 40 North Carolina counties are subject to Section 5 of the Voting Rights Act. However, many people were upset about the actions of Jenkins and the Republicans. The following is a sampling of some of the reaction to Judge Jenkins:

> Judge Knox V. Jenkins, Jr.'s rejection of redistricting maps drawn by the N. C. General Assembly and the substitution of his own maps is a blatant case of politically motivated judicial activism. Drawing redistricting maps is delegated to the state legislature by the N.C. Constitution. It's up to the courts to decide whether those maps meet constitutional mandates—and to send them back if they do not. (Editorial from Asheville Citizen-Times, 6/3/02)

All of this judicial activity delayed the primary, which was originally scheduled for May, until September. Not surprisingly, the plans were beneficial for the Republicans. With a major GOTV effort, the Republicans were able to take advantage of the plans. They were able to pick up seven seats in the Senate. Meanwhile the House is divided 60-60, with the speaker's chair being held jointly by a Democrat and a Republican.

Conclusion

I started by pointing out the value of looking to the states to help us understand race and politics at this moment of our nation's history. This examination of the 2002 elections in North Carolina helps to support this. For instance, by focusing on the U.S. Senate race, I showed that serious strains exist between the Democratic Party and Black Americans, its most loyal constituency. Obviously, the issues discussed here are revealed in hundreds of campaigns and elections throughout the nation. But the North Carolina race was especially important because of the attention it received from scholars and analysts outside the state.

The tendency of the party to engage in its own brand of deracialization is ominous and potentially cataclysmic for Democratic Party politics at all levels. This is not hyperbole because it reveals that the party is unwilling or unable to address how race plays out in party politics. The party wants loyalty yet it works against viable African American candidates, fails to effectively mobilize the Black electorate, and it too quickly points a finger at Blacks when Democrats experience losses. By doing this, the party gives tacit acknowledgement and acceptance to white racialized voting by ensuring that in certain elections, especially those involving majority white voting districts, Blacks do not carry the party banner. The example of the selection of Bowles by the Democratic Party is just one way to do this. As opposed to these tactics, the party could directly confront the challenges posed by changes in the party. For example, the party could take creative measures to expand and solidify its base without sacrificing traditional party values. In addition, it could attempt to transform, through education and outreach, the racial reasoning of many white voters. Moreover, Black leadership must make a more forceful demand for changes in the approach. The party will not do change on its own, especially as long as Blacks continue to offer uninterrupted support for Democratic candidates. But change must come because many Black office-seekers and voters are becoming increasingly frustrated with a political party that treats its most loyal constituent group with such disdain. But all of this shows that, "Ain't No Party Like a Democratic Party."

Although I spent less time on the role of Judge Jenkins, I believe the precedent he established is equally important. Here a judge, handpicked by Republicans, greatly extended the role of the courts in redistricting. Two observations are important here. First, it seems a bit hypocritical for Republicans to decry judicial activism while applauding this unprecedented action by this Superior Court judge. Second, in my judgement and others, the enduring legacy of Republican political ascendancy is control of the judiciary. This is certainly the case in North Carolina. And as of this writing the Bush Administration is making plans to appoint federal judges and Supreme Court justices that reflect their conservative judicial philosophy. Considering that the federal judiciary, especially the U.S. Supreme Court, is hostile to what had been accepted interpretations of the U.S. constitution and the Voting Rights Act, the action by the judge from Johnston County is as ominous as the issues mentioned regarding the Democratic Party.

As noted, at the outset, I said that this article was not designed to be a comprehensive examination of the events and developments mentioned about. I have kept that promise. Much was left out of this analysis here. That means there is much more to be done. But I believe that the present work calls attention to important matters that deserve the attention of leaders, politicians, activists, and scholars alike.

Notes

1. The discussion of the election was taken from various news accounts from the Raleigh *News and observer*, the Durham *Herald-Sun* and the *Charlotte Observer*.
2. The workplace reforms were a direct response to a devastating fire at a Hamlet, north Carolina chicken plant where 25 workers were killed.
3. In fact, some Blacks, especially some prominent Black ministers, also questioned Blue's electability. But none of them had the political wherewithal to do anything about it. However, the party did.
4. The electability issue was also raised when Gantt ran for the Senate in 1996. He sought the Democratic nomination against former Glaxo executive Charlie Sanders who is white. Many thought Sanders had a better chance against Helms although he had never held elect-

ed office and had a very spotty record of voting in elections.
5. In fact, one of Bowles' campaign ads showed a picture of him with former Senate minority leader, Republican Trent Lott. Although this was well before Lott's unfortunate comments praising Strom Thurmond's 1948 Dixiecrat campaign for president, the Black community abhorred this ad.
6. Interestingly, Dole did not merely concede the Black vote to Bowles, she sought the support of African American ministers and she attended and addressed the state meeting of the National Association for the Advancement of Colored People.
7. Similar to the discussion of the election, the following was taken from various news accounts from the Raleigh *News and Observer*, the Durham *Herald-Sun* and the *Charlotte Observer*.
8. This is the term given to North Carolina Democrats who consistently support Jesse Helms for Senate.
9. Ellis was the founder of the National Congressional Club, which was responsible for helping Jesse Helms win 6 of his 8 Senate elections from 1972-1992.
10. Jenkins later removed himself from the case. The defendant in the case was freed after being wrongfully accused.

References

Black, Earl and Merle Black. *The Rise of Southern Republicans*. Cambridge: Belknap Press of Harvard University. 2002.

Citrin, Jack, Donald Philip Green and David O. Sears. "White Reactions to Black Candidates: When Does Race Matter." *Public Opinion Quarterly*. Vol. 54: 74-96. 1990.

Edsall, Thomas Byrne and Mary D. Edsall. *Chain Reaction: The Impact of Race, Rights and Taxes on American Politics*. New York: W. W. Norton. 1992.

McCormick, Joseph, II, and Charles E. Jones. "Conceptualization of Deracialization: Thinking Though the Dilemma," In Dilemmas of Black Politics: Issues of Leadership and Strategy, ed. Georgia A. Persons, 65-84. New York: Harper Collins, 1993.

Reeves, Keith. *Voting Hopes or Fears? White Voters, Black Candidates and Racial Politics in American*. New York: Oxford University Press. 1997.

Schneider, William. "Say Hello to NASCAR Dads," The *National Journal*. July 13, 2002.

Proportional Representation and Black Political Representation and Influence in America: An Alternative to the Single Member District Strategy

Bob Holmes

The issue of fair representation for African Americans has been a matter of concern and much debate for more than 50 years. Many scholars have examined this problem.[1] More than 90 percent of Black state legislators were elected from majority black districts that were drawn based on the Voting Rights Act (VRA) of 1965. The VRA and the 1982 amendments have been the primary mechanism to ensure that protected racial minorities would have access to representation by drawing majority-minority districts. For example, in 1991-1992, Congressional districts with majority black voters were drawn in Alabama, North Carolina, South Carolina and Virginia and these states elected their first black Congresspersons in the 20th Century. However, in the 1993 case of Shaw vs. Reno, the U.S. Supreme Court rules that drawing irregularly shaped districts based primarily on racial factors could be constitutionally suspect.

The Shaw ruling threatened to reverse many of the advances made during the previous two decades toward fair representation that had been made by African Americans and other minorities protected under the VRA. Then in the Georgia case of Miller vs. Johnson (1995), the court ruled by a 5-4 vote that race could not be the primary factor in drawing majority-minority legislative districts. This made it more difficult for the Department of Justice to protect or enhance minority political representation. Subsequently, several majority-minority districts have been successfully challenged by white plaintiffs and many more districts seem vulnerable to challenges based on the Shaw decision. There is the fear that the successful use of the VRA during the decade of the 1970s, 1980s, and early 1990s to allow minorities to elect the candidates of their choice, resulting in hundreds of victories by candidates from minority communities, is now in serious jeopardy as a remedy for minority vote dilution.

The key problem for the 21st century is to find a strategy that will enable minorities to maintain or enhance their representation given the likelihood of a conservative Supreme Court majority that will most likely follow the Shaw decision in future redistricting/reapportionment cases. And since drawing of new legislative districts as occurred in 2001-2002 and will be repeated in each decade hereafter, alternatives to the single member district electoral system need to be examined to help ensure future fair representation for minorities. The keys to changing an electoral system are research, litigation and community mobilization. This chapter will explore the use of proportional representation election systems, such as cumulative voting, limited voting, and preference (or choice) voting,[2] as an alternative strategy to achieve fair representation and political influence for minorities in political jurisdictions in multi-member legislative bodies at all levels of government. While there are some examples of minority candidates being elected to federal, state and local political offices in non-minority districts, such as former U.S. Senator Edward Brooke (Massachusetts), Governor L. Douglas Wilder (Virginia), and Mayor David Dinkens (New York City), the fact is that racially polarized voting occurs in the overwhelming majority of political jurisdictions in the nation and it is still very difficult for African Americans to win elections in a single member district system, particularly in at-large election systems, which requires winning a majority of the vote.

Proportional representation (PR) voting systems are used by almost all of the world's major democracies, including all of the Western European countries, except Great Britain. Under PR, representatives are elected from multi-seat districts in approximate proportion to the number of votes received and this outcome helps to ensure that political parties or candidates will win the approximate percent of legislative seats that reflects their level of electoral support. A candidate need not come in first to win a seat. Thus different ethnic or racial groups, ideological based interest groups or political parities can have representation in legislative bodies comparable to their percent of the electorate casting ballots.

In contrast, in the United States the use of the "winner take all" single member district means a losing candidate who receives 49.9 percent of the vote will leave his/her block of supporters unrepresented. Voters sense this and many do not vote for the candidates they like, because he does not stand a realistic chance of winning, but vote instead for their second choice ("lesser of two evils") because they stand the best chance of winning. Proponents of PR assert that this is a major reason why the U.S. have such a low voter turnout, that there is a growing interest in third parties, that many elections are not competitive, that 70 percent of Americans believe they are not well represented by the officials who are elected and that there will be continuing political and legal battles over minority voting rights, racial and political gerrymandering as well as fair representation.[3]

A growing number of voting rights experts and advocates, such as Lani Guinier, have advocated the use of PR as a "race neutral" method to provide fair representation for political minorities in competitive elections. And even conservative Black Supreme Court Justice Clarence Thomas indicated his support for PR in a concurring opinion in Holder v. Hall, which involved a Supreme Court ruling that the size of county commissions in Georgia would not have to be increased to ensure the creation of a majority-minority Single member district. He stated that single member districts was a political choice, but that multi-member districts had along political tradition in the U.S. to elect state legislators and city councils. In his words:

> the decision to rely on single-member geographic districts as a mechanism for conducting elections is merely a political choice—and one that we might reconsider in the future. . . . Already, some advocates have criticized the current strategy of creating majority-minority districts and have urged the option of other voting mechanisms—for example, cumulative voting or a system using transferable votes [e.g., preference voting]—that can produce proportional results without requiring division of the electorate into racially segregated districts. At least one court, in fact, has already abandoned districting and has opted instead for cumulative voting on a county-wide basis as a remedy for a Voting Rights Act violation. The district Court for the District of Maryland recently reasoned that, compared to a system that divides voters into districts according to race, "[c]umulative voting is less likely to allow themselves," thereby avoiding government involvement in the process of segregating the electorate. . . . If such a system can be ordered under the act that would prevent federal courts from requiring it for elections to state legislatures as well.

PR requires fewer votes to win a seat in a multi-member district than in a winner-take-all system and votes can be gathered from a larger area, which makes it easier for a racial minority to win seats without having to racially gerrymander districts. Thus, PR offers a method of addressing the Miller v. Johnson (1995). To convert the current electoral system from the single member winner-take-all type to PR would require changes in federal, state and local laws to permit the system to be used to elect representatives to city councils, school boards, county commissions, state legislatures and the U.S. House of Representatives.

Critics of the single member district system assert that it is unfair and undemocratic because it denies representation to a large number of voters, it limits voter choices, and it encourages political and racial gerrymandering. It produces legislative bodies that do not accurately reflect the views of the public, it discourages competition, it discriminates against third parties, it creates obstacles to the election of political minorities and it discourages voter participation.[4]

As Justice Thomas has written, many local and state political jurisdictions in the U.S. have used PR as early as the 19th century. For example, cumulative voting was used to elect the Illinois House of Representatives from 1870 to 1980; limited voting is used in Jamesville, North Carolina to elect county commissioners; and preference voting was used in Cincinnati between 1925-1957 to elect the city council; it has been used since 1941 in Cambridge (Massachusetts) to elect city council members; and more recently to elect local school board members in New York City. The two states with the largest number of political jurisdictions that are currently using some type of PR electoral system are Alabama (30) and Texas (50). Texas has the largest political jurisdiction to adopt PR, the Amarillo School District with 150,000, and held its first election under this new system in May 2000. African American and

Latino candidates won two seats on the seven member school board with less than 20 percent of the population.

The issue of fair representation is at the core of democracy. Thus, it is important to explore ways that the political system can be changed to better represent its people in government and to promote increased participation in elections.[5]

There is a relative paricity of research on PR in terms of its actual impact on African Americans. Most of the extant literature focuses on philosophical discussions about the advantages of PR versus the single member district electoral method. We are interested in determining whether PR is a potentially useful electoral system for ensuring fair black political representation and other improvements in a democratic system. Lani Guinier wrote in *Lift Every Voice* that,

> "Election reform, including PR, is not primarily about electoral rules. It is not simply about getting more people of color and women into office. It is about transforming how power itself is exercised and shared. It is about opening up a different kind of political conversation, as elections become forums for voters to express their ideas and choose their representative. It is about giving citizens their due. . . . After all, democracy takes place when the silent find their voice, and when we begin to listen to what they have to say."[6]

It is Guinier's vision and goals that the proponents of PR are seeking to achieve. Among the scholars who have examined the topic are Richard Engstrom, Edward Still and Jason F. Kirksey, who wrote: "With limited and cumulative voting, minority groups may be provided with electoral opportunities based on the extent to which they are politically cohesive, rather than the extent to which they are residentially segregated." And Jerome Gray, Field Director of the Alabama Democratic Conference, stated that African American voters were able to successfully force local political jurisdictions to change election mechanisms to achieve fair representation in local government. In 1986, the ADC successfully settled a class action suit that permitted 30 political jurisdictions to utilize PR to elect school boards, city councils and county commissions beginning with the 1988 election. African Americans have been elected in each political jurisdiction since PR was adopted. The next section which provide some data and an historical perspective of the experience of other political jurisdictions using PR as related to African American representation.[7]

In Illinois, cumulative voting was used from 1880-1970 to elect members of the state legislature. An important outcome of this electoral reform was that Senator Emile Jones, who became Senate Minority Leader was elected from a three member district which had only a 28 percent African American population at the time of his first election in 1972. The City of Cincinnati used choice/preference voting to elect its city council from 1924-1955 with a population that was less than 20 percent black; there were always one or two African Americans on the Council. Prior to the adoption of PR, there was no person of color on the Council, but soon afterwards their legislative representation was approximately proportionate to their population. In 1957, PR was repealed and replaced by an at-large, winner take all election method to elect a nine member council. It should be noted that the motive for the adoption of the new system was the fear of whites that black city councilman Theodore Berry might receive the highest number of first preference votes and become the presiding officer/mayor. It is alleged that preventing the election of a black mayor was the impetus for eliminating PR. After 1957, the population grew steadily to 38 percent but no blacks were elected to the Council during the first three elections after the new at-large system was adopted. Subsequently, no more than two blacks were elected to the Council prior to the 1993 election.[8]

In Amarillo, Texas, no Black or Latino had been elected to serve on the seven member school board for more than 20 years in a city that had a combined African American and Hispanic speaking population of approximately 20 percent. The Mexican-American Legal Defense Fund (MALDEF), the League of United Latin American Citizen's (LULAC) and the NAACP Legal Defense and Education Fund filed a voting rights suit. A settlement was reached to adopt cumulative voting as a remedy to achieve minority political representation. As indicated, 50 political jurisdictions have enacted cumulative voting in Texas and in 1995, President Bush signed legislation to permit all school boards to use cumulative and limited voting.[9] In the 2000 election for the Amarillo School Board, one Black and one Latino were elected to serve.

Four political scientists examined minority representation resulting from modified PR elections (cumulative and limited voting) in several local elections during the 1990s in the U.S. Concerning African Americans, they said,

> Our data provide evidence that modifying local at-large elections with cumulative voting offers the promise of minority representation at levels similar to those found under single member districts. These findings should be encouraging to those interested in facilitating minority representation without relying upon the acrimonious process of drawing districts on the basis of race. Previous research has established that minorities do win seats under these modified plans. Our purpose was to identify how the seats—population relationship under cumulative voting/limited voting compares to those produced under other plans. For African Americans, representation from CV/LV elections compares favorably to that obtained from SMD and is more proportionate than representation under unmodified at large.[10]

However, for Latinos the election results were not proportionate because of three factors: (1) few Latino candidates ran for office; (2) a lower percent of adult Latinos voter turnout in elections; and (3) a higher threshold of inclusion was used in the CV plans adopted in the 30 political jurisdictions where they were the largest minority (typically two or three seats requiring a 25 or 33 percent threshold.*)

In Illinois, three State House members were elected from multi-member districts under the cumulative voting method in the primary and general elections from 1870-1980. Black candidates were first elected in the House beginning in 1984 (3) until 1980 (15) in larger numbers than would have been possible under single member district voting. The numbers more than tripled from the 1952 (4) to 1968 (13) in the House and from one in 1964 (Senators were elected from single member districts comprised of three House districts) to 4 in 1966. Many were elected from white majority districts, such as Emile Jones who won in a 28 percent Black three member district. However, a major limitation was that there were few districts outside of Chicago in the state where African Americans represented a threshold of 25 percent. The history of cumulative voting in Illinois suggests that dispersed, populations such as blacks in much of the South, Asians and Hispanics throughout the nation could achieve greater descriptive representation in legislative bodies. Asian Americans and Latinos in much of the country would do well with cumulative voting and proportional systems.[11]

As indicated above, Alabama has had extensive experience with Cumulative and

Limited Voting. Participant observer Jerome Cray assessed the 1986-1998 experience related to the Dillard v. Crenshaw County et. al litigation of 1986.[12] Gray is the State Field Director of the Alabama Democratic Conference (ADC) and was directly involved in the case which challenged 180 Alabama political jurisdictions that had at-large elections. The first time PR was used in the state was to elect the 32 member Executive Committee of the Conecuh County Democratic Party 1971; two districts elected 15 members each at-large from numbered posts by majority vote. This replaced the electoral system of electing two members each from 16 precincts. The 1971 change had not been pre-cleared by the U.S. Department of Justice and was invalidated. Rather than propose 32 single member districts (SMDs), civil rights Birmingham Attorney Edward Still proposed limited voting as a remedy and it was accepted. In the 1982 election, blacks increased the representation from 10 percent (3 members) to 40 percent (12 members).

After litigation, voter education and political mobilization were the other two key components that contributed to the success of the new systems. Flyers were prepaid which explained how limited voting worked. The ADC and County NAACP chapter recruited candidates in each precinct with a black population at or above the 25 percent political threshold. Sample ballots were distributed in churches and neighborhoods containing instructions on how to limit voting. And several meetings and training sessions were held to allow precinct leaders and voters to practice in mock elections.[13] Gray asserted that the electoral success with the Democratic Executive Committee convinced the ADC and attorneys that alternative voting systems should be a remedy option to settle other litigation involving at-large elections. The Dillard case involved 180 cities and counties based on factors, such as black population totals/percentages, the degree of concentration and dispersal, voter registration, level of political organization and economic conditions. A key effort was made to increase the number of seats from five to seven in the governing bodies (school boards, councils and commissions), but were only successful in seven cases. With one exception, blacks were elected in all cities where the number of seats were increased. The jurisdictions were all small, 16 had populations less than 25 percent and only one had a black majority and generally were very poor communities and were also declining in population (17 lost population between the 1980 and 1990 census). Overall, two-thirds of the communities have elected black officials to public office and only one political jurisdiction over 25 percent has failed to elect a candidate of their choice.

Gray seemed very pleased with Alabama's experience with PR's use to increase black political representation. He expressed this sentiment in the following words:

With a sixteen-year history and electoral record of using alternative voting in Alabama, it can be said with some certainty that these systems, overall, have worked well. Indeed, given the state's history of racial segregation and discrimination, black voter denial, average family median income, and level of education, one is moved to say that if alternative voting systems have been used successfully in Alabama to help elect more blacks to public office since 1982, then it ought to work elsewhere. The advantages of alternative voting systems as they worked in Alabama are enumerated below:

1. They eliminate the requirement of jurisdictions having to redistrict themselves every ten years after a census.

2. They eliminate numbered places and the majority vote requirement.

3. Minority candidates and women often benefit greatly from these systems because they allow minority and women voters to "plump" their limited or cumulative votes in a block in support of candidates that they prefer.

4. The delectability of good candidates under these systems is not skewed unduly toward incumbents or candidates with the most money.

5. Strong minority candidates are able to win under these systems even with less resources and political connections.

6. It facilitates the establishment and/or use of voting centers for local elections.

7. It saves jurisdictions a lot of money in that no runoff elections are required.

8. It saves money for the jurisdictions. They will never have to pay lawyers and demographers to assist them in drawing redistricting plans.

9. Increase the potential pool of good minority candidates to run and win simply because they do not restrict or limit winnable candidate selection to the majority black district(s).

10. All the minority voters throughout the jurisdiction (in the city or county) always have the opportunity to vote and help elect the minority candidate(s) of their choice.

A study of the increase in black representation in state legislatures and Congress during the 1980s and early 1990s showed that in 1992, the vast majority of African Americans serving in the state legislatures (89 percent) and Congress (9 percent) are present majority black districts.[14] In 1992, fewer African Americans actually represented majority white districts than in 1990. And Bernard Grofman, one of the prominent expert witnesses and scholars on voting rights issues surmised that black legislative representation seems destined to decline unless new creative and innovative strategies are utilized to address the series of 1990's ruling by the court which found "reverse racism" and discriminatory intent in the drawing of majority black districts.[15] One course of action is to explore alternatives to the SMD method of electing legislative bodies. Since state legislatures have the responsibility for redistricting/reapportionment after each decennial census, it seems important to understand their attitudes on PR. In recent years, more African American legislators have expressed an interest in PR.

African American legislators in Georgia, Texas and Tennessee have proposed PR legislation recently while others in Florida, Massachusetts, South Carolina and Alabama have requested information PR from the Center for Voting and Democracy, the premier organization supporting PR in the U.S. This writer conducted a survey of a sample of the membership of the National Black Caucus of State Legislators, and the findings are based on the responses of 106 of the 575 members of the organization. A demographic profile shows 62 percent were male and 32 percent female; 60 percent were between 40-59 years and 17 percent above 60; 60 percent had tenure of less than 10 years and 27 percent 11-20 years; 72 percent represented urban areas, 14 percent rural and 9 percent suburban; 79 percent had majority black constituencies, 10 percent majority white and 8 percent mixed.

Concerning PR related issues, 81 percent had not been involved in multi-seat PR election districts and only 12 percent had. 42 percent were familiar with the PR concept and 41.5 percent were unfamiliar with PR; 91.59 percent desired more information about PR and only 3.8 percent did not want any; 80 percent said such information would be helpful to them in future reapportionment/redistricting, 18 percent were uncertain about its usefulness; 19 percent were aware of court rulings on PR and 70 percent were unaware; 64% didn't know if legal restrictions prevented PRs use in their state, and 13 percent were aware of such impediments; 31 percent believed PR would facilitate the election of minorities, 40 percent said they did not know the impact and 11 percent said PR would make it more difficult to elect people of color and women; 82 percent said the issue had never been debated in their state legislature; only 28 percent said they favored multi-party multi-member district electoral system with plurality elections, 36 percent opposed such an electoral method and 33 percent did not have a position on the issue; only 29 percent said demographic changes would make it more difficult to draw single member majority black districts after the next census, 49 percent said it would be more difficult; 63.1 percent of males said alternatives to the SMD should be explored and 64.7 percent of females agreed; legislators age 50-59 were the most likely (62.5 percent to support PR compared to 57.1 percent for age 40-49) and only 33.3 percent in age 30-39.

The survey results indicate that while there is a significant interest among black legislators to learn more about PR, however, there are major challenges in educating them about the positive impacts that PR can have on African American electoral opportunities to increase their political representation.[16] At the Congressional level, Mel Watt of North Carolina and former Congressperson Cynthia McKinney of Georgia were among the most ardent supporters of PR for election of the U.S. House of Representatives. It is no coincidence that both have been "victims" of major reductions in their districts as a result of Supreme Court decisions. Congressman James Clyburn during his tenure as Chair of the Congressional Black Caucus of South Carolina was a strong advocate. McKinney introduced legislation in 1995 and in the 2000 session HR1173 by Watt and others would lift the 1967 ban against multi-seat elections for the U.S. House. Even some affirmative action opponents such as Republican Tom Campbell of California have supported the legislation. Former Congressman McKinney spoke in favor of HR1173 from the well of the House noting that

"Most of the democratic world long ago abandoned one-seat district representation in favor of proportional systems in "super districts" with more than one member. I have long been convinced of the merits of proportional representation, which is why I twice introduced the Voters' Choice Act, a forerunner of the States' Choice of Voting Systems Act. It would have restored the opportunity to use proportional systems to elect their delegations to the House—a power they held as recently as the 1960s. It's potential appeal is broad enough that in announcing my 1995 bill, I had beside me the directors of the U.S. Term Limits, the Committee for the Study of the American Electorate and the National Women's Political Caucus. The discussion on proportional representation must begin in earnest as public discontent increases, voter turnout decreases and representation of our diversity is challenged in court."[17]

The debate over PR has begun in the late 1990s as several government reform organizations have become concerned about political aberration and low voter turnout, the growing opposition to large campaign contributions in the electoral process and the increase in criticism of political and racial gerrymandering, consequently, more people have become more interested in alternative election systems.

Douglas Amy[18] is among the most insightful writers on PR. He says voter turnout in the U.S. is among the lowest in the world with less than 50 percent in non-Presidential election years and barely 60 percent in Presidential elections. In contrast, European nations have 80 percent-90 percent of their eligible electorate who vote. There are several other indicators of dissatisfaction with the SMD electoral method and why there is a need for reform. While many people seem oblivious to the outmoded, unfair and undemocratic structural nature of the electoral system, but they constantly complain about the poor quality or lack of good choices among candidates, the almost automatic reelection of incumbents and the pernicious nature of special interest money in political campaigns. Amy says the worldwide trend has been for old and new democracies to abandon SMD in favor of PR.

While PR was used in some state and local political jurisdictions in the U.S. in the 1800s and there was a renewed interest in the early part of the 20th century as several major cities such as New York (Adam Clayton Powell, Jr. was elected to the Council under PR), Cleveland and Cincinnati. A third wave of interest occurred in the 1990s with the Supreme Court decisions on redistricting among political pundits, elected officials, federal courts and university scholars began to search for options. Numerous articles appeared in academic journals as well as the print media, such as *Atlantic Boston Globe, Christian Science Monitor, Chicago Tribune, New York Times, New Yorker, New Republic, San Francisco Chronicle, The Nation, Time* and the *Washington Post*. Many civil rights leaders such as Jesse Jackson of Operation PUSH and Dr. Joseph E. Lowery, former President of the SCLC and now Chair of the Leadership Conference on Civil Rights have advocated PR. Several national organizations such as the Center for Voting and Democracy and the Southern Center for Studies in Public Policy have emerged and provided education materials and workshops on PR for elected officials and community leaders. During 2001-2002 the League of Women Voters and its 50 state chapters examined PR as part of its focus on electoral reform and held numerous forums. Congressmen, such as James Clyburn, Cynthia McKinney and Mel Watts introduced legislation to repeal the 1967 statute which prohibits elections of members of the U.S House from multi-member districts, and state legislators have introduced bills in their states to permit use of PR. The Republican governor of Illinois appointed a Blue Congressman to examine whether PR should be reinstituted in that state to elect the state legislatures by cumulative voting as done for over a century from 1970-1980.[19] Also, organizations and individuals across a broad spectrum of political ideology of whites have begun to seriously consider PR. For example, the Georgia Municipal Association and the Association of County Commissioners of Georgia have created committees to research and examine the issue primarily because it would reduce the expensive litigation that occurs after each redistricting cycle and reduce attendant political and racial conflicts within their communities. The Conservative U.S. Term Limits Committee and the National Women's Political Caucus both endorsed former Congresswoman McKinney's 1995 Voter Choice Act legislation. And as one writer stated:

> Clarence Thomas and Lani Guinier don't agree on much. So when the arch-conservative Supreme Court Justice and the Clinton Administration nominee who was dumped as too radical (she was labeled "quota queen" the xxx of her advocacy of PR to achieve black political representation), find common ground, we should

take notice. Both agree that some version of proportional representation is an attractive way out of one of the most mind-numbing legal and philosophical puzzles of democratic representation."[20]

Ironically, it was the Supreme Courts' Shaw v. Reno and Miller v. Johnson decisions which declared unconstitutional the drawing of racially based and often oddly shaped single member districts, such as Mel Watt's snake like Congressional 160 mile district from Charlotte to Durham along I-85, that provided the impetus for the renewed interest in PR. This method of increasing the number of black elected officials was based on findings that white polarized, block-voting prevented the election of blacks in majority white districts and while opponents argued drawing black majority districts amounted to "racial apartheid" (Editorial Board of the Atlanta Constitution), "racial balkanization" (Justice Thomas) and "political apartheid" (Justice Sandra Day O'Connor) and "racial gerrymandering" (plaintiffs' lawyers) and violated the 14th Amendment Equal Protection Clause for white voters and prevented the races from forming "common ground" and coalitions in the electoral process.

The debate over how best to achieve fair political representation for African Americans is similar to the debate about affirmative action in business, education and employment—how to create opportunities for minorities without establishing preferences or so-called quotas. In the 1990s, the debate became increasingly racially divisive as education admission and minority business enterprise programs (see Croson v. Richmond 1989) were declared unconstitutional because they were racial based preferences or quotas which violated the 14th amendment equal protection clause. Justice Thomas solution to the dilemma in the area of voting rights is PR, the same one for which Lani Guinier advocated. He said;

"cumulative voting and other non-district based methods of effecting proportional representation are simply more efficient and straightforward mechanisms for achieving what has already become our tacit objective: roughly proportional allocation of political power according to race."[21]

It seems that Lani Guinier may prove to have been a prophet who was ahead of her time. Her ideas offered in the previous decade are now being given increasing attention.

The reason that persons of diverse political philosophies seem to be "strange political bed fellows" when it comes to PR, is that voters don't have to be grouped based on the idea that race or skin color alone determines common political interests. And white Democrats don't have to fear a zero sum outcome in which the political empowerment of blacks in one political area will result in the political weakness in the adjacent area i.e. creating a majority district would "bleach" a neighboring area and create a Republican district. The potential benefits of PR have led dozens of local political jurisdictions in Alabama and Texas to settle voting rights cases without adopting the traditional remedy that is backed by such political opposites as Lani Guinier and Clarence Thomas, it seems likely that PR will become more acceptable and used as a remedy to resolve future redistricting political struggles.

There is a plethora of literature on PR that has documented its success in increasing minority political representation. Some of the most important writings on PR and Minority Representation are: Douglas J. Amy: *Real Choices, New Voices: The Case for Proportional Representation Elections in the*

United States (New York: Columbia University Press: 2002). Chapter 5 which shows how the SMD results in under representation of people of color on legislative bodies. Blacks are 15 percent of the population, but have less than two percent of elected officials. Many studies show that where PR is used this unfair under representation has been somewhat remedied. Center for Voting and Democracy, *Voting and Democracy Report* (Washington, D.C., CVD, 1995) contains several case studies such as Robert Bischetto "Cumulative Voting at Work in Texas" (the effectiveness of cumulative voting in enhancing Latino Political representation in 15 Texas communities); Jason Kirskey et al "Cumulative Voting in an Alabama County: (documents how Bobby Agee, an African American mortician, was elected to the seven member Commission in Chilton County which has a ten percent black population and subsequently, has served twice as Chair of that Commission); Edward Still and Pamela Karlan, "Cumulative Voting and the Voting Rights Act: Amicus Curiae in a Maryland Voting Rights Case" (shows how cumulative voting was suggested and adopted by a federal district court as the remedy in a county on the eastern shore of Maryland which resulted in the first African Americans being elected); Clarence Thomas, "Justice Thomas on Proportional Voting Systems: Excerpts from Concurring Opinion in Holder v. Hall (summarized Thomas's philosophy that PR is an appropriate race neutral remedy for voting rights redistricting cases; Lani Guinier, *Lift Every Voice* (New York: Simon and Shuster, 1998) Chapter 5 (shows why PR is the best hope for creating diverse representation in government); Wilma Rule and Joseph Zimmerman (eds), *United States Electoral Systems: Their Impact on Women and Minorities* (New York: Greenwood Press, 1993) contains many important chapters like Richard L. Engstrom, "Alternative Judicial Election Systems: Solving the Minority Dilution Problem (proposes PR to remedy the under representation of African American judges who are frequently elected in majority white circuits at-large); Edward Still, "Cumulative Voting and Limited Voting in Alabama" (shows the growth of black political representation in cities and counties in Alabama after these two electoral methods were adopted as remedies); and Leon Weaver and Judith Brum, "Proportional Representation in New York City Community School Boards (shows how Blacks and Hispanics were elected to membership in rough approximation to their percentage of their school district population after this electoral reform was used); and Southern Center for Studies in Public Policy and Center for Voting and Democracy, *Fair Representation: Alternative Election Systems Manual* (Atlanta: SCSPP, 2000) is a "How To" primer on PR which explains the keys to changing election systems, key concepts with a glossary, advantages and disadvantages of cumulative voting, limited voting and preference voting methods of PR, education, choosing the best system to empower minorities, addressing common concerns about PR and PR materials (sample ballots maps and organization resources).

These readings are particularly useful in showing both the philosophical basis for PR as well as documenting the many successful uses of PR in increasing minority representation. (For other readings on the topic, see Appendix A).

Conclusion

The U.S. Supreme Court's rejections of minority majority districts in several Congressional redistricting cases indicated SMDs would be an unconstitutional method to create Black districts to increase fair representation. For the past decade, voting rights leaders have criticized the Court for "standing the Voting Rights Act on its head." Since the primary method for increasing Black legislative representation had been creating majority Black districts. There are basically three options: (1) accept the Supreme Court decisions which suggests a race-neutral approach to redistricting which in essence would result in denial of Black representation similar to the situation that existed in the South prior to the enactment of the Voting Rights Act of 1965 when no blacks were in Congress and only a handful in state legislatures; (2) continue to push the majority minority district plans to preserve and expand minority representation and face the likely prospect that the Supreme Court will rule in favor of challenges; or (3) consider PR as a strategy that has been shown to be acceptable to federal judiciary and has a track record favorable to increasing representation for political and racial minorities.[22]

The literature cited documents the positive impact of PR as a viable solution to fair representation for African Americans which can be described as race-neutral and be supported by a diverse political ideological coalition. There would no longer be a need to draw gerrymandering districts to include a majority of Black voters. Furthermore, it would enhance the prospects in political jurisdictions where blacks will never become a majority and where white voter polarization exists. The beauty of PR is that a minority which reaches the political threshold of inclusion can elect a candidate or candidates of their choice regardless of how the majority population votes. Thus, it would seem that PR may offer the best opportunity among the extant option available to achieve African American fair representation in the 21st century and beyond.

Notes

1. SCSPP and Center for Voting and Democracy. *Alternative Election Systems Manual 2001.*
2. "Legislative Black Caucus in Georgia" and "Black Mobilization in Georgia" in *The New Georgia Encyclopedia* (forthcoming 2003).
3. "Reapportionment/Redistricting Politics in Georgia: the 1990s and 2001-2002; Reflections of Participant Observer" David Botsitis (ed), *Voting Rights and Redistricting.* (Washington DC: Joint Center for Political and Economic Studies: 2003 forthcoming.)
4. "Alternative Election Systems and the African American Community" in Franklin D. Jones and Michael O. Adams (eds), *Readings in American Political Issues* (2nd ed.), Kendall/Hunt (forthcoming 2003).
5. "The Georgia Legislative Black Caucus: An Analysis of a Legislative Subgroup" *Journal of Black Studies* (vol. 30, no. 6, July 2000).
6. "A Survey of Members of the National Black Caucus of State Legislators on Alternatives to Single Member Districts" *Endarch,* Spring 2000.
7. Reapportionment Strategies in the 1990s" in Bernard Grofman (ed.), *Race and Redistricting in the 1990s* (NY: Agathon Press), 1998.
8. "Reapportionment Politics in the 1990's: The Case of Georgia" in Georgia Persons (ed.), *Race and Representation* (New Brunswick: Transaction Press, 1997).
9. "Georgia's Reapportionment/Redistricting Process in 1995" *National Political Science Review,* Volume VI, 1997.

Appendix A

"Proportional Representation: A Tool for Empowering Minorities and the Poor." *Poverty and Race,* Vol. 3, No. 5 (Sept./Oct. 1994), 1-2, 10. Washington, D.C.: Poverty and Race Research Council.

Anderson, John, "A Better Approach to Boosting Minority Representation?" *The Christian Science Monitor,* July 6, 1993, 18.

Anderson, John, "A Way to End 'Political Apartheid.'" USA Today, August 3, 1994, p. 9A.

Applebome, Peter, "Guinier Ideas, Once Seen as Odd, Now Get Serious Study." *The New York Times,* April 3, 1994, E5.

Briffault, Richard, "Lani Guinier and Dilemmas of American Democracy." *Columbia Law Review,* Vol. 95, 1995, 418-472.

Brischetto, Robert, "Cumulative Voting and Latino Representation: Exit Surveys in Fifteen Texas Communities." *Social Science Quarterly* 78, no. 4, p. 973.

Brockington, David, Todd Donovan and Shaun Bowler. "Minority Representation under Cumulative and Limited Voting." *The Journal of Politics* 60, no. 4 (Nov. 1998), p. 1108-25.

Buckley, Stephen. "Unusual Ruling in Rights Case: Md. County Must Use Cumulative Voting," *The Washington Post,* April 6, 1994.

Brunham, Robert. "Reform, Politics, and Race in Cincinnati: Proportional Representation and the City Charter Committee, 1924-1959." *Journal of Urban History.* Vol. 23, No. 2 (1997): 131.

Cohen, Frank. "Proportional versus Majoritarian Ethnic Conflict Management in Democracies." *Comparative Political Studies.* Vol. 30. (October 1997), 607-30.

Cole, Richard and Delbert Taebel. "Cumulative Voting in Local Elections: Lessons from the Alamagordo Experience," *Social Science Quarterly* 73, no. 1 (March 1992): 194-201.

Engstrom, Richard L. "Modified Multi-Seat Election Systems As Remedies for Minority Vote Dilution." *Stetson Law Review,* Vol. 21, No. 3, Summer 1992, 743-770.

_____. "The Single Transferable Vote: An Alternative Remedy for Minority Vote Dilution." *University of San Francisco Law Review,* Vol. 27, Summer 1993, 781-813.

Engstrom, Richard and Charles Barrilleaux, "Native Americans and Cumulative Voting: The Sisseton-Wahpeton Sioux." *Social Science Quarterly, Vol. 72, No. 2,* June 1991, pp. 388-393.

Guinier, Lani. *The Tyranny of the Majority: Fundamental Fairness in Representative Democracy.* New York: Free Press, 1994.

_____. "The Triumph of Tokenism: The Voting Rights Act and the Theory of Black Electoral Success. *Michigan Law Review,* Vol. 89, No. 5, March 1991, 1077-1154.

Hertzberg, Hendrik. "Along Racial Lines." *The New Yorker,* April 4, 1994, 7.

Hill, Steven. "Warring for the Heart of the Voting Rights Act." *The Christian Science Monitor,* June 25, 1996.

Hoffman, Matthew. "Time to Scrap District-Based Voting." *Roll Call,* June 27, 1996.

Kaplan, David. "Alternative Election Methods: A Fix for a Besieged System?" *Congressional Quarterly,* April 2, 1994, 812-813.

McKinney, Cynthia. "Keep It Simple." *Boston Review,* March/April 1998. http://www-polisci.mit.edu/bostonreview/BR23.1/

The Nation. "Wronging Voting Rights." *The Nation.* July 8, 1996. Editorial.

Pildes, Richard and Donoghue, Kristen. "Cumulative Voting in the United States." *The University of Chicago Legal Forum*, Vol. 1995, 241-313.

Raspberry, William. "Super Districts—Without the Image Problem." *Washington Post*, June 27, 1996.

Raspberry, William. "The Balkanization of America." *The Washington Post*, July 7, 1995, op-ed page.

Reding, Andrew. "Making Every Vote Really Count." *Los Angeles Times*, July 17, 1994, M5.

Rule, Wilma and Joseph F. Zimmerman (eds.). *Electoral Systems in Comparative Perspective: Their Impact on Women and Minorities.* Westport, CT: Greenwood Press, 1994.

Shugart, Matthew S. "Minorities Represented and Unrepresented" in *Electoral Systems in Comparative Perspective: Their Impact on Women and Minorities*, edited by Rule and Zimmerman. Westport, CT: Greenwood Press, 1994.

———. "Cumulative Voting as a Remedy in Voting Rights Cases." *National Civic Review* Vol. 84 (Fall/Winter 1995): 337-346.

Taagepera, Rein. "Beating the Law of Minority Attrition," in *Electoral Systems in Comparative Perspective: Their Impact on Women and Minorities*, edited by Rule and Zimmerman. Westport, CT: Greenwood Press, 1994.

Taebel, Delbert A., Richard Engstom and Richard Cole. "Alternative Electoral Systems as Remedies for Minority Vote Dilution," *Hamline Journal of Public Law and Policy*, Vol. 11, Spring 1990, pp. 19-29.

USA Today, "A Route to Fairer Voting." *USA Today*, June 30, 1995, p. 12A.

Van Biema, David. "One Person, Seven Votes." *Time*, April 25, 1994, 42-43.

Notes

1. Among the many recent studies that have explored this issue are: Chandler Davidson (ed), *Minority Vote Dilution* (1984); Bernard Grofman, et. al., *Minoritiy Representation and the Quest for Voting Equality* (1992); Chandler Davidson and Bernard Grofman (eds), *Quiet Revolution in the South: The Impact of the Voting Rights Act 1965-1990* (1995); Georgia Persons (ed), *Race and Representation* 1997); Bernard Grofman (ed), *Race and Redistricting in the 1990s* (1998); and David T. Cannon, *Race, Redistricting and Representation* (1999).

2. *Cumulative Voting*—voters cast as many votes as there are seats, but are not limited to giving a candidate one vote. Voters can concentrate their votes on one or more candidates and winning candidates are determined by a simple plurality of votes cast.

   Limited Voting—voters cast fewer votes than the number of seats and winners are determined by totaling all votes cast. The greater the difference between the number of votes and the number of seats, the greater the opportunities for fair representation.

   Preference Choice Voting—voters rank as many candidates as they wish and candidates win by reaching a "victory threshold" of 1st choice votes divided by the number of votes equal to the number of seats. Ballots are transferred to the next highest vote getter.

3.

4. Douglas Amy, *Proportional Representation: The Case for a Better Election System* (Northampton: Cresent Street Press, 1997), 3.

5. A study by Professors Shaun Bowles (University of California Riverside), David Brockington (University of Twente) and Todd Donovan (Western Washington State University) found that there was a 5 percent greater turnout of voters in cumulative voting local elections in the U.S. than in majoritarian/plurality elections paper presented at American Political Science Association Annual Meeting 1997 (available from the author), "Election Systems and Voter Turnout: Experiments in the United States."
6. (New York: Simon and Shuster, 1998).
7. "Limited and Cumulative Voting in Alabama" in Georgia Persons (ed); Race and Representation (New Brunswick: Transaction Publishers 1999), *Winning Fair Representation in At-Large Elections: Cumulative and Limited Voting in Alabama Local Elections* (Atlanta: Southern Regional Council, 1999)
8. For an excellent history of Cincinnati's experiment with PR see Robert Burnham, "Reform, Politics, and Race in Cincinnati: Proportional Representation and the City Charter Committee" 1924-1959, *Journal of Urban History,* vol 23, no. 2, January 1999, 131-163.
9. See Robert Brischetto, Cumulative Voting at Work in Texas, in Center for Voting and Democracy, *Voting and Democracy Report 1995,* (Washington, D.C.: CVD, 1995), 61-65.
10. See David Brockington, Todd Donovan, Shaun Bowles and Robert Birshetto, Minority Representation Under Cumulative and Limited Voting," *The Journal of Politics,* vol 60, no. 4 (number 1978) 1108-1025.
* The threshold of inclusion is the lowest percent vote that a voting group needs to guarantee a chance of electing the candidate of their choice. For example, if a city council, county commission or school board had 3 members, 25 percent would be the threshold, but for a seven member body only 12.5 percent would be needed.
11. See Southern Center for Studies in Public Policy and Center for Voting and Democracy, *Alternative Election Systems Manual* (Atlanta: SCSPP, 2000), 30.
12. *Winning Fair Representation in At-Large Elections: Cumulative Voting and Limited Voting in Alabama Local Elections* (Atlanta: CVD and SRC 1999).
13. Gray, op. cit, 3-4.
14. Wayne Arden, Bernard Grofman and Lisa Hudley, "The Impact of Redistricting in African American Representation in the U.S. Congress and State Legislatures in the 1990s," in Georgia Persons (ed) Race and Representation (New Brunswick: Transaction Publishers 1997), 43.
15. Bernard Grofman (ed) "Race and Redistricting in the 1990s" (New York: Agathan Press, 1998).
16. Bob Holmes, "A Preliminary Discussion on Alternative Electoral Systems and Black Legislators: A National Survey," ENDARCH (Spring 2000) 31-48.
17. Rep. Cynthia McKinney, Roll Call, February 14, 2000, http://www.natholyoke.edu/acad/polit/damy/articles/mckinney2.htm
18. See Douglas J. Amy, Proportional Representations the Case for a Better Election System (North Hampton: Cresent Street Press, 1997) and Real Choices/New Voices (New York and Columbia University Press, 2002)
19. IGPA of University of Illinois', "Illinois Assembly on Political Representation and Alternative Electoral Systems," Final Report and Background Papers; Spring 2001.

20. E. Joshua Rosenkranz, "The Case for Proportional Representation," Boston Review, March/April 1998-http://www-polisci.mit.edu/bostonreview/PR 23.1/
21. Ibid.
22. Douglas J. Amy, "Fair Representation for Racial Minorities: Is Proportional Representation the Answer?" http://www.mtholyoke.edu/read/polit/demy/articles/minority.htm

PART THREE

Issues in Institutional Politics

The conservative state of governmental institutions has never been more prevalent. Institutions of government are led by individuals who are committed to a conservative political agenda, who threaten minority rights, health care, employment opportunities and even the election of progressive members of Congress. Moreover, conservatives are now in a position to do real damage to civil rights and civil liberties by packing the federal courts with more right-wingers who are approved for ideological zealotry instead of their judicial intellect. For the average citizen and student of governmental institutions it becomes more confusing when we see the President being selected by the U.S. Supreme Court and not the other way around.

To help us make some sense out of this nonsense, we have selected a group of articles that address some of the challenges that these institutions present for ethnic minorities.

Mfanya D. Tryman and Reginald Knight, "The Federal Courts and Higher Education Desegregation in Mississippi: The Ayers' Case," examines the history of racial segregation and discrimination in Mississippi in reference to the state's Historically Black Colleges and Universities; (HBCUS) by analyzing the federal courts' role in Ayers v. Fordice. This article provides interesting insights into the plans and policy recommendations proposed by the federal courts in reference to equal funding and desegregation of Mississippi's institutions of higher learning.

Shaka T. Jones, "The Power of the Jurist: An Examination of Jury Nullification and Its Use as a Tool for Political Advancement of African Americans," analyzes the recent debate over the legal issue of jury nullification. Jones argues that the "knowing and deliberate rejection of evidence or refusal to apply the law either because a jury wants to send a message about some social issue that is larger than the case itself or because a result dictated by law is contrary to the jury's sense of justice, morality or fairness," may be assessed as a possible tool for the political liberation for Black Americans;

Nancy C. Cornwell, "Dismantling Racial Profiling: The ACLU's Arrest of the Racism Campaign," Journal of Intergroup Relations, vol XX, no 1, Spring 2002, 16–33. A description and analysis of the constitutional and civil liberties concerns raised by the practice of racial profiling through the description of the ACLU's campaign against racial profiling;

American Civil Liberties Union, "Report on the Anniversary of *Furman v. Georgia.*" This is a comprehensive review of the capital punishment debate that is designed to educate the public concerning the controversy surrounding the death penalty. It analyzes the relevant death penalty issues with the most up-to-date facts and data;

Francisco A. Villarruel and Nancy E. Walker, "Invisible Latino Youth Find Injustice System," from Joint Center for Political and Economic Studies. Villarruel and Walker address the disparities and inequities that exist in the incarceration of Latino youth in America. They reveal that the incarceration rates of Latino youth are often hidden in the official statistics that examine racial disparities in the nation's criminal justice system;

"Clarence Thomas and His Latino Clone." This article describes the conservative judicial decision making of Black U.S. Supreme Court Justice Clarence Thomas. Specifically, it analyzes the legal reasoning of Mr. Justice Thomas in the appeal of a capital punishment conviction of a Black Texas man sentenced to death by a predominantly white jury. Mr. Thomas, the lone dissenter in the case argued that there was no racial bias against the Black defendant and the case lacked "anything remotely resembling clear and convincing evidence of purposeful discrimination";

Charles E. Jones, "The New Nadir of African American Congressional Participation, revision of article from 1st ed. An analysis of the role played by the Congressional Black Caucus in the legislative process;

Marilyn Davis' "Cynthia McKinney's Struggle to Win Reelection Against All Odds." This essay analyzes the failure of Black Georgia Congresswoman Cynthia McKinney to win reelection in a hotly contested Democratic primary. Davis' article provides an interesting commentary on how a strange coalition of white Democrats, some Black Democrats, and crossover Republicans helped nominate a centrist Black woman, Denise Majette to defeat an outspoken and "controversial" incumbent Black congresswoman McKinney. Also McKinney was criticized for a public statement questioning the role of the George W. Bush administration in the Iraqi War;

Byrdie A. Larkin's "Earl Hilliard v. Artie Davis: Globalization of Alabama Politics," examines the charge that the Middle East conflict led to the defeat of Black incumbent Earl Hilliard in Alabama's 7th Congressional district. Larkin's essay reveals that Arthur Davis received 79 percent of his $1.3 million campaign contributions from out-of-state donations. More importantly, $200,000 came from the New York state area from pro-Israeli groups. These contributors did not like Earl Hilliard's position on Israel. Specifically, he was targeted for defeat for his opposition to a non-binding resolution supporting Israel and condemning Palestinian suicide bombers. Larkin argues that the campaign was also globalized with Congressman Hilliard's out-of-state contributions from Arab-American groups.

The Federal Courts and Higher Education Desegregation in Mississippi: The Ayers Case in Perspective

Mfanya D. Tryman and Reginald Knight

Introduction

The history of racial segregation in Mississippi has had a long and storied past in all areas of public life, including education. One of the most controversial educational issues that arose concerned the Ayers desegregation case that was filed by Jake Ayers in 1975. The major grievance of the plaintiff was that the state of Mississippi continued to support the doctrine of "separate but equal" in higher education in monitoring Historically Black Colleges and Universities (HBCUS) and Historically White Colleges and Universities (HWCUS). It was maintained that HBCUs were receiving unequal funding compared to their white counterparts. The case had been in federal court since 1975. From 1975 to 1987 when the case went to trial, there were several attempts at closure with an out of court settlement. The U.S. Supreme Court in the spring of 1992 ruled that Mississippi indeed continued to use a dual system of higher education. The vote was 8–1; with the only dissenting vote being that of Justice Antonin Scalia (Ayers v. Fordice, 1992). Ayers was remanded to Mississippi Federal District Court for remedy.

Throughout the spring of 1992 until the spring of 1994, there were several major proposals that recommended that the old remnants of segregation in higher education in Mississippi be dismantled by a group of involved parties. The proposals came from the plaintiffs, the Institute of Higher Learning (IHL), pejoratively known as the College Board, the United States Department of Justice, an informal committee of average citizens appointed by the state government, and a subcommittee of the Mississippi state senate.

This paper has several major goals. The first goal is to provide a more extensive outlook of the legal history of the Ayers case. The second goal is to analyze the different policy proposals by the various participants and discuss the implications of the different resolutions in reference to desegregation in higher education. The third goal is to examine the scope of higher education since the ruling of the United States Supreme Court, by taking into account the four legal areas that were constitutionally suspect and the paradox it created. The final goal is to discuss the settlement that was reached between the parties and the different funding sections of the settlement.

The History of Ayers

The state of Mississippi, like many other states of the Old Confederacy, continuously practiced *de jure* segregation until the 1960s. Mississippi created three HBCUs for African American students. The HBCUs that were created were Alcorn State University (ASU) in Lorman, Jackson State University (JSU) in Jackson, and Mississippi Valley State University (MVSU) in Itta Bena. Mississippi HBCUs met the constitutional conditions of the doctrine of "separate-but-equal racial dogma" established by the Taney Court in one of the most recognized cases known as *Plessey v. Ferguson* in 1896 (*Plessey v. Ferguson, 1896*). There were three important legal confrontations that assisted in ending the use of the separate but equal doctrine in the state of Mississippi. The first of the three was the *Brown v. Board of Education of Topeka, Kansas* (*Brown v. Board*, 1954) in the mid-fifties. Second, the racial integration of the University of Mississippi in 1962 by James Meredith with the assistance of federal marshals and third, Title VI of the 1964 Civil Rights Act (which requires the federal government to cut federal funds off with entities that do not desegregate).

In spite of these events, the state of Mississippi continually defied the federal law regarding desegregation with a large amount of opposition. In the case of *Adam v. Richardson* in 1973 that was filed by the NAACP Legal Defense Fund, it called for the federal government under Title VI of the 1964 Civil Rights Act to discontinue appropriations for any state that still functioned under a segregated system of higher education. Thus, the state of Mississippi unwillingly submitted its first Proposal of Compliance for four-year institutions to the Department of Health, Education, and Welfare (HEW). Nonetheless, the plan was vague, it still accentuated freedom of choice, and there was no participation from Mississippi's black population. Following a year of bickering between the state of Mississippi and the Department of Health, Education, and Welfare, a modified plan was agreed upon. According to Title VI regulations there were requirements for an inclusive proposal for both junior colleges as well as senior colleges. Therefore, the state of Mississippi had only fulfilled partial compliance with the requirements (Adams, 1993).

As a result, the Department of Health, Education, and Welfare submitted the Mississippi case to the United States Department of Justice to see if compliance with Title VI had been satisfied. In the early 1970s, the state of Louisiana along with Mississippi were the only two states in the *Adams* case that had the dubious honor of not making significant steps in ending racial segregation in their state higher education systems. Afterwards, the Department of Justice filed suit against the state of Louisiana in March 1974. The state of Mississippi was the only state that had no significant racial desegregation design that was complete in its nature. In May of 1974, the Black Mississippian's Council on Higher Education (BMCHE) an organization of approximately two dozen black activists, chose to devise their own plan that would correct the discrepancies that were in the state of Mississippi plan. BMCHE then attempted to submit their proposal to HEW before HEW had accepted the amended Third Plan of Compliance by the state of Mississippi. Consequently, the case of *Wade v. Mississippi* was decided in 1974. The Wade case had been filed by the Lawyers Committee for Civil Rights Under Law based in Washington D.C. The defendant in the case was the United States Department of Agriculture. It coordinated the U.S. Agricultural Extension Service at two of Mississippi's Universities, Mississippi State University and Alcorn State University (Adams, 1993). The *Wade* case attempted to force the extension service to desegregate and was later added to the Department of Justice to widen its influence, without informing the BMCHE. As Adams notes:

> Although the decision in Wade was handed down in 1974, the case remained active in order that implementation of the decree could be monitored. In mid-February, 1975, the DOJ filed a petition to enter the case as a plaintiff (thereby being on both sides at the same time). It sought to reopen the suit and expand the focus to include both the senior and the junior colleges, thereby hoping to kill two unconstitutional birds with one judicial stone. The Council, at the time, was apparently unaware of DOJ plans to enter Wade. Unwilling to let the DOJ get judicial ratification of HEW's accepted solution to the senior college system of segregation, the Council decided to bring suit itself. (Adams, 1993 p. 278).

During this time in 1975 the late Jake Ayers, Sr. filed a lawsuit on behalf of his son, Jake Ayers, Jr., who at the time was still attending high school, along with 20 other black plaintiffs in the case that was originally known as *Ayers v. Waller* (the governor at the time was Waller). There were other plaintiffs such as Louis Armstrong, who later became a councilman on the Jackson City Council, and Bennie Thompson, who now serves as the only black U.S. Congressman in Mississippi (Ayers v. Allain, 1987). The United States also intervened as a plaintiff, claiming that desegregation of the higher education system was a violation of the Equal Protection Clause of the 14th Amendment and Title VI of the Civil Rights Act of 1964. On the legal front, the Federal District Court undertook the case while negotiations were conducted between the plaintiff and defendant.

However, the parties could not reach an agreement before the case was finally set for a trial. The plaintiffs argued that racially discriminatory practices in a dual system of higher education continued to exist. The plaintiffs also argued that this system was used to hinder blacks in admissions and enrollment, university staff composition, the provision and maintenance of facilities, operation of branch programs, the allocation of land grant functions, funding curricular offerings, placement of programs, and the composition of the Board of Trustees and its staff. The defendant insisted that the Board of Trustees and each of the universities had continued to maintain good faith, non-racial and non-discriminatory and operational policies in reverence to students, faculty, and staff. As a result, the defendant disputed that there had not been any additional responsibility other than to destroy state-enforced segregation. The state also argued that their education policies were not accountable for those aspects of racial stigma that still survived at the various universities. (Clarion-Ledger, 1990)

In the time period that followed, the Institution of Higher Learning created different admissions standards for HBCUs and HWCUs based on ACT scores. Thus, HWCUs had higher admissions requirements. In 1981, the IHL distributed mission statements for the three larger and predominantly white schools, the University of Mississippi (UM or Ole Miss), the University of Southern Mississippi (USM), and Mississippi State University (MSU), which were defined as comprehensive universities. Jackson State was classified as an urban university, and ASU, MVSU, and two other white schools, Delta State University (DSU) and the Mississippi University for Women (MUW) were classified as regional universities. The comprehensive (white) universities had the largest enrollments, the most programs, the best facilities, and received most of the state funding.

The case went to trial in 1987. The Federal District Court proceeded to rule in favor of the defendant, in this case the state of Mississippi. The Federal District Court declared that the state of Mississippi's educational policies that had directed the higher education system did not violate the 14th Amendment of the U.S. Constitution and did not reinforce the racial identification of individual universities, which was a result of individual free choice rather than racial segregation policies (Ayers v. Allain, 1987). The decision also made a distinction among primary and secondary education and that of post-secondary education on the inability of a state to designate college attendance regions and the choices available of a college student in making a decision about attending a particular university (Ayers v. Allain, 1987). Therefore, the state allowed all students the opportunity to attend a university of his or her choice. As a result of the ruling, Federal District Judge Neal Biggers the presiding judge dismissed the lawsuit.

The plaintiffs, BMCHE, then appealed the decision to the Fifth Circuit Court of Appeals in New Orleans. As a result, a three-judge panel of the Fifth Circuit Court overturned the decision and ruled in favor of the plaintiffs in February of 1990 ruling, that Mississippi had continued to function under a segregated system of higher education. The judges, in a 2-1 voted, ruled that a race-neutral admissions policy would not suffice. Therefore, Mississippi would have to create measures that would ensure that blacks would enroll at HWCUs and that whites would enroll at HBCUs. The Circuit Court decided that Mississippi's procedure for funding HBCUs did not remedy the historical injustices and under funding HBCUs. Thus, Judge Biggers was ordered to conduct more proceedings in the suit. The Circuit Court also ruled that until the "the badge of inferiority" which had impacted the images of black students was removed, only then would they be free to choose and the remnants of segregation eliminated (United States Court of Appeals, 1990).

In unanimity, IHL asked for the entire Fifth Circuit Court of Appeals to reassess the ruling of the three-judge panel. After a period of seven months, the entire Fifth Circuit Court of Appeals presented their findings. Their findings concluded that the three-judge panel erred in their constitutional finding, thus ruling in favor of the state of Mississippi. The majority decision declared that "the state of Mississippi had indeed adopted and implemented the race-neutral policies for running its colleges and universities, and that the students had free choice in attending college (United States Court of Appeals, 1990).

As a result, the plaintiffs in the Ayers case then decided to appeal to the United States Supreme Court, in which they were joined in an *amicus curiae* brief filed by the United States Department of Justice. In November of 1991, the case of *United States v. Fordice* was disputed before the United States Supreme Court and a decision was passed down in June 1992. The United States Supreme Court declared, in an 8-1 vote, with one dissenting vote by Justice Scalia, that the ruling of the lower courts did not apply the correct legal criterion in ruling that Mississippi was in compliance with federal law. When the right legal criterion is applied, the Court argued, it would be determined that there are still several remnants of Mississippi's dual system of higher education, which affect desegregation. The court also explained that those aspects were "constitutionally suspect" and prohibited an individual's choice of schools. As a result the Courts explained, it continuously added on to the racial identification of Mississippi's eight public universities. In addition, the state of Mississippi would have to validate such guidelines that could be challenged on remand under the more stringent standard or remove them (Syllabus, United States v. Fordice, 1992).

In Justice Scalia's dissenting vote against the majority 8–1 opinion, he presented a contemptuous argument against the decision and its reasoning. He argued with the majority decision that it was unconstitutional for discriminatory barriers to remain, but that the Constitution did not require equal funding between HBCUs and HWCUs and that the ACT should require a closer examination. Scalia also rejected the *Green* standard in higher education. He argued that the Court standard for desegregation was vague and complicated to follow and that it left little or no realistic direction for the lower courts to take. Scalia suggested that the Bazemore requirement for desegregation as "the discontinuation of discriminatory practices and the adoption of a race-neutral admissions policy" was adequate. (Davis, 1993, pp. 447–448). In the case of *Green v. County School Board* (1968) the Court decided that the practice of *de jure* segregation in public school systems burdens the school with the constitutional responsibility to discontinue racial segregation as a policy, and to move toward desegregation. As a result of the Green decision, the school board implemented a "freedom of choice plan for students" to decide upon the school they wanted to attend, but only 15 percent of the black students attended previously all-white schools, and there was no record of any whites who attended all-black schools. Therefore, the courts ordered the school to adopt a unitary school system expeditiously (*Green v. County Board of New Kent County*, VA., 391 U.S. 430, 88 S.Ct. 1689, 20 L.td. 2d 716 1968).

When Ayers was remanded to Federal District Court, the U.S. Supreme Court argued that there were four areas that were constitutionally suspect regarding the Fifth and Fourteenth Amendments and that they must be questioned because they had the same effect as *de jure* segregation. The first area that had to be questioned was in admissions and the continued use of the ACT (American College Testing) score by the state as the most important factor for admission to HWCUs and HBCUs, which required a higher ACT score to receive admission to HWCUs. The ACT was first used in 1963, and a minimum of 15 was required for admission to flagship universities. The average white student scored 18 while the average black student scored seven. However the ACT had racist origins,[1] and was used to prohibit Blacks' admission to HWCUs. The second area that the Supreme Court questioned was the duplication of programs—there was no logical reasoning for offering the same educational programs at HWCUs and HBCUs. However, this was a result of the "separate but equal" doctrine practiced during segregation. The third area that the Supreme Court questioned was the Mission Statement that was created by the College Board in 1981, which reinforced the policy of *de jure* racial segregation system previously in existence. Last but not least, the fourth area that the court found constitutionally suspect was the number of educational institutions and whether or not Mississippi's management of the eight universities in an effort to meet constitutional muster affects student choice, reinforces the practice of *de jure* segregation and whether or not one or more schools could be combined to eliminate the vestiges of *de jure* segregation (Syllabus, United v. Fordice 1992).

Optional Designs

As a result of the Court's ruling, a number of state agencies and committees submitted their own plans for improvement. This included IHL the Ayers Lay Advisory Board Initial Report of Recommendations, devised by a group of individuals that were appointed by the Governor at that time, Fordice, and other officials, the Senate Fees, Salaries and Administration Interim Subcommittee on the Ayers Case, the U.S. Department of Justice. Each plan included the option of either merging or closing down HBCUs. By categorizing colleges and the universities by their mission, there were also attempts to move programs from one university to another. One example was to allow JSU to take over the professional schools of medicine and dentistry from the University of Mississippi, which was located in the city of Jackson (Defendant, *Ayers v. Fordice,* 1992; Bishop, 1992, Report of the Senate Subcommittee, 1992; Kanengiser, Simmons, and Walton, 1993). However, the Justice Department plan was more lenient toward HBCUs and would also give them control over certain doctoral programs.

The Senate listed four reasons for the closing of a college or university. These are as follows: (1) the decline in university enrollment, which has other affects on a school; (2) the cost of monitoring buildings on campus is not cost-beneficial and it would take more money to close them than to keep them open; (3) fiscal problems that may impact expansion or would continue to have a negative effect on the status quo; and (4) changing the university mission of one or more schools would result in a duplication of services and constituencies (Senate Subcommittee, 1992). The Senate Subcommittee points out that the College Board may respond to these conditions in one of four ways. These reactions may include: (1) changing the policies to prevent the declining conditions, (2) consolidating weaker schools with stronger schools; (3) changing the missions of the universities to legitimize the system; and (4) as a last option, eliminate one or more of the institutions (Senate Subcommittee, 1992).

One of the 11 southern states of the Old Confederacy, and the two contiguous states that border the old Confederacy of public four-year institutions, only the state of Kentucky has a smaller number of colleges and universities that are equal to Mississippi's number of universities and colleges. Kentucky and Mississippi have eight universities based on 1990 data. The state of Texas has the most with 40. The state of Florida has the most population per college/university with about 1,267,100. West Virginia has the least population per college/university with about 154,750. The state of Mississippi is near the average with one college/university per 382,945, population with 327,625. For the most part the state of Mississippi is not inconsistent with the southern average of universities and colleges per/population. However, the states of Arkansas and West Virginia have more colleges and universities, but a smaller population that the state of Mississippi. Arkansas has 10 universities and colleges, but with only a population of about 2,406,000 while the state of West Virginia also had 10 institutions of higher learning with only a state population 1,857,000. As a matter of fact, there are only a total of five states—Arkansas, Alabama, Oklahoma, South Carolina, and West Virginia, who had a smaller ration of population per colleges and universities than Mississippi. The full data for these statistics are found in Table 1. The states are part of the Southern Regional Educational Board.

The U.S. Circuit Court of Appeals containing Alabama in 1994 decided in support of Alabama A&M, and HBCU, over Auburn University, an HWCU, because in three crucial areas they found discrimination, thus ordering a new trial in Federal District Court. One of the areas found that Alabama's HWCUs discriminated against African Americans and deterred them from enrolling at those schools because there were no courses offered that related to black studies. The second area included whether Alabama's policies of distributing funds to land grant institutions like Auburn and Alabama A&M was a result of the past history of the *de jure* segregation system. The third and final area included whether Alabama mission statements for colleges and universities were associated with segregation in college enrollment. The issues that arose in Alabama, interestingly enough, were comparable to those in Mississippi.

The parties in the Ayers case once again attempted to settle out of court during the spring of 1994. However, there was a gag order imposed by Federal District Court Judge Biggers, in which the parties involved had to meet in private discussing any public issues that would affect all Mississippians.

Table 1
Southern State Populations and Public Four-Year Schools

STATE	POPULATION	NO. OF COLL./UNIV.	POP. PER RES. UNIV.*	POP. PER COLL./UNIV.	POP. PER RES. UNIV.
ALA	4,118,000	18	2	228,778	2,059,000
ARK	2,406,000	10	1	240,600	2,406,000
FL	12,671,000	10	3	1,267,100	4,223,667
GA	6,436,000	19	3	338,737	2,145,333
KY	3,727,000	8	2	465,875	1,863,500
LA	4,382,000	14	1	313,000	4,382,000
MD	4,694,000	14	2	335,286	2,347,000
MS	2,621,000	8	3	327,625	837,667
NC	6,571,000	16	3	410,688	2,190,333
OK	3,224,000	14	2	230,286	1,612,000
SC	3,512,000	12	2	292,667	1,756,000
TN	4,940,000	10	2	494,000	2,470,000
TX	16,991,000	40	8	424,775	2,123,875
VA	6,098,000	15	4	406,533	1,524,500
WV	1,857,000	12	1	154,750	1,857,000
Average, SREB		15	2.6	382,945	2,160,205
NA**	248,239,000	595	—	417,208	—

Source: Almanac, The Chronicle of Higher Education, September 5, 1990

* Research universities are those which award a large number of doctorates, primarily the Ph.D
** The Nation

Even though there were three blacks on the College Board, the public reacted with disapproval and the meetings did not go as well as many expected. Also, IHL met with all five presidents of the HWCUs, presumably to exchange and discuss strategies for the negotiations. There were many that criticized the actions of IHL members because none of the three black presidents of HBCUs were invited to the meeting. However, IHL responded by stating that the HWCUs were defendants in the case and they had to meet with the appropriate individuals. As a result, this incident reflected the racial symbolism of the old *de jure* system of segregation in the state of Mississippi. In March of 1994, because of the commotion and uproar associated with the incident with the white presidents, IHL also agreed to meet with the presidents from the HBCUs. As a result of the gag order, little is known about the meetings that were held. Yet, the role of HBCUs in the Ayers case is ironic because they are at once one of the defendants of the state, yet reflect the concerns of the plaintiffs who will benefit the most from educational parity.

During 1995, Judge Biggers handed down a ruling after another trial in Federal District Court. Although the main objective was to make funding equitable for HBCUs the litigation turned into a "reverse desegregation" suit as well, with stipulations related to economic incentives enhancing HBCUs in order to attract white students. During that same year, HWCUs were prohibited from using the ACT score as the primary tool for admissions of students, which was used in the past to reject blacks. Therefore, admissions would now have to be based on a variety of factors including ACT scores, high school grades and class rank. Jackson State would receive $20 million additional dollars to upgrade facilities beginning in 1996. Judge Biggers also rejected the proposal to close MVSU and merge the student population with Delta State since there was no evidence to show that the proposal would be educationally efficient. He also refused the College Board proposal to combine MUW with Mississippi State University 25 miles away. In regards to both of the proposed mergers, Judge Biggers ruled that there was no way to promote desegregation by combining the institutions. Jackson State University would also receive new graduate programs and doctoral programs in the disciplines of social work, urban planning and business and the College Board would also consider expanded programs for a law school, an engineering school, and a school of pharmacy. Furthermore, the College Board was forbidden to promulgate any policies that would delay desegregation efforts. In conclusion, a special three-member committee would be drafted to observe the desegregation efforts with the parties involved submitting proposed names to Judge Biggers (Kanegiser, 1995).

Progress and the Desegregation Mission

In the period from 1992–2000, Kirk Fordice served as the governor corresponding with most of the Ayers years of litigation. Governor Fordice also threatened to use the National Guard (a tactic used by segregationist governors during the 1960s) rather than increase taxes, before he would agree with the Supreme Court in the Ayers case (Shaffer, 1994). In 1996, Fordice also appointed four white male businessmen to fill positions on the College Board, which replaced four members, one of whom was black and one who was a woman. As a result, there was public outrage among many black leaders and educational constituencies. Fordice contended that blacks were only using race as an issue to disagree with his all-white appointees (Wagster, 1996).

In 1998, three years after the last Ayers ruling, Judge Biggers queried to find out why only such a small number of black freshmen were enrolling at Mississippi's eight public universities. He also inquired as to whether it was a result of HBCUs raising their admission standards or the results of a solution that IHL developed, which also included freshmen enrolling in developmental programs in the summer prior to entering college as a regular student. The number of black freshmen dropped dramatically to 21.4 percent from 1995 to 1997 when the new policies were implemented. Also during this time period the enrollment at HWCUs of black freshmen remained stagnant while experiencing a drastic decline at HBCUs. However, during this two year interval the overall enrollment of black students increased by 7 percent (The Chronicle, 1998). While there was a decline at HBCUs in freshmen enrollment, one of the positive results of the Ayers case is that JSU in 1998 was scheduled to add new programs in engineering, health, business, and education, while MVSU and DSU would create joint programs, with MVSU enhancing existing programs in business, education, and technology.

The Mississippi state legislature in 1999 appropriated 4.8 million dollars to begin expanding and strengthening academic programs at HBCUs and their operations as required by order of the Federal Court to desegregate and attract white students. As a result, JSU received funding to build new schools of business and engineering in an attempt to draw more white students as a follow-up of the Ayers decision. During the 1998-99 school year, Federal District Court Judge Biggers stopped a proposal to take a two-year college on the Gulf Coast of Mississippi and turn it into a four-year college. Plaintiffs in the Ayers case had argued that the money to create the new college would reduce the needed money for the HBCUs in their effort to attract white students and to improve their programs simultaneously (*The Chronicle*, 1999).

One technique of assessing the efforts of racial desegregation and educational parity is to compare the graduation rate at HWCU's and HBCU's institutions. Table 2 shows the graduation rate of the three HBCUs and the three largest HWCUs for the 1998-99 academic school year. The table shows that at two of the three HWCUs, MSU and the University of Mississippi graduation rates more than double that of two of the three HBCUs, JSU and MVSU. HWCUs have significantly higher graduation rates compared to HBCUs.

While graduation rates are revealing, the actual impact of racial desegregation of HWCUs and HBCUs tells us even more. Tables 3 and 4 show the number of blacks and whites at "other race" schools in 1994 and 1999 and the magnitude of racial desegregation efforts over that time period.

During the period beginning in the fall of 1994 to the fall of 1999, desegregation efforts increased amongst Mississippi's eight major universities, which often had mixed results. At two of the three HBCUs the number of whites attending those universities began to decrease. Alcorn State University enrollment for white students dropped from 165 (6 percent) to 134 (4.7 percent) in 1999, while the

Table 2
Graduation Rates from the Largest White/Black Universities, 1998-99

Mississippi State University	49%
University of Mississippi	49%
University of Southern Mississippi	40%
Alcorn State University	34%
Jackson State University	29%
Mississippi Valley State University	25%

Source: The Chronicle of Higher Education, Almanac Issue, August 27, 1999, p. 96.

Table 3
Enrollment by Race in Mississippi's Eight Universities, 1994

UNIVERSITY	WHITE	%	BLACK	%	OTHER	%	TOTAL
Alcorn State	165	6.0	2,557	93.3	20	.7	2,742
Delta State	2,902	74.1	964	24.6	51	1.3	3,917
Jackson State	168	2.7	5,882	94.5	174	2.8	6,224
Mississippi State	11,135	78.3	2,061	14.5	1019	7.2	14,215
MUW	2,295	79.5	688	22.8	40	1.3	3,023
Mississippi Valley St.	15	0.7	2,165	99.2	2	0.1	2,182
U. of Mississippi	8,767	84.0	980	9.4	688	6.6	10,435
UMMC	1,529	84.1	162	8.9	126	6.9	1,817
USM	10,445	80.1	2079	15.9	523	4.0	13,047
TOTAL	**37,421**	**65.0**	**17,538**	**30.4**	**2,643**	**4.6**	**57,602**

Source: Peterson's 1996, 4-Year Colleges, 25th Edition, pp. 655–664.

TABLE 4
Enrollment by Race in Mississippi's Eight Universities, 1999

UNIVERSITY	WHITE	%	BLACK	%	OTHER	%	TOTAL
Alcorn State	134	4.7	2,706	94.3	31	1.1	2,871
Delta State	2,863	70.1	1,166	28.5	57	1.4	4,086
Jackson State	162	2.5	6,050	95.2	142	2.2	6,354
Mississippi State	12,202	75.9	2,724	16.9	1,150	7.2	16,076
MUW	2,045	69.3	810	27.4	98	3.3	2,953
Mississippi Valley St.	103	4.1	2,388	95.2	18	0.7	2,509
U. of Mississippi	9,650	82.2	1,401	11.9	695	5.9	11,746
UMMC	1,435	80.6	167	9.4	179	10.1	1,781
U. of Southern Miss.	10,898	75.9	2,786	19.4	666	4.6	14,350
TOTAL	**39,492**	**63.0**	**20,198**	**32.2**	**3,036**	**4.8**	**62,726**

Source: Peterson's 2000, 4-Year Colleges, 30th Edition, Princeton, N.J., pp. 491–99.

black enrollment only increased 1 percent, going from 2,557 to 2,706. JSU enrollment for white students dropped from 168 (2.7 percent) white to 162 (2.5 percent), while the black enrollment increased from 5,882 (94.5 percent) to 6,050 (95.2 percent). MVSU was the only HBCU to gain more white students during this time period, rising from 15 students (0.7 percent) in 1994 to 103 (4.1 percent) in 1999. Of significant interest, the College Board was willing to make the sacrificial lamb in consolidating MVSU, which had the best desegregation record within that five-year time span. (See Table 4.)

All of the state's HWCUs had a greater increase in black enrollment in actual numbers as well as a percent of the total student population. Paradoxically, Mississippi University of Women, the former all-white and all-women's school, proved to have the largest increase in black enrollment, rising over a five-year span with a 4.6 percent increase from 688 (22.8 percent) in 1994 to 810 (27.4 percent) in 1999. Delta State University was second in the percentage of African American student enrollment during this time period with 964 (24.6 percent) in 1994 and rising to 1,166 (28.5 percent) in 1999, a 3.9 percent increase. USM had the third largest increase among the HWCUs in percent over the five-year time span, jumping from 2,079 (15.9 percent) in 1994 to 2,786 (19.4 percent) in 1999, which was a 3.5 percent increase. USM had the highest enrollment of African Americans among state HWCUs in 1999. USM also had the largest increase in the number of African Americans over that five-year period, with approximately 707 more in 1999 than in 1994. USM is located in an ideal site. It is only 90 miles southeast from Jackson, the capitol, and about 60 miles from the Gulf Coast, which makes it attractive to vacationers as an alternative resort and which also has a large number of casinos. One of the main state highways (Hwy 49) also passes through the city of Hattiesburg, which connects USM with Jackson to the north and the Gulf Coast to the south.

UMMC (University of Mississippi Medical) trains most of the state of Mississippi's doctors and physicians and represents an extension campus for the University of Mississippi in Jackson, which mostly white students attend. Although it is not an independent university it is often identified separately in order to measure its progress with regard to students. In 1994, there were only 162 (8.9 percent) blacks enrolled at UMMC. In 1999, the enrollment for blacks only increased by five students and they constituted only 9.4 percent of the entire student body. During the same span, the number of white students decreased, dropping from 1,529 (84.1 percent) to 1,435 (80.6 percent). The largest increase came from the "Other" category, mostly Asian Americans and African Americans that had an enrollment of 126 (6.9 percent) students in 1994, but rose to 179 (10.1 percent) in 1999. However, only the main flagship campus showed considerable progress in the number of black students, the branch has failed to attract significant numbers of black students pursuant to desegregation efforts at UMMC.

In the entire public university system, white students consisted 65 percent of the total in 1994, while blacks only constituted about 30.4 percent, with 4.6 percent in the "Other" category. Despite making up 30.4 percent of the 17,538 black students enrolled, 10,604 (60 percent) attended HBCUs with only 6,934 (40 percent) attending HWCUs. In 1999, blacks only comprised 32.2 percent, while whites constituted 63 percent, and the "Other" category made up 4.8 percent. In fact, of the total of 20,198 blacks enrolled at four-year colleges and universities in the state, 11,144 (55 percent) were attending HBCUs, while only 9,054 (45 percent) were attending HWCUs. Hence, a majority of blacks in higher education still attend the HBCU, even though the public university system saw an increase of 5 percent of black students at HWCUs over the five-year time span under discussion here and 2 percent more in the entire state system. In the state of Mississippi, blacks are 37 percent of the state population.

At the same time schools in Mississippi have continued to be comparably segregated; only MVSU ranked among the top 14 HBCUs as one of the most segregated in 1994. Table 5 reveals that Valley ranked in the top 14 and was tied with Dilliard and Morehouse with 99.3 percent of their enrollment African American.

During the same time in 1994, not one of Mississippi's HBCUs ranked among the top 14 in regards to racial desegregation, that is, the percentage of white students enrolled.

Table 5
Top Black Enrollments at HBCUs, 1994

SCHOOL	STUDENTS	BLACK	%BLACK
Tougaloo College (Miss)	1105	1105	100%
Lane College (Tenn.)	667	667	100%
Allen University (S.C.)	256	256	100%
Livingstone College (N.C.)	836	835	97.9%
J.C. Smith University (N.C.)	1413	1409	99.7%
Miles College (Ala.)	1068	1065	99.7%
Morris College (Ala.)	889	886	99.7%
Fisk University (Tenn.)	872	869	99.7%
LeMoyne-Owen College (Tenn.)	1436	1430	99.6%
Barber-Scotia College (N.C.)	432	430	99.5%
Selma University (Ala.)	206	205	99.5%
Morehouse College (Ga.)	2992	2972	99.3%
Mississippi Valley State U. (Miss.)	2182	2166	99.3%
Dillard University (La.)	1675	1663	99.3%

Source: U.S. Department of Education, National Center for Educational Statistics, *The Digest of Education Statistics,* 1996.

Table 6 also reflects broad differences among HBCUs with regards to desegregation. In West Virginia, Bluefield State at one end of the continuum had a total enrollment of 2,609 students in 1994, and of that total 92 percent or 2,390 were white. On the other end of the continuum, Norfolk State University, a HBCU in Virginia, had an enrollment of 8,667 students in 1994 and 17 percent or 1,475 were white.

On the other hand, when comparing the state of Mississippi's HWCUS to the top HBCUs in regards to desegregation in 1994, the smallest schools, DSU and MUW, are the only two that rank among the top HBCUs in regards to racial desegregation. At Delta State

Table 6
Top White Enrollments at HBCUs, 1994

SCHOOL	STUDENTS	WHITE	%WHITE
Bluefield State (West Va.)	2609	2390	92%
West Virginia State	4519	3864	86%
Lincoln University (Mo.)	3512	2476	70%
Kentucky State	2563	1274	50%
Langston University (Okla.)	3408	1357	39%
Tennessee State	8180	2637	32%
Fayetteville State (N.C.)	4109	1261	31%
Delaware State	3381	995	29%
Elizabeth State (Del.)	2099	519	25%
Harris-Stowe State (Mo.)	1757	407	23%
Maryland-East Shore	2925	658	22%
Winston-Salem State (N.C.)	2915	653	22%
Bowie State (Md.)	4896	1033	21%
Norfolk State (Va.)	8667	1475	17%

Source: U.S. Department of Education, National Center for Educational Statistics, *The Digest of Education Statistics*, 1996.

there were 24.6 percent black students and MUW had 22.8 percent black students.

In the spring of 2001, the College Board and the U.S. Department of Justice, along with private plaintiffs met and negotiated a settlement. The settlement was subsequently sent to Judge Biggers for approval. Biggers explained that the state of Mississippi legislature would have to agree to the plan because the state legislature would have to appropriate the funding as well (Kanengiser, 2002). On January 18, 2002, a final settlement was agreed upon when the Mississippi state legislature voted in favor of a settlement that would provide 503 million dollars in funding for HBCUs over a 17-year period. The Mississippi House voted 100 to 20 in favor of the resolution, while the Senate voted 33–10 to commit to the appropriation plan. Overall, the vote in both houses combined was 133–30 or 77 percent for the settlement and 23 percent against the settlement proposed. The plan would include $245 million for academic programs, $83 million which had already been spent on Ayers programs the last three years, new facilities which would cost $75 million,

$55 million for new endowments, $35 million for private endowments, and $6.25 million for summer development courses and programs, and $2.5 million for lawyers fees. In 2002, $16.9 million was guaranteed in appropriations for academic programs, $20.2 million from 2002–2008, $13.5 million from 2009–2014, and $6.7 million from 2015–2018 (Sawyer 2002).

However, the ruling requires Alcorn, Jackson State, and Mississippi Valley to obtain a 10 percent non-black enrollment before they can divide up the private endowments. (Kanengiser, 2001, p. 1A, 6A). Presumably, what began as an equal funding case resulted in a desegregation case, ironically with the onus put on HBCUs to integrate and attract a numerical portion of white students, in an era when quotas are under attack. Interestingly, the Federal Courts are questioning racial desegregation in elementary and secondary public schools. In Mississippi, efforts of racial desegregation are more complicated because of the tremendous fiscal woes and declining state revenues.

Summary and Conclusion

There are a variety of factors that may incite a push for racial desegregation in Mississippi's institutions of higher learning. One of the most obvious players has been the Federal Courts and plaintiffs. Present and future governors, state legislatures, the financial woes of the state, and the political pressures from different interest groups may also accelerate or decelerate the process of racial desegregation. The resistance to end racial desegregation and the willingness to support institutions promulgating racial segregation in the past has cost the state of Mississippi millions of dollars. This situation has had a major impact on a poor state like Mississippi. The hundreds of millions of dollars to equalize funding and bring parity to HBCUs with their white counterparts, has come at great costs.

In conclusion, the U.S. Supreme Court found four areas in which the Mississippi higher education system was suspect, which included admissions, program duplication, mission statements, and the number of universities. One of the goals of Ayers is to eliminate biases in admissions at HWCUs. However, program duplication has not been addressed. There are programs that still exist that promote the doctrine of "separate but equal." The state of Mississippi has chosen to add and develop programs that would attract white students to HBCUs. For example, Jackson State will be adding new doctoral degree programs in business and engineering to attract white students. The District Court did not decrease the number of colleges and universities and the question of adequate funding remains. However, Mississippi is not atypical of its southern counterparts on this issue.

There should be more emphasis on eliminating program duplication at HWCUs and HBCUs that have not facilitated racial desegregation since these programs were designed by IHL to perpetuate racial segregation. There are universal admissions criteria that have been developed to prevent the indigenous biases of the ACT and SAT tests. The use of standardized exam scores can be only used as one factor in the admission process. Furthermore, admissions criteria must consider the use of a student's grade point average and graduation class rank.

The question of HBCUs and HWCUs reaching parity is questionable in light of the historical discrepancies and the fact that 503 million dollars is a small amount. HBCUs have always had open admissions and never had a policy of racial discrimination. Yet, as the result of the Ayers case, the burden for racial desegregation has fallen upon them.

References

Adams, John Quincy, "Through the Looking Glass and What the Court Finds There: The Political Setting of United States v. Fordice," *Mississippi Law Journal*, Vol. 62, No. 2, Winter 1993, pp. 276-77.

Ayers v. Allain, 674 F. Supp. 1526 (1987).

Ayers v. Fordice, 112, S. Ct., 2744 (Thomas, C. concurring), (1992).

Edward S. Bishop, Sr., et al., *Ayers Lay Advisory Board Initial Report of Recommendations*, December 9, 1992, p. 10.

The Clarion-Ledger, "Mississippi's Universities Still Segregated," February 7, 1990.

The Chronicle of Higher Education, August 28, 1998, p. 80.

The Chronicle of Higher Education, Almanac Issue, August 27, 1999, pp. 95–96.

The Chronicle of Higher Education, Almanac Issue, September 5, 1990.

Fish, Stanley, "Affirmative Action and the SAT," *The Journal of Blacks in Higher Education*, No. 2, Winter 1993/1994, p. 83.

Davis, Robert N., "The Quest for Equal Education in Mississippi: The Implications of United States v. Fordice," *Mississippi Law Journal*, Vol. 62, No. 2, Winter 1993, 99. 447–448.

Defendant, Board of Trustees of State Institutions of Higher Learning's Proposed Remedies, *Ayers v. Fordice*, Civil Action No. GC75-9-13-0, United States District Court for the Northern District of Mississippi, October 22, 1992, p. 7.

Green v. County Board of New Kent County, VA., 391 U.S. 430, 88 S.Ct. 1689, 20 L.td. 2d 716 (1968).

Jaschik, Scott, "Victory for Black Colleges," *The Chronicle of Higher Education*, Vol. XL, No. 27, 1994, pp. 20–21.

Kanengiser, Andy, Grace Simmons and Steve Walton, "No Closures in New Ayers Plan," *The Clarion-Ledger*, December 30, 1993, p. 9A.

Kanengiser, Andy, "Ayers ruling spares Valley, MUW," *The Clarion Ledger*, 1995, p. 12.

Kanengiser, Andy, "Judge questions Ayers plan," *The Clarion Ledger*, May 9, 2001, p. 1A, 6A. Kanengiser, Andy, "Critics still questioning final outcome," The Clarion Ledger, January 19, 2002, p. 8A

Peterson's 1996, 4 Year Colleges, 25th Edition, Princeton, N.J., pp. 655–664.

Peterson's 2000, 4 Year Colleges, 30th Edition, Princeton, N.J., pp. 491–99.

Plessey v. Ferguson, 163 U.S. 537 (1896).

Report of the Senate Fees, Salaries and Administration Interim Subcommittee on the Ayers Case, Presented to Lieutenant Governor Eddie Briggs and the Mississippi State Senate, December 1992, pp. 1–8, *passim*.

Sawyer, Patrice, "Senate vote seals deal in college suit," *The Clarion Ledger*, January 19, 2002, p. 1A, 8A.

Shaffer, Steve, "Mississippi: Friends and Neighbors Fight the 'Liberal' Label," in *The 1992 Presidential Election in the South*, edited by Robert P. Steed, Laurence W. Moreland, and Tod A. Baker, Westport: Praeger Publishers, 1992.

United States Court of Appeals, the Fifth Circuit from *Reply to Supplemental Brief on Defendants-Appellees on Rehearing En Banc*, 88-4103, February 17 and 18, 1990, pp. 3–5.

United States Department of Education, National Center for Education Statistics, *The Digest of Education Statistics*, 1996.

United States v. Fordice, Syllabus, *Reporter of Decisions*, No. 90-1205, Together with No. 90-6588, *Ayers et al. V. Fordice*, June 26, 1992, p. iv.

Emily Wagster, "Fordice rips Senate over nominees," *The Clarion-Ledger*, July 21, 1996, p. 1A.

The Power of the Jurist: An Examination of Jury Nullification and Its Use as a Tool for Political Advancement of African Americans

Shaka T. Jones
Attorney

Introduction

In the United States of America one of the most powerful and important functions a citizen has is serving on a jury. It is in their capacity as jurors that the people decide who is right and who is wrong, who is granted freedom and who is denied liberty. This is especially true in America's criminal justice system, where the jury's verdict of guilty or not guilty carries a tremendous amount of weight.

Recently, how a jury should wield this power has sparked a tremendous debate. This primarily has to do with the legal phenomenon known as jury nullification. Jury nullification is defined as a jury's "knowing and deliberate rejection of the evidence or refusal to apply the law either because the jury wants to send a message about some social issue that is larger than the case itself or because a result dictated by law is contrary to the jury's sense of justice, morality, or fairness."[1] The power of a jury to nullify law arises from a judicial system built upon a structured democratic law making process, an established principal of juror sovereignty, and the rules of law that prohibit double jeopardy. The combination of these principals create a system that allow a jury to acquit a defendant in a criminal trial regardless of how compelling the evidence against the defendant may be. If the jury, despite the fact that the defendant is guilty of the crime for which he has been tried, exonerates the defendant, the defendant cannot be tried again. Of equal importance is the fact that the jury will not face any repercussion for their verdict.

Throughout American history various groups have used the power of jury nullification to give social commentary on current events, protest perceived injustices within the law, or to further the goals of a particular group. This essay will provide a brief summary of the English trial origins of jury nullification, the history of its use in America, and why it is an excellent vessel for African Americans to combat a racially unjust criminal judicial system.

The History of Jury Nullification

In the mid 17th century a radical reformist group in England known as the Levellers led by John Liburne were the first to assert that juries possessed the right to decide the law.[2] Liburne was arrested and charged with treason for publishing pamphlets that opposed the harsh rule imposed by the government.[3] At his trial Liburne advanced the theory that the law that was accused of violating was unlawful in itself. Despite the fact that there was no foundation in English common law to support Liburne's argument, his principals struck a chord with the jury and they subsequently acquitted Liburne of the charges.[4]

In 1653, the English government brought more charges against Liburne for violating the provisions of an exile imposed upon him. In his second trial, Liburne expanded his theory of jury supremacy even further claiming that juries not only had the right to declare that a statute was not valid under English fundamental law, but that a jury possessed the power to acquit the defendant if they determined that the punishment prescribed was unduly harsh compared to the acts of the defendant.[5] Liburne was acquitted once again, however, he was imprisoned following the trial and died shortly thereafter.

The next major development in the jury nullification dialogue arose from the opinion of the Court of Common Pleas in the *Bushel's* case.[6] Two Quakers, William Penn and William Mead, were arrested in London and charged with unlawful assembly and disturbing the peace after preaching to a large crowd in the city streets. Edward Bushel was a juror at their trial.[7] Penn and Mead both admitted that they had assembled the crowd to preach and pray, but argued that the proper question to be decided was not whether they were actually guilty of the indictment, but whether the indictment was legal.[8] At the close of the trial, the judge warned the jurors that they would be punished if they refused to convict the defendants. Nevertheless, the jurors chose to acquit the defendants.

The trial judge immediately fined the jurors for their insurrection. Bushel refused to pay the fine and the judge put him in jail. Bushel then petitioned the Court of Common Pleas for a writ of habeas corpus.[9] The court ruled in Bushel's favor, establishing the premise that jurors may not be fined or imprisoned for the outcome of their verdicts.[10] The official opinion of the court, written by Chief Justice Vaughan, explained that because both judge and jury are capable of making mistakes, it would be unfair to punish jurors for their decisions when judges face no similar punishment.[11] Although Chief Justice Vaughan's opinion did not recognize the jury's right to nullify the law, it effectively bestowed a power upon the jury to generate a verdict inconsistent with either the law or facts presented at trial.

In the American colonies, jury nullification was used to oppose the tyrannical rule of the British. The case that initiated the debate on jury nullification in America was the *Zenger* trial of 1735. The trial took place in New York, which at the time was still a colony under British rule. John Peter Zenger was charged with seditious libel for printing a newspaper that published political views contrary to the then governor William Crosby. Zenger was defended by Andrew Hamilton who argued that Zenger was innocent because everything that he had published was true. However, at that time truth was not an acceptable defense against a charge of seditious libel, and the judge instructed the jury as such. In spite of this, the judge allowed Hamilton to advance a jury nullification argument before the jury.[12] The nullification argument was well received by the jury, and they found Zenger innocent of the charges, notwithstanding the judge's inference that they should convict.

The *Zenger* case was one of many cases taking place in early American colonies where juries used their power to nullify the law to oppose British rule and advance their causes. In the years leading up to the American Revolution, colonial juries often refused to enforce laws they saw as unjust such as the Navigation Acts, smuggling laws, and laws against seditious libel.

In the hundred years following the Revolutionary War, the jury's power to openly nullify the law was eroded, primarily due to the growth of professionalism in the legal field. Judges were now seen as better equipped to interpret the law. Furthermore, since a democratic system was in place to determine what the law would be there was no need to use the jury as a means to oppose tyrannical rule. The turn away from a judicial system based on a jury's sovereignty to decide both the law and the facts of a case was officially endorsed by the United States Supreme Court when it rendered its opinion in *Sparf v. United States* in 1895.

Herman Sparf and Hans Hansen were crewmen on an American ship sailing to Tahiti in 1893. They were accused of killing a fellow sailor on the ship and throwing his body overboard.[13] After the prosecution presented a case with no strong direct evidence against them[14] but which contained an overwhelming amount of circumstantial evidence,[15] the jury convicted the men of murder and they were sentenced to death.[16] The men appealed the decision citing that the trial judge had erred in refusing to instruct the jury that it could find Sparf and Hansen guilty of manslaughter rather than murder. During the original trial the defendants requested that the judge instruct the jury that though the indictment was for a charge of murder, the defendants could be convicted of murder, manslaughter or attempted murder or attempted manslaughter.[17] The trial judge refused to instruct the jury as the defendants requested and instead impressed upon the jury that the only verdicts that the jury could return under the law were guilty of murder or not guilty of murder.[18]

The Supreme Court upheld the trial judge's instructions to the jury. Justice Harlan writing for the majority argued that in American courts it was the duty of the judge to interpret the law and the duty of the jury to apply the law as instructed by the judge to the facts.[19] A system where the jury was given a right to interpret the law as well as the facts would result in a "government of men" rather than a "government of laws"[20], thus eroding the "stability of public justice."[21]

The *Sparf* case is still seen as the leading case dealing with the issue of jury nullification today. This has brought about an interesting debate in recent times over whether juries have the right to use jury nullification or if it is simply a power that they possess as a byproduct from the structure of the American criminal justice system. However, when looking at the case history on this issue in the years after the *Sparf* decision, it is clear that criminal juries possess the power to nullify the law and acquit defendants no matter how strongly the evidence may point towards a conviction.[22]

The Modern View on Nullification

The jury's power of nullification in criminal trials stems from a unique combination of legal safeguards. The principal source is the Fifth Amendment of the Constitution, which provides protection from double jeopardy[23], which prohibits the government from retrying a person for a crime once they have been acquitted. This, along with the various procedural elements of a criminal trial, effectively guarantees that a criminal trial verdict of not guilty is not subject to review or reversal under any circumstances.

Although juries clearly possess the power to nullify the law, courts have consistently held that they do not have the right to use that power.[24] This is an important distinction that is enforced by judges using various tactics to prevent jurors from exercising their power to nullify the law. The most effective such tactic is preventing the criminal defendant from informing the jury that they possess the power to nullify the law. Since jury nullification is a topic not widely discussed outside of legal circles, the majority of the American public does not realize the power that they possess. By refusing to allow the jury to be informed about their defacto power to nullify the law and instead giving them instructions that their decision to convict or acquit must be based on the law as the judge interprets it, a judge can effectively keep jurors from willfully returning a verdict contrary to the law.

The Political Use of Nullification

The next major question in the debate over jury nullification is whether it should be used in today's criminal justice system as a means for furthering the political goals of various groups. This is a topic that brings about strong opinions from those who oppose jury nullification as well as those who support it.

Those who are in the camp opposing the use of jury nullification for the advancement of political goals have several valid points in their favor, the strongest of which is the current state of the law, which as discussed above denies juries the right to nullify the law. Opponents of nullification contend that if juries exercise their nullification power, they are effectively undermining the democratic process. The American criminal justice system is governed by laws made by various federal and state legislative bodies that have been elected by a majority of voters through the democratic process of government. Therefore, the laws in place are a reflection of the majority's wishes, and if a jury nullifies the law, it is usurping the power that the voting public has in the lawmaking process. Thus, the argument that jury nullification is an undemocratic use of power is a compelling one.

I agree that juries possess a power and not a right to nullify the law, and that by exercising that power juries are effectively undermining the criminal justice system. Nevertheless, I am in favor of a plan proposed by Paul Butler advocating the use of limited jury nullification to advance the interests of African Americans. The main thrust of Professor Butler's plan is that African Americans should use their power to nullify the law in cases where other African Americans are charged with nonviolent or victimless crimes thus resulting in a subversion of a racially biased criminal justice system, forcing the government to come up with a more just system.[25]

While I am theoretically in favor of a criminal justice system based on an established set of laws that judge each defendant the same regardless of his race I cannot ignore the results that the current American criminal justice system produces. In 1992, African Americans accounted for 12.4 percent of the population in the United States[26], but represented 30.3 percent of all arrests.[27] African Americans also accounted for 44.1 percent of all jail inmates[28] and 48 percent of those under the jurisdiction of state and federal correctional authorities.[29] These statistics are troubling to say the least. There is no real credible evidence that African Americans as a group are more prone to criminal behavior than any other racial group. This begs the question as to why their representation in the criminal justice system is so disproportionate to the other racial groups in American society.

I believe that the answer to this question lies in the methods used to deal with crime in today's criminal justice system. Prisons in America have seemed to forsake the notion of rehabilitation and instead have become a warehousing system of human beings who are seen to be a threat to society. The irony in this is that many individuals who serve time in prison are often much more prone to crime, particularly violent crime, than they were when they first entered the prison walls. This warehousing system poses a particularly strong threat to the African American community. Due to the fact that an unproportionately high percentage of African Americans are under criminal justice supervision, particularly African American males, a vicious self-perpetuating cycle is created. African Americans are seen as public enemy number one, a threat to all of society and must be ruled with an iron fist. This leads to an incorrect perception that the reason so many African Americans are behind bars due to their naturally strong criminal tendencies.

Moreover, members of the African American community who have committed crimes are not given the opportunity to become rehabilitated. They are instead placed in a prison system that often turns them into an institutionalized being that is incapable of ever functioning properly in society, which in turn increases the likelihood of their recidivism when released from prison. This cycle created by the warehousing syndrome harms the African American community directly in two ways. First, it takes an individual who may or may not have been dangerous to the community, exponentially increase his capacity for violent and criminal behavior and then effectively turns him loose on the African American community (seeing that it is unlikely he will live in a non African American community when he is released). Secondly, it increases the already disproportionate percentage of the African American population under the supervision of the criminal justice system.

Critics of the use of jury nullification for advancing the political goals of African Americans point to the remedies already in place in the government such as seeking help from representatives in our legislative bodies as a method to achieve a more just system of criminal laws. I agree that these remedies could prove effective and I am not suggesting that African Americans abandon the use of the traditional democratic process to further their goals, however, I believe that the time it would take for such methods alone to have a meaningful impact on the criminal justice system would be monumental, certainly more than my own lifetime. I do not see the need for African Americans to endure the injustices heaped upon them by the criminal justice system, and I certainly cannot in good conscience endorse any plan of action that I feel would prolong these injustices.

There are also those who may argue that if African Americans begin to use their power as jurists to advance their political cause, a government backlash will ensue that will seek to reduce the role of juries in the criminal justice system and cause an erosion of rights. While I do not prescribe to this train of thought, I am willing to assume the risk that there may be some backlash against nullification. I do not believe that any restrictions put on juries in criminal trials would put African

Americans in a worse position than they are already in.

Conclusion

In spite of the proposed risks or warnings from opponents of jury nullification, I am strongly in favor of African Americans using it in a limited manner to acquit members of the African American community who have been charged with nonviolent or victimless crimes. This option should only be exercised when there is a reasonable likelihood that the defendant is capable of functioning as a positive contributing member of the African American society as a whole. I believe that jury nullification when effectively and carefully used in this manner, can serve to remove the burdensome unjust yoke placed upon African Americans by the current criminal justice system.

Notes

1. BLACK'S LAW DICTIONARY 862 (7th ed. 1999).
2. Thomas A. Green, *Verdict According to Conscience: Perspectives on the English Criminal Trial Jury* 1200-1800, at 153 (1985).
3. Id. at 170.
4. Id. at 175.
5. Id. at 159.
6. *Bushel's Case*, 124 English Reporter 1006 (1670).
7. Green, supra note 2, at 221.
8. Id. at 223.
9. *Bushel's Case*, 124 English Reporter 1006 (1670).
10. Green, supra note 2, at 200.
11. Id. at 237.
12. James Alexander, *A Brief Narrative of the Case and Trial of John Peter Zenger* 75 (Stanley Katz ed., 1963).
13. *Sparf v. United States*, 156 U.S. 51 (1895).
14. Id. at 111 (Gray, J., dissenting).
15. Id. at 53.
16. Id. at 52.
17. Id. at 59.
18. Id. at 60.
19. Id. at 102.
20. Id. at 103.
21. Id. at 106.
22. See, e.g., *Scarpa v. DuBois*, 38 F.3d 1 (1st Cir. 1994), cert. denied, 115 S. Ct. 940 (1995); United States v. Dougherty, 473 F.2d 1113, (D.C. Cir. 1972); State v. Green, 458 N.W.2d 472 (Neb. 1990); State v. Ragland, 519 A.2d 1361 (N.J. 1986).
23. U.S. Cont. amend. V.
24. See, e.g. *United States v. Gaudin*, 115 S. Ct. 2310 (1995); *United States v. Powell*, 469 U.S. 57 (1984); *Scarpa v. Dubois*, 38 F.3d 1 (1st Cir. 1994), cert. denied, 115 S. Ct. 940 (1995); *United States v. Krzyske*, 836 F.2d 1013 (6th Cir.), cert. denied, 488 U.S. 832 (1988); *United States v. Trujillo*, 714 F.2d 102 (11th Cir. 1983); *United States v. Washington*, 705 F.2d 489, (D.C. Cir 1983); *State v. Hendrickson*, 444 N.W.2d 468, (Iowa 1989); *Commonwealth v. Leno*, 616 N.E.2d 453, (Mass. 1993); *People v. Demers*, 489 N.W.2d 173, (Mich. Ct. App.1992)(per curiam); *State v. Rangland*, 519 A.2d 1361, (N.J. 1986); *People v. Weinberg*, 631 N.E.2d 97 (N.Y. 1994).
25. Paul Butler, *Racially Based Jury Nullification: Black Power in the Criminal Justice System*, 105 Yale L.J. 677 (1995).
26. See U.S. Department of Commerce, *Economics & Statistics Administration Bureau of the Census, Statistical Abstract of the United States 1994*, at 13.
27. Id at 205.
28. See U.S. Department of Justice, Bureau of Justice Statistics, *Sourcebook of Criminal Justice Statistics 1993* at 592.
29. Id at 606.

Dismantling Racial Profiling: The ACLU's "Arrest the Racism" Campaign

Nancy C. Cornwell

Ask anyone. They know what it is. Some know it by the name of racial profiling. Others call it Driving While Black (DWB). White people read and hear about it in the media. Blacks, Hispanics and other people of color live with it. The "corrosive evil" (King, 1986, p. 623) of "America's original sin" (Wallis, 1988, p. 9) once temporarily submerged under a collective denial of the privileged has reemerged into the public consciousness under the catchy, media-friendly acronym of DWB. This particularly egregious form of racial profiling occurs when law enforcement officers use minor traffic violations as a "pretext for stopping, searching and sometimes arresting motorists because of their race" (Moss, 2001, p. 36).

A 1999 Gallup poll suggests that people's awareness of racial profiling as a social problem is growing with 59 percent of the American public viewing racial profiling as a problem. While racial profiling is arguably not limited to police activities, its use by law enforcement agencies has attracted the most attention. And the use of racial profiling by police has become a flash point for civil rights advocates in particular. Even so, 89 percent of those surveyed in the Gallup poll think that the police should not use racial profiling as a law enforcement technique (Gallup Poll, 1999). While awareness and condemnation of the practice may have crossed color lines, the degree to which racial profiling undermines public confidence in law enforcement—one of the social costs of racial profiling—is more split along racial lines. In the words of one civil rights worker, "With the Gallup survey showing African Americans three times more likely than whites to view police unfavorably or as being unfair, it is

---

From *The Journal of Intergroup Relations*, Volume XXIX, No. 1 by Nancy C. Cornwell. Copyright © 2002 by Journal of Intergroup Relations. Reprinted by permission.

clear that racial profiling has created a crisis in confidence in communities of color" (ACLU, December 9, 1999). Thus, racial profiling is recognized as a practice worthy of public scrutiny by the American public overall, but the negative impact of racial profiling is still borne by people of color.

The pressing constitutional and civil liberties concerns raised by the practice of racial profiling has attracted the attention and resources of numerous organizations that focus on problems of racial inequality and civil liberties violations. This paper will outline one such organization's efforts. The American Civil Liberties Union (ACLU) has become actively involved with the problem of racial profiling because of the 14th Amendment equal protection clause and the 4th Amendment protection against unreasonable search and seizure. But the efforts to combat racial profiling are complex and multi-faceted. For example, from a political perspective, it is not so clear what should be done about racial profiling, for the practice of it is wrapped up, albeit in a highly problematic way, with ongoing public and legislative pressure for law enforcement agencies to crack down on drug-related illegal activity.

The challenge facing civil liberties organizations is how to simultaneously address specific incidents of racial profiling as well as the larger judicial and legislative issues also presented by racial profiling. In other words, racial profiling ultimately needs to be addressed as a form of direct and indirect racism. Each requires a different set of reform efforts and pose different challenges for civil libertarians.

This essay will begin with a brief contextual description of racial profiling both as a form of systemic (indirect) racism and a specific (direct) racist practice that violates individual's civil rights. Then, the efforts of the ACLU will be outlined as an example of how one civil liberties organization is attempting to fight racial profiling. In particular, the litigation efforts, legislative efforts and public education efforts will be reviewed.

The ACLU is used as the focus of this discussion because its efforts to redress racial profiling extend back to 1997 and it has consciously structured its efforts to fight racial profiling in a multi-faceted effort at both the state and national levels. Starting in 1997, the ACLU put racial profiling at the top of their civil rights agenda and initiated the "Arrest the Racism" campaign. This campaign attempts to navigate and respond to both racial profiling as a practice that violates individual's civil rights and racial profiling as a continued reflection of ongoing racism in America.

The Practice of Racial Profiling: Direct Racism

The practice of racial profiling certainly predates the implementation of specific drug trafficking policies in the late 1990s. Yet, it was when the Drug Enforcement Agency developed the Drug Courier Profile (Trende, 2000), which included a program of "random" traffic stops on interstate highways, that this particularly egregious violation of civil rights entered the public sphere. To exacerbate the problem, these profiles were widely adopted by other police agencies (Harris, 1999a). The Drug Courier Profile provided a variety of indicators for law enforcement officers to use in determining whom to "randomly" stop along interstates thought to be courier routes for illegal drugs. In essence the Drug Courier Profile is largely a list of criteria to use in helping identify possible drug traffickers. However, some of the criteria are contradictory. For example, the profile lists being first off the plane, being the last off the plane, using a one way ticket, using a round trip ticket, traveling alone, traveling with someone, acting too nervous, acting too calm, etc. The problem with which we are all now so clearly aware, is that race both explicitly and implicitly became one of the Profile indicators. Yet, there is no statistical connection between drug trafficking and race. Nevertheless, the disproportionate arrest and prosecution of African Americans is well documented. For example, comprising just 12 percent of the population and 13 percent of drug users, they make up 38 percent of those arrested for drug offenses, 59 percent of those convicted of drug use (and 63 percent of those convicted of drug trafficking). As a result, people of color were, and continue to be, disproportionately singled out in these traffic stops (Bureau of Justice Statistics, 1998).

In spite of the lack of meaningful evidence for connecting race and drug trafficking, the practice of racial profiling is structured such that its pattern of abuse is characterized by a spiraling quality that results in accelerating violations of civil rights for people of color. Harris (2001) describes how the spiral works:

> Because police will target black drivers for drug crimes, they will find it disproportionately among black drivers. This means that more blacks will be arrested, prosecuted, convicted, and jailed, which of course will reinforce the idea that blacks are disproportionately involved in drug crimes, resulting in a continuing motive and justification for stopping more black drivers as a rational way of using resources to catch the most criminals. (p. 16)

As with other racist practices that become integrated into social structures and ultimately transparent, racial profiling can be difficult to nail down because it occurs, in part, within the larger effort to respond to increasing public and political pressure to deal with drug trafficking. So discourse about the problem of racial profiling can easily slip into rhetoric about how race is not a conscious factor in traffic stops or that skin color is one of the factors that "fits" the drug profile. It is that kind of rhetoric that reflects the way in which racial profiling must also be conceptualized and addressed as a form of systemic or indirect racism.

The Systemic Roots of Racial Profiling

In a letter to U.S. Attorney General, Janet Reno, Laura Murphy, Legislative Director for the ACLU's Washington office, wrote, "Racial profiling is caused by racism. It has been exacerbated and legitimized by the war on drugs but it precedes the war on drugs and is prevalent throughout the country" (ACLU, June 4, 1999). Ira Glasser, former National ACLU Executive Director stated back in 1999 "It is time for our national leaders to realize that this is not about a few 'bad apples.' It's about the whole tree, right down to the roots" (ACLU, December 1999). It can be hard at times to fully understand the way systemic, institutionalized racism has followed us into the new century. It is more comforting to think that the 1960s civil rights movement dismantled the superstructure of racism, leaving for those in the decades that followed the task of addressing isolated pockets of racism, individual racist activities and enforcing antiracist legislation enacted during the transformative struggles of the 1960s. In that light, racial profiling might, at first, appear to be the unfortunate activities of a handful of racist law enforcement officers, a few misguided police policies or, at worst, the sign of a corrupt police force in need of retraining. Yet, racial profiling can also be theorized as an apparent manifestation of ongoing racist practices that more often remain silent and embedded in the very way social institutions are constructed to privilege some (in this case those in positions of power) at the expense of others (who are less powerful). As Barendt (1991) argues, "Institutional racism as practiced today with subtlety and sophistication often seems both innocent and innocuous unless it is recognized as the successor in disguise to the deliberate and direct institutional racism of the past" (p. 83).

The exposure of the practice of racial profiling, the extensive use in law enforcement practices, and the way racial profiling has been constructed as a "normal" law enforcement strategy, reveal that deeply ingrained institutionalized racism continues. To view racial profiling within the larger social, political and economic context of ongoing racist practices expands the public imagination beyond the need for isolated reform to a space where, conceivably, racial profiling can be addressed as part and parcel of larger structures of institutionalized racism. In other words, it would be remiss to neglect the place of racial profiling within an ongoing manifestation of continued systemic and institutionalized racist practices in American society. Any effort to redress the practice of racial profiling must at some level recognize the role racial profiling plays in perpetuating ongoing racist social, political, legal and economic structures in this country.

Likewise, any attempt to eliminate racial profiling would necessitate an approach that attempts to address both the specific violations of individual civil rights and work to dismantle the larger institutionalized practices. One particular effort along these lines is the ACLU's "Arrest the Racism" campaign. This campaign works to eliminate racial profiling in a multi-faceted approach that grapples with the problem on a specific and systemic level. The next section of this article explores this campaign with a focus on the way the "Arrest the Racism" initiative responds to the complex issues surrounding racial profiling.

The ACLU *and the* "Arrest the Racism" *Campaign*

It was not until the ACLU (and the NAACP) were formed in the early 1920s that the Bill of Rights was even enforced in this country. Today, the ACLU is just one of numerous organizations committed to eliminating all forms of racism. The organization has designed a campaign to address both the specific harms associated with racial profiling as well as link these injuries and recommended reforms to larger practices of institutional racism. The organization has more than 300 chapters across the nation and an annual budget of more than $40 million from contributions by its 275,000 members. The range of activities that make up the focus of the "Arrest the Racism" campaign are varied and reflect the complex nature of this pressing civil rights issue.

The launch of the "Arrest the Racism" campaign started with a 1999 letter to U.S. Attorney General, Janet Reno, calling on her office to investigate police use of racial profiling (ACLU, June 4, 1999). The letter included specific suggestions for funding and law enforcement training. It also suggested 5 specific actions to combat racial profiling:

1. Passage of the federal Traffic Stops Statistics Study Act (HR 1443, S 861);

2. Require that agencies receiving federal money for drug interdiction to collect race data on stops and searches;

3. Require that agencies receiving federal money for drug interdictions use "indicators of drug activity" as part of legitimate traffic stops, not as a pretext for traffic stops;

4. Require that the attorney general's office review all federally funded drug interdic-

tion training programs for explicit or implicit racist practices;

5. Require that agencies receiving federal money for drug interdiction programs implement measures to prevent, identify and remedy practices that violate the Fourth Amendment protection against unreasonable search and seizure (ACLU, June 4, 1999).

These recommendations set the stage for the "Arrest the Racism" campaign, an initiative which consists of three general strategies: (1) legislative efforts for statistical documentation of racial profiling, (2) public education, and (3) judicial remedies. In combination, these three efforts target the direct and indirect racism associated with racial profiling.

Legislative Efforts: Statistical Documentation of Racial Profiling

There is no federal legislation requiring data collection on racial profiling. However, the lack of legislation is not the result of a lack of effort on the part of several Congressional members. Representative John Conyers (D-MI) has been introducing legislation requiring data collection since 1997. For example, the 1997 "Traffic Stops Act" required that the Justice Department collect statistics on the frequency with which African Americans are pulled over in police traffic stops. While federal legislation lags, the growing number of racial profiling lawsuits is increasing pressure for legislative action. Consider the following incident that led to the first ACLU racial profiling lawsuit.

On August 13, 1998, Army Sergeant First Class Rossano V. Gerald and his 12-year-old son, Gregory, entered Oklahoma on Interstate 40. They were on their way to a family reunion. Once in Oklahoma, the police stopped Gerald and his son two times within 30 minutes. The first time, Gerald was cautioned not to follow another car so closely, but was not issued a citation. The second stop was under the pretense of not signaling a lane change. Gerald declined the trooper's request to search is car; what followed led to Gerald filing a complaint with the ACLU. According to the ACLU complaint, the state troopers:

- Warned SFC Gerald and his son that dogs would attack them if they attempted to "escape;"
- Illegally claimed that state law allowed them to conduct a car search without his consent;
- Shut off a video evidence camera halfway through the search;
- Placed SFC Gerald and his son in a closed car with the air conditioner off in the summer heat;
- Isolated 12-year-old Gregory for questioning in a car with a barking drug dog [without Gerald's consent]; and
- Refused to follow Army protocol and advise SFC Gerald's commanding officer of the stop (ACLU, May 18, 1999).

In the end, Gerald was released with a warning ticket. His car was left in disarray after the officers commented, "We ain't good at repacking" (ACLU, May 18, 1999).

This lawsuit filed by the ACLU generated much press attention but was just one of several other ACLU lawsuits filed in Maryland, New Jersey and Illinois. In addition to the pressure for legislation these lawsuits signal something deeper: a shift in the evidence surrounding racial profiling. While there are plenty of anecdotal stories of racial profiling, like the one described above (see, for example, Harris, 1999b), there is now growing statistical evidence that people of color are subjected to traffic stops more often than Whites. Highway studies in Maryland and New Jersey conducted by Temple University researcher John Lamberth include evidence of racial profiling by state police (Buckman & Lamberth, 1999; Harris, 1999a). The *Wichita Eagle* newspaper study found that in 1997 and 1998 17.8 percent of motorists ticketed in the city were black. On nearby interstates 19.5 percent of tickets were given to Blacks. However, the city consisted of only 12 percent Blacks (ACLU, January 21, 2000a). Likewise, in the Village of Mount Prospect, Illinois, up to 50 percent of those arrested from 1994 to 1999 were Hispanic, though Hispanics make up only 6 percent of the population (ACLU, January 19, 2000).

While the number of community-based studies are growing, the ACLU continues to lobby aggressively for federal legislation requiring the statistical documentation of racial profiling practices. Recent efforts include the "Traffic Stops Statistics Act," introduced by Sen. Thomas Daschle in January, 2001, (which did not emerge from the Senate Judiciary Committee, although hearings were held in April of 2001) (Seidenstein, 2001), and the "End Racial Profiling Act of 2001" (S.989/H.R. 2074). The most recent legislation, introduced by democratic senators from New York, Wisconsin, New Jersey and Michigan, is currently stalled in respective Senate and House subcommittees (ACLU, August 8, 2001). Over the past two years, however, the introduction of federal legislation has drawn media attention to racial profiling. Additionally, in mid-1999, President Clinton signed an executive order requiring federal law enforcement agencies to collect data, but to date, there remains no federal legislation in place that requires police agencies to gather statistics on traffic stops.

Nevertheless, efforts at the federal level, litigation of numerous racial profiling lawsuits and pressure from state based civil rights organizations have spurred similar legislative measures at the state level, often with the active support from state ACLU chapters. These efforts have been more successful. There are nine states, including Kansas, Connecticut, Washington, North Carolina, Rhode Island, Tennessee and Missouri, with legislation requiring data collection (ACLU, August 8, 2001). Another 24 states are at various stages of introducing or implementing similar legislation. Additionally, numerous city and municipal police departments (e.g., San Diego, Ann Arbor, Dearborn, Lansing, San Jose, Houston, Philadelphia, and Pittsburgh) are collecting data. Stamford, Connecticut was the first community to formally ban racial profiling, stating in its policy that racial profiling is "unethical and improper" and a violation of civil rights (ACLU, January 18, 2000).

This is not to suggest that data collection has not bet with some resistance by some law enforcement agencies and government officials. Prior to its eventual passage in mid-2000, the Rhode Island Senate Judiciary Committee grappled with the particulars of the racial profiling bill, specifically disagreeing on the kind of information that would be gathered during traffic stops as well as the kinds of statistical information that would ultimately be made public (ACLU, May 19, 2000). In mid-2000, San Jose was the battleground for two Senate bills on racial profiling that were vetoed by Gov. Gray Davis (the only sitting governor to do so) (ACLU, June 21, 2000). The one that ultimately passed did not require the collection of racial data (ACLU, May 21, 2000).

L.A. County Sheriff Lee Baca refused the local Board of Supervisor's request that his department track the ethnicity of drivers that his deputies stop. Baca argued that the complex computer programming was unreasonable and the effort would require 50,000 hours of extra work annually. However, 70 other California agencies have managed to comply with similar data collection requests (ACLU, January 21, 2000a).

While there has been a distinct focus on introducing legislation to compel law enforcement agencies to collect racial profiling data, the impact of voluntary efforts should not be minimized. State police around the country (e.g., Washington, Michigan and Florida) have started to collect their own data (Harris, 2001). For example, Michigan gathers data whether or not a ticket was issued or whether the vehicle was searched. The state also notes the search was consensual or based on probable cause. This is a significant commitment on the part of the Michigan State Police given that they make about 830,000 traffic stops and issue about 400,000 tickets a year (ACLU, December 10, 1999). In Michigan, as in other states across the country, disputes remain about who will interpret the data. Community leaders obviously support an independent evaluation of the data, while police agencies are concerned that the data collection will be used against them unfairly (Moss, 2002). For example, the ACLU of Michigan has criticized the Michigan State police for not obtaining an independent analysis and presenting the results only from a statewide perspective. When the data are broken down by district, problem areas in the state become evident (Moss, 2002).

This kind of voluntary collection of statistical data at the agency level is probably the most widespread and successful effort thus far to document the practice of racial profiling. Some members of police agencies have even testified that they were instructed in profiling techniques and claim racial profiling "is just a symptom of racism in the [New Jersey] State Police" (Seidenstein, 2001. P. 3).

In spite of the increasing willingness of some law enforcement agencies to voluntarily collect data, "Almost universally, police . . . don't believe that racial profiling is going on or is much of an issue here. But when you talk to people of color, it is an immense problem" (ACLU, May 28, 2000). One of the most public and political debates over racial profiling involved the New Jersey State Police and Governor Christie Whitman. Data released in April 1999 showed that 80 percent of the drivers pulled over on the New Jersey Turnpike were minorities (ACLU, July 24, 2000). One New Jersey Turnpike victim, Dr. Elmo Randolph, an African American dentist was stopped over 100 times in a five year period. Randolph stated, "The police searched my car and I had to prove to the troopers that being an African-American man in a nice car doesn't mean that I am a drug dealer or a car thief" (ACLU, October 25, 2001). Ultimately, Gov. Whitman admitted her police force routinely stopped drivers on the basis of race, leading to President Clinton's executive order for data collection by federal law enforcement agencies (ACLU, June 15, 2000). While New Jersey's problems with racial profiling may have received a substantial amount of public attention, problems continue within the state law enforcement agencies. For instance, a 1999 report documented racial profiling by the New Jersey State Police and increased numbers of pending lawsuits involving racial profiling resulted in the governor's admission of institutionalized racial profiling practice in New Jersey law enforcement. What resulted was an agreement with the Department of Justice to remedy the problem of racial profiling in the state. Yet incidents of profiling continue to be documented as recently as April, 2001 (ACLU,

October 10, 2001). Furthermore, the state of New Jersey has not moved forward on remedies for victims of racial profiling. This has prompted the ACLU to move forward with legal action charging that several top state officials "acted with deliberate indifference rather than attempting to stop the practice" (ACLU, January 11, 2002).

In short, problems with traffic-based racial profiling continue to plague law enforcement practices. In addition to legal remedies for victims, the ACLU is pushing hard for increased state-enforced data collection. Questions arise regarding whether the voluntary efforts to collect data on traffic stops are revealing any useful information. Reports of data collection studies are beginning to be released. San Jose Police Department was one of the first in California to voluntarily agree to collect data on traffic stops and the first police department to voluntarily release the results of the study. They released their preliminary report, based on three months of data, which revealed that Latino drivers account for 31 percent of San Jose's residents and 43 percent of drivers stopped by police. Furthermore, Blacks make up 4.5 percent of the population and 7 percent of drivers stopped. By comparison, Whites make up 43 percent of the population but 29 percent of the stops. Finally, Asian Americans make up 21 percent of the population and 16 percent of the stops. In other words, the data collection that has occurred has helped substantiate the anecdotal complaints of many people of color traveling the nation's highways.

More recently the ACLU's "Arrest the Racism Campaign" has raised awareness about racial profiling practices that go beyond "driving while black." Consider the experiences of Yvette Bradley, a 33-year-old advertising executive. The ACLU filed a federal lawsuit after the U.S. Customs Service allegedly targeted Yvette Bradley and several other African American women returning from Jamaica for search and interrogation by Customs agents. According to the lawsuit, "Bradley was led to a room at the airport and instructed to place her hands on the wall while an officer ran her hands and fingers over every area of her body, including her breast and the inner and outer labia of her vagina" (ACLU, May 12, 2000). During congressional hearings on U.S. Customs Service practices, victims of race-motivated customs inspections described numerous similar experiences. In addition to these anecdotal testimonies, a General accounting Office study revealed that almost 70 percent of the people subjected to searches upon entering the United States were people of color. Black female U.S. citizens were nine times more likely to be searched (ACLU, November 5, 2001). Black and Latino Americans were four times as likely as white Americans to be x-rayed (ACLU, April 2001). As a result of these U.S. Customs Service practices, legislation was introduced in mid-2000 requiring the Customs Service to report the race, national origin and gender of all the people searched (ACLU, June 26, 2000).

In summary, it is clear that data collection is essential to a statistical punctuation to the litany of personal testimonies about racial profiling. And while some law enforcement agencies are voluntarily collecting data, it is clear that state and federal legislation is needed to create a compulsory, institutional mandate and structure for data collection. Thus far, the data gathered suggest racial profiling practices are remarkably widespread and pervasive. The degree with which they are consistently present in federal, state, and community suggests a level of systemic racism. While this may be unconscious and unintentional, it demands a comprehensive effort to successfully eradicate the underlying structures and policies that have made it a normal police practice. So while individual communities slowly begin to address racial profiling with varying degrees of willingness, the words spoken by San Jose Police Chief William Lansdowne, upon the release of the city's racial profiling data ring clear, "This is a small step in a very long journey" (ACLU, December 18, 1999).

Public Education Campaigns

It would be hard to find someone who had not heard the phrase, "Driving While Black." The ACLU has worked at the state and national level to raise public awareness of the problem. The kinds of complex work associated with lobbying legislators or filing lawsuits tend not to attract public attention. However, some of the particular experiences of racial profiling victims have captured the public eye, and in combination with media campaigns, have successfully brought racial profiling to the forefront of public discourse.

In addition to the Reno letter mentioned earlier, "Arrest the Racism" started with a strong public awareness campaign that included magazine advertisements, particularly targeting magazines with African American readership. The ACLU also established a toll-free hotline an interactive website designed to facilitate reports of racial profiling. The ACLU designed and distributed 50,000 "Driving While Black or Brown" kits to people attending the McDonald's Heritage Bowl in Atlanta, Georgia and continues to distribute them by the thousands throughout the country. The kit includes a sample letter to Congress urging support for federal legislation, stickers with the ACLU toll-free racial profiling hotline, and ACLU bust card (wallet-sized explanation of what to do if stopped by police), and other information detailing ACLU activities in the campaign against racial profiling (ACLU, December 14, 1999). The kits have been translated into both Spanish and Arabic, and different ACLU affiliates have developed specialized outreach programs to reach targeted communities, like in Dearborn, Michigan which has the largest Arabic population outside of the Middle East (Moss, 2002).

The ACLU also worked with DeVito/Verdi Advertising to develop a print campaign targeting what then Executive Director, Ira Glasser described as "the vast majority of 'persuadables' in the middle: people who are highly likely to share the ACLU's core values even if they don't agree with all of its policies" (ACLU, June 2, 2000). In one of these ads, published *The New York Times* Sunday magazine and in *The New Yorker,* there were side-by-side pictures of Martin Luther King (left) and Charles Manson (right). The text begins with "The man on the left is 75 times more likely to be stopped by the police while driving than the man on the right." Additionally, the ACLU has launched radio and television public service announcements targeting Latino and African American communities. The 1999 radio campaign netted more than 1,000 calls to the toll-free hotline (ACLU, August 21, 2000). The public awareness campaign continues targeting specific problems and geographical regions. Towards the end of 2001, the ACLU launched a newspaper, billboard and radio advertising campaign designed to raise awareness of continued problems of racial profiling in New Jersey. The ads include information on how to file a complaint via the toll-free hotline or through the organization's website.

Litigation Efforts

In fact, it was one of the magazine ads spotted by Rossan Gerald that prompted his contact with the ACLU leading ultimately to the first ACLU racial profiling lawsuit

(*Gerald v. Oklahoma Department of Public Safety*, 1999). Given the large number of complaints documented by the ACLU and the statistical data indicated widespread racial profiling, it is not surprising that there is a surge in litigation. New Jersey alone has more than 20 state and federal district court cases pending since 1999. The ACLU is involved in two of them in New Jersey and 11 other lawsuits spread across Maryland, Indiana, Oklahoma (described above), Illinois, and Florida. One of the cases, *White v. Williams* (1999), raises the question of whether several key New Jersey state officials, including a New Jersey Supreme Court Justice, a former attorney general and the superintendent of the state police, knew about the problem of racial profiling and did nothing to redress it (in other words, acted with "deliberate indifference").

But litigation is not the only strategy employed by the ACLU to combat racial profiling. It is, rather, a last resort. Typically, litigation serves several specific purposes. These include: (1) to seek remedies for victims of racial profiling when other efforts have failed; (2) to raise awareness of the racial profiling by litigating the more egregious cases; (3) to use the judicial system to force state enforcement agencies to respond to pervasive racial profiling practices; and (4) to increase pressure for legislative action. These litigious efforts, combined with the extensive legislative pressure and public education campaigns, provide the key elements of the ACLU's multi-faceted effort to combat the direct and indirect problems of racism as manifesting in the practice of racial profiling. Litigation has made a "huge difference in massing support for Conyer's legislation and for many state bills introduced around the country" (Moss, 2002).

Even with numerous cases available for litigation, racial profiling cases are difficult to win. After 1996 U.S. Supreme Court decision, *Whren v. United States*, it is more difficult to successfully litigate racial profiling cases as an unconstitutional violation of the Fourth Amendment protection against unreasonable search and seizure. To get around the limits placed by *Whren*, one must prove no traffic violation occurred or that the police "overstep[ped] law regarding consent or plain view" (ACLU of Michigan, 2001, p. 19). The problem is that the vast majority of traffic-based racial profiling stops involve minor infractions of traffic laws. These infractions are used as a pretext for targeting drivers of color. But if there is a traffic infraction involved *Whren* makes it extremely difficult to claim an unconstitutional violation of Fourth Amendment rights.

State Level Efforts: The Michigan Example

The structure of the ACLU is such that in addition to the national organization, there are autonomous state and regional chapters that focus on civil liberties, civil rights, public education, and most recently, racial profiling. Complaints received by the national website are forwarded to the relevant state chapters for follow-up. Since 1999, the ACLU of Michigan has committed extensive resources to racial profiling. Its Executive Director currently serves as chair of an innovative coalition that includes over 20 community and civil rights organizations and over 20 law enforcement agencies such as the FBI, State police, Office of the United States Attorney, Immigration and Naturalization and U.S. Customs. The ACLU of Michigan also obtained funding for a full-time staff lawyer to work exclusively on racial profiling documentation, education and litigation needs within the state. With the support of numerous foundations, the Michigan ACLU has established a racial profiling project "dedicated primarily to educating the public, lawyers, judges, and law enforcement officials about the problem and potential solutions" (ACLU of Michigan, 2001, p. 2).

Several Michigan law enforcement agencies have been willing to collect data, and there have been numerous meetings between law enforcement agencies and civil rights organizations to develop recommendations for redressing racial profiling. The Michigan State police released the analysis of 134, 656 stops between January 1 and March 31, 2000. The data showed a disproportionate percentage of black men being stopped in metro Detroit. Cars driven by black men were searched without consent more often than any other group. They also received 45 percent of the tickets while only representing 32 percent of the area population (ACLU, July 21, 2000).

There remains significant contention over the interpretation of the data collected by Michigan law enforcement agencies. Some data are being analyzed internally by the police agencies, and some police departments have hired outside consultants (ACLU of Michigan, 2001). The ACLU of Michigan is working closely with police agencies throughout the state to develop means of data collection and interpretation that will be credible to communities. For example, the affiliate has worked closely with the Ann Arbor police, Washetaw County Sheriff's Department and the Grand Rapids police to review data collections methods and participate in the interpretation process. According to Kary Moss, Executive Director of the ACLU of Michigan, the results have been positive. In Ann Arbor for example, the police department has created a new set of training guidelines for its officers after one report indicated profiling in certain areas of the region (Moss, 2002). In other parts of Michigan, data interpretation remains contentious. In Lansing, for example, the ACLU of Michigan has questioned the police department's interpretation of their racial profiling data. They have pointed out that "even if the police paint a positive picture, if the sentiment in the community is that profiling is a problem, then the lack of trust between the police and community is only exacerbated by law enforcement refusal to undertake a good faith [effort] to collect and analyze the data" (Moss, 2002).

To help establish independent analysis and consistency in data collection, Michigan State Representative Buzz Thomas introduced a bill in May of 2001 that, if passed, would establish some of the strongest racial profiling laws in the nation (Michigan House Democratic Caucus, 2001). Specifically this bill would:

- Define racial profiling as the "detention, interdiction or other disparate treatment" of a person on the basis of race or ethnicity, and make it illegal;
- Require police to record and report the race of drivers they stop, including those searched;
- Create an attorney general's division to oversee and investigate police stop and search patterns; and
- Develop procedures to discipline police departments guilty of racial profiling. (Arellano, 2001)

The ACLU is also suing the Michigan police for racial profiling associated with the race-based stops of at least 21 black teenagers on bikes in response to a bike theft (ACLU of Michigan, 2000). This case, filed in April 2001, rests on the constitutional protection against unreasonable stops and searches. What makes this case a compelling test case for the Michigan chapter is that a large number of victims were involved in over 100 incidents in a 3-year period. Furthermore a February 1996 memo from the former chief of police directed police officers to investigate black youth riding in certain Eastpointe subdivisions (Arellano, 2001).

Another high profile Michigan racial profiling case, known as "swimming while black," involved six African American children who were victims of racial profiling at an Ann Arbor pool. A patron at the pool reported a cell phone stolen and the pool manager singled out these children, ordering them to stay until the police arrived. With the police present, the owner of the cell phone searched the children's bags to no avail. No white children were searched. To avoid costly litigation, the ACLU of Michigan is currently assisting the city of Ann Arbor in their efforts to: (1) implement an affirmative action plan; (2) provide regular diversity training for city employees; (3) plan programs to educate teenagers about their constitutional rights; and (4) reach acceptable compensation for the six children that were targeted because of their race (ACLU of Michigan, November 12, 2001).

Michigan provides a good case study of how the state chapters of the ACLU, often in collaboration with other civil rights and social justice organizations such as the NAACP, mirror and often lead the framework of the national initiative. The ACLU of Michigan, in particular, has devoted significant resources to initiate data collection, collaborative and cooperative relationships between state agencies and civil rights groups, public education, legislative lobbying and carefully chosen litigation efforts. These coordinated efforts reflect an understanding of the multifaceted nature of racial profiling—its direct harm to its victims as well as its reflection of ongoing racist social and institutional structures. Through these efforts, the ACLU of Michigan has developed "many strong relationships across cultural and ethnic boundaries, establishing bridges that have improved the organization's capacity to influence public policy" (Moss, 2002). Moss describes the "big picture" by suggesting the ACLU has "targeted a difficult issue using a creative combination of strategies that include a strong grassroots component," as evidenced by the work of state affiliate chapters that function with great autonomy and often help shape or lead the national agenda.

> That freedom, and the affiliates connection to a variety of grassroots organizations, ensures that the work of the national office is informed by the perspective of those most affected by [racist practices]. It also enables the affiliates to put resources into the most serious problem affecting the people of that state, problems which may vary strongly in degree and intensity throughout the country. (Moss, 2002)

Conclusion

The perpetuation of racism in the United States lies in it ability to be masked under the cover of normalized social, economic, cultural and professional practices as well as illusory notions of substantive legal equality and protection. The reality of racism is reflected in the current practice of racial profiling. We live in a society that has accomplished a legal structure of formal equality under the law and embraced, for the most part, the lessons to be learned from the civil rights movement. We continue to look upon other societies and cultures that continue racist and other discriminatory practices as unenlightened. In this context, it seems almost remarkable that racial profiling could flourish under any conditions. Yet, in spite of the growing public condemnation of traffic-based racial profiling, the events of September 11th have signaled a shift in discourse about the practice. A country shaken to the core by an unprecedented breach of its domestic security now faces the test of its commitment to the human value of civil liberties. Travelers who look Middle

Eastern have been removed from domestic flights at the behest of other passengers (ACLU, November 8, 2001). U.S. American citizens or immigrants have been targeted for verbal or physical abuse, primarily because of their ethnic identity. Even more troubling are the implications for racial profiling that may result from the expanded search and seizure powers U.S. Customs official will gain with the passage of the Customs Border Security Act (H.R. 3129). The Act would "expand the immunity of customs officials in ways that would make it nearly impossible for a person to seek redress from an unconstitutional research" (ACLU, November 5, 2001).

It will require tremendous effort on the part of civil liberties and human rights organizations to continue to respond to specific acts of racial profiling in light of the current climate in the United States. These efforts must include educating community members about the American legal system and their constitutional rights, challenging unconstitutional provisions of anti-terrorist legislation and responding aggressively to racial profiling that occurs under the guise of "homeland security." The practice of racial profiling does not happen in a vacuum; they very fact that it can happen is a sign of deeper problems. This is why it remains equally important for organizations dedicated to human rights and civil liberties as well as push this country's citizens to push toward a deeper understanding of the cultural, institutional and systemic roots of racism that remain imbedded in the collective consciousness of the U.S. American psyche.

References

ACLU, (1999, May 18). Black army sergeant files lawsuit after terrifying race profiling stop in Oklahoma. ACLU [On-line]. Available: http://www.aclu.org/news/1999/n051899c.html

ACLU, (1999, June 4). ACLU letter to Attorney General Reno on police practices. ACLU [On-line]. Available: http://www.aclu.org/congress/1060499a.html

ACLU, (1999, December 9). New poll shows public overwhelmingly disapproves of racial profiling. ACLU [On-line]. Available: http://www.aclu.org/news/1999/n120999a.html

ACLU, (1999, December 10). Michigan state police join national push to collect race data on traffic stops. ACLU [On-line]. Available: http://www.aclu.org/news/1999/w121099c.html

ACLU, (1999, December 14). ACLU to distribute 50,000 racial profiling resource kits at black college Super Bowl. ACLU [On-line]. Available: http://www.aclu.org/news/1999/w121499b.html

ACLU, (1999, December 18). Policy and community react to San Jose traffic stop data. ACLU [On-line]. Available: http://www.aclu.org/news/1999/w121899a.html

ACLU, (1999, December). "Arrest the Racism": Racial profiling in America, campaign background information. ACLU [On-line]. Available: http://www.aclu.org/profiling/background/index.html

ACLU, (2000, January 18). Connecticut city celebrates M.L.K. Day by banning racial profiling. ACLU [On-line]. Available: http://www.aclu.org/news/2000/w01900a.html

ACLU, (2000, January 19). Federal judge calls for Justice Department investigation of racial profiling in Illinois town. ACLU [On-line]. Available: http://www.aclu.org/news/2000/w01900a.html

ACLU, (2000a, January 21). Kansas legislature tackles racial profiling. ACLU [On-line]. Available: http://www.aclu.org/news/2000/w012100a.html

ACLU, (2000b, January 21). L.A. County elected officials blast sheriff's failure to address DWB. ACLU [On-line]. Available: http://www.aclu.org/news/2000/w012100b.html

ACLU, (2000, May 12). ACLU sues U.S. Custom Service over degrading search in case of "Flying While Black." ACLU [On-line]. Available: http://www.aclu.org/news.n051200a.html

ACLU, (2000, May 19). Legislators "confident" on prospects for Rhode Island DWB bill. ACLU [On-line]. Available: http://www.aclu.org/news/2000/wo51900a.html

ACLU, (2000, May 21). California newspapers blast Governor's DWB deal. ACLU [On-line]. Available: http://www.aclu.org/news/2000/w052100a.html

ACLU, (2000, May 28). Cape Cod police agencies face demands for DWB data. ACLU [On-line]. Available: http://www.aclu.org/news/2000/w052800a.html

ACLU, (2000, June 2). Provocative new ACLU advertising series uses American icons in message of racial profiling. ACLU [On-line]. Available: http://www.aclu.org/news/2000/n60200a.html

ACLU, (2000, June 15). NAACP Chairman Julian Bond calls "evil practice" of racial profiling a problem in all 50 states. ACLU [On-line]. Available: http://www.aclu.org/news/2000/w026500b.html

ACLU, (2000, June 21). CHP officers predict California DWB compromise will lead to more ticketing of minorities. ACLU [On-line]. Available: http://www.aclu.org/news/2000/w062100a.html

ACLU, (2000, June 26). Racial profiling report calls for judicial review of border searches: Shows need for legislation. ACLU [On-line]. Available: http://www.aclu.org/news/2000/n062800a.html

ACLU, (2000, July 21). State police in Michigan more likely to search African American men. ACLU [On-line]. Available: http://www.aclu.org/news/2000/w072100b.html

ACLU, (2000, July 24). States focus on data collection as legislative response to racial profiling. ACLU [On-line]. Available: http://www.aclu.org/news/2000/w072400c.html

ACLU, (2000, August 21). In new radio and television PSA campaign, ACLU urges victims of racial profiling to fight back. ACLU [On-line]. Available: http://www.aclu.org/news/2000/n082100a.html

ACLU, (2001, April). End racial profiling in the nation's airports. ACLU [On-line]. Available: http://www.aclu.org/action/airprofile107.html

ACLU, (2001, August 8). Legislation addresses racial profiling. ACLU [On-line]. Available http://www.aclu.org/action/dwb107.html

ACLU, (2001, October 10. New Jersey's victims of racial profiling call for justice and closure. ACLU [On-Line]. Available http://www.aclu.org/news/2001/n101001b.html

ACLU, (2001, October 25). ACLU unveils new ad campaign to end racial profiling in New Jersey. ACLU [On-line]. Available: http://www.aclu.org/news/2001/n102501a.html

ACLU, (2001, November 5). Keep customs officers accountable! ACLU [On-Line]. Available: http://www.aclu.org/action/customs107.html

ACLU, (2001, November 8). Northwest Airlines apologizes to civil rights groups. ACLU {On-line]. Available: http://www.aclumich.org/press$20releases/PR-14-nov-01.html

ACLU, (2001, November 10). Racial equality. ACLU of Michigan {On-line]. Available: http://www.aclumich.org/issues/racial.html

ACLU, (2002, January 10). Court says ACLU NJ racial profiling cases can include claims that officials acted with "deliberate indifference" to discrimination. ACLU [On-line]. Available: http://www.aclu.org/news/2001/n011002b.html

ACLU of Michigan, (2000). ACLU legal docket. ACLU of Michigan [On-line].

Available: http://www.aclumich.org/docket/docket2000.htm#RACIAL JUSTICE

ACLU of Michigan, (2001). Destination Justice: Driving while Black and the struggle to end it. Training manual on file with author.

Arellano, A. (2001, February 1). Strong profiling proposal in works. *Detroit Free Press*. Available: http://freep.com/news/mich/profile1-2001-201.html.

Arellano, A. (2001, April 10). ACLU says Eastpointe targets blacks on bikes. *Detroit Free Press*, p. 1A.

Barendt, J. (1991). *Dismantling racism: The continuing challenge to white America*. Minneapolis, MN: Augsburg.

Buckman, W., & Lamberth, J. (1999). Challenging racial profiles: Attacking Jim Crow on the interstate. [On-line] Available: http://whbuckman.com/profiling/championart.html

Bureau of Justice Statistics. (1998). U.S. Dept of Justice, Sourcebook on Criminal Justice Statistics 1997, 338, 442 Tables 4.10 and 5.46 (1998). As cited in Harris, D. (2001). Law Enforcements Stake in Coming to grips with Racial Profiling. 3 Rutgers Race & L. Rev. 9-38, 17 (2001).

Gallup Poll. (1999). Gallup [On-line]. Available: http://www.gallup.com/poll/releases/pre991209.ssp

Gerald v. Oklahoma Department of Public Safety. (1999). ACLU [On-line]. Available: http://www.aclu.org/court/gerald/oklahoma-complaint.html

Harris, D. (1999a). The stories, the statistics, and the law: Why "Driving while Black" matters, *Minnesota Law Review*, 84, 265-326.

Harris, D. (1999b, June). Driving while Black. Racial profiling on our nation's highways, ACLU [On-line] Available: http://www.aclu.org/profiling/report/index.html

Harris, D. (2001). Law enforcement's stake in coming to grips with racial profiling. *Rutgers Race & Law Review, 3*, 9-38.

King Jr., M.L. (1986). Where do we go from here: Chaos or community? In J. E. Washington (Ed.), *A testament of hope: The essential writings of Martin Luther King* (p. 623). San Francisco: Harper and Row.

Michigan House Democratic Caucus (2001, May 31). Rep. Thomas introduces legislation to end racial profiling in Michigan. *Michigan House Democratic Caucus* [On-line].

Moss, K. (2001). Destination: crossroads. *Michigan Bar Journal, 80*(1), 36-42.

Moss, K. (2002, January, 15). Personal communication.

Seidenstein, R. (2001, April 16). Racial profiling: Tales of woe, pleas for reform. *The New Jersey Lawyer*, p. 3.

Trende, S. P. (2000). "Why modest proposals offer the best solution for combating racial profiling. *Duke Law Journal*, 331-380.

Wallis, J. (1988). *America's original sin: A study guide on white racism*. Washington, D.C.: Sojourners Resource Center.

White v. Williams. (1999). No. 99-CV-2240 (JAP). Available: http://lawlibrary.rutgers.edu/fed/.html

Whren v. United States, 116 S. Ct. 1769 (1996).

Report on the Anniversary of *Furman v. Georgia*

Three Decades Later: Why We Need a Temporary Halt on Executions

American Civil Liberties Union

In the landmark 1972 case *Furman v. Georgia*, the Supreme Court struck down the death penalty statutes of Georgia and Texas, ruling that the manner in which the penalty was imposed throughout the country constituted cruel and unusual punishment in violation of the Eighth and Fourteenth Amendments.[1] In his concurring opinion, Justice Stewart wrote:

> These death sentences are cruel and unusual in the same way that being struck by lightning is cruel and unusual. For, of all the people convicted of rapes and murders in 1967 and 1968, many just as reprehensible as these, the petitioners are among a capriciously selected random handful upon whom the sentence of death has in fact been imposed . . . I simply conclude that the Eighth and Fourteenth Amendments cannot tolerate the infliction of a sentence of death under legal systems that permit this unique penalty to be so wantonly and so freakishly imposed.[2]

The court commuted the sentences of all 629 death row prisoners in the country, and, in rendering all existing statutes invalid, in effect suspended the use of the death penalty.

Four years later in *Gregg v. Georgia*, the court upheld Georgia's newly revised death penalty statute beginning the "modern era" of the death penalty.[3] In response to *Gregg*, *Furman*, and other decisions, states established new and "objective" sentencing procedures designed to ensure that the death penalty would be imposed fairly. Executions resumed in 1977. As of June 2003, 38 states,

---

From American Civil Liberties Union Report on the Anniversary of *Furman v. Georgia*. Copyright © by ACLU. Reprinted by permission.

the federal government, and the military have death penalty statutes on their books, 855 prisoners have been executed and nearly 4,000 men, women and youthful offenders—83 people on death row are there for committing crimes while under the age of 18—remain under a death sentence.[4]

A careful review of the last thirty years shows that despite efforts at reform, the death penalty is as arbitrary as it was in 1972. The problems: one hundred and eight exonerated people have been released from death row, the death penalty remains primarily the province of the poor, and racial and geographic disparity in sentencing continues. This report discusses some of the most pervasive systemic flaws that continue to plague death penalty systems:

- wrongful conviction of the innocent,
- inadequate counsel,
- geographic disparity, and
- racial and socioeconomic bias.

It concludes that there are reasons for another temporary halt to executions while individual states reexamine their statutes and their performance.

The Death Penalty Punishes Innocent People

On April 8, 2002, Ray Krone was released from prison in Arizona after DNA evidence proved that he was not responsible for the murder of a Phoenix bartender. Krone became the 100th person exonerated since 1973 after having been on death row. Convicted twice for a brutal murder, largely because of forensic testimony that a bite on the victim matched his teeth, Krone spent ten years in prison, two of them on death row.

> "NO MATTER HOW CAREFUL courts are, the possibility of perjured testimony, mistaken honest testimony, and human error remain all too real. We have no way of judging how many innocent persons have been executed but we can be certain that there were some.... Surely there will be more as long as capital punishment remains part of our penal law."
>
> —Justice Byron White in his concurrence in <u>Furman v. Georgia</u>, 1972.[5]

The DNA evidence that ultimately proved his innocence also implicated the real murderer.

Unfortunately, Mr. Krone's story is not unique. As of June 2003, 108 people have been released from death row in 25 states, more than half in the last 10 years. That works out to be one person exonerated for every eight people executed, or an average of four people a year.[6]

Proponents of the death penalty often suggest that this indicates our criminal justice system is working. However, in many of the 108 cases it was good luck—not the system—that established innocence. Often, it was people outside the system who proved their innocence. For example, it was journalism students at Northwestern University whose work led to the release of several death row inmates in Illinois, including Anthony Porter, who came within two days of execution. It was a fluke that Mr. Porter was not executed. The students had previously decided not to investigate Mr. Porter's case due to insufficient time before his scheduled execution date. However, Mr. Porter got a last minute stay from the court to determine his competency, an issue completely unrelated to his innocence. The students decided to look into his case and located the real killer, who confessed on videotape to the murder. Nearly presiding

Exonerations 1973-present
(Total=108)

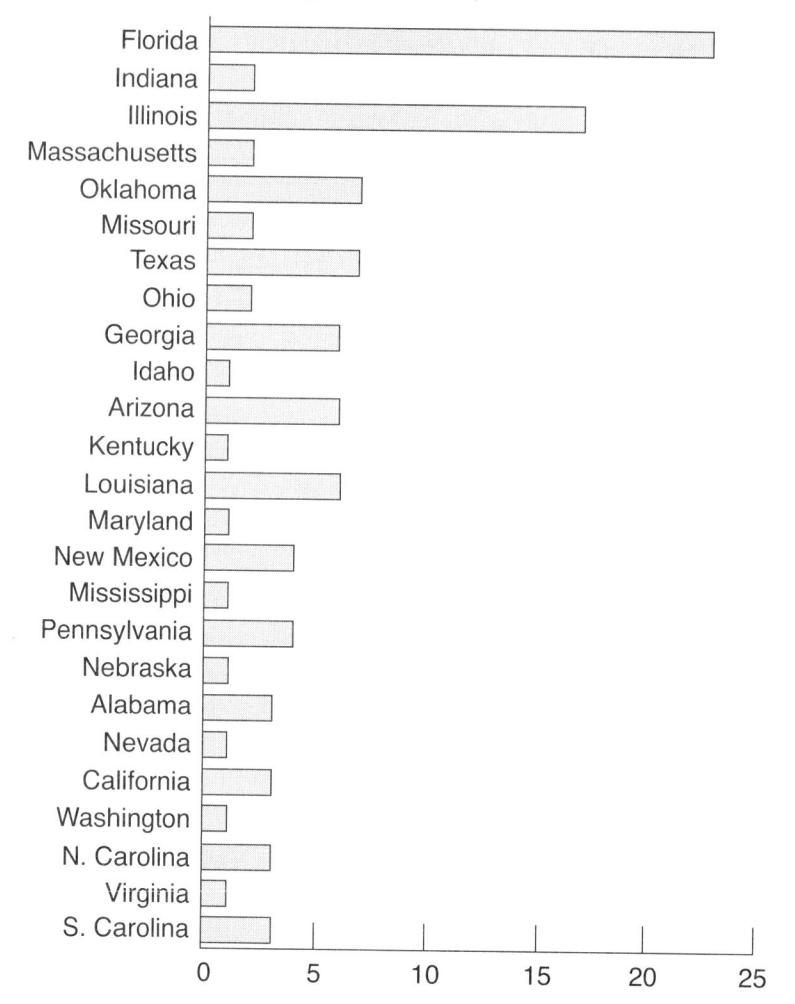

Florida	~23
Indiana	~2
Illinois	~17
Massachusetts	~2
Oklahoma	~7
Missouri	~2
Texas	~7
Ohio	~2
Georgia	~6
Idaho	~1
Arizona	~6
Kentucky	~1
Louisiana	~6
Maryland	~1
New Mexico	~4
Mississippi	~1
Pennsylvania	~4
Nebraska	~1
Alabama	~3
Nevada	~1
California	~3
Washington	~1
N. Carolina	~3
Virginia	~1
S. Carolina	~3

This information is taken from Death Penalty Information Center's Website at: http://www.deathpenaltyinfo.org/article.php?did=412&scid=6

over the execution of an innocent man convinced Governor George Ryan of the need to impose a moratorium on executions.[7]

Likewise, students in an investigative journalism class at Webster University uncovered evidence of prosecutorial misconduct and helped get a new trial for a Louisiana death row inmate.[8] If it had not been for the work of these students, innocent people would have been killed. In other instances, coverage in the media has led to exposing mistaken death penalty convictions—such as the movie "The Thin Blue Line" which exposed Randall Dale Adams' innocence.[9]

> **WHO IS INNOCENT?**
>
> There has been much debate surrounding the use of the term "innocent" to describe those exonerated from death row. Proponents of the death penalty often argue that many of those wrongfully convicted, who are later released because of legal innocence, may have committed the crime. The Death Penalty Information Center (DPIC)—the organization that keeps track of innocence cases—includes people who have been convicted and sentenced to death and were either acquitted at a re-trial, had all charges dropped, or were given an absolute pardon by the governor based on new evidence of innocence.[10]

The list of 108 is a conservative one. It excludes people who are almost certainly innocent. It does not include Sonya "Sunny" Jacobs, whose story is portrayed in the play "The Exonerated." Ms. Jacobs was present at the murder of two Florida State Troopers, but was in the back seat of the car shielding her children, and did not even observe the crime. She was convicted, sentenced to death, and spent 17 years in a maximum-security facility, based on the testimony of the co-defendant, who later confessed to being the actual killer. The only other person who testified against her was a cellmate who claimed that Ms. Jacobs had confessed to killing the officers. This witness later recanted on national television, claiming that the prosecutor had offered her an early release for her testimony.[11] However, after the appellate court overturned her conviction the state of Florida refused to dismiss the charges against her and threatened to try her again. Wanting to avoid another trial, and having served nearly two decades in prison, Ms. Jacobs agreed to a plea, whereby she has a conviction on her record for a less serious crime, but is free to maintain her innocence. Because of this conviction, she does not meet the DPIC's definition of "innocent". Her partner, Jesse Tafero, was convicted based on the same evidence. Unfortunately, Mr. Tafero was executed before the evidence of his innocence was revealed. Adding Ms. Jacobs and Mr. Tafero to the list would bring the total number of exonerees to 110.[12]

Executing the Innocent

No one has yet been able to prove conclusively that an innocent person has been executed during the modern era, although most believe it has happened. A June 2002 CNN/USA Today/Gallup Poll found that 80 percent of Americans believe an innocent person has been executed in the United States in the past five years.[13]

There is no way to tell how many of the more than 800 people executed since 1976 may have been found innocent if further investigation had been done into their cases. Attorneys and court officials generally do not continue investigation into claims of innocence after a person is put to death. There are, however, a few cases where strong claims of innocence existed and the prisoner was still put to death. Mr. Tafero, mentioned above, is one example. Another is Roger Coleman, who was convicted of the rape and murder of his sister-in-law without any witnesses, motive, or fingerprints. Blood and semen tests matched Coleman's, but were not unique to him. Mr. Coleman asserted his innocence to the end. After his execution, more sophisticated DNA testing became available that might prove Mr. Coleman's innocence, but the state of Virginia has continued to oppose requests by his attorneys to retest the evidence.[14] Another case may be that of Shaka Sankofa (aka Gary Graham) who was convicted and sentenced to death based on the testimony of an eyewitness who observed the crime at night from her car from a distance. Two other eyewitnesses claimed that Mr. Sankofa was not the killer; an expert who evaluated the case said that under the conditions existing at the time of the crime, the witness could not have made a positive identification. Unfortunately, Mr. Sankofa was executed even though no court had ever heard the testimony of the other two eyewitnesses or the expert.[15]

The Benefits, and Limits, of DNA

Although there has been much attention surrounding DNA testing, only 13 death row prisoners of the 108 have been exonerated through DNA testing.[16] Many people falsely believe that DNA testing is a panacea that guarantees innocent people will not be put to death. But DNA testing is usually not able to determine the killer. There may not be any physical evidence to test, either because none was collected from the crime scene, or because it has since been destroyed. If the suspect is a person that the victim knew, there may be legitimate explanations for why the physical evidence was at the crime scene.

DNA testing is also only as effective as the people conducting the tests. In 2003, the Houston Police Department's lab came under attack because of ongoing gross negligence and fabrication of results. That led the FBI to purge the results of all DNA tests taken at that lab from the national DNA database.[17] Dozens of convictions from that jurisdiction have been called into question.

Still, DNA testing is an essential tool in proving innocence in some cases. In Illinois, five of the 17 people released from death row were released because of DNA evidence.[18] DNA has been especially useful in rape cases, where testing semen left at the crime scene can conclusively exclude innocent people.

Unfortunately, many prisoners do not have access to testing. Pending bi-partisan federal legislation—the Innocence Protection Act—sponsored by Senators Patrick Leahy (D-VT), Susan Collins (R-ME) and Gordon Smith (R-OR) and Representatives William Delahunt (D-MA) and Ray LaHood (R-IL), would ensure that DNA testing is available to all who have credible claims of innocence. It would also require states to examine their indigent defense systems and establish minimum competency standards. Testifying before the House Judiciary Committee, Representative Delahunt observed, "Our criminal justice system is not working as it should when innocent people are convicted of serious crimes and then spend decades—or have even reached the end of death row—before the mistakes, if ever, are caught."[19]

The risk of executing an innocent person is not only horrific; it is the ultimate indicator that America's criminal justice system is broken. However, not all government officials believe that preventing the execution of an innocent person is paramount. Some prosecutors place so much importance on securing a conviction, and protecting the finality of that conviction, that doubts about the person's guilt or innocence become secondary. Frank Jung, an assistant to Missouri Attorney General Jay Nixon, recently told the Missouri Supreme Court that it should not concern itself with mounting evidence that death row inmate Joseph Amrine might be innocent. One judge asked Jung, "Is it not cruel and unusual punishment to execute an innocent person?" Jung responded, "If there is no underlying constitutional violation, there is not a right to relief."[20] The prosecutor is saying that as long as a person was convicted at a fair trial, then even if that person was later found to be innocent, he could still be executed. Truth is not as important as process. Similarly, the actions of the Virginia prosecutors objecting to further investigation of the Coleman case show how far some prosecutors may go to prevent investigation of the truth.

> "Not only does capital punishment fail in its justification, but no punishment could be invented with so many inherent defects. It is an unequal punishment in the way it is applied to the rich and to the poor. The defendant of wealth and position never goes to the electric chair or to the gallows."
> —Justice Douglas from his concurrence in <u>Furman v. Georgia</u>, 1972.[21]

The Death Penalty Is Discriminatory

Inadequate Counsel

There are many factors that contribute to convicting innocent people such as prosecutorial and police misconduct, mistaken eye-witness identification, lying jailhouse snitches and false confessions. Yet the factor that probably accounts for the most wrongful convictions is inadequate defense counsel, a problem that falls most heavily on the poor.

March 18, 2003 marked the 40th anniversary of the *Gideon v. Wainwright* decision, in which the Supreme Court ruled that the constitution required that indigent people charged with felonies who could not afford to hire a lawyer would be appointed one at public expense.[22] Not all public defenders or court-appointed counsel are incompetent. Many are excellent lawyers; however, they are usually hampered by limited resources. They often do not have the resources to hire experts who are necessary to provide a competent defense in complex capital cases. They almost never have the same amount of resources as the prosecutor who is seeking the death penalty.

The Supreme Court has not made sure that the counsel provided under *Gideon* are competent. There are major problems in capital cases. In 2002, the Court upheld the death sentences in a Virginia case where the lawyer had previously represented the murder victim and in a Tennessee case where the lawyer did not ask the jury to spare his client's life.[23] Other courts have ruled that counsel was competent in cases where the lawyer was unaware of the governing law or was intoxicated. A Texas case made national news when the state courts and the Fifth Circuit Court of Appeals held that it was not ineffective assistance of counsel for the attorney to sleep during the trial. The court sitting *en banc* reversed that ruling, but five of the 14 judges dissented and would have allowed the defendant to be executed.[24]

Delma Banks, Jr.

A recent case the epitomizes the problems of inadequate representation is that of Delma Banks, Jr., which the Supreme Court accepted for review on April 21, 2003. Delma Banks, Jr. received such poor representation that former FBI director and United States District Court Judge William Sessions intervened and asked the Supreme Court to temporarily stay his execution. Judge Sessions argued that the constitutional issues raised in Mr. Banks' petition called into question the reliability of the guilty verdict and the death sentence and the criminal justice system as a whole: "when a criminal defendant is forced to pay with his life for his lawyer's errors, the effectiveness of the criminal justice system as a whole is undermined."[25]

Delma Banks, Jr. is an African-American man who was charged in 1980 with murder for killing Richard Whitehead, a white man, in Texarkana, Texas. The only "evidence" against Banks was the testimony of an informant who in exchange for his testimony received $200 and the dismissal of an arson charge that could have resulted in his life sentence as a habitual offender.

> "When a criminal defendant is forced to pay with his life for his lawyer's errors, the effectiveness of the criminal justice system as a whole is undermined."[25]
>
> —United States District Court Judge William Sessions

Banks' lawyer did not vigorously cross-examine the informant, nor did he investigate the case. Had he done so, he would have learned of strong evidence that Banks was in another city at the time of the crime.

Banks was convicted and sentenced to death after a one-day trial in which the prosecutors systematically removed all African-Americans from the jury—again not challenged by Banks' attorney. At the sentencing hearing, Banks' lawyer did not challenge the state's claim that his client posed a "future danger to society"—a requirement for a death sentence in Texas—even though Banks had no criminal record or history of violence.

No Competency Standards

Few if any states provide sufficient funds to compensate lawyers for their work and most do not have meaningful competency standards for an attorney to meet in order to defend a capital murder suspect. In 2003, the American Bar Association (ABA) published revised Guidelines for the Appointment and Performance of Defense Counsel in Death Penalty Cases that include: requiring the attorneys to have abilities, expertise and skills in representing clients in capital cases; providing two attorneys, an investigator and mitigation specialist in every case; and providing full funding of the defense and eliminating statutory caps or flat fees.[26] According to the ABA, no state has yet established standards that meet its minimum requirements.

State Studies of Indigent Defense

Reports on indigent defense have recently been done in Texas, Georgia, North Carolina, Pennsylvania, and Tennessee. The Texas study, Lethal Indifference, conducted by the Texas Defender Service, found that the quality of legal representation is abysmal for death row prisoners both at the trial and appeals levels.[27]

The study found that judges often appointed defense attorneys based on their reputation for rapidly moving cases through the system, instead of for their competence and experience. Judges even appointed attorneys who have been disciplined, such as in the case of Leonard Rojas. He was appointed an appellate attorney who had been disciplined three times by the state bar and been given two probated suspensions. (A probated suspension allows an otherwise suspended attorney to continue representing clients.) The study concluded that death row prisoners, "face a one-in-three chance of being executed without having the case properly investigated by a competent attorney or without having any claims of innocence or unfairness heard."

Texas is not alone in providing inadequate counsel for death penalty cases. The Tennessee Supreme Court reviewed all death sentences post-*Furman* and found that in one-fourth of those cases, attorneys did not submit evidence that might persuade a jury to impose a prison sentence instead of death.[28] In Philadelphia, 60 percent of all capital cases went without proper investigation or experienced attorneys.[29] In fact, a March 2003 report prepared for the Pennsylvania Supreme Court by an appointed commission had such grave concerns about the quality of representation in that state that it recommended an overhaul of the entire system.[30] It also found that people of color were affected to a greater degree by the problems of indigent defense because of their overrepresentation in the criminal justice system. The concerns of racial bias led the commission to recommend a moratorium in the report it prepared on behalf of the court.[31]

In December 2002, at the request of the Georgia Supreme Court Chief Justice's Commission on Indigent Defense, the Spangenberg Group issued a 100-page report on the state's failure to provide adequate representation for indigent people. Supplementing that report was a series of recommendations reported by the Commission on Indigent Defense. Although the recommendations did not focus specifically on needs in death penalty cases, they are applicable. Recommended reforms include: increasing funding for indigent defense, including shifting funding from the counties to the state; establishing multi-county public defender offices that would operate throughout a judicial circuit; adopting principles to govern the system of providing legal services to indigent criminal defendants; and adopting performance standards for defense attorneys.[32]

According to a report just released by the Common Sense Foundation of North Carolina, Life and Death Lottery: Capital Defendants and the Lawyers Who Fail Them, no fewer than 35 prisoners currently on death row in North Carolina—one out of every six—were represented by lawyers who had been disbarred, suspended or otherwise disciplined by the state.[33] That list did not include at least four prisoners who had already been executed. One of those prisoners was Michael McDougall, who had been represented by Jerry Paul. A judge reviewing the case found that Paul "acted unethically or even criminally" while defending his client.[34]

The problem of ineffective counsel for those on death row has been so pronounced that two Supreme Court Justices have publicly remarked on it, an unusual practice for high court judges. Supreme Court Justice Ruth Bader Ginsburg said, *"I have yet to see a death case among the dozens coming to the Supreme Court on eve-of-execution stay applications in which the defendant was well represented at trial . . . People who are well represented at trial do not get the death penalty."*[35] Justice Sandra Day O'Connor expressed similar concerns when addressing the Minnesota Women Lawyers, stating, *"[perhaps] it's time to look at minimum standards for appointed counsel in death cases and adequate compensation for appointed counsel when they are used."*[36]

When a person faces the death penalty, effective counsel can mean the difference between life and death. A system that executes people based on their inability to afford adequate representation rather than the nature of the crime committed is both arbitrary and discriminatory. Justice and fairness require that every defendant in a capital case receive a competent and zealous defense.

Discrimination Against the Poor

Whether the death penalty is biased against poor people, apart from the issue of incompetent counsel and inadequate defense resources, has not been thoroughly studied. However, over 90 percent of those sentenced to death are indigent. There are a handful of middle-class defendants, and upper-class defendants are virtually non-existent. Although not the focus of the study, a 2002 Maryland study on the death penalty found that 90 percent of the people on death row in Maryland were indigent.[37]

The Economic Background of the Victim

The issue of how much the victim's socioeconomic status affects the result of the case has not been widely studied either.

However, in one study commissioned by the Nebraska legislature, The Disposition of Nebraska Capital and Non-Capital Homicide Cases (1973–1999): A Legal and Empirical Analysis, researcher David Baldus found that defendants who killed victims with high socioeconomic status were almost six times more likely to be sentenced to death than those whose victims had low socioeconomic status.[38] According to Baldus, "this is a classic example of disparate treatment, that is, people are being treated differently on the basis of factors that have nothing whatever to do with their culpability but rather on the socioeconomic status of the victim that they have killed. It's a system-wide influence that exists in both the major urban counties and it exists in greater Nebraska, and you can see it in the decisions of both the prosecutors and the sentencing judges."

The Death Penalty Is Arbitrary

Geographic and Racial Disparities

Where the crime occurs and whom one kills, as much as the nature of the crime, are determining factors in who receives a death sentence. Death penalty statutes differ widely from state to state. Some states, such as Florida, have many aggravating factors that make a defendant eligible for the death penalty. Other states, like New Hampshire, have fewer. In Maryland, felony murder—an unintentional murder that occurs in the course of a serious crime—is not a capital crime, but in New Jersey it is. In 22 states, people who commit homicides while under the age of 18 are eligible for capital punishment, but in the other 16 death penalty states juveniles are ineligible for the death penalty. The federal government does not have the juvenile death penalty.

Of the more than 800 executions carried out since 1977, 82 percent were carried out by only ten states: Alabama, Arkansas, Florida, Georgia, Louisiana, Missouri, Oklahoma, South Carolina, Texas, and Virginia.[40] Texas and Virginia alone accounted for more than half of those executions. While Texas has executed over 300 people in the past 27 years, a number significantly higher than any other state, 12 other death penalty states performed only one, or no, executions in that time.

Disparities within States

However, even within the same state, some counties or municipalities bring more capital cases than others. The prevalence of geographic disparity in the death penalty system has been frequently demonstrated over the past two decades, including a 1995 survey by the *New York Times* and a 1999 survey by *USA Today*.

USA Today reported that the odds that a convicted killer will be sentenced to death vary dramatically from county to county within many states.[41] For example, Hamilton County, Ohio, which includes Cincinnati, had 50 people on death row at the time but prosecutors in Franklin County had sent only 11 people to death row, even though the county's

> "When the punishment of death is inflicted in a trivial number of the cases in which it is legally available, the conclusion is virtually inescapable that it is being inflicted arbitrarily. Indeed, it smacks of little more than a lottery system."
>
> —Justice Brennan from his concurrence in Furman v. Georgia, 1972.[39]

Race of Victims in Death Penalty Cases

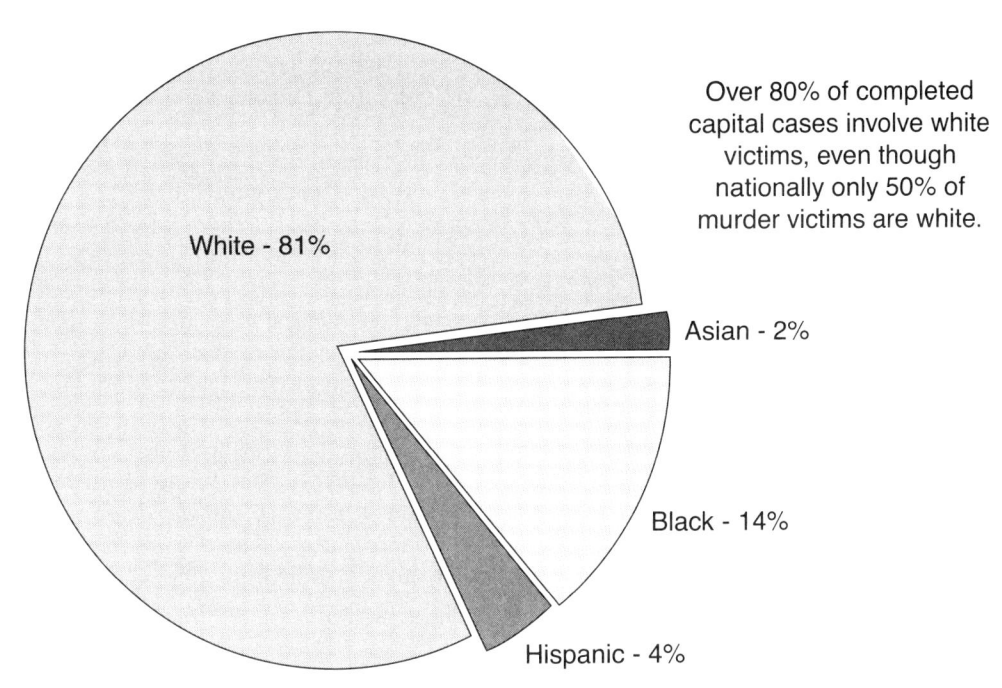

White - 81%
Asian - 2%
Black - 14%
Hispanic - 4%

Over 80% of completed capital cases involve white victims, even though nationally only 50% of murder victims are white.

This information is taken from the Death Penalty Information Center, http://www.deathpenaltyinfo.org/article.php?scid=5&did=184#inmaterace.

population was 14 percent larger than Hamilton's and it had twice as many murders. In New York, accused killers were more likely to face a death sentence if the crime occurred outside of New York City and its suburbs, even though 83 percent of the state's murder convictions come from that region.

Tiny Baldwin County of Georgia also showed signs of geographic disparity. Although the population of the county was approximately 42,000, it had five people on death row, a number that exceeded that of Fulton County, population 722,400. The study concluded that, "the willingness of the local prosecutor to seek the death penalty seems to play by far the most significant role in determining who will eventually be sentenced to death."

Harris County Texas, where Houston is located, accounts for 140, nearly a third, of the state's death row inmates. Prosecutor Johnny Holmes has a special death squad that tries a capital case about every three weeks. Dallas, with a higher murder rate, has only 37 people on death row.[42]

In the fall of 2002, the University of Maryland released a comprehensive report on a study that examined all the death eligible cases in Maryland from 1978 (the year Maryland reinstated the death penalty following *Gregg*) to 1999.[43] The study documented geographic and racial disparities in the prosecution of death cases in Maryland, concluding that prosecutorial discretion was a key factor in determining who receives the death penalty. For example, prosecutors in Baltimore

County were 13 times more likely to seek the death penalty in an eligible case than those in Baltimore City, the state's largest city. Baltimore County was also found to be five times more likely to seek the death penalty in an eligible case than was Montgomery County and three times more likely than was Anne Arundel County.

In addition to the Maryland study, the Nebraska Crime Commission found that prosecutors in the urban counties of Omaha and Lincoln were more likely to seek the death penalty and refuse plea bargains than those in the more rural counties of Nebraska.[44] The study found that over the past 16 years, the odds were 2.4 times as great that prosecutors in a major urban county would seek the death penalty than those in a rural area.

Studies from both Pennsylvania and North Carolina demonstrated similar disparities. Of the people sentenced to death in Pennsylvania, more than half came from Philadelphia County, where people were sentenced to death at a rate 11 times greater than were those in the Harrisburg area, even though Philadelphia only accounts for 14 percent of the state's total population.[45] Two North Carolina counties accounted for 40 and 42 percent of all capital cases respectively. People who lived in those counties were 2.8 times more likely to face capital charges than those in the county with the lowest rate.[46]

Race of the Victim

Study after study has shown that people who kill whites are more likely to get a death sentence than people who kill blacks. In some places, blacks who kill whites are the most likely to end up on death row. This discrepancy is revealed even more when one considers that 86 percent of white victims were killed by whites and 94 percent of black victims were killed by blacks.[47]

The University of Maryland study found the probability that a state's attorney will seek the death penalty is 1.6 times higher when the victim is white than for a black homicide victim, even after considering case characteristics and jurisdiction issues. Blacks who kill whites are 2.5 times more likely to be sentenced to death than whites who kill whites, and 3.5 times more likely than blacks who kill blacks."[48] The two counties with the highest incidence of charging capital cases and sentencing defendants to death—Baltimore and Hartford—are also the two jurisdictions with the highest instance of white victim and black defendant homicides.

In 2001, a report released by the New Jersey Supreme Court found disturbing evidence regarding race and the death penalty.[49] The report stated, "There is unsettling statistical evidence indicating that cases involving killers of white victims are more likely to progress to a penalty phase than cases involving killers of African-American victims." The American Civil Liberties Union of Virginia released a report in 2000 that found race to be a controlling factor in the way the death penalty is administered.[50] The ACLU's study, which was based on 20 years worth of data, found that capital murder defendants in Virginia who murdered whites were more likely to be sentenced to death than those who murdered blacks.

In addition, according to a report by the Texas Defender Service, of the 301 prisoners executed in the State of Texas between 1982 and 2003, 78 percent were put to death for crimes involving white victims. In 21 percent of the cases, a black defendant was convicted of killing a white person. Only 11 percent of defendants sentenced to death were convicted of killing black men, even though black men accounted for 23 percent of murder victims in Texas.[51]

Findings by the General Accounting Office (GAO)

These recent studies confirm what a study conducted by the General Accounting Office (GAO) found more than a decade ago. The GAO reviewed 28 empirical studies on race and the death penalty from around the country. It found that in 82 percent of the studies, the race of the victim was a decisive factor in determining the likelihood of receiving the death penalty. Those who murder whites were more likely to be sentenced to death than those who murdered blacks.[52]

One of the most compelling studies reviewed was the Baldus study, which examined the death penalty in Georgia. After reviewing 2,400 cases over a seven-year period, the study concluded that defendants whose victims were white were more than four times more likely to receive the death penalty than others who committed crimes of similar severity. This study was submitted as evidence by the defendant in the case of *McCleskey v Kemp*.[53] The Court did not dispute the accuracy of the findings that in Georgia, defendants who killed whites were four times more likely to be sentenced to death than those who killed non-whites, but it ruled that in order for a defendant to make a successful appeal he or she would have to provide "exceptionally clear proof" that the decision makers had acted with discriminatory intent in his or her case. The GAO found the Baldus study to be valid and it found studies contradicting it to be invalid.

Dr. Issac Unah, author of the North Carolina study that found that defendants whose victims are white are 3.5 times more likely to be sentenced to death, came to the

Almost All Prosecutors Responsible for the Death Penalty Are White

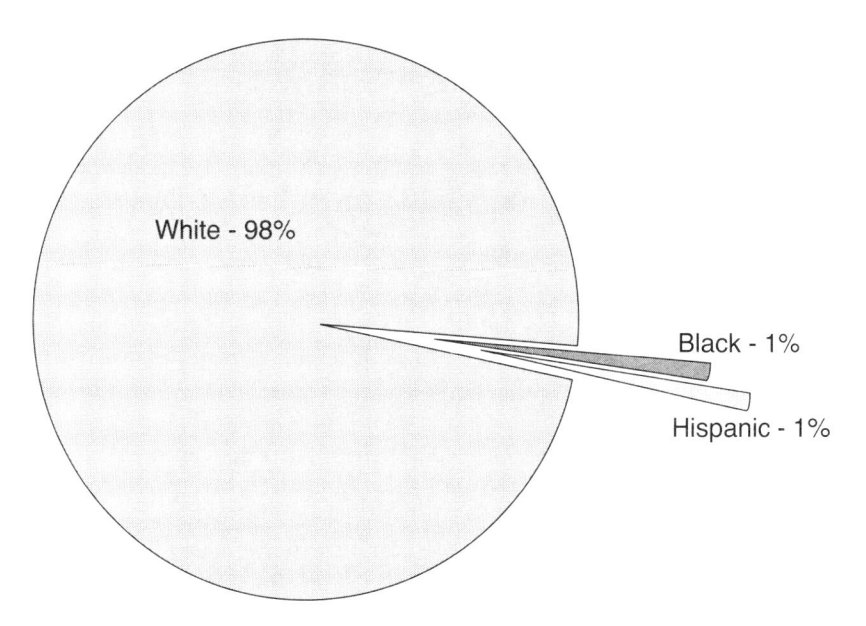

- White - 98%
- Black - 1%
- Hispanic - 1%

Race of District Attorneys in Death Penalty Cases

STATE	White DAs	Black DAs	Hispanic DAs	STATE	White DAs	Black DAs	Hispanic DAs
Alabama	39	1	0	Nebraska	89	0	0
Arizona	15	0	1	Nevada	17	0	0
Arkansas	24	0	0	N. Hampshire	10	0	0
California	55	0	3	New Jersey	20	1	0
Colorado	21	0	1	New Mexico	9	0	5
Connecticut	12	0	0	New York	61	1	0
Delaware	3	0	0	N. Carolina	37	2	0
Florida	19	0	1	Ohio	87	1	0
Georgia	45	1	0	Oklahoma**	26	0	0
Idaho	44	0	0	Oregon	36	0	0
Illinois	102	0	0	Pennsylvania	67	0	0
Indiana	90	1	0	South Carolina	15	1	0
Kansas	104	1	0	South Dakota	66	0	0
Kentucky	56	0	0	Tennessee	31	0	0
Louisiana	39	1	0	Texas	137	0	11
Maryland	23	2	0	Utah	29	0	0
Mississippi	21	1	0	Virginia	113	8	0
Missouri	115	0	0	Washington	39	0	0
Montana**	56	0	0	Wyoming	22	0	0
				TOTAL	1794	22	22
					97.5%	1.2%	1.2%

The information for these graphs was taken from the Death Penalty Information Center's "The Death Penalty In Black and White: Whose lives, Who Decides" http://www.deathpenaltyinfo.org/article.php?scid=45&did=539

sobering observation that, "[i]n sum, no matter what analyses we have performed, and no matter what stage of the process we have examined, the fact that the homicide victim is a white person turns out to operate as a "silent aggravating circumstance" that makes death significantly more likely to be imposed."[54]

The Role of Prosecutors and Judges

One of the likely factors contributing to the racial discrepancies is the lack of diversity among the decision makers. Almost all of the prosecutors making the key decision about whether to seek the death penalty are white. Professor Jeffrey Pokorak of St. Mary's University School of Law collected data regarding the race and gender of the government officials empowered to prosecute criminal offenses, and, in particular, capital offenses, from all 38 states that use the death penalty. The study was concluded in February 1998. It revealed that only one percent of the District Attorneys in death penalty states are black, and only one percent are Hispanic. The remaining 97.5 percent are white, and almost all of them are male.[55]

Chattahoochee County, Georgia, a county where prosecutors vigorously pursue the death penalty, presents a microcosm of the all-white judicial process. An evaluation of the death penalty cases in that county revealed that while black people were 65 percent of homicide victims, 85 percent of the capital trials were for white-victim cases. In potentially capital cases, the district attorney sought the death penalty on average 34.3 percent of the time when the victim was white, but only 5.8 percent of the time when the victim was black. This percentage broke down further: the district attorney sought the death penalty 38.7 percent of the time when the defendant was black and the victim white, 32.4 percent when both defendant and victim were white, 5.9 percent when both defendant and victim were black, and never when the defendant was white and the victim black.[56]

Stephen Bright, of the Southern Center for Human Rights in Atlanta, a prominent capital litigator, illustrated the way that race affects outcomes in criminal cases in Chattahoochee County:

> [A]n investigation of all murder cases prosecuted . . . from 1973 to 1990 revealed that in cases involving the murder of a white person, prosecutors often met with the victim's family and discussed whether to seek the death penalty. In a case involving the murder of the daughter of a prominent white contractor, the prosecutor contacted the contractor and asked him if he wanted to seek the death penalty. When the contractor replied in the affirmative, the prosecutor said that was all he needed to know. He obtained the death penalty at trial. He was rewarded with a contribution of $5,000 from the contractor when he successfully ran for judge in the next election. The contribution was the largest received by the District Attorney. There were other cases in which the District Attorney issued press releases announcing that he was seeking the death penalty after meeting with the family of a white victim. But prosecutors failed to meet with African-Americans whose family members had been murdered to determine what sentence they wanted. Most were not even notified that the case had been resolved. As a result of these practices, although African-Americans were the victims of 65 percent of the homicides in the Chattahoochee Judicial District, 85 percent of the capital cases in that circuit were white victim cases.[57]

Jury Selection

Another area where race plays a role is jury selection. At least one in five of all black prisoners executed since 1976 were convicted by all-white juries. Although the Supreme Court has ruled that jurors cannot be excluded on the basis of race, certain prosecutors have been found to remove African-Americans from juries believing that they are less likely to impose the death penalty than whites. During the 1997 election campaign for Philadelphia's District Attorney, it was revealed that one of the candidates had produced, as an assistant district attorney, a training video for new prosecutors in which he instructed them about whom to exclude from the jury, noting that "young black women are very bad" on the jury for a prosecutor, and that "blacks from low-income areas are less likely to convict." The training tape also instructed the new recruits on how to hide the racial motivation for their jury strikes.[58]

African-American jurors who find themselves to be the only person of color on a jury are sometimes pressured to convict or impose a death sentence. Both Louis Jones and Walanzo Robinson were convicted by juries composed of eleven whites and one black. Both men were sentenced to death. In both cases, the sole black juror later alleged that he or she was pressured to follow other jurors and change their vote.[59] Similarly, Abu-Ali

Percentage of Cases in Which Death Sentence Was Sought:
in Chattahoochee Judicial District, by Race of Defendant and Victim

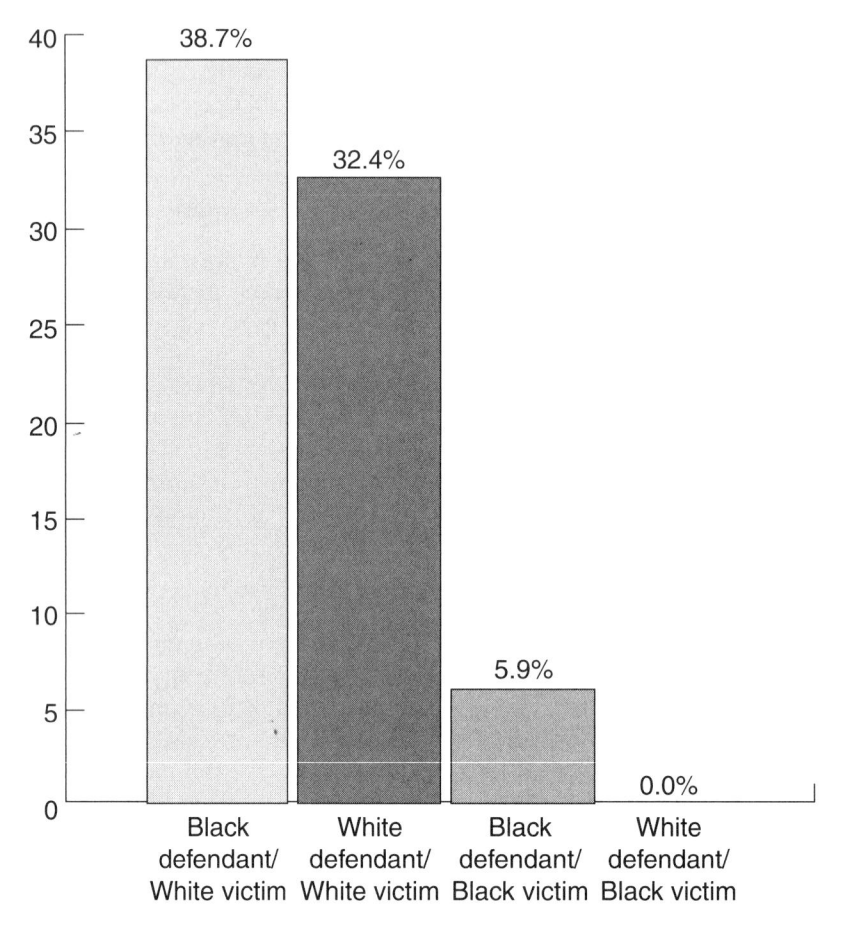

- Black defendant/White victim: 38.7%
- White defendant/White victim: 32.4%
- Black defendant/Black victim: 5.9%
- White defendant/Black victim: 0.0%

Taken from Chattahoochee Judicial District: BUCKLE OF DEATH BELT: The Death Penalty in Microcosm. Death Penalty Information Center
http://www.deathpenaltyinfo.org/article.php?scid=45&did=540

Abdur'Rahman, also African-American, was sentenced to death by a jury composed of eleven whites and one black, even though his county's population was approximately 23 percent black. The Supreme Court heard Abdur'Rahman's case on December 10, 2002; however, the case was dismissed without a ruling and returned to the lower court. Abdur'Rahman is scheduled to be executed in Tennessee on June 18, 2003.[60]

These three cases are not unique. According to a federal court decision in Alabama reviewing a death penalty case, the Tuscaloosa District Attorney's Office had a "standard operating procedure ... to use the peremptory challenges to strike as many blacks as possible from the venires in cases involving serious crimes."[61] In Philadelphia, prosecutors were shown to have struck 52 percent of potential black jurors, but only 23 percent of other potential jurors.[62]

Unfortunately, there has been very little progress in addressing the overt racial disparities that continue to affect the imposition of the death penalty. Only recently have responses begun to materialize. The Racial Justice Act, which allows a capital defendant to use statistical evidence to show that race influenced the decision to seek the death penalty in his or her case, was twice passed by the United States House of Representatives, but was defeated each time by the Senate. In 1998, Kentucky became the first state to pass a Racial Justice Act. Other states have tried, but none have been successful at getting such legislation passed.

Disparity in the Federal Death Penalty

Racial bias in the death penalty is not limited to the state systems. A Department of Justice report found racial disparities in the federal death penalty.[63] The report revealed that, in the past five years, 80 percent of the cases submitted by federal prosecutors for review involved racial minorities as defendants. In more than half of those cases, the defendant was black. Currently, 19 out of the 25 prisoners on federal death row are people of color. Attorney General John Ashcroft contends that there is no evidence of racial discrimination in the federal death penalty, but in spite of the fact that he promised Congress that he would commission a follow-up study on these disparities, as of 2003, three years after the initial report was released, the study has still not been completed.

Despite the strong evidence of racial disparities in the federal death penalty system, in March 2003, Louis Jones, who was African-American, was put to death for the murder of a white woman. On the day of his execution Senator Russell Feingold stated, "Today, more than two years after the United States Department of Justice released a survey showing geographic and racial disparities in the federal death penalty, we still do not have an explanation why who lives and who dies in the federal system appears to relate to the color the defendant's skin . . . . Attorney General John Ashcroft pledged to continue this study, but we still await the results . . . Today, with the execution of Mr. Jones, our federal criminal justice system has taken a step backward. Our goals of fairness and equal justice under law were not met . . ."[64]

The influence of race on the death penalty is pervasive, to say the least, influencing all aspects of a capital trial. Race has proven to act as an insidious aggravating circumstance when the death penalty is being considered, and this bias is unacceptable. Whether you favor the death penalty or not, there is no looking past the fact that the race of the defendant, victim, prosecutor, and jury play an overwhelming role in determining who will receive a death sentence.

Conclusion

Governor Ryan's decision in 2000 to impose a moratorium on executions in his state, until he could be sure that innocent people were not going to die, opened the door to confronting the problems in Illinois' death penalty system. In one of his last acts as governor, he commuted the sentences of 163 death row prisoners to life in prison and pardoned four others. At a speech at Northwestern University he said, "Our capital system is haunted by the demon of error: error in determining guilt and error determining who among the guilty deserves to die."[65]

Although his successor Governor Rod Blagojevich criticized Governor Ryan's broad grant of clemency, he announced in April 2003 that he would continue the moratorium. "The decision for me on an issue like lifting the moratorium won't be driven by what happens in the state Senate or the House," Blagojevich said. "It will be driven by whether or not the system in Illinois has been reformed in such a way where we can have no doubt that we're (not) going to make any mistakes. And it begs the question of whether we can ever get to a point in Illinois that we can feel comfortable with that."[66]

The Illinois example has prompted other jurisdictions to examine their death penalty systems. In May 2002, then Maryland Governor Paris Glendenning imposed a moratorium on executions until the University of Maryland death penalty study was completed. In January of 2003, the study was released and demonstrated racial and geographic bias in the implementation of the death penalty. Unfortunately, his successor, Governor Robert Ehrlich, lifted the moratorium upon taking office in January 2003. The Maryland legislature failed to pass a moratorium bill by one vote in the Senate and had sufficient votes to pass it in the Assembly, although Governor Ehrlich had said he would veto the measure. However, he has promised to study the issue and has asked Lieutenant Governor Michael Steele to be in charge of the study.

The North Carolina Senate passed a moratorium bill in May and the house will take the issue up in June. Across the country, hundreds of local city councils, businesses and religious organizations have passed resolutions in support of a moratorium and more than two million have signed petitions.

This momentum demonstrates the growing awareness of systemic problems in the death penalty system. For many, time is running out. Thousands face execution now, many of whom received death sentences at trials plagued with error, tainted by bias and represented by unqualified lawyers. Some of those people are innocent. Based on past trends, the number of innocent people currently on death row likely exceeds 100. Equity demands that executions cease until the systems can be thoroughly examined and those with claims of innocence can have a fair day in court.

The ACLU remains skeptical that the unfairness that has plagued the death penalty for so long can ever be completely eliminated. But as long as the death penalty remains public policy basic decency requires all citizens of good will to try.

In 1994, conservative Justice Harry A. Blackmun, who had voted with the dissent in the *Furman* case, announced that he regretted the decision he made when he voted with the majority to reinstate the death penalty in *Gregg*. He wrote, "Twenty years have passed since this Court declared that the death penalty must be imposed fairly, and with reasonable consistency, or not at all, and, despite the effort of the states and courts to devise legal formulas and procedural rules to meet this daunting challenge, the death penalty remains fraught with arbitrariness, discrimination, caprice, and mistake."[67]

The Supreme Court in *Furman* held that death penalty laws must be narrowly drafted to punish the worst offenders. Yet factors like the quality of legal representation, class, geography, and race powerfully influence the outcome in capital cases. These factors are unrelated to the severity of the crime or the individual merits of the defendant and should not determine who lives and who dies. The same arbitrariness and discrimination present at the time of the *Furman* decision persist today.

Like the Court did in *Furman*, states and the federal government must temporarily halt executions while necessary changes are made.

Notes

1. Furman v. Georgia, 408 U.S. 238, 239–40 (1972).
2. Id. at 309-310 (Stewart, J., concurring).
3. Gregg v. Georgia, 428 U.S. 153, 207 (1976).
4. Death Penalty Information Center at http://deathpenalty-info.org/article.php?scid=8&did=146 and http://deathpenaltyinfo.org/article.php?did=205&scid=27.
5. See note 1 at 367–68 (White, J., concurring).
6. The Death Penalty Information Center keeps an updated tab of executions and demographics of death row populations. For additional information, please visit http://www.deathpenaltyinfo.org.
7. Id.
8. Jim Suhr, "Students Get Man a New Trial: Journalism Class Uncovers the Lies in Death Row Case," Houston Chronical, August 11, 2001; Douglas Holt & Flynn McRoberts, "Porter Fully Savors 1st Taste of Freedom: Judge Releases Man Once Set for Execution," Chicago Tribune, February 6, 1999.
9. For a complete list of those exonerated from death row, visit: http://www.deathpenaltyinfo.org/article.php?scid=6&did=110.
10. Definition taken from "Innocence and the Death Penalty: assessing the Danger of Mistaken Executions," Staff Report by the Subcommittee on Civil and Constitutional Rights, Committee on the Judiciary, One Hundred Third Congress, First Session, Issued October 21, 1993. Find report at: http://www.deathpenalty-info.org/article.php?scid=45&did=535hompson.
11. See note 9, "Released from Death Row, Possible or Probable Innocence," http://www.deathpenaltyinfo.org/article.php?scid=6&did=111#Released ASK.
12. Id.
13. CNN/USA Today Gallup Poll Release, June 30, 2000.
14. Leonard Pitts Jr., "In Death Penalty Cases, the Truth Won't Set You Free," Houston Chronical, March 17, 2003; John Aloysium Farrell, "Court Bars DNA Test in 1981 Killing, Bid to Investigate Va. Execution Fails," The Boston Globe, November 2, 2002.
15. Jim Dwyer, "Gore's Ghost of a Campaign," New York Daily News, June 25, 2000.
16. See note 9.
17. Steve McViker & Roma Khanna, "All HPD Cases will be Purged from State, U.S. DNA Databases," Houston Chronical, March 25, 2003.
18. American Bar Association, "Death Penalty Symposium: A Call to Action: A Moratorium on Executions: The Imposition of the Death Penalty is Fraught with Error: Where Do We Go From Here?" New York Law Review, Spring 2002.
19. Testimony of William Delahunt (D-MA) in support of the Innocence Protection Act before the Judiciary Committee of the U.S. House of Representatives, June 20, 2000.
20. Barbara Shelly, "A system in need of repair," The Kansas City Star, February 8, 2003.
21. See note 1 at 251-252 (Douglas, J., concurring).
22. Gideon v. Wainwright, 372 U.S. 335 (1963).
23. Stephen B. Bright, "Turning Celebrated Principles into Reality," The Champion,

January/February 2003, at 6 referring to Mickens v. Taylor, 122 S.Ct. 1237 (2002) and Bell v. Cone, 122 S.Ct. 1843 (2002).
24. Id.
25. The Justice Project, "Prosecutorial Misconduct and Ineffective Counsel: The Case of Delma Banks, Jr.," profile on Delma Banks at http://justice.policy.net/proactive/newsroom/release.vtml?id=33663.
26. American Bar Association. Guidelines for the Appointment and Performance of Defense Counsel in Death Penalty Cases. Revised Edition. February 2003. See http://www.abanet.org/death-penalty.
27. "Lethal Indifference: The Fatal Combination of Incompetent Attorneys and Unaccountable Courts in Texas Death Penalty Appeals," The Texas Defender Service, December 3, 2002. Report available at: http://justice.policy.net/proactive/newsroom/release.vtml?id=32477.
28. State v. Melson, 772 S.W. 2d 417, 421 (Tenn. 1989).
29. Dieter, Richard C., "Killing For Votes: The Danger of Politicizing the Death Penalty," Death Penalty Information Center," October 1995.
30. "Final Report of the Pennsylvania Supreme Court Committee on Racial and Gender Bias in the Justice System," March 4, 2003, at http://www.courts.state.pa.us/Index/Supreme/biasreport.htm.
31. Id. At 221.
32. Georgia Judicial Branch, Indigent Defense Commission Reports, at http://www.georgiacourts.org/aoc/idreports.html.
33. Common Sense Foundation of North Carolina, "Life and Death Lottery: Capital Defendants and the Lawyers Who Fail Them," October 2002.
34. Liz Chandler, "Lawyers, Inadequate Defense Cited in a Third of Death Case Reversals," The Charlotte Observer, September 11, 2000.
35. Joseph L. Rauh Lecture at the David A. Clarke School of Law of the University of the District of Columbia, "In Pursuit of the Public Good: Lawyers Who Care," April 9, 2001.
36. Justice Sandra Day O'Connor, Remarks at the Meeting of the Minnesota Women Lawyers, July 2, 2001.
37. The University of Maryland, "An Empirical Analysis of Maryland's Death Sentencing System With Respect to Race and Legal Jurisdiction," January 2003 at http://justice.policy.net/proactive/newsroom/release.vtml?id=32881.
38. David Baldus, "The Disposition of Nebraska Capital and Non-Capital Homicide Cases (1973–1999): A Legal and Empirical Analysis," Commissioned by the State of Nebraska, October 2001 at http://justice.policy.net/proactive/newsroom/release.vtml?id=23960.
39. See note 1 at 293 (Brennan, J., concurring).
40. The U.S. Justice Department, "The Federal Death Penalty System: A Statistical Survey (1988–2000)," September 12, 2000 at http://justice.policy.net/proactive/newsroom/release.vtml?id=18720.
41. Gary Fields, Richard Willing, "Geography of the Death Penalty," USA Today, December 20, 1999.
42. Id.
43. See note 37.
44. Pam Belluck, "Nebraska Said To Use Death Penalty Unequally," The New York Times, August 2, 2001.
45. See note 30.
46. Jack Boger; Isaac Unah, "Race and the Death Penalty in North Carolina An Empirical Analysis: 1993\–1997," University of North Carolina, April 16, 2001. Report available at: http://www.

deathpenaltyinfo.org/article.php?scid=19&did=246.
47. The Death Penalty Information Center maintains statistics on racial disparity in application of the death penalty. For additional information, please visit http://www.deathpenaltyinfo.org/article.php?did=105&scid=5.
48. See note 37.
49. Judge David S. Baime, "Report to the Supreme Court: Systemic Proportionality Review Project," New Jersey, August 13, 2001. Report available at: http://justice.policy.net/proactive/newsroom/release.vtml?id=24361.
50. American Civil Liberties of Virginia, "Unequal, Unfair, and Irreversible: The Death Penalty in Virginia," December 2000. Report available at: http://members.aol.com/aclu-va/.
51. Texas Defender Service, "A State of Denial: Texas Justice and the Death Penalty," October 2000. Report available at http://www.deathpenaltyinfo.org/article.php?did=221&scid=19.
52. U.S. General Accounting Office, "Death Penalty Sentencing: Research Indicates Patterns of Racial Disparities," February 1990.
53. McCleskey v. Kemp 481 U.S. 279 (1987).
54. See note 46.
55. Jeffrey Pokorak, "Probing the Capital Prosecutor's Perspective: Race and Gender of the Discretionary Actors," Cornell Law Review, February 1998.
56. David Margolick, "In Land of Death Penalty, Accusations of Racial Bias," The New York Times, July 10, 1991.
57. Stephen Bright, "Discrimination, Death and Denial: The Tolerance of Racial Discrimination in Infliction of the Death Penalty," 35 Santa Clara Law Review, 433, 453-54 (1995) (emphasis added).
58. Dick Dieter, "The Death Penalty in Black and White: Who Lives Who Dies," Death Penalty Information Center, 1998. Available at: http://www.deathpenaltyinfo.org/article.php?scid=45&did=539.
59. Amnesty International, "U.S. Death By Discrimination: The Continuing Role of Race in Capital Cases" April 24, 2003. Available at: http://justice.policy.net/proactive/newsroom/release.vtml?id=34201.
60. Id.
61. See note 58 citing Jackson v. Thigpen, 752 F. Supp. 1551, 1554 (N.D. Ala. 1990), rev'd in part and aff'd in part, sub nom. Jackson v. Herring, 42 F.3d 1350 (11th Cir. 1995).
62. See note 58.
63. See note 40.
64. Statement of Senator Russell Feingold on the Federal Execution of Louis Jones, Before the U.S. Senate, March 18, 2003.
65. Jeff Flock, "'Blanket Communication' Empties Illinois Death Row," CNN News, January 13, 2003.
66. Rick Pearson, "Governor says ban to stay on death penalty but gambling may be expanded," The Chicago Tribune, April 24, 2003.
67. Callins v. Collins, 114 S. Ct. 1127, 1129 (1994) (Blackman, J., dissenting).

"Invisible" Latino Youth Find Injustice in the Justice System

Gross Disparities Tip of the Iceberg

Francisco A. Villarruel and Nancy E. Walker

During the 2000 presidential campaign, both political parties drew upon the motto of the Children's Defense Fund: "Leave no child behind." The stark reality is, however, that too many Latino youth are being left behind—behind bars, where they become "invisible."

Yet, while Latino youth are often overlooked, they are overrepresented at every stage of the justice system. Compared to non-Latino White youth, Latino youth are arrested more often, detained more often, waived to criminal court as adults more often, and incarcerated more often and for longer periods of time, even when charged with the same crimes.

Our report, *¿Dónde está la justicia? A Call to Action on Behalf of Latino and Latina Youth in the U.S. Justice System*, documented that Latino youth in Los Angeles County in 1998 were 1.8 times as likely as White youth to be arrested for felony offenses. When charged with a drug offense, a Latino youth was 13 times more likely than a White youth with a similar history to be sentenced to prison—and likely to be incarcerated, on average, nearly five months longer for the same drug offense.

According to Human Rights Watch, Latino youth were confined in institutional placements at higher rates than Whites in 39 states during 2000. Among those states, the Latino rate was two to three times the White rate in nine states; three to six times the rates of White youth in eight states; and seven to 17 times the rates of White youth in four states. Further, between 1983 and 1991, the percentage of Latino youth in public detention centers increased by 84 percent, compared to an eight percent increase for White youth and a 46 percent increase for youth overall.

Reprinted from *Focus Magazine*. March/April 2003. Copyright © 2003 by Joint Center for Political and Economic Studies, www.jointcenter.org Reprinted by permission.

While the available data indicate that there are gross disparities in the system, what we see is only the tip of the iceberg. If the United States required a uniform procedure across jurisdictions for calculating the number of Latino youth at every stage of the justice system, the results would be even more disturbing.

For example, In *Masking the Divide: How Officially Reported Prison Statistics Distort the Racial and Ethnic Realities of Prison Growth*, Barry Holman reported that separating race from ethnicity results in dramatic differences in prison demographics. With more than 47,000 Latino prisoners counted nationally as White in 1985, it appeared that there were 4 percent more White prisoners (52 percent) than non-White (48 percent), according to the report issued by the Alexandria, VA-based National Center on Institutions and Alternatives. However, when Latinos were removed from the White category, non-White prisoners outnumbered White prisoners by 15 percent. Moreover, between 1985 and 1997 the divide between the percent of the prison population that was White and non-White doubled to 30 percent.

National, state, and local data collection systems mask the divide in various ways. First, Latino youth are seriously undercounted in state databases because race is not separated from ethnicity. As a result, approximately 96 percent of Latinos are categorized as "White" or "other," thus inflating the number of "White" youth who are recorded as incarcerated and seriously masking the overrepresentation of Latino youth in the system.

Take Florida as an example: Latino youth constitute 15 percent of the state's population. The state's justice system intake forms provide five racial categories ("White," "African-American," "Native American," "Asian," and "Other"), but no category for ethnicity. Therefore, Latino youth are forced into one of the five racial categories provided by the state.

The result? Only 2 percent of individuals are categorized as "Other," with most Latinos disappearing into the "White" category. These youth thus become invisible in the state's databases.

In addition, states use different procedures for identifying Latino youth, so conducting cross-state comparisons becomes difficult, if not impossible. Arizona and New Mexico allow youth to categorize themselves, using both race and ethnicity as defining variables. California and North Carolina require corrections professionals to assign youth to racial categories, with no clear guidelines for including information on ethnicity. In California, some state workers report using skin tone as the defining variable. In Ohio, Latino youth are considered biracial, but ethnicity is not considered separately from race. As a result, Latinos become invisible in these systems, hidden in race categories that do not recognize Latino or Hispanic heritage.

Why is this problem important? First and foremost, it matters because current data collection systems seriously undercount Latino youth, thus inappropriately minimizing the magnitude of disproportionality and disparate treatment.

Also, the Latino population is growing rapidly, particularly its youth. Census data reveal that the Latino population in the U.S. grew by 58 percent from 1990 to 2000. Given these trends, it seems more likely that the problems associated with Latino youth in the justice system will increase rather than diminish.

In spite of this steady population growth, as Mart'n M. Ahumada, founding president of the National Association for Hispanic Education (NAHE), points out, "Latinos still lack the clout to tout and act upon that demographic distinction." With state-of-the art technology to manage information systems and an alleged embracing of cultural diversity, "it is incomprehensible that our juvenile justice system continues to distort data and condone unfair treatment of Latino youths," he adds.

In addition to the regular criminal justice system, the Immigration and Naturalization Service incarcerates thousands of Latino youth each year, often for lengthy periods of time under punitive conditions, even though in most instances they are not charged with any crime other than being in the United States without proper documentation.

Example: Alfredo Lopez Sanchez, a 16-year-old from Guatemala, was locked alone in a hotel room for five weeks with no one to talk to, no change of clothes, and nothing to read while the INS worked to deport him. Alfredo had never been charged with any crime, but he was held in jails and other

Rate of Confinement in Juvenile Detention Facilities by Race

State	White	Black	Latino	Black/White Ratio	Latino/White Ratio	State	White	Black	Latino	Black/White Ratio	Latino/White Ratio
AL	112	242	96	2.2	0.9	MT	128	434	245	3.4	1.9
AK	111	316	302	2.8	2.7	NE	222	1145	465	5.2	2.1
AZ	80	357	139	4.5	1.7	NV	163	473	126	2.9	0.8
AR	94	283	112	3.0	1.2	NH	129	551	205	4.3	1.6
CA	100	502	169	5.0	1.7	NJ	42	377	109	9.1	2.6
CO	121	453	296	3.7	2.5	NM	73	234	118	3.2	1.6
CT	56	334	208	6.0	3.8	NY	82	385	158	4.7	1.9
DE	23	127	15	5.5	0.6	NC	83	196	45	2.4	0.5
DC	7	51	9	7.0	1.2	ND	102	381	687	3.7	6.7
FL	141	337	101	2.4	0.7	OH	92	371	185	4.0	2.0
GA	135	314	72	2.3	0.5	OK	136	306	114	2.2	0.8
HI	61	68	88	1.1	1.5	OR	147	413	299	2.8	2.0
ID	156	263	179	1.7	1.1	PA	115	687	515	6.0	4.5
IL	89	285	67	3.2	0.8	RI	94	584	226	6.2	2.4
IN	143	489	196	3.4	1.4	SC	111	269	64	2.4	0.6
IA	138	762	275	5.5	2.0	SD	181	2667	1283	14.8	7.1
KS	117	587	210	5.0	1.8	TN	141	322	144	2.3	1.0
KY	120	470	244	3.9	2.0	TX	105	302	117	2.9	1.1
LA	82	372	55	4.5	0.7	UT	145	705	240	4.9	1.7
ME	125	272	279	2.2	2.2	VT	74	646	436	8.8	5.9
MD	73	261	79	3.6	1.1	VA	114	397	149	3.5	1.3
MA	113	393	276	3.5	2.4	WA	110	502	248	4.6	2.3
MI	89	369	647	4.1	7.2	WV	105	398	361	3.8	3.4
MN	97	491	198	5.0	2.0	WI	72	629	222	8.7	3.1
MS	126	233	224	1.8	1.8	WY	249	1092	515	4.4	2.1
MO	130	388	131	3.0	1.0	**U.S.**	105	350	159	3.3	1.5

Rates per 100,000 youths under age 18.
Source: Human Rights Watch, 2002, calculated from Census 2000 data

detention facilities in four states. He was shackled and handcuffed to chains around his waist because, as an illegal alien, he had been labeled a "threat risk." Alfredo was moved eight times without prior notification of his lawyer.

Gross injustices for Latino youth are common in the criminal justice system, but it doesn't have to be this way. Bias and unfair practices can be changed, if the political will exists to do so. By methodically reforming their systems, increasing the use of alternatives to detention, adding bilingual and culturally competent staff, including families in system-wide reform, and addressing the issue of racial and ethnic overrepresentation head on, officials in Santa Cruz, California, significantly reduced the number of Latino youth in detention. Similarly, despite the fact that in 1994 there was stark overrepresentation of youth of color in Multnomah County (Portland), Oregon, by 2000 these disparities had declined to the point where youth of all races were equally likely to be detained, and the overall detention rate had dropped by two-thirds to 22 percent.

These examples demonstrate what can be done when politicians and criminal justice officials target racial and ethnic bias in the system. It is possible for the justice system to live up to its name.

Clarence Thomas and His Latino Clone: The Dollar's Global Death-Grip

Bush Must Co-sign for Turkey Money

Clarence Thomas is number one—*the* most backward, reactionary, bloodthirsty, Black people hater on the U.S. Supreme Court. The pride of Pinpoint, Georgia has added yet another superlative to dazzle the Black-appointed-faces-in-high-places crowd. In defiance of storerooms of evidence, bravely disregarding all standards of human decency, and with clear-eyed contempt for legal process, Thomas has registered a singular achievement as a representative of "the race," one he need not share with any of his colleagues on the High Court.

Alone among the nine Persons in Black, Thomas stood firm against a new hearing and possible new trial for a Black Texas man sentenced to death by a jury of nine whites, one Asian, one Hispanic and an African American in 1986. Lawyers for Thomas Miller-El presented damning evidence that the Dallas prosecutor's office pursued a *policy* of excluding minorities from juries. As the *New York Times* reported on February 13, 2002:

> Statements from several black prospective jurors who were struck from the Miller-El trial are included in the clemency petition, along with a 1986 article in *The Dallas Morning News* citing a 1963 internal memo in the district attorney's office advising prosecutors who were picking juries: "Do not take Jews, Negroes, Dagos, Mexicans or a member of any minority race on a jury, no matter how rich or how well educated."

That language was later dropped, but in the early 1970s the office used a training manual that included a memo from a

---

From *The Black Commentator*, No. 31, February 27, 2003 with permission.

Dallas County prosecutor, Jon Sparling, containing advice on jury selection: "You are not looking for any member of a minority group which may subject him to oppression—they almost always empathize with the accused."

The 1970s memo was still in circulation when Miller-El went on trial for the murder of a Holiday Inn employee.

Even a Supreme Fool could see that Miller-El had been victimized by a system programmed to kill Black defendants. The sheer weight of the evidence of racial manipulation of the jury selection process convinced Antonin Scalia, the Neanderthal who served as Thomas' early mentor on the court, to relent. There was "a close rather than a clear" chance that El-Miller might prevail in an appeal to the Fifth U.S. Circuit Court, said Scalia, according to the *Washington Post*. Justice Anthony Kennedy wrote for the majority.

> Justice Kennedy said Mr. Miller-El had clearly shown that the evidence of bias was at least debatable. Not only did the prosecution remove most black prospective jurors, but black members of the panel were subjected to more searching questioning on their views of the death penalty in what Justice Kennedy said could fairly be seen as an effort to build a record justifying their removal.

However, nothing could shake the resolve of the man from Pinpoint, quoted in the February 26 edition of the *New York Times*:

> The lone dissenter was Justice Clarence Thomas, who said Mr. Miller-El had not met even the relatively low threshold that the majority emphasized today. "The simple truth" is that proof of racial bias is circumstantial at best, lacking "anything remotely resembling clear and convincing evidence of purposeful discrimination," Justice Thomas said.

This is the humanoid affliction brought down upon us by the Republican Party, which only Divine Providence can remove. Clarence Thomas is 54 years old. He serves for life.

Back in 1991, a sorry pack of Black back door feeders rushed to Clarence Thomas' side during his confirmation hearings, hurrumphing that the young political operative with the barest of judicial credentials should be given a chance to prove himself. Like the Spook Who Sat By the Door in the novel, Thomas would show his true Black colors once the U.S. Senate punched his lifetime ticket, they grinned greasily.

In our January 30 discussion of "race traitors," we speculated that "some of us would cheer if a Black were appointed Lord High Executioner of African Americans." We misspoke; the position was already filled. Clarence Thomas *is* Lord High Executioner of Blacks. It takes eight white people to hold him back.

Clone of Clarence

BC hosted a brief but interesting EmailBox dialogue, early this month, on the exploding Hispanic presence in the southern United States. A number of Black readers took offence at suggestions that the "Black-white paradigm" of race relations in the U.S. was outdated, now that Latinos outnumber African Americans. Simply put, the Black responders told our Chicano guest commentator that the newcomers should learn some lessons about white American racism from folks with a few centuries of experience on the subject, before they declared the Black worldview an anachronism. (See *"Plain Language on Blacks and Hispanics,"* February 6.)

Clearly, some Hispanics are repeating the most backward aspects of the tortuous Black experience as they attempt to reinvent the race relations wheel. The question of changing paradigms is misdirected. It is the racists of the White Man's Party who impose the rules of the grotesque game, and they are now playing the same tricks on Hispanics that proved effective in suppressing and confusing Black Americans.

The Miguel Estrada spectacle is like watching a rerun of the Clarence Thomas confirmation, poorly dubbed in Spanish. Estrada, too, is a young (41), Hard Right political operative with few qualifications for the federal bench. Like pre-confirmation Thomas, Estrada has refused to say much of anything substantial about his legal opinions, and lies when he does speak.

In terms of social background, Estrada bears no comparison to Clarence from Pinpoint. He is the U.S.-educated scion of the Honduran elite, with no connection to the barrios of the U.S. or the shantytowns of his native land. But that doesn't matter, because *white people are the ones who always deal and play the race card.* And sure enough, the old racial mojo is working fine. The Hispanics are split, and the Democrats are in agony.

As 41 Democratic Senators prepared to filibuster against confirmation of yet another reactionary colored man with life tenure, Thomas patron Senator Orrin Hatch (R-Utah) denounced the Estrada opposition as *"anti-Latino."* The old trickster was encouraged by the League of United Latin American Citizens (LULAC), which had endorsed Estrada for no coherent reason other than his surname.

"It was just very difficult for us not to support the guy, given his impeccable credentials," said Hector Flores, president of the Texas-based group. "It's the American dream, rising up from Honduras the way he has. The battle isn't whether he's conservative; it's that he represents Latinos, whether we like him or not."

Estrada held down assistant positions in the U.S. Attorney's office for the Southern District of New York and the U.S. Solicitor General's office, and is a partner at a high-powered Washington firm. His qualifications to sit on the U.S. Court of Appeals for the District of Columbia Circuit are comparatively weak. LULAC's Flores has an "American dream" dancing in his own head and, like Black Clarence Thomas supporters of the previous decade, he will populate it with whomever of his ethnic group the White Man's Party offers.

The other mainline Latino organizations—the Puerto Rican Legal Defense and Educational Fund, the Southwest Voter Registration Project and the House Hispanic Caucus—are having as little success with determined Latino dupes as did the national African American organizations back in 1991. Brown fools walking in the footsteps of Black fools, all the while declaring that their new day has dawned.

New paradigm? No, just a new bunch of suckers. White supremacy may well have a brown defender to keep the Black one company on the High Court deep into the century.

War Against the Euro

The London Sunday Observer took note of the "quiet emergence of the 'petroeuro,'" this week, part of the growing realization that the unfolding U.S. military encirclement and impending occupation of Middle Eastern oil fields is directly linked to maintaining the American dollar as the preeminent oil currency. As Dr. Sonja Ebron explained in last week's analysis, "Why African Americans Should Oppose the War," the U.S. economy would suffer a devastating crash were the dollar's value not "*backed by oil*, which allows our Treasury to simply print money as needed to finance our debt."

The Sunday Observer's Faisal Islam agrees. "The U.S. can carry on printing money—effectively IOUs—to fund tax cuts, increased military spending, and consumer spending on imports without fear of inflation or that these loans will be called in," he writes. "It's probably the nearest thing to a 'free lunch' in global economics."

It is also ample cause for a war to "shock and awe" the people of the planet and prevent oil producing nations from considering a switch to the euro as a petroleum currency, a move that would be in the best interests of many producers. Middle East oil nations engage in more reciprocal trade with Europe than with the United States. The Observer's Faisal also reports that "the Bank of China and the Russian Central Bank are both rumored to be waiting for the best moment to increase the holdings of euros."

By exposing itself as a would-be global dictator, the United States may be accelerating the very thing that it seeks to prevent: a mad dash *away* from the dollar. As Dr. Ebron put it in her February 20 analysis, "Far from staving off disaster, our arrogance may instead compel OPEC to 'go euro' *en masse*, taking many oil-consuming nations with them by force of economics. And a trade war with Europe will lend the *coup de grace* to our economy."

Yellow Times contributor Paul Harris writes that the "reason for the drive against Iraq is Bush's war against Europe." Harris dates the current crisis to November, 2000, when Saddam Hussein began accepting only euros for Iraq's oil, threatening a status quo in which "the U.S. essentially owns the world's oil for free." Harris concludes:

> The point of Bush's war against Iraq, therefore, is to secure control of those oil fields and revert their valuation to dollars, then to increase production exponentially, forcing prices to drop. Finally, the point of Bush's war is to threaten significant action against any of the oil producers who would switch to the euro.
>
> In the long run, then, it is not really Saddam who is the target; it is the euro and, therefore, Europe. There is no way the United States will sit by idly and let those upstart Europeans take charge of their own fate, let alone of the world's finances.

In this context, the shockingly crude behavior of George Bush and his pirates towards the French and Germans becomes more understandable.

Long term oil availability has never been an acute concern for the people who rule America—if it were, Bush would not be offering tax breaks for gas guzzling SUVs, defying the rest of the planet over global warming, or putting the physical safety of the oil fields themselves in jeopardy. It is not in the interest of a single nation on the planet to seriously disrupt the flow of oil—the producing states least of all. However, U.S. *hegemony* in the world is based on keeping oil prices tied directly and exclusively to the dollar. This is the artificial arrangement at the heart of the empire—the "national interest" for which millions will die in Permanent War until the pirates are removed from power.

Black Lawmakers in the Lead

"The path that the U.S. is going ... will destabilize the world as it is destabilizing the Middle East," Texas Black Congresswoman Sheila Jackson-Lee told CNN, this week. Reflecting overwhelming African American distrust of U.S. war policy—historically and in the current madness—Black lawmakers have assumed leadership of the resistance to Bush's machinery of destruction.

Led by Rep. John Conyers (D-MI), the dean of the Congressional Black Caucus, six members challenged in federal court Bush's right to invade Iraq without specific congressional authorization. "The Iraq Resolution passed by Congress on October 3, 2002, did not declare war and unlawfully ceded to the President that decision," said Rep. Jesse Jackson Jr. (D-IL), one of the plaintiffs. "Historical records show that the framers of the Constitution sought to ensure that U.S. presidents did not have the power of European monarchs to single-handedly declare and wage war." Representatives Sheila Jackson-Lee, Jim McDermott (D-WA), and Jose Serrano (D-NY) joined in the suit.

Former Georgia Congresswoman Cynthia McKinney lent her considerable prestige to a Canadian-based effort to expose the U.S. as "home of the largest arsenal of weapons of mass destruction." McKinney has signed on as an honorary weapons inspector for the Rooting Out Evil project. In a letter of support, she wrote:

> Certainly, the United States under the leadership of George W. Bush qualifies as a misguided missile, dangerous to global peace and security. You are right to begin your campaign in the U.S. because it is here that the world's largest stockpiles of weapons of mass destruction including nuclear, conventional, biological, and chemical weapons are situated. At the same time, the American people are paying a dear price for the U.S. focus on militarization at home and abroad. This focus impoverishes the American people, insults our fundamental values, and diminishes our spirit and moral character.
>
> The economics of war are hurting the American people. And the Bush government is becoming a global threat. There was a time when America was loved around the world. Now, it is feared. Now is the time for all good people of conscience to act.

A Rooting Out Evil team last week staged a visit to the Edgewood Chemical and Biological Center, in Maryland, to bring public attention to the "dangerous chemical and biological agents being developed and stored at the facility."

Even the doggedly domestic-oriented NAACP is assuming the role of global citizen. As a new non-governmental organization (NGO) affiliate of the United Nations, the civil rights group will host an "America's Summit" at its annual meeting in Miami, in July. "The world is much smaller today," said executive director Kweisi Mfume. "Many more issues are cross-linked between the domestic and international realms. And the issue of Third World development resonates particularly with our constituency."

NAACP chairman Julian Bond spoke for the organization at the February 15 anti-war rally in New York City, sounding much as he did four decades ago as a leader of the staunchly anti-Vietnam War Student Non-violent Coordinating Committee (SNCC):

> We Americans must ask ourselves today, are we prepared for the consequences and after effects of an attack on Iraq—continued destabilization of the region, the deaths of American fighting women and men, the deaths of thousands upon thousands of innocent Iraqis, the collapse of regimes, however undemocratic, which now support us, near permanent occupation by our soldiers of a defeated Iraq and the millions upon millions required to bring it stability? If we really favor regime change, we ought to begin right here at home.

Veteran activist Ron Daniels is coordinating a February 28 action to "surround the U.S. State Department with a massive Prayer Circle for Peace before leaving on an urgent Prayer Pilgrimage for Peace to Iraq." Daniels explains the mission.

In my capacity as Executive Director of the *Center for Constitutional Rights*, since September of 2002, I have been working to build an African American lead, multi-racial, ecumenical coalition of faith leaders opposed to the war. Dr. James Forbes, Senior Pastor of Riverside Church in New York, Rev. Tyrone Pitts, General Secretary of the Progressive Baptist Convention, Rev. Herbert Daughtry, pastor of House of the Lord Church in Brooklyn and founder of the National Black United Front, former Congressman Walter Fauntroy, pastor of New Bethel Baptist Church in Washington, D.C. and President of the National Black Leadership Roundtable, Imam Mahdi Bray, President of the MAS Freedom Foundation in D.C. and Rev. John Mendez, former Chairman of the Racial Justice Working Group of the National Council of Churches from Winston Salem, N.C. are among the African American faith leaders who have participated in the coalition. . . .

Taken together, it is clear that Black voices for peace and justice are increasing as Bush and company push forward with their misadventure in Iraq. In the coming days and months ahead, however, more and more Black voices must come to the forefront to stridently say no to war and yes to justice and peace. As Martin Luther King put it, "when machines . . . and profit motives and property rights are considered more important than people, the giant triplets of racism, materialism, and militarism are incapable of being conquered." Black voices for peace and justice can be decisive in ending militarism, not only in this country but the entire planet!

This is a righteous Faith-based Initiative, bearing no resemblance to George Bush's slavery-time religion.

Coalition of the Bribed

The Bush administration finds international allies in the same way that it attracts African Americans to the GOP: it bribes them. As this issue was going to press, the legislature of overwhelmingly Muslim Turkey was about to decide how many billions of dollars it will take to buy its participation in the war on Iraq—an invasion that more than 95 percent of the Turkish people oppose. An important sticking point is Turkish insistence that Bush sign off on the deal, personally, since the U.S. is famous around the globe for reneging on its promises once its goals have been achieved. (Native Americans could have warned the world about this reflexive behavior.)

The figures bandied about range to upwards of $30 billion. All that is certain is that, as with all U.S. foreign "aid" deals, much of the money must be spent with corporate friends of the regime in Washington.

At $30 billion, the Turkish deal would be *twice* the amount spent annually on federal Temporary Aid to Needy Families—the program once known as welfare.

In all its dimensions, the Bush War is depraved.

Post-1994: The New Nadir of African-American Congressional Participation

Charles E. Jones

The dawn of the 20th century marked the beginning of the extended absence of African-Americans from the congressional arena. On his departure from the House of Representatives in 1901, Congressmember George White (R-NC), the last African-American elected in the 19th century (1898-1901), defiantly declared: "This, Mr. Chairman, is perhaps the Negro's temporary farewell to the American Congress; but let me say Phoenix-like he will rise up someday and come again. These parting words are on behalf of the outraged, heartbroken, bruised and bleeding, but God fearing, people" (Clayton, 1964: 37). Representative White's prediction eventually materialized, as it was not until the 1928 election of Oscar Depriest (R-IL) before another African-American entered Congress. During this nearly thirty-year absence of Black representation from this institution, people of African descent in America not only lacked descriptive representation in Congress, but substantive representation as well, given the prevailing sentiments of white supremacy, de jure segregation and the political influence of the Ku Klux Klan.

Ironically, as we begin the 21st century, we are now witnessing disturbing developments concerning African-American congressional participation. While these developments cannot be said to be nearly as severe as those occurring during the first nadir; they, nevertheless, remain discomforting, invoking a political dé jà vu that suggests African-Americans may be on the verge of entering a period of decline in congressional representation. This is ironic, given that the number of Black members of Congress (40) in the last decade of the 20th century was at its peak. While the first nadir in Black congressional participation involved the total disappearance of African-Americans from Congress, this second decline is more elusive: we have the image of Black congressional representation, given the number of Black lawmakers, but the reality is the emasculation of African-American congressional representation, which characterizes the current predicament of the Congressional Black Caucus (CBC).

This essay seeks to identify the key political and congressional dynamics that account for the current decline of African-American congressional participation. It analyzes those factors, developments and trends that undergird the diminished influence of African-American congressional participation. The chapter begins by examining the Congressional Black Caucus's role as a racial legislative subgroup that was formally created to serve as a vehicle for the collective interests of the African American community. It then discusses the "golden years" of the CBC in order to illuminate the CBC's relative impotency during the last five Congresses (104th thru 108th). Finally, the essay concludes by discussing the future prospects of the Congressional Black Caucus.

CBC: *Collective African-American Congressional Participation*

Formally organized in 1971, the Congressional Black Caucus represents the primary mechanism for collective African-American congressional participation (Singh, 1998). It is an informal organization with a national constituency, which means that it has an "identifiable, self-conscious, relatively stable unit(s) of interacting members whose relationships are not officially prescribed by statutes of and rules" (Fiellin, 1962: 76). Other examples of informal organizations with national constituencies include the Congressional Hispanic Caucus and the Caucus on Women's Issues. Unofficial legislative caucuses have long been actors on the congressional landscape. During the 1970s, however, the prevalence of legislative caucuses increased due to congressional reform that emphasized decentralizing power in the House of Representatives. However, the creation of the Congressional Black Caucus did not stem from this congressional trend. Its formation was directly a result of "an outgrowth of the Black power movement's call for racial solidarity and independent black organizations" (Walton and Smith, 2000:182). In short, external political dynamics, rather than internal congressional factors account for its creation. Given the more political circumstances surrounding its birth and that Black members of Congress are the highest elective officeholders, the CBC mandate has been undergirded by a racial imperative— an obligation to advance the collective political objectives and racial interests of the African-American community.

The Congressional Black Caucus (CBC) has generally been viewed as one of the most effective legislative caucuses in the House of Representatives. The CBC has served as a model of political action to other Black politicians, including African-American state legislators who have attempted to replicate its structure and tactics at the state level. Moreover, the CBC was the impetus for the formation of the short-lived Parliamentary Black Caucus in Great Britain (Jones, 1999). The CBC's ability to "institutionalize" collective African-American political participation during the past three decades (1971 to 2003) contributes to its reputation as an effective legislative caucus. Five attributes help to explain its ability to "institutionalize" the congressional participation of Black Americans. These attributes include: permanence, goal-agreement, specialization of tasks, auxiliary support mechanisms and fundraising capabilities (Polsby, 1968).

In order for an organization to become institutionalized, it must first establish some degree of permanence. The CBC constitutes one of the oldest informal organizations in Congress. Its longevity underscores its permanence as a stable actor within the congressional process. During its over thirty year existence, only two African-American Congressmembers—Senator Edward Brooks (R-MA) and Representative J.C. Watts (R-OK)—refused official membership in the CBC. Its leadership is organized hierarchically, with a chairperson, two vice-chairs, a secretary and a whip. CBC leadership of the 108th Congress (2003-2004) includes Elijah Cummings, chair; Sheila Jackson, vice-chair; Corrine Brown, second vice-chair; Danny Davis, secretary; and Barbara Lee, whip.

The CBC's permanence can largely be attributed to the "goal agreement" among its members, a second attribute that contributes to the CBC institutionalization. "Goal agreement" means that CBC members share a commitment to promoting the collective interests of all African-Americans in the congressional arena, rather than just the interest of citizens within their individual congressional districts. "Goal agreement" among CBC members is not always automatic. At times, CBC members' commitment to a racial collective orientation can be threatened by competing factors, such as the tendency of members of Congress to focus on the needs of constituents from their own congressional district. Congressional scholar Marguerite Barnett has perceptively observed that CBC members are indeed "caught between pressures to represent blacks collectively and constraints dictated by individual political circumstances" (1977: 26). Moreover, Leroy Rieselbach argues "that specific institutional arrangements in Congress are increasingly compelling the CBC to resolve its crisis in favor of ordinary legislative politics" (1995: 133). In short, these scholars suggest that ordinary legislative politics—the reward and punishment system within Congress—may at times discourage CBC members from pursuing a collective racial orientation in policymaking. However, their assessment overlooks a racial imperative that helps to prevent the demise of the CBC. In other words, if Black Congressmembers believe they have a racial obligation to the African-American, then Black lawmakers will be more likely to act in ways that benefit African-Americans as a whole. In this sense, a racial imperative is positive for the CBC, as it helps to ensure that if CBC members experience an "identity crisis" and/or confront objectives that compete with pursuing the "racial imperative," then the "identity crisis" is more likely to be temporary, rather than permanent (Menifield and Jones, 2001).

A third attribute that contributes to the CBC institutionalization is the existence of auxiliary support mechanisms, which means additional support systems that aid the organization. In 1976, the CBC created its primary auxiliary support mechanism—The Congressional Black Caucus Foundation (CBCF). The Congressional Black Caucus Foundation (CBCF) serves as the educational research arm of the CBC. The CBC Foundation conducts policy research and coordinates a fellowship program for graduate students and scholars. It is governed by an independent Board of Directors who is also responsible for fundraising for the CBC.

In addition to the Congressional Black Caucus Foundation, the CBC's three-member staff served as a second auxiliary support mechanism until its abolishment in 1994 by the Republican-controlled House, which eliminated congressional staff support for legislative caucuses. The CBC staff had several responsibilities, such as publishing the CBC newsletter, providing legislative briefings to CBC members, organizing CBC forums and task force meetings, conducting legislative research and participating with the CBC Foundation to coordinate its fellowship program (Singh, 1998: 66-67).

A fourth essential attribute to CBC institutionalization is the "specialization of tasks." This refers to an organization's internal ability to organize its workload into an efficient division of labor. More complex organizations are more likely to exhibit a "specialization of tasks" than simpler ones. The CBC's task force system represents an example of this attribute. The CBC task force system consists of African-American professional and policy experts who assist CBC members in formulating legislation that benefits the African-American community. A task force—which is also known as the CBC "brain trust"—is designated for each policy area of importance to the interest of African-Americans. Along with task forces, the CBC handles its workload by using an elaborate subcommittee system. Each CBC member is assigned to chair a CBC subcommittee that coincides with the CBC members' respective standing committee assignment in the House. Also, the chair of the CBC subcommittee is charged with developing a CBC task force to complement his/her respective subcommittee.

The final attribute that contributes to CBC institutionalization is fundraising. The CBC's annual "Legislative Weekend"—usually held in September in Washington, D.C.—has become its signature fundraising event. The highly popular and successful event is one of the premiere affairs of the Black upper middle-class social-political circuit. The CBC "Legislative Weekend" is comprised of receptions, fashion shows, luncheons, concerts and an awards banquet. According to congressional observers (Singh, 1998: 69), "the CBC consistently ranked among the best-financed and highest-spending of all caucuses." To offset mounting criticism concerning the overly social aspect of its "Legislative Weekend," CBC members have placed greater emphasis on sponsoring legislative workshops and task force meetings (Trescott, 1981: B1). Before 1994, additional funding was garnered from CBC members' $5,000-a-year dues to help finance caucus activities. However, when Republicans won control of Congress in 1994, they sponsored rule changes that prevented legislative caucuses from using members' dues as a source of income.

"Golden Years" of CBC Influence: 103rd Congress (1993-94)

The 1992 congressional elections dramatically altered the membership composition of the United States Congress. Redistricting, anti-incumbent sentiments and the Clarence Thomas-Anita Hill debate all contributed to the election of the most heterogeneous class of junior legislators in the history of Congress (Carpin and Fuchs, 1993; Hershey, 1993). Traditionally excluded groups, such as women and racial minorities, significantly expanded their congressional representation in the 103rd Congress (1993–94). Female candidates captured forty-seven districts in the House of Representatives and acquired four new seats in the Senate, increasing the total number of female senators to six. In addition, the congressional representation of both Asian-Americans and Hispanic-Americans reached historic proportions. Six Asian-Americans won seats in Congress while 19 individuals of Hispanic descent were elected. Similarly, African-Americans also significantly benefited from the 1992 congressional elections. The number of Black Congress-members expanded from 26 to 40 members. This unprecedented growth in African-

American Congress members included the first African-American female, Carol Mosely-Braun (D-IL), ever elected to the United States Senate (See Table 1).

The 18 Black newcomers of the 103rd Congress represented the largest Black delegation ever elected to Congress. In order to compare this historic class with earlier Black lawmakers, data were collected for all African-Americans who served from the 1928 election of Oscar DePriest to the end of the 103rd Congress in 1992. During this time frame (1928-1992), 50 African-Americans were elected to the United States Congress. The data reveal that the 1993 Black freshman class differs from previous African-American members of Congress.

Unlike previous Black lawmakers, the 1993 freshman class has a conspicuous absence of former ministers and civil rights activists among its ranks, denoting a significant departure from past Black congressional participation (See Table 2). Former Black legislators, such as Clayton Powell (D-NY), Andrew Young (D-GA), Walter Fauntroy (D-D.C.), William Gray (D-PA) and Floyd Flake (D-NY) exemplify this tradition. The prominence of ministers and civil rights activists is one of the few differences between the occupations of Black and non-black legislators (Jones 1987a, 224-225). What accounts for the relative absence of ministers and civil rights activists among the 1993 Black freshman class? One explanation may stem from

Table 1

African-American Freshman Members of the 103rd Congress (1993–94)

Name	District
1. Carol Moseley-Braun	(D-IL, Senator)
2. Earl F. Hilliard	(D-AL, 7th)
3. Walter R. Tucker III	(D-CA, 37th)
4. Corrine Brown	(D-FL, 3rd)
5. Carrie Meek	(D-FL, 17th)
6. Alcee Hastings	(D-FL, 23rd)
7. Sanford Bishop	(D-GA, 2nd)
8. Cynthia McKinney	(D-GA, 11th)
9. Bobby L. Rush	(D-IL, 1st)
10. Mel Reynolds	(D-IL, 2nd)
11. Cleo Fields	(D-LA, 4th)
12. Albert R. Wynn	(D-MD, 4th)
13. Eva Clayton	(D-NC, 1st)
14. Melvin Watt	(D-NC, 12th)
15. James E. Clyburn	(D-SC, 6th)
16. Eddie Bernice Johnson	(D-TX, 30th)
17. Robert C. Scott	(D-VA, 3rd)
18. Bennie Thompson	(D-MS, 2nd; elected 4/13/93 to succeed Secretary of Agriculture Mike Espy)

Source: Joint Center for Political and Economic Studies, "Political Trend Letter" *Focus* 21(2): 1–3.

modernization developments within African-American politics that have weakened the function of the Black church to serve as a vehicle for the political recruitment of political leadership.

All but one of the newly elected Black legislators previously occupied either appointed or elective political offices (See Table 2). Prior political experience also distinguishes the newcomers of the 103rd Congress and highlights the freshman class's distinctiveness from previous African-American congressional representation. Nearly fifty-six (56%) of the 1993 delegation served as former state legislators, compared to forty percent (40%) of the African-Americans who served before the 103rd Congress. Black members of Congress of the earlier era (1928–1992) were either political amateurs or former city council members. By contrast, the 1993 Black freshman class accrued significant legislative experience at the state level, where many had been ten-year veterans. Their prior political experience ensured a certain level of knowledge and expertise that would serve to enhance their legislative effectiveness. CBC veteran John Lewis (GA-5) explained, "they aren't newcomers to the job like a lot of us were. They have command of issues and will be able to hit the ground running" (Smothers, 1992: A17).

Table 2 indicates that the African-Americans elected to the 103rd Congress were a highly educated group. All 18 newcomers earned baccalaureate degrees and (89%) of them possessed post-graduate degrees. The degree of formal education among the 1993 freshman class was higher than that of previous Black lawmakers, where 60 percent (60%) earned advance degrees (See Table 2). Nevertheless, the high level of formal education among both junior and senior African-American legislators (1928–1992) remains congruent with the educational attributes of congressional members in general (Keffe, 1980: 56; Rieselbach, 1973: 33).

The data also revealed a continuation of a prior pattern of African-American female congressional participation. Beginning with the 93rd Congress (1973–74), the proportion of Black female legislators has been typically larger than its white counterparts (Jones, 1987a: 225). Among the first-time CBC members, women comprised 33 percent of the delegation, doubling the percentage (16 percent) of previous Black female Congressmembers (See Table 2). Notwithstanding this divergence between the two groups, the gender attribute remains "one of the more striking differences when one compares blacks and whites in Congress" (Smith, 1981:209).

Both the 1993 African-American members of Congress and their pre-1993 counterparts were similar regarding their party affiliation. One hundred percent of the eighteen first-timers were Democrats, compared to ninety-two percent (92%) of the early group of Black legislators (See Table 2). Former Congressman Gary Franks (R-CT), was the lone African-American Republican of the 103rd Congress.

The unprecedented growth in the size of the Congressional Black Caucus membership during the 103rd Congress to forty members provided a sufficient numerical base to enhance CBC influence. Yet, paradoxically, this growth also represented a potential threat to the CBC's active orientation. The data indicate that the career patterns of the junior delegation of African-American legislators coincided with the attributes of the transethnic politician (Kilson, 1989). Political observer Richard Cohen contends that the new generation of Black Congressmembers "are pragmatic, articulate and young. They have government and business experience, not solely the civil rights profiles" (Cohen, 1987, 2432). This trend poses challenges to CBC unity and to necessary resources for organizational effectiveness.

Another potential threat is the diversification within congressional districts represented

Table 2
Comparison of Selected Background Characteristics of African-Americans of Congress, 1928–1994

Characteristic	CBC Freshmen (103rd Congress) (N=18)	African-American Members of Congress (1928-1992) (N=50)
Gender:		
Male	67% (12)	84% (42)
Female	33% (6)	16% (8)
Education:		
Advanced Degree	89% (16)	60% (30)
College Graduate	11% (2)	28% (14)
Cumulative	100% (18)	88% (44)
Non-College Graduate	—	12% (6)
Occupation:		
Attorney/Judge	44% (8)	34% (17)
Teacher	28% (5)	12% (6)
Public Official	11% (2)	10% (5)
Educational Admin.	11% (2)	2% (1)
Minister	—	10% (5)
Civil Rights Activist	—	2% (1)
Real Estate	—	8% (4)
Business	6% (1)	—
Social Worker	—	4% (2)
Accountant	—	2% (1)
Labor Official	—	4% (2)
Librarian	—	2% (1)
Radio Station Program Dir.	—	2% (1)
Medical Practitioner	—	2% (1)
Mortician	—	4% (2)
Newspaper Publisher	—	2% (1)
Prior Political Experience:		
None	6% (1)	18% (9)
Appointed	22% (4)	10% (5)
Elective	72% (13)	72% (36)
Party Affiliation:		
Democratic	100% (18)	92% (46)
Republican	—	8% (4)

Source: Biographic Directory of the American Congress: 1774-1989. Washington, D.C.: U. S. Government Printing Office, 1990. Barone, Michael, and Grand Ujifusa. Almanac of American Politics. Washington, D. C.: National Journal, 1972–1994.

by CBC members. Before the election of the historic (103rd) junior African-American congressional delegation, CBC members served similar constituencies who tended to be overwhelmingly Black, largely poor and drawn from northern urban districts. The homogeneity of CBC-held districts was shattered by Black lawmakers elected to the 103rd Congress. Several of the CBC newcomers represented southern rural congressional districts that threaten cohesion among the CBC membership.

When the CBC significantly expanded its membership following the 1992 congressional elections, it also enhanced the descriptive representation of African-Americans (Pitkin, 1967: 10–11). Descriptive representation means that the composition of Congress should correspond to the demographic make-up of the American public. In the case of African-Americans, the 1992 congressional elections reduced the discrepancy between the proportion of the African-Americans (12 percent) and the African-American composition within the House of Representatives (9 percent). The addition of eighteen newcomers not only energized the Caucus but also redistributed the organizational workload of its membership. New Junior CBC members supplied the much needed personnel to convert the CBC's enhanced descriptive representation into a more meaningful substantive representation.

Substantive representation became more likely after the 1992 elections because the increased number of Black lawmakers allowed the CBC to disperse a greater number of its members throughout the various decisionmaking structures within the House of Representatives. CBC members served on a broader array of House committees. During the 103rd Congress (1993–94), CBC members occupied seats on all twenty-two standing committees (with the exception of Natural Resources). Two junior CBC members, Carrie Meek and Mel Reynolds, secured "exclusive committee" assignments on Appropriation and Ways and Means, respectively (Bositis, 1993; Lusane, 2001). Freshmen appointments to these influential House committees—even in the post-1974 reform Congress—were extremely rare. (For example, in 1983, former CBC member Alan Wheat (D-MO) managed to acquire a seat on the powerful House Rules committee).

CBC's expanded sphere of influence enhanced the "integrative" function of the unofficial legislative subgroup. In the midst of a decentralized congressional arena "informal groups, whatever the basis for establishment, can integrate a wide range of social, economic and political considerations relating to the group's shared concerns and formulate a consistent policy response" (Stevens, Hammond and Mulhollan, 1981: 13). Enhancing this function increases the CBC's capacity to influence the policy process. The successful CBC efforts in preserving the status of the subcommittee on Africa during the reorganization process of the Foreign Affairs Committee was one example of the growing influence of the CBC. (JCPES, 1993a: 1).

The CBC's newfound clout was also reinforced by its membership participation in the committee and party leadership structure. CBC members chaired three full standing committees and 17 subcommittees. Most notably, Ronald Dellums chaired the House Armed Services Committee. Dellums was one of the most progressive members of the House of Representatives and his ascendancy to the chair of the Armed Services Committee was especially significant because of his key role in shaping the post-cold war American military (Browning, 1993a: 1220). In addition, CBC members held seats on several important Democratic Party organs, including four positions on the 22-member Democratic Steering and Policy Committee, as well as six seats on the Democratic National Congressional Campaign committee.

The CBC's expanded membership also enabled the organization to maximize its bargaining leverage. The CBC could rely on its dependable block of 38 votes (Gary Franks, the lone CBC Republican, seldom voted with the Caucus majority). This allowed the CBC to expand its political clout. The CBC's ability to deliver a 38-member bloc of votes in the gridlock of the contemporary congressional process becomes a critical political resource. Bloc voting permits the CBC to maximize its influence in the deliberations of the House (Fiellin, 1962). The enhanced influence of the CBC was witnessed in the passage of the Clinton administration budget legislation. Cunningham observed, "there are 38 Democratic members of the Black Caucus, and without their votes, the House version of the deficit-reduction bill would not have passed. Hence, Democratic leaders are displaying new respect for what may be the party's most cohesive force on its left wing" (1993: 1711). CBC budgetary support was contingent upon the inclusion of several non-negotiable provisions, including an earned income tax credit, increased funding for immunizations, and empowerment zones (Browning, 1993b: 1925).

In short, several positive developments were associated with the expansion of CBC membership during the 103rd Congress. Enhanced descriptive representation, an expanded sphere of influence, and increased voting strength represented valuable strategic resources of the CBC as they advocated on behalf of their national racial constituency. However, the CBC's newfound clout of CBC was short-lived. After its two-year period—its "golden years"—of exercising congressional clout, the CBC moved from its finest hour to a relatively impotent actor in Congress. The next section examines those factors that help to explain the decline of CBC influence in the congressional process.

Key Factors for the Decline of CBC Influence (1995–2003)

External political events, emerging trends and congressional reform converged to circumscribe CBC influence during the last five Congresses (104th thru 108th). Adverse factors which came to threaten CBC effectiveness include: (1) the prominence of the transethnic legislator; (2) the Republican Party takeover of Congress; (3) congressional reform which adversely impacted informal legislative organizations; and (4) increased competition among African-American congressional office seekers.

From 1995 to 2003, the time period of the recent demise of CBC influence, twenty African-Americans entered Congress. Since the election of the historic 1993 class, the size of the African-American congressional delegation has remained rather stable. The CBC has been unable to significantly expand its membership beyond its all-time high of forty members, which it achieved in the 103rd Congress. Since that time, there has been a one-member decrease in the total number of Black lawmakers. Despite the importance of incumbency in Congress, three Black Congressional incumbents lost their seats during Congressional elections. In 1998, Senator Carol Mosley-Braun (D-IL) failed to retain her U.S. Senate seat. The Mosley-Braun loss meant the disappearance of African-Americans from the Senate landscape and a return to prevailing patterns of racial exclusion in the upper chamber. During the entire 20th century, African-Americans have held Senate seats only twice. Besides Mosley-Braun, Edward Brooke (R-MA), a two-term Republican Senator (1967–1979) was the only other African-American to serve in the Senate during the last century.

Nearly all twenty Black House members (95 percent) elected from 1994 to 2002 (the

104th through 108th Congresses) were Democrats, a trend consistent with previous patterns of African-American representation (See Table 3). The one exception from the post-1994 classes of Black legislators was Congressmember J. C. Watts, a former all-American college quarterback and conservative businessman, who served as a Republican (Watts, 2002). The African-American females among the twenty members in the post-1994 cohort also parallel the previous pattern of a higher rate of participation than their white counterparts. In this post-1994 cohort, 40 percent of the congressional newcomers were female (See Table 4). Moreover, the 20 Black legislators who served during the 104th through the 108th Congresses shared similar educational and occupational attributes of their Black predecessors. All but one of the 20 post-1994 Black lawmakers (95 percent) graduated from college and 90 percent earned post-baccalaureate degrees. As noted earlier, this high level of educational attainment among the post-1994 African-American congressional members was congruent with the formal education of their white counterparts. Similarly, lawyers (35 percent), educators (25 percent) and business (20 percent) were occupations that were overrepresented among this group (See Table 4).

Table 3
African-American Members of the 104th through 108th Congresses (1995–2004)

Name	District	Year Elected
1. Elijah Cummings	MD-07	1994
2. Chaka Fattah	PA-02	1994
3. Sheila Jackson-Lee	TX-18	1994
4. J. C. Watts	OK-04	1994
5. Jesse Jackson, Jr.	IL-02	1995
6. Julia Carson	IN-10	1996
7. Carolyn Cheeks Kilpatrick	MI-15	1996
8. Danny K. Davis	IL-07	1996
9. Harold E. Ford, Jr.	TN-09	1996
10. Juanita Millender-McDonald	CA-37	1996
11. Barbara Lee	CA-09	1998
12. Gregory Meeks	NY-06	1998
13. Stephanie Tubbs-Jones	OH-11	1998
14. William L. Clay, Jr.	MO-01	2000
15. Diane Watson	CA-32	2000
16. Artur Davis	AL-07	2002
17. Denise Majette	GA-04	2002
18. Kendrick Meek	FL-17	2002
19. David Scott	GA-13	2002

Source: Congressional Quarterly Weekly Report 49 (Jan. 2, 1993), p. 10; *Congressional Quarterly Weekly Report* 49 (Jan. 16, 1993), p. 12; and *Congressional Quarterly Weekly Report* 53 (Jan. 24, 1997), p. 28; Amer, Mildred L., "Black Members of United States Congress: 1789-2001, *CRS Report for Congress*, http:*www.senate.gov/reference/resources/pdf/RL30378.pdf*; "Congressional Black Caucus of the 107th United States Congress," *http://www.house.gov/ebjohnson/cbcmembers4.htm*; *Congressional Quarterly Weekly*, Vol. 60, Iss. 43, (Nov. 9, 2002): 18.

Table 4

Selected Social Characteristics of African American Congressmembers: 104th–108th Congresses (1995–2004)

Characteristics	(n=20)
Gender	
Male	60%
Female	40%
Religion	
Baptist	60%
African Methodist Episcopalian	5%
Protestant	5%
Other	15%
Missing Data	15%
Education	
Post-College Graduate	90%
College Graduate	95%
Non-College Graduate	5%
Occupation	
Law	35%
Business	20%
Education	25%
Clergy	0%
Agriculture	0%
Medicine	0%
Public Service	15%
Other	5%
Education	
Democratic Party	95%
Republication Party	5%
Prior Political Experience	
Elective	80%
Appointive	5%
None	15%

Source: Michael Barone and Grant Ujifusa, *The Almanac of American Politics* (Washington, DC. *National Journal*, editions: 1996, 1998, 2000); "Special Report Election 2002: New Representatives," *Congressional Quarterly Weekly*, Vol. 60, Issue 43 (Nov. 9, 2002): 18.

As with the historic 1993 Black congressional class, ministers and civil rights activists were relatively absent among the 20-member cohort elected after 1993. Jesse Jackson, Jr. (D-IL) was the only former civil rights activist among this group. Moreover, political amateurs among the 20-member delegation were virtually non-existent (See Table 4). Only three of the 20 Congressmembers—Jesse Jackson, Jr. (D-IL), Harold Ford, Jr. (D-TN) and Artur Davis (D-AL)—lacked prior elective or appointive experience. Eighty percent (80 percent) of the post-1994 Black congressional delegation held elective office, with (60 percent) previously served as state legislators.

Another emerging pattern among the African-American members of Congress serving from 1995 through 2004 is the second-generation succession of office by a family member. Fifteen percent of the cohort under study succeeded one of their respective parents in Congress. Two father-son combinations are the Clays of Missouri's 1st Congressional District (William Clay, Sr. was a CBC founding member) and the Fords who have represented Tennessee's lone majority Black district (13th) since 1975. Kendrick Meek succeeded his mother Carrie in Florida's seventeenth congressional district. Jesse Jackson, Jr. the namesake of one of the most well-known African-American leaders of the post-civil rights era, is the fourth son of a prominent Black leader to occupy a seat in Congress. The phenomenon of African-American career politicians who are succeeded by a family member is a development that reflects the continuity of African-American participation in the post-civil rights era.

The social background of the post-1994 cohort personifies the "transethnic legislator," which was also identified earlier with the historic 1993 Black congressional class. These empirical findings show that African-American members of Congress elected between 1994 and 2002, like their 1993 counterparts, mark a significant departure from the previous patterns of Black congressional representation. Consequently, this new generation of CBC members can be expected to exacerbate organizational tension within the CBC, a tension stemming from the quest of CBC members to locate the optimal balance between serving the collective interests of the African-American community versus serving the needs of their respective congressional districts.

The 1994 Congressional elections significantly altered the political fortunes of the CBC. During these mid-term elections, the Republican candidates won a majority of seats within the 435-member House of Representatives. This victory allowed the Republicans to regain control over the House leadership after a 40-year absence. Not since 1954 had there been a Republican Speaker of the House of Representatives. The majority Republican House of Representatives severely limited the political opportunities of the CBC membership.

The political party has a central role in the congressional process. It is the principal organizing mechanism of Congress. The majority political party determines the leadership positions in the two-chamber legislative body. As the majority party, the Republican Party determines leadership positions in the House of Representatives, including the Speaker of the House, House Majority Leader and the Majority Whips. In addition, the majority party selects committee chairs, determines the number of committee members from the minority party and formulates the legislative agenda.

Consequently, the 1994 congressional elections transformed the Democratic Party into the new "minority" party, which resulted in their loss of chamber leadership in the House and their control of the House committees during the 104th Congress. With a Republican-led majority in the 104th Congress, the status of the African-American members changed drastically. CBC members changed from a "minority within a majority party" to a "minority within a *minority* party"—a predicament that did not bode well for African-American lawmakers. With the Republican victory, for example, the CBC lost the chair position of three standing committees and the chair position of seventeen subcommittees acquired during the historic 103rd Congress. For the first time in the CBC's history, its absence from committee chair positions was due to the minority status of the Democratic Party, rather than a lack of seniority among its members.

The CBC's newfound "minority within a minority party" status also decreased its leverage within the Democratic Party. Since the Democratic Party was the "out party" rather than the governing party, the Democratic Party placed less emphasis on forging majority coalitions with fellow Democratic Party members to pass legislation. In other words, Democratic Congressmembers had less need to seek CBC votes, given the Democratic Party's minority status in the House. While CBC members still maintained seats on various Democratic Party caucuses and committees, such as the Democratic Steering and Policy Committee, their appointments on these entities were rendered ineffective by the Democrats' minority status.

Several political scholars note the adverse impact of the Republican Party on the political fortunes of the Congressional Black Caucus. Barbour and Wright argue that the "Black Caucus lost a good deal of its political muscle with the Republican takeover of Congress" (2001: 263). Walton and Smith conclude that "with a Republican majority, the Black Caucus becomes a minority within a minority with little bargaining power, since the conservative Republican majority will ignore the liberal minority, just as the Democratic majority ignored the Republican minority when it controlled the House (Walton and Smith, 1999: 200).

With control over the House of Representatives, the Republican Party also had the prerogative and authority to determine the governing procedures of the legislative chamber. Immediately upon assuming the House leadership after a 40-year absence, the new Republican Speaker of the House Newt Gingrich and his fellow GOP colleagues adopted a flurry of rule changes, changes which included significantly expanding the power of the Speaker of the House, restricting the tenure of committee chairs and virtually abolishing the 1973–1974 subcommittee Bill of Rights (Seelye, 1997: A18; Davidson, 1995). The Republicans passed section 22 of House Resolution 6, a new regulation that formally disbanded legislative service organizations in the House (Salant, 1995: 1483; Hammond, 1998: 209–212). Section 22 eliminated all congressional funding, office space and staff for legislative service organizations, in effect severing the lifeline for many informal legislative groups.

One purpose of the Republican assault on legislative service organizations was to neutralize opposition to its leadership. Congressional scholar Susan Webb Hammond noted that "some believe the Speaker, Newt Gingrich (R-GA) saw caucuses as threats to the leadership centralization that he sought to put in place in the House" (Hammond, 1998: 210). Similarly, other political analysts have observed that "several of the most effective legislative service organizations, including the Black Caucus, the Hispanic Caucus and the Womens Caucus were closely tied to the Democratic Party" (Ginsberg, Lowi and Weir, 1997: 415).

The Republican move to abolish congressional support for informal legislative organizations severely hampered the effectiveness of the CBC. Donald Payne (D-NJ), the newly elected CBC chair, understood the saliency of this Republican tactic when he declared on the House floor that Section 22 " is not about reform. It is a blatant move to put a gag on minorities and others who may differ in the opinion from the new majority party" (Hammond, 1998: 211).

Increased electoral competition among African-American congressional office seekers constitutes the fourth and final factor diminishing CBC effectiveness during the last five Congresses. Traditionally, African-American incumbents, like all incumbents, enjoy a high rate of reelection. Indeed, Congressional scholars Roger H. Davidson and Walter J. Oleszek note that "since World War II, on average 93 percent of incumbent representatives and 80 percent of incumbent senators running for reelection have been returned to office (Davidson and Oleszek, 2000, 61). Heretofore, it was not unusual for CBC incumbents to run unopposed or face weak opposition.

However, during the 2002 Presidential and Congressional elections, the incumbent advantage did not hold true for two Black incumbents, as evidenced by the failed elections of Cynthia McKinney (GA-04) and Earl Hilliard (AL-07). Both McKinney and Hilliard, who were ten-year veterans, lost primary elections to Democratic challengers. McKinney lost a highly publicized race to a state judge Denise Majette, while Hilliard failed to win a run-off election against Artur Davis, a Harvard-trained federal prosecutor who lacked prior elective experience.

Both defeated incumbents were generally viewed as legislators who were predisposed to promoting a collective racial orientation. As House members, both McKinney and Hilliard had very liberal voting records. Since joining the CBC as a member of the historic 103rd CBC freshman class, Cynthia McKinney had garnered a reputation as one of the CBC's most progressive members. Under her leadership, CBC "brain trusts" conducted hearings on the

COINTELPRO actions that led to the unjust incarceration of African-American political activists (*Nation Time*, 2000: 1–3; Umoja, 1998). McKinney possessed a forthright, provocative political style that many viewed as confrontational. Representative Hilliard also possessed a proclivity toward a collective racial orientation. He advocated the creation of a National Commission on Slavery and Reparations: "It's often said that you can't fault the offspring of slaveholders. I would say that's incorrect because (some of) the offspring are still living off the wealth created by the labor of my ancestors. They are still benefiting from the work of my forefathers (Barone and Ujifusa, 1999: 93).

Neither incumbent was protected in the redistricting process that established the boundaries for their congressional districts in the subsequent 2002 elections. Both Hilliard and McKinney lost key sectors of their respective support base in the redistricting process (Davis, 2003; Larkin, 2003). Two of the largest counties (Montgomery and Lowndes) carried by Hilliard in the 2000 congressional elections were eliminated from the newly drawn district (Larkin, 2003: 4). Similarly, in response to a court mandate, Democratic state legislators reconfigured McKinney's fourth congressional district by offsetting a solid base of African-American support in south DeKalb with less sympathetic white voters from the county's northern region (Davis, 2003).

As a result of their weaker electorate base and perceived political vulnerabilities, the two CBC incumbents were more susceptible to formidable opposition. The strength of their respective challenges, however, had less to do with the opponents' outstanding credentials than with intense Jewish and out-of-state opposition (Edwards, 2002; Basu, 2002; Davis, 2003; Larkin, 2003). Artur Davis, a political novice, and Denise Majette, a political enigma who personifies the emerging transethnic politician, are not the typical viable candidates who unseat ten-year incumbents.

Instead, foreign policy concerns, particularly the Middle East, nationalized the contests in Georgia's fourth and Alabama's seventh congressional districts. This nationalization of their campaigns altered conventional features of congressional elections. For example, challengers seldom raise more campaign funds than incumbents. However, the challengers of both McKinney and Hilliard proved to be the exception. Both Majette and Davis garnered war chests larger than that of the two sitting incumbents. Each opponent raised approximately 1.1 million dollars, in which the bulk came from out-of-state sources (Davis, 2003; Larkin, 2003). For example, approximately 80 percent of Davis's campaign funds came from Jewish groups and individual contributions from out-of-state (Larkin, 2003).

Factors other than the pro-Israel lobby also adversely impacted the reelection bid of Congresswoman McKinney, who has been a targeted candidate since she entered office. She declared, "ever since I came to Congress in 1992, there are those who have been trying to silence my voice. I've been told to 'sit down and shut up' over and over again. Well, I won't sit down and I won't shut up until the full and unvarnished truth is placed before the American people (Eversley, 2000: A1). After rebutting several Republican efforts to unseat her, including twice defeating an African-American GOP nominee Sunny Warren, McKinney was the victim of a Republican Party crossover voting in the 2002 Democratic primary elections (Wooten, 2002: H4; Cook, 2002a: A1; Smith, 2002a: A1). Approximately, 35,000 Republicans crossed over to the Democratic Party primary election to cast votes for McKinney's opponent Denise Majette.

A final divergence from previous dynamics of congressional elections evident in the defeat of the two CBC incumbents was the lack of Democratic Party campaign assistance to McKinney and Hilliard. Congressional incumbents usually receive campaign assistance from the Democratic Party leadership. Both CBC incumbents complained that they did not receive adequate support from the Democratic Party (Cook, 2000b: D3; Larkin, 2003). Notwithstanding the Democratic Party's reluctance to support these two embattled incumbents, both McKinney and Hilliard contributed to their own failed reelection bids. McKinney made several controversial statements concerning the September 11 terrorist attack, while Hilliard mobilized Jewish opposition by visiting Libya in 1997 and exhibiting a record of poor constituency service.

Conclusion

The CBC's current predicament in the 108th Congress (2003–2004) is undoubtedly its weakest moment since its formation in 1971. The CBC operates in a unified government in which the Republican Party controls both the legislative and executive branches of government. Heretofore, CBC members' majority party status helped to offset a Republican presidency. Presently, CBC influence is severely limited by a lack of formal power in a Republican majority Congress and minimum access to a GOP-controlled White House.

Several troubling developments have further diminished the political clout exercised by the CBC during the last five Congresses, the 104th through the 108th. Republicans initiated a congressional reform that served to abolish informal congressional organizations. Second, we see the emergence of a new style of African-American Congressmember whose orientation may be contrary to the CBC's racial collective raison d'etre. Indeed, if this new wave of CBC members succumbs to the needs of their respective congressional districts at the expense of the racial imperative for all Black Americans, it may render the CBC a muted version of its Black power imperative (Menifield and Jones, 2001: 23). Finally, CBC effectiveness is also minimized by an increase in electoral competition among Black congressional office seekers. During this period, two ten-year CBC veterans lost their seats to challengers who were substantially supported by the pro-Israel lobbying interests.

One consequence of the CBC's diminishing influence over the course of the last five Congresses (104th through the 108th) has been the voluntary retirement of several Black Congressmembers. Several CBC members have opted to retire rather than serve in a legislative body with such limited opportunities to exercise influence. Among these retirees are Kweisi Mfume, Ronald Dellums and William Clay. The impact of these developments has culminated into a new nadir of African-American congressional participation. Perhaps the characterization of this period as a second nadir is somewhat of a hyperbole when compared to an earlier era that had the total absence of African-American formal representation in the legislative body. However, this assessment is linked to the precepts of the Black power imperative—namely, the ability of the CBC to improve the conditions of the collective African-American community.

While acknowledging the grave implications of the aforementioned dynamics that adversely impact the fortunes of the CBC, it would be premature to dismiss the CBC as a future vehicle of Black empowerment. Membership in Congress permits African-American lawmakers to provide valuable constituency service to individuals in their respective districts. Second, the African-American presence in the legislative arena ensures that the CBC engages in the function of constructive opposition. The CBC remains the most progressive liberal block within Congress. It has been and continues to serve as the "conscience of Congress." Finally, if and when the Democrats return to power in the House of Representatives, the CBC membership is poised to capture chair positions of powerful committees, such as the Judiciary Committee (John Conyers) and Ways and Means (Charles Rangel). In the meantime, however, the CBC is haunted by limited opportunities to exercise muscle on behalf of the African-American community.

References

Barbour, Christine and Gerald C. Wright. 2001. *Keeping the Republic: Power and Citizenship in American Politics*. Boston: Houghton Mifflin Co.

Barone, Michael and Grant Ujifusa, eds. 1999. *Almanac of American Politics 2000*. Washington, DC: National Journal.

Barnett, Marguerite Ross. 1977. "The Congressional Black Caucus and the Institutionalization of Black Politics." *Journal of Afro-American Issues*. 5: 201–226.

Basu, Moni. 2002. "Pro-India Lobby Credited in McKinney's Drubbing." *Atlanta Journal-Constitution*. August 23, D8.

Bositis, David A. 1993. *The Congressional Black Caucus in the 103rd Congress*. Washington, DC: Joint Center for Political and Economic Studies.

Browning, Graeme. 1993a. "Dellums' Turn." *National Journal* 25:1220–1224.

Browning, Graeme. 1993b. "Flex Time." *National Journal* 25:1921–1925.

Carpin, Michael X. and Ester R. Fuchs. 1993. "The Year of the Woman? Candidates, Votes and the 1992 Elections." *Political Science Quarterly* 108: 29–35.

Clayton, Edward. 1964. *The Negro Politician*. Chicago: Johnson.

Cohen, Richard. 1987. "New Breed for Black Caucus." *National Journal* 19: 2432–2435.

Cook, Rhonda. 2002a. "'Crossover Voting Push on to Oust McKinney." *Atlanta Journal-Constitution*. August 9, pp. A1 and A16.

Cook, Rhonda. 2002b. "McKinney Blames Defeat on D-E-M-S." *Atlanta Journal-Constitution*. September 13, p. D3.

Cunningham, Kitty, 1993. "Black Caucus Flexes Muscle on Budget—And More." *Congressional Quarterly Weekly Report*. July 3: 1711–1715.

Davidson, Roger. 1995. "Congressional Committees in the New Reform Era: From Combat to Contract." In *Remaking Congress: Change and Stability in the 1990's*. James A. Thurber and Roger H. Davidson, editors. Washington, DC: CQ Press.

Davidson, Roger H. and Walter J. Oleszek. 2002. *Congress and Its Members*. Washington, DC: CQ Press.

Davis, Marilyn A. 2003. "Cynthia McKinney's Struggle to Win Re-election Against All Odds." In *Readings in American Politics*. Franklin D. Jones, editor. Dubuque: IA: Kendall Hunt Publications.

Edwards, Bob. 2002. "Profile: Factors Contributing to Earl Hilliard's Loss in Alabama's Democratic Primary." Morning Edition. National Public Radio transcript. July 2.

Eversley, Melanie. 2002. "McKinney Said She Won't Shut Up on Sept. 11, Claims She Was Wrongly Derided." *Atlanta Journal-Constitution*. May 17, p. A2.

Fiellin, Allan. 1962. "The Function of Informal Groups in Legislative Institutions." *Journal of Politics* 24: 75–90.

Ginsberg, Benjamin, Theodore J. Lowi and Margaret Weir. 1997. *We The People: An Introduction to American Politics. Shorter Edition*. New York: W.W. Norton.

Gugliotta, Greg. 1999. "Term Limits on Chairman Shake Up House." *Washington Post*. March 22, p. A4.

Hammond, Susan Webb. 1998. *Congressional Caucuses in National Policymaking*. Baltimore: Johns Hopkins University Press.

Hershey, Marjorie R. 1993. "The Congressional Elections." In *The Election of 1992*. Gerald M. Pomper et al., editors. Chatham, NJ: Chatham Publishers, pp. 157–189.

Joint Center for Political and Economic Studies. 1993a. "The CBC: More Power and Influence." Political Trendletter in *Focus 21* (2): 1–2.

Jones, Charles E. 1999. "A Dream Deferred: The Aborted Efforts of the Parliamentary Black Caucus in Great Britain." *National Political Science Review* 7: 37–52.

Jones, Charles E. 1987. "An Overview of the Congressional Black Caucus: 1970–1985." In *Readings in American Political Issues*. Franklin D. Jones and Michael O. Adams, editors. Dubuque, IA: Kendall Hunt Publishing Co.

Keffe, William J. 1980. *Congress and the American People*. Englewood Cliffs, NJ: Prentice Hall.

Kilson, Martin. 1989. "Problems of Black Politics." *Dissent* 36: 526–34.

Larkin, Byrdie A. 2003. "Earl Hilliard vs. Artur Davis: The Globalization of Alabama State Politics." Paper presented at the Annual Conference of the National Conference of Black Political Scientists. Oakland, CA. March 13–15.

Lusane, Clarence. 2001. "Unity and Struggle: The Political Behavior of African American Members of Congress." *The Black Scholar* 24 (4): 16–27.

Menifield, Charles E. and Charles E. Jones. 2002. "African-American Representation in Congress, Then and Now." In *Representation of Minority Groups in the US: Implications for the Twenty-First Century*. Charles E. Menifield, editor. Boston, MA: Austin and Winfield Publishers, pp. 13–36.

Nation Time: The Voice of the New Afrikan Liberation Front. 2000. "A Small Step Forward: CBC Hosts Hearings and Political Prisoners" Winter, p. 3.

Pitkin, Hanna. 1967. *The Concept of Representation*. Berkeley: University of California Press.

Polsby, Nelson W. 1968. "The Institutionalization of the U.S. House of Representatives." *American Political Science Review* 62: 144–168.

Rieselbach, Leroy N. 1973. *Congressional Politics*. New York: McGraw-Hill.

Riselbach, Leroy. 1995. "The Evolving Congressional Black Caucus: The Reagan-Bush Years." In *Blacks and the American Political System*. Huey L. Perry and Wayne Parents, editors. Gainsville, FL: University of Florida Press, pp. 130–161.

Salant, Jonathan D. 1995. "LSOs Are No Longer Separate, the Work Almost Equal." *Congressional Quarterly Weekly Report* 53 (May 27): 1483.

Singh, Robert. 1998. *The Congressional Black Caucus: Racial Politics in the U.S. Congress*. Thousand Oaks, CA: Sage Publications.

Smith, Ben. 2002. "How Majette Beat McKinney." *Atlanta Journal-Constitution*, August 22, pp. A1 and A10.

Smith, Robert C. 1981. "The Black Congressional Delegation." *Western Political Quarterly* 34: 203–221.

Smothers, Ronald. 1992. "Black Caucus in Congress Gains in Diversity and

Experience." *New York Times,* November 10: A17.

Steelye, Katherine. 1999. "Congressional Memo: New Speaker, New Style, Old Problem," *New York Times,* March 12, A18.

Stevens, Arthur G., Susan W. Hammond, and Daniel P. Mulhollan. 1981. "Changes in Decision-Making in the Congressional System: An Examination of the Role of Informal Groups." Paper presented at the Annual Meeting of the Western Political Science Association, Denver, CO.

Thurber, James and Roger H. Davidson, eds. 1995. *Remaking Congress: Change and Stability in the 1990s.* Washington, D.C.: CQ Press.

Trescott, Jacqueline. 1981. "The Gloom Amid the Glitter: The Black Caucus Politics and Parties." *Washington Post.* September 28, p. B1.

Umoja, Akinyele O. 1998. "Set Our Warriors Free: The Legacy of the Black Panther Party and Political Prisoners." In *Black Panther Party Reconsidered.* Charles E. Jones, editor. Baltimore, MD: Black Classic Press, pp. 417–441.

Walton, Hanes and Robert C. Smith. 2000. *American Politics and the African-American Quest for Universal freedom.* New York: Longman.

Watts, J.C. 2002. *What Color is a Conservative: My Life and My Politics?* New York: Harper Collins.

Wooten, Jim. 2002. "Republicans can help boot McKinney." *Atlanta Journal-Constitution.* August 4, p. H4.

Cynthia McKinney's Struggle to Win Reelection Against All Odds

Marilyn A. Davis, Ph.D.
Spelman College

Introduction

Cynthia McKinney: A Decade of Service in the Face of Political and Legal Opposition

After the 1990 Census, the Georgia legislature's redistricting plan that was precleared by the Department of Justice (DOJ) created the Eleventh Congressional District. Cynthia McKinney won the seat, but her district was the target of multiple political and legal challenges. Political challenges were from a well-financed White Republican male and a Black Republican woman. Legal challenges were the *Shaw* inspired cases of *Miller v. Johnson* and *Abrams v. Johnson*. Her experience reveals the continuous struggle over the place of the Black vote at the end of the twentieth century.

A major push developed to challenge congressional districts before the 1996 presidential election. News stories report that the push was funded, in large part by Augusta's "Old Money," i.e., cotton merchants, textile factory owners, and doctors. They were aligned against a Black woman whose district included Kaolin Country, the site of a dispute where Black farmers were involved in a battle to extract themselves from disadvantageous contracts under which they received substantially less than fair market value for Kaolin clay.

Five white voters from the Eleventh District sued various state officials in the United States District Court for the Southern District of Georgia. Their suit alleged that the district was a racial gerrymander and thus a violation of the Equal Protection Clause as interpreted in *Shaw v. Reno*. On December 13, 1994, just five weeks after her election to a second term, McKinney would hear a three-judge panel rule in favor of the white voters saying that the Georgia legislature had violated the U.S. Constitution when it specifically set out to design the majority-Black Eleventh Congressional District.

The United States Supreme Court agreed, and delivered the opinion *Miller v. Johnson*. Associate Justice Anthony Kennedy wrote that race was the predominant factor motivating the drawing of the Eleventh District, and a majority of the Court voted to invalidate McKinney's majority-Black Eleventh Congressional District. The next round of redistricting began with the creation of the Fourth Congressional District in December 1995. Once the district map was redrawn, McKinney's constituency changed. Once 64 percent Black, it would now be 33 percent Black. Now running in a white-majority district, she faced three elections with three opponents in the Democratic party primary and run-off, and a well-financed white male Republican challenger in the general election. The racial crossover vote was called "solid" in a 65 percent white district. In the newly drawn district, she prevailed against Republican John Mitnick, with 58 percent of the vote. Campaign finance became critical in the 1996 reelection bid. The challenger spent more than six hundred thousand dollars; McKinney spent one million dollars. Her incumbency, the access to money, and the quality of her organization jelled, and she won in a white-majority district.

Even though Representative McKinney received some white votes in the newly-drawn, majority-white district in 1996, voting was racially polarized. In the Democratic primary, she received 13 percent of the white vote and large majorities of Black votes. Black voter turnout was 31 percent, while white voter turnout was only 11 percent, a figure attributed to stay-at-home white voters or white participation in the Republican primary.

In the general election there was more crossover voting, but also a continuing pattern of bloc voting was present. Most Blacks voted for the Black Democratic incumbent, while about 70 percent of whites voted for the white Republican challenger, Mitnick. In 1996, McKinney won easily with 58 percent of the vote. But she lost all of the county's Republican-leaning precincts in north and central DeKalb, plus 27 majority-white precincts that consistently vote Democratic. The campaign was especially harsh; both campaigns accused the other of employing racial politics to seek advantage. Playing the race card in this situation was complicated by the parallel and delicate condition of Black-Jewish relations in Atlanta. It is very difficult to separate Black-Jewish relations from the acrimonious competition between Democrats and Republicans in the Eleventh District.

In 1998, a Black Republican woman, Sunny Warren, challenged Representative Cynthia McKinney. In this contest, McKinney won back most of the Democratic-leaning, majority-white precincts she had lost in 1996. In that election, Warren garnered 40 percent of the vote, the highest of any Republican candidate in DeKalb and the third highest vote total of any African-American Republican running for Congress in the United States. In the 2000 election, Sunny Warren challenged Representative McKinney once again. Warren ran a campaign that painted McKinney as a racially polarizing politician who was also unresponsive to many Black constituents. The Republican challenger's support in northern DeKalb was overwhelming. Warren swept predominantly white northern DeKalb precincts, including some traditionally Democratic precincts, but pulled no more than 30 percent of the vote in six southern and eastern Dekalb Black precincts.[1] The stage was now set for a formidable challenge in 2002 to the Black Democrat, Congresswoman McKinney. That challenge would come from another Black woman. This time it would be a Democrat with an incomparable campaign war chest, funded by Jewish, Indian, and conservative groups who were angered by the congresswoman's positions on national and international issues.

Georgia's Renewed Struggle with Race, Ideology and Discrimination in Voting

"We're through with the Democrats," and "It looks like the Republicans wanted to beat me more than the Democrats wanted to keep me," said Georgia Congresswoman Cynthia McKinney after her August loss in the Democratic primary election. The remark calls attention to the historically tenuous, unstable nature of Democratic, biracial coalition politics in the state. It also provides context for a study of the strange coalition of White Democrats, some Black Democrats, and crossover Republicans that nominated ideologically centrist Black woman, Denise Majette to run in the Fourth Congressional District's general election. The Democratic primary election alone drew national attention and money.[2] Four essential forces contributed to Majette's victories in the primary and general elections. They were: (1) extremely generous campaign contributions from American Jewish and other donors inside and outside the state; (2) strong Republican crossover voting[3] in the Democratic primary election; (3) a "McKinney backlash" campaign encouraged in large part by news articles, reports, polling, and editorials in *The Atlanta Journal-Constitution;* and (4) an indifferent Democratic and civil rights leadership at the national and state levels. Additional problems for Rep. McKinney were low South DeKalb voter turnout and her inability to energize her Democratic base—as she had done in the past. Various factors converged to give Majette an election advantage. The Majette victory in the primary seemed to be a bellwether for the November referendum on Democratic incumbents, Senator Max Cleland and Governor Roy Barnes. After McKinney's defeat, many Democratic voters who helped make the difference for Cleland in 1996 and Barnes in 1998 were grumbling and upset that Democratic and civil rights leaders failed to support McKinney's reelection to maintain her seat and considerable seniority in the House committee system.[4] However, mutiny by DeKalb County's Democratic voters failed to materialize in the general election. Instead, Cleland carried the county with 72.41 percent of the vote and Barnes received 73.58 percent of the vote there. Voter turnout in the county was 58 percent.[5] Election results in African-American and White voting districts (precincts) for the Fourth Congressional District's Democratic and Republican primaries, Republican runoff election, and the general election are described in Table 1 at the end of the chapter. They demonstrate how race, gender, partisan affiliation, and income[6] influenced voter participation.

Precinct Support for the Democratic Primary Candidates

Denise Majette received 68 percent of the vote in the Democratic primary election. Her support came from North DeKalb and portions of South and East DeKalb, specifically Stone Mountain, which has the highest median incomes in the county. Majette carried racially mixed and affluent neighborhoods along Stone Haven Drive and Monteagle Trace, and Sandstone Estates. She made a strong showing in seven predominantly Black and other minority precincts, including two that now exist in North DeKalb. Cynthia McKinney garnered 42 percent of the vote. Her strong support by more than a two to one ratio was in considerably less affluent South DeKalb that is on the county's border with south Atlanta. This was a significant drop from the nine to one ratios she had received in other elections. Eastland favored McKinney by a ratio of four to one.

Gresham Park supported her by a ratio of five to one. Terry Mill voted for her by a ratio of six to one. In some voting districts in DeKalb, Majette ran competitively with McKinney across a string of Black-majority central DeKalb precincts. Along Memorial Drive and in Clarkston, Majette ran evenly with McKinney in several precincts that McKinney carried by a three to one or better ratio in the 2000 election. The total vote for Majette in the general election was 77 percent; for van Auken it was 22 percent.[7]

Voter Turnout and Outcome in the Democratic Primary Election

Fifty percent of DeKalb voters, not including those in seven Gwinnett County precincts in the Fourth District, voted in the Democratic primary. Race and ideology were the primary issues in this election. Turnout in 56 voting districts that are ninety-nine percent Black was considerably lower at 44 percent. Congresswoman McKinney won all of these precincts and received 77.2 percent of the vote in them. Challenger Majette won all 48 voting districts that are 99 percent White. Turnout in these precincts was 52.1 percent, which was slightly higher than the district as a whole. Voter turnout by Blacks and Whites was the determining factor in the Democratic primary outcome. There was racial polarization in the voting of both Blacks and Whites. Black and White voters demonstrated racial reflexivity, bloc voting, and racial crossover voting in the same election.

For the first time, the Democratic Party did not exclusively use churches and civil rights leaders to increase the participation of African Americans in the election.[8] Instead, party organizers used small teams to target 300 important voting districts in Fulton, DeKalb, and Clayton counties. There were more than one thousand volunteers to help compensate for any significant decline in South DeKalb County voter turnout, where McKinney supporters, who were defeated in the August primary, had threatened to stay home or vote Republican.[9]

In the most critical race of her political life, McKinney was unable to rally the constituents she had served for a decade. On primary election night, McKinney called the office of Governor Roy Barnes,[10] to say, "You need to get your staffers out of my opponent's [Majette's] headquarters." Governor Barnes dismissed the accusation, as did Calvin Smyre, the "first Black" chairman of the Georgia Democratic Party[11]. Race, voting discrimination,[12] and conservatism have been dominant themes in Georgia's history. These themes resurfaced through the prominent role the Republican Party played in the 2002 primary election, as a large voting bloc and less a traditional political party. More than 37,000 Republican voters devised a strategy in early August for defeating Congresswoman McKinney by crossing over in the August 20 primary to vote for McKinney's Democratic challenger, Denise Majette[13]. Georgia allows crossover voting in the primary election because the state has an open primary system. Georgia voters do not register with a political party, as they do in 29 states. So Georgians can choose to vote in either the Republican or Democratic primary. Although crossover voting is rare and poorly organized in most congressional primaries, it was successful in the Fourth Congressional District's primary election as a result of the effective strategies funded by Jewish and other groups, planned and executed by two conservative advocacy groups. They are New Leadership for DeKalb, a political action committee (PAC), and the Southeastern Legal Foundation, a conservative organization that successfully initiated and won lawsuits against affirmative action programs in education, employment, and government contract side-asides. The New Leadership group estimated Republican voters could swing the vote to Majette if 3,000 to 5,000 voted a Democratic ballot. Sentiments expressed by a local leader of the Southeastern Legal Foundation (SLF) group[14] demonstrate how a significant number of Fourth District Republicans who live in North DeKalb County feel. Their attitudes demonstrate that race, discrimination, and conservative ideology unite in their minds to spur efforts to disenfranchise Democratic voters in the district, by completely distorting the purpose of the primary election, through financial and partisan intervention. A local SLF leader expressed "horror" when he "landed in Cynthia McKinney's district." With regard to the pivotal 2002 primary race, he rationalized "a Republican is unlikely to win the heavily Democratic district but McKinney must go, no matter what," and "made the decision to make a change" from "probably one of the worst out-of-control, left-wing people in Congress." In a similar vein, White House spokesman Scott McClellan declared, "The fact that she [McKinney] questions the president's legitimacy shows a partisan mind-set beyond all reason."

Furthermore, there were many Jewish, pro-Israel, Indian, and pro-India contributors who were upset by statements and votes made by incumbent Congresswoman McKinney[15]. Their outrage galvanized around a public statement McKinney made questioning the role of the George W. Bush administration in the terrorist events of September 11, 2001.[16] These "offended" groups contributed much of the more than $1.1 million Majette[17] raised for the primary and general election campaigns. This was 58 percent greater than the approximately $640,000 McKinney's campaign organization raised. Since McKinney won her first election in the Fourth Congressional District, there has been a concerted effort by conservatives to provide substantial financial support to *any* McKinney challenger. The Majette fund was an enormous sum for a congressional primary race. Conservatives contributed about fifteen thousand dollars through a web site dubbed "goodbyecynthia," established a phone bank to mobilize Republicans and others to vote for the Democratic challenger, Denise Majette, and sent out tens of thousands of fliers in the district[18].

The Character of the 2002 Electoral Competition: The Campaign and the Outcome

Issues

Issues dominated only the Democratic primary election campaign, not the Republican primary, runoff, and general election campaigns. The major issues were candidate personality and style, campaign contribution sources, the work records of the candidates, and the "true" partisan affiliation of the Democratic challenger. Print and electronic media, state party and civil rights leaders significantly influenced popular interpretations of the candidates' personality and style.

Style

The major local newspaper, local television stations, national newspapers, national public radio (NPR), and state party leadership characterized McKinney as a polarizing maverick whose confrontational style was inappropriate for an elected official. Conversely, media and state party leaders emphasized the personable qualities of Majette and offensive qualities of McKinney to the exclusion of any emphasis on hard decision making in office on the part of McKinney, e.g., her pro-environment voting record.[19] As Davis and Willingham have written elsewhere, media cast certain African-American candidates as genial and tolerant conciliators. "In large part because of these characterizations, [Majette] could chance a campaign geared to [her] personality, to the 'bigger picture' of things, conducted 'above the fray.'"[20] She was described as an inclusive moderate with a consensus approach to politics, thereby earning financial support from United States Senator Zell Miller, who described McKinney's criticism of President Bush as "loony" and "dangerous and irresponsible." Unlike the state's party leadership, some civil rights leaders offered more balanced personal descriptions of the Congresswoman. For instance, during a campaign visit to Atlanta, Rev. Jesse Jackson described McKinney as a "cutting-edge politician," who "Georgia would do well to keep in office." Jackson expressed appreciation for her work "whether it be work in Africa or asking tough questions about what we did not know about September 11."[21] Rev. Andrew Young who "so often assumed the duties of mediator," told the campaigns of McKinney and challenger Denise Majette that he was going to sit this primary election out." He "really didn't want to get involved because [he admired] Cynthia and her outspokenness and strength, but [he] also [admired] Denise."[22] Some civil rights leaders ineffectively supported McKinney. For instance, only a few people gathered to hear Rev. Jesse Jackson, Rev. Joseph Lowery, Minister Louis Farrakhan, and Martin Luther King, III at Stoneview Elementary School. This voting district is 72 percent Black. Two years earlier, more than 1,800 people voted at the precinct in the general election for Cynthia McKinney. On primary election day, only 169 people cast ballots at the same precinct, and McKinney received 72 percent of the ballots cast. Some civil rights and labor union leaders enthusiastically supported McKinney.[23] Minister Farrakhan promised "we are going to fight . . . for you."[24] A local AFL-CIO labor union leader encouraged "union members in the Fourth Congressional District to support McKinney in her reelection in any and every way."[25] Media, more than leaders, adversely affected the image of the incumbent. By far, newspaper coverage was the major image detractor for the McKinney reelection campaign. The *Atlanta Journal-Constitution* incessantly attacked the incumbent. Outraged by Representative McKinney's remarks about the Bush administration's handling of the "greatest single security failure in American history," the newspaper described her as "a fringe lunatic, well outside the congressional mainstream." It failed in an attempt to negatively portray McKinney using public opinion poll results. "When the newspaper conducted a poll on its web site, asking whether readers believed the Bush administration or the congresswoman, it found an even split and discontinued the poll."[26]

Newspaper editorials and endorsements proved more effective tools of attack. Republican commentator, Jim Wooten, of the *Atlanta Journal-Constitution* openly promoted the Republican crossover vote for Majette and against McKinney.[27] In the August 11 Democratic primary election endorsement for Denise Majette, the newspaper described Cynthia McKinney's words as "irresponsible—indeed, wildly irrational—rhetoric" that "alienated many of her constituents." Conversely, Majette is characterized as a "bright and thoughtful Yale Law School graduate, a moderate candidate who can well represent the needs of a diverse district."[28] In the November 1 general election endorsement, the newspaper continued to refer to McKinney as "divisive and irresponsible," even though she was not a candidate in the general election. The *Atlanta Journal-*

Constitution's endorsement described Majette as having "grown on the campaign trail, showing a command of the issues and a confidence in her judgments, that she did not have at the beginning of the season, and being a "much better representative of her district than her Republican opponent, Cynthia van Auken."[29] The local newspaper's rationale for its Majette endorsement is shear propaganda and contradictory. Four months later, the paper describes her as having much to learn before she can speak out more forthrightly on many issues. Her positions on subjects ranging from education to health care to fighting terrorism have not been worked out yet. The only issue that Majette is forthright about is support for President Bush's war with Iraq, and a short war is hoped for.[30]

In a final effort to place blame for Cynthia McKinney's unsuccessful reelection bid solely on her shoulders, the newspaper claimed to have conducted an "analysis" of the DeKalb County voters who cast ballots in the Fourth District Democratic congressional primary, and found the Republican crossover was not key in McKinney's loss. Voting statistics demonstrate that Republican crossover was in fact the key in McKinney's loss. There was also a belief among some McKinney critics that she failed to recognize and represent the increasing international diversity of her district. This phenomenon is not demonstrated in voter registration. Ninety-seven percent of 4th district voters are Black and White. Only three percent of the electorate are Hispanic, Asian, and other nationalities. Fifty-two percent of the voters in the district are Black. Thirty-one percent of the district's voters are Black women and twenty-one percent are Black men. Forty-five percent of the voters are White. Twenty-four percent are White women and twenty-one percent are White men. So the diversity issue that the local newspaper and other critics negatively tied to the McKinney defeat is not demonstrated at the ballot box. Rather, it is the fact that leaders must respond to public opinion, which reflects the attitudes of voters and nonvoters alike. This fact may also cause people to devalue the vote because they have reservations about whether voting works in the sense of producing the public policies they want.[31]

Campaign Finance

Comparable to the Alabama reelection campaign of Congressman Earl Hilliard against a heavily-funded Artur Davis, the McKinney-Majette contest appeared to be a proxy Middle Eastern conflict in the form of outside campaign funding and influence.[32] Much of Majette's funds raised during the summer months of the campaign came from out-of-state Jewish donors and more than half of McKinney's funds came from out-of-state Arab and Muslim donors.

A Campaign Issue: Is a Democrat Really a Republican in Sheep's Clothing?

While challenger Majette's campaign focused on issues of economic development, infrastructure, childcare, and health care, the major issue raised by incumbent Democratic Representative Cynthia McKinney was Majette's "true" partisan affiliation. According to *Osburn v. Cox*[33], "the Republican-backed Majette voted for extreme right wing Republican Alan Keyes in the 2000 Republican presidential primary, supported Michael Bowers in the 1998 Republican gubernatorial primary, accepted campaign contributions from known Republicans and those known to encourage Republican crossover voting, and maintains many Republican beliefs and positions."

A Campaign Issue: Do Legislators Work Hard and Do Judges Run Ethical Courtrooms?

In a contentious televised debate between the Democratic primary candidates, challenger Majette questioned incumbent McKinney's record as an ineffective lawmaker who brought in only $365 million to her district, compared to Fifth District Congressman John Lewis, who brought five times that amount to his district. Majette also accused McKinney of being unresponsive to constituents and having shepherded through only three pieces of legislation, including two non-binding resolutions, in her 10 years in Congress. The incumbent countered that her challenger's court record was less than exemplary. Then-state judge Majette allegedly lied about the existence of court transcripts to conceal a mistake she made concerning the protection of a defendant's rights. Interestingly, some people who know Majette say her newcomer's hesitation, as she prepares to take a seat in the House, fits the demeanor of the former jurist, whose staff still calls her "Judge."

Moreover, McKinney charged during the primary election campaign that Majette was ambivalent on affirmative action because she opposed reparation for slavery.[34] Majette supports affirmative action.[35]

A major campaign issue was whether Majette was recruited to run for office. Early campaign comments by Majette in February 2002 suggested that her goal was to run McKinney out of Congress. However, as Majette prepares to take office, she insists that this was not her goal. She argues that the goal was never about being against anything. It was about offering herself in service to benefit the larger community. Majette briefly considered running in the new 13th district which touches 11 metro Atlanta counties including a portion of DeKalb, but opted not to because it made perfect sense for her to run in the district where she lives.[36] Because of David Scott's financial and name-recognition advantages, it would have been much more difficult for Denise Majette to defeat him than it was to defeat Cynthia McKinney. She would have faced an uphill battle against David Scott.

In the general election, Black precincts voted solidly for Democrat Denise Majette according to Table 1. She received 93 percent of the vote in these precincts and their turnout increased to 52 percent. Interestingly, this was the same percentage of support White precincts gave Majette in the primary election. Such a turnout level for the 56 Black precincts would have significantly helped Cynthia McKinney in the Democratic primary. There was little racial crossover voting for Republican Cynthia van Auken in the 56 Black precincts. White precinct support for Black Democrat Denise Majette declined to 62 percent in the general election contest with White Republican Cynthia van Auken. Voter turnout in the 48 White precincts increased to 62.7 percent in the general election. These election results demonstrate continued racial polarization and racial reflexivity among the district's electorate, no matter who the Black candidate is. It is obvious that White voters financially supported and strategically used Denise Majette in the Democratic primary to get Cynthia McKinney out of Congress. Cynthia van Auken received more White voter support than Denise Majette did in seven racially reflexive White precincts—Austin, Dunwoody, Dunwoody Library, Kingsley, Mount Vernon, Shallowford, and Vanderlyn. However, racial crossover voting was evident in eight White precincts in the Republican primary runoff. Black Republican Catherine Davis won Briarlake, Briarcliff, Coralwood, Emory South, Henderson Mill, Midvale, Northlake, and Scott. There was little to no interest in the Republican primary

Table 1
2002 Election Results

Democratic Primary Election August 20, 2002

Denise Majette	Votes	
DeKalb	66,467	
Gwinnett	2,145	
Total for Majette	68,612	58.3 percent

48 White Precincts 30,299 (92.4 percent) Voter Turnout 52.2 percent
56 Black Precincts 7,146 (20.9 percent) Voter Turnout 44.0 percent

Cynthia McKinney	Votes	
DeKalb	48,798	
Gwinnett	260	
Total for McKinney	49,058	41.7 percent

48 White Precincts 2,263 (6.90 percent) Voter Turnout 52.2 percent
56 Black Precincts 26,554 (77.2 percent) Voter Turnout 44.0 percent

Republican Primary Election August 20, 2002

Catherine Davis	Votes	
DeKalb	1,787	
Gwinnett	123	
Total for Davis	1,910	34.1 percent
Barbara Pereira	**Votes**	
DeKalb	1,434	
Gwinnett	81	
Total for Pereira	1,515	27.1 percent
Cynthia van Auken	**Votes**	
DeKalb	2,067	
Gwinnett	102	
Total for van Auken	2,169	38.8 percent

Republican Primary Runoff Election September 10, 2002

Catherine Davis	Votes
DeKalb	780
Gwinnett	36

Table 1
Continued

	Votes
Total for Davis	816 38.7 percent
48 White Precincts	353 (31.9 percent) Voter Turnout 1.9 percent
56 Black Precincts	75 (63.6 percent) Voter Turnout 1.7 percent

Cynthia van Auken	*Votes*
Dekalb	1,250
Gwinnett	42
Total for van Auken	1,292 61.3 percent
48 White Precincts	700 (63.3 percent) Voter Turnout 1.9 percent
56 Black Precincts	39 (33.0 percent) Voter Turnout 1.7 percent

General Election November 5, 2002
U.S. Rep 4th District

	Total
Number of Precincts	171
Precincts Reporting	171 100 percent
Total Votes	150,556

Denise Majette	*Votes*
DeKalb	115,994
Gwinnett	2,041
Total for Majette	116,003 77.05 percent
48 White Precincts	25,989 (62.0 percent) Voter Turnout 62.7 percent
56 Black Precincts	36,064 (93.0 percent) Voter Turnout 52.1 percent

Cynthia van Auken	*Votes*
DeKalb	33,197
Gwinnett	2,004
Total for van Auken	33,198 22.05 percent
48 White Precincts	15,030 (37.8 percent) Voter Turnout 62.7 percent
56 Black Precincts	2,142 (5.5 percent) Voter Turnout 52.1 percent

Source: Secretary of State, Georgia Election Results, Official Results of the August 20, 2002 Primary Election, United States Representative—4th District, Democrat and Republican. Secretary of State, Georgia Election Results, Official Results of the September 10, 2002 Primary Runoff Election, United States Representative—4th, Republican. Secretary of State, Georgia Election Results, Official Results of the November 5, 2002 General Election.

runoff. White voters sat this one out. Voter turnout in the Republican primary runoff was less than two percent of the registered voters in the 4th District. Whites voted in the Democratic primary election to get McKinney out of Congress and voted in the general election to put a centrist Black Democrat in Congress. There was considerably less effort on the part of activists and civil rights groups to mobilize the Black vote for the 2002 Democratic primary election and the general election. A strong Black voter turnout coupled with strong Black voter support for Cynthia McKinney would have significantly enhanced her chances for re-election to Congress.

Congresswoman Denise Majette Prepares to Take a Seat in the U.S. House

Fourth District representative-elect Denise Majette attended orientation meetings in December at the Capitol rotunda in Washington. She plans to focus on constituent services with a diverse group of veterans from the political or campaign staffs of former Senators Sam Nunn and Max Cleland, the state Democratic Party and Mayor Shirley Franklin to manage the district and Washington offices like well-oiled machines. All members of Congress provide services in their state or district, to constituents, and to local and distant special interests. Constituents who ask a member for help in dealing with the federal bureaucracy get special attention from the member's staff because a response can earn a vote next election.[37] She is seeking appointment to the House Transportation and Infrastructure and Financial Services committees in an effort to secure more federal funding for the district. In particular, Majette says she will seek more funding for the Centers for Disease Control and Prevention and Emory University's medical complex.[38] Her request for funding is to help the local economy, and help nationally and globally in controlling the spread of AIDS and countering bio-terrorism threats against the United States.

The Roles of Congresswoman Majette: The Representative Advocate, the Effective Colleague, and the Cue-Taker?

The local newspaper as a political enigma, who defines her politically in an unusual sound bite, describes Denise Majette. In terms of her political ideology, she is quoted as saying, "If you look at these things on a continuum, who you are is one end and who you never want to become is on the other end. You have to decide how far you go to becoming that which you don't want to become, and at some point you draw a line in the sand and say, I'm not going any farther." Nearly four months after Majette defeated Congresswoman Cynthia McKinney in the Democratic primary, she continues to make implicit references to the provocative statements attributed to McKinney that angered many people in the district. Majette is described by friends as a person who never speaks without lengthy consideration of what she is going to say, as she ponders a question before answering it. Majette takes a deliberative approach to political issues. She takes time to understand an issue and is fully aware that she does not know it all. She is willing and eager to be educated by others with more knowledge.[39] Majette may be willing to apprentice in the House because she acknowledges that she has much to learn before she can speak out more forthrightly on issues ranging from education to health care to fighting terrorism. However, the newly elected congresswoman must make a quick and clear transition from campaigning to governing. If Majette wants to be a representative House member, she must decide whom or what to represent.[40] Her belief about learning from others will have implications for her voting in the House. To vote on a bill's merits, Congresswoman Majette may resort to cue-taking, that is looking to trusted colleagues of either party who share her political orientation on the issue at hand for guidance on how to vote.[41] Her newcomer hesitation to step on too many toes before taking office fits the role of the colleague who stresses efficiency (she wants her office to run like a well-oiled machine) over ideology. Senator Hubert Humphrey (D-Minn.) described this role when he said "Don't let your ideology embitter your personal relationships." This traditional rule was probably best summarized in the axiom of the legendary Speaker of the House Sam Rayburn who said "If you want to get along, go along." Such restraint and civility have recently declined considerably in the House and the Senate.[42] Even if representative-elect Denise Majette adopts a style of civility, that is, a respect for social order which is especially important in a democracy where there is a diversity of opinion on issues, no member of Congress can be typical of the district population in gender, since the population is equally male and female.[43] African American women comprise about 20 percent of the House membership. Denise Majette has a potential advantage for this reason. The similarity of this member of the House and her constituents may be very important for representativeness. Only time will tell whether or not Majette's tenure acknowledges this situation. She must govern. The election campaign has ended.

Notes

1. Marilyn A. Davis, "The Survival of Cynthia McKinney in Georgia's Fourth Congressional District," in Alex W. Willingham, editor, *Beyond the Color Line? Race, Representation, and Community in the New Century*, New York: Brennan Center for Justice at NYU School of Law, 2002, pp. 24–38.
2. Each vote Majette received cost twenty dollars in campaign contributions. Patrick martin and Barry Grey, "Behind the defeat of Georgia Congresswoman: Republican right, Israel lobby unite to silence criticism of 'anti-terror' war," World Socialist Web Site, 28 August 2002, pp. 1–4.
3. Crossover voting occurs when voters who typically vote in one primary strategically choose to vote in the other. The crossover effort was significant as voter turnout in the Republican primary election was only eight percent.
4. McKinney is the senior Democrat on the human rights subcommittee of the International Relations Committee, and would have chaired that panel in the event that she won reelection and the Democrats won back control of the House in November.
5. Secretary of State, Georgia Election Results, Official Results of the November 5, 2002 General Election.
6. According to the 2000 census, DeKalb County has a growing middle class and is ranked fifth among the nation's most affluent Black communities. It is necessary for political scientists to more closely examine the implication of: 1) "a growing middle class which has replaced a serious and active mass base of support in the working population;" and 2) "more youthful affluence that is apparently Independent, with little to no allegiance to the old guard leadership of the civil rights era."
7. Statement of Vote, DeKalb County General Primary and Nonpartisan Election—August 20, 2002; Ben Smith, "How Majette beat McKinney," *The*

Atlanta Journal-Constitution, August 22, 2002, pp. A1 & A10.
8. Rhonda Cook and Bill Torpy, "Fourth District rivals go to church," *The Atlanta Journal-Constitution*, August 19, 2002, pp. C1 and C4.
9. Jim Galloway, "Georgia voters make a drastic change," *The Atlanta Journal-Constitution*, November 6, 2002, p. A15.
10. Incumbent Barnes was defeated in the general election by Democrat-turned-Republican Sonny Perdue. Perdue is Georgia's first Republican governor-elect since Reconstruction.
11. Rhonda Cook, "McKinney blames defeats on D-E-M-S," *The Atlanta Journal-Constitution*, September 13, 2002, p. D3.
12. Discrimination is voter dilution through White bloc crossover voting under the Voting Rights Act of 1965, *Thornburg v. Gingles* (1986), and *California Democratic party v. Jones* (2000) According to *California Democratic party v. Jones* (2000), when a State prescribes an election process that gives a special role to political parties, it endorses, adopts, and enforces the discrimination against Negroes that the parties . . . bring into the process—so that the parties' discriminatory action becomes state action under the Fifteenth Amendment.
13. Rhonda Cook, " 'Crossover' voting push on to oust McKinney," *The Atlanta Journal-Constitution*, August 19, 2002, p. A1 & A16.
14. Financed by billionaire Richard Mellon Scaife, who wrote to former Democratic House Minority Leader Richard Gephardt demanding that he remove McKinney from her positions on the Armed Services and International Relations Committees. See Patrick Martin and Barry Grey, "Behind the defeat of Georgia Congresswoman: Republican right, Israel lobby united to silence criticism of 'anti-terror' war," World Socialist Web Site, 28 August 2002, pp. 1-4.
15. Moni Basu, "Pro-India lobby credited in McKinney's drubbing," *The Atlanta Journal-Constitution*, August 23, 2002, p. D8.
16. Congresswoman McKinney's opposition to the Bush Administration apparently had two sides. She voted in favor of the post-September 11 resolution that authorized President Bush to take military action in Afghanistan, although she opposed the Patriot Act, which gave the president expanded powers to suspend civil liberties under specific conditions at home. Then, Representative McKinney criticized President Bush for opposing an independent investigation into the terrorist attacks.
17. She contributed thirty-five thousand dollars of her own money to the campaign.
18. Rhonda Cook, " 'Crossover' voting push on to oust McKinney," *The Atlanta Journal-Constitution*, August 19, 2002, pp. A1 & A16.
19. The Sierra Club, the League of Conservation Voters, and the American Lands Campaign endorsed her reelection campaign and provided financial support for it because of her vote against a Nevada nuclear waste dump, a vote against presidential fast track trade authority which could allow trade deals that circumvent environmental health and safety laws, a vote to protect a wildlife refuse from oil drilling, and a vote to close a loophole that permitted sport-utility vehicles (SUVs) and other light trucks to follow lower fuel economy standards than cars. Cynthia McKinney has been mentioned as a possible Green Party presidential or vice presidential

candidate because of her solid vote on the environment. See Melanie Eversley, "Environmentalists show support for McKinney," *The Atlanta Journal-Constitution,* July 21, 2002, p. A6 and the Associated Press article, "McKinney urged to run for president," *The Atlanta Journal-Constitution,* September 12, 2002, p. B3.

20. See Marilyn Davis and Alex Willingham, "Andrew Young and the Georgia State Elections of 1990," in Georgia Persons (ed.), *Dilemmas of Black Politics: Issues of Leadership and Strategy,* New York: HarperCollins, 1992, pp. 147–175.

21. Rick Badie, "Jackson endorses McKinney," *The Atlanta Journal-Constitution,* August 12, 2002, p. B3.

22. Bill Torpy and Melanie Eversley, "McKinney recycles endorsements," *The Atlanta Journal-Constitution,* August 20, 2002, pp. B3.

23. Jim Galloway, "Outspoken Democrat ousted after 10 years in Congress," *The Atlanta Journal-Constitution,* August 21, 2002, pp. A1 and A12.

24. Bill Torpy, "Farrakhan to stump for McKinney," *The Atlanta Journal-Constitution,* August 16, 2002, p. D4.

25. "Gun group, labor back Georgians," *The Atlanta Journal-Constitution,* August 4, 2002, p. D2.

26. Patrick Martin and Barry Grey, "Behind the defeat of Georgia Congresswoman: Republican right, Israel lobby unite to silence criticism of 'anti-terror' war," World Socialist Web site, 28 August 2002, pp. 1–4.

27. See Jim Wooten, "Conservative blacks align with GOP," *The Atlanta Journal-Constitution,* August 20, 2002, p. A22 and Jim Wooten, "Republicans can help boot McKinney," *The Atlanta Journal-Constitution* August 4, 2002, p. H4.

28. "Cream of the crop in races for House," *The Atlanta Journal-Constitution,* August 11, 2002, p. F8.

29. "These picks for U.S. House would serve Georgia well," *The Atlanta Journal-Constitution,* November 1, 2002, p. A22. Cynthia van Auken is White and a homemaker, educator, and small business owner who placed first in the Republican primary and won the Republican runoff against Catherine Davis, who is African-American and a human resources professional. In November, van Auken lost the general election. Electoral support for the candidates in three elections is included below.

30. Ben Smith, "Majette treads carefully," *The Atlanta Journal-Constitution,* December 15, 2002, p. D5.

31. David Edwards and Alessandra Lippucci, *Practicing American Politics: An Introduction to American Government,* New York: Worth Publishers, 1998, p. 194.

32. Philip Shenon, "In Georgia a Race Too Close to Call," *The New York Times,* August 19, 2002, p. A10.

33. This October 26, 2002 lawsuit filed on behalf of Cynthia McKinney requests that she be named the primary election victor because the Republican Party's crossover voting violates the Fourteenth and Fifteenth Amendments to the United States Constitution and the Voting Rights Act of 1965.

34. Rhonda Cook, "McKinney undecided on whether to attend TV debate with Majette," *The Atlanta Journal-Constitution,* August 7, 2002, p. B5.

35. Ben Smith, "Majette treads carefully," *The Atlanta Journal-Constitution,* December 15, 2002, p. D5.

36. Ben Smith, "Majette treads carefully," *The Atlanta Journal-Constitution,* December 15, 2002, p. D5.

37. David Edwards and Alessandra Lippucci, *Practicing American Politics: An Introduction to Government,* New York: Worth Publishers, 1998, p. 404.
38. Ben Smith, "Majette treads carefully," *The Atlanta Journal Constitution,* December 15, 2002, p. D5.
39. Ben Smith, "Majette treads carefully," *The Atlanta Journal-Constitution,* December 15, 2002, p. D5.
40. Edwards and Lippucci, p. 401.
41. Edwards and Lippucci, p. 422.
42. Edwards and Lippucci, pp. 403–404.
43. Edwards and Lippucci, p. 401.

References

Badie, Rick, "Jackson endorses McKinney," *The Atlanta Journal-Constitution,* August 12, 2002, p. B3.

Basu, Moni, "Pro-India lobby credited in McKinney's drubbing," *The Atlanta Journal-Constitution,* August 23, 2002, p. D8.

Cook, Rhonda, " 'Crossover' voting push on to oust McKinney," *The Atlanta Journal-Constitution,* August 9, 2002, pp. A1 and A16.

Cook, Rhonda, "McKinney blames defeats on D-E-M-S," *The Atlanta Journal-Constitution,* September 13, 2002, p. D3.

"Cream of the crop in races for House," *The Atlanta Journal-Constitution,* August 11, 2002, p. F8.

Davis, Marilyn and Alex Willingham, "Andrew Young and the Georgia State Elections of 1990," in Georgia Persons (ed.), *Dilemmas of Black Politics: Issues of Leadership and Strategy,* New York: HarperCollins, 1992.

Edwards, David and Alessandra Lippucci, *Practicing American Politics: An Introduction to American Government,* New York: Worth Publishers, 1998.

Eversley, Melanie, "Environmentalists show support for McKinney," *The Atlanta Journal-Constitution,* July 21, 2002, p. A6.

Galloway, Jim, "Georgia voters make a drastic change," *The Atlanta Journal-Constitution,* November 6, 2002, p. A15.

Galloway, Jim, "Outspoken Democrat ousted after 10 years in Congress," *The Atlanta Journal-Constitution,* August 21, 2002, pp. A1 and A12.

"Gun group, labor back Georgians," *The Atlanta Journal-Constitution,* August 4, 2002, p. D2.

Martin, Patrick and Barry Grey, "Behind the defeat of Georgia Congresswoman: Republican right, Israel lobby unite to silence criticism of 'anti-terror' war," World Socialist Web Site, 28 August 2002, pp. 1–4.

"McKinney urged to run for president," *The Atlanta Journal-Constitution,* September 12, 2002, p. B3.

Pohlmann, Marcus D. and Michael P. Kirby, *Racial Politics at the Crossroads: Memphis Elects Dr. W.W. Herenton,* Knoxville: The University of Tennessee Press, 1996.

Secretary of State, Georgia Election Results, Official Results of the August 20, 2002 Primary Election, United States Representative—4th District, Democrat.

Secretary of State, Georgia Election Results, Official Results of the August 20, 2002 Primary Election, United States Representative—4th District, Republican.

Smith, Ben, "How Majette beat McKinney," *The Atlanta Journal-Constitution,* August 22, 2002, pp. A1 and A10.

Smith, Ben, "Majette treads carefully," *The Atlanta Journal-Constitution,* December 15, 2002, pp. D1 and D5.

Statement of Vote, DeKalb County General Primary and Nonpartisan Election— August 20, 2002.

Secretary of State, Georgia Election Results, Official Results of the September 10, 2002

Primary Runoff Election, United States Representative—4th District, Republican.

Secretary of State, Georgia Election Results, Official Results of the November 5, 2002 General Election, United States Representative—4th District.

Shenon, Philip, "In Georgia a Race Too Close to Call," *The New York Times*, August 19, 2002, p. A10.

"These picks for U.S. House would serve Georgia well," *The Atlanta Journal-Constitution*, November 1, 2002, p. A22.

Torpy, Bill and Melanie Eversley, "McKinney recycles endorsements," *The Atlanta Journal-Constitution*, August 20, 2002, p. B3.

Willingham, Alex W., editor, *Beyond the Color Line? Race, Representation, and Community in the New Century*, New York: Brennan Center for Justice at NYU School of Law, 2002.

Wooten, Jim, "Conservative blacks align with GOP," *The Atlanta Journal-Constitution*, August 20, 2002, p. A22.

Wooten, Jim, "Republicans can help boot McKinney," *The Atlanta Journal-Constitution*, August 4, 2002, p. H4.

Globalization of Alabama Politics

Byrdie A. Larkin

Just prior to the 2003 Alabama Democratic Party run off primary, I was interviewed by a local media outlet concerning the possible impact of the Middle Eastern conflict on the vote for the democratic nominee for the Seventh Congressional District. The district is the only majority minority congressional district in Alabama and was represented by Earl Hilliard since its creation and his election 1992. Hilliard is a longtime civil rights and political figure in Alabama who served in the Alabama State Senate from 1974 to his election to congress. His runoff primary opponent was Artur Davis a 35-year-old Harvard law school graduate, federal prosecutor and lawyer in private practice. As a native of Alabama and political science professor in my home state, I did not believe nor did I see evidence that the voters in the 7th district were deciding on whom to vote for based on the candidate's positions on U.S. foreign policy towards Israel or the Middle East in general. In the aftermath of the national hoopla of the campaign and election results plus repeated questions from my out of state colleagues, I thought the idea of the globalization of Alabama state politics could withstand a second look. Certainly a congressional election in Alabama could have national implications for domestic as well as foreign policy in a divided Congress with single digits margins of control. While local voters may not be concentrating on those issues, supporters of those issues can introduce themselves financially into the campaigns and affect the outcome. That appears to be case in the race for the Seventh District.

In the 2002 Democratic Party primary for the 7th congressional incumbent, Earl Hilliard led the field winning 45.74 percent. He was followed by Artur Davis (43.06 percent) and Sam Wiggins (11.02). Davis had unsuccessfully challenged Hilliard in 2000 losing by a margin of 58 to 34 percent. This time Hilliard was forced into a run off election where he lost to Davis 56 to 44 percent. But was this the result of introducing Middle Eastern politics into the race?

Living in Alabama I have not known foreign policy issues as decisive issues in Alabama elections, especially in the 7th district. The political flyers and allegations by both the Davis and Hilliard camps caused little furor among voters who appeared to be concerned about the bleak conditions dominating their lives. Alabama's Black Belt, found in this district, is one of the poorest regions in

Table 1
Selected Alabama Democratic Party Primary Results from 2000 and 2002

Year	2000		2002		
COUNTY	DAVIS	HILLIARD	DAVIS	HILLIARD	WIGGINS
CHOCTAW	1072	1541	1739	2593	733
CLARK	77	150	782	1126	387
DALLAS	2927	6508	4244	5772	1187
GREENE	1163	1403	1655	1588	194
HALE	1196	2948	3417	1498	695
JEFFERSON	6462	6998	19596	18938	4163
MARENGO	1687	2282	2962	2523	698
PERRY	931	2544	1142	2666	525
PICKENS	224	304	1422	1100	491
SUMTER	497	1770	2058	2471	617
TUSCALOOSA	1667	2038	4703	3175	686
WILCOX	878	2442	699	2774	933
LOWNDES	112	2004	. . .	. . .	. . .
MONTGOMERY	1080	3281	. . .	. . .	. . .
TOTAL	20133	36249	43519	46225	11313

Source: Alabama Secretary of State, Elections Division.

Table 2
Results of Hilliard/Davis Run off Election 2002

County	Davis	Hilliard
Choctaw	2385	2160
Clark	777	941
Dallas	5724	4982
Green	2167	1141
Hale	1888	2466
Jefferson	24191	17879
Marengo	2398	1910
Perry	1377	2228
Pickens	1540	698
Sumter	2478	1722
Tuscaloosa	6480	2540
Wilcox	989	2495
Total	52394	41162

Source: Alabama Secretary of State, election Division.

Table 3

Selected Socio-Economic Data Alabama Congressional District 7

Items	Total	African-American	White
Total Population	635,300	393,907	228,688
Median Family Income	26,672	$25,985	$46,8875
Per Capita Income	14,684	$11,858	$19,7879
Poverty Status			
Educational Attainment			

Source: American Fact Finder, factfinder.census.gov.

the country and is home to six of the 100 poorest counties in the U.S.

How did this contest become one that spawned both national and international interests? During the run off election and in the aftermath of the defeat of Hilliard, several African-American activist, social scientists, and political leaders sought to explain Hilliard's defeat as the result of targeting African-American politicians who adopted positions on Middle Eastern politics different from those of AIPAC and Jewish interests. An online news service, Blackelectorate.com wrote, "Irrespective of the everyday concerns of Alabama's 7th district, and Mr. Davis or Rep. Hilliard's responsiveness to such, AIPAC hopes to determine who represents Black people in Alabama on the basis of the political candidates' position on Israel."

Eric Ture Muhammad of The Final Call linked the pro-Israeli funding of black opponents to Congresspersons Cynthia McKinney of Georgia and Earl Hilliard of Alabama to the election troubles of the two. He also explained what Hilliard had done to earn the wrath of the pro-Israeli Groups in the U.S. and why this was yet another issue in what some see as the growing rift between Blacks and Jews in the United States.

In a fundraising appeal from Davis supporters, David Kahn and Jeffrey Synder wrote, "We have a very important opportunity in Alabama to help challenger Artur Davis (D) to defeat an incumbent five-term congressman, Earl Hilliard (D-AL-7) who has not been a friend of the U.S./Israel relationship . . . Hilliard has been extremely dangerous to not only our community but the U.S./Israel relationship. As chairman of the Black Caucus, he has lobbied members of the Black Caucus to oppose initiatives supporting Israel . . ."

Washington Watch reported, "the Democratic (run off) in Alabama's Seventh Congressional District is being closely watched by Israel's supporters who view it as a chance to unseat an incumbent with ties to Arab countries and a spotty record of support for the Jewish state."

Noting the growing intensity of the black Jewish divide, noted political scientist Ronald Walters, Director of the African American leadership Institute of the University of Maryland, he quoted as saying,

"Its (Jews role in Alabama and Georgia elections) being discussed both at the political level and in the streets . . . while the pragmatic people have been trying to keep a lid on it the brothers and sisters in the street are up the wall."

Arab American and Arab voices internationally expressed their views on the election. Articles were written to publicize what pro Israeli groups were doing in the election and why those groups opposed Hilliard. Typical was an article written by respected national pollster, James Zogby, who wrote a well circulated article, "A Congressional Election to Watch: the Middle East Conflict in Alabama's Seventh." Zogby wrote, "On June 4th 2002, voters in the Seventh Congressional District of Alabama's primary elections will do more than determine the political future of democratic congressman Earl Hilliard, they also will determine whether, once again, pro-Israeli groups around the U.S. will be able to claim that they defeated a supporter of Palestinian rights."

The international news service Aljazeerah carried a story, "AIPAC's Bid to Defeat Hilliard is Neo-McCarthyism." In it Hasan A. El-Najjar wrote, "Alabama voters should know that unseating their representative would only serve Israel, not the 7th district of their state. More important, Americans should be alerted to the tactics used by pro-Israel groups in their nationwide efforts to pressure members of Congress to vote for resolutions that serve Israel, not the U.S. interests."

Sarah Maserati of the conservative National Review Online characterized the primary runoff as a ". . . sideline skirmish in the war on terror." She basically described Hilliard as terrorist sympathizer and said, Artur Davis is a liberal Democrat. Earl Hilliard, though just as liberal, has voted for school prayer and against gun control. But school prayer and the Second Amendment can take the sacrifice. Anything to make Cynthia McKinney a little lonelier."

While lively and important, I do not believe the debate on U.S. foreign policy was primary in the defeat of Earl Hilliard by Artur Davis. I have identified four factors that contributed to his defeat. They are:

1. The 2000 round of redistricting that significantly altered the make up of the 7th district
2. The conduction of campaigns by Hilliard and Davis including the role of out of state funding
3. The stewardship of Earl Hilliard as a U.S. congressman
4. Goal setting by the Alabama Democratic party

Redistricting

When the 7th district was created in 1990 as a majority minority district (70% African-American, 28.7 percent Anglo) it included most of Birmingham, Alabama's rural black belt, and the most western neighborhoods of Montgomery. After the 2000 round of redistricting, the new 7th district comprised of only 60 percent of the old 7th. Two counties that were Hilliard strongholds, Montgomery and Lowndes, were removed and replaced by parts of two counties (Jefferson and Tuscaloosa) where Davis had run strong in 2000. Hilliard opposed the new map because he said it hurt him tremendously. "It puts me (Hilliard) in a whole new area and changes my district drastically. Forty percent of the voters are new to me." On the other hand, Davis said the new map favored him because of the elimination of Montgomery and Lowndes County. In the 2000 democratic primary in Lowndes and Montgomery counties, Hilliard outpolled Davis 5,321 to 2,192 or 70.6 to 29.2 percent in Lowndes and

Montgomery counties. The two large counties where Davis fared better and which became a larger portion of the new 7th were won by Hilliard, 9,036 to 8,129 or 52 to 47.3 percent.

The Campaign and the Issue of Money

In the 2000 primary, Davis had conducted a campaign as a representative of the new style of African-American leader challenging what he characterized as the non responsiveness of the old guard to the critical problems of African-Americans. This challenge has been described by Ronald Walters as " . . . a consistent attempt by the establishment to create a Black leadership that would be absent on major public policy issues that would be non-threatening on the racist treatment of blacks and that would not march and raise hell in the "old" civil rights style to challenge the system." Of the new leaders Walters states, "They dare not violate in clear words the actual Black consensus on basic issues."

But the Davis challenge was not an anomaly to Alabama politics. Old line members of city councils in Birmingham (2001) and Montgomery (1999) endorsed by the long time politically dominant American Democratic Conference (ADC) and the Jefferson county Citizen Coalition lost to political newcomers.

A lot less money was raised and spent in the 2000 election than the 2002 race. According to reports, in 2000 Hilliard was better funded than Davis. He raised $431,146 while Davis raised $83,208. Two years later the tables were turned. Davis collected $1,567,429 to Hilliard's $812,209. Both Davis (79 percent) and Hilliard (63 percent) received most of their funding from out of state sources. More than $200,000 of contributions to Davis came out of the New York area alone. Pro Israeli groups were the single largest contributor to Davis, $206,595. However, a large portion of the individual donations ($1,231,231) or 79 percent accounted for 79 percent of the contributions to Davis. Much of these were raised at Jewish fund raisers. The Congressional Black Caucus PAC and Arab American groups and individuals contributed far less to Hilliard. Individual contributions accounted for only 33.8 percent of his contributions and PACs 33.8 percent.

The timing of the contributions may have been crucial to the election outcome. There was a surge in donations to Davis after the first primary. Hilliard was reported to have $108,139 on hand as compared to Davis, $117,993. It was during the run off that the issue of Jewish support for Davis and Hilliard's record on Middle Eastern affairs became important. A flyer entitled, "Davis and the Jews," surfaced as a product of Friends of Hiliard with Hilliard misspelled and shortened versions of the names of former Hilliard associates. Hilliard denied any connection to the flyer and charged it was being used by Davis as a fund raiser in the Jewish community. With his new found wealth Davis altered his campaign strategy. He saturated the air waves with numerous slick TV ads that were critical of Hilliard's link to Arab causes and Hilliard's record in Congress. The commercials also addressed the issues of education, health insurance and the economy. Voters were constantly reminded of the ethical lapses of Congressman Hilliard and what the Davis camp called his ineptness to deliver services to the 7th district. Using television was a first for the 7th district which was used to the radio and mass mailings of previous Hilliard campaigns.

At the same time, Davis funded grassroots organizations in the Black Belt who supported his campaign and received the endorsement of the mayor of Birmingham, Bernard Kincaid and influential community leaders like

African-American businessman and lawyer Donald Watkins.

For whatever reasons, Hilliard was slow to respond to the Davis campaign. Some observers have noted the "late start" by Hilliard's campaign, once a low key operation came to life in the last ten days of the run off election. It exhibited slicker and more frequent television commercials, a celebrity bus tour and a huge infusion of cash. One campaign junket through what should have been Hilliard stronghold revealed Davis signs and materials far exceeded Hilliard campaign material. This pattern was also prevalent in those new areas of the district where Hilliard had never campaigned. Donald Watkins, also head of the Voter News Network, an organization of independent voters believed that the Hilliard campaign strategy was outdated. Al LaPierre, former Alabama Democratic Party Director noted that it is not enough to appeal to organizations like the Alabama Democratic Conference and New South. Most African-American Alabama state legislators are members of one or both of these groups and they did not protect Hilliard's interest in the legislature during redistricting. Their reliability in the election should have received much more scrutiny by Hilliard as he developed his campaign strategy. While Hilliard demanded and did get some support from national democrats and African-American leaders it was not enough to alter the results.

Stewardship and Ethics

Even before his 1992 election to Congress, Hilliard was plagued by ethical baggage. In 1999, the House of Representatives Ethics Committee opened an investigation into the financial dealings of Hilliard. The Committee's formal inquiry focused on allegations that Hilliard improperly made loans from campaign funds to several employees in 1993 and 1994; used his congressional office in Birmingham as a campaign office from 1992–1998 and failed to disclose his ownership interest in Hilliard's and Company, Inc. and the Birmingham Greater Golf Associates, Inc. and its successor company, Birmingham Recreation, Inc.

In 2001, the Ethics committee reprimanded and rebuked Hilliard for irregularities in his handling of campaign funds. Its actions were the subject of numerous Davis campaign ads during the runoff.

A long time civil rights activist and pioneer, Hilliard are not able to successfully confront the charge of inadequate representation. The constant refrain of what have you done for me lately resonated loudly with the voters. The older political and party structures that supported Hilliard's rise to power had lost much of their influence and they too were searching for new and different leaders. The style of leadership appeared distant as it relied on the logic of dues paying in the earlier civil rights and political struggles as a prerequisite for holding office.

Democratic Party

Finally, what role did the Democratic Party, both national and state play in the outcome of Alabama's 7th congressional district race? The most crucial function of major United States political parties is to win elections. Hence, party members spend much time and energy on the election process. Parties select candidates, provide money to local, state and national races, and arrange administrative support at all levels of electoral competition. State party organizations play a pivotal role to the party's structure and success. They organize elections and provide the Electoral College votes to win the presidency; they also supervise the various functions vital to state parties, such as fund raising, identifying potential candidates, providing election services, developing campaign strategies and leading the effort in reapportionment matters.

State parties usually avoid openly supporting candidates in their primaries but have been known to favor incumbents when they are challenged. In the later stages of the primary, Hilliard let it be known that he expected support from the national and state party leadership. However, Hilliard must have felt something about the relationship between him and his party leadership when the party did not protect his (the lone democratic congressperson from Alabama) majority base in the reconfiguration of his district. Although the district remained a safe democratic and majority minority district, 63 instead of 70 percent minority, it was just more attractive to the challenger Davis. Party leaders noted that the reconfigurations of the 7th district were part of a plan to increase democratic representation in the U.S. House of Representatives. The population shift would increase the percent of blacks in the 3rd congressional district from 25.3 percent to 32.7 percent and the percent of democratic voters from 51.1 to 57 percent. In so doing, party leaders thought they would increase the opportunities of winning the 3rd district which was previously held by Republican Congressman Bob Riley. The strategy did not work as Republicans held on to the seat and heard Davis talk about a congressional delegation working more closely together for Alabama.

Were Alabama voters from one of the nation's poorest areas so interested in Middle Eastern policy that they rejected a five term congressman? I think not. The victorious camp says the election was about the delivery of services and improving the conditions in the impoverished 7th district. On the other hand Hilliard, who eventually endorsed Davis, believed that his stance on middle Eastern politics and the influence of Jewish contributions probably cost him the election. However, most of what occurred during the campaign should have been expected by Hilliard. At the very least he should have been prepared to respond to the type of campaigning levied against him. Some have argued the charge of Jewish influence was overblown or misplaced and if AIPAC and Jewish organizations saw the chance to eliminate a congressperson that they felt was unfriendly to their interests, they had every right to do so. It is up to black voters and communities to organize and protect their interests. In this election, I believe they made a choice based on their interpretation of their interests.

Notes

1. AIPC goes to Alabama to Protect Israel's Black Vote," *BlackElectorate.com,* June 2, 2002.
2. Eric Ture Muhammad, "With Pro-Israeli Funding Candidates Put reps. Hilliard, McKinney in Run offs," *Final Call,* June 18, 2002.
3. Larry Brook, "Loser in Vote Blames Jews," *Jewish News of Greater Phoenix,* July 12, 2002, vol. 54. No. 43. Also see Mary Orndoff, "Hilliard, Davis Race Goes to Voters."
4. James Zogby, "A Congressional Election to Watch: the Middle East conflict in Alabama's Seventh," *Washington Watch,* May 27, 2002. For example see Jason Maoz, "Lieberman Gave a Thousand Dollars to Whom?" *Jewish Press Online,* posted 1/29/2003; Larry Brook, "Loser in Vote blames Jews," Jewish News of Greater Phoenix, July 12, 2002; also complete an internet search on Earl Hilliard and Jewish newspapers.
5. Larry Bivens, "Some Blacks Blame Jews for Election Defeats," *Montgomery Advertiser,* September 15, 2002. Also see

Ron Walters, "the New Negativism of Black Leadership," *www.blackpressusa.com/op.ed*
6. Zogby, op cit.
7. Hassan A El-Najjar, "AIPAC's Bid to Defeat Hilliard is Neo-McCarthism," *www.aljazeerah.info/editorial/May%202002.*
8. Sarah Maserati, "Hilliard's Battle," National Review Online, *www.nationalreview.com,* June 25, 2002.
9. Mary Orndoff, "Hilliard, Davis Race Goes to Voters," Al.com, June 25, 2002.
10. Walters, op cit.
11. Sharon Childs-Long, "Black Voters showing Signs of Independence," Voter News Network, December 2001, vol 1, Issue 10.
12. For totals visit *www.opensecrets.org/politicians* Summary and see reports for Earl Hilliard and Artur Davis for the 2000 and 2002 election cycles
13. Donna Leinward, "House to Investigate Hilliard," Montgomery Advertiser, September 24, 1999.
14. Sen. Bill Armistead, "DNC Pushes Redistricting in Alabama," suppressed-news.com, February 8, 2002. Mike Cason, "Area Districts May Change," Montgomery Advertiser, January 23, 2002.

PART 4

Foreign and Domestic Policy

In the post September 11 environment, it seem as though the American government is seizing the opportunity to exploit this tragedy by using deceit and out right lies to terrorize foreign governments through invasion and occupation with no justification based on a real threat to national security. On the domestic front, right-wingers both in and out of government advocate a dismantling of many of the true pillars of American progress in reference to the rights of individual. Moreover, an atmosphere of conservative arrogance permeates the corridors of government in reference to helping those who cannot help themselves. To be sure, these are challenging times for the poor and racial minorities.

To help us put things in perspective we have included some interesting articles that speak directly to the consequence, American foreign and domestic policies.

Foreign

Hoda M. Zaki's, "The Birth of a Global Anti-Racist Community at the World Conference against Racism, Racial Discrimination, Xenophobia and Related Intollerence," analyzes the historical and contemporary efforts to convene international conferences to discuss the issue of racial discrimination and inequality. Zaki's article focuses on the Non-Governmental Organization Forum in which she attended as a delegate of the Arab American Institute. She gives a first person account of the reactions of the U.S. Government and media to the Palestian-Israeli conflict as it was debated at the NGO Forum;

Elisabeth Reichert, "The Universal Declaration of Human Rights—Only a Foundation," *The Journal of Intergroup Relations*, vol. Spring 2002 pp. 34-49. This article is an introduction to the history and development of the Universal Declaration of Human Rights. Reinhert analyzes the Universal Declaration of Human Rights in an attempt to establish a model standard of conduct applicable to every individual and government to basic human rights;

Mack H. Jones' "War Terror, the Quest for Domination and Resistance," provides a critical assessment of America's "war on terrorism," in the aftermath of the September 11, 2001 attacks on the World Trade Center of New York. Jones' article is particular useful in placing the September 11 attacks in a theoretical and systematic context that assesses the actions of the terrorists and the U.S. Government's response which included the eventual invasion and occupation of Iraq. Lastly, this article is very useful in the explanation of public opinions held by African-Americans in reference to the "war on Iraq";

On the domestic policy front we included a number of pieces that specifically address domestic policy implications for African-Americans.

Domestic

Margaret C. Simms, "No Matter the Measure, Black Poverty Is High," analyzes the latest U.S. Census Bureau's data on income and poverty in the United States. She reveals that the indices for states in the U.S. with over one million African-Americans, suggests a reversal of economic progress for African Americans. More importantly, the comparative data revealed that African American's households had the highest poverty rate (22.7 percent) of all groups in 2001;

Armstrong Williams, "Politics Mondays: School Vouchers," and the *Black Commentator's* **"Shoving Vouchers down D.C.'s Throat,"** provides an interesting debate on the often divisive issue of school vouchers;

Lastly, we provide Thurgood Marshall's opinion in the Bakke case to set up the Clarence Thomas opinion in the Grutter case to see how the second African-American appointed to the U.S. Supreme Court judicial philosophy is antithetical to the interest of minorities.

The Birth of a Global Anti-Racist Community at the World Conference against Racism, Racial Discrimination, Xenophobia and Related Intolerance

Hoda M. Zaki
Hood College

Introduction

A number of global conferences on colonialism and racism were held in the 20th century. Before the establishment of the United Nations (UN), Africans and blacks in the New World held Pan-African Congresses to discuss these mutual problems. These meetings helped to foster African national movements for independence. In 1955 in Bandung, Indonesia, the heads of the newly sovereign nations of Africa, Asia, and the Middle East met to discuss world peace and development issues. From the Bandung Conference emerged the Non-Aligned Movement, which addressed the problems of development, world peace, and the Cold War from the perspective of the developing world.[1]

The UN also has convened a number of global conferences on topics of concern to the international community, such as the global environment, children's rights, and hunger. When the UN targets a particular issue and calls a global conference to discuss this problem, it hopes to suggest solutions and to establish benchmarks by which progress toward achieving the desired end can be measured. Although the final documents to emerge from

Reprinted by permission of the author.

such conferences are non-binding, they are often used as benchmarks to make governments accountable for their progress toward achieving the agreed-upon goals.

Racial discrimination has been a topic of deep concern to the international community, and the focus of three UN sponsored conferences. These conferences have been in response to a series of UN declarations and actions deploring racial discrimination. In 1963, the UN adopted the "Declaration on the Elimination of All Forms of Racial Discrimination," in which it declared that racial discrimination violated the principles of the UN Charter. Almost ten years later, the UN General Assembly designated 1971 as the International Year to Combat Racism and Racial Discrimination, and specified that the next three decades, from 1973 to 2001, should be targeted toward the elimination of racism. The final year of the third decade, 2001, was named by the UN as the International Year of Mobilization Against Racism.

The first two world conferences on racism were held in 1973 and 1983 in Geneva, Switzerland, and focused primarily upon the ways to eradicate racial discrimination in South Africa, which at the time was governed under the racist ideology of apartheid, promoting a sustained a policy of racial separation. The third UN-sponsored world conference on racism was held over a two-week span in late August 2001, in Durban, South Africa. Durban is a bustling city, home to the busiest port in Africa. It is known for its beaches and its well-developed tourist industry. Choosing to hold the conference in South Africa was a significant and celebratory decision. South Africa, long a symbol of extreme racial oppression, had become since its liberation from apartheid and the establishment of majority rule, a progressive democracy. Today, South Africa has one of the most progressive constitutions with reference to its guarantees for full racial equality.

This third UN sponsored conference on racism was actually composed of three conferences: the first one was an international Youth Summit, the second was the Non-Governmental Organization (NGO) Forum of the World Conference Against Racism, Racial Discrimination, Xenophobia, and Related Intolerance, and the third conference, composed of the world's governmental leadership, met at the World Conference Against Racism, Racial Discrimination, Xenophobia and Related Intolerance (WCAR). Together, these three meetings were known as the 3rd World Conference Against Racism, Racial Discrimination, Xenophobia, and Related Intolerance (WCAR). Each of the three conferences was to deliberate and craft two documents: a Declaration of Principles and the more action-oriented Program of Action. This was the third time world leaders were gathered in a UN sponsored conference to discuss ways to combat racism, and as it turned out, the third time the U.S. government stayed away.

The focus of my article will be the NGO Forum, which I attended as a delegate of the Arab American Institute, a civil rights organization for Arab Americans. I will describe some of the events that took place at this meeting that brought together a remarkable group of activists committed to fighting injustice in their communities. I will then assess two of the most significant accomplishments of the NGO Forum, the reactions of the U.S. government and media to the WCAR, and the attention given to the Palestinian-Israeli conflict as it played itself out at the NGO Forum. I then conclude with some thoughts about the significance of the WCAR as we chart our way through the 21st century.

The NGO Forum was organized by the NGOs with the assistance of the UN. NGOs are known as non-profit organizations in the United States, and are voluntary organizations established for reasons other than profit. NGOs represent a segment in society known as "civil society," that layer of organizations existing between individuals and their governments. Their activities often supplement government services. They can be religious, economic, social, or political in nature. NGOs have played an increasingly important role in global affairs over the past decade, and it was felt that the global NGO community had a perspective and an agenda distinct and different from those of governments.

Preparing for the NGO Forum of the WCAR

The UN and the NGOs spent 15 months planning for this conference, and held a number of pre-conference planning meetings called "PrepCom" meetings in Strasbourg, France, Santiago, Chile, Dakar, Senegal, and Tehran, Iran. At the first PrepCom, the motto for the WCAR was adopted: "United to Combat Racism: Equality, Justice, Dignity," and five broad objectives were chosen for the conference. These objectives were: (1) to understand the history and sources of the current manifestations of racism, discrimination and intolerance; (2) to ascertain who were and are its victims; (3) to suggest ways to protect victims while working to eradicate racism; (4) to provide remedies to racism at all levels; and (5) to suggest strategies to achieve equality.[2] Much additional important work was accomplished at the PrepComs, such as selecting the specific issues the conference needed to address. Twenty-five issues were chosen, ranging from the trafficking of women and religious intolerance, to migrants rights, reparations, and hate crimes.[3] Twenty-five commissions were set up to deliberate upon these issues and to formulate the ideas and language for the final documents. Many of the NGOs worked together in caucuses, of which there were 40.

The PrepComs were venues of intense lobbying by the NGOs. It was in response to the lobbying done by some groups that the decision was made that the conference would have a broader focus than racial discrimination. This time, it would include other forms of discrimination perpetrated on the basis of disability, gender, religion, sexual orientation, xenophobia, and all other excuses for intolerance devised by humanity. At the PrepComs, U.S. blacks were instrumental in putting the discrimination against Latin American blacks, and the issue of reparations, on the table.[4]

Many of the NGO's did a great deal of preparatory work for the Durban meeting, gathering information and writing reports which they distributed at the conference.[5] Many NGOs around the world and in the U.S. who were unable to pay for the travel, accommodation and registration expenses (registration alone cost $100), received funding from the UN. The UN came under some criticism for its lack of funding and support staff to organize the conference, when compared to other global conferences.[6] Notwithstanding these shortcomings, the NGO Forum turned out to be a truly global representation of human rights activists, and an exceptional opportunity to meet with individuals who ordinarily one could not come into contact with.

The NGO Forum of the WCAR

At the NGO Forum, the vanguard of the world's NGO leadership committed to eradicating all forms of intolerance met to talk, strategize, and make recommendations they wished to include in the two final documents, the Declaration of Principles and a Program of Action. These documents were to be shared with the UN Commissioner for Human Rights, Mary Robinson, who was then to share it with the world leaders.

This was the first time delegates from the NGOs from around the world were gathered at a global conference to discuss racism and discrimination. Six thousand NGO delegates representing 2,000 NGOs came to the conference,[7] many of them taking long and dangerous journeys to travel to Durban in order to promote their issues. Some groups braved hostility and displeasure from their own governments, who wished to deny their existence.[8] At Durban religious orders, international and domestic labor unions, international student unions, professional associations, women's groups, children's rights groups, and organizations designed to protect and further migrant workers' rights and those of indigenous populations in Native Americans in North and South America, sent delegates if not delegations. These are only a few examples of the organizations represented at Durban.

NGOs from the United States were very well represented at the NGO Forum and played an important part in the weeklong dialogue that took place. U.S. organizations such as the American Friends Service Committee, and the Leadership Conference on Civil Rights, a coalition of 180 groups, sent large delegations. The Congressional Black Caucus was in attendance. Some of the speakers were well-known U.S. human and civil rights activists such as Angela Davis, Danny Glover, and Jesse Jackson.

International human rights activists spoke and participated, such as the President of South Africa, Thabo Mbeki, Rigoberta Menchu, and the President of Cuba, Fidel Castro. President Mbeki had played an important role in the South African struggle for freedom and equality in South Africa, and he addressed the audience at the opening session. Rigoberta Menchu is the first and most prominent spokesperson to bring to the world's attention the plight of the Mayan Indians in Guatemala through the publication of her autobiography and her political work. She is active in the movement of indigenous Americans in North and South America.[9] Decades ago, President Castro led a successful movement to overthrow a corrupt political regime in Cuba, and established the current socialist regime in Cuba. He had come to attend the world governments' WCAR, and he was the key speaker at the conference's final session. Many of the delegates attending the NGO Forum also attended the World Conference and were able to address world leaders in panels and plenary sessions.[10]

The venue where much of the action took place was a cricket stadium, Kingsmead Cricket Stadium, which is in the center of the city and is surrounded by shopping centers, museums, schools, colleges and parks. In the stadium's central arena, half dozen large tents were set up to accommodate panels of speakers. Translators and headphones were available to translate many of the panel discussions in a number of languages. Smaller tents were placed around the perimeter of the stadium to allow a variety of caucuses, such as the African and African Descendants Caucus, a place to meet and discuss lobbying and voting activities. At a short distance from the stadium, two large exhibition halls were filled with tables to allow organizations to display their materials, much of it educational in nature. Every day, hundreds of attendees wandered through the aisles to browse through the materials and to talk to representatives of organizations from every continent, from the African National Congress to Out, a South African organization for lesbian, gay, bisexual and transgendered rights.

The NGO's pursued a number of different ways to communicate their agendas: some focused on working within the thematic commissions, while others held workshops, gave briefings, and organized panels. Workshops were held all over the city, in museums, schools, hotels, art centers, the aquarium, and in technical colleges. The Congressional Black Caucus held a briefing in the City Hall's chambers; in fact, Durban's City Hall was completely given over to the conferees.

One of the most moving panels I attended was a human rights hearing hosted by the Center for Women's Global Leadership, based in New Jersey, which has been active for over a decade in the field of women's human rights. For six hours we heard testimonies from women who were and are subjected to many forms of discrimination, from Roma bride-selling in Serbia and the treatment accorded to black women in prisons in the United States, to Haitian women migrant workers in the Dominican Republic who often are not allowed to give birth in public hospitals, and who if admitted, are segregated in hospital wards. Migrant women workers in Malaysia testified to working conditions in which wages were withheld and physical abuse was common. Women from the Congo and Guatemala described the horrors of sexualized violence they are forced to endure during times of war. A Palestinian grandmother and her granddaughter testified to the difficulties of living in refugee camps for three generations. Twelve testimonies in all were given, some by the women who had gone through the experiences they described. At times, there was not a dry eye in the audience. As powerful as the testimonies were, what struck many in the audience were the commonalities of women's experiences, the intersection of xenophobia, racism, and gender discrimination, and the ability of the women who testified to transform their pain into organizing for change.

One of the most enriching aspects of the conference was the cultural activity that took place throughout the conference. A 10-day Film Festival Against Racism, free and open to the public, took place in three locations around the city. Films and documentaries were shown from Canada, Mali, Senegal, South Africa, and the United States, to name a few of the countries, and film directors such as Ousmane Sambene, Haile Gerima, and Akin Omotoso were present to talk about their works. Musical and theatrical productions took place in different locations in the city at night by artists such as Hugh Masekela, Miriam Mekeba, and Johnny Clegg. Dance and musical performances punctuated the day's events, and were held on stages near the stadium and around the city. In the evenings, receptions and dinners were hosted by various groups, which allowed delegates to talk and socialize well into the night.

Significant Accomplishments of the NGO Forum of the WCAR

While many significant events took place at the NGO Forum, I will highlight only two. First and foremost was the adoption by the conference of the resolution that slavery was a crime against humanity. Resolution Number 64 states:

> We affirm that the Trans-Atlantic Slave Trade and the enslavement of Africans and African Descendants was a crime against humanity and a unique tragedy in the history of humanity, and that its roots and bases were economic, institutional, systemic and transnational in dimension.[11]

Although this declaration was seen by its supporters as long overdue and the first step to a longer process of remedying past injustices, it was a significant accomplishment to have it included in the final documents of the NGO Forum. A milder version of the resolution was passed and included in the final document of the world governmental WCAR, where significant resistance to it was mounted by the former colonial European governments, who feared this declaration would lead to legal and economic repercussions for their governments and economic institutions.[12]

The resolution designating slavery as a crime against humanity can be traced, in part, to a recommendation taken in April of 2002 at the 58th Session of the UN Commission of Human Rights. At this meeting, a resolution was passed that formally established a Working Group for African Descendants in the Diaspora. This decision has been characterized by the supporters of reparations for slavery in the organization All For Reparations and Emancipation (AFRE) as being "... the first official recognition of the collective existence of the descendants of enslaved Africans by the international community. It offers an opportunity for leaders of Afro Descendant peoples to work in unity, under one internationally recognized identity, in order to gain reparations and restoration."[13] African, U.S. blacks and West Indians who composed the African and African Descendants Caucus collaborated and lobbied successfully in Durban to have slavery defined as a crime against humanity in the final declaration.

This resolution was only one of many passed by the NGO Forum. The NGO Forum's Declaration and Program of Action is 72 pages long and contains 473 resolutions. The governmental WCAR Declaration and Program of Action, voted on by representatives of world nation states, are 56 pages long and contain 219 resolutions.[14] Examples of the resolutions would include the NGO Forum urging States to construct their criminal justice systems to make sure that all individuals had fair and equal access to it, especially those of African descent; urging for an end to racial profiling; calling for more resources to be put into anti-racist education; and for victims of discrimination to have better and more resources put at their disposal. These documents provide a framework to aid the struggle against racism and related intolerances, especially for those individuals and groups who work in countries whose governments participated in the WCAR. If benchmarks are established at global conferences, NGOs can use them to push their governments for additional funding and agitate for social change.

The second significant accomplishment to take place is related to the first, but is more intangible: it was the conversation that took place between, and the links forged by, the global activists. The conference was a site for delegates to learn and to share; the communication and dialogue that took place was exceedingly important in providing a shared consciousness of discrimination and its impact upon its victims, as the delegates crafted and voted on the final documents of the conference. Delegates shared information about their particular groups, evaluated the tactics they used, and discussed future strategies.

This dialogue worked to do two things: first, to present the issues of a particular group to those assembled in Durban. The WCAR was an opportunity to inform and gain sympathy of the world's public opinion, and many groups seized that opportunity and used it well. Three groups were particularly effective in presenting their cases to the NGO Forum and to the world stage: the Dalits, known colloquially as the "Untouchables" of India; the Roma peoples or the Travelers, the preferred terminology for a group usually known as the "Gypsies," and the Palestinians. The Roma delegation, for example, described their experiences of racial discrimination and violence they are forced to endure in Kosovo, Italy, and Slovakia at the hands of skinheads and law enforcement officials. In some countries, the Roma are segregated in housing and education, in others, they are subject to ethnic cleansing. Much of this information was new to many delegates, who left the conference aware and sympathetic to these groups.

Second, the dialogue between delegates at the workshops and panels about racism, intolerance and xenophobia also included a more theoretical and prescriptive dimension, where the roots of intolerance, its consequences, and the methods best used to eradicate it, was debated. Delegates described intolerance and discrimination as ubiquitous and not an affliction found in only the poorer nations. For example, in a panel dedicated to the discussion of hate crimes committed against Asians globally, organizers of Asian communities in Great Britain discussed how they had to deal with anti-Muslim skinhead groups and the police. They characterized this form of discrimination as "Islamophobia." This was a term new to many in the audience, who in a few weeks were to identify a wave of Islamophobia in the U.S. after the events of September 11, 2001. At the same panel, a representative of an Asian American civil rights group discussed hate crimes perpetrated against Asians in the U.S., and how Asian Americans are viewed as perpetual foreigners. The treatment of Asians in Canada was the subject of another presentation at the panel; there, Asians are on the receiving end of harsh treatment especially with regard to immigration and detention laws. Such discriminatory treatment was seen as a deep-rooted fear that some Canadians have about an Asian influx into Canada.

The convener of the panel, Karen Narasaki of the National Asian Pacific American Legal Consortium (NAPALC), noted that she went to Durban aiming to insert into the final documents her understanding of the sustained link between xenophobia and racism. For her and her organization, the rights of immigrants and migrants needed to be placed on the world's agenda.

She stated in an essay: "It is important that people understand how Asian descendants fit in on a global level. When racial issues are talked about globally, they are still black and white. We are trying to get countries to acknowledge [that] [y]es, there are these issues of Asian descendants who face discrimination."[15] She also came away from Durban with new ideas:

> We were really looking at Durban to see what will help us in our future work. We found interesting programs to explore. For example, language access issues are already in international law. European countries recognize the rights of language minorities. I want to see that extended to migrants. We want to see how certain European policies make sense here in the U.S. Would they fit here?[16]

At the conference, many groups defined racism and intolerance as a contagious disease that could be contained, rooted out and conquered. A bright red headband distributed by a Guyanese group dedicated to children's rights summarized this can-do attitude best: "I am a race-free zone," it proclaimed in large black letters, and many conferees wore these headbands during the debates. Many groups accepted the notion of the intersectionality of race, class and gender. And the solutions to discrimination advanced by different groups included reparations and the truth and reconciliation commissions, adopted in South Africa and in some Latin American countries, which stands in sharp contrast to a Nuremberg-style of court-room justice. For many of the delegations, racial discrimination was seen as the hardest discrimination to endure and eradicate, and groups wishing to promote their cause would often present their experiences with oppression as that of racial discrimination.

Ideas about the sources and reasons for racial discrimination have traveled from continent to continent throughout the 20th century. Theoretical advances made by U.S. groups in our national struggle for human rights have been found useful by other groups in other continents, who used them to define their particular situations. The Dalits, for example, described casteism as a form of racial discrimination.[17] Yet six decades ago, some U.S. social scientists imported and used the concept of caste to explain Jim Crow in the U.S. South.[18] And it is pertinent to remember that Durban, South Africa, was the venue where Mahatma Gandhi lived for many years and first used the principles of satyagraha, which were to deeply influence Martin Luther King, Jr.

As a result of this intense dialogue, it was clear to many delegates that there were a number of crosscutting issues that connected them to others around the world who also were committed to making their societies just and equitable. Some of the unresolved human rights issues connecting the U.S. to the rest of the world include the following: the death penalty, gender discrimination, the discrimination against indigenous populations, the lack of migrant workers' rights, the consequences of slavery, the growth of the prison-industrial complex which includes the racial make-up of the inmate population and also, the INS detention camps and the corporate move to exploit a vulnerable population, and lastly, Islamophobia. As Clarissa Rojas, a U.S. delegate for INCITE Women of Color Against Violence, an organization in San Francisco, California, stated a few months after the conference:

> Going to Durban has impacted my work here in a number of ways.... We are really beginning to see that if we are working for social justice issues and if we are committed to a post-Durban strategy, there is no way to consider issues without a transnational focus. It's kind of a double consciousness.... The U.S. is almost in everybody's back yard. We have this incredible presence in the world. Yet here we are blinded by that reality. We need to not just learn about the world, but about the connections between us and the world and what we are doing in [the] world.[19]

This realization of globally shared oppressions is especially important in the U.S., where successive government administrations have repeatedly presented its racial problems as domestic and regional in nature, and therefore, limited in terms of its scope and seriousness. Typically, successive administrations since the mid-20th century have portrayed the problems of race in U.S. society as not being systemic to the social structure, but as aberrations to U.S. democracy.[20]

The conferences in Durban gave its participants a sense of belonging to a global community dedicated to the eradication of discrimination. At the NGO Forum, this community allowed the delegates to see connections and compare solutions, and the opportunity to learn from each other. Thus, the decision of the U.S. government to boycott the WCAR was greeted by the delegates with consternation and dismay, although not with surprise from the U.S. delegates. To many observers, the U.S. government's decision to pull out of Durban was a confirmation of its reluctance to engage in a fruitful discussion with the rest of the world on these issues.

The Reactions of the U.S. Government and Media to the WCAR

As mentioned earlier, the U.S. government did not attend the first two UN-sponsored conferences on racism, and it maintained its isolationist stance by boycotting the WCAR. The position of the U.S. government during the conference planning period was that it would not participate should Israel be singled out for criticism for its treatment of the Palestinians. Of particular concern to the administration was the resuscitation by Arabs and Palestinians of a UN General Assembly resolution passed years ago stating Zionism was similar to apartheid, and was a form of racism.

In the months leading up to the conference, U.S. civil rights groups pressured the Bush administration to send a high level delegation with Secretary of State, Colin L. Powell at its head.[21] As the summer of 2001 unfolded, it became evident that the Bush administration was becoming increasingly ambivalent about sending a high-level delegation. A few days before the conference, the decision was made that Secretary of State Colin L. Powell would not attend. Instead, a mid-level ranking delegation would be sent, headed by Representative Tom Lantos, (D-Calif) a ranking Democrat in the House International Relations Committee and a Holocaust survivor.[22] After a couple of days in Durban, however, the administration withdrew even this delegation from the WCAR, citing a proposed resolution condemning Israel as its reason. This proposed resolution, said Secretary of State Colin L. Powell, led him to believe the conference could not be a success. He stated he made this decision to quit the conference "with regret."[23] The delegation from Israel was the only other country to walk out with the U.S.[24]

The fact that the U.S. government decided to boycott the governmental WCAR was a source of deep disappointment for the representatives of the NGOs delegates, world leaders, and U.S. citizens at home and in Durban.[25] Those in Durban were repeatedly asked to explain how the most powerful government in the world could absent itself from a world gathering of this nature and significance. Groups of U.S. delegates demonstrated in the streets, chanting "Shame, shame, U.S.A." Some held placards stating "U.S. Citizens DEMAND U.S. Participation in WCAR."[26] U.S. civil rights groups interpreted the stance of the U.S. government as disingenuous. They maintained there were two less obvious reasons for the administration's refusal to attend Durban: one was its discomfort in discussing racial discrimination within its own borders at a world arena, and two, it did not want to discuss the issue of reparations.[27]

The position of the U.S. government was generally supported by the mass media in the U.S. Even before the events of September 11th, 2001, the representation of the WCAR by the U.S. media had been unfavorable.[28] Some opinion editorials pointed out how certain African leaders were racist;[29] others pointed to the constitutional guarantees in the U.S. that allowed movements such as the Civil Rights Movement to take place as proof of the superiority of U.S. democratic institutions.[30]

One example of this attitude toward the WCAR is seen in Bob Herbert's opinion-editorial. On September 7, columnist Bob Herbert in the *New York Times* described the conference as "doomed to irrelevance from its inception." The problems of intolerance, he said, "are much too big and much to complex and intractable to be seriously addressed by a UN conference." Many of the delegates themselves were bigots, he noted, such as the attackers of Israel, and "you can't launch a global fight against racism from a base of bad faith and hypocrisy." How can you fight intolerance, he asked, "with a resolution"? For Herbert, the solutions to the problems of intolerance need to be "creative" and formulated by "mature and open-minded individuals." There are "no easy solutions of any kind, and certainly not to the watered-down-one-size-fits-all proclamations of a worldwide convocation against racism."[31]

Conservative pundits seized on the events of September 11 to marginalize Durban as ineffectual and irrelevant even further. Shelby Steele at the Hoover Institution, wrote on September 17 that before September 11, he was going to characterize Durban as "absurd", but now he saw it as "trivial" and a "bizarre little conference." Steele saw a connection between Durban and September 11th. The conferees, he said, embraced an ideology of victimization with "almost [a] religious embrace" because it was only through their protestations that racism was alive, that they could excuse their rank inferiority and "ineffectuality in the face of freedom. . . ." Western culture, noted Steele, was "rich and utterly decisive" and the greatness of this culture was directly responsible for its success. For Steele, the West should have "a profound commitment to fairness. . . . After this, America and the West should unapologetically pursue their self-interest, . . ."[32] While some local newspapers held different views,[33] the major newspapers' analyses of Durban helped to bolster the U.S. government's position to boycott the WCAR. In the final analysis, such uncritical support helps to perpetuate a growing suspicion and distrust around the world about the U.S. government's foreign policy and its inability to collaborate effectively with other nations to solve global problems.[34]

The U.S. government after September 11th has continued to work against the resolutions passed in Durban and the individuals who endorsed them. One example is the action of the U.S. government against Mary Robinson, the former president of Ireland and the former UN High Commissioner for Human Rights. Because Mary Robinson, at the time the UN High Commissioner for Human Rights, had endorsed the declarations of the WCAR, had been supportive of compensations for slavery, and had taken stands on the Middle East that were unpopular with the U.S. government, it lobbied very hard, and successfully, to drive her out of her position. Her contract was not renewed.[35]

The Middle East Conflict and the WCAR

The Palestinian delegation to the NGO Forum came from many sectors of the Palestinian civil and human rights organizations. They came prepared to present their case forcefully, and they did so. They described their experiences in Israel as being a severe form of racism, and that they were a people under siege. They pointed out their lack of freedom of movement, their inability to practice the right to self-determination, and the lack of political equality in all aspects of their lives under Israeli occupation as proof of a deep-seated racial discrimination on the part of the Israeli state. Indeed, the Palestinian delegation was not sure that their leader Yassir Arafat, would be permitted to travel to Durban by the Israeli government. It is important to keep in mind that in the summer of 2001, an undeclared war was unfolding between the Israeli state and the Palestinians. The events in the Middle East and the starkly different positions held by both sides led to a great deal of tension erupting between delegates of the opposing sides. I observed pro-Israeli hecklers in the audience challenge a long-standing group of Jewish orthodox rabbis who spoke out against the Israeli government's policy. Heated arguments between pro-Palestinian and pro-Israeli delegates led to an exchange of fisticuffs on more than one occasion. Palestinians interrupted a news conference held by Jewish civic groups, and reports of intimidation of Jewish delegates were lodged with the organizers of the conference. Both sides, in their zeal to establish their national legitimacy, did not observe established rules of procedure. Mary Robinson expressed concern and condemnation of such activities, but felt that the conference was not derailed as the "rich texture" of the conference's discussions outweighed the "discordant voices."[36] Many others echoed this observation.[37]

However, the Palestinian delegation was often misrepresented in the U.S. media as hijacking the NGO Forum and impeding a real discussion of racism.[38] It did not in fact do so: the vast majority of the delegates from around the world were already in sympathy with the Palestinians, their lack of human and civil rights, and their status as the longest-existing group of refugees in history. This open and global sympathy for the Palestinians greatly upset the U.S. pro-Israeli delegates in Durban, such as the Anti-Defamation League. Such delegates found themselves to be a highly criticized minority, and they subsequently characterized their experiences in Durban as anti-Semitic in nature.[39] However, other Jewish delegates from Israel who were critical of their own government did not complain of anti-Semitism while in Durban. The emotional intensity of the Palestinian and pro-Israeli forces foreshadowed the events which were to take place in the following year in that region. For these groups Durban was not just a place to think and talk about racism, it was also a battlefield.

While the discussion around the Middle East was contentious, the Palestinian-Israeli issue was only one of many difficult issues dealt with at the conference. The politics of the WCAR included other controversial issues. Two of the other major issues of contention were first, the issue of which groups should be included as victims of racism, xenophobia and related intolerance, and the historical issues surrounding slavery and its aftermath. The second issue was that of the definition of the trans-Atlantic slave trade, colonialism, slavery and reparation.[40] Notwithstanding the attempts to stifle dialogue, the debates went on at Durban, and the conference dealt with the many topics placed on its agenda.

Conclusion: Politics and Hope

The venue of the Durban conferences, South Africa, was a constant reminder of how society can be transformed for the better if we use politics as an agent of change. During the conference, it was remarked upon frequently that ten years ago, many of the conferees would not have been able to enter and use City Hall. In fact, holding such a conference a decade ago would have been impossible in South Africa. Yet, during the conference Durban's City Hall sported a huge banner over its front portals, welcoming its guests, and proclaiming its solidarity with the world's anti-racist forces. On a personal note, I observed how delegates from around the world had more faith in the power of politics to affect change than many of us from the U.S. had; hope burns brighter abroad even though the struggle for human rights in the U.S. has won some important advances.

This lesson about politics and hope was reinforced by many small incidents I observed during that week. While waiting for one of the workshops to begin, I viewed an exhibit dedicated to the history of apartheid in Durban, and the various aspects of the pass system. While I was there a group of young South African schoolgirls entered, and began to listen to the tape explaining the pass system. The thought occurred to me that had the struggle in South Africa not been successful in dismantling apartheid, these young school children would have learned about the pass system by living it, instead of learning about it by going to a museum.

Globalization has given birth to its dissenters, and it is in conferences such as the NGO Forum of the WCAR and its documents where one finds the most trenchant criticisms of globalization and the most comprehensive hopes for a more just global society. At the NGO Forum, we did not agree as to the causes of racism and related intolerances, or as to their remedies. But if South Africa, which a few years ago was the most racist of all nations, is today one of the most progressive countries in terms of its constitutional guarantees for human equality, then we, too, can struggle and hope to win the battle against racism. Durban gave us a sense that winning the fight against all forms of intolerance is a distinct possibility and not a utopian dream.

The Durban conferences engendered a sense of empowerment, hope and optimism that were grounded in the realization of shared work and commitments. It was a realization of the strength in our numbers. Many of us took away from the NGO Forum a sense of hope because we felt we were part of a larger, global movement committed to working against all forms of intolerance and for human rights. This dialogue, and sharing of ideas, tactics, and strategy, is an important step in the consolidation of global progressive forces that need to be able to come together to talk about goals and strategies. In fact, such a conference should be seen as a progressive counterpart to the consolidation of the forces of global capitalism, which meet far more frequently and have more resources at their disposal.

Conferences are convened to accomplish a specific set of goals, and international conferences are no exception. While at a conference, delegates share their views, learn from each other, and take new ideas home. At some conferences, a specific set of recommendations are crafted, voted upon, and adopted by the attendees. Global conferences are logistically the most difficult to convene, given the distances many of the delegates have to travel, the prohibitive costs involved, the languages that need to be translated instantaneously in order for communication to take place, and the difficulties in accommodating large numbers of people. Yet all conferences, be they global, regional, national or local, create for its attendees a sense of community engendered by a shared sense of mission, and which can often create a momentum for social change. At the NGO Forum, a fleeting community of 10 days duration was created out of shared interests, passions, and the sheer exhilaration of living in a country that recently had taken enormous strides toward achieving a just and egalitarian society. This sense of support and community still exists. Many NGOs here and around the world continue to work toward the elimination of discrimination and new injustices created in the wake of September 11th. We must not let this global conference on oppression be marginalized; it was a significant moment where those whose lives have been distorted by various systems of oppression had a rendezvous with each other. Hopefully, Durban will be remembered as the site and catalyst for the rebirth of a long-dormant, global, anti-racist civic community.

Appendix

Twenty-nine topics were given specific attention in the NGO Program of Action. These were:

African/African Descendants; Slave Trade and Slavery; Reparations; Anti-Semitism; Arab and Middle East [Islamophobia]; Asians and Asian Descendants; Caste and Discrimination Based on Work and Descent; Criminal Justice and Judicial Systems; Colonialism and Foreign Occupation; Persons With Disabilities; Education; Ethnic and National Minorities and Groups; Environmental Racism; Gender; Globalization; Hate Crimes; Health and HIV/AIDS; Indigenous Peoples; Labor; Media and Communication; Migrants and Migrant Workers; Palestinians and Palestine; Refugees, Asylum Seekers, Stateless and Internally Displaced Persons; Religious Intolerance; Roma Nation; Sexual Orientation; Young People and Children; The Girl Child; and Trafficking.

References

All for Reparations and Emancipation. "Progress For Reparations and Emancipation." Press release on 6 May 2002, pp. 1-3. Accessed on http://www.ncobps-575W@ncat.edu on 5/13/2002.

American Friends Service Committee. "Durban and Beyond: A Report on the American Friends Service Committee's Involvement in the 3rd World Conference Against Racism, Racial Discrimination, Xenophobia and Related Intolerance." Board Supporting Paper #14. No place, n.d.

"Call to Eradicate Discrimination and Intolerance Marks Conclusion of World Conference Against Racism," 8 September 2001. NY: Department of Public Information, News and Media Services Division. Accessed on http://www.un.org/WCAR/pressreleases/rd-d45.html on 9/11/01.

Constable, Pamela. "Mideast Dominates Racism Meeting." *The Washington Post* 1 September 2001, A-1, A-22.

_____. "Slavery's Legacy: Divisions on How To Make Amends: Debate at World Racism Conference Focuses on Apologies vs. Reparations." *The Washington Post* 2 September 2001, A-16.

_____. "Israel, U.S. Quit Forum On Racism." *The Washington Post* 4 September 2001, A-1, A-16.

Crossette, Barbara. "Global Look at Racism Hits Many Sore Points." *The New York Times* 4 March 2001.

_____. "Rights Leaders Urge Powell to Attend U.V. Racism Conference." *The New York Times* 11 July 2001, A-9.

Cushman, John H. Jr. "U.S. Delegates In Durban Practiced Minimalism." *The New York Times* 4 September 2001, A-8.

Dalit Caucus Handout No. 1. "Caste Discrimination Against Dalits is Racial Discrimination: Work and Descent based Caste Discrimination against Dalits is Racial Discrimination." No place, n.d.

"Declaration of the World Conference Against Racism, Racial Discrimination, Xenophobia and Related Intolerance." Accessed on http://www.icare.to/31decwebversion.html on 3/21/2002.

Dollard, John. Caste and Class in a Southern Town. NY: Doubleday, 1957.

Dudziak, Mary L. "Desegregation as a Cold War Imperative." *Stanford Law Review* 41 (November 1988): 61-120.

Esedebe, P. O. *Pan-Africanism: The Idea and the Movement, 1776-1963*. Washington, DC: Howard University Press, 1982.

Fears, Darryl. "Threat to Boycott U.N. Race Talks Praised, Attacked." *The Washington Post* 1 August 2001, A-3.

"Forecast: High Winds, Hot Air." Editorial of *The Washington Post* 28 August 2001, A-14.

Herbert, Bob. "Doomed to Irrelevance." *New York Times* 6 September 2001, A-27.

Hoagland, Jim. "Speak Out Against Mugabe's Racism." *The Washington Post* 26 August 2001, B-7.

International Human Rights Law Group. "Combating Racism Together: A Guide to Participating in the UN World Conference Against Racism." Washington, DC: International Human Rights Law Group, June 2001.

———, convener. "Report of the US Leadership Meetings on the World Conference Against Racism."

———. "Bellagio Consultation on the UN World Conference Against Racism." Convened by Gay J. McDougall. January 2000.

International Possibilities Unlimited. *Journey to Durban.* Silver Spring, MD: n.d.

King, Albert I. "What Durban Could Learn From Jim Nabrit." *The Washington Post* 1 September 2001, A-29.

Lawyers' Committee for Civil Rights Under Law. "Global Injustice: An Overview of Racism, Racial Discrimination, Xenophobia, and Related Intolerance: Produced in Preparation for the United Nations World Conference Against Racism, Racial Discrimination, Xenophobia, and Related Intolerance in Durban, South Africa." Washington, DC: Lawyers' Committee for Civil Rights Under Law, July 2001.

Leadership Conference on Civil Rights. "American Dream? America Reality! A Report on Race, Ethnicity and the Law in the United States In Preparation for the Initial Country Review of the United States by the United Nations Committee on the Elimination of Racial Discrimination." Washington, DC: Leadership Conference on Civil Rights and Lawyers' Committee for Civil Rights Under Law, 2001.

"A Mean-Spirited Conference." Editorial, *The New York Times* 17 August 2001, A-18.

Menchu, Rigoberta. *I, Rigobeta Menchu: An Indian Woman in Guatemala.* Translated and ed. by E. Borgos-Debray.

"Missing the boat at Durban." Editorial in *The Berkshire Eagle* 31 August 2001, A-6.

Morin, Richard. "World Image of U.S. Declines." *The Washington Post* 5 December 2002. A-26.

Narasaki, Karen. "Personal Experiences at the WCAR." Accessed on http://ww.ngoworldconference.org/ach010701.html on 3/21/2002.

Perlez, Jane. "Powell Will Not Attend Racism Conference in South Africa." *The New York Times* 28 August 2001, A-7.

Polakow-Suransky, Sasha. "A Politics of Denial." *The American Prospect* 13 1 (January 1-14, 2002).

Raheem, T. Abdul. *Pan Africanism: Politics, Economy, and Social Change in the Twenty First Century.* NY: New York University Press, 1996.

Rojas, Clarissa. "Personal Reactions to the WCAR, 28 February 2002." Accessed on http://www.ngoworldconference.org/arch022802.html on 3/21/2002.

Sipress, Alan. "Powell To Avoid Racism Forum." *The Washington Post* 27 August 2001, A-1, A-12.

Slevin, Peter. "Decision to Skip N.N. Meeting Lamented." *The Washington Post* 28 August 2001, p. A-4.

Steele, Shelby. "War of the Worlds." *The Wall Street Journal* 17 September 2001.

Swarns, Rachel L. "Walkout Staged by U.S. and Israel at Racism Talks." *The New York Times* 4 September 2001, A-1, A-8.

———. "At Race Talks, Delegates Cite Early Mistrust." *The New York Times* 5 September 2001, A-1, A-8.

———. "Overshadowed, Slavery Debate Boils in Durban." *The New York Times* 6 September 2001, A-1, A-12.

———. "Rancor and Powell's Absence Cloud Racism Parley." *The New York Times* 31 August 2001, A-3.

Themba-Nixon, Makani. "Durban Diary: Up Close and Black at the World Conference Against Racism." Accessed on http://www.seeingblack.com on 3/13/2002.

TransAfrica Forum. "United Nations World Conference Against Racism, Racial

Discrimination, Xenophobia and Related Intolerance." Washington, DC: Trans-Africa Forum, October 2001.

Transnational Racial Justice Initiative, compiler. "The Persistence of White Privilege and Institutional Racism in U.S. Policy: A Report of the U.S. Government Compliance with the International Convention on the Elimination of All Forms of Racial Discrimination." Oakland, California: Transnational Racial Justice Initiative, March 2001.

Tupaj Amaru. "Causes and origin of racial discrimination." Submitted at the World Conference Against Race, Racial Discrimination, Xenophobia and Related Intolerance. 31 May 2001.

"WCAR: Next Steps In A Painful Journey?" The Network of Alliances Bridging Race & Ethnicity (NABRE) accessed on http://www.jointcenter.org/nabre/whatsnew/wcar on 12/15/2001.

WCAR NGO Forum Declaration. 3 September 2001. Accessed from http://www.icare.to/31decwebversion.html.

Williams, Ian. "Bush's Hit List At the United Nations." *Foreign Policy in Focus* (2001) Accessed on http://www.alternet.org 13 May 2002.

Wright, Richard. *The Color Curtain: A Report on the Bandung Conference* with a Foreword by Gunnar Myrdal and an Afterword by Amritjit Singh. NY: World Publishing Company, 1956; reprint edition, Jackson, Mississippi: Banner Books, University Press of Mississippi, 1994.

Notes

1. For information about Pan-Africanism, consult P.O. Esedebe, *Pan Africanism: The Idea and the Movement, 1776-1963* (Washington, DC: Howard University press, 1982); and T. Abdul Raheeem, *Pan Africanism: Politics, Economy and Social Change in the Twenty First Century* (NY: New York University Press, 1996). For an analysis of the Bandung conference, see Richard Wright, *The Color Curtain: A Report on the Bandung Conference* with a Foreword by Gunnar Myrdal and an Afterword by Amritjit Singh (NY: World Publishing Company, 1956; Jackson, Mississippi: Banner Books, University Press of Mississippi, 1994).

2. See International Human Rights Law Group, *Combating Racism Together: A Guide to Participating in the UN World Conference Against Racism,* (Washington, DC: International Human Rights Law Group, June 2001), p.5.

3. For a complete listing of the issues that were discussed and voted upon at the NGO Forum see the Appendix.

4. Barbara Crossette, "Global Look at Racism Hits Many Sore Points," *The New York Times* 4 March 2001.

5. Examples of such reports to come out of the US would include: American Friends Service Committee, "Durban and Beyond: A Report on the American Friends Service Committee's Involvement in the 3rd World Conference Against Racism, Racial Discrimination, Xenophobia and Related Intolerance," Board Supporting Paper #14, (n.d.); Transnational Racial Justice Initiative, compiler, "The Persistence of White International Convention on the Elimination of All Forms of Racial Discrimination," (Oakland, California: Transnational Racial Justice Initiative, March 2001); "Report of the US Leadership Meetings on the World Conference Against Racism," convened by the International Human Rights Law Group, which held three meetings in 2000, in Atlanta, San Francisco, and Phoenix; International Human Rights Law Group, "Bellagio Consultation on

the UN World Conference Against Racism," convened by Gay J. McDougall with the support of The Rockefeller Foundation (January 2000); International Possibilities Unlimited (IPU), *Journey to Durban* (Silver Spring, MD, n.d); Lawyers' Committee for Civil Rights Under Law, "Global Injustice: An Overview of Racism, Racial Discrimination, Xenophobia, and Related Intolerance: Produced in Preparation for the United Nations World Conference Against Racism, Racial Discrimination, Xenophobia, and Related Intolerance in Durban, South Africa," (Washington, DC: Lawyers' Committee for Civil Rights Under Law, July 2001); Leadership Conference on Civil Rights, "American Dream? America Reality! A Report on Race, Ethnicity and the Law in the United States In Preparation for the Initial Country Review of the United States by the United Nations Committee on the Elimination of Racial Discrimination," (Washington, DC: Leadership Conference on Civil Rights and Lawyers' Committee for Civil Rights Under Law, 2001); and TransAfrica Forum, "United Nations World Conference Against Racism, Racial Discrimination, Xenophobia and Related Intolerance," (Washington, DC: TransAfrica Forum, October 2001).

6. Makani Themba-Nixon, "Durban Diary: Up Close and Black at the World Conference Against Racism," p.7. Accessed on http://www.seeingblack.com on 3/12/2002; Karen Narasaki, "Personal Experiences at the WCAR," originally posted to CAMBIO, http://www.ngoworldconference.org/arch0107 02.html, accessed on 3/21/2002, pp. 1-3.

7. American Friends Service Committee, "Durban and Beyond," p.2.

8. Sasha Polakow-Suransky, "A Politics of Denial," *The American Prospect* 13, 1 (January 1-14, 2002).

9. See Menchu's autobiography for a moving account of the conditions of her people and her evolution as a political activist: Rigoberta Menchu, *I Rigoberta Menchu: An Indian Woman in Guatemala* trans. and ed. E. Borgos-Debray (get data)

10. "Call to Eradicate Discrimination and Intolerance Marks Conclusion of World Conference Against Racism," 8 September, Department of Public Information, News and Media Services Division, New York. Accessed on http://www.un.org/WCAR/pressreleases/rd-d45.html on 9/11/01.

11. NGO Forum Declaration, 3 September 2001, p.10. It may be accessed at http://www.icare.to/31decwebversion.html.

12. Resolution Number 13 in the "Declaration of the WCAR" states: "We acknowledge that slavery and the slave trade, including the transatlantic slave trade, were appalling tragedies in the history of humanity not only because of their abhorrent barbarism but also in terms of their magnitude, organized nature and especially their negation of the essence of the victims, and further acknowledge that slavery and the slave trade are a crime against humanity and should always have been so, especially the transatlantic slave trade and are among the major sources and manifestations of racism, racial discrimination, xenophobia and related intolerance, and that Africans and people of African descent, Asians and people of Asian descent and indigenous peoples were victims of these acts and continue to be victims of their consequences." "Declaration of the World Conference Against Racism, Racial Discrimination, Xenophobia and

Related Intolerance," http://www.icare.to/31decwebversion.html accessed on 3/21/2002, p.6. Many considered it watered-down because it made no mention of the economic underpinnings of slavery.

13. All For Reparations and Emancipation, "Progress in the International Reparations Effort," press release on 6 May 2002, pp. 1-3, accessed at http://www.ncobps-575W@ncat.edu on 5/13/2002. AFRE can be accessed on the Internet at http://www.afre-ngo.org

14. These documents may be accessed at http://www.icare.to/31decwebversion.html

15. Narasaki, pp. 3-4.

16. Ibid., p.4.

17. See the Dalit Caucus Handout: No. 1 "Caste Discrimination Against Dalits is Racial Discrimination: Work and Descent based Caste Discrimination against Dalits is Racial Discrimination," n.p., n.d.; and "Causes and origin of racial discrimination," Contribution submitted by the Indian Movement "Tupaj Amaru," at the World Conference Against Racism, Racial Discrimination, Xenophobia and Related Intolerance, 31 May 2001.

18. John Dollard, *Caste and Class in a Southern Town* (Doubleday, 1957)

19. Clarissa Rojas, "Personal Reactions to the WCAR, 28 February 2002," originally posted to CAMBIO, http://www.ngoworldconference.org/arch022802.html, accessed on 3/21/2002.

20. For a historical perspective on how the U.S. government represents its internal problems abroad, see Mary L. Dudziak, "Desegregation as a Cold War Imperative," *Stanford Law Review* 41 (November 1988): 61-120.

21. Barbara Crossette, "Rights Leaders Urge Powell to Attend U.N. Racism Conference," *New York Times* 11 July 2001, p. A-9.

22. John H. Cashman, Jr., "U.S. Delegates In Durban Practiced Minimalism," *The New York Times* 4 September 2001, p. A-8; Jane Perlez, "Powell Will Not Attend Racism Conference in South Africa," *New York Times* 28 August 2001, p. A-7; Alan Sipress, "Powell To Avoid Racism Forum," *Washington Post* 27 August 2001, pp. A-1, A-12.

23. Pamela Constable, "Israel, U.S. Quit Forum On Racism," *The Washington Post* 4 September 201, pp. A-1, A-16.

24. Rachel L. Swarns, "Walkout Staged by U.S. and Israel at Racism Talks," *New York Times* 4 September 2001, pp. A-1, A-8.

25. Peter Slevin, "Decision to Skip U.N. Meeting Lamented," *The Washington Post* 28 August 2001, p. A-4.

26. Swarns, "Walkout Staged by U.S. and Israel at Racism Talks," pp. A-1, A-8.

27. Darryl Fears, "Threat to Boycott U.N. Race Talks Praised, Attacked," *Washington Post* 1 August 2001, p. A-3.

28. See Rachel L. Swarns, "At Race Talks, Delegates Cite Early Mistrust," *New York Times*, 5 September 2001, p. A-1, A-8; "Forecast: High Winds, Hot Air," an editorial of *The Washington Post* 28 August 2001, A-14; "A Mean-Spirited N.N. Conference," editorial, *The New York Times* 17 August 2001, p. A-18.

29. Jim Hoagland, "Speak Out Against Mugabe's Racism," *The Washington Post* 26 August 2001, p. B-7.

30. Albert I. King, "What Durban Could Learn From Jim Nabrit," *The Washington Post* 1 September 2001, p. A-29.

31. Bob Herbert, "Doomed to Irrelevance," *The New York Times* 6 September 2001, p. A-27.

32. Shelby Steele, "War of the Worlds," *The Wall Street Journal,* 17 September 2001.
33. See for example, the editorial "Missing the boat at Durban," *The Berkshire Eagle* 31 August 2001, p. A-6.
34. Richard Morin, "World Image of U.S. Declines," *The Washington Post* 5 December 2002, p. A-26.
35. Ian Williams, "Bush's Hit List At the United Nations," *Foreign Policy in Focus* (2001). Accessed on http://www.alternet.org on 13 May 2002.
36. Mary Robinson quoted in Rachel L. Swarns, "Rancor and Powell's Absence Cloud Racism Parley," *The New York Times* 31 August 2001, p. A-3.
37. Even those delegates who felt that the attention to the Palestinian-Israeli dispute was too time-consuming acknowledged that valuable discussions on other issues took place. See Narasaki, p.3.
38. See for example, Pamela Constable, "Mideast Dominates Racism Meeting," *The Washington Post* 1 September 2001, pp. A-1, A-22.
39. See the statement by Stacy Burdett of the Anti-Defamation League in "WCAR: Next Steps In a Painful Journey?" on the Network of Alliances Bridging Race & Ethnicity (NABRE) site on http://www.jointcenter.org/nabre/whatsnew/wcar accessed on 12/15/2001.
40. See Pamela Constable, "Slavery's Legacy: Divisions on How To Make Amends: Debate at World Racism Conference Focuses on Apologies vs. Reparations," *Washington Post* 2 September 2001, p. A-16; Rachel L. Swarns, "Overshadowed, Slavery Debate Boils in Durban," *New York Times* 6 September 2001, pp. A-1, A-12; American Friends Service Committee, "Durban and Beyond."

The Universal Declaration of Human Rights— Only a Foundation

Elisabeth Reichert

Human rights is a relatively new term, with its beginning stage of use occurring in 1945 after the end of the Second World War (Morsink, 1999). This catastrophic even, in which barely any corner of the world had escaped unscathed, provided a catalyst for peoples and governments everywhere to create a mechanism by which to prevent a recurrence. The result of this effort to create a more stable and peaceful world order culminated in 1948 with the Universal Declaration of Human Rights (Morsink, 1999).

The Universal Declaration was nothing short of a revolution in thought—instead of each nation being the master of its own domain, universal principles or rules now appeared. A set of guidelines sanctioned by a higher authority, at least in theory, would inhibit nations from violating the agreed upon human rights. No longer could a nation simply do what it wanted to its own citizens or those of other nations. The Universal Declaration would set minimum standards of conduct for governments all over the world (Economist, 1998; Press, 2000).

In spite of efforts before the Universal Declaration to establish a model standard of conduct applicable to every individual and government, no prior document could match the Universal Declaration in scope or participation. The development and eventual fruition of the Universal Declaration exemplifies how individuals and groups from diverse backgrounds mutually produced an extraordinary document that transcends customary borders. While many nations violate human rights contained in the declaration, pressure for countries to adhere to the declaration exists. Individuals or governments who ignore or vio-

From *The Journal of Intergroup Relations*, Volume XXIX, No. 1 by Elisabeth Reichert. Copyright © 2002 by Journal of Intergroup Relations. Reprinted by permission.

late human rights can face diminished reputations and scorn (Economist, 1998). Even with its shortcomings, the Universal Declaration of Human Rights certainly ranks as one of the most esteemed accomplishments in political, social, economic and cultural history.

This article explains that the concept of human rights emanates from all corners of the world, not just the Western world. Although not all countries existing in 1948 voted to approve the Universal Declaration of Human Rights, no country voted against the declaration. Some countries abstained from voting because they disapproved of particular sections of the document. Despite the significance of a universal set of human rights, the declaration has merely formed a beginning point for infusing human rights into everyday life. A multitude of human rights documents have expanded upon the declaration to form a broad body of human rights principles applicable to governments and individuals everywhere.

The first part of the article presents a brief explanation of provisions contained within the Universal Declaration of Human Rights. The next section traces historical beginnings of human rights to 1945, with a subsequent section detailing events after 1945 up to the adoption of the Universal Declaration of Human Rights by the United Nations. The last part of the article explains essential terminology used in describing human rights instruments that have been drafted after the declaration.

Three Generations of Human Rights

A brief summary of the Universal Declaration of Human Rights reveals three distinct sets, or generations, of human rights. The first set or generation lists political and individual freedoms (Reichert, 2001). The right to a fair trial, freedom of speech and religion, freedom of movement and assembly, and guarantees against discrimination, slavery and torture fall within these political and civil human rights (United Nations, 1948, Articles 2-15). These rights are often referred to as negative rights in that they restrict the role of government. In other words, government or other authority shall refrain from doing a certain act. This *shall not* set of guidelines emphasizes non-interference by government, or a negative position.

Another set of human rights in the declaration embodies so-called positive rights (Reichert, 2001). This set of rights attempts to ensure each resident of a country an adequate standard of living based on the resources of that country. Under this second set of human rights, everyone "has the right to a standard of living adequate for the health and well-being of himself and of his family, including food, clothing, housing and medical care and necessary social services." In addition, "motherhood and childhood are entitled to special care and assistance" and everyone has the right to a free education at the elementary level (United Nations, 1948, Articles 16-27). These rights are termed positive in that governments and individuals must take action to preserve these rights. In other words, governments *shall* provide these rights.

Of course, the distinction between negative and positive human rights can be viewed as contrived. If governments shall not restrict free speech or discriminate against gender or race, who monitors whether government satisfied these negative rights? Obviously governments must affirmatively act to prevent violations of free speech and discrimination. That requires positive acts on the part of government. Still, whether contrived or not, in discussions about human rights, a distinction between negative and positive human rights continues to exist.

A last set of human rights involves collective rights among nations. This set of rights is the least developed among the three types of human rights. Under the 1948 declaration, everyone "is entitled to a social and international order in which the rights and freedoms" listed in the document can be fully realized (United Nations, 1948, Article 28). Essentially, promotion of collective human rights requires intergovernmental cooperation on world issues, like environmental protection and economic development. One group of countries should not dictate conditions to another group when these conditions would inhibit the growth or prosperity of the other group. Industrialized countries should not take advantage of less economically developed countries by exploiting resources. The third set of human rights indicates that solidarity among nations and individuals forms a core value of the declaration.

Reference to three generations, or sets of human rights, may actually inhibit understanding of those rights and the concept of indivisibility. With three different sets of rights, an issue can easily arise as to priority of rights. Are political and civil rights more important than economic, social and cultural rights or international solidarity? Can human rights even be logically separated into different sets? Unfortunately, the notion of different sets of human rights continues to exist. A better approach is to avoid reference to different sets, and acknowledge that human rights are equally important.

Historical Beginnings of Human Rights

The Universal Declaration of Human Rights did not arise out of a vacuum. Early civilization produced religious codes that established standards of conduct for fairly homogenous groups within limited territorial jurisdictions (National Coordination Committee for UDHR50, 1998). By requiring humans to treat fellow humans with dignity and help provide for each other's needs, many religions are precursors to human rights (p. 1). In varying degrees, Judaism, Christianity, Buddhism, Confucianism and Islam all stress what would now be called human rights. These religions emphasize the necessity of fairness from political authorities and the distribution of economic resources to those in need (Ife, 2001; Laquer & Rubin, 1979; McKinney & Park-Cunningham, 1997; van Wormer, 1996; Wronka, 1998).

In ancient times, philosophers had written about equality and justice. Over two thousand years ago, philosophers, including Plato and Socrates, explored the realm of basic, inalienable rights of man, which in those times literally meant man (Wronka, 1998). Women's rights as human rights came much, much later (Reichert, 1996, 1998). The Greek philosopher Aristotle wrote that an unjust man is a man who is not content to have an equal share with others (Wronka, 1998, p. 43). Since the unjust thing is the unequal thing, it is obvious that there must be a mean between greater and less inequality. If then the unjust is the unequal, the just is the equal. The Romans developed *The Twelve Tables*, which stresses the necessity for a proper trial, the presentation of evidence and proof, and the illegality of bribery in judicial proceedings (Wronka, 1998, p. 46).

In 1215, a cornerstone of human rights came into existence when English nobles, bishops and archbishops forced [the then reigning] King John to end his abuses against his subjects. The subjects drafted a document known as the Magna Carta, which King John signed. The Magna Carta prohibited a sovereign taking of property without due process and detention without a legal judgment by peers—the forerunner of trial by jury. The document also highlighted the importance of family and provided for safety from abusive treatment.

Another concept behind the development of human rights is natural law, which holds that a certain order in nature provides norms for human conduct. St. Thomas Aquinas wrote that natural law was humanity's "participation" in the comprehensive eternal law (Hall, 1992, p. 581). People could grasp certain self-evident principles of practical reason, which correspond to the various goods toward which human nature inclined. Natural law was a standard for human laws: unjust laws in principle did not bind in conscience. During the 17th century, European philosophers advocated for what they viewed as the natural rights of the citizens—the idea that people by their nature have certain basic rights that precede the establishment of any government (Hall, 1992, p. 590). Two early modern political philosophers, Thomas Hobbes and John Locke, explored the theme of natural rights. Hobbes and Locke stated that the source of natural law was not a set of naturally ordered ends of human well being and fulfillment, but an innate desire for self-preservation (Hall, 1992, p. 581). Out of this theme, Hobbes and Locke erected a new doctrine known as *natural rights*. The desire for self-preservation in a state of nature led to the establishment of a social contract, the foundation of civil society. The fundamental duty of government, according to Locke, became the protection of rights to life, liberty and property. This concept of natural rights went beyond theoretical views of man and society and aimed to establish actual rules of conduct. Initially, these natural rights focused on freedom of the press, with subsequent attention to freedom of thought in politics and religion. Abolition of slavery and a more humane treatment of criminals also formed part of the natural rights movement (Rawls, 1993).

Uprisings in the late 18th century against government and royalty in France and the American colonies engendered considerable discussion as to how nations should treat citizens. Until this period, privileged males occupied center stage in discussion about concepts of human rights, with most, if not all the rights being solely for men. However, in 1787, philosopher Condorcet published a treatise on the rights of women, holding that women had the same *natural rights* as men (Staub-Bernasconi, 1998). During the French Revolution of 1789, women were extremely active in the fight against an old feudal regime. Women led demonstrations that forced the king from his palace at Versailles. Women's groups in Paris demanded the same political rights as men, as well as change in marriage laws, and improvements in women's social conditions.

One of the most outspoken advocates for women's rights during the French Revolution was Olympe de Gouges. Two years after the revolution, she published a declaration on the rights of women and demanded the same rights for women as men. In 1793, a backlash occurred, and the French government beheaded Olympe de Gouges and banned further political activity by women. The tragic irony in the beheading of de Gouges becomes evident within the context the French Declaration of the Rights of Man and Citizen adopted by the French government in 1789 (Staub-Bernasconi, 1998). That declaration referred only to men and specified numerous negative rights, including freedom from excessive punishment, freedom of thought and religion, and freedom to speak, write and print. Only later would women be specifically recognized as entitled to basic human rights and freedoms.

At the time of the French revolution, the U.S. colonists had recently completed their own uprising against the British. Out of this revolt came various documents expounding on the rights of man, including the Declaration of Independence and later the U.S. Constitution. The Declaration of Independence held certain rights, life, liberty and the pursuit of happiness, as *self-evident*. A key part of the U.S. Constitution, placed immediately after articles defining the mechanical functioning of the newly formed U.S. government, became known as the Bill of Rights (U.S. Constitution, 1787). The Bill of Rights consists of amendments to the body of the Constitution and specifies certain civil and political rights. For instance, in the first amendment of the Bill of Rights, government shall make no law respecting an establishment of religion or prohibiting the free exercise of religion (U.S. Constitution, 1787, Amend. I). Government may not abridge the freedom of speech, or of the press; or the right of the people peaceable to assemble. The people also have the right to petition the Government for a redress of grievances. Other amendments guarantee the right of the people not be subjected to unreasonable searches (Amend. IV), and cruel and unusual punishment (Amend. VIII). Nobody has to testify against herself or himself and government may not take "life, liberty, or property, without due process of law" (Amend. V).

The Bill of Rights in the U.S. Constitution took a major step in defining and limiting government action in political and civil matters. However, what the Bill or Rights and the U.S. Constitution omitted were guarantees of economic and social needs. It took another revolution of sorts to focus on this aspect of the human existence.

In the late 18th and early 19th centuries, the age of industrialization began in England, Europe and the United States. In these parts of the world, people left their agricultural based activities to find work in factories, often working long hours in unsanitary conditions. Factory owners frequently exploited their workers, paying them little for their efforts. Children, too, would work at an early age in the factories. Of course, many accepted these circumstances as the normal course of events for that time period. Opposition, though, to exploitation of labor in the industrialized world began to emerge in the middle of the 19th century. Karl Marx and Friedrich Engels produced the Communist Manifesto in opposition to what they saw as exploitation of the working class by owners of factories and other means of production (Wronka, 1998). The manifesto outlined the class struggle against capitalists and the eventual takeover of the means of production by workers. While many of the predictions of Marx and Engels never came about, the underlying theme of their writings resulted in greater attention to the less economically fortunate of the world.

In the late 19th century, governments in Europe began to support the development of social welfare as social activists recognized the inadequacy of an individual response to broad economic problems, like massive poverty (Wronka, 1998). At this time, social workers began to join together, to share ideas and experience, to develop their practice and to express a collective response to the issues they encountered.

The First World War and its aftermath in the early 20th century led to a greater attention on the interdependence of humankind. A shared desire to condemn warfare and develop institutional frameworks for international cooperation took form. Establishment of the League of Nations and the International Labor Organization and the inception of social welfare organizations, such as the International Conference of Social Welfare, supported this new mood of international, regional and national collaboration. Among social workers, the establishment of intergovernmental organizations, such as the International Committee of Schools of Social Work and International Permanent Secretariat of Social Workers, paralleled this collaboration. During this period, social work organizations began to establish the basis for a social work profession and create social work values for their practice. This international promotion of social work formed a key concept that social work values could transcend borders, a notion that would manifest itself in the drafting of the Universal Declaration a few years later. However, while concepts of human rights underpinned the value base of social work, no formal teaching on human rights issues occurred (Center for Human Rights, 1994).

In spite of recognition about the dangers of war, especially after the immense destruction of the First World War, European countries almost immediately became embroiled again in armed battle. The budding international organizations had limited support and no real enforcement powers. For instance, the League of Nations encountered obstacles from the onset because the United States withdrew its membership (Alexander, 1996). The League became little more than a forum in which European countries could discuss world issues. Enforcement of decisions remained absent.

In 1939, the Second World War began involving even more countries and areas of the world. Even before the end of this war in 1945, many groups devoted attention to notions of human rights (Morsink, 1999; Wronka, 1998). Wartime conferences in London, Moscow, the United States and Yalta by major countries aligned against Germany issued declarations about the failure of the League of Nations. They emphasized the need to develop a "United Nations" to maintain international peace and security. In 1941, U.S. President Franklin D. Roosevelt enunciated four freedoms: freedom of speech and expression, freedom of worship, freedom from want (i.e., economic security) and freedom from fear (e.g., international peace). Three years later, President Roosevelt asked Congress to explore the means for implementing an Economic Bill of Rights, including the rights to a useful and remunerative job; sufficient income to provide adequate food, clothing and recreation; decent home; medical care; retirement, disability and unemployment security; and good education. All of these concepts contributed to the soon to be Universal Declaration of Human Rights (Morsink, 1999; Wronka, 1998).

Construction of the Universal Declaration of Human Rights might appear to have been primarily a European and United States project. However, this was not the case. Other regions of the world have developed their own laws, principles, religions that, in many ways, had much in common with concepts eventually included in the Universal Declaration. For instance, in China, elements of classical Confucian though formed a basis for modern human rights doctrines (Ganjian & Gang, 1995, p. 36). In South America, 19th century movements led by Simon Bolivar and others provided later impetus for contributions to human rights principles. In the Soviet Union, the Soviet Constitution of 1936 contained numerous references to civil, political, economic and social rights (Wronka, 1998).

Indigenous peoples, such as the Native Americans, also contributed concepts of freedom, peace and democracy to the development of human rights (Wronka, 1998 p. 70). However, during the 19th century, European countries and, to a lesser extent the United States, began massive colonization of indigenous peoples in Africa and parts of Asia. The degree of political and civil freedom varied according to the colonizers. In Australia and the United States, the new citizens began a massive decimation of indigenous populations, the idea being that these populations were inferior and had little to contribute to the needs of a modern, western country (Alexander, 1996; Brown, 1970; Hughes, 1987). Unfortunately, colonization and expulsion of indigenous peoples did much to silence the voices of these groups.

Developments after 1945

The Second World War ended in Europe in May 1945 with the defeat of Germany and in August 1945 with the defeat of Japan. Devastation from the war had become so great that, at its end, individuals and governments from every corner of the globe realized a repeat would probably spell the end of humankind. The search for universal principles of conduct now began in earnest.

Until 1945, the notion of state sovereignty dominated international relations (Economist, 1998). Within its borders, a state controlled its own affairs. A state generally did not interfere in the affairs of another state; states did to their own nationals as each saw fit. Of course, this respect for non-interference in the affairs of other states did not prevent colonizing and destruction of other peoples who had no defined national boundaries. African, American, Australian and other aborigines generally found themselves on the losing end of better-armed westerners who arrived from European nations to expand their own sovereign reach.

After the end of the Second World War, however, the concept that a state or nation had total control over its own affairs mellowed. Extreme nationalism gave way to a more global consciousness where the international community would not remain silent when egregious abuses occurred within a particular country. The primary issue then became one of defining rights, abuses and other universal principles by which every country would subscribe.

In June 1945, in San Francisco, the United States, Soviet Union, France, Cuba, Chile, Panama and many other countries laid the groundwork for the creation of a United Nations (Morsink, 1999). The United Nations Charter pledges the organization to reaffirm faith in fundamental human rights, and Article I of the Charter cites "promoting and encouraging respect for human rights and for fundamental freedoms for all without distinction as to race, sex, language or religion" (Economist, 1998, p. 10). As part of this Charter, participants agreed to establish a Commission of Human Rights. Before the creation of this commission in 1946, the term human rights had not been a commonly used expression. While the development of human rights principles had been occurring for centuries, the actual use of the term human rights only found expression in 1945.

A universal declaration of rights ranked high on the agenda of this new organization known as the United Nations. However, many governments were reluctant to accept detailed provisions concerning human rights. The Soviet Union had it Gulags, or labor camps for those who spoke against the government; the United States had its numerous racial problems; the Europeans had their colonial empires (Buergenthal, 1988). All of these circumstances could be viewed as contrary to human rights principles. Consequently, establishing a strong international mechanism for protecting human rights could work against the interests of these major blocs. Certainly, the Soviets did not want human rights inspectors examining their labor camps and the dissidents inhabiting the camps. The United States did not want human rights examiners questioning near apartheid conditions, especially in the South. And European countries had no interest in allowing human rights monitors checking out exploitative activities in their African and Asian colonies.

Fortunately, an impetus for a more detailed and comprehensive set of rights than desired by the major blocs existed in the form of private institutions now commonly known as non-governmental organizations (NGO's) (Farer, 1989, p. 195). According to John Humphrey, first Director of the Division of Human Rights at the United Nations, without the efforts of a few deeply committed delegates and representatives of 42 private organizations serving as consultants, human rights would have received only a passing reference. With promotion of human rights by the NGO's and dedicated countries, by 1947, the international consensus for human rights became an aggressive one.

The Commission on Human Rights held its first session in early 1947, electing Eleanor Roosevelt as president and Rene Cassin from France as vice-present. The member commission included representatives from Australia, Belgium, Byelorussia Soviet Socialist Republics, Chile, China, Egypt, France, India, Iran, Lebanon, Panama, Philippine Republic, United Kingdom, United States of America, Union of Soviet Socialist Republics, Uruguay and Yugoslavia. The commission drafted an initial document on human rights containing numerous articles on the rights and duties of individuals. The document covered political, social and economic rights, with differing viewpoints on how much influence should be extended to each set of rights. In June 1948, the commission completed the draft declaration, and the entire General Assembly of the United Nations began debating the draft (Morsink, 1999).

At the time the commission submitted its draft declaration on human rights to the General Assembly, the United Nations consisted of fifty-six countries. Most of these countries were located in North and South America, Europe, and the Soviet Union. A few Arabic countries were also members, but Africa and Asia had little representation because of colonization by European countries. Only later, beginning in the late 1950's, did colonized territories begin the path toward independence and membership in the United Nations.

In spite of this limited membership within the United Nations in 1948, a spirited debate surrounded the draft declaration. Many countries agreed to the necessity of enforcement provisions that would ensure compliance with human rights principles. Countries did not want an organization that would be as impotent as the League of Nations. Obtaining agreement that countries should give human rights more than lip service was perhaps the easiest point to discuss. The U.S. contingent focused on political and civil rights, desiring no guarantee to economic and social rights. This viewpoint simply matched common U.S. strains of thought about government and society: Nobody owes anybody a job, unemployment benefits or medical care. Why should governments be responsible for those items? Yet, government should stay out of religion, refrain from censorship, and ensure numerous other safeguards against governmental interference in the liberty of its citizens. On the other hand, the Soviet Union viewed free speech and other political rights, U.S. American style, as anathema to their society. Instead, distribution of economic and social benefits to all citizens was a priority. Other countries, like Saudi Arabia, weighed in with objections to provisions on the right to change religion and equal right to marry, believing this would conflict with marriage laws in most Muslim countries. The Union of South Africa objected to numerous provisions in the draft document because those provisions could be used to attack its apartheid system of segregating citizens. Chile, often serving as a spokesperson for the Latin American contingent of the commission, believed that economic and social rights had to be assured, thereby making a return to fascism impossible.

The final draft of the document that would become the Universal Declaration of Human Rights bore the unmistakable stamp of the horrific experiences of the recent war. Rene Cassin, the French delegate, stated that "the last war had taken on the character of a crusade for human rights" and that the declaration was most urgently needed as a protest against oppression (Morsink, 1999, p. 37).

On December 10, 1948, the General Assembly of the United Nation adopted the Universal Declaration of Human Rights. The declaration passed unopposed by the entire Soviet bloc, Saudi Arabia and South Africa abstained from voting because of objections to certain provisions within the declaration (Morsink, 1999).

The Universal Declaration of Human Rights was not a legally binding document given the difficulty of enforcing it against powerful countries like the United States and the Soviet Union. Yet, it did set a common precedent for universal human rights. The significance of this step cannot be underestimated. From this point forward, human rights have made astonishing inroads into the vocabularies of social workers, philosophers, educators, political leaders, lawyers, and many other groups.

Terminology of Human Rights Documents

After the adoption of the Universal Declaration of Human Rights, numerous instruments have expanded upon particular sections and topics contained within the declaration. For instance, the International Covenant on Civil and Political Rights and the International Covenant on Econcomi, Social and Cultural Rights, aim to make provisions of the declaration enforceable by countries that approved the covenants. However, to understand the significance of these and other documents relating to human rights, familiarity with human rights terminology becomes crucial. Significant terms include declaration, covenant, treaty, platform, ratification and customary international law. For purposes of understanding human rights, knowledge of the finer points of international law is not necessary. A brief introduction suffices for understanding the significance of a particular document and the legal standing of provisions contained in the document.

Declaration. In respect to human rights documents, a declaration presents a formal and solemn non-binding statement listing general principles and broad obligations (Center for Human Rights, 1994, p. 14). For instance, the Universal Declaration of Human Rights contains many statements on human rights with the goal of encouraging countries to recognize human rights. However, the declaration does not impose any specific requirement on a particular country or nation to actually comply with the declaration. The non-binding nature of a declaration may appear detrimental in promoting human rights. After all, words are cheap. However, a declaration does indicate a position on human rights issues. Any country signing a declaration definitely states to other countries that it intends to abide by the declaration and make efforts to put principles contained in the declaration into practice. By signing a declaration and making no effort to comply with the declaration, a country is, at a minimum, showing bad faith and running a risk of losing respect within the international community.

Afghanistan provides a recent example of the loss of respect resulting from a blind eye to human rights principles. Afghanistan belongs to the United Nations and has accepted principles contained in the Universal Declaration of Human Rights. Yet, among other human rights abuses, the Taliban government of that country openly placed restrictions on women that inhibited their education, employment and other benefits. Even after allowing for a culturally specific interpretation of human rights principles, Afghanistan clearly violated many provisions of the universal declaration. A direct consequence of those violations was a lack of international respect for the ruling government of Afghanistan. The vast majority of countries had no diplomatic relations with Afghanistan and entertained little contact with the country. This isolation and failure to at least acknowledge some provisions within the Universal Declaration worked to the detriment of most Afghan citizens. Declarations commonly address human rights issues and allow countries the opportunity to gather and discuss current areas of concern. Countries within the United Nations often schedule conferences on human rights topics with the goal of presenting a declaration on the various topics. These conferences can often be controversial, as conflict frequently arises among participants over particular language within the declaration. For instance, in a recent conference on racism, the United States objected to positions taken concerning Israel and walked out of the conference (Swarns, 2001).

The importance of declarations should not be underestimated, even if countries pay no more than lip service to statements within the declarations. By merely signing on to a specific position concerning human rights issues, a country and its government does indicate intent to follow that position. Individuals and groups can at least point to the declaration in shaping policies that their government should be pursuing.

Covenant, Convention and Treaty. In contrast to the non-binding nature of a declaration, the United Nations has adopted the use of various instruments that impose specific obligations on those countries signing and ratifying the instruments. Those instruments are known as covenants, conventions and treaties.

Generally, a covenant on human rights principles serves as a promise between two or more countries that they will enforce provisions of the covenants with specific laws (Campbell Black, 1968). A convention is an international agreement that contains provisions to promote or protect specific human rights or fundamental provisions (Center for Human Rights, 1994, p. 14). Covenants and conventions relating to human rights documents generally require a specified number of countries to agree to the document before the document becomes effective. A treaty is much like a covenant or convention but may not require any specific number of signatures before becoming effective. Other than a declaration, human rights instruments generally are classified as a covenant or convention but would also fall within the definition of treaty.

A key distinction between a covenant, convention or treaty and a declaration is that of obligation. Countries signing a covenant, convention or treaty intend to bind themselves to provisions within the document, whereas countries signing a declaration merely indicate their intent to follow provisions within the declaration. The language of a covenant, convention or treaty generally imposes obligations upon a State or country to ensure and undertake certain human rights, whereas the language of a declaration focuses more on the need to recognize particular human rights.

Accession and Ratification. When a country signs a human rights covenant or convention, that country must either *accede to* or *ratify* the covenant or convention before provisions within the document become a legally binding instrument in that country. The terms *accession* and *ratification* relate to the means by which a country expresses consent to be bound by the document, with technical distinctions between those terms best left to international lawyers.

In the United States, a treaty, including a covenant or convention, becomes legally binding upon its ratification, as opposed to accession. Under the U.S. Constitution, the President has the power, with the advice and consent of the Senate to make treaties, provided two-thirds of the Senate present concur with the treaty (U.S. Constitution, 1787, Article II). As noted above, a covenant or convention on human rights would be viewed as a treaty. Therefore, in the United States, before any human rights covenant or convention can become legally binding, a two-thirds majority of the U.S. Senate must vote for the covenant or convention. This required approval by the Senate can result in a President signing a human rights covenant or convention for consideration by the Senate, which might then delay approval of, or even refuse to approve, the document. For instance, in 1978, President Carter submitted the human rights document known as the International Covenant on Civil and Political Rights to the Senate. Yet, the Senate did not ratify the covenant until 1992 (Newman, Weisbrodt, Frank, & David, 1996). In some cases, a President may sign a treaty, but the Senate may never ratify the treaty. At the time President Carter submitted the covenant on civil and political rights to the Senate, he also submitted the International Covenant on Economic, Social and Cultural Rights. However, the Senate has never ratified that covenant nor does ratification of that instrument by the Senate appear likely at this time.

Another point to note concerning a state's acceptance of a covenant or convention involves the practice of some countries to place "reservations" on particular provisions within the document. A reservation expresses the intent of a state to modify or use a different standard from a particular provision of a covenant or convention. Under commonly accepted laws regarding treaties, a state may place a reservation on a treaty unless the treaty specifically prohibits or limits reservations (Vienna Convention, 1969, Article 19). In cases which the treaty does not prohibit or limit reservations, a State may place a reservation on the treaty provided the reservation is not incompatible with the object and purpose of the treaty.

Customary International Law. In addition to a country acceding to or ratifying a covenant or convention on human rights, another process exists by which a country can be legally bound to follow human rights principles. This process is known as customary international law and essentially means that a particular rule has become so matter-of-fact all over the world that all countries should enforce the rule. Certain human rights, particularly some of those listed in the Universal Declaration, probably qualify as customary international law and, therefore could be enforceable in all countries. In the United States, a federal court held that a foreign national could sue in a U.S. court for civil damages allegedly caused from torture perpetrated by a Paraguayan national (*Filartiga v. Pena-Irala*, 1980). The court considered the human right to be free from torture as binding on all countries:

> For although there is no universal agreement as to the precise extent of the "human rights and fundamental freedoms' guaranteed to all by the [United Nations] Charter, there is at present no dissent from the view that the guaranties include, at a bare minimum, the right to be free from torture. This prohibition has become part of customary international law, as evidenced and defined by the Universal Declaration of Human Rights. (p. 882)

The court did not indicate that all human rights contained in the Universal Declaration met the standard of customary international law. Rather, courts would need to examine the particular right at issue and then determine whether that right qualified as part of customary international law.

The intricacies of international law obviously exceed the scope of this article, however, human rights workers should understand the concept of customary international law and it applications to human rights principles. If virtually every country accepts a particular human right as being fundamental to the human existence, then that right could become part of customary international law and enforceable. From a human rights perspective, going to court to enforce a human right may appear distasteful. However, the point here is to recognize the importance of human rights and the reasons why those rights are basic to the human condition.

Conclusion

The Universal Declaration of Human Rights clearly set a milestone in the development of global humanity and common ground for existence. The declaration culminated from input by many different cultures and societies. This multiplicity of voices in drafting human rights instruments has continued after the adoption of the document.

Even though the Universal Declaration ranks as nothing short of miraculous, the declaration represents only an initial building block in the incorporation of human rights into everyday life. Subsequent documents relating to human rights continually appear, with high hopes of obtaining necessary approval from governmental and non-governmental forces.

Clearly the process of drafting and obtaining acceptance of a human rights document involves numerous factors. The initial wording of the document contains its own set of challenges, with some countries or groups wanting a particular wording to satisfy their own political or social agenda. After the inevitable tug of war over language of a covenant or convention comes the vote on the document. Will enough countries in the General Assembly of the United Nations vote to adopt the instrument? If so, then comes the subsequent process of putting the instrument into effect, which requires a specific number of countries accepting the instrument as the law of their lands. It is important to note that acceptance of the document as law does not prevent a country from placing reservations on the treaty. If a country wants to generally accept the treaty but does not like a particular provision, then that country may reserve enforcement of that provision. Finally, after ratification of the treaty, a country has to decide whether the treaty is self-implementing or requires specific legislation to implement the terms of the treaty. The United States has usually viewed UN treaties as requiring specific legislation to implement the treaty. In other words, an individual who might be affected by the treaty could not simply refer to the treaty in a court of law but would need to refer to specific legislation indicating the treaty applies. If that legislation does not exist, the individual could not rely on the treaty for legal support.

With all the ins and outs relating to human rights documents, a person might wonder how any document ever sees the light of day. Yet, substantial efforts in drafting new documents and revising existing documents continue as a means of improving political, social, economic and cultural situations around the world. This dedication by many individuals, groups and governments reveals an importance of basic principles to varying professions, directly and indirectly, related to human rights advocacy.

References

Alexander, T. (1996). *Unraveling global apartheid*. Cambridge, MA: Polity Press.

Brown, D. (1970). *Bury my heart at wounded knee. An Indian history of the American west*. New York: Holt Rinehart & Winston.

Buergenthal, T. (1988). *International human rights law*. St. Paul, MN: West.

Boulding E. (1992). *The underside of history* (Vol 2). Newbury Park, CA: Sage Publications.

Campell Black, H. (1968). *Black's Law Dictionary: Definitions of the terms and phrases of American and English jurisprudence, ancient and modern* (4th ed.). St. Paul, MN: West Publishing Co.

Center for Human Rights (1994). *Human rights and social work. A manual for schools of social work and the social work profession [Training Series No. 1]*. Geneva: United Nations.

Gangjian, D., & Gang, S. (1995). Relating human rights to Chinese culture: The fourth paths of the Confucian analects and the four principles of a new theory of benevolence. In F. Davis (Ed), *Human rights and Chinese values* (pp. 35-55). Hong Kong: Oxford University Press.

Economist. (1998, December 15). Human-rights law, pp. 4-16.

Economist (2001, August 18-24). Special report on human rights: Righting wrongs, pp 18-20.

Farer, T. (1989). The United Nations and human rights: More than a whimper. In R. P. Claude & B. H. Weston (Eds.), *Human rights in the world community* (pp. 194-208). Philadelphia: University of Pennsylvania Press.

Filartiga v. Pena-Irala, 630 F2d. 876, 1980.

Hall, K. (Ed.) (1992). *The Oxford companion to the Supreme Court of the United States*. Oxford, England: Oxford University Press.

Hughes, R. (1987). *The fatal shore: The epic of Australia's founding*. New York: Alfred A. Knopf.

Ife, J. (2001). *Human rights and social work: Towards rights based practice*. Cambridge, MA: Cambridge University Press.

Laqueur, W., & Rubin, B. (Eds.). (1979). *The human rights reader*. Philadelphia, PA: Temple University Press.

McKinney, C. M., & Park-Cunningham, R. (1997). Evolution of the social work profession: An historical review of the U.S. and selected countries, 1995. *In Proceedings: 28th Annual Conference, New York State Social Work Education Association* (pp. 3-9). Syracuse, NY: New York State Social Work Education Association.

Morsink J. (1999). *The Universal Declaration of Human Rights*. Philadelphia: University of Pennsylvania Press.

National Coordinating Committee for UDHR50. (1998). Franklin and Eleanor Roosevelt Institute home page [Online]. Available: http://www.udhr50.org/history/timeline.htm

Press, E. (2000). (December 25) Human rights-the next step. *The Nation*, pp. 13-18.

Rawls, J. (1993). *Political liberalism*. New York: Columbia University Press.

Reichert E. (1996). Keep on moving forward: NGO Forum on women, Beijing, China. *Social Development Issues, 18*(1), 61-71.

Reichert E. (1998). Women's rights are human rights: A platform for action. *International Social Work, 15*(3), 177-185.

Reichert, E. (2001). Placing human rights at the center of the social work profession. *The Journal of Intergroup Relations, XXVIII*(1), 43-50.

Staub-Bernasconi, S. (1998). Soziale Arbeit als Menschenrechtsprofession in A. Woehrle (Hg), *Profession and Wissenschaft Sozialer Arbeit, Positionen in einer Phase der generellen Neuverortung and Spezifika* (pp. 305-332). Cenaurus: Pfaffenweiler.

Swarns, R. (2001), (September 9). Conference calls for reversing consequences of slavery:

UN meeting on racism ends in controversy. *St. Louis Dispatch*, pp. A1, A10.

United Nations. (1948). *Universal declaration of human rights.* New York: Author.

United Nations. (1987). *Human rights: Questions and answers:* New York: Author.

United Nations. (1994). *Human rights and social work: A manual for schools of social work and the social work profession* (Professional Training Series No. 4). New York: Author.

van Wormer, K. (1997). *Social welfare: A world view.* Chicago: Nelson Hall Publishers.

Vienna Convention on the Law of Treaties, 1969. 1155 U.N.T.S. 331, U.S. No. 58 (1980) reprinted in 8 I. L. M. 679 (1969) entered into force January 27, 1980.

Wronka, J. (1998). *Human rights and social policy in the 21st century: A history of the idea of human rights and comparison of the United Nations Universal Declaration of Human Rights with United States federal and state constitutions* (Rev. ed.). Lanham, MD: University Press of America.

Rebuilding America's Defenses

Strategy, Forces and Resources for a New Century

Donald Kagan and Gary Schmitt
Project Co-Chairmen

Thomas Donnelly
Principal Author

Introduction

The Project for the New American Century was established in the spring of 1997. From its inception, the Project has been concerned with the decline in the strength of America's defenses, and in the problems this would create for the exercise of American leadership around the globe and, ultimately, for the preservation of peace.

Our concerns were reinforced by the two congressionally-mandated defense studies that appeared soon thereafter: the Pentagon's Quadrennial Defense Review (May 1997) and the report of the National Defense Panel (December 1997). Both studies assumed that U.S. defense budgets would remain flat or continue to shrink. As a result, the defense plans and recommendations outlined in the two reports were fashioned with such budget constraints in mind. Broadly speaking, the QDR stressed current military requirements at the expense of future defense needs, while the NDP's report emphasized future needs by underestimating today's defense responsibilities.

Although the QDR and the report of the NDP proposed different policies, they shared one underlying feature: the gap between resources and strategy should be resolved not by increasing resources but by shortchanging strategy. America's armed forces, it seemed, could either prepare for the future by retreating

---

From www.newcentury.org by Donald Kagan, Gary Schmitt and Thomas Donnelly. Copyright © by Project for the New American Century. Reprinted by permission.

from its role as the essential defender of today's global security order, or it could take care of current business but be unprepared for tomorrow's threats and tomorrow's battlefields.

Either alternative seemed to us shortsighted. The United States is the world's only superpower, combining preeminent military power, global technological leadership, and the world's largest economy. Moreover, America stands at the head of a system of alliances which includes the world's other leading democratic powers. At present the United States faces no global rival. America's grand strategy should aim to preserve and extend this advantageous position as far into the future as possible. There are, however, potentially powerful states dissatisfied with the current situation and eager to change it, if they can, in directions that endanger the relatively peaceful, prosperous and free condition the world enjoys today. Up to now, they have been deterred from doing so by the capability and global presence of American military power. But, as that power declines, relatively and absolutely, the happy conditions that follow from it will be inevitably undermined.

Preserving the desirable strategic situation in which the United States now finds itself requires a globally preeminent military capability both today and in the future. But years of cuts in defense spending have eroded the American military's combat readiness, and put in jeopardy the Pentagon's plans for maintaining military superiority in the years ahead. Increasingly, the U.S. military has found itself undermanned, inadequately equipped and trained, straining to handle contingency operations, and ill-prepared to adapt itself to the revolution in military affairs. Without a well-conceived defense policy and an appropriate increase in defense spending, the United States has been letting its ability to take full advantage of the remarkable strategic opportunity at hand slip away.

With this in mind, we began a project in the spring of 1998 to examine the country's defense plans and resource requirements. We started from the premise that U.S. military capabilities should be sufficient to support an American grand strategy committed to building upon this unprecedented opportunity. We did not accept pre-ordained constraints that followed from assumptions about what the country might or might not be willing to expend on its defenses.

In broad terms, we saw the project as building upon the defense strategy outlined by the Cheney Defense Department in the waning days of the Bush Administration. The Defense Policy Guidance (DPG) drafted in the early months of 1992 provided a blueprint for maintaining U.S. preeminence, precluding the rise of a great power rival, and shaping the international security order in line with American principles and interests. Leaked before it had been formally approved, the document was criticized as an effort by "cold warriors" to keep defense spending high and cuts in forces small despite the collapse of the Soviet Union; not surprisingly, it was subsequently buried by the new administration.

Although the experience of the past eight years has modified our understanding of particular military requirements for carrying out such a strategy, the basic tenets of the DPG, in our judgment, remain sound. And what Secretary Cheney said at the time in response to the DPG's critics remains true today: "We can either sustain the [armed] forces we require and remain in a position to help shape things for the better, or we can throw that advantage away. [But] that would only hasten the day when we face greater threats, at higher costs and further risk to American lives."

The project proceeded by holding a series of seminars. We asked outstanding defense specialists to write papers to explore a variety of topics: the future missions and requirements of the individual military services, the role of the reserves, nuclear strategic doctrine and missile defenses, the defense budget and prospects for military modernization, the state (training and readiness) of today's forces, the revolution in military affairs, and defense-planning for theater wars, small wars and constabulary operations. The papers were circulated to a group of participants, chosen for their experience and judgment in defense affairs. (The list of participants may be found at the end of this report.) Each paper then became the basis for discussion and debate. Our goal was to use the papers to assist deliberation, to generate and test ideas, and to assist us in developing our final report. While each paper took as its starting point a shared strategic point of view, we made no attempt to dictate the views or direction of the individual papers. We wanted as full and as diverse a discussion as possible.

Our report borrows heavily from those deliberations. But we did not ask seminar participants to "sign-off" on the final report. We wanted frank discussions and we sought to avoid the pitfalls of trying to produce a consensual but bland product. We wanted to try to define and describe a defense strategy that is honest, thoughtful, bold, internally consistent and clear. And we wanted to spark a serious and informed discussion, the essential first step for reaching sound conclusions and for gaining public support.

New circumstances make us think that the report might have a more receptive audience now than in recent years. For the first time since the late 1960s the federal government is running a surplus. For most of the 1990s, Congress and the White House gave balancing the federal budget a higher priority than funding national security. In fact, to a significant degree, the budget was balanced by a combination of increased tax revenues and cuts in defense spending. The surplus expected in federal revenues over the next decade, however, removes any need to hold defense spending to some preconceived low level.

Moreover, the American public and its elected representatives have become increasingly aware of the declining state of the U.S. military. News stories, Pentagon reports, congressional testimony and anecdotal accounts from members of the armed services paint a disturbing picture of an American military that is troubled by poor enlistment and retention rates, shoddy housing, a shortage of spare parts and weapons, and diminishing combat readiness.

Finally, this report comes after a decade's worth of experience in dealing with the post-Cold War world. Previous efforts to fashion a defense strategy that would make sense for today's security environment were forced to work from many untested assumptions about the nature of a world without a superpower rival. We have a much better idea today of what our responsibilities are, what the threats to us might be in this new security environment, and what it will take to secure the relative peace and stability. We believe our report reflects and benefits from that decade's worth of experience.

Our report is published in a presidential election year. The new administration will need to produce a second Quadrennial Defense Review shortly after it takes office. We hope that the Project's report will be useful as a road map for the nation's immediate and future defense plans. We believe we have set forth a defense program that is justified by the evidence, rests on an honest examination of the problems and possibilities, and does not flinch from facing the true cost of security. We hope it will inspire careful consideration and serious discussion. The post-Cold War world will not remain a relatively peaceful place if we continue to neglect foreign and defense matters. But serious attention, careful thought, and the willingness to devote adequate resources to maintaining America's military strength can make the world safer and American strategic interests more secure now and in the future.

Key Findings

This report proceeds from the belief that America should seek to preserve and extend its position of global leadership by maintaining the preeminence of U.S. military forces. Today, the United States has an unprecedented strategic opportunity. It faces no immediate great-power challenge; it is blessed with wealthy, powerful and democratic allies in every part of the world; it is in the midst of the longest economic expansion in its history; and its political and economic principles are almost universally embraced. At no time in history has the international security order been as conducive to American interests and ideals. The challenge for the coming century is to preserve and enhance this "American peace."

Yet unless the United States maintains sufficient military strength, this opportunity will be lost. And in fact, over the past decade, the failure to establish a security strategy responsive to new realities and to provide adequate resources for the full range of missions needed to exercise U.S. global leadership has placed the American peace at growing risk. This report attempts to define those requirements. In particular, we need to:

Establish four core missions for U.S. military forces:

- defend the American homeland;
- fight and decisively win multiple, simultaneous major theater wars;
- perform the "constabulary" duties associated with shaping the security environment in critical regions;
- transform U.S. forces to exploit the 'revolution in military affairs;"

To carry out these core missions, we need to provide sufficient force and budgetary allocations. In particular, the United States must:

Maintain nuclear strategic superiority, basing the U.S. nuclear deterrent upon a global, nuclear net assessment that weighs the full range of current and emerging threats, not merely the U.S.-Russia balance.

Restore the personnel strength of today's force to roughly the levels anticipated in the "Base Force" outlined by the Bush Administration, an increase in active-duty strength from 1.4 million to 1.6 million.

Reposition U.S. forces to respond to 21st century strategic realities by shifting permanently-based forces to Southeast Europe and Southeast Asia, and by changing naval deployment patterns to reflect growing U.S. strategic concerns in East Asia.

Modernize current U.S. forces selectively, proceeding with the F-22 program while increasing purchases of lift, electronic support and other aircraft; expanding submarine and

(continued)

surface combatant fleets; purchasing Comanche helicopters and medium-weight ground vehicles for the Army, and the V-22 Osprey "tilt-rotor" aircraft for the Marine Corps.

Cancel "roadblock" programs such as the Joint Strike Fighter, CVX aircraft carrier, and Crusader howitzer system that would absorb exorbitant amounts of Pentagon funding while providing limited improvements to current capabilities. Savings from these canceled programs should be used to spur the process of military transformation.

Develop and deploy global missile defenses to defend the American homeland and American allies, and to provide a secure basis for U.S. power projection around the world.

Control the new "international commons" of space and "cyberspace," and pave the way for the creation of a new military service—U.S. Space Forces—with the mission of space control.

Exploit the "revolution in military affairs" to insure the long-term superiority of U.S. conventional forces. Establish a two-stage transformation process which

- maximizes the value of current weapons systems through the application of advanced technologies, and,

- produces more profound improvements in military capabilities, encourages competition between single services and joint-service experimentation efforts.

Increase defense spending gradually to a minimum level of 3.5 to 3.8 percent of gross domestic product, adding $15 billion to $20 billion to total defense spending annually.

Fulfilling these requirements is essential if America is to retain its militarily dominant status for the coming decades. Conversely, the failure to meet any of these needs must result in some form of strategic retreat. At current levels of defense spending, the only option is to try ineffectually to "manage" increasingly large risks: paying for today's needs by short-changing tomorrow's; withdrawing from constabulary missions to retain strength for large-scale wars; "choosing" between presence in Europe or presence in Asia; and so on. These are bad choices. They are also false economies. The "savings" from withdrawing from the Balkans, for example, will not free up anywhere near the magnitude of funds needed for military modernization or transformation. But these are false economies in other, more profound ways as well. The true cost of not meeting our defense requirements will be a lessened capacity for American global leadership and, ultimately, the loss of a global security order that is uniquely friendly to American principles and prosperity.

I.

Why Another Defense Review?

Since the end of the Cold War, the United States has struggled to formulate a coherent national security or military strategy, one that accounts for the constants of American power and principles yet accommodates 21st century realities. Absent a strategic framework, U.S. defense planning has been an empty and increasingly self-referential exercise, often dominated by bureaucratic and budgetary rather than strategic interests. Indeed, the proliferation of defense reviews over the past decade testifies to the failure to chart a consistent course: to date, there have been half a dozen formal defense reviews, and the Pentagon is now gearing up for a second Quadrennial Defense Review in 2001. Unless this "QDR II" matches U.S. military forces and resources to a viable American strategy, it, too, will fail.

These failures are not without cost: already, they place at risk an historic opportunity. After the victories of the past century—two world wars, the Cold War and most recently the Gulf War—the United States finds itself as the uniquely powerful leader of a coalition of free and prosperous states that faces no immediate great-power challenge.

The American peace has proven itself peaceful, stable and durable. It has, over the past decade, provided the geopolitical framework for widespread economic growth and the spread of American principles of liberty and democracy. Yet no moment in international politics can be frozen in time; even a global *Pax Americana* will not preserve itself.

Paradoxically, as American power and influence are at their apogee, American military forces limp toward exhaustion, unable to meet the demands of their many and varied missions, including preparing for tomorrow's battlefield. Today's force, reduced by a third or more over the past decade, suffers from degraded combat readiness; from difficulties in recruiting and retaining sufficient numbers of soldiers, sailors, airmen and Marines; from the effects of an extended "procurement holiday" that has resulted in the premature aging of most weapons systems; from an increasingly obsolescent and inadequate military infrastructure; from a shrinking industrial base poorly structured to be the "arsenal of democracy" for the 21st century; from a lack of innovation that threatens the technological and operational advantages enjoyed by U.S. forces for a generation and upon which American strategy depends. Finally, and most dangerously, the social fabric of the military is frayed and worn. U.S. armed forces suffer from a degraded quality of life divorced from middle-class expectations, upon which an all-volunteer force depends. Enlisted men and women and junior officers increasingly lack confidence in their senior leaders, whom they believe will not tell unpleasant truths to their civilian leaders. In sum, as the American peace reaches across the globe, the force that preserves that peace is increasingly overwhelmed by its tasks.

This is no paradox; it is the inevitable consequence of the failure to match military means to geopolitical ends. Underlying the failed strategic and defense reviews of the past decade is the idea that the collapse of the Soviet Union had created a "strategic pause." In other words, until another great-power challenger emerges, the United States can enjoy a respite from the demands of international leadership. Like a boxer between championship bouts, America can afford to relax and live the good life, certain that there would be enough time to shape up for the next big challenge. Thus the United States could afford to reduce its military forces, close bases overseas, halt major weapons programs and reap the financial benefits of the "peace dividend." But as we have seen over the past decade, there has been no shortage of powers around the world who have taken the collapse of the Soviet empire as an opportunity to expand their own influence and challenge the American-led security order.

Beyond the faulty notion of a strategic pause, recent defense reviews have suffered from an inverted understanding of the military dimension of the Cold War struggle between the United States and the Soviet Union. American containment strategy did not proceed from the assumption that the Cold War would be a purely military struggle, in which the U.S. Army matched the Red

Army tank for tank; rather, the United States would seek to deter the Soviets militarily while defeating them economically and ideologically over time. And, even within the realm of military affairs, the practice of deterrence allowed for what in military terms is called "an economy of force." The principle job of NATO forces, for example, was to deter an invasion of Western Europe, not to invade and occupy the Russian heartland. Moreover, the bipolar nuclear balance of terror made both the United States and the Soviet Union generally cautious. Behind the smallest proxy war in the most remote region lurked the possibility of Armageddon. Thus, despite numerous miscalculations through the five decades of Cold War, the United States reaped an extraordinary measure of global security and stability simply by building a credible and, in relative terms, inexpensive nuclear arsenal.

Over the decade of the post-Cold-War period, however, almost everything has changed. The Cold War world was a bipolar world; the 21st century world is—for the moment, at least—decidedly unipolar, with America as the world's "sole superpower." America's strategic goal used to be containment of the Soviet Union; today the task is to preserve an international security environment conducive to American interests and ideals. The military's job during the Cold War was to deter Soviet expansionism. Today its task is to secure and expand the "zones of democratic peace;" to deter the rise of a new great-power competitor; defend key regions of Europe, East Asia and the Middle East; and to preserve American preeminence through the coming transformation of war made possible by new technologies. From 1945 to 1990, U.S. forces prepared themselves for a single, global war that might be fought across many theaters; in the new century, the prospect is for a variety of theater wars around the world, against separate and distinct adversaries pursuing separate and distinct goals. During the Cold War, the main venue of superpower rivalry, the strategic "center of gravity," was in Europe, where large U.S. and NATO conventional forces prepared to repulse a Soviet attack and over which nuclear war might begin; and with Europe now generally at peace, the new strategic center of concern appears to be shifting to East Asia. The missions for America's armed forces have not diminished so much as shifted. The

	Cold War	*21st Century*
Security system	Bipolar	Unipolar
Strategic goal	Contain Soviet Union	Preserve *Pax Americana*
Main military mission(s)	Deter Soviet expansionism	Secure and expand zones of democratic peace; deter rise of new great-power competitor; defend key regions; exploit transformation of war
Main military threat(s)	Potential global war across many theaters	Potential theater wars spread across globe
Focus of strategic competition	Europe	East Asia

threats may not be as great, but there are more of them. During the Cold War, America acquired its security "wholesale" by global deterrence of the Soviet Union. Today, that same security can only be acquired at the "retail" level, by deterring or, when needed, by compelling regional foes to act in ways that protect American interests and principles.

This gap between a diverse and expansive set of new strategic realities and diminishing defense forces and resources does much to explain why the Joint Chiefs of Staff routinely declare that they see "high risk" in executing the missions assigned to U.S. armed forces under the government's declared national military strategy. Indeed, a JCS assessment conducted at the height of the Kosovo air war found the risk level "unacceptable." Such risks are the result of the combination of the new missions described above and the dramatically reduced military force that has emerged from the defense "drawdown" of the past decade. Today, America spends less than 3 percent of its gross domestic product on national defense, less than at any time since before World War II—in other words, since before the United States established itself as the world's leading power—and a cut from 4.7 percent of GDP in 1992, the first real post-Cold-War defense budget. Most of this reduction has come under the Clinton Administration; despite initial promises to approximate the level of defense spending called for in the final Bush Administration program, President Clinton cut more than $160 billion from the Bush program from 1992 to 1996 alone. Over the first seven years of the Clinton Administration, approximately $426 billion in defense investments have been deferred, creating a weapons procurement "bow wave" of immense proportions.

The most immediate effect of reduced defense spending has been a precipitate decline in combat readiness. Across all services, units are reporting degraded readiness, spare parts and personnel shortages, postponed and simplified training regimens, and many other problems. In congressional testimony, service chiefs of staff now routinely report that their forces are inadequate to the demands of the "two-war" national military strategy. Press attention focused on these readiness problems when it was revealed that two Army divisions were given a "C-4" rating, meaning they were not ready for war. Yet it was perhaps more telling that *none* of the Army's ten divisions achieved the highest "C-1" rating, reflecting the widespread effects of slipping readiness standards. By contrast, *every* division that deployed to Operation Desert Storm in 1990 and 1991 received a "C-1" rating. This is just a snapshot that captures the state of U.S. armed forces today.

These readiness problems are exacerbated by the fact that U.S. forces are poorly positioned to respond to today's crises. In Europe, for example, the overwhelming majority of Army and Air Force units remain at their Cold War bases in Germany or England, while the security problems on the continent have moved to Southeast Europe. Temporary rotations of forces to the Balkans and elsewhere in Southeast Europe increase the overall burdens of these operations many times. Likewise, the Clinton Administration has continued the fiction that the operations of American forces in the Persian Gulf are merely temporary duties. Nearly a decade after the Gulf War, U.S. air, ground and naval forces continue to protect enduring American interests in the region. In addition to rotational naval forces, the Army maintains what amounts to an armored brigade in Kuwait for nine months of every year; the Air Force has two composite air wings in constant "no-fly zone" operations over northern and southern Iraq. And despite increasing worries about the rise of China and instability in Southeast Asia, U.S. forces are found almost exclusively in Northeast Asian bases.

Yet for all its problems in carrying out today's missions, the Pentagon has done almost nothing to prepare for a future that promises to be very different and potentially much more dangerous. It is now commonly understood that information and other new technologies—as well as widespread technological and weapons proliferation—are creating a dynamic that may threaten America's ability to exercise its dominant military power. Potential rivals such as China are anxious to exploit these transformational technologies broadly, while adversaries like Iran, Iraq and North Korea are rushing to develop ballistic missiles and nuclear weapons as a deterrent to American intervention in regions they seek to dominate. Yet the Defense Department and the services have done little more than affix a "transformation" label to programs developed during the Cold War, while diverting effort and attention to a process of joint experimentation which restricts rather than encourages innovation. Rather than admit that rapid technological changes makes it uncertain which new weapons systems to develop, the armed services cling ever more tightly to traditional program and concepts. As Andrew Krepinevich, a member of the National Defense Panel, put it in a recent study of Pentagon experimentation, "Unfortunately, the Defense Department's rhetoric asserting the need for military transformation and its support for joint experimentation has yet to be matched by any great sense of urgency or any substantial resource support.... At present the Department's effort is poorly focused and woefully underfunded."

In sum, the 1990s have been a "decade of defense neglect." This leaves the next president of the United States with an enormous challenge: he must increase military spending to preserve American geopolitical leadership, or he must pull back from the security commitments that are the measure of America's position as the world's sole superpower and the final guarantee of security, democratic freedoms and individual political rights. This choice will be among the first to confront the president: new legislation requires the incoming administration to fashion a national security strategy within six months of assuming office, as opposed to waiting a full year, and to complete another quadrennial defense review three months after that. In a larger sense, the new president will choose whether today's "unipolar moment," to use columnist Charles Krauthammer's phrase for America's current geopolitical preeminence, will be extended along with the peace and prosperity that it provides.

This study seeks to frame these choices clearly, and to re-establish the links between U.S. foreign policy, security strategy, force planning and defense spending. If an American peace is to be maintained, and expanded, it must have a secure foundation on unquestioned U.S. military preeminence.

II.

Four Essential Missions

America's global leadership, and its role as the guarantor of the current great-power peace, relies upon the safety of the American homeland; the preservation of a favorable balance of power in Europe, the Middle East and surrounding energy-producing region, and East Asia; and the general stability of the international system of nation-states relative to terrorists, organized crime, and other "non-state actors." The relative importance of these elements, and the threats to U.S. interests, may rise and fall over time. Europe, for example, is now extraordinarily peaceful and stable, despite the turmoil in the Balkans. Conversely, East Asia appears to be entering a period with increased potential for instability and competition. In the Gulf, American power and presence has achieved relative external security for U.S. allies, but the longer-term prospects are murkier. Generally, American strategy for the coming decades should seek to consolidate the great victories won in the 20th century—which have made Germany and Japan into stable democracies, for example—maintain stability in the Middle East, while setting the conditions for 21st-century successes, especially in East Asia.

A retreat from any one of these requirements would call America's status as the world's leading power into question. As we have seen, even a small failure like that in Somalia or a halting and incomplete triumph as in the Balkans can cast doubt on American credibility. The failure to define a coherent global security and military strategy during the post-Cold-War period has invited challenges; states seeking to establish regional hegemony continue to probe for the limits of the American security perimeter. None of the defense reviews of the past decade has weighed fully the range of missions demanded by U.S. global leadership: defending the homeland, fighting and winning multiple large-scale wars, conducting constabulary missions which preserve the current peace, and transforming the U.S. armed forces to exploit the "revolution in military affairs." Nor have they adequately quantified the forces and resources necessary to execute these missions separately and successfully. While much further detailed analysis would

---

Homeland Defense. America must defend its homeland. During the Cold War, nuclear deterrence was the key element in homeland defense; it remains essential. But the new century has brought with it new challenges. While reconfiguring its nuclear force, the United States also must counteract the effects of the proliferation of Ballistic missiles and weapons of mass destruction that may soon allow lesser states to deter U.S. military action by threatening U.S. allies and the American homeland itself. Of all the new and current missions for U.S. armed forces, this must have priority.

Large Wars. Second, the United States must retain sufficient forces able to rapidly deploy and win multiple simultaneous large-scale wars and also to be able to respond to unanticipated contingencies in regions where it does not maintain forward-based forces. This resembles the "two-war" standard that has been the basis of U.S. force planning over the past decade. Yet this standard needs to be updated to account for new realities and potential new conflicts.

Constabulary duties. Third, the Pentagon must retain forces to preserve the current peace in ways that fall short of conduction major theater campaigns. A decade's experience and the policies of two administrations have shown that such forces must be expanded to meet the needs of the new, long-term NATO mission in the Balkans, the continuing no-fly-zone and other missions in Southwest Asia, and other presence missions in vital regions of East Asia [sic]. These duties are today's most frequent missions, requiring forces configured for combat but capable of long-term, independent constabulary operations.

Transform U.S. Armed Forces. Finally, the Pentagon must begin now to exploit the so-called "revolution in military affairs," sparked by the introduction of advanced technologies into military systems; this must be regarded as a separate and critical mission worthy of a share of force structure and defense budgets.

be required, it is the purpose of this study to outline the large, "full-spectrum" forces that are necessary to conduct the varied tasks demanded by a strategy of American preeminence for today and tomorrow.

Current American armed forces are ill-prepared to execute these four missions. Over the past decade, efforts to design and build effective missile defenses have been ill-conceived and underfunded, and the Clinton Administration has proposed deep reductions in U.S. nuclear forces without sufficient analysis of the changing global nuclear balance of forces. While, broadly speaking, the United States now maintains sufficient active and reserve forces to meet the traditional two-war standard, this is true only in the abstract, under the most favorable geopolitical conditions. As the Joint Chiefs of Staff have admitted repeatedly in congressional testimony, they lack the forces necessary to meet the two-war benchmark as expressed in the warplans of the regional commanders-in-chief. The requirements for major-war forces must be reevaluated to accommodate new strategic realities. One of these new realities is the requirement for peacekeeping operations; unless this requirement is better understood, America's ability to fight major wars will be jeopardized. Likewise, the transformation process has gotten short shrift.

To meet the requirements of the four new missions highlighted above, the United States must undertake a two-stage process. The immediate task is to rebuild today's force, ensuring that it is equal to the tasks before it: shaping the peacetime environment and winning multiple, simultaneous theater wars; these forces must be large enough to accomplish these tasks without running the "high" or "unacceptable" risks it faces now. The second task is to seriously embark upon a transformation of the Defense Department. This itself will be a two-stage effort: for the next decade or more, the armed forces will continue to operate many of the same systems it now does, organize themselves in traditional units, and employ current operational concepts. However, this transition period must be a first step toward more substantial reform. Over the next several decades, the United States must field a global system of missile defenses, divine ways to control the new "international commons" of space and cyberspace, and build new kinds of conventional forces for different strategic challenges and a new technological environment.

War, Terror, the Quest for Domination and Resistance

Mack H. Jones
Clark Atlanta University

On September 11, 2002 the United States, the only remaining super power in the world, was attacked by a heretofore obscure, at least to the general public, band of terrorists. Using highjacked American airliners as bombs the terrorists destroyed a major symbol of American capitalism, the twin towers of the World Trade Center in New York. The United States quickly identified al-Qaida and its leader Osama bin Laden as the perpetrator, declared unconditional war against al-Qaida and terrorism in general, and unleashed a withering counter attack that routed the Taliban and destroyed al-Qaida base camps in Afghanistan. President George W. Bush described the war against terrorism as a battle of good against evil and declared that there was no middle ground, that the war involved every solitary county on the planet. Other countries, according to the president, were either with the United States or with the terrorists. Thus the United States declared a world war not only for itself but for the rest of humankind as well, a unilaterally declared world war, as it were. The next step in the war against terror, Bush asserted, would be a war for regime change in Iraq. This was clearly an unprecedented act that could have far reaching consequences for the future of the world. Under these foreboding circumstances those of us in the academy have a responsibility to help the world understand this new reality being thrust upon us. We need to understand why and how so-called terrorism became a major factor in world politics and what implications it might have on our collective future. To develop such an understanding we might begin by placing September 11 in an appropriate theoretical and systemic context that may provide a basis for understanding both the actions of the terrorists and the American response including the proposed

---

Copyright © Mack H. Jones. Reprinted by permission of the author.

invasion and occupation of Iraq. In this paper I am also concerned with the African American response to all of this and the implications for Black politics. I offer this essay as a modest contribution toward that end.

I begin by affirming a principle that should underlie all social analysis. That principle says that the truth is the whole, that there is an interrelatedness among all forces, social political, economic, cultural, secular, and spiritual and that they all come together in various ways to create existing social reality. That is to say that to understand the meaning and significance of any single event or development we must understand how it fits in to the ongoing stream of history as well as how it fits into the systemic patterns manifested at any given historical moment. And, of course, any and every understanding of social reality begins with a frame of reference or conceptual scheme that orders our perceptions. Thus to understand September 11, the immediate American response, the proposed American conquest and occupation of Iraq, and the long range campaign against terrorism, we have to first of all lay bare our frame of reference and then put events in their proper systemic and historical contexts.

The Systemic Context

Let me begin by identifying certain critical dimensions of social reality of the international system that gave rise to terrorism and counter-terrorism. Perhaps the most salient fact about the environment from which these issues arise is the gross and growing inequalities among the peoples and nations of the world. It is a world in which the richest 20 percent of the population is 61 times better off than the poorest 20 percent and the gap between the richest and poorest is growing. The ratio was 30 times in 1960. That richest 20 percent, as we all know, are mostly the people of Europe and North America. The depth of inequality is further dramatized by the fact that, according to Forbes Magazine, the 200 most wealthy individuals have personal wealth (around one trillion dollars) that is greater than the gross domestic product of all but five countries in the world, U.S., China, Japan, India, and Germany. The assets controlled by that 200 are greater than the GDP of the entire African continent.

The cleavage between the rich countries of the North and the poor countries of the South, the so-called Third World, is a second critical dimension of the current international system. There is an inequitable international division of labor between the rich countries of the North and the poor countries of the South, a division of labor in which the peoples and nations of color serve as sources of cheap labor and primary commodities, including minerals and ores necessary for sustaining the industrial societies of the West, and as markets for western goods and industrial and financial capital. In this system, the price of primary commodities remains stagnant or actually decline while the price of industrial goods and related services continues to rise. This means that the poor countries of the South must continue to produce more and more to buy less and less from the North. And when the countries of the South cannot pay their international bills they are forced to borrow from the West; and then to service their debts, they are required to cut back on vital social services at home such as education and health care. In the process the poor countries become poorer and poorer and the quality of life of their people continues to deteriorate. Third World citizens trained as engineers, doctors, skilled craftsmen and craftswomen are reduced to impoverished beggars. As the lone superpower the United States serves as the international banker and policeman responsible for maintaining this inequitable international order.

A third critical dimension of the existing international order is the role and behavior of the ruling classes of the countries of the South who in a dance of death with the West collude with their patrons from the West in the exploitation of their own people. Rather than pursuing indigenously generated strategies for development they are content to follow the dictates of the North, and to resort to further repression when their rule is challenged by their subjects. Such was the case with Mobutus, the Abachis, the Duvaliers, the Somozas, the Sukarnos and others.

A fourth critical factor is the white supremacist attitudes of the middle age white men from Europe and North America who assume that they have the right and duty to dictate what economic and political systems the people of the so-called Third World should follow. They are quick to use their economic and military advantages to insure compliance by the poor countries of the South. And we must acknowledge that recently in the United States a smattering of women and men of color have been included in this fraternity of self anointed rulers and that have exhibited the same arrogance of the white men who appointed them to positions of authority. Cases in point are Condoleezza Rice, National Security advisor to President George W. Bush and Secretary of State, Colin Powell.

A fifth critical dimension is the transformation of the international system from a bi-polar to a uni-polar one. The two military alliances that dominated the world during the period of the cold war, NATO and the Warsaw pact, have been reduced to one, NATO. Parenthetically, it is interesting to note that during the Cold War, these two antagonistic alliances of competing white nations were bitter enemies. But once the West triumphed over the Soviet led communist bloc, NATO did not declare victory and disband. Instead it moved to have the former communist governments incorporated into NATO, bringing practically all of the nations of European heritage under one military alliance. A relevant question is against whom are they allied. At any rate, the demise of the communist bloc meant that the poor countries of the South could no longer create independent space for themselves by playing one bloc against the other. In the unipolar world they are now obliged to defer to the dictates of the West or suffer the consequences.

To a certain extent this was true also during the bi-polar era. The West led by the United States always strove to prevent the rise of indigenous political movements in the poor countries that would seek an independent non-capitalist path of development; and if such movements somehow managed to come to power as they did in Guatemala in 1954, Chile in 1973, Angola in 1975, and more recently Venezuela, the West led by the United States would seek to undermine or overthrow them. And if the government of a client state was challenged by a popular movement of its subjects, the United States was always ready, willing and able to step in and help the reactionary government put down any popular uprising.

Moreover over the past 50 years the United States has used an extensive array of tactics to maintain Western dominance in the South, including providing arms and counter insurgency training for Third World despots, supporting or orchestrating coup d'tats, and endorsing political assassinations and other forms of terror. There is also credible evidence that chemical and bacteriological warfare has been used by U.S. supported agents, particularly in efforts to defeat the Cuban revolution. I will say more about that shortly.

A final factor that conditions the world of September 11 is the Low Intensity Conflict (LIC) doctrine adopted by the United States during the 1980s. At that time, the makers of U.S. foreign policy concluded that the chief threat to American foreign policy interests would come from progressive movements in the Third World and developed a military-politico strategy designed to meet the presumed threat.

In a 1988 report entitled *Discriminate Deterrence*, the Commission on Integrated Long-Term Strategy that included members such as Zbigniew Brzezinski, Samuel Huntington, and Henry Kissinger, asserted that:

> Nearly all the armed conflicts of the past forty years have occurred in what is vaguely referred to as the Third World: the diverse countries of Asia, the Middle East, Africa, Latin America, and the eastern Caribbean. In the same period, all the wars in which the United States was involved—either directly with its combat forces or indirectly with military assistance—occurred in the Third World. (P.13)

The Commission speculated that in the future the major threats to American interests would occur in the same arena and called for restructuring the military to meet such future threats. The response was the low intensity conflict doctrine to be applied as Klare argues "... where the United States is either trying to bolster a client government against a revolutionary upheaval or fostering a counterrevolutionary insurgency against an unfriendly Third World Regime." (Klare and Kornbluh 1988, p. 7)

This followed a 1986 final *Report Of the Joint Low Intensity Conflict Project* that advanced guidelines for the application of low-level war fighting in the Third World. Proponents of the LIC doctrine argued that to be successful, they had to fight their war on two levels, one for the hearts and minds of the people at home to overcome the so-called Vietnam syndrome and the other on battle fields in third world countries. The battle for the hearts and minds was called *the campaign to garner grass-roots support for renewed intervention in Third World countries.* As one deputy secretary of the Air Force told senior officers at a National Defense University conference, "I think the most critical special operations mission we have today is to persuade the American public that the Communists are out to get us." (Quoted in Klare and Kornbluh, p. 15).

Consistent with the LIC doctrine, the entire U.S. military posture was reconfigured to fight anticipated wars in the Third World, wars expected to have no moral limitations. As another LIC theorist argued ". . . national leaders and the public must understand that low-intensity conflicts do not conform to democratic notions of strategy or tactics. Revolution and counterrevolution develop their own morality and ethics that justify any means to achieve success. Survival is the ultimate morality." As Neil Livingstone told senior US officers in 1983, ". . . the dirty little wars are not pretty, but if we shrink back from harsh and brutal measures, . . . we abrogate our ability to engage successfully in low-level conflict." (Klare, 15). Among Livingstone's suggestion for success were restrictions on media access to foreign war zone, diminished congressional oversight of LIC operations, and the employment of bounty hunters to track down and assassinate suspected terrorists. And according to an army training manual LIC itself employs tactics ". . . . ranging from diplomatic, economic, and psycho-social pressures through terrorism and insurgency." (U.S. Army, TRADOC Pamphlet No. 525-44, p.2, Quoted in Klare, p. 53).

Initially the LIC doctrine, at least for public consumption, was based on the premise that Third World insurgencies were instigated by the international communist movement led by the Soviet Union. However, now that the international communist movement has receded as a threat and several erstwhile Warsaw Pact nations are now considered American allies, the communist fig leaf has been removed. The real reason for LIC and continuing American intervention in the Third World is their strategic importance and the fact that the West is not only dependent on certain critical Third World resources such as oil, columbium, cobalt, and zinc, to name but a few, but the West insists on having access to these resources on its own terms. Terrorists have succeeded communists as the bogeyman in the Western struggle to maintain its dominance. Terrorists are now the evil doers, fanatics without a cause. Fanatics, we are told, who are simply envious of our good fortune and democratic ways.

The foregoing is at least part of the systemic context within which we have to understand both the rise of terrorism directed at the United States and the American response to it. Now let me turn to the theoretical and historical contexts which may help us understand the use of violence by terrorist groups and the American response.

Theoretical Context

Violence is a primary technique used by all international actors be they nation states, governments in exile, liberation movements, or irredentist sects. All, at one time or another, resort to violence to achieve their objectives. The form that violence takes, the particular violent technique that actors use, is a function of resources at their disposal and what they believe to be the vulnerabilities of their perceived enemy. To be blunt about it, international actors use what they have and what they think will work against their enemy. Terrorism is a weapon of the militarily weak used to exploit vulnerabilities of a stronger adversary and as the American LIC doctrine asserts its use contravenes traditional notions of morality.

An important question to ponder is: are some forms of violence permissible and others to be prohibited? Are their different rules governing the use of violence by nation-states and non-nation-state actors? Is it permissible for nation-states to use violence to achieve foreign policy objectives but not for non-nation-state actors who oppose the policies of nation states? When nation states use cruise missiles and smart bombs, deploy land, and antipersonnel mines to achieve their foreign policy objectives, killing thousands of people in the process, is that permissible? Is it permissible to use special forces to invade another country as was done in Panama and Grenada?

A related question is what nations are allowed to have so-called weapons of mass destruction? What are the criteria used to make that determination? What are we to make of a situation when one country says that it is prepared to use its weapons of mass destruction to destroy another country suspected of trying to obtain such weapons? Is it to say that it is OK for U.S., Britain, France, Israel and Russia to have such weapons because they will only use them in the right situation or on the right people? Other countries cannot have them because they will use them at the wrong time or on the wrong people? Who are the right people and who are the wrong people?

To elaborate further on the context of September 11, let us review the actual use of violence by the united States in the Third World over the past forty or fifty years because it is that history of violence that establishes the historical context in which September 11 arose.

Brief History of Recent U.S. Violence in the Third World

Since WWII, the U.S. has a long history of using violence against those said to be threats to American interests in the third World, and the number of persons killed runs in the hundreds of thousands if not more. Let me cite briefly 12 selected examples, the dirty-dozen, from this extensive catalog of violent intervention by the United States:

1. Coup in Iran that installed the Shah in 1952, eventually 70,000 lives lost in insurrections against Shah.
2. Guatemala 1954 coup against democratically elected government 120,000 deaths.
3. The assassination of Patrice Lumumba in the Congo in 1960 and the subsequent enthronement and support for the decades of barbarous rule by Mobutu; this also contributed to the long running civil war in Angola.
4. Dominican Republic coup 1965, 3000 deaths.
5. Coup in Indonesia 1965, 800,000 ensued.
6. Invasion of Grenada in 1983 and the death of several hundred people.
7. El Salvador and support for brutal regime 1980, 80,000 deaths.
8. Mined Harbors and supported Contra War in Nicaragua 1984 30,000 deaths.
9. Invasion of Panama 1989, search for erstwhile ally Noriega and 8,000 deaths.
10. The blockade and indiscriminate bombing of Iraq after the Gulf War that has cost the lives of 500,000 children.
11. The coup against the legally elected Allende regime in Chile in 1973 that eventually cost more than 70,000 lives.
12. The 40-year war of terror against the Cuban Revolution:
    - 7 attempts to assassinate Fidel Castro;
    - blowing up of Cuban airline in flight in October 1976 killing all 73 on board by Orlando Bosch, Hernan Ricardo, and Freddy Lugo. Both Bosch and Ricardo had demonstrated ties to the CIA. Bosch, an internationally recognized terrorist was convicted for committing terrorist acts in the United States in 1968. He was subsequently pardoned by President George Bush Sr.;
    - the 1971 poisoning of the swine population in Cuba (See Warren Hickle and William Turner, *The Fish is Red*, also *Newsday* Jan. 9, 1977);
    - germ warfare against sugar cane crop (*Covert Action Bulletin*, Summer 1982);
    - Dengue flu virus spread in Cuba, 1981, Covert Action Bulletin, Summer 1982, p. 28-31).

The U.S. sponsored terrorist campaign against Cuba is easily the most flagrant use of terrorism in the post WW II world.

It should be noted that several of the leaders who eventually became targets of US as terrorists were at one time armed, used, and supported by the US. This includes Saddam Hussein, Noriega, and Bin Laden. All were allies and presumably internationally accepted leaders until they were no longer useful to American foreign policy makers.

So what are we to make of all of this? Did September 11 transform the world? What was different when the world woke up on September 12? Was it the use of violence? Certainly not. Was it the death of innocents? Certainly not. As I have demonstrated, the use of violence for political objectives was a long established and accepted principle in international politics. And what is more, since the 1980s US foreign policy has been based on the assumption that it was at war with third world interests. The killing of civilians, collateral damage they call it in the Pentagon, was also a long accepted principle. The several thousand people killed in Nicaragua and Panama, for example, were collateral damage, as were those killed in Afghanistan. So what was different? The difference was that the United States has long rained violence on people throughout the Third World, but the US felt that it was insulated from and immune to violence on its own territory. However September 11 demonstrated that was mistaken. What was thought to be a one way street to the bombing fields of the Third World suddenly became a two lane highway with one lane coming back to the U.S. Violence was no longer something that the US visited on other people exclusively. It began to be a boomerang.

What has been the American response? Rather than reflect on our posture in the world and our complicity in the circumstances that led to September 11, the U.S. has declared war and its intention to use its superior military might to wipe out those who oppose it and to declare to the world that there are only two sides, either you are with us or you too are the enemy. But who is the enemy? How do others in the world view these developments? Let me quote three foreign sources, one from the Americas, one from Asia and one from Africa.

From the Americas, Radio Havana opined:

> But who is the "enemy?" The enemy are successive Washington administrations that have for more than five decades promoted terrorism on an enormous scale across the globe. Administrations that have trained international military personnel in techniques of torture and terrorism in its meek-sounding School of the Americas. Administrations that have for 40 years permitted and supported terrorist attacks against its island neighbor whose only crime was to advocate a different socio-political system. Administrations that introduced the world to nuclear holocaust, to carpet bombing, to horrendous use of phosphorous and napalm bombs. Administrations that maintain an economic blockade that is directly responsible for the loss of hundreds of thousands of Iraqi children's lives. Administrations that support one of the most repressive, brutal and racist regimes on earth with massive flows of money and weapons to use against the Palestinian people. Administrations that financed the Latin American dictatorships of the eighties and then later "apologized" for some of the unspeakable crimes they committed in the name of "democracy."

No solution will be forthcoming in the destruction of those deemed responsible. The enemy will still be there because the enemy comes from within. The CIA supported Noriega, Marcos, Sukarno, the Shah, Idi Amin, Mobuto, the Contra, Pinochet, the Argentinian generals, d'Aubuison, Somoza, Batista, Stroessner et al—the list is long and represents the obliteration of hundreds of thousands of civilian lives. In Panama 2,000, in Nicaragua 30,000, in El Salvador 75,000, in Guatemala over 150,000, in Indonesia 300,000.

The people of the U.S. can surely no longer remain immune from the terrorism their governments provoke, promote and tolerate in their name. After the rage, the hatred, and the clamouring for vengeance have subsided, the time for reflection must come. War should be declared on the real threats to humanity: AIDS, racism, neo-colonialism, ruthless free market profiteering and Washington's "democracy" of domination. That way the poverty and desperation that creates the kind of hatred of the U.S. that leads to such unspeakable acts of terrorism will be avoided. The security and welfare of the United States clearly depends on social justice for all. There must be a change in this U.S. psyche of isolation and pre-eminence or we shall all be brought to the brink of disaster once more. (Radio Havana, Cuba)

The sentiments expressed in the message from Cuba is echoed in a column from India:

I belong to the uncivilized part of the world. I am not ashamed to conceal the fact that my first reaction on seeing the destruction of the Pentagon and WTC Towers was jubilation. For that matter, it was the reaction of the overwhelming majority of our people. The mighty power on earth was slapped on it's face!

But, when we witnessed the T.V. images of people jumping from the towers, wailing women and people running for their lives. . . . we really felt bad. Especially, when we realized that a sizable section of the people killed were ordinary workers, we were back to our senses. Because you know, we are not civilized enough to watch this horror on the T.V. Screen, munching Chocolates and sipping Coke, as America did during the "Operation - Desert Storm."

First it was "Terror on America," Then "War on America," Now it is "America's new War". U.S. Marines and F.B.I. sleuths are landing in Pakistan. Standing in the midst of rubbles, putting his arms around the shoulder of a fireman, American President declares war. It reminds me of the Hollywood Trash "Independence Day." But the reality is far more vulgar than the illusion. I am surprised to see that the civilized people of America are politically more naive than the illiterate peasants of India.

The fact that the 'Evil' itself was created by the 'Good' is not relevant here. All Evil is Good when it serves the Empire. Saddam is fine when he remains an instrument to attack Iran. Noriega is fine until he defies the Empire. Thus when the Empire so desires it will bomb any country. In 1986 it bombed Libya and killed unknown number of people including Gadaffi's child. It was a retribution for a bomb blast in a Berlin Discotheque in which two American Marines died. Involvement of Libyan Govt. in the blast is yet to be proved. . . . In 1998, a pharmaceutical factory in Sudan was bombed. Number of deaths unknown. The factory was accused of manufacturing chemical weapons for Terrorists. The owner is suing the U.S. now. The accusation against the factory is yet to be proved. . . . (Maruthaiyam, "Evil Empire—Innocent Civilians," *Puthiya Kalachakra, indymedia, September 22, 2001*, Tamil Nadu, South India)

Finally the analysis coming from Nigeria, a leading African country is virtually the same as that from Asia and the Americas:

On September 11, 2001, an unpopular position was taken by a courageous few in clamor for justice. The World is confused, afraid and every one is talking, guessing and debating on what would happen next. The president of the United States of America George Bush (alas Baby Bush) is angry, spitting fire and demanding forcefully for a "must" support from the

NATO countries. NATO has evoked article 5 and now, we are looking at WWIII as they claim. The fight now is the "HAVES" against the "HAVE NOTS." America and Europe against Africa, Asia, the Middle East etc. . . . [the intention is] to keep them busy, hungry, impoverished, confused and subdued. What does the US think, that in an unjust and undemocratic world created by them and NATO, with people hungry, angry and dying that there would be PEACE? No, it is not possible as much as we all clamor to stop terrorist attacks, condemn it with all of our might the fact remains that as long as the World remains unequal in this era of feminist, ethnic and general people's campaign for equality activities are still grossly unequal. It is sad though that America speaks of revenge with so much aggression and that apart from NATO States all others are prime suspects and considered enemies. (Annie Brisibe, "Who Dares the Untouchables, The Myth of American Supremacy, *Nigeria World,* September 20, 2001)

These lengthy quotations from the international press reveal that the rest of the world, especially the impoverished people of the Third World, understand the history of imperialism and exploitation and they assign primary culpability to the United States. Only the American people, particularly white males, believe their own propaganda. Many appear to have no understanding of what the government has done and continues to do in their name. African Americans, as the discussion below of the impending war on Iraq will show, are much more knowledgeable about, and critical of American foreign policy toward the Third World.

War, Iraq, Bush, and African Americans

Following its successful campaign to drive the Taliban from power and destroy Al Qaida base camps in Afghanistan, the Bush administration broadened its war on terror to include a planned invasion of Iraq. Even though no link between the perpetrators of the September 11 attacks and Iraq was established, to justify the planned invasion, the Bush administration initiated a spirited propaganda campaign to convince the American public that Saddam Hussein regime was part of an international terrorist network and a threat to American interests. The two highest ranking African Americans in the administration, Secretary of State, Colin Powell, and National Security Adviser, Condoleezza Rice, have been key players in the propaganda offensive. Rice has been a peripatetic participant on Sunday morning talk shows and news programs trying to influence domestic opinion while Powell has done the heavy lifting on the international front. Powell's role has been especially important because he has consistently received the highest approval ratings among all American public officials and therefore lends credibility to the administration both at home and abroad.

Thus, when a preponderant majority of the Security Council declined in early 2003 to support the American call for an invasion of Iraq, Powell was dispatched to the UN to make the case. Prior to his appearance, a Gallup poll analyst had proclaimed that Powell remained the most popular political figure in America with 88 percent expressing a favorable view of him and only 6 percent an unfavorable one. In the same poll Bush's ratings were 70 percent favorable and 28 percent unfavorable. (Poll Analyses, Sept. 30, 2002) Furthermore, polling data had shown that Americans did not trust the Bush administration to be honest about the Iraqi situation. Forty-nine percent had said that it was very likely, 14 percent, or somewhat likely, 35 percent, that the administration would present inaccurate information, and 58 percent believed that it was very likely, 22 percent, or somewhat likely, 36 percent, that the Bush administration would conceal evidence that did not support the American position. (Poll Analysis Feb. 4, 2003) Immediately prior to his address to the Security Council, close to nine in 10 Americans said Powell's speech would be important in determining their view about an attack on Iraq, and more Americans, 63 percent vs. 24 percent, chose Powell over Bush as the leader they trusted more in making decisions about U.S.–Iraq policy. (Poll Analyses, Feb. 4, 2003).

Using an array of audiovisual aids, Powell told a rapt Security Council that "... every statement I make today is backed up by sources, solid sources. These are not assertions. What we're giving you are facts and conclusions based on solid intelligence." In making the Bush administration case for war, Powell made the major claims against Iraq. He asserted that: (1) Iraq used mobile bio-chemical laboratories to conceal its illicit weapons and deceive weapon inspectors; (2) that Iraq had advanced notice of inspection schedules and he presented satellite photos said to show Iraqis sanitizing a prohibited bio-chemical site after they knew that inspectors were coming; (3) that a known terrorist allied with Iraq was running a "poison factory" producing bio-chemical weapons in a compound in northern Iraq; and (4) A few days later appearing before the Senate Budget Committee Powell offered the coup de grace when he reported that a then yet-to-be-released bin Laden tape established beyond a show of doubt the fraternal link between bin Laden and Hussein as comrades in terror.

Powell's presentation had the intended impact on American public opinion. Polling data showed that following his address support for invading Iraq among the American people rose from 58 percent to 63 percent. Powell, the believable African American, had turned the tide for war. The American press was effusive in its praise for Powell for having exposed the alleged Iraqi hypocrisy.

Outside the United States, however, the response was different. One of the solid sources that Powell had relied on was a British intelligence report the solidity of which quickly came into question. The British report, it turned out, had been cobbled together from a graduate student thesis with data more than ten years old and from other previously published academic papers. None of the sources had been acknowledged by either the British or Powell. Further undermining Powell's credibility, the UN chief weapons inspector challenged the veracity of the data on mobile bio-chem labs and the claim that Iraqis had advanced notice about inspection sites and schedules. (Guardian UK, Feb. 5, 2003) And contributing to further embarrassment, international journalists inspecting the reputed poison factory found that the ". . . terrorist factory was nothing of the kind—more of a dilapidated collection of concrete outbuildings at the foot of a grassy sloping hill. There is a bakery. There is no sign of chemical weapons anywhere—only the smell of paraffin and vegetable ghee used for cooking." (The Observer, Feb. 9, 2003). Finally the Bin Laden tape, rather than demonstrating solidarity between Bin Laden and Hussein, called upon Bin Laden's followers to oppose both the United States and the "socialist" Hussein regime.

To date, I have seen no published response from Powell about challenges to his data. We can only speculate, was he set up or did he knowingly present false information to the Security Council and Senate Budge Committee? Was Harry Belafonte on the mark when he accused Powell of willingly carrying water for the imperialist?

Whatever the answers to these questions may be, it is clear that the positions of Rice and Powell are not shared by most African Americans. Black public opinion, major Black organizations and important Black leaders have all voiced opposition to the proposed war. For example, a recent poll shows that while 58 percent of whites support invading Iraq, 56 percent of African Americans (and 60 percent of Hispanics) are opposed to it. (Poll Analyses, Jan. 30, 2003). Black leadership has also gone on record in opposition to the proposed invasion. The leader of the Nation of Islam, Minister Louis Farrakhan, among the first to publicly opposed the war, sent a letter of concern to President Bush in December 2001 stating his opposition to U.S. policy. The NAACP Board of Directors confirmed its opposition to the war in early 2003. At a national meeting of Black clergy in February 2003 with some 8000 in attendance and broadcast on C-Span the ministers announced their opposition to the proposed war. (Final Call, Feb. 20, 2003). The Congressional Black Caucus in October 2002 passed a resolution opposing a "unilateral first strike" against Iraq and later three of its members, Jesse Jackson, Jr, Sheila Jackson Lee, and John Conyers, joined three other Congresspersons in a suit to enjoin President Bush from going to war without the Congressional consent. Congressman Charles Rangel of New York suggested that the rush to war would not be so brisk if the sons and daughters of the privileged classes were conscripted for military service and called for reinstatement of the draft to dramatize his point. Finally, the city Council of New York endorsed the decision of a local group to change the name of Black History Month to "Black Protest for Peace Month" to highlight Black opposition to the proposed war.

Thus, as the foregoing recitation shows, African Americans oppose the proposed war overwhelmingly. Many African Americans have always been wary of the imperialist policies of the United States toward the Third World and have striven to distance themselves from them. African Americans try to convince Third World people that we do not share the imperial designs of the typical white American. However, at this critical historical moment when the United States asserts that it has the right and duty to use preemptive war to force its will on the people of the Third World, when Nelson Mandela charges that Bush's policies will lead to a holocaust, and when Winnie Mandela contemplates being part of a human shield to protect Iraqi children from the impending American onslaught the Black faces that the world will see supporting the planned invasion and occupation will be Colin Powell and Condoleezza Rice.

Whither Black Power?

References

Bardach, Louise, *Cuba Confidential*. New York, Random House, 2002.

Farrakhan, Louis, "A Letter to George W. Bush, Dec. 1, 2001, *FinalCall.com*

Featherston, Drew and Cummings, James, "Outbreak of Swine Fever Linked to CIA, *Newsday* (New York), January 9, 1977.

Harding, Luke, "Revealed: Truth Behind U.S. Poison Factory Claim, *The Observer* (UK), Feb. 9, 2003

Hinkle, Warren, *The Fish is Red*, New York, Harper Collins, 1981.

Jones, Jeffrey, Poll Analyses, Jan. 30, 2003, Blacks, Postgraduates Among Groups Most Likely to Oppose Iraqi Invasion, Gallup News Service.

Klare, Michael and Kornbluh, Peter, *Low Intensity Warfare*, New York, Pantheon Books, 1988.

Moore, David, Poll Analyses, Sept. 30, 2002, "Powell Remains Most Popular Figure, Gallup News Service.

—Poll Analyses, Feb. 4, 2003, "Powell UN Appearance Important to Public, Gallup News Service.

—Poll Analyses, Feb. 11, 2003, "Public Rallying Around Bush Call For War," Gallup News Service.

Muhammad, Nisa, "Black Clergy: War is Not the Answer, solve problems at home, FinalCall.com, Feb. 20, 2003.

Plesch, Dad, "US Claim Dismissed by Blix, *The Observer* (UK), Feb. 5, 2003.

Schapp, Bill, "The 1981 Cuba Dengue Epidemic, Covert Action Bulletin (Summer 1982), pp 28-31.

No Matter the Measure, Black Poverty Is High

Margaret C. Simms

Each year the U.S. Census Bureau releases the latest data on money income and poverty in the United States. When the 2001 income and poverty figures were announced late last year, few were surprised that the numbers indicated a reversal of economic progress for a number of groups.

In 2001, 32.9 million individuals in the U.S.—which is 11.7 percent of the population—fell below the poverty line. This was the first increase in the poverty rate since 1993, with 1.3 million more people in poverty than in 2000. Although the poverty rate increased only among non-Hispanic White households, the number of Hispanics in poverty increased by 300,000. The poverty rate did not change significantly among African American households; nevertheless, they had the highest poverty rate (22.7 percent) of all groups.

Median income also declined in 2001, with household income falling by 2.2 percent in real terms, that is, when adjusted for inflation. Most groups and most regions shared in the reversal; only the median income of Hispanics was unchanged. The steepest drop in household income was among Asians and Pacific Islanders (6.4 percent), followed by African Americans (3.4 percent). For African American households, this marked the first decline in income in 20 years.

Changes in both poverty rates and income reflect changes in employment and earnings. The poverty rate increased most among the working-age population (18-64) and among married-couple families, which typically have one or two wage earners. In fact, Black married-couple families were the only group to experience an increase in both the numbers in poverty and the proportion of families in poverty.

Annual income and poverty figures based on income are only two measures of economic status. Another important, but less frequently measured, indicator of economic well-

---

Reprinted from *Focus Magazine,* January/February 2003. Copyright © 2003 Joint Center for Political and Economic Studies, www.jointcenter.org Reprinted by permission.

being is assets. In a report released about the same time as the Census Bureau reports, the Corporation for Enterprise Development (CFED) offers a state-by-state assessment of asset growth and examines state initiatives to promote or support asset accumulation by individuals and families.

Asset Poverty

Assets are an extremely important aspect of economic well-being. While the tendency is to think of savings and wealth accumulation for the purposes of building "nest eggs" for children's education or for retirement, liquid assets also provide the cushion households need during times of unemployment. It is in this context that CFED developed a different measure of well-being, in the form of asset poverty. They define asset poverty as insufficient assets to sustain the household at the federal poverty level for a period of three months. By this measure, 25.5 percent of all U.S. households would have been poor in 1998, a rate more than double the more commonly recognized rate for income poverty.

The asset poverty measure is one of 30 asset measures presented in CFED's State Asset Development Report Card study. Among the others are financial assets, home-ownership capital, human capital, business capital and blank access. They also include access to health insurance. In addition, the study includes an analysis of 36 policy measures that states can take to help families build assets or protect them against depleting assets during economic adversity. These include policies directed toward financial asset building and improved bank access, affordable homeownership, human capital development, and small business development. Protective measures such as wage protection, health insurance, and property protection are included as well.

Good First Step

The authors of the report acknowledge that some of the data utilized are not definitive, as state level data for some measures are not readily available or may not have been collected since the mid-1990s. In some cases, the analysts have used proxies for the actual measure or estimated the values. The Survey of Income and Program Participation was the major source, but the analysts also re-weighed the sample data using the Current Population Survey in order to estimate the relevant population groups. Despite its shortcomings, the study is a good first step in assessing how well different groups are doing and how much they are assisted by their state's overall policy environment. The written report provides a summary analysis of each state and tables ranking the states on each of the asset outcomes and protection measures. There is an interactive version on the CFED website, which allows you to generate detailed state-specific tables on the various measures.

A major contribution of the CFED report is its cross-state analysis of asset accumulation and policy environments. They find that in 49 of the 50 states, asset poverty is greater than income poverty. In general, states in the Midwest tended to have higher asset outcomes and those in the Northeast had better policies for asset accumulation. The Southern states, on average, did quite poorly. Three-quarters of the states had a grade of "D" or "F" on the asset outcome measure, and over 60 percent of states earned less than a "C" in the effectiveness of their policies.

Significant asset gaps exist between White and non-White households in all 28 states for which race-specific calculations could be made. In most states, the ratio of White to non-White was greater than three-to-one. The smallest gap existed in Mississippi, where non-White poverty rates were "only" twice those of White families. The widest gaps were

Asset Indices for States with over One Million African Americans, 2000

State	African American Population, 2000	Household Mean Net Worth (1999 dollars)	Asset Inequality by Race (White/non-White ratio)[1]	Asset Poverty by Race (White/non-White ratio)[2]
Alabama	1,155,930	92,858	3.73	0.40
California	2,263,882	131,913	2.30	0.49
Florida	2,335,505	117,023	2.57	0.37
Georgia	2,349,542	89,855	4.40	0.39
Illinois	1,876,875	118,146	2.93	0.34
Louisiana	1,451,944	88,614	4.11	0.32
Maryland	1,477,411	138,422	3.50	0.38
Michigan	1,412,742	122,900	3.73	0.44
Mississippi	1,033,809	79,552	4.00	0.57
New Jersey	1,141,821	145,243	3.97	0.30
New York	3,014,385	103,177	4.39	0.30
North Carolina	1,737,545	100,561	3.28	0.48
Ohio	1,301,307	113,481	3.46	0.38
Pennsylvania	1,224,612	117,385	4.90	0.33
South Carolina	1,185,216	97,521	4.85	0.53
Texas	2,404,566	81,314	3.07	0.54
Virginia	1,390,293	122,320	5.02	0.42

[1]Asset inequality by race means that in Alabama, for example, White households have 3.73 times the mean net worth of non-White households.

[2]Asset poverty by race means that in Alabama, for example, White households are 40 percent as likely to be asset poor as non-White households.

Source: Compilation based on Corporation for Enterprise Development report. Population numbers from U.S. Census Bureau.

in the Northeastern states, with Connecticut having nearly four-to-one. To some extent, these gaps reflect the relative wealth of the Northeastern states versus those in the South. In other words, in places where fewer people are wealthy, the gap between White and non-White tends to be smaller, because Whites there are more likely to have modest levels of assets.

The smallest gap in wealth existed in Tennessee. But even in this state, Whites still had twice the assets of non-Whites. The largest gap was in Virginia, home to nearly 1.4 million African Americans. There, Whites had over five times the assets of non-Whites.

The ranking of states on their policies produced an "honor roll" of five states that received "A's" on asset outcomes and asset policies—Maine, Minnesota, Oregon, Vermont, and Washington. But none of these five states have large African American populations.

Examining the 17 states with over one million African Americans produces an interesting picture of similarities and contrasts. Eight of the 17 are in the South, while seven are in the Northeast and Midwest. Only two are outside those regions (Texas and California). In only three of the Southern states was average net worth (assets minus debts) over $100,000, while such levels were almost universal in the states outside the South. There was no regional difference in the asset poverty ratio (Whites to non-Whites) with ratios ranging from .30 to .54 outside the South and from .32 to .57 in the Southern states. When it comes to overall ratings in terms of asset outcomes and supportive policies for their residents, the Southern states fall short. None of them received a grade of "B" or better in terms of outcomes, and only one (North Carolina) got a "B" or better in terms of their policies. While no state with a large African American population ranked in the top 10 states in asset outcomes, four of them did rank in the top 10 in the effectiveness of their policies to support asset building. None of these states was in the South.

What Can Be Done?

Given this current period of economic uncertainty and the likelihood that most individuals will have to undergo several economic transitions in their lives, it is important for government to support the efforts of families and individuals to build wealth. Most of the recent federal policy has focused on changes in the Social Security system, but the CFED report places more emphasis on approaches that would build a range of more flexible assets, such as individual development accounts. They also call for states to make their budgets more transparent so that outsiders can determine how well they may be supporting asset development through tax expenditures.

Politics Mondays: School Vouchers

Armstrong Williams

President Bush's fiscal budget for 04' includes $756 million for school choice programs.

That's good news for the nation's minority students who, according to a recent study by the Manhattan Institute, drop out of high school at a disproportionate rate.

The report, which calculated the graduation rates for the fifty largest districts in America, found that 44 percent of African-American students and 46 percent of Latino students drop out of high school, compared to just 22 percent of white students. There is a logical progression: a lack of education equals a racial achievement gap equals a lack of economic integration equals ugly stereotypes about how minorities are lazy and unintelligent. For these reasons, improving the graduation rates among minority students should be considered one of the primary goals of the civil rights movement.

There is ample evidence that vouchers could help redress this disparity by giving parents and children more educational options while holding public schools accountable for their performance. But for reasons of self-preservation, members of the public school Cosa Nostra continue to oppose school vouchers.

That's what Education Secretary Rod Paige confronted last week when he met with D.C. school officials to discuss strengthening education in the nation's capitol.

Predictably, the school officials chaffed at the idea of accountability. "Vouchers drain critical dollars from neighborhood schools and divert attention form the reform effort already under way. . . ." said school board members in a written statement. And because schoolteachers represent one of the largest unions in the country, the Democratic Party continues to underwrite their tired rhetoric. "You are not going to see our government participate in a government sponsored voucher program," proclaimed the District's Democratic mayor, Anthony Williams.

Meanwhile, the needs of countless school children—mostly of color—fall by the wayside.

So, why are so many minorities dropping out of high school? That's the question I asked Dr. Jay Greene, the researcher who carried out the study for The Manhattan Institute.

Politics Mondays: School Vouchers by Armstrong Williams. Used by permission of the author.

"I suspect that part of the problem is that too many in the education establishment believe that African-American students cannot really do much better and so they tolerate a system with incredibly low graduation rates for black students. If expectations for African-American performance were much higher and if African-American students had access to the same range of educational options available to affluent whites, including private school options," Greene concluded, "African-American graduation rates would be much higher."

This arbitrary shaping of our youth is occurring in poor, urban school districts across the country. According to the 2000 National Assessment of Education Progress (NAEP) test, 63 percent of black, inner city 4th graders and 58 percent of urban Hispanic 4th graders are unable to demonstrate a "basic" proficiency in reading.

There is ample evidence that this is an urban problem. But geography is not destiny.

Rather than blaming the families for failure, we need to focus on ensuring that the education system offers solutions. That means breaking apart those conditions that con young minorities into feeling trapped, despondent, without a future. We need to direct these efforts at disadvantaged elementary schoolers. Most of all, we need to consider the public education system in poor urban neighborhoods as something other than an unalterable fact. That means embracing true change of the school voucher variety, rather than reinforcing the status quo by simply throwing more money at the problem.

Then, perhaps we can achieve a public school system that works as well for minority students as it does for the rest of us.

Shoving Vouchers Down D.C.'s Throat

The Black Commentator

The white man in the White House has his Black operatives running up and down the streets of Washington, D.C., waving millions of dollars in private school voucher money—and nobody's taking the bribe. Mayor Anthony A. Williams says, No. Bush says, No matter. The city school board says, No. The White House doesn't hear them. A poll shows that overwhelming majorities of the public reject vouchers. Bush insists it is his compassionate duty to foist the scheme on the recalcitrant natives, anyway.

There can no longer be any doubt: The Bush push for school vouchers has been definitively exposed as a phony issue, an invention of Right think tanks and their hired Black hustlers that has only the thinnest support among the people who are the supposed beneficiaries. Nobody ever marched for vouchers.

Congress set aside $75 million to fund vouchers programs in seven or eight cities, part of $756 million in so-called "school choice" money in Bush's 2004 budget. The U.S. Supreme Court has ruled that voucher programs are constitutional. So is sex, but that doesn't make it mandatory. A Zogby poll taken in November showed that 76 percent of D.C. residents—and a whopping 85 percent of Blacks—reject vouchers. It is a sentiment of longstanding—back in 1981, nine out of ten D.C. voters turned down a voucher tax credit scheme. DC's elected representatives are speaking for their constituents. To the Bush crew, this is a mere technicality.

The elected school board issued a written statement: "Vouchers drain critical dollars from neighborhood schools and divert attention from the reform effort already under way in the DCPS System." So Bush sent in his Education HNIC, Rod Paige, to browbeat the Mayor. Clearly, the voucher scheme is being presented as an offer that cannot be refused with impunity.

After the meeting, Paige spokesman Dan Langan tried to put the best spin on the con-

---

From *The Black Commentator*, No. 29, February 13, 2003 with permission.

versation, indicting to the *Washington Post* that the Mayor was amendable to putting the voucher money in a non-profit "entity" for distribution to families. That's not the way Mayor Williams remembered it. "He is not in support of that at all," said mayoral spokesman Tony Bullock. No means no.

The Bush operatives whispered a different story, forcing the Mayor's man to speak more expansively. "We needed that face-to-face [meeting with Mr. Paige] to agree to disagree," Bullock told the *Washington Times*. "And we wanted to do so in ways that didn't prevent us from accessing funding for other school-choice programs offered. But you are not going to see our government participate in a government-sponsored voucher program. Once you have moved past that immovable position, we are really flexible about school choice and have a proven track record with it."

Gangster Conservatism

An illiterate person can read between those lines. Bush is threatening to punish D.C.'s public schools unless he is given a green light for his private voucher showcase. Washington maintains one of the nation's most extensive charter public school networks—the implicit target of Republican political retribution.

Like the rest of urban America, D.C. is in need of . . . everything. Even the unwanted programs favored by the powerful are not rejected, lightly. However, "The notion of skirting the public officials by finding a private entity [for vouchers] is both insulting to public officials in the District of Columbia and treating the District in a way no other city or state is treated," said Washington's non-voting Congressional Representative Eleanor Holmes Norton. "And we will not be treated unequally. We demand equal treatment when it comes to federal funds."

Bush is attempting to steamroll D.C. because he can—and because it is Black. In the process, he is demonstrating that the voucher scam is a foreign political object that must be forced down the throats of Black America. The Hard Right plan to showcase the wonders of educational privatization in the nation's capital has gone awry, and been revealed as its opposite: a thuggish display of the administration's contempt for democracy in general, and the rights of Black children, parents and voters, in particular.

... and the Last Shall Be First

Washington's Democrats are gearing up to mount a bum rush of their own, one that could change the political and racial texture of the coming primary season.

The formal American presidential selection process begins in the glaringly white environs of New Hampshire and becomes progressively more distorted as the primary schedule lurches along. If a unanimous D.C. City Council gets its way, Washington will preempt New Hampshire to hold the nation's first primary on January 10, 2004, giving its Black (and relatively progressive white) electorate first whack at the candidates.

Just as Iowa farmers demand that candidates take firm positions on hog prices, Democrats who want to break out of the pack with D.C.'s convention votes in hand and momentum in their campaigns will be pressed on full voting rights for Washington. This is not a local issue: in addition to a fully privileged U.S. Representative, the District would elect two U.S. Senators.

D.C. Democracy Fund Executive Director Sean Tenner informs us that the City Council will hold public hearings on its historic "first in the nation" legislation on Wednesday, February 19. The measure, introduced by Councilman Jack Evans and supported by

Mayor Williams and the entire City Council, including Republicans may well overcome initial resistance from the National Democratic Party. As Tenner wrote in last week's *Black Commentator*:

> The city's activists and politicians are fed up with 200 years of second-class status and are asserting themselves in ways that would have previously seemed unthinkable. Along with Evans, D.C. Council Chair Linda Cropp (D) went on the radio and stated she would fight to hold the primary regardless of opposition from Congress. "This is a local matter that should be decided locally," Cropp said. "They may be able to keep us (delegates) from being seated but they cannot keep us from voting."

The Democrat's Sharpton Dilemma

Nobody savors the prospect of a "D.C. first" primary season more than Rev. Al Sharpton, who would be favored to win. Instead, Sharpton this week found himself having to admit to Iowa farmers that he has not yet developed a full-fledged agricultural policy, but will put together "a progressive farm agenda in Iowa" by sometime next month. According to the *Des Moines Register*, Sharpton considers himself not just the only Black in the contest, but one of the few real Democrats. "We have far too many people who will be coming through Iowa that are elephants in donkey clothes," he said.

Sharpton is also probably the best speaker and quickest mind in the bunch—bad news for those who seek to marginalize his candidacy. The "Black Hope" of this crowd is Carolyn Moseley-Braun, former Senator from Illinois who, the theory goes, would split the African American vote.

Chicago Sun-Times columnist Mark Brown caught Sharpton's act last weekend. He thinks Moseley-Braun is outclassed:

> Sharpton has the potential to be hugely popular with black voters all across the country, possibly enough to win a southern primary or two in a crowded field. And, believe it or not, he might even attract a small following among white voters looking for somebody to "tell it like it is."
>
> Apparently others had started to figure out the same thing and became the source of some of the encouragement for Moseley-Braun's sudden interest in the presidency. It's the old divide-and-conquer strategy that is well-known in Chicago ward politics. If the first black woman in the U.S. Senate can dilute some of Sharpton's support, he becomes a non-factor.
>
> But if Moseley-Braun is going to enter the fray with Sharpton, she'd better bring her "A" game if she doesn't want to look like a fool.

Columnist Mark Brown titled his piece, "Sharpton not the dullest tool in the shed"—a strangely backhanded compliment.

Of course, Black excellence is circumscribed by the practice of comparing Blacks only to other Blacks, allowing inferior white contenders to shine, undeservedly. Sharpton should be measured against presidential standards, such as those set by George Bush:

> "The war on terror involves Saddam Hussein because of the nature of Saddam Hussein, the history of Saddam Hussein and his willingness to terrorize himself."— Grand Rapids, Mich., January 29.

Now, that's a dull tool.

Affirmative Business Actions

It may surprise some readers to learn that the publishers of The Black Commentator give corporate America much of the credit for the limited gains of affirmative action in the U.S. Although big business certainly did not welcome Dr. Martin Luther King and his movement, it was corporate planners who realized that southern cities like Atlanta would be doomed to remain provincial backwaters while in the grip of Jim Crow.

Once a mega-corporation decides on a course of even limited diversity among its tens of thousands of employees, the imperatives of corporate policy—matched with corporate power—can move significant numbers of lives in new directions. People's activism provides the *push* for social change but, once corporate institutions have been forced into motion, they exert a powerful *pull* on everything around them. Specifically, corporations have tremendous influence on American higher education, which has been molded over generations to service corporate demands.

For this reason, *Black Commentator* is not surprised that corporations are prominent supporters of the besieged affirmative action program at the University of Michigan. As the *February 11 Washington Post* reports:

> Among the organizations and individuals who are planning to submit friend-of-the-court briefs supporting the university are several dozen Fortune 500 companies, the nation's elite private universities and colleges, the AFL-CIO, the American Bar Association—and a list of former high-ranking military officers and civilian defense officials, according to attorneys involved in the case....
>
> So powerful is this consensus that much of big business, a major component of the Republican Party's political coalition, is parting company with President Bush, who has sided with the white students challenging Michigan's admissions programs as a form of "reverse discrimination." Bush's brief agreed that diversity was a "paramount" goal—but said Michigan should pursue it by race-neutral means.

The White Man's Party is a mechanism for gaining political support among the racist American majority for the economic policies of rich. It promises many things to people who—very much like the clinically insane—operate in a false reality; huge numbers of whites believe they are victimized by affirmative action, based on no personal evidence whatsoever. Conversely, the corporate planner's job is to see the world clearly, adjust to it, and influence the future to his company's advantage.

Corporations understand that Black people will not allow the clock to be turned back. These executives see no profit in fighting the tides of history. Corporate defense of affirmative action is a testament to Black American tenacity—recognition of our will to resist.

Unearned Privilege

For a lawyerly approach to affirmative action, we highly recommend Kimberle W. Crenshaw's excellent piece at *NorthStar Network*—a new and valuable Black political resource.

Attorney Crenshaw is a nationally recognized expert on critical race theory and Professor of Law at UCLA Law School and Columbia University Law School. Her treatise is titled, The Preference of White Privilege.

> Affirmative Action is often misunderstood as a preference, while the real preferences that happen every day are virtually ignored in a discourse that uses stereotypes

and race baiting to do its work. Consider the experiences of Dr. Martin Luther King, Jr. and George Bush, two names that will certainly come up in the conservative assault on affirmative action. We know that tests tend to under-predict the performance of certain members of the population, especially people of color.

Dr. King's score on the GRE placed him in the bottom percentile of all test takers, yet he is probably the most gifted orator and one of the most brilliant visionaries of the 20th century. Think about all the other would be gifted orators, surgeons, lawyers, teachers, and business people whose potential remain tragically wasted by unwarranted reliance on such an artificial benchmark of merit as a test score. One the other hand, when we think about preferences, let's consider our president, whose SAT score was 150 points below the average Yale matriculant. And who no doubt benefited from his pedigree.

This form of privileging constitutes a preference, the kind that is most responsible for excluding the wealth of talent that would otherwise gain access to higher education while maintaining white hegemony. This simply shows the hypocrisy of the argument against affirmative action; it's really not about equal opportunity or merit at all. It is largely a racially coded, and delimited diatribe that trains attention on those aspects of educational policy that are least responsible for the current state of educational mis-opportunity.

The Black-White War Divide

It would require a multidisciplinary assemblage of experts to undertake a meaningful study of why Blacks are underrepresented at anti-war rallies. Two facts are, however, undeniable: the Black public has consistently opposed U.S. military adventures during the past 40 years, and current African American political leadership—elected and institutional—is generally reflective of that popular opposition.

For these reasons, *Black Commentator* felt justified in describing as *The Four Eunuchs* those Black congresspersons that voted for Bush's war powers resolution, in October. We knew with absolute certainty that Harold Ford (TN), William Jefferson (LA), Sanford Bishop (GA) and Albert Wynn (MD) had acted in scornful disregard of the sentiments of the overwhelming majority of their Black constituents and a significant minority of white voters in their districts—ironically, the same white voters most likely to have supported *them.*

An *Atlanta Journal-Constitution/Zogby America poll* released this past weekend shows that less than a quarter of Blacks (23 percent) support Bush's war against Iraq, versus 62 percent of the white public. 64 percent of Blacks surveyed "somewhat or strongly oppose" the planned attack, while 13 percent "aren't sure" what to think.

The bloodthirstiness of white American males is astounding: 68 percent of men surveyed are gung ho, indicating that the white male pro-war cohort soars somewhere in the high seventies. Less than half of all women favor war.

Hispanics polled nearly as warlike as whites. When asked the general question on war, 60 percent support it.

The lack of empathy with Iraqis as human beings marks white American males as a collective danger to the species. Zogby pollsters asked: Would you support or oppose a war against Iraq if it meant thousands of Iraqi civilian casualties? A solid majority of white men answered in the affirmative, as did more than a third of white women. Only seven percent of African Americans favored a war that would kill thousands.

Hispanics lost some of their bloodlust when confronted with the prospect of mass

Iraqi civilian casualties; only 16 percent are willing to support such an outcome.

Bush No Stand-Up Guy

As Black Harlem Congressman Charles Rangel pointed out in a recent television interview, George Bush spent months in hiding during the Vietnam War, absenting himself from his Air National Guard unit long enough to have earned a non-privileged officer five years at Leavenworth. "There have been a lot of people who have stood up for this country and I don't think that President Bush has been in that number," said Rangel, a Korean War veteran, Iraq war opponent, and sponsor of a bill to bring back compulsory national service.

Peace Weekend

The Brits are headlining Rev. Jesse Jackson for this weekend's anti-war demonstration, in London. Jackson believes that British public opinion may be "more critical" to averting war than U.S. public opposition.

Jackson challenged British Prime Minister Tony Blair, Bush's principal yes-man in Europe, to "use his talents" to find a peaceful solution. Speaking to the British newspaper *The Independent*, Jackson said:

> I think the people of Britain must pressure [Tony Blair]. He has dug his heels in, but in a democracy while leaders speak, people speak louder and people over the world are impressed by the demonstrations of the people of London. It was the same with the demonstrations in London over the freeing of Nelson Mandela. They have left a very powerful impression on people around the world. There is no future in war. The [London] marchers help the chance of people. The [world] will be looking at them.

Jackson also sent an open letter to Saddam Hussein, whom he met prior to the 1991 Gulf War. "Once more, I call on you with our countries on the verge of war, just as I did 12 years ago. Once more, we face a war of terrible consequence. One more, I appeal to you to act now to avoid the impending catastrophe," Jackson wrote. "Once more the fate of your country lies in your hands. I beseech you to act now, boldly, destroy your weapons to avoid a catastrophic war."

Organizers expect the Hyde Park demonstration to be Britain's biggest since the end of World War Two. Protests are planned in at least 300 cities, worldwide.

New York police got a judge's permission to confine hundreds of thousands of demonstrators to a strip of midtown Manhattan, Saturday. United for Peace and Justice organizers had planned to march to the United Nations headquarters, but police argued that the crowd would pose a danger to public safety and the security of the UN. "We are appalled by this attack on our basic First Amendment rights," said the organizers, calling the quarantine "an attempt to stifle the growing opposition to Bush's war."

Actor Danny Glover and South African Bishop Desmond Tutu accused New York officials of acting in solidarity with Bush's war aims. "If we were marching in support of war or in celebration of Saint Patrick's Day or some other celebration, we would have been granted a permit immediately," *said Glover*. "It is tragic that this city, which prides itself on leading the world as a cultural center, would not allow a march at this time."

Bishop Tutu compared Republican Mayor Michael Bloomberg's New York to apartheid-era South Africa, adding that New York "will probably be the only city in the world on February 15 that will not be permitting its citizens and others to express a differing point of view."

ACLU lawyers say the city has not allowed any demonstrations south of 59th Street since September 11.

NAACP chairman Julian Bond and Martin Luther King III will also address the rally. San Francisco will be the site of a major demonstration on Sunday.

War Day

The A.N.S.W.E.R. coalition, which spearheaded the demonstrations in Washington and San Francisco on October 26 and January 18, is in the role of supporting player for this weekend's events. A.N.S.W.E.R. organizers are already busy preparing for War Day, itself.

"We do not believe that war is inevitable," said the coalition. "However, if the war starts we must be organized to resist and disable the war machine." The group urges activists to gather for emergency protests at preselected sites in their localities on the day that war begins, and to prepare for a "*Convergence on White House*," March 1.

Opinion in Bakke

Thurgood Marshall

Supreme Court of the United States
REGENTS OF the UNIVERSITY OF CALIFORNIA, Petitioner,
v.
Allan BAKKE.

No. 76-811.

Argued Oct. 12, 1977.
Decided June 28, 1978.

White male whose application to state medical school was rejected brought action challenging legality of the school's special admissions program under which 16 of the 100 positions in the class were reserved for "disadvantaged" minority students. School cross-claimed for declaratory judgment that its program was legal. The trial court declared the program illegal but refused to order the school to admit the applicant. The California Supreme Court, 18 Cal.3d 34, 132 Cal.Rptr. 680, 553 P.2d 1152, affirmed the finding that the program was illegal and ordered the student admitted and the school sought certiorari. The Supreme Court, Mr. Justice Powell, held that: (1) the special admissions program was illegal, but (2) race may be one of a number of factors considered by school in passing on applications, and (3) since the school could not show that the white applicant would not have been admitted even in the absence of the special admissions program, the applicant was entitled to be admitted.

Affirmed in part and reversed in part.

Mr. Justice Brennan, Mr. Justice White, Mr. Justice Marshall and Mr. Justice Blackmun filed an opinion concurring in the judgment in part and dissenting.

Mr. Justice White filed a separate opinion.

Mr. Justice Marshall filed a separate opinion.

Supreme Court of the United States; Regents of the University of California v. Allan Bakke #76-811.

Mr. Justice Blackmun filed a separate opinion.

Mr. Justice Stevens concurred in the judgment in part and dissented in part and filed an opinion in which Mr. Chief Justice Burger, Mr. Justice Stewart and Mr. Justice Rehnquist joined.

* * *

Mr. Justice MARSHALL.

I agree with the judgment of the Court only insofar as it permits a university to consider the race of an applicant in making admissions decisions. I do not agree that petitioner's admissions program violates the **2798 Constitution. For it must be remembered that, during most of the past 200 years, the Constitution as interpreted by this Court did not prohibit the most ingenious and pervasive forms of discrimination against the Negro. Now, when a State acts to remedy the effects of that legacy of discrimination, I cannot believe that this same Constitution stands as a barrier.

I

A

Three hundred and fifty years ago, the Negro was dragged to this country in chains to be sold into slavery. Uprooted from his homeland and thrust into bondage for forced labor, *388 the slave was deprived of all legal rights. It was unlawful to teach him to read; he could be sold away from his family and friends at the whim of his master; and killing or maiming him was not a crime. The system of slavery brutalized and dehumanized both master and slave.[1]

The denial of human rights was etched into the American Colonies' first attempts at establishing self-government. When the colonists determined to seek their independence from England, they drafted a unique document cataloguing their grievances against the King and proclaiming as "self-evident" that "all men are created equal" and are endowed "with certain unalienable Rights," including those to "Life, Liberty and the pursuit of Happiness." The self-evident truths and the unalienable rights were intended, however, to apply only to white men. An earlier draft of the Declaration of Independence, submitted by Thomas Jefferson to the Continental Congress, had included among the charges against the King that

"[h]e has waged cruel war against human nature itself, violating its most sacred rights of life and liberty in the persons of a distant people who never offended him, captivating and carrying them into slavery in another hemisphere, or to incur miserable death in their transportation thither." Franklin 88.

The Southern delegation insisted that the charge be deleted; the colonists themselves were implicated in the slave trade, and inclusion of this claim might have made it more difficult to justify the continuation of slavery once the ties to England were severed. Thus, even as the colonists embarked on a *389 course to secure their own freedom and equality, they ensured perpetuation of the system that deprived a whole race of those rights.

The implicit protection of slavery embodied in the Declaration of Independence was made explicit in the Constitution, which treated a slave as being equivalent to three-fifths of a person for purposes of apportioning representatives and taxes among the States. Art. I, § 2. The Constitution also contained a clause ensuring that the "Migration or Importation" of slaves into the existing States would be legal until at least 1808, Art. I, § 9, and a fugitive slave clause requiring that when a slave escaped to another State, he must be returned on the claim of the master, Art. IV, § 2. In their declaration of the principles that were to provide the cornerstone of the new Nation, therefore, the Framers made it plain that "we the people," for whose protection the constitution was designed, did not include those whose skins were the wrong color. As Professor John Hope Franklin has observed Americans "proudly accepted the challenge and responsibility of their new political freedom by establishing the machinery and safeguards that insured the continued enslavement of blacks." Franklin 100.

The individual States likewise established the machinery to protect the system of slavery through the promulgation of the Slave **2799 Codes, which were designed primarily to defend the property interest of the owner in his slave. The position of the Negro slave as mere property was confirmed by this Court in <u>Dred Scott v. Sandford, How. 393, 15 L.Ed. 691 (1857)</u>, Holding that the Missouri Compromise—which prohibited slavery in the portion of the Louisiana Purchase Territory north of Missouri—was unconstitutional because it deprived slave owners of their property without due process. The Court declared that under the Constitution a slave was property, and "[t]he right to traffic in it, like an ordinary article of merchandise and property, was guaranteed to the citizens of the United *390 States...." <u>Id., at 451</u>. The Court further concluded that Negroes were not intended to be included as citizens under the Constitution but were "regarded as beings of an inferior order . . . altogether unfit to associate with the white race, either in social or political relations; and so far inferior, that they had no rights which the white man was bound to respect. . . ." <u>Id., at 407</u>.

B

The status of the Negro as property was officially erased by his emancipation at the end of the Civil War. But the long-awaited emancipation, while freeing the Negro from slavery, did not bring him citizenship or equality in any meaningful way. Slavery was replaced by a system of "laws which imposed upon the colored race onerous disabilities and burdens, and curtailed their rights in the pursuit of life, liberty, and property to such an extent that their freedom was of little value." <u>Slaughter-House Cases, 16 Wall. 36, 70, 21 L.Ed. 394 (1873)</u>. Despite the passage of the Thirteenth, Fourteenth, and Fifteenth Amendments, the Negro was systematically denied the rights those Amendments were supposed to secure. The combined actions and inactions of the State and Federal Governments maintained Negroes in a position of legal inferiority for another century after the Civil War.

The Southern States took the first steps to re-enslave the Negroes. Immediately following the end of the Civil War, many of the provisional legislatures passed Black Codes, similar to the Slave Codes, which, among other things, limited the rights of Negroes to own or rent property and permitted imprisonment for breach of employment contracts.

Over the next several decades, the South managed to disenfranchise the Negroes in spite of the fifteenth Amendment by various techniques, including poll taxes, deliberately complicated balloting processes, property and literacy qualifications, and finally the white primary.

Congress responded to the legal disabilities being imposed *391 in the Southern States by passing the Reconstruction Acts and the Civil Rights Acts. Congress also responded to the needs of the Negroes at the end of the Civil War by establishing the Bureau of Refugees, Freedmen, and Abandoned Lands, better known as the Freedmen's Bureau, to supply food, hospitals, land, and education to the newly freed slaves. Thus, for a time it seemed as if the Negro might be protected from the continued denial of his civil rights and might be relieved of the disabilities that prevented him from taking his place as a free and equal citizen.

That time, however, was short-lived. Reconstruction came to a close, and, with the assistance of this Court, the Negro was rapidly stripped of his new civil rights. In the words of C. Vann Woodward: "By narrow and ingenious interpretation [the Supreme Court's] decisions over a period of years had whittled away a great part of the authority presumably given the government for protection of civil rights." Woodward 139.

The Court began by interpreting the Civil War Amendments in a manner that sharply curtailed their substantive protections. See, *e.g., Slaughter-House Cases, supra* ; United States v. Reese, 92 U.S. 214, 23 L.Ed. 563 (1876); United States v. Cruikshank, 92 U.S. 542, 23 L.Ed. 588 (1876). Then in the notorious Civil Rights Cases, 109 U.S. 3, 3 S.Ct. 18, 27 L.Ed. 835 (1883), **2800 the Court strangled Congress' efforts to use its power to promote racial equality. In those cases the Court invalidated sections of the Civil Rights Act of 1875 that made it a crime to deny equal access to "inns, public conveyances, theatres and other places of public amusement." Id., at 10, 3 S.Ct., at 20. According to the Court, the Fourteenth Amendment gave Congress the power to proscribe only discriminatory action by the State. The Court ruled that the Negroes who were excluded from public places suffered only an invasion of their social rights at the hands of private individuals, and Congress had no power to remedy that. Id., at 24-25, 3 S.Ct., at 31. "When a man has emerged from slavery, and by the aid of beneficent legislation has shaken off the inseparable concomitants of that *392 state," the Court concluded, "there must be some stage in the progress of his elevation when he takes the rank of a mere citizen, and ceases to be the special favorite of the laws. . . ." Id., at 25, 3 S.Ct., at 31. As Mr. Justice Harlan noted in dissent, however, the Civil War Amendments and Civil Rights Acts did not make the Negroes the "special favorite" of the laws but instead "sought to accomplish in reference to that race . . .—what had already been done in every State of the Union for the white race— to secure and protect rights belonging to them as freemen and citizens; nothing more." Id., at 61, 3 S.Ct., at 57.

The Court's ultimate blow to the Civil War Amendments and to the equality of Negroes came in *Plessy v. Ferguson,* 163 U.S. 537, 16 S.Ct. 1138, 41 L.Ed. 256 (1896). In upholding a Louisiana law that required railway companies to provide "equal but separate" accommodations for whites and Negroes, the Court held that the Fourteenth Amendment was not intended "to abolish distinctions based upon color, or to enforce social, as distinguished from political equality, or a commingling of the two races upon terms unsatisfactory to either." Id., at 544, 16 S.Ct., at 1140. Ignoring totally the realities of the positions of the two races, the Court remarked:

"We consider the underlying fallacy of the plaintiff's argument to consist in the assumption that the enforced separation of the two races stamps the colored race with a badge of inferiority. If this be so, it is not by reason of anything found in the act, but solely because the colored race chooses to put that construction upon it." Id., at 551, 16 S.Ct., at 1143.

Mr. Justice Harlan's dissenting opinion recognized the bankruptcy of the Court's reasoning. He noted that the "real meaning" of the legislation was "that colored citizens are so inferior and degraded that they cannot be allowed to sit in public coaches occupied by white citizens." Id., at 560, 16 S.Ct., at 1147. He expressed his fear that if like laws were enacted in other *393 States, "the effect would be in the highest degree mischievous." Id., at 563, 16 S.Ct., at 1148. Although slavery would have disappeared, the States would retain the power "to interfere with the full enjoyment of the blessings of freedom; to regulate civil rights, common to all citizens, upon the basis of race; and to place in a condition of legal inferiority a large body of American citizens. . . ." *Ibid.*

The fears of Mr. Justice Harlan were soon to be realized. In the wake of *Plessy*, many States expanded their Jim Crow laws, which had up until that time been limited primarily to passenger trains and schools. The segregation of the races was extended to residential areas, parks, hospitals, theaters, waiting rooms, and bathrooms. There were even statutes and ordinances which authorized separate phone booths for Negroes and whites, which required that textbooks used by children of one race be kept separate from those used by the other, and which required that Negro and white prostitutes be kept in separate districts. In 1898, after *Plessy*, the Charlestown News and Courier printed a parody of Jim Crow laws:

"'If there must be Jim Crow cars on the railroads, there should be Jim Crow cars on the street railways. Also on all passenger boats.... If there are to be **2801 Jim Crow cars, moreover, there should be Jim Crow waiting saloons at all stations, and Jim Crow eating houses.... There should be Jim Crow sections of the jury box, and a separate Jim Crow dock and witness stand in every court—and a Jim Crow Bible for colored witnesses to kiss.'" Woodward 68.

The irony is that before many years had passed, with the exception of the Jim Crow witness stand, "all the improbable applications of the principle suggested by the editor in derision had been put into practice—down to and including the Jim Crow Bible." *Id.*, at 69.

Nor were the laws restricting the rights of Negroes limited *394 solely to the Southern States. In many of the Northern States, the Negro was denied the right to vote, prevented from serving on juries, and excluded from theaters, restaurants, hotels, and inns. Under President Wilson, the Federal Government began to require segregation in Government buildings; desks of Negro employees were curtained off; separate bathrooms and separate tables in the cafeterias were provided; and even the galleries of the Congress were segregated. When his segregationist policies were attacked, President Wilson responded that segregation was "'not humiliating but a benefit'" and that he was "'rendering [the Negroes] more safe in their possession of office and less likely to be discriminated against.'" Kluger 91.

The enforced segregation of the races continued into the middle of the 20th century. In both World Wars, Negroes were for the most part confined to separate military units; it was not until 1948 that an end to segregation in the military was ordered by President Truman. And the history of the exclusion of Negro children from white public schools is too well known and recent to require repeating here. That Negroes were deliberately excluded from public graduate and professional schools—and thereby denied the opportunity to become doctors, lawyers, engineers, and the like—is also well established. It is of course true that some of the Jim Crow laws (which the decisions of this Court had helped to foster) were struck down by this Court in a series of decisions leading up to <u>Brown v. Board of Education, 347 U.S. 483, 74 S.Ct. 686, 98 L.Ed. 873 (1954)</u>. See, *e.g.*, <u>Morgan v. Virginia, 328 U.S. 373, 66 S.Ct. 1050, 90 L.Ed. 1317 (1946)</u>; <u>Sweatt v. Painter, 339 U.S. 629, 70 S.Ct. 848, 94 L.Ed. 1114 (1950)</u>; <u>McLaurin v. Oklahoma State Regents, 339 U.S. 637, 70 S.Ct. 851, 94 L.Ed. 1149 (1950)</u>. Those decisions, however, did not automatically end segregation, nor did they move Negroes from a position of legal inferiority to one of equality. The legacy of years of slavery and of years of second-class citizenship in the wake of emancipation could not be so easily eliminated.

*395 II

The position of the Negro today in America is the tragic but inevitable consequence of centuries of unequal treatment.

Measured by any benchmark of comfort or achievement, meaningful equality remains a distant dream for the Negro.

A Negro child today has a life expectancy which is shorter by more than five years than that of a white child.[2] The Negro child's mother is over three times more likely to die of complications in childbirth,[3] and the infant mortality rate for Negroes is nearly twice that for whites.[4] The median income of the Negro family is only 60% that of the median of a white family,[5] and the percentage of Negroes who live in families with incomes below the poverty line is nearly four times greater than that of whites.[6]

**2802 When the Negro child reaches working age, he finds that America offers him significantly less than it offers his white counterpart. For Negro adults, the unemployment rate is twice that of whites,[7] and the unemployment rate for Negro teenagers is nearly three times that of white teenagers.[8] A Negro male who completes four years of college can expect a median annual income of merely $110 more than a white male who has only a high school diploma.[9] Although Negroes *396 represent 11.5% of the population,[10] they are only 1.2% of the lawyers, and judges, 2% of the physicians, 2.3% of the dentists, 1.1% of the engineers and 2.6% of the college and university professors.[11]

The relationship between those figures and the history of unequal treatment afforded to the Negro cannot be denied. At every point from birth to death the impact of the past is reflected in the still disfavored position of the Negro.

In light of the sorry history of discrimination and its devastating impact on the lives of Negroes, bringing the Negro into the mainstream of American life should be a state interest of the highest order. To fail to do so is to ensure that American will forever remain a divided society.

III

I do not believe that the Fourteenth Amendment requires us to accept that fate. Neither its history nor our past cases lend any support to the conclusion that a university may not remedy the cumulative effects of society's discrimination by giving consideration to race in an effort to increase the number and percentage of Negro doctors.

A

This Court long ago remarked that

"in any fair and just construction of any section or phrase of these [Civil War] amendments, it is necessary to look to the purpose which we have said was the pervading spirit of them all, the evil which they were designed to remedy. . . ." <u>Slaughter-House Cases, 16 Wall., at 72</u>.

It is plain that the Fourteenth Amendment was not intended to prohibit measures designed to remedy the effects of the *397 Nation's past treatment of Negroes. The Congress that passed the Fourteenth Amendment is the same Congress that passed the 1866 Freedmen's Bureau Act, an Act that provided many of its benefits only to Negroes. Act of July 16, 1866, ch. 200, 14 Stat. 173; see *supra*, at 2800. Although the Freedmen's Bureau legislation provided aid for refugees, thereby including white persons within some of the relief measures, 14 Stat. 174; see also Act of Mar. 3, 1865, ch. 90, 13 Stat. 507, the bill was regarded, to the dismay of many Congressmen, as "solely and entirely for the freedmen, and to the exclusion of all other persons. . . ." Cong.Globe, 39th Cong., 1st Sess., 544 (1866) (remarks of Rep. Taylor). See also *id.*, at 634-635 (remarks of Rep. Ritter); *id.*, at App. 78, 80-81 (remarks of Rep. Chanler). Indeed, the bill was bitterly opposed on the ground that it "undertakes to make the negro in some respects . . . superior . . . and gives them favors that the poor white boy in the North cannot get." *Id.*, at 401 (remarks of Sen. McDougall). See also *id.*, at 319 (remarks of Sen. Hendricks); *id.*, at 362 (remarks of Sen. Saulsbury); *id.*, at 397 (remarks of Sen. Willey); *id.*, at 544 (remarks of Rep. Taylor). The bill's supporters defended it—not by rebutting the claim of special treatment—but by pointing to the need for such treatment:

**2803 "The very discrimination it makes between 'destitute and suffering' negroes, and destitute and suffering white paupers, proceeds upon the distinction that, in the omitted case, civil rights and immunities are already sufficiently protected by the possession of political power, the absence of which in the case provided for necessitates governmental protection." *Id.*, at App. 75 (remarks of Rep. Phelps).

Despite the objection to the special treatment the bill would provide for Negroes, it was passed by Congress. *Id.*, at 421, 688. President Johnson vetoed this bill and also a subsequent bill that contained some modifications; one of his principal *398 objections to both bills was that they gave special benefits to Negroes. 8 Messages and Papers of the Presidents 3596, 3599, 3620, 3623 (1897). Rejecting the concerns of the President and the bill's opponents, Congress overrode the President's second veto. Cong.Globe, 39th Cong., 1st Sess., 3842, 3850 (1866).

Since the Congress that considered and rejected the objections to the 1866 Freedmen's Bureau Act concerning special relief to Negroes also proposed the Fourteenth Amendment, it is inconceivable that the Fourteenth Amendment was intended to prohibit all race-conscious relief measures. It "would be a distortion of the policy manifested in that amendment, which was adopted to prevent state legislation designed to perpetuate discrimination on the basis of race or color." Railway Mail Assn. v. Corsi, 326 U.S. 88, 94, 65 S.Ct. 1483, 1487, 89 L.Ed. 2072 (1945), to hold that it barred state action to remedy the effects of that discrimination. Such a result would pervert the intent of the Framers by substituting abstract equality for the genuine equality the Amendment was intended to achieve.

B

As has been demonstrated in our joint opinion, this Court's past cases establish the constitutionality of race-conscious remedial measures. Beginning with the school desegregation cases, we recognized that even absent a judicial or legislative finding of constitutional violation, a school board constitutionally could consider the race of students in making school-assignment decisions. See Swann v. Charlotte-Mecklenburg Board of Education, 402 U.S. 1, 16, 91 S.Ct. 1267, 1276, 28 L.Ed.2d 554 (1971); McDaniel v. Barresi, 402 U.S. 39, 41, 91 S.Ct. 1287, 1288, 28 L.Ed.2d 582 (1971). We noted, moreover, that a

"flat prohibition against assignment of students for the purpose of creating a racial balance must inevitably conflict with the duty of school authorities to disestablish dual school systems. As we have held in *Swann*, the Constitution does not compel any particular degree of *399 racial balance or mixing, but when past and continuing constitutional violations are found, some ratios are likely to be useful as starting points in shaping a remedy. An absolute prohibition against use of such a device—even as a starting point—contravenes the implicit command of Green v. County School Board, 391 U.S. 430 [88 S.Ct. 1689, 20 L.Ed.2d 716] (1968), that all reasonable methods be available to formulate an effective remedy." Board of Education v. Swann, 402 U.S. 43, 46, 91 S.Ct. 1284, 1286, 28 L.Ed.2d 586 (1971).

As we have observed, "[a]ny other approach would freeze the status quo that is the very target of all desegregation processes." McDaniel v. Barresi, *supra*, 402 U.S. at 41, 91 S.Ct. at 1289.

Only last Term, in *United Jewish Organizations v. Carey*, 430 U.S. 144, 97 S.Ct. 996, 51 L.Ed. 229 (1977), we upheld a New York reapportionment plan that was deliberately drawn on the basis of race to enhance the electoral power of Negroes and Puerto Ricans; the plan had the effect of diluting the electoral strength of the Hasidic Jewish community. We were willing in *UJO* to sanction the remedial use of a racial classification even though it disadvantaged otherwise "innocent" individuals. In another case last Term, **2804 *Califano v. Webster*, 430 U.S. 313, 97 S.Ct. 1192, 51 L.Ed.2d 360 (1977), the Court upheld a provision in the Social Security laws that discriminated against men because its purpose was "'the permissible one of redressing our society's longstanding disparate treatment of women.'" *Id.*, at 317, 97 S.Ct. at 1195, quoting *Califano v. Goldfarb*, 430 U.S. 199, 209 n. 8, 97 S.Ct. 1021, 1028, 51 L.Ed.2d 270 (1977) (plurality opinion). We thus recognized the permissibility of remedying past societal discrimination through the use of otherwise disfavored classifications.

Nothing in those cases suggests that a university cannot similarly act to remedy past discrimination.[12] It is true that *400 in both *UJO* and *Webster* the use of the disfavored classification was predicated on legislative or administrative action, but in neither case had those bodies made findings that there had been constitutional violations or that the specific individuals to be benefited had actually been the victims of discrimination. Rather, the classification in each of those cases was based on a determination that the group was in need of the remedy because of some type of past discrimination. There is thus ample support for the conclusion that a university can employ race-conscious measures to remedy past societal discrimination, without the need for a finding that those benefited were actually victims of that discrimination.

IV

While I applaud the judgment of the Court that a university may consider race in its admissions process, it is more than a little ironic that, after several hundred years of class-based discrimination against Negroes, the Court is unwilling to hold that a class-based remedy for that discrimination is permissible. In declining to so hold, today's judgment ignores the fact that for several hundred years Negroes have been discriminated against, not as individuals, but rather solely because of the color of their skins. It is unnecessary in 20th-century America to have individual Negroes demonstrate that they have been victims of racial discrimination; the racism of our society has been so pervasive that none, regardless of wealth or position, has managed to escape its impact. The experience of Negroes in America has been different in kind, not just in degree, from that of other ethnic groups. It is not merely the history of slavery alone but also that a whole people were marked as inferior by the law. And that mark has endured. The dream of America as the great melting pot has *401 not been realized for the Negro; because of his skin color he never even made it into the pot.

These differences in the experience of the Negro make it difficult for me to accept that Negroes cannot be afforded greater protection under the Fourteenth Amendment where it is necessary to remedy the effects of past discrimination. In the *Civil Rights Cases, supra*, the Court wrote that the Negro emerging from slavery must cease "to be the special favorite of the laws." 109 U.S., at 25, 3 S.Ct., at 31, see *supra*, at 2800. We cannot in light of the history of the last century yield to that view. Had the Court in that decision and others been willing to "do for human liberty and the fundamental rights of American citizenship, what it did . . . for the protection of slavery and the rights of the masters of fugitive slaves," 109 U.S., at 53, 3 S.Ct., at 51 (Harlan, J., dissenting), we would not need now to permit the recognition of any "special wards."

Most importantly, had the Court been willing in 1896, in *Plessy v. Ferguson,* to hold that the Equal Protection Clause forbids differences in treatment based on race, we would not be faced with this dilemma in 1978. We must remember, however, that **2805 the principle that the "Constitution is colorblind" appeared only in the opinion of the lone dissenter. 163 U.S., at 559, 16 S.Ct., at 1146. The majority of the Court rejected the principle of color-blindness, and for the next 58 years, from *Plessy* to *Brown v. Board of Education,* ours was a Nation where, *by law,* an individual could be given "special" treatment based on the color of his skin.

It is because of a legacy of unequal treatment that we now must permit the institutions of this society to give consideration to race in making decisions about who will hold the positions of influence, affluence, and prestige in America. For far too long, the doors to those positions have been shut to Negroes. If we are ever to become a fully integrated society, one in which the color of a person's skin will not determine the opportunities available to him or her, we must be willing *402 to take steps to open those doors. I do not believe that anyone can truly look into America's past and still find that a remedy for the effects of that past is impermissible.

It has been said that this case involves only the individual, Bakke, and this University. I doubt, however, that there is a computer capable of determining the number of persons and institutions that may be affected by the decision in this case. For example, we are told by the Attorney General of the United States that at least 27 federal agencies have adopted regulations requiring recipients of federal funds to take "'*affirmative action* to overcome the effects of conditions which resulted in limiting participation . . . by persons of a particular race, color, or national origin.'" Supplemental Brief for United States as *Amicus Curiae* 16 (emphasis added). I cannot even guess the number of state and local governments that have set up affirmative-action programs, which may be affected by today's decision.

I fear that we have come full circle. After the Civil War our Government started several "affirmative action" programs. This Court in the *Civil Rights Cases* and *Plessy v. Ferguson* destroyed the movement toward complete equality. For almost a century no action was taken, and this nonaction was with the tacit approval of the courts. Then we had *Brown v. Board of Education* and the Civil Rights Acts of Congress, followed by numerous affirmative-action programs. *Now,* we have this Court again stepping in, this time to stop affirmative-action programs of the type used by the University of California.

Notes

1. The history recounted here is perhaps too well known to require documentation. But I must acknowledge the authorities on which I rely in retelling it. J. Franklin, From Slavery to Freedom (4th ed. 1974) (hereinafter Franklin); R. Kluger, Simple Justice (1975) (hereinafter Kluger); C. Woodward, The Strange Career of Jim Crow (3d ed. 1974) (hereinafter Woodward).
2. U.S. Dept. of Commerce, Bureau of the Census, Statistical Abstract of the United States 65 (1977) (Table 94).
3. *Id.,* at 70 (Table 102).
4. *Ibid.*
5. U.S. Dept. of Commerce, Bureau of the Census, Current Population Reports, Series P-60, No. 107, p. 7 (1977) (Table 1).

6. Id., at 20 (Table 14).
7. U.S. Dept. of Labor, Bureau of Labor Statistics, Employment and Earnings, January 1978, p. 170 (Table 44).
8. *Ibid.*
9. U.S. Dept. of Commerce, Bureau of the Census, Current Population Reports, Series P-60, No. 105, p. 198 (1977) (Table 47).
10. U.S. Dept. of Commerce, Bureau of the Census, Statistical Abstract, *supra,* at 25 (Table 24).
11. Id., at 407-408 (Table 662) (based on 1970 census).
12. Indeed, the action of the University finds support in the regulations promulgated under Title VI by the Department of Health, Education, and Welfare and approved by the President, which authorize a federally funded institution to take affirmative steps to overcome past discrimination against groups even where the institution was not guilty of prior discrimination. 45 CFR § 80.3(b)(6)(ii) (1977).

Opinion in Grutter

Clarence Thomas

Cite as: 539 U.S. ___ (2003)

Opinion of THOMAS, J.

SUPREME COURT OF THE UNITED STATES

No. 02-241

BARBARA GRUTTER, PETITIONER *v.* LEE BOLLINGER ET AL.

ON WRIT OF CERTIORARI TO THE UNITED STATES COURT OF APPEALS FOR THE SIXTH CIRCUIT

[June 23, 2003[

JUSTICE THOMAS, with whom JUSTICE SCALIA joins as to Parts I–VII, concurring in part and dissenting in part.

Frederick Douglass, speaking to a group of abolitionists almost 140 years ago, delivered a message lost on today's majority:

"[I]n regard to the colored people, there is always more that is benevolent, I perceive, than just, manifested towards us. What I ask for the negro is not benevolence, not pity, not sympathy, but simply *justice*. The American people have always been anxious to know what they shall do with us . . . . I have had but one answer from the beginning. Do nothing with us! Your doing with us has already played the mischief with us. Do nothing with us! If the apples will not remain on the tree of their own strength, if they are worm-eaten at the core, if they are early ripe and disposed to fall, let them fall! . . . And if the negro cannot stand on his

---

Supreme Court of the United States; Barbara Grutter v. Lee Bollinger et al, #02-241.

own legs, let him fall also. All I ask is, give him a chance to stand on his own legs! Let him alone! . . . [Y]our interference is doing him positive injury." What the Black Man Wants: An Address Delivered in Boston, Massachusetts, on 26 January 1865, reprinted in 4 The Frederick Douglass Papers 59, 68 (J. Blassingame & J. McKivigan eds. 1991) (emphasis in original).

Like Douglass, I believe blacks can achieve in every avenue of American life without the meddling of university administrators. Because I wish to see all students succeed whatever their color, I share, in some respect, the sympathies of those who sponsor the type of discrimination advanced by the University of Michigan Law School (Law School). The Constitution does not, however, tolerate institutional devotion to the status quo in admissions policies when such devotion ripens into racial discrimination. Nor does the Constitution countenance the unprecedented deference the Court gives to the Law School, an approach inconsistent with the very concept of "strict scrutiny."

No one would argue that a university could set up a lower general admission standard and then impose heightened requirements only on black applicants. Similarly, a university may not maintain a high admission standard and grant exemptions to favored races. The Law School, of its own choosing, and for its own purposes, maintains an exclusionary admissions system that it knows produces racially disproportionate results. Racial discrimination is not a permissible solution to the self-inflicted wounds of this elitist admissions policy.

The majority upholds the Law School's racial discrimination not by interpreting the people's Constitution, but by responding to a faddish slogan of the cognoscenti. Nevertheless, I concur in part in the Court's opinion. First, I agree with the Court insofar as its decision, which approves of only one racial classification, confirms that further use of race in admissions remains unlawful. Second, I agree with the Court's holding that racial discrimination in higher education admissions will be illegal in 25 years. See *ante,* at 31 (stating that racial discrimination will no longer be narrowly tailored, or "necessary to further" a compelling state interest, in 25 years). I respectfully dissent from the remainder of the Court's opinion and the judgment, however, because I believe that the Law School's current use of race violates the Equal Protection Clause and that the Constitution means the same thing today as it will in 300 months.

I

The majority agrees that the Law School's racial discrimination should be subjected to strict scrutiny. *Ante,* at 14. Before applying that standard to this case, I will briefly revisit the Court's treatment of racial classifications.

The strict scrutiny standard that the Court purports to apply in this case was first enunciated in *Korematsu* v. *United States,* 323 U.S. 214 (1944). There the Court held that "[p]ressing public necessity may sometimes justify the existence of [racial discrimination]; racial antagonism never can." *Id.,* at 216. This standard of "pressing public necessity" has more frequently been termed "compelling governmental interest,"[1] see, *e.g., Regents of Univ. of Cal.* v. *Bakke,* 438 U.S. 265, 299 (1978) (opinion of Powell, J.). A majority of the Court has validated only two circumstances where "pressing public necessity" or a "compelling state interest" can possibly justify racial discrimination by state actors. First, the lesson of *Korematsu* is that national security constitutes a "pressing public necessity," though the government's use of race to advance that objective must be narrowly tailored. Second, the Court has recognized as a compelling state interest a government's effort to remedy past discrimination for which it is responsible. *Richmond* v. *J. A. Croson Co.*, 488 U. S. 469, 504 (1989).

The contours of "pressing public necessity" can be further discerned from those interests the Court has rejected as bases for racial discrimination. For example, *Wygant* v. *Jackson Bd. Of Ed.*, 476 U. S. 267 (1986), found unconstitutional a collective-bargaining agreement between a school board and a teachers' union that favored certain minority races. The school board defended the policy on the grounds that minority teachers provided "role models" for minority students and that a racially "diverse" faculty would improve the education of all students. See Brief for Respondents, O. T. 1984, No. 84–1340, pp. 27–28; 476 U. S., at 315 (STEVENS, J., dissenting) ("[A]n integrated faculty will be able to provide benefits to the student body that could not be provided by an all-white, or nearly all-white faculty"). Nevertheless, the Court found that the use of race violated the Equal Protection Clause, deeming both asserted state interests insufficiently compelling. *Id.*, at 275–276 (plurality opinion); *id.*, at 295 (White, J., concurring in judgment) ("None of the interests asserted by the [school board] . . . justify this racially discriminatory layoff policy").[2]

An even greater governmental interest involves the sensitive role of courts in child custody determinations. In *Palmore* v. *Sidoti*, 466 U. S. 429 (1984), the Court held that even the best interests of a child did not constitute a compelling state interest that would allow a state court to award custody to the father because the mother was in a mixed-race marriage. *Id.*, at 433 (finding the interest "substantial" but holding the custody decision could not be based on the race of the mother's new husband).

Finally, the Court has rejected an interest in remedying general societal discrimination as a justification for race discrimination. See *Wygant, supra,* at 276 (plurality opinion); *Croson,* 488 U. S., at 496–498 (plurality opinion); *id.*, at 520–521 (SCALIA, J., concurring in judgment). "Societal discrimination, without more, is too amorphous a basis for imposing a racially classified remedy" because a "court could uphold remedies that are ageless in their reach into the past, and timeless in their ability to affect the future." *Wygant, supra,* at 276 (plurality opinion). But see *Gratz* v. *Bollinger, ante,* p. ___ (GINSBURG, J., dissenting).

Where the Court has accepted only national security, and rejected even the best interests of a child, as a justification for racial discrimination, I conclude that only those measures the State must take to provide a bulwark against anarchy, or to prevent violence, will constitute a "pressing public necessity." Cf. *Lee* v. *Washington,* 390 U. S. 333, 334 (1968) (*per curiam*) (Black, J., concurring) (indicating that protecting prisoners from violence might justify narrowly tailored racial discrimination); *Croson, supra,* at 521 (SCALIA, J., concurring in judgment) ("At least where state or local action is at issue, only a social emergency rising to the level of imminent danger to life and limb . . . can justify [racial discrimination]").

The Constitution abhors classifications based on race, not only because those classifications can harm favored races or are based on illegitimate motives, but also because every time the government places citizens on racial registers and makes race relevant to the provision of burdens or benefits, it demeans us all. "Purchased at the price of immeasurable human suffering, the equal protection principle reflects our Nation's understanding that such classifications ultimately have a destructive impact on the individual and our society." *Adarand Construction, Inc.* v. *Peña,* 515 U. S.

200, 240 (1995) (THOMAS, J., concurring in part and concurring in judgment).

II

Unlike the majority, I seek to define with precision the interest being asserted by the Law School before determining whether that interest is so compelling as to justify racial discrimination. The Law School maintains that it wishes to obtain "educational benefits that flow from student body diversity," Brief for Respondents Bollinger et al. 14. This statement must be evaluated carefully, because it implies that both "diversity" and "educational benefits" are components of the Law School's compelling state interest. Additionally, the Law School's refusal to entertain certain changes in its admissions process and status indicates that the compelling state interest it seeks to validate is actually broader than might appear at first glance.

Undoubtedly there are other ways to "better" the education of law students aside from ensuring that the student body contains a "critical mass" of underrepresented minority students. Attaining "diversity," whatever it means,[3] is the mechanism by which the Law School obtains educational benefits, not an end of itself. The Law School, however, apparently believes that only a racially mixed student body can lead to the educational benefits it seeks. How, then, is the Law School's interest in these allegedly unique educational "benefits" *not* simply the forbidden interest in "racial balancing," *ante,* at 17, that the majority expressly rejects?

A distinction between these two ideas (unique educational benefits based on racial aesthetics and race for its own sake) is purely sophistic—so much so that the majority uses them interchangeably. Compare *ante,* at 16 ("[T]he Law School has a compelling interest in attaining a diverse student body"), with *ante,* at 21 (referring to the "compelling interest in securing the *educational benefits* of a diverse student body" (emphasis added)). The Law School's argument, as facile as it is, can only be understood in one way: Classroom aesthetics yields educational benefits, racially discriminatory admissions policies are required to achieve the right racial mix, and therefore the policies are required to achieve the educational benefits. It is the *educational benefits* that are the end, or allegedly compelling state interest, not "diversity." But see *ante,* at 20 (citing the need for "openness and integrity of the educational institutions that provide [legal] training" without reference to any consequential educational benefits).

One must also consider the Law School's refusal to entertain changes to its current admissions system that might produce the same educational benefits. The Law School adamantly disclaims any race-neutral alternative that would reduce "academic selectivity," which would in turn "require the Law School to become a very different institution, and to sacrifice a core part of its educational mission." Brief for Respondents Bollinger et al. 33–36. In other words, the Law School seeks to improve marginally the education it offers without sacrificing too much of its exclusivity and elite status.[4]

The proffered interest that the majority vindicates today, then, is not simply "diversity." Instead the Court upholds the use of racial discrimination as a tool to advance the Law School's interest in offering a marginally superior education while maintaining an elite institution. Unless each constituent part of this state interest is of pressing public necessity, the Law School's use of race is unconstitutional. I find each of them to fall far short of this standard.

III

A

A close reading of the Court's opinion reveals that all of its legal work is done through one conclusory statement: The Law School has a "compelling interest in securing the educational benefits of a diverse student body." *Ante*, at 21. No serious effort is made to explain how these benefits fit with the state interests the Court has recognized (or rejected) as compelling, see Part I, *supra*, or to place any theoretical constraints on an enterprising court's desire to discover still more justifications for racial discrimination. In the absence of any explanation, one might expect the Court to fall back on the judicial policy of *stare decisis*. But the Court eschews even this weak defense of its holding, shunning an analysis of the extent to which Justice Powell's opinion in *Regents of Univ. of Cal.* v. *Bakke*, 438 U. S. 265 (1978), is binding, *ante*, at 13, in favor of an unfounded wholesale adoption of it.

Justice Powell's opinion in *Bakke* and the Court's decision today rest on the fundamentally flawed proposition that racial discrimination can be contextualized so that a goal, such as classroom aesthetics, can be compelling in one context but not in another. This "we know it when we see it" approach to evaluating state interests is not capable of judicial application. Today, the Court insists on radically expanding the range of permissible uses of race to something as trivial (by comparison) as the assembling of a law school class. I can only presume that the majority's failure to justify its decision by reference to any principle arises from the absence of any such principle. See Part VI, *infra*.

B

Under the proper standard, there is no pressing public necessity in maintaining a public law school at all and, it follows, certainly not an elite law school. Likewise, marginal improvements in legal education do not qualify as a compelling state interest.

1

While legal education at a public university may be good policy or otherwise laudable, it is obviously not a pressing public necessity when the correct legal standard is applied. Additionally, circumstantial evidence as to whether a state activity is of pressing public necessity can be obtained by asking whether all States feel compelled to engage in that activity. Evidence that States, in general, engage in a certain activity by no means demonstrates that the activity constitutes a pressing public necessity, given the expansive role of government in today's society. The fact that some fraction of the States reject a particular enterprise, however, creates a presumption that the enterprise itself is not a compelling state interest. In this sense, the absence of a public, American Bar Association (ABA) accredited, law school in Alaska, Delaware, Massachusetts, New Hampshire, and Rhode Island, see ABA–LSAC Official Guide to ABA-Approved Law Schools (W. Margolis, B. Gordon, J. Puskarz, & D. Rosenlieb, eds. 2004) (hereinafter ABA–LSAC Guide), provides further evidence that Michigan's maintenance of the Law School does not constitute a compelling state interest.

2

As the foregoing makes clear, Michigan has no compelling interest in having a law school at all, much less an *elite* one. Still, even assuming that a State may, under appropriate circumstances, demonstrate a cognizable interest in having an elite law school, Michigan has failed to do so here.

This Court has limited the scope of equal protection review to interests and activities that occur within that State's jurisdiction. The Court held in *Missouri ex rel. Gaines* v.

Canada, 305 U. S. 337 (1938), that Missouri could not satisfy the demands of "separate but equal" by paying for legal training of blacks at neighboring state law schools, while maintaining a segregated law school within the State. The equal protection

> "obligation is imposed by the Constitution upon the States severally as governmental entities—each responsible for its own laws establishing the rights and duties of persons within its borders. It is an obligation the burden of which cannot be cast by one State upon another, and no State can be excused from performance *by what another State may do or fail to do.* That separate responsibility of each State within its own sphere is of the essence of statehood maintained under our dual system." *Id.,* at 350 (emphasis added).

The Equal Protection Clause, as interpreted by the Court in *Gaines,* does not permit States to justify racial discrimination on the basis of what the rest of the Nation "may do or fail to do." The only interests that can satisfy the Equal Protection Clause's demands are those found within a State's jurisdiction.

The only cognizable state interests vindicated by operating a public law school are, therefore, the education of that State's citizens and the training of that State's lawyers. James Campbell's address at the opening of the Law Department at the University of Michigan on October 3, 1859, makes this clear:

> "It not only concerns *the State* that every one should have all reasonable facilities for preparing himself for any honest position in life to which he may aspire, but it also concerns *the community* that the Law should be taught and understood.... There is not an office *in the State* in which serious legal inquiries may not frequently arise.... In all these matters, public and private rights are constantly involved and discussed, and ignorance of the Law has frequently led to results deplorable and alarming.... [I]n the history of *this State,* in more than one instance, that ignorance has led to unlawful violence, and the shedding of innocent blood." E. Brown, Legal Education at Michigan 1859-1959, pp. 404-406 (1959) (emphasis added).

The Law School today, however, does precious little training of those attorneys who will serve the citizens of Michigan. In 2002, graduates of the University of Michigan Law School made up less than 6% of applicants to the Michigan bar, Michigan Lawyers Weekly, available at http://www.michiganlawyersweekly.com/barpassers0202.cfm,barpassers0702.cfm (all Internet materials as visited June 13, 2003, and available in Clerk of Court's case file), even though the Law School's graduates constitute nearly 30% of all law students graduating in Michigan. *Ibid.* Less than 16% of the Law School's graduating class elects to stay in Michigan after law school. ABA–LSAC Guide 427. Thus, while a mere 27% of the Law School's 2002 entering class are from Michigan, see University of Michigan Law School Website, available at http://www.law.umich.edu/prospectivestudents/Admissions/index.htm, only half of these, it appears, will stay in Michigan.

In sum, the Law School trains few Michigan residents and overwhelmingly serves students, who, as lawyers, leave the State of Michigan. By contrast, Michigan's other public law school, Wayne State University Law School, sends 88% of its graduates on to serve the people of Michigan. ABA–LSAC Guide 775. It does not take a social scientist to conclude that it is precisely the Law School's status as an elite institution that causes it to be a way-station for the rest of the country's lawyers, rather than a training ground for those who will remain in Michigan. The Law School's decision to be an elite institution does little to advance the welfare of the people of Michigan or any cognizable interest of the State of Michigan.

Again, the fact that few States choose to maintain elite law schools raises a strong inference that there is nothing compelling about elite status. Arguably, only the public law schools of the University of Texas, the University of California, Berkeley (Boalt Hall), and the University of Virginia maintain the same reputation for excellence as the Law School.[5] Two of these States, Texas and California, are so large that they could reasonably be expected to provide elite legal training at a separate law school to students who will, in fact, stay in the State and provide legal services to its citizens. And these two schools far outshine the Law School in producing in-state lawyers. The University of Texas, for example, sends over three-fourths of its graduates on to work in the State of Texas, vindicating the State's interest (compelling or not) in training Texas' lawyers. *Id.,* at 691.

3

Finally, even if the Law School's racial tinkering produces tangible educational benefits, a marginal improvement in legal education cannot justify racial discrimination where the Law School has no compelling interest in either its existence or in its current educational and admissions policies.

IV

The interest in remaining elite and exclusive that the majority thinks so obviously critical requires the use of admissions "standards" that, in turn, create the Law School's "need" to discriminate on the basis of race. The Court validates these admissions standards by concluding that alternatives that would require "a dramatic sacrifice of . . . the academic quality of all admitted students," *ante,* at 27, need not be considered before racial discrimination can be employed.[6] In the majority's view, such methods are not required by the "narrow tailoring" prong of strict scrutiny because that inquiry demands, in this context, that any race-neutral alternative work "'about as well.'" *Ante,* at 26–27 (quoting *Wygant,* 476 U. S., at 280, n. 6). The majority errs, however, because race-neutral alternatives must only be "workable," *ante,* at 27, and do "about as well" *in vindicating the compelling state interest.* The Court never explicitly holds that the Law School's desire to retain the status quo in "academic selectivity" is itself a compelling state interest, and, as I have demonstrated, it is not. See Part III–B, *supra.* Therefore, the Law School should be forced to choose between its classroom aesthetic and its exclusionary admissions system—it cannot have it both ways.

With the adoption of different admissions methods, such as accepting all students who meet minimum qualifications, see Brief for United States as *Amicus Curiae* 13–14, the Law School could achieve its vision of the racially aesthetic student body without the use of racial discrimination. The Law School concedes this, but the Court holds, implicitly and under the guise of narrow tailoring, that the Law School has a compelling state interest in doing what it wants to do. I cannot agree. First, under strict scrutiny, the Law School's assessment of the benefits of racial discrimination and devotion to the admissions status quo are not entitled to any sort of deference, grounded in the First Amendment or anywhere else. Second, even if its "academic selectivity" must be maintained at all costs along with racial discrimination, the Court ignores the fact that other top law schools have succeeded in meeting their aesthetic demands without racial discrimination.

A

The Court bases its unprecedented deference to the Law School—a deference antithetical to strict scrutiny—on an idea of "educational autonomy" grounded in the First Amendment. *Ante*, at 17. In my view, there is no basis for a right of public universities to do what would otherwise violate the Equal Protection Clause.

The constitutionalization of "academic freedom" began with the concurring opinion of Justice Frankfurter in *Sweezy* v. *New Hampshire*, 354 U. S. 234 (1957). Sweezy, a Marxist economist, was investigated by the Attorney General of New Hampshire on suspicion of being a subversive. The prosecution sought, *inter alia*, the contents of a lecture Sweezy had given at the University of New Hampshire. The Court held that the investigation violated due process. *Id.*, at 254.

Justice Frankfurter went further, however, reasoning that the First Amendment created a right of academic freedom that prohibited the investigation. *Id.*, at 256–267 (opinion concurring in result). Much of the rhetoric in Justice Frankfurter's opinion was devoted to the personal right of Sweezy to free speech. See, *e.g., id.*, at 265 ("For a citizen to be made to forgo even a part of so basic a liberty as his political autonomy, the subordinating interest of the State must be compelling"). Still, claiming that the United States Reports "need not be burdened with proof," Justice Frankfurter also asserted that a "free society" depends on "free universities" and "[t]his means the exclusion of governmental intervention in the intellectual life of a university." *Id.*, at 262. According to Justice Frankfurter: "[I]t is the business of a university to provide that atmosphere which is most conducive to speculation, experiment and creation. It is an atmosphere in which there prevail 'the four essential freedoms' of a university—to determine for itself on academic grounds who may teach, what may be taught, how it shall be taught, and who may be admitted to study.'" *Id.*, at 263 (citation omitted).

In my view, "[i]t is the business" of this Court to explain itself when it cites provisions of the Constitution to invent new doctrines—including the idea that the First Amendment authorizes a public university to do what would otherwise violate the Equal Protection Clause. The majority fails in its summary effort to prove this point. The only source for the Court's conclusion that public universities are entitled to deference even within the confines of strict scrutiny is Justice Powell's opinion in *Bakke*. Justice Powell, for his part, relied only on Justice Frankfurter's opinion in *Sweezy* and the Court's decision in *Keyishian* v. *Board of Regents of Univ. of State of N. Y.*, 385 U. S. 589 (1967), to support his view that the First Amendment somehow protected a public university's use of race in admissions. *Bakke*, 438 U. S. at 312. *Keyishian* provides no answer to the question whether the Fourteenth Amendment's restrictions are relaxed when applied to public universities. In that case, the Court held that state statutes and regulations designed to prevent the "appointment or retention of 'subversive' persons in state employment," 385 U. S., at 592, violated the First Amendment for vagueness. The statutes covered all public employees and were not invalidated only as applied to university faculty members, although the Court appeared sympathetic to the notion of academic freedom, calling it a "special concern of the First Amendment." *Id.*, at 603. Again, however, the Court did not relax any independent constitutional restrictions on public universities.

I doubt that when Justice Frankfurter spoke of governmental intrusions into the independence of universities, he was thinking of the Constitution's ban on racial discrimination. The majority's broad deference to both the Law School's judgment that racial aesthetics leads to educational benefits and its stubborn refusal to alter the status quo in admissions methods finds no basis in the Constitution or decisions of this Court.

B

1

The Court's deference to the Law School's conclusion that its racial experimentation leads to educational benefits will, if adhered to, have serious collateral consequences. The Court relies heavily on social science evidence to justify its deference. See *ante*, at 18–20; but see also Rothman, Lipset, & Nevitte, Racial Diversity Reconsidered, 151 Public Interest 25 (2003) (finding that the racial mix of a student body produced by racial discrimination of the type practiced by the Law School in fact hinders students' perception of academic quality). The Court never acknowledges, however, the growing evidence that racial (and other sorts) of heterogeneity actually impairs learning among black students. See, *e.g.*, Flowers & Pascarella, Cognitive Effects of College Racial Composition on African American Students After 3 Years of College, 40 J. of College Student Development 669, 674 (1999) (concluding that black students experience superior cognitive development at Historically Black Colleges (HBCs) and that, even among blacks, "a substantial diversity moderates the cognitive effects of attending an HBC"); Allen, The Color of Success: African-American College Student Outcomes at Predominantly White and Historically Black Public Colleges and Universities, 62 Harv. Educ. Rev. 26, 35 (1992) (finding that black students attending HBCs report higher academic achievement than those attending predominantly white colleges).

At oral argument in *Gratz* v. *Bollinger*, *ante*, p. ___, counsel for respondents stated that "most every single one of [the HBCs] do have diverse student bodies." Tr. Of Oral Arg. in No. 02–516, p. 52. What precisely counsel meant by "diverse" is indeterminate, but it is reported that in 2000 at Morehouse College, one of the most distinguished HBC's in the Nation, only 0.1% of the student body was white, and only 0.2% was Hispanic. College Admissions Data Handbook 2002–2003, p. 613 (43d ed. 2002) (hereinafter College Admissions Data Handbook). And at Mississippi Valley State University, a public HBC, only 1.1% of the freshman class in 2001 was white. *Id.*, at 603. If there is a "critical mass" of whites at these institutions, then "critical mass" is indeed a very small proportion.

The majority grants deference to the Law School's "assessment that diversity will, in fact, yield educational benefits," *ante*, at 16. It follows, therefore, that an HBC's assessment that racial homogeneity will yield educational benefits would similarly be given deference.[7] An HBC's rejection of white applicants in order to maintain racial homogeneity seems permissible, therefore, under the majority's view of the Equal Protection Clause. But see *United States* v. *Fordice*, 505 U. S. 717, 748 (1992) (THOMAS, J., concurring) ("Obviously, a State cannot maintain . . . traditions by closing particular institutions, historically white or historically black, to particular racial groups"). Contained within today's majority opinion is the seed of a new constitutional justification for a concept I thought long and rightly rejected—racial segregation.

2

Moreover one would think, in light of the Court's decision in *United States* v. *Virginia*, 518 U. S. 515 (1996), that before being given license to use racial discrimination, the Law School would be required to radically reshape its admissions process, even to the point of sacrificing some elements of its character. In *Virginia*, a majority of the Court, without a word about academic freedom, accepted the all-male Virginia Military Institute's (VMI) representation that some changes in its "adversative" method of education would be required with the admission of women, *id.,* at 540, but did not defer to VMI's judgment that these changes would be too great. Instead, the Court concluded that they were "manageable." *Id.,* at 551, n. 19. That case involved sex discrimination, which is subjected to intermediate, not strict, scrutiny. *Id.,* at 533; *Craig v. Boren,* 429 U. S. 190, 197 (1976). So in *Virginia,* where the standard of review dictated that greater flexibility be granted to VMI's educational policies than the Law School deserves here, this Court gave no deference. Apparently where the status quo being defended is that of the elite establishment—here the Law School—rather than a less fashionable Southern military institution, the Court will defer without serious inquiry and without regard to the applicable legal standard.

C

Virginia is also notable for the fact that the Court relied on the "experience" of formerly single-sex institutions, such as the service academies, to conclude that admission of women to VMI would be "manageable." 518 U. S., at 544–545. Today, however, the majority ignores the "experience" of those institutions that have been forced to abandon explicit racial discrimination in admissions.

The sky has not fallen at Boalt Hall at the University of California, Berkeley, for example. Prior to Proposition 209's adoption of Cal. Const., Art. 1, §31(a), which bars the State from "grant[ing] preferential treatment . . . on the basis of race . . . in the operation of . . . public education,"[8] Boalt Hall enrolled 20 blacks and 28 Hispanics in its first-year class for 1996. In 2002, without deploying express racial discrimination in admissions, Boalt's entering class enrolled 14 blacks and 36 Hispanics.[9] University of California Law and Medical School Enrollments, available at http://www.ucop.edu/acadadv/datamgmt/lawmed/law-enrolls-eth2.html. Total underrepresented minority student enrollment at Boalt Hall now exceeds 1996 levels. Apparently the Law School cannot be counted on to be as resourceful. The Court is willfully blind to the very real experience in California and elsewhere, which raises the inference that institutions with "reputation[s] for excellence," *ante,* at 16, 26, rivaling the Law School's have satisfied their sense of mission without resorting to prohibited racial discrimination.

V

Putting aside the absence of any legal support for the majority's reflexive deference, there is much to be said for the view that the use of tests and other measures to "predict" academic performance is a poor substitute for a system that gives every applicant a chance to prove he can succeed in the study of law. The rallying cry that in the absence of racial discrimination in admissions there would be a true meritocracy ignores the fact that the entire process is poisoned by numerous exceptions to "merit." For example, in the national debate on racial discrimination in higher education admissions, much has been made of the fact that elite institutions utilize a so-called "legacy" preference to give the children of alumni an advantage in admissions. This, and other, exceptions to a "true" meritocracy give the lie to protestations that merit admissions are in fact the order of the day at the Nation's universities. The Equal Protection Clause does not, however, prohibit the use of unseemly legacy preferences or many other kinds of arbitrary admissions procedures. What the Equal Protection Clause does prohibit are classifications made on the basis of race. So while legacy preferences can stand under the Constitution, racial discrimination cannot.[10] I will not twist the Constitution to invalidate legacy preferences or otherwise impose my vision of higher education admissions on the

Nation. The majority should similarly stay its impulse to validate faddish racial discrimination the Constitution clearly forbids.

In any event, there is nothing ancient, honorable, or constitutionally protected about "selective" admissions. The University of Michigan should be well aware that alternative methods have historically been used for the admission of students, for it brought to this country the German certificate system in the late-19th century. See H. Wechsler, the Qualified Student 16–39 (1977) (hereinafter Qualified Student). Under this system, a secondary school was certified by a university to that any graduate who completed the course offered by the school was offered admission to the university. The certification regime supplemented, and later virtually replaced (at least in the Midwest), the prior regime of rigorous subject-matter entrance examinations. *Id.*, at 57–58. The facially race-neutral "percent plans" now used in Texas, California, and Florida, see *ante*, at 28, are in many ways the descendents of the certificate system.

Certification was replaced by selective admissions in the beginning of the 20th century, as universities sought to exercise more control over the composition of their student bodies. Since its inception, selective admissions has been the vehicle for racial, ethnic, and religious tinkering and experimentation by university administrators. The initial driving force for the relocation of the selective function from the high school to the universities was the same desire to select racial winners and losers that the Law School exhibits today. Columbia, Harvard, and others infamously determined that they had "too many" Jews, just as today the Law School argues it would have "too many" whites if it could not discriminate in its admissions process. See Qualified Student 155–168 (Columbia); H. Broun & G. Britt, Christians Only: A Study in Prejudice 53–54 (1931) (Harvard).

Columbia employed intelligence tests precisely because Jewish applicants, who were predominantly immigrants, scored worse on such tests. Thus, Columbia could claim (falsely) that "'[w]e have not eliminated boys because they were Jews and do not propose to do so. We have honestly attempted to eliminate the lowest grade of applicant [through the use of intelligence testing] and it turns out that a good many of the low grade men are New York City Jews.'" Letter from Herbert E. Hawkes, dean of Columbia College, to E. B. Wilson, June 16, 1922 (reprinted in Qualified Student 160–161). In other words, the tests were adopted with full knowledge of their disparate impact. Cf. *DeFunis* v. *Odegaard,* 416 U. S. 312, 335 (1974) (*per curiam*) (Douglas, J., dissenting).

Similarly no modern law school can claim ignorance of the poor performance of blacks, relatively speaking, on the Law School Admissions Test (LSAT). Nevertheless, law schools continue to use the test and then attempt to "correct" for black underperformance by using racial discrimination in admissions so as to obtain their aesthetic student body. The Law School's continued adherence to measures it knows produce racially skewed results is not entitled to deference by this Court. See Part IV, *supra*. The Law School itself admits that the test is imperfect, as it must, given that it regularly admits students who score at or below 150 (the national median) on the test. See App. 156–203 (showing that, between 1995 and 2000, the Law School admitted 37 students— 27 of whom were black; 31 of whom were "underrepresented minorities"—with LSAT scores of 150 or lower). And the Law School's *amici* cannot seem to agree on the fundamental question whether the test itself is useful. Compare Brief for Law School Admission Council as *Amicus Curiae* 12 ("LSAT scores . . . are an effective predictor of students' performance in law school") with Brief for Harvard Black Law Students Association et al. as *Amici Curiae* 27 ("Whether [the LSAT] measure[s] objective merit . . . is certainly questionable").

Having decided to use the LSAT, the Law School must accept the constitutional burdens that come with this decision. The Law School may freely continue to employ the LSAT and other allegedly merit-based standards in whatever fashion it likes. What the Equal Protection Clause forbids, but the Court today allows, is the use of these standards hand-in-hand with racial discrimination. An infinite variety of admissions methods are available to the Law School. Considering all of the radical thinking that has historically occurred at this country's universities, the Law School's intractable approach toward admissions is striking.

The Court will not even deign to make the Law School try other methods, however, preferring instead to grant a 25-year license to violate the Constitution. And the same Court that had the courage to order the desegregation of all public schools in the South now fears, on the basis of platitudes rather than principle, to force the Law School to abandon a decidedly imperfect admissions regime that provides the basis for racial discrimination.

VI

The absence of any articulated legal principle supporting the majority's principal holding suggests another rationale. I believe what lies beneath the Court's decision today are the benighted notions that one can tell when racial discrimination benefits (rather than hurts) minority groups, see *Adarand*, 515 U. S., at 239 (SCLIA, J., concurring in part and concurring in judgment), and that racial discrimination is necessary to remedy general societal ills. This Court's precedents supposedly settled both issues, but clearly the majority still cannot commit to the principle that racial classifications are *per se* harmful and that almost no amount of benefit in the eye of the beholder can justify such classifications.

Putting aside what I take to be the Court's implicit rejection of *Adarand's* holding that beneficial and burdensome racial classifications are equally invalid, I must contest the notion that the Law School's discrimination benefits those admitted as a result of it. The Court spends considerable time discussing the impressive display of *amicus* support for the Law School in this case from all corners of society. *Ante*, at 18–19. But nowhere in any of the filings in this Court is any evidence that the purported "beneficiaries" of this racial discrimination prove themselves by performing at (or even near) the same level as those students who receive no preferences. Cf. Thernstrom & Thernstrom, Reflections on the Shape of the River, 46 UCLA L. Rev. 1583, 1605–1608 (1999) (discussing the failure of defenders of racial discrimination in admissions to consider the fact that its "beneficiaries" are underperforming in the classroom).

The silence in this case is deafening to those of us who view higher education's purpose as imparting knowledge and skills to students, rather than a communal, rubberstamp, credentialing process. The Law School is not looking for those students who, despite a lower LSAT score or undergraduate grade point average, will succeed in the study of law. The Law School seeks only a facade—it is sufficient that the class looks right, even if it does not perform right.

The Law School tantalizes unprepared students with the promise of a University of Michigan degree and all of the opportunities that it offers. These overmatched students take the bait, only to find that they cannot succeed in the cauldron of competition. And this mismatch crisis is not restricted to elite institutions. See T. Sowell, Race and Culture

176–177 (1994) ("Even if most minority students are able to meet the normal standards at the 'average' range of colleges and universities, the systematic mismatching of minority students begun at the top can mean that such students are generally overmatched throughout all levels of higher education"). Indeed, to cover the tracks of the aestheticists, this cruel farce of racial discrimination must continue—in selection for the Michigan Law Review, see University of Michigan Law School Student Handbook 2002–2003, pp. 39–40 (noting the presence of a "diversity plan" for admission to the review), and in hiring at law firms and for judicial clerkships—until the "beneficiaries" are no longer tolerated. While these students may graduate with law degrees, there is no evidence that they have received a qualitatively better legal education (or become better lawyers) than if they had gone to a less "elite" law school for which they were better prepared. And the aestheticists will never address the real problems facing "underrepresented minorities,"[11] instead continuing their social experiments on other people's children.

Beyond the harm the Law School's racial discrimination visits upon its test subjects, no social science has disproved the notion that this discrimination "engender[s] attitudes of superiority or, alternatively, provoke[s] resentment among those who believe that they have been wronged by the government's use of race." *Adarand*, 515 U. S., at 241 (THOMAS, J., concurring in part and concurring in judgment). "These programs stamp minorities with a badge of inferiority and may cause them to develop dependencies or to adopt an attitude that they are 'entitled' to preferences." *Ibid.*

It is uncontested that each year, the Law School admits a handful of blacks who would be admitted in the absence of racial discrimination. See Brief for Respondents Bollinger et al. 6. Who can differentiate between those who belong and those who do not? The majority of blacks are admitted to the Law School because of discrimination, and because of this policy all are tarred as undeserving. This problem of stigma does not depend on determinacy as to whether those stigmatized are actually the "beneficiaries" of racial discrimination. When blacks take positions in the highest places of government, industry, or academia, it is an open question today whether their skin color played a part in their advancement. The question itself is the stigma—because either racial discrimination did play a role, in which case the person may be deemed "otherwise unqualified," or it did not, in which case asking the question itself unfairly marks those blacks who would succeed without discrimination. Is this what the Court means by "visibly open"? *Ante,* at 20.

Finally, the Court's disturbing reference to the importance of the country's law schools as training grounds meant to cultivate "a set of leaders with legitimacy in the eyes of the citizenry," *ibid.,* through the use of racial discrimination deserves discussion. As noted earlier, the Court has soundly rejected the remedying of societal discrimination as a justification for governmental use of race. *Wygant*, 476 U. S., at 276 (plurality opinion); *Croson,* 488 U. S., at 497 (plurality opinion); *id.,* at 520–521 (SCALIA, J., concurring in judgment). For those who believe that every racial disproportionality in our society is caused by some kind of racial discrimination, there can be no distinction between remedying societal discrimination and erasing racial disproportionalities in the country's leadership caste. And if the lack of proportional racial representation among our leaders is not caused by societal discrimination, then "fixing" it is even less of a pressing public necessity.

The Court's civics lesson presents yet another example of judicial selection of a theory of political representation based on skin color—an endeavor I have previously rejected. See *Holder v. Hall,* 512 U. S. 874, 899 (1994) (THOMAS, J., concurring in judgment). The majority appears to believe that broader utopian goals justify the Law School's use of race, but "[t]he Equal Protection Clause commands the elimination of racial barriers, not their creation in order to satisfy our theory as to how society ought to be organized." *DeFunis,* 416 U. S., at 342 (Douglas, J., dissenting).

VII

As the foregoing makes clear, I believe the Court's opinion to be, in most respects, erroneous. I do, however, find two points on which I agree.

A

First, I note that the issue of unconstitutional racial discrimination among the groups the Law School prefers is not presented in this case, because petitioner has never argued that the Law School engages in such a practice, and the Law School maintains that it does not. See Brief for Respondents Bollinger et al. 32, n. 50, and 6–7, n. 7. I join the Court's opinion insofar as it confirms that this type of racial discrimination remains unlawful. *Ante,* at 13–15. Under today's decision, it is still the case that racial discrimination that does not help a university to enroll an unspecified number, or "critical mass," of underrepresented minority students is unconstitutional. Thus, the Law School may not discriminate in admissions between similarly situated blacks and Hispanics, or between whites and Asians. This is so because preferring black to Hispanic applicants, for instance, does nothing to further the interest recognized by the majority today.[12] Indeed, the majority describes such racial balancing as "patently unconstitutional." *Ante,* at 17. Like the Court, *ante,* at 24, I express no opinion as to whether the Law School's current admissions program runs afoul of this prohibition.

B

The Court also holds that racial discrimination in admissions should be given another 25 years before it is deemed no longer narrowly tailored to the Law School's fabricated compelling state interest. *Ante,* at 30. While I agree that in 25 years the practices of the Law School will be illegal, they are, for the reasons I have given, illegal now. The majority does not and cannot rest its time limitation on any evidence that the gap in credentials between black and white students is shrinking or will be gone in that timeframe.[13] In recent years there has been virtually no change, for example, in the proportion of law school applicants with LSAT scores of 165 and higher who are black.[14] In 1993 blacks constituted 1.1% of law school applicants in that score range, though they represented 11.1% of all applicants. Law School Admission Council, National Statistical Report (1994) (hereinafter LSAC Statistical Report). In 2000 the comparable numbers were 1.0% and 11.3%. LSAC Statistical Report (2001). No one can seriously contend, and the Court does not, that the racial gap in academic credentials will disappear in 25 years. Nor is the Court's holding that racial discrimination will be unconstitutional in 25 years made contingent on the gap closing in that time.[15]

Indeed, the very existence of racial discrimination of the type practiced by the Law School may impede the narrowing of the LSAT testing gap. An applicant's LSAT score can improve dramatically with preparation, but such preparation is a cost, and there must be sufficient benefits attached to an improved score to justify additional study. Whites scoring between 163 and 167 on the LSAT are routinely rejected by the Law School, and thus whites aspiring to admission at the Law School have every incentive to improve their score to levels above that range. See App. 199 (showing that in 2000, 209 out of 422 white applicants were rejected in this scoring range).

Blacks, on the other hand, are nearly guaranteed admission if they score above 155. *Id.,* at 198 (showing that 63 out of 77 black applicants are accepted with LSAT scores above 155). As admission prospects approach certainty, there is no incentive for the black applicant to continue to prepare for the LSAT once he is reasonably assured of achieving the requisite score. It is far from certain that the LSAT test-taker's behavior is responsive to the Law School's admissions policies.[16] Nevertheless, the possibility remains that this racial discrimination will help fulfill the bigot's prophecy about black underperformance—just as it confirms the conspiracy theorist's belief that "institutional racism" is at fault for every racial disparity in our society.

I therefore can understand the imposition of a 25-year time limit only as a holding that the deference the Court pays to the Law School's educational judgments and refusal to change its admissions policies will itself expire. At that point these policies will clearly have failed to "'eliminat[e] the [perceived] need for any racial or ethnic'" discrimination because the academic credentials gap will still be there. *Ante,* at 30 (quoting Nathanson & Bartnika, The Constitutionality of Preferential Treatment for Minority Applicants to Professional Schools, 58 Chicago Bar Rec. 282, 293 (May–June 1977)). The Court defines this time limit in terms of narrow tailoring, see *ante,* at 30, but I believe this arises from its refusal to define rigorously the broad state interest vindicated today. Cf. Part II, *supra.* With these observations, I join the last sentence of Part III of the opinion of the Court.

* * *

For the immediate future, however, the majority has placed its *imprimatur* on a practice that can only weaken the principle of equality embodied in the Declaration of Independence and the Equal Protection Clause. "Our Constitution is color-blind, and neither knows nor tolerates classes among citizens." *Plessy* v. *Ferguson,* 163 U. S. 537, 559 (1896) (Harlan, J., dissenting). It has been nearly 140 years since Frederick Douglass asked the intellectual ancestors of the Law School to "[d]o nothing with us!" and the Nation adopted the Fourteenth Amendment. Now we must wait another 25 years to see this principle of equality vindicated. I therefore respectfully dissent from the remainder of the Court's opinion and the judgment.

Notes

1. Throughout I will use the two phrases interchangeably.
2. The Court's refusal to address *Wygant's* rejection of a state interest virtually indistinguishable from that presented by the Law School is perplexing. If the Court defers to the Law School's judgment that a racially mixed student body confers educational benefits to all, then why would the *Wygant* Court not defer to the school board's judgment with respect to the benefits a racially mixed faculty confers?
3. "[D]iversity," for all of its devotees, is more a fashionable catch-phrase than it is a useful term, especially when something as serious as racial discrimination is at issue. Because the Equal Protection Clause renders the color of one's skin constitutionally irrelevant to the Law School's mission, I refer to the Law School's interest as an "aesthetic." That is, the Law School wants to have a certain appearance, from the shape of the desks and tables in its classrooms to the color of the students sitting at them.

    I also use the term "aesthetic" because it underlines the ineffectiveness of racially discriminatory admissions in actually helping those who are truly underprivileged. Cf. *Orr v. Orr,* 440 U. S. 268, 283 (1979) (noting that suspect classifications are especially impermissible when "the choice made by the State appears to redound . . . to the benefit of those without need for special solicitude"). It must be remembered that the Law School's racial discrimination does nothing for those too poor or uneducated to participate in elite higher education and therefore presents only an illusory solution to the challenges facing our Nation.

4. The Law School believes both that the educational benefits of a racially engineered student body are large and that adjusting its overall admissions standards to achieve the same racial mix would require it to sacrifice its elite status. If the Law School is correct that the educational benefits of "diversity" are so great, then achieving them by altering admissions standards should not compromise its elite status. The Law School's reluctance to do this suggests that the educational benefits it alleges are not significant or do not exist at all.

5. Cf. U. S. News & World Report, America's Best Graduate Schools 28 (2004 ed.) (placing these schools in the uppermost 15 in the Nation).

6. The Court refers to this component of the Law School's compelling state interest variously as "academic quality," avoiding "sacrifice [of] a vital component of its educational mission," and "academic selectivity." *Ante,* at 27–28.

7. For example, North Carolina A&T State University, which is currently 5.4% white, College Admissions Data Handbook 643, could seek to reduce the representation of whites in order to gain additional educational benefits.

8. Cal. Const., Art. 1, §31(a), states in full:

"The state shall not discriminate against, or grant preferential treatment to, any individual or group on the basis of race, sex, color, ethnicity, or national origin in the operation of public employment, public education, or public contracting." See *Coalition for Economic Equity* v. *Wilson,* 122 F. 3d 692 (CA9 1997).

9. Given the incredible deference the Law School receives from the Court, I think it appropriate to indulge in the presumption that Boalt Hall operates without violating California law.

10. Were this Court to have the courage to forbid the use of racial discrimination in admissions, legacy preferences (and similar practices) might quickly become less popular—a possibility not lost, I am certain, on the elites (both individual and institutional) supporting the Law School in this case.

11. For example, there is no recognition by the Law School in this case that even with their racial discrimination in place, black *men* are "underrepresented" at the Law School. See ABA–LSAC Guide 426 (reporting that the Law School has 46 black women and 28 black men). Why does the Law School not also discriminate in favor of black men over black women, given this underrepresentation? The answer is, again, that all the Law School cares about is its own image among know-it-all elites, not solving real problems like the crisis of black male underperformance.

12. That interest depends on enrolling a "critical mass" of underrepresented minority students, as the majority repeatedly states. *Ante,* at 3, 5, 7, 17, 20, 21, 23, 28; cf. *ante,* at 21 (referring to the unique experience of being a "racial minority," as opposed to being black, or Native American); *ante,* at 24 (rejecting argument that the Law School maintains

a disguised quota by referring to the total number of enrolled underrepresented minority students, not specific races). As it relates to the Law School's racial discrimination, the Court clearly approves of only one use of race—the distinction between underrepresented minority applicants and those of all other races. A relative preference awarded to a black applicant over, for example, a similarly situated Native American applicant, does not lead to the enrollment of even one more underrepresented minority student, but only balances the races within the "critical mass."

13. I agree with JUSTICE GINSBURG that the Court's holding that racial discrimination in admissions will be illegal in 25 years is not based upon a "forecast," *post*, at 3 (concurring opinion). I do not agree with JUSTICE GINSBURG's characterization of the Court's holding as an expression of "hope." *Ibid.*

14. I use a score of 165 as the benchmark here because the Law School feels it is the relevant score range for applicant consideration (absent race discrimination). See Brief for Respondents Bollinger et al. 5; App. to Pet. for Cert. 309a (showing that the median LSAT score for all accepted applicants from 1995–1998 was 168); *id.*, at 310a–311a (showing the median LSAT score for accepted applicants was 167 for the years 1999 and 2000); University of Michigan Law School Website, available at http://www.law.umich.edu/prospectivestudents/Admissions/index.htm (showing that the median LSAT score for accepted applicants in 2002 was 166).

15. The majority's non sequitur observation that since 1978 the number of blacks that have scored in these upper ranges on the LSAT has grown, *ante,* at 30, says nothing about current trends. First, black participation in the LSAT until the early 1990's lagged behind black representation in the general population. For instance, in 1984 only 7.3% of law school applicants were black, whereas in 2000 11.3% of law school applicants were black. See LSAC Statistical Reports (1984 and 2000). Today however unless blacks were to begin applying to Law School in proportions greater than their representation in the general population, the growth in absolute numbers of high scoring blacks should be expected to plateau, and it has. In 1992, 63 black applicants to law school had LSAT scores above 165. In 2000, that number was 65. See LSAC Statistical Reports (1992 and 2000).

16. I use the LSAT as an example, but the same incentive structure is in place for any admissions criteria, including undergraduate grades, on which minorities are consistently admitted as thresholds significantly lower than whites.